W F

People in Organizations

An Introduction to Organizational Behavior

McGRAW-HILL SERIES IN MANAGEMENT

Fred Luthans and Keith Davis, Consulting Editors

ALLEN   The Management Profession

ARNOLD AND FELDMAN   Organizational Behavior

BENTON   Supervision and Management

BUCHELE   The Management of Business and Public Organizations

CASCIO   Managing Human Resources: Productivity, Quality of Work Life, Profits

CLELAND AND KING   Management: A Systems Approach

CLELAND AND KING   Systems Analysis and Project Management

DALE   Management: Theory and Practice

DAVIS AND FREDERICK   Business and Society: Management, Public Policy, Ethics

DAVIS AND NEWSTROM   Human Behavior at Work: Organizational Behavior

DAVIS AND NEWSTROM   Organizational Behavior: Readings and Exercises

DEL MAR   Operations and Industrial Management: Designing and Managing for Productivity

DOBLER, LEE, AND BURT   Purchasing and Materials Management: Text and Cases

DUNN AND RACHEL   Wage and Salary Administration: Total Compensation Systems

FELDMAN AND ARNOLD   Managing Individual and Group Behavior in Organizations

FINCH, JONES, AND LITTERER   Managing for Organizational Effectiveness:
   An Experiential Approach

FLIPPO   Personnel Management

GERLOFF   Organizational Theory and Design: A Strategic Approach for Management

GLUECK AND JAUCH   Business Policy and Strategic Management

GLUECK AND JAUCH   Strategic Management and Business Policy

GLUECK AND SNYDER   Readings in Business Policy and Strategy from *Business Week*

HAMPTON   Management

HAMPTON   Inside Management: Readings from *Business Week*

HICKS AND GULLETT   Management

HICKS AND GULLETT   Modern Business Management: A Systems and Environmental Approach

HICKS AND GULLETT   Organizations: Theory and Behavior

HODGETTS   Effective Supervision: A Practical Approach

JAUCH AND TOWNSEND   Cases in Strategic Management and Business Policy

JOHNSON, KAST, AND ROSENZWEIG   The Theory and Management of Systems

KARLINS   The Human Use of Human Resources

KAST AND ROSENZWEIG   Experiential Exercises and Cases in Management

KAST AND ROSENZWEIG   Organization and Management: A Systems and Contingency Approach

KNUDSON, WOODWORTH, AND BELL   Management: An Experiential Approach

KOONTZ, O'DONNELL, AND WEIHRICH   Essentials of Management

KOONTZ, O'DONNELL, AND WEIHRICH   Management

People in Organizations

An Introduction to Organizational Behavior

THIRD EDITION

Terence R. Mitchell

Edward E. Carlson Professor of Business Administration and Professor of Psychology
University of Washington

James R. Larson, Jr.

Asssociate Professor of Psychology
The University of Illinois at Chicago

McGRAW-HILL BOOK COMPANY
New York   St. Louis   San Francisco   Auckland   Bogotá   Hamburg
London   Madrid   Mexico   Milan   Montreal   New Delhi   Panama
Paris   São Paulo   Singapore   Sydney   Tokyo   Toronto

This book was set in Goudy Old Style by Better Graphics (ECU). The editors were Kathleen L. Loy and Peggy Rehberger; the designer was Joan Greenfield; the production supervisors were Diane Renda and Fred Schulte. The photo editor was Inge King. The drawings were done by J & R Services, Inc. R. R. Donnelley & Sons Company was printer and binder.

Illustration credits appear on pages 585–587. Copyrights included on this page by reference.

PEOPLE IN ORGANIZATIONS:
An Introduction
to Organizational Behavior

234567890 DOCDOC 8943210987

ISBN 0-07-042534-5

Library of Congress Cataloging-in-Publication Data

Mitchell, Terence R.
  People in organizations.

  (McGraw-Hill series in management)
  Includes bibliographies and index.
  1. Organization. 2. Organizational behavior.
I. Larson, James R.   II. Title.   III. Series.
HD31.M478 1987   658.3   86-20043
ISBN 0-07-042534-5

About the Authors

TERENCE R. MITCHELL is the Edward Carlson Professor of Business Administration and Psychology at the University of Washington. He holds an Advanced Diploma in Public Administration from Exeter University, and received his M.A. and Ph.D. in social psychology from The University of Illinois at Urbana-Champaign. Professor Mitchell's currrent research interests are in the areas of leadership, motivation, and decision making. He has published numerous articles on these topics in *Organizational Behavior and Human Decision Processes, Academy of Management Journal, Academy of Management Review,* and *Journal of Applied Psychology.*

JAMES R. LARSON, JR. is an Associate Professor of Psychology at The University of Illinois at Chicago. He received his Ph.D. in social psychology from the University of Washington, and has taught at Rutgers University, Barnard College, and in the Graduate School of Business at Columbia University. Professor Larson's research interests are in the areas of leader behavior, social perception, and performance feedback processes. He has published articles on these topics in *Organizational Behavior and Human Decision Processes, Journal of Applied Psychology, Journal of Applied Social Psychology,* and *Journal of Personality and Social Psychology.*

To SKM, FFL, and FFF:

for their intellectual and emotional sustenance—TRM

To IRG:

for the encouragement to start this project, and the time to finish it—JRL

Contents

Preface

It has been 5 years since the second edition of *People in Organizations* was published, and 9 years since the first edition appeared. In that time a significant amount of progress has been made in the field of organizational behavior. Research has continued on many fronts, and some important new developments have occurred in areas such as motivation, leadership, decision making, and job stress. These developments, along with our own careful analysis of the two previous editions, prompted this revision.

The appearance of any new edition of a textbook implies that the book has undergone a certain amount of change. In the case of *People in Organizations*, however, the change has been substantial. In this third edition we have not only brought the book up to date, we have also made a number of fundamental changes in its orientation and coverage.

First, we have made a major effort to increase the research thrust of the book. Both of us are strongly committed to the idea that the practice of management is most effective when it is informed by the results of carefully conducted, systematic research. Consequently, we have rewritten and updated every chapter in the book to emphasize current research and its practical implications. Over 700 research studies are cited—more than twice the number cited in the second edition. Nearly one third of these have come into the literature since the second edition was published. We describe some of these studies in detail so that the reader can get a sense of how research in organizational behavior is conducted.

To balance this research orientation, we have also added numerous examples of practical applications. While increasing the overall length of the book, these examples help the reader to better understand the material and its usefulness. We have also included a "Special Report" in every chapter. These special reports come directly from prominent newspapers, magazines, and applied business journals, and they illustrate the application of significant research findings.

Near the end of each chapter can be found one other new feature we have added to this edition. Every chapter ends with two concluding sections, one labelled "Implications for Practice," and the other "Implications for Research." Whereas the former summarizes the major practical implications of the material covered in the chapter, the latter outlines areas where our understanding of the behavior of people in organizations is still incomplete and needs to be supplemented with further empirical research.

Finally, there have also been substantial changes in topic coverage. There is a brand new chapter on job stress (Chapter 7), as well as major new sections on (a) the open systems view of organizations, (b) perceptual and cognitive biases in judgment and decision making, (c) work motivation (d) the development of group norms and their impact on behavior, (e) group decision making, (f) political processes in organizations, (g) the socialization of new employees, (h) strategies for organizational change, and much much more. In short, this edition represents a complete overhaul of the text.

This edition was improved by the helpful comments of a number of individuals who read preliminary drafts of the manuscript. We would especially like to thank:

Hrach Bedrosian, New York University; Warren Blank, Maharishi International University; Dennis L. Dossett, University of Missouri; Maureen Fleming, University of Montana; Charles Hobson, Indiana University; Harriet A. Kandelman, University of Portland; Kathryn Lewis, California State University, Chico; James McFillen, Bowling Green State University; Gregory B. Northcraft, University of Arizona; Robert Paul, Kansas State University; Anson Seers, University of Alabama; Pamela Specht, University of Nebraska; Susan Taylor, University of Maryland; Ken Thompson, University of Arkansas; and John A. Wagner, Michigan State University.

Several people also helped in preparing the manuscript. In particular, we would like to thank Pam Martin for her tireless efforts on the word processor. Her expert skill, careful attention to detail, and unfailing good cheer made her a joy to work with. We would also like to thank Gauri Bhosley and Donna Hayes for their help in assembling and proofreading the final manuscript. Because of their efforts, we were able to concentrate more of our own energies on the actual writing of this edition.

Terence R. Mitchell
James R. Larson, Jr.

People in Organizations

An Introduction
to
Organizational Behavior

Part One

Foundations

A central theme running throughout this book is that people's behavior is jointly caused by their own personal characteristics and the setting in which they find themselves. Since our interest is in organizational behavior, we will focus on organizational settings. Empirical research has uncovered a number of general rules and relationships, and in this book we review these findings.

However, before we can begin this review, we must first lay the foundations upon which the book rests. In order to understand the behavior of people in organizations, we must know more about two things: (1) people—in particular, the basic nature of human beings, and (2) organizations—why they form and what they consist of. These topics are covered in Part 1.

The introductory chapter (Chapter 1) is meant to give the reader some insight into our goals in writing this book, as well as our biases as authors. Briefly stated, the purpose of this book is to examine the general principles of human behavior in organizations and to show how these principles can be adopted to solve a wide variety of organizational problems. The first chapter also provides the rationale for the structure of the book.

Chapter 2, "Understanding People," examines several basic aspects of human nature. We start out by discussing a number of important philosophical and empirical questions, such as: Are humans a unique species? What is our capacity for change? To what extent is our behavior externally caused (i.e., regulated by the situation) versus internally caused (i.e., regulated by internal processes such as instincts or personality)? In general, we conclude that people are unique, that they are influenced by both internal and external factors, and that they are capable of great change. We then discuss in some detail the major mechanism of change—learning. Particular emphasis is placed on learning in organizational settings.

Finally, Chapter 3, "Understanding Organizations," focuses on the setting in which organizational behavior takes place. The chapter begins with a discussion of the reasons for the existence of organizations and some of the problems that modern organizations face (e.g., size, complexity). A large part of the chapter is then devoted to examining the various elements that make up an organization. The chapter concludes by emphasizing the importance of understanding how these various elements fit together to form a cohesive whole.

Chapter 1

Introduction

Chapter Outline
  I. The Field of Organizational Behavior
 II. Format of the Text
III. Underlying Philosophy
 IV. Content and Outline

Knowledge is the only instrument of production that is not subject to diminishing returns.

—J. M. CLARK

Before proceeding into the substantive content of this text, the reader should be aware of the book's educational objectives, its structure, and its 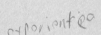 philosophical underpinnings. *People in Organizations* was written with four major goals in mind. First, it is meant to be an empirically based survey of the field. It provides a broad overview of what is known about human behavior in organizational settings. Second, it is designed to be easy and enjoyable to read. Both the language and format emphasize this goal. Third, the underlying philosophy is optimistic. Organizations can be very productive and satisfying places for people to work. Finally, the content is organized so that later chapters build on the material presented in earlier chapters. The purpose of this first chapter is to discuss these four goals in more detail.

THE FIELD OF ORGANIZATIONAL BEHAVIOR

There was a time not long ago when the business schools and management departments in most colleges and universities offered only one introductory course with a behavioral emphasis. Typically, that course would cover a

3

potpourri of topics, ranging from principles of general management to principles of human behavior. During the last 25 years, however, these various areas have become much more distinct and well defined. The result has been that most business schools now offer separate courses in general management, organizational theory, personnel, and *organizational behavior*.

During the same period a parallel trend occurred in psychology departments. It used to be that most psychology departments offered only one course directly applicable to business settings. That course, called *industrial psychology*, focused primarily on issues concerning employee selection, training, placement, and performance appraisal. However, driven in part by a perceived need to be more relevant, psychology departments began to offer specialized courses in such applied areas as work motivation, group decision making, and leadership. The latter are all central topics in what is today called *organizational behavior*.

Briefly defined, organizational behavior is a field that is oriented toward developing a better understanding of human behavior and using that knowledge to help people be more productive and satisfied in organizational settings. The primary values characterizing this field include (1) an emphasis on establishing cause-and-effect relationships, (2) a commitment to change, (3) a humanistic concern for people, (4) a concern for organizational effectiveness, and (5) a reliance on empirical research and the scientific method (Cummings, 1978). These five values make organizational behavior unique as a field of study. The focus is on individual and group behavior in organizations, principles are based on empirical research, and there is a definite applied orientation.

It is important to recognize that some of the values listed above are relatively new, having developed only as the field itself developed. For example, the emphasis on research and the scientific method was not always as strong as it is today. During the past quarter century, there has been a dramatic growth in the number of empirical studies that have been conducted. So much so, in fact, that new scientific journals have been founded just to accommodate the increased volume. For example, for many years *The Academy of Management Journal* published papers covering the broad spectrum of management thought. Both research and theoretical papers were included on topics that were varied in their emphasis. However, in 1975 the *Journal* split into two publications: *The Academy of Management Review* and *The Academy of Management Journal*. The *Review* publishes theoretical and review papers, while the *Journal* is devoted exclusively to empirical research. Many of these empirical studies deal with individual and group behavior, and thus fall under the heading of organizational behavior.

Unfortunately, textbooks in the field do not always reflect this change toward a more empirical orientation. They may cover all the right topics, but they often do not give the reader much of a feel for the vast amount of research that has been done. *People in Organizations* is different in this respect. It is an *empirically based review* of what we know about individual and group behavior in organizational settings and how this knowledge can be applied to increase the effectiveness and satisfaction of organizational participants.

A second goal in writing the book was to produce a text that students would both enjoy and learn from at the same time. The book is designed to be a learning tool. With this goal in mind, the following format was adopted. First, each chapter begins with an outline. This outline not only lists the topics that are covered in the chapter but also helps the reader see how these topics fit together.

Second, throughout each chapter we weave into our discussion of theory and research numerous practical examples and short stories that help to illustrate the points that are being made. There is also a short case study at the end of each chapter that gives the readers a chance to apply the concepts that have been learned. Finally, cartoons, quotations, photographs, and advertisements are used throughout the book to highlight various points.

Third, in many cases our discussion of specific research studies is sufficiently detailed to give the reader a clear idea of how the study was actually conducted. We also provide full citations for all the sources we use. These are listed at the end of each chapter. The interested reader who wishes to pursue some topic in more detail or verify the basis for statements made in the chapter can easily do so by using these citations. Most of the sources can be located in any good college or university library.

Finally, at the end of each chapter there is a summary of the major points that were discussed, along with several discussion questions to help direct the reader's thinking about the topic. Also, at the end of each chapter, we have included two sections: one on implications for practice, and one on implications for research. The purpose of the former is to offer additional suggestions about how the ideas presented in the chapter can be applied in an organizational setting. The latter points out areas in which our understanding is still incomplete and where further empirical research is needed.

In short, everything has been done with an eye toward making the text an integrated learning tool that is also informative and enjoyable to use.

UNDERLYING PHILOSOPHY

No textbook can be written without being influenced by the particular biases of the authors. Some material is included, and some is not; some concepts and theories are discussed in detail, while others are mentioned only briefly. In the following paragraphs, some of our biases are openly discussed so that the reader can be aware of the philosophical premises on which the text is based. This knowledge enables readers to put the material in its proper perspective.

The first issue to consider is our perception of our responsibility as textbook writers. We do not view this book merely as a forum for presenting our own ideas or research, nor do we see it as a treatise supporting one orientation or another. Rather, it is an attempt to organize and integrate material drawn from the entire field. When our own experience or research is discussed, it is only because this experience illustrates a particular point well. We view our role to be that of reviewers and organizers. As such, our objective is to provide you with as clear and concise a picture of this complex field as is possible.

Within this framework, however, the reader will find that we have a distinctly optimistic bias. We believe that organizations can be very satisfying settings in which to work. Furthermore, we believe that those organizations and work settings that are not now satisfying can be changed. In Chapter 2, "Understanding People," and in other discussions throughout the text, the point is made that humans have a great capacity for change. Because some of our behavior is under our own control and some of it is influenced by the environment, both individuals and the social institutions in which they work share the responsibility for implementing change. But change *is* possible, which means that when it is necessary, we do have the capacity for improving the quality of life at work.

Another bias we have concerns the practical implications of the book. We strongly believe that the ideas presented in each chapter are useful and that they can be applied in everyday work settings. To help illustrate this point we have given numerous examples that show the relevance of the material to particular situations. In addition, at the end of each chapter we have provided a section entitled "Implications for Practice," which discusses how some of the most important concepts from the chapter can be put to use.

At the same time, however, we also recognize that organizations are extremely complex social entities and that it is impossible to offer specific solutions that will apply in every circumstance. Thus we place a great deal of emphasis on learning how to properly *diagnose* various situations. For example, suppose you are faced with a problem of low employee morale or poor performance. The answer is not simply to give everyone a raise, punish them, or automatically use any other "off the shelf" solution. First you must discover more about the problem. What is it that your employees find dissatisfying? Are there technical or communication problems that are causing the poor performance? Do all employees understand exactly what is expected of them? It is only when you have thoroughly diagnosed the problem that you can begin to apply the basic principles of human behavior to tailor a solution that fits the unique circumstances at hand.

Finally, we believe that in addition to learning about what is known in a particular field, it is also useful for students to have a sense of what is not known. As in most areas of inquiry, we as social scientists do not understand everything there is to know about the behavior of individuals and groups in organizations. There are large gaps in our understanding. We point out some of these gaps in the section at the end of each chapter entitled "Implications for Research." We feel that this section is useful in part because it conveys the idea that we do not yet have all of the answers. Thus, we should be open to new ideas and new ways of managing people, and we should be willing to test these ideas out in careful empirical research. With continued research the gaps in our knowledge will begin to close. As they do, the new knowledge that is generated can be put to use to make the lives of people in organizations more productive and satisfying.

CONTENT AND OUTLINE

It is often difficult for students to figure out why chapters appear in a text where they do. The particular order of the material can be a mystery. The rationale presented below is designed to convey the logical basis used for structuring *People in Organizations.*

First, we have made the assumption that if one wants to understand human behavior in organizations, one must be exposed to some information about both human nature and the organizational environment. The first section of the book reviews these topics. Chapter 2 discussed some underlying principles of human nature—in particular, why humans are a unique and changeable species. Chapter 3 examines the organizational environment and discusses the various elements that make up "the organization." Of special concern is the way in which these elements fit together.

The second set of chapters (Part 2) is designed to investigate *individual behavior* in more detail. What do all human beings bring to the organization? What is unique about any one individual? Chapter 4 discusses the topics of perception and personality, and Chapter 5 discusses attitudes. Chapter 6, which focuses on motivation, is in many ways the foundation for the rest of the book. It examines why people choose to do what they do—what motivates them. Finally, Chapter 7 discusses the topic of job stress and what can be done about it.

In Part 3, the focus switches to the *social environment.* The emphasis is on how the individual behaves when dealing with others. Chapter 8 provides an overview of groups—how they form and develop, and their strong and weak points. Chapter 9 focuses on three ways that people learn what behaviors are expected and rewarded in the social setting, that is, through roles, norms, and status differences. Chapter 10 discusses the communication process and how it can be more effective.

Once we have a firm understanding of why people behave the way they do, both alone and in groups, we can begin to discuss how to use this knowledge to change people's behavior and increase effectiveness. We can discuss how one *gets things done* in an organization. Part 4 covers this topic. Chapter 11 describes individual decision making, while Chapter 12 deals with decision making in groups. Chapters 13 and 14 focus on ways to change people's behavior, either through the use of power and politics, or through the use of leadership.

Part 5 also emphasizes change, but from a somewhat different perspective. While Part 4 covers change as a result of either individual or interpersonal action, Part 5 discusses ways in which an organization, through its personnel policies, its key managers, and its general approach to institutional change, can *increase organizational effectiveness.* Chapter 15 deals with the classical functions of personnel—selection, placement, performance appraisal, and rewards. Chapter 16 discusses the line manager's role in socializing new employees, managing poor performers, and managing effective employees. Finally, Chapter 17 presents a number of general organizational change strat-

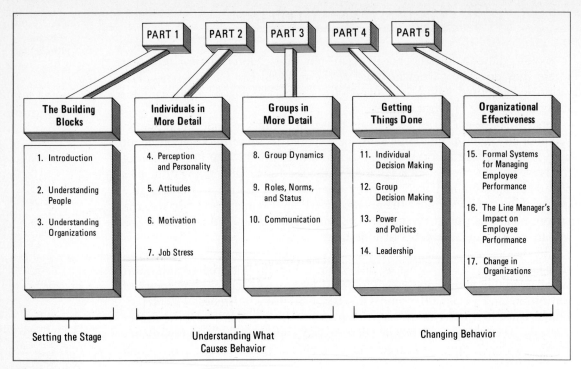

FIGURE 1-1
The structure
of the book.

egies that can be used to increase the overall effectiveness of an organization. The structure of the book is outlined in Figure 1-1.

Reference

Cummings, L. L. (1978). Towards organizational behavior. *Academy of Management Review, 3,* 90–98.

Chapter 2

Understanding People

Knowledge about what man has been and is can protect the future
—MARGARET MEAD

W hen we think about organizations, we often think about the various ways they can be designed and run. The possibilities seem endless. They can be run in a very bureaucratic fashion, with many rules, regulations, and standard operating procedures, or they can be run in a rather loose and informal way. They can be highly centralized, with most decisions made by a few individuals at the top, or they can be decentralized, with important decisions made by many individuals throughout the organization. They can be structured in such a way that jobs are narrowly defined, with each person in

9

the organization performing relatively few tasks, or structured so that everyone performs a wide variety of tasks. And they can be designed so that employees are responsible for and rewarded on the basis of their own individual performance, or so that group performance and teamwork are rewarded.

These and many other possibilities will be discussed in more detail in Chapter 3. For now it is important only to recognize that all of these various approaches to designing and running organizations involve either implicit or explicit assumptions about human nature. They involve certain basic assumptions about what motivates organizational members, and these basic assumptions in turn suggest ways to reward people, provide leadership, maintain control, manage performance, and so on. Our goal in the present chapter is to describe the current thinking of social scientists with respect to some basic questions about human nature.

One fundamental question is whether people should be viewed negatively, as naturally lazy and self-serving, or positively, as self-motivated. Proponents of the first position argue that people are rather lazy and need to be pushed, controlled, and kept under surveillance, never to be trusted to put in a good day's work by themselves. Many of the classical approaches to designing and running organizations made these types of assumptions. Economic rewards were the only ones considered, and close, autocratic supervision was suggested.

At the other extreme are human-relations theorists who have a positive view of human nature. Employees are seen as striving for personal and social well-being. If left alone, they will work hard for the intrinsic satisfaction of a job well done. Jobs should therefore be challenging and allow the individual employee to be creative.

A closer inspection of the positive–negative dichotomy seems to raise more questions than it answers. The terms *positive* and *negative* are obviously value-laden. Other issues related to human nature seem to be less emotionally charged and more relevant for decisions about organizational design. For example, one would like to know how flexible or changeable people actually are. Is their nature fixed or malleable? To what extent can training be used to modify their behavior? Can we really change people once they join the organization? An equally important topic that is frequently debated by social scientists is whether the causes of behavior are internal or external. Those that argue for external events tend to see the environment and immediate situational variables as causes of behavior. Those that believe in internal causes use personality traits as their explanations. To the degree that internal explanations are true, the organizational processes of selection and placement become crucial. It would be very important to select the right people initially and place them in the right jobs, since there would be little chance of changing them later. On the other hand, if external events are the major cause of behavior, then the proper organizational environment could produce those behaviors deemed to be appropriate. By changing the situation one could change a person's behavior.

Note that this internal–external distinction places our earlier positive and negative positions in the internal category. The positive and negative labels refer to an internal disposition—human beings come programmed one way or the other. The external category implies that learning (i.e., our experience with our environment) causes our behavior.

A related issue deals with the uniqueness of human beings. Are we clearly different from our animal ancestors, or are we guided by and subject to the same urges as animals? Also important is the question of uniqueness *among* human beings. Just how different are we from each other? If we are all very different, and if much of our behavior cannot be predicted, an organization must build in flexibility to handle our complex unique characteristics. However, if we are all basically the same, we can treat everyone alike (a boon for designers of any system).

The debates over these questions are far from over. They raise some profound philosophical and practical issues. There is, however, some consensus among social scientists on these topics, and we will briefly review the evidence that led to these positions. We will be concerned with the following questions.

1. Are humans unique?
2. How much and what kind of change can occur in people?
3. Are we controlled by internal or external processes?
4. Is our capacity for learning and change unlimited?

The conclusions we will draw from these discussions will point up two key facts: (1) learning is the central mechanism by which people change their behavior, and (2) most people are capable of large amounts of change.

THE UNIQUENESS OF HUMAN BEINGS

Man is a predator whose natural instinct is to kill with a weapon.
—Robert Ardry

Over 100 years ago Charles Darwin published his revolutionary works *The Origin of Species* (1859) and *The Descent of Man* (1871). Darwin argued that human beings evolved just like other animals, and that the laws of selection and evolution are as applicable for humans as they are for animals. In 1871 Darwin went even further, claiming that there are no fundamental differences in the higher mental processses of humans and animals. He noted that animals seem to possess intelligence and memory as well as learning and problem-solving abilities. The differences that do exist, Darwin felt, are quantitative (i.e., differences in degree) rather than qualitative (i.e., differences in kind). Thus, in Darwin's view, human beings are not unique. Rather, we share a common heritage with other animal species, and as a consequence of this heritage, we behave in fundamentally similar ways.

Darwin's theory of evolution has had a tremendous impact on the biological and social sciences during the last century. It has spawned the growth of whole new fields of inquiry, the most recent of which is sociobiology. *Sociobiology* is the systematic study of the biological basis of all forms of social behavior, in all kinds of organisms, including humans (Wilson, 1978). Sociobiologists have argued quite persuasively that many aspects of human social behavior may

FIGURE 2-1
A question of
major importance
is the degree to
which human
beings are unique
from their animal
ancestors.

have deep-seated biological roots. Included are our tendencies toward aggressiveness and altruism, as well as features of our sexual behavior. For example, Wilson (1978) suggests that the nearly universal taboo against incest may have biological underpinnings. He notes that animals seem naturally to avoid incestuous relationships without evidence of external pressure from other members of their species. Furthermore, in human populations, unrelated children who are raised together from a very young age (e.g., on a kibbutz) later in life show no strong sexual attraction toward one another (when presumably there would be no taboo against such relationships). Perhaps, then, there are subtle biological forces connected with early childhood development that guide this aspect of our sexual behavior. If so, our social customs and laws regarding incest would seem to be largely superfluous.

Although many dimensions of human behavior may be organized by genes shared with closely related animal species (e.g., primates, and mammals more generally), it is also apparent that some aspects of our behavior are not shared by animals. Perhaps the most obvious is our degree of language development. Our ability to use linguistic symbols far exceeds what is found among animals. While it is true that many animals communicate with one another, there is little evidence that they can make known anything more than simple emotional reactions. This seems to be true even for chimpanzees, the most intelligent of the animal species. Research has shown that chimpanzees can learn a rudimentary form of sign language (e.g., Gardner & Gardner, 1975). These chimps, if continuously trained from an early age, can learn approximately 400 different signs, and can string them together in sentencelike sequences. However, the sort of language sophistication reached by the best of these apes is little beyond what we expect from a 3-year-old child. Thus, while language development may not be completely unique, it is many magnitudes more sophisticated in humans than has been illustrated in the best animals.

There are also differences in the way humans adjust to their environment. We clearly control and manipulate our environment in ways that facilitate adaptation. For most species, an inhospitable environment means either a change in the species or death. Humans, on the other hand, will change the environment to suit their needs. This is a basic difference which in many respects can be seen as the reason we have survived and prospered as a species. Again, while there is evidence that many animals do use rudimentary tools, the difference between humans and animals on this dimension is great.

Where does this leave us with respect to the uniqueness of the human race? A position somewhere between the two extremes seems to be most widely held. While it is true that our animal ancestry may have more to do with our current behavior than was previously believed, it is also true that there are certain dimensions that clearly differentiate our species from others. An understanding of animal behavior is not sufficient to understand human behavior.

These conclusions also help us to answer the second "uniqueness" question pertaining to the variability *within* the human species. Since we are not all governed by some easily describable set of behavior patterns, it is argued that humans are also not all alike. Individuals are unique not only with respect to other species, but also with respect to their own species. We have all observed that people are different physically, emotionally, and intellectually. The questions of interest are how do they become that way? and what are the common elements of the human experience? There are differences—but there are also similarities. To understand how this uniqueness occurs and whether it overshadows our similarities, we must understand how people develop and change.

THE CONTINUITY OF GROWTH

One often hears the old saw "You can't teach an old dog new tricks" with reference to human beings. The essence of this statement is that with age we become more rigid—more fixed in our behavior patterns and habits. It becomes increasingly difficult to learn new skills and behaviors.

The implications for organizations are obvious. Most organizations need and desire some degree of flexibility, especially in our current complex, rapidly changing environment. Yet, some people believe that our older, more senior, people (who often hold more responsible positions) are less flexible than other, younger employees. If this is true, we may be placing the people with the least flexibility in the very positions in which flexibility is needed most. The adage about old dogs and new tricks needs to be thoroughly examined.

There is evidence from a number of sources that suggests we do in fact become more rigid with age. Some of this evidence focuses on characteristics of people that make it difficult to change, while other evidence focuses on aspects of the environment. We review both types of evidence.

Personal Characteristics

One set of personal characteristics that inhibit change are personality traits. *Personality traits* are defined as enduring behavioral dispositions that persist across time and situations. Thus, when an individual is described as shy, extroverted, or ambitious, these labels suggest that the person will behave in a certain way and will do so consistently. Personality traits develop very early in life and are assumed to be fixed by late adolescence.

A second source of personal constancy comes from social-psychological theories of attitudes and attitude change. The basic tenet of these theories is that humans strive for cognitive consistency or balance. We try to hold beliefs and attitudes that do not contradict one another. When a contradiction does occur, we are uncomfortable and feel motivated to reduce or eliminate the contradiction. We build up over time a very complex, interrelated structure of beliefs and attitudes that are supportive of our behavior. This structure is hard to change bit by bit, since we are more likely to reject any single new item of inconsistent information than to change the whole cognitive structure.

Finally, there is some evidence that we selectively expose ourselves to information and people that already support our views. We tend not to seek out discrepant information or attitudes. Nor do we often seek out other people who are very different from ourselves. Thus, our personality traits and cognitive structures are constantly being bolstered and supported by the information and people to which we are exposed. This process reduces the possibilities for change.

Environmental Characteristics

There are also aspects of the *situation* that reduce the likelihood of change. First, the interpersonal environment stays fairly constant for most of us. Our friends, relatives, neighbors, and acquaintances tend to stay the same. While this circle may occasionally incorporate new people and discard others, there is more constancy than change.

This constancy is also true of the groups to which we belong. Our churches, social clubs, and recreational groups provide stability. These groups encourage stability by enforcing norms and roles. Within most social settings, including the work environment, there are some fairly well-known rules about how people should behave in general (norms), and how specific people in particular positions should behave (roles). There is a lot of pressure on all of us not to deviate from these norms and roles. To do so would encourage a reprimand or rejection by other group members. No one wants to be a social outcast.

At a somewhat broader level of analysis is our cultural environment. There are certain expectations about what behaviors are acceptable in the United States. For example, Americans are very time-oriented, and punctuality is seen as a good characteristic. The same type of behavior in some other cultures might be less important. Such general cultural expectations also reduce the individual's ability to change.

In summary, the evidence seems to suggest that it may in fact be hard to teach an old dog new tricks. There are both personal and environmental pressures that reduce change and increase constancy. What implications does this have for organizations? It is unlikely that most organizations will be able to change the basic personality structure of their employees. On the other hand, management does have some control over the organizational environment. Rules, regulations, policies, rewards, chains of command, and other formal aspects of the organization's structure can be modified. Communication lines can be influenced, as can the types of people who are selected to join the organization. Some social aspects of the situation can also be modified.

What this analysis suggests is that the crucial question is whether human behavior is controlled more by internal characteristics, such as our genetic background and personality traits, or by external characteristics, such as the environment and social setting. If behavior is mostly controlled by internal characteristics, there is probably little that can be done by organizations to change people's behavior. Most employees join organizations at the earliest in their late teens or early twenties, and by then their personality traits are pretty well established. The best an organization could do in this case would be to *select* and *place* people wisely. If, on the other hand, behavior is mostly controlled by external factors, people would be capable of great change. The organization could influence a great deal of behavior by changing the environment. The next section examines this debate in more detail.

INTERNAL VERSUS EXTERNAL DETERMINANTS OF BEHAVIOR

Men's natures are alike, it is their habits that carry them far apart
—CONFUCIUS

The controversy over internal versus external determinants of behavior exists in many forms and is relevant for many other topics in human behavior. At one extreme, some believe that almost everything is learned and can therefore be attributed to the environment. If we can control the environment, we can control the individual. This is the external position. Those opposed to this view have suggested a number of internal mechanisms as causes of behavior, such as instincts, personality traits, beliefs, and thought processes. We will briefly review the arguments for three internal mechanisms and present a tentative conclusion with respect to this issue.

Instincts versus the Environment

Earlier in this century, much of human social behavior was described as instinctive (e.g., McDougall, 1908). *Instincts* are defined as internally generated drives to activity. These drives are hereditary and genetically programmed. Instincts were proposed for aggression, shyness, curiosity, gregariousness, and cleanliness. There were instincts suggested for just about everything, including the liking for apples. What started out as a scientific explanation of behavior soon turned into a word game. To describe all behavior as caused by instincts does little to help our understanding of why the behavior occurs.

The reaction of many American social scientists was to go to the opposite extreme. They argued that almost all behavior is learned and environmentally (externally) determined. John Watson, who was the founder of this position (called *behaviorism*), went so far as to say that if you gave him a healthy infant, he could train the child to be any type of specialist one might select—doctor, lawyer, beggarman, or thief (1924). This position asserts that just about any behavior can be learned and strengthened with the proper rewards and environmental circumstances. For most of this century the behaviorist position or some variant of it has dominated much of social science.

The research evidence on the instinct position suggests that perhaps a few neural patterns are instinctual, and that specific behaviors do occur in response to specific stimuli. For example, there is some evidence that infants have instinctual preferences for certain types of visual stimuli. Also, the work of Piaget (1970) suggests that intelligence and cognitive development pass through a series of genetically regulated stages. Finally, there are numerous linguists who believe language development is greatly influenced by inborn determinants. But these examples account for only a small proportion of the richness of our behavior. The prevailing view is that most behavior is not instinctual in nature.

In more recent years, the instinct position has been combined with evolutionary notions to form the emerging discipline of sociobiology (e.g., Barash, 1979; Wilson, 1975). As we suggested previously, sociobiology asserts that social behavior has biological and evolutionary roots. The underlying idea is that people behave in ways that will preserve their genes and increase the probability that their progeny will survive and prosper. Instead of suggesting that specific mechanisms such as instincts exist in all humans, sociobiologists suggest that evolution over the years has tended to favor those individuals demonstrating certain social behaviors (e.g., avoiding incestuous relationships). These arguments have caused lots of controversy, and the debate is currently a popular topic.

While most social scientists agree that the principles of evolutionary theory are important for understanding the survival of animal species, they are less sure about the explanatory power of evolutionary notions for understanding specific human social behaviors (Campbell, 1975). The important point to emphasize, however, is that sociobiology and evolutionary theory see behavior development as an interactive process between the species and the environment. Thus, there is a recognition of the fact that the environment plays a major role in shaping behavior.

Personality versus the Environment

A somewhat different internal explanation of behavior is concerned with personality traits. The debate here focuses on whether behavior is caused by enduring personal characteristics or by external environment events. Personality theory is different from the instinct argument because most personality theorists believe that one's personality is partly learned (i.e., not due to genetic factors). The differences from the environment position are twofold. First, most personality theorists believe that personality is formed at a fairly early age. They argue, therefore, that it is long-forgotten past environmental events that determine our present behavior. Environmentalists, on the other hand, hold that more immediate and current external events cause behavior. Second, personality theorists believe that traits are fairly enduring and consistent. Therefore, a person who is shy in one situation should be shy in all situations. By contrast, the environmentalists hold that someone can be shy in one setting and outgoing in another; it all depends on the demands of the situation.

Over the last 20 years there has been a great deal of research on this problem. Early on during this period a very strong case was made for the environmentalist position (e.g., Mischel, 1968). At that time, there seemed to be little solid empirical evidence for behavioral consistency across situations, and what evidence did exist suggested that personality traits had only a weak influence on behavior. On the basis of this finding, many social scientists jumped on the environmentalist bandwagon, and even today hold steadfastly to that position. More recently, however, there has been a growing body of research that counters the strict environmentalist position (e.g., Epstein & O'Brien, 1985; Funder & Ozer, 1983; Sarason, Smith, & Diener, 1975; Woodruffe, 1984). Some of this research has involved measuring the effects of personality traits and situational variables simultaneously in the same study. The results indicate that personality traits do significantly influence behavior, and that the magnitude of their influence can often be just as great as that of situational factors.

Based on the most current evidence, therefore, it seems that both personality traits and situational variables must be taken into account in order to explain human behavior. We should not focus on either one to the exclusion of the other. However, this does not eliminate the possibility that under some conditions either personality traits or situational factors might predominate. The question that needs to be answered is, under what conditions do personality traits exert the greatest influence on behavior, and under what conditions do situational factors exert the greatest influence?

Cognitions versus the Environment

The third and final set of internal mechanisms we will discuss concerns people's cognitive activities. The strict behaviorist believes in environmental determinism: All noninstinctual behavior is caused by past and present environmental events. To understand someone's behavior, all we have to know is the individual's past responses to similar stimulus situations and the rewards or punishments that followed those reponses. There is no reference to internal cognitive events such as attitudes, beliefs, or values as causes of behavior.

The cognitive viewpoint says that, yes, the environment is important, as are past rewards and punishments, but it is our cognitive interpretations of the environment (e.g., our evaluations, memories, and expectations) that actually cause our behavior. The behaviorist view might best be represented as a stimulus–response model (S–R), and the cognitive view by a stimulus–organism–response model (S–O–R). Both approaches see learning and the environment as having a major impact on behavior. However, the cognitive position says that there is an intermediate step between the external environmental stimulus and the response.

This intermediate step is the cognitive processing and evaluation of the environment. The important point is that this cognitive process is *not the same as the* environment. Our cognitions are biased by self-serving motives, a fallible memory, and limited information-processing skills. Our cognitive representation of the environment in many cases may be similar to the actual environment, but it may also be different in some interesting and significant ways. Thus, the cognitive and environmentalist positions might lead to very different predictions about an individual's behavior if the individual's evaluation of the situation is substantially different from what really exists.

Today there are relatively few researchers who adhere to the extreme environmentalist point of view: most reject the notion that behavior can be completely explained by external environmental events and contingencies. There is ample evidence that in some cases cognitive events are better predictors of behavior.

To summarize, most social scientists have moved a long way toward an environmentalist position. However, few have gone all the way to the extreme position of environmental determinism, the belief that all behavior can be explained solely by past and present external events. Although instincts are seldom seen as determinants of behavior, there is still a strong belief that human beings are cognitively active processors and evaluators of the environment, and that personality and cognitive activity influence our behavior. Thus, internal causes of behavior are still important. Our final question deals with the limitations of these cognitive activities.

HUMAN LIMITATIONS

An analysis of the internal-versus-external-cause-of-behavior question raises one additional issue. If behavior were completely determined by internal factors, the amount of change and growth possible for each individual would be severely limited. On the other hand, if behavior were determined solely by the environment, the capacity of human beings to change would be almost unlimiited. Given the right environment, people could become anything they wanted.

The social implications of the latter position are extremely important. If that position is correct, large numbers of people who have been disadvantaged because of their genetic background (e.g., race) could be helped to overcome their disadvantage. Furthermore, performance in school, on the job, and in other areas of competence could be attributed to the environment. Poor performance, according to this position, is simply the result of an impoverished environment. In order to improve performance, one needs only to make the appropriate environmental changes. Thus, organizations could have a powerful impact on the behavior of their employees through educational and training programs and through careful design of the work environment. And society in general could increase the skills and abilities of its members by allocating resources to environmental (e.g., educational) programs. Much of the social and political reform of the 1960s reflected this type of thinking.

As we have seen, the answer to the internal-versus-external question seems to lie somewhere between the two extremes. Our behavior is strongly influenced by the environment, but internal factors are also important and must be taken into consideration. The implication is that while human beings do have a great capacity to change and grow, that capacity is not infinite. People as individuals do have physical and psychological limits.

A few examples might help. In the area of judgment and decision making, we find that human beings are somewhat limited. People are only able to deal with a few dimensions of information at a time. More complex inputs cause confusion and overload. Similarly, there are limits to what we can store and remember. We do not have unlimited memory capacity. Further, research shows that we make a number of systematic errors in processing information. We tend to be too cautious in reevaluating data, we do not use all of the information available, and that which we do use often has less of an impact than it optimally should. While some improvement in judgment and decision making is possible, we will probably never be able to completely overcome these errors and limitations.

Review

An examination of all the issues raised so far reveals two broad views of human behavior. One view holds that behavior is mostly caused by instincts, genetic background, and personality traits that are formed at an early age. According to this view, change is very difficult for the individual, and one's capacity for growth is severely limited. Some social scientists still hold this view today. The opposite is that much of our behavior is learned through our interactions with the environment, that current events are important, and that even though there are some limitations on our capacities, we are capable of great amounts of change. This is the more widely accepted view.

While these issues are far from settled, there is a growing consensus that the environment has a substantial effect on our behavior. The implications for organizations are important. If large areas of human behavior are modifiable, training and organizational design can have a profound impact on the behavior of the members of an organization. Thus, it becomes imperative that we understand the basic processes by which these changes come about.

UNDERSTANDING BEHAVIOR: LEARNING

One thorn of experience is worth a whole wilderness of warnings.
—JAMES RUSSELL LOWELL

Much of our behavior in organizations is learned behavior. We learn a variety of technical and interpersonal skills that help us to function successfully. Frequently, these are skills and behaviors that we did not have before we entered a particular organization (e.g., running a lathe or giving orders to subordinates). Learning implies a basic change in our behavior. We are able to do something we could not do before.

In the next few pages we will attempt to define and describe some of the basic concepts of learning. Many new terms will be introduced, and it may be difficult at first to remember all of them. However, most of the terms and concepts discussed will appear again in other chapters, and you should soon be familiar with them.

One preliminary point is worth mentioning. In an earlier section we emphasized that while each human being is unique, there are common elements to the human experience. Learning is one of these elements. Learning processes are basically similar for most people. *What* we learn may be drastically different due to our different environments, but *how* we learn is pretty much the same. It is a process common to the human condition.

A Definition of Learning

Learning can be defined as a relatively permanent change that occurs in a person as a result of experience, making possible a corresponding change in that person's behavior (Gagné, 1984). Because it occurs in response to experience, this change is distinguished from changes that occur as a function of physiological forces or maturation. Let us take a closer look at several aspects of this definition.

First, learning involves change. It is concerned with the acquisition of new knowledge or skills. Second, it is based on experience. That is, some sort of interaction with the environment is necessary. This may involve repetition or practice, as well as receiving feedback (e.g., from a teacher or trainer) about what is being done well or poorly. Both practice and feedback facilitate the learning process. Finally, in most cases learning results in a fairly permanent change. As we shall see, however, unless we have the opportunity to practice the behavior and to receive periodic feedback, the learning may eventually disappear.

What is Learned

A wide variety of things are learned in organizational settings. First, motor skills often need to be learned. A crane operator must learn a unique set of coordinated arm and leg movements in order to accurately maneuver heavy loads through a construction site, and a surgeon must learn the fine hand and finger movements that are so vital to success in the operating room. Second, technical knowledge also needs to be learned. Knowing how to type (a motor skill) is only part of what is required in order to operate a computer. A general understanding of the overall system and the commands for running specific programs is also necessary. A great deal of technical information must be learned in order to function successfully in many jobs. Imagine, for example, the various types of technical knowledge that must be mastered by electricians, accountants, and airline pilots.

Third, interpersonal skills must be learned. Organizations are made up of people, and the ability to get along with others is essential. Interpersonal skills are especially important for those in supervisory and managerial positions. Katz (1974) notes that the ability to work effectively with other people and to foster cooperation and motivation in them is critical to the success of every manager, from the supervisor on the manufacturing plant floor to the chief executive. Finally, attitudes are also learned in organizations. Employees learn from their peers the "proper" attitude toward management, managers develop distinct attitudes toward unions, and we all learn attitudes toward our immediate supervisors and our work. Attitudes are not something that the organization necessarily *requires* its employees to learn, but they are learned just the same. And, like motor skills, technical information, and interpersonal skills, attitudes can have a significant impact on both the behavior of individuals and the performance of the organization as a whole.

How Learning Occurs in Organizations

All organizations expect new employees to have mastered at least some skills before they are hired. These are the skills one learns in school. In addition, some individuals are hired because of the special technical skills they have acquired (e.g., engineers, physicians, attorneys). But a great deal of learning also occurs within the organization. Some of this learning occurs in the context of formal training programs. Organizations often assess the special technical skills and abilities that are needed by their employees and provide training in these areas whenever this seems feasible. Often they also provide interpersonal training. For example, they might offer seminars for supervisors on how to give performance feedback or how to set performance goals and manage by objectives. Training might even involve teaching cultural values and norms, especially when an understanding of values and norms that differ from the employee's own is important for his or her on-the-job-performance. Consider, for example, the training needs of a multinational corporation that regularly rotates managers through assignments in various foreign countries. The manager's understanding of the customs of the foreign country may have a strong influence upon his or her ability to do business. Organizations can provide training to help their managers learn these customs. As an illustration of how this might be done, look at Figure 2-3. This figure displays two frames from a set of training materials designed to teach Americans the cultural values and customs of Greece (Fiedler, Mitchell, & Triandis, 1971). The trainee reads a large number of these stories (from 150 to 300), answers

FIGURE 2-2
Organizations
sometimes provide
their employees
with specialized
technical training.

2-1

Rob Johnson and his wife had been in Greece for about 4 weeks and were having a wonderful time. Rob was a visiting Fulbright scholar at Athens College and had met a number of Greeks during his first few weeks there. Rob and his wife decided to have a dinner party for all their new Greek friends. They asked about what time the Greeks eat in the evening, and they were told 9:00 P.M. The invitations were made for everyone to come at 9:00 P.M. for cocktails and dinner. Mrs. Johnson figured everyone could have a drink or two and that dinner would be served at 9:45. However, by 9:45 only half of the guests had arrived and the dinner got cold. By 10:30 when everyone had arrived, both Rob and his wife were very upset and angry and the atmosphere was very strained.

How Would You Account for the Tardiness of the Greek Guests?

X **1.** The Greek conception of time is different from the American conception of time.

Go to page 2-3

2. The guests were outgroup members; consequently, they had no desire to be prompt.

Go to page 2-4

3. Such behavior is rare in Greece. Most Greeks are quite prompt.

Go to page 2-5

4. In Greece it is impolite to require all guests to arrive at the same time. The guests resented this requirement and they expressed their resentment by arriving late.

Go to page 2-6

2-3

You selected 1: The Greek conception of time is different from the American conception of time.

Correct: Greeks do not emphasize promptness nearly so much as Americans. For a Greek a social invitation for 9:00 P.M. means "around 9:00" rather than "exactly at 9:00." However, not all Greeks use "Greek time." Many nontraditional and urban Greeks use American criteria. As a result half of those invited may arrive promptly and the other half 1 1/2 hours later. Be prepared for this much variety.

Go to page 3-1

FIGURE 2-3
Two frames from the Greek Assimilator, a programmed instruction text for Americans working in Greece.

questions about each one, and receives feedback on what is correct and why. This type of cultural training has been shown to produce better interpersonal relations between Americans and people from the foreign country studied, better adjustment, and in some cases, better overall performance (Mitchell, Dossett, & Fiedler, 1972).

Although formal training programs are quite common in organizations, they actually represent only a small fraction of the total learning that occurs. Most learning occurs in a much more informal and haphazard manner. Let's take a close look at the two processes involved in informal learning.

Associative Learning

Some of the learning that takes place in organizations, especially the learning of attitudes, takes place by means of what is known as *associative learning* (also called *classical conditioning*). Associative learning occurs whenever a neutral stimulus is systematically paired (associated) with another stimulus that by itself elicits a strong reaction. The stimulus that elicits the strong reaction is called the *unconditioned stimulus*. The strong reaction is referred to as the *unconditioned response*. The neutral stimulus is called the *conditioned stimulus*. After the conditioned stimulus is paired several times with the unconditioned stimulus, the conditioned stimulus will begin to elicit the same sort of response

Are Whizzes Washed Up at 35?

Professional football players expect it: ten or twelve years after college, their reflexes go, they slow down, younger players overtake them. But at the Massachusetts Institute of Technology recently, some 800 representatives from government, industry and academe were told that the same fate befalls, of all people, engineers. Particularly in the fast-moving fields of computer science and electrical engineering, former whizzes who are now middle-aged were described as fighting a losing battle to keep from falling behind intellectually. All too often, M.I.T. Electrical Engineering Professor Louis Smulin told the Oct. 2 symposium, engineers "are washed up by the time they are 35 or 40, and new ones are recruited from the universities." Said C. Gordon Bell, vice president at Digital Equipment Corp.: "The young engineers coming in are sharper than older engineers. Sometimes they blow the older engineers away."

Each year some 10,000, or 5% of the nation's electrical engineers, transfer out of their field, many because they feel useless or technologically obsolescent. Yet by 1985 the U.S. is expected to suffer from a shortage of more than 100,000 engineers. This gap cannot be closed by increasing the output of engineering schools, which are at their production limit. As Ray Stata, president of Analog Devices, told the M.I.T. symposium, "Our only viable strategy for coping is for industry to increase the productivity, retention and competence of those engineers already engaged in the professions."

To this end, the symposium considered a yearlong study by a four-man M.I.T. committee chaired by M.I.T. Professor of Engineering Robert M. Fano. The committee's conclusion: "The problems we are facing cannot be solved simply by incrementally improving and expanding current educational programs. A quantum jump is needed, amounting to a revolution in engineering education." The committee proposed a new alliance between industry and academe under which, on company time and at company expense, engineers would continue their graduate-level education in at least one 15-week course per year. Universities should adopt residency requirements flexible enough so that graduate-level courses could be taught at the workplace. It recommended that as much as 10% of engineers' working time be devoted to continuing education.

At present, joint education projects are sponsored by only a few computer and high-technology firms, including AT&T, Bell Telephone Labs, General Electric, RCA and Wang, and even fewer universities, notably Stanford. The computer and electronics firm Hewlett-Packard in Palo Alto, Calif., encourages its engineers to take six course hours a week on the firm's time. Says President John Young, "Sure, we lose six hours a week, but in exchange our engineers usually manage to get their job done, and the new knowledge they get from the course will inevitably help." Of course, continuing education for engineers is already stressed by the Japanese, who, it seems, cannot learn enough. Sitting in the audience at M.I.T. last week was none other than Koji Kobayashi, chairman of Japan's Nippon Electric Corp. He took notes.

as does the unconditioned stimulus; that is, the previously neutral stimulus becomes *conditioned* to elicit the response.

Let's take an example. Suppose you work in the documents department of a large computer manufacturing firm. Your job is to write some of the technical documentation that accompanies the equipment. Typically, a document goes through several drafts and is read by a number of people to make sure it is accurate and easy to understand. Once a document is finalized, it is distributed to other members of the organization. At that point, as far as you are concerned, the job is finished. However, every document must ultimately be approved by the director of your department, and all too often she sends things back to be rewritten. Sometimes her complaints are justified, but just as frequently the changes she wants seem petty and do not really improve the document's quality. This rewriting is an annoyance. It means that you have to drop what you are doing (the director always wants you to have the revision done by yesterday!) and get back into some complex material that you may not have worked with for quite some time. Furthermore, you are still expected to meet your current deadlines for the work that you have put aside in order to do the rewrite. Thus, the director's request for a rewrite is a stimulus that causes a rather strong negative response in you.

Recently, the director has taken up a new strategy for informing you that a rewrite is necessary. She makes a few margin notes in the document, explains them to her secretary, and has her secretary come down to your office (two floors below) to give you the bad news. The director's secretary is new on the job. You met her when she was first hired, and at the time she seemed nice enough. But you've had no interaction with her except when she comes to your office to explain the director's request for a rewrite. The first time this happened you didn't think much of it. Sure, you were a little bothered by having to do another rewrite, but you didn't give the secretary much thought one way or the other. Over the course of time, however, you begin to see a pattern. The only time the director's secretary is ever on your floor is when she brings down a request for another rewrite. Previously, the director's secretary was a neutral or perhaps even slightly positive stimulus. Now, however, her presence is being systematically paired with those annoying requests for revisions, and after a time you begin to feel a negative reaction every time you see her walk in your direction. The director's secretary (the conditioned stimulus) has been systematically associated with an event (the unconditioned stimulus) that causes a strong negative response in you (the unconditioned response), and as a consequence you developed a distinct disliking for her. This new disliking is called a *conditioned response*.

Thus, negative attitudes toward people, things, and activities can be learned if they are systematically paired with other stimuli that cause unpleasant reactions. Positive attitudes can be learned in essentially the same way, as long as the unconditioned stimulus elicits a positive reaction. For example, we might expect employees to develop positive attitudes toward the payroll clerk who hands them their weekly paycheck.

The problem with associative learning is that it is a difficult process to control in organizations. It is hard to arrange for the systematic pairing of conditioned and unconditioned stimuli. Also, it is a very inefficient method for learning things other than attitudes (e.g., motor and interpersonal skills, and technical information). This does not mean that associative learning does not occur. What it does mean, however, is that it is difficult for organizations to make active use of the associative learning process. This is not a limitation of *instrumental learning,* the second learning process we will consider.

Instrumental Learning

Most learning that takes place in organizations takes place through the process of *instrumental learning* (also called *operant conditioning*). Instrumental learning occurs whenever an individual's behavior is followed by some event that either increases or decreases the probability that the behavior will be repeated. Events that increase the probability that a behavior will be repeated are called *reinforcers*. Events that decrease the probability that a behavior will be repeated are called *punishers*. Again, let's consider an example.

Back in the documents department, you wonder how to get around the rewrite problem. You have more than your share of work to do, and you certainly don't need to be wasting time on unnecessary revisions. You try a number of things, including having more people read the preliminary drafts, but nothing seems to help. The director still asks you to make some sort of revision in at least one out of every three documents you produce. Then something interesting happens. You are way behind on a project and miss an assigned deadline by nearly 3 weeks. Deadlines in the documents department are structured so that everyone in the company who needs to see and/or approve a document has several weeks to look it over before it has to be sent to the printers. This time, however, because you were so late getting it done, the director of the documents department has only 2 days to look it over. You send your final draft up to her office and wait to see what happens. Five days later, you suddenly realize that you haven't seen the director's secretary all week. Apparently the director approved the document without requiring a revision. As it turns out, because of a backlog of work, each of the next three documents you write also miss their assigned deadlines and get to the director's office very late. And none of them are sent back for revision! Maybe you have discovered something. The next project you work on is completed on time, but you decide to test out your hunch. You hold onto the final draft until just 3 days before it needs to go to the printer. Then you send it up to the director's office. Again, there is no request for a revision. Furthermore, no one has said anything to you about having missed the deadlines. You have learned that if you delay getting the document to the director until just before she needs to sign off on it, you are unlikely to get a request for a revision. Said differently, the absence of a request for a rewrite has increased the probability that you will delay the delivery of your final drafts to the director in the future. Delaying the drafts is thus *instrumental* for avoiding rewrite requests.

We should point out that in the examples above we have presented a cognitive orientation to the learning process. Recall that cognitive theorists hold that environmental events affect behavior through their influence on cognitions. If as a consequence of your behavior (e.g., delaying the delivery of a document to the director) something happens that you *like* (e.g., you are not asked to make any revisions), you will be more likely to engage in the same behavior next time because you *expect* the same consequence to occur again. However, a strict behaviorist would take a somewhat different approach. A behaviorist would not refer to cognitive events such as liking or expecting. Instead, he or she would simply say that if the consequences of a behavior increase the probability that that behavior will be repeated in the future, reinforcement has occurred. If they decrease the probability that it will be repeated, punishment has occurred. The behaviorist would make no reference to cognitive events.

While the differences between the cognitive and behaviorist viewpoints are important from a philosophical perspective (and we will discuss this in more detail in Chapter 6 when we talk about employee motivation), they are somewhat less important from a practical standpoint, especially with regard to learning. Thus, although we prefer to use a cognitive framework to describe much of the learning that goes on in organizations, we acknowledge that a strictly behavioral framework could also be used.

Some Important Distinctions

There are a number of distinctions that are important to make with regard to instrumental learning. These include the distinction between learning and performance, between positive and negative reinforcement, between intrinsic and extrinsic reinforcers, between primary and secondary reinforcers, and between generalization, discrimination, and extinction.

Learning versus Performance. One very important distinction is between learning and performance. When we use the term *learning,* we usually mean the acquisition of a *capacity* to perform a behavior. Whether or not that behavior is actually performed, however, is quite another thing. For example, when we say that a truck driver has learned how to load his or her vehicle effectively, we mean either that the driver knows the proper strategies for making the most effective use of the space on the truck, or knows what needs to be done in order to get the truck loaded quickly. However, it seems unlikely that the driver will actually perform these behaviors unless it is in his or her best interest to do so. Similarly, an insurance agent may have learned that the best way to retain existing accounts is to provide prompt service. Yet, that agent may not be inclined to give prompt service if his or her company offers much larger commissions for getting new customers than for retaining old ones. The point is, learning and performance are two very different things. Performance implies not only that the proper behavior has been learned, but also that the individual is sufficiently motivated to engage in that behavior.

In this connection it should be noted that reinforcement and punishment are relevant to *both* learning and performance. However, the methods of reinforcement and punishment that are most effective for learning are not necessarily the same as those that are most effective for performance. Consider, for example, the effectiveness of various *schedules of reinforcement.* A schedule of reinforcement specifies the timing and administration of rewards. There are many possible schedules. A reward might be given every time the desired behavior occurs (e.g., every time an employee comes to work on time, he or she get a $2 bonus). Alternatively, the reward might be given every other time the behavior occurs, or every tenth time it occurs. Or, the reward might by given only after a set period of time has elapsed (e.g., much the way weekly paychecks are administered). In general, the reinforcement schedules that are most effective for helping people learn new behaviors are those that provide frequent reinforcement and do so immediately after the desired behavior has occurred. Once the behavior is learned, however, such a schedule may or may not be optimal for motivating people to high levels of performance. For example, in one study it was shown that employees react much more positively to a less frequent (and more variable) schedule of monetary reinforcement than to one that reinforces them every single time the desired behavior occurs (Sarri & Latham, 1982). We discuss the research evidence concerning sched-

ules of reinforcement, motivation, and performance in much greater detail in
Chapter 6.

27

Chapter 2:
Understanding
People

Positive versus Negative Reinforcement. Recall that a *reinforcer* is defined as
any event that increases the probability that a target behavior will be repeated.
Reinforcement can occur in two different ways. One way is to present the
individual with an attractive or desirable stimulus. This is called *positive
reinforcement.* Giving an employee a bonus for high performance is a good
example of positive reinforcement. The other way reinforcement can occur is
to remove a noxious or undesirable stimulus from the environment. This is
called *negative reinforcement.* In our initial example of instrumental learning in
the documents department, the elimination of the annoying requests for
revisions was an example of negative reinforcement. Note that negative
reinforcement still *increases* the probability that a behavior will be repeated.
Thus, negative reinforcement should not be confused with punishment, which
is an event that *decreases* the probability that a behavior will be repeated.

negative =
removal of
a painful
stimulus

The distinction between positive reinforcement, negative reinforcement,
and punishment is depicted in Figure 2-4. As can be seen, both reinforcement
and punishment can occur in two ways. Reinforcement can occur either by
presenting a desirable stimulus (positive reinforcement) or by removing an
undesirable stimulus (negative reinforcement). Punishment can occur either
by presenting an undesirable stimulus (e.g., giving a reprimand), or by removing a desirable stimulus (e.g., docking pay). Although punishment can occur
in two different ways, we usually *do not* use the terms *positive* and *negative
punishment.*

Research comparing the effectiveness of positive reinforcement, negative
reinforcement, and punishment has shown that punishment is the least effective method for promoting both learning and performance (Sims, 1980). The

	Desirable Stimulus	Undesirable Stimulus
Present Stimulus	Positive reinforcement	Punishment
Remove Stimulus	Punishment	Negative reinforcement

FIGURE 2-4
Both positive and
negative reinforce-
ment increase the
likelihood that a
behavior will be
repeated. Punish-
ment decreases
the likelihood that
a behavior will be
repeated.

reason is that, by itself, punishment does not necessarily provide a clear idea about what behaviors are needed in order to do something correctly. Punishment indicates only what the incorrect behavior is. Thus, if punishment is to be effective at all as a method of promoting learning, it must be accompanied by a clear explanation of what behavior is *correct*. Further, if punishment is employed, it should be (1) delivered immediately after an incorrect or undesirable behavior occurs, (2) delivered after every single occurrence of the incorrect or undesirable behavior, and (3) used in conjunction with the positive reinforcement of correct or desirable behaviors (Arvey & Ivancevich, 1980).

Intrinsic versus Extrinsic Reinforcers.   Another distinction that is commonly made is between intrinsic and extrinsic reinforcers. *Intrinsic reinforcers* are reinforcers that come as an inherent consequence of doing a task. Responsibility and achievement are often described as intrinsic reinforcers. *Extrinsic reinforcers,* by contrast, are reinforcers that are not an inherent consequence of a task. Pay, promotions, and fringe benefits are examples of extrinsic reinforcers.

Consider the possible intrinsic and extrinsic reinforcements that a builder might get for completing the construction of a house. The completion of the house will result in a number of extrinsic consequences that do not naturally flow from the activity of building. Many of these will be financial in nature. Financial rewards are clearly extrinsic to the act of building a house, since it is easy to conceive of someone building a house without being paid. However, there are also rewards that come just as a function of completing the project, such as a sense of accomplishment and pride in a job well done. These are considered to be intrinsic rewards because they are a natural consequence of the building behavior itself. Much of the research on organizational reward systems, as we shall see, divides rewards into these extrinsic and intrinsic categories (e.g., financial bonuses versus interesting assignments).

Primary versus Secondary Reinforcers. Another distinction that is commonly made is between primary and secondary reinforcers. *Primary reinforcers* are those rewards that are innately satisfying to the individual because they reduce basic physiological drives. Food for a hungry individual is a good example. *Secondary reinforcers* are consequences that are satisfying because they were initially paired with primary reinforcers. They are learned rewards (as opposed to being innately satisfying). Most rewards in organizational settings are secondary reinforcers. An example of secondary reinforcement would be a hungry child associating food with the warm cuddling it receives from its mother. Later, the warm cuddling becomes satisfying in itself. (This is another example of associative learning.) Rewards such as affection and approval may later become important secondary reinforcers in an organizational setting.

Generalization, Discrimination, and Extinction. The final set of distinctions we wish to make concerns three consequences for learning of systematic reinforcement and nonreinforcement in a variety of situations. Consider the following scenario. In order to put yourself through school, you take a job as the night manager in a small local grocery store. You are responsible for the operation of the store from 6 P.M. (when the store manager goes home) until closing time. Because you want to do well and please the store manager, you resolve to make every effort to ensure that when you leave for the night the store is in order and ready for business the next day. One thing you decide to do is organize for the manager a summary of each evening's transactions. This involves tallying the cash register receipts, sorting the checks to be deposited, and doing a cash inventory. The manager responds to your initiative by praising your behavior and expressing his appreciation for the effort you have expended. Thus, you learn that initiative is rewarded in this job.

You then decide to see what you can do about the general appearance of the store. You spend an hour or two each night straightening up the merchandise on the shelves. You also make sure that someone polices the parking lot and sidewalks outside the store so that there is no litter blowing about. Again, your efforts are met with praise by the manager. Thus, you have learned that your initiative is valued not only with respect to the nightly paperwork, but also with respect to other aspects of the store's operation. The process of learning that a type of behavior applies in more than one situation is known as *generalization.*

Your next move is to attack the mess in the stockroom. The problem is that there is not enough floor space in the stockroom for the volume of backstock the store needs to carry. You judge that this problem can be solved by installing some shelving, so that much of the space high up on the walls can be used. You place an order with a local company to put the shelving in, and you leave a note for the manager explaining what you have done. This time your initiative is not well received. Instead of praising you, the manager chews you out for taking an action involving a capital expenditure without consulting him. Thus, you have learned that your initiative is rewarded, but only in some situations. This process is referred to as *discrimination learning,* and it occurs whenever a behavior is rewarded in some situations but not in others. The individual learns to discriminate between those situations in which the behavior is rewarded and those in which it is not rewarded. Where it is rewarded, the behavior is more likely to be repeated. Where it is not rewarded, it is less likely to be repeated.

After a period of time, the store manager is promoted and moved to another location, and a new person is brought in to fill the manager's job. The new manager never seems to say anything (one way or the other) about the initiative you take, even though you have made several changes since she arrived. Sooner or later, this lack of reinforcement may cause you to stop showing initiative. This process is referred to as *extinction.* The nonreinforcement of behavior will decrease the probability that that behavior will be repeated again, and continued nonreinforcement may ultimately cause the behavior to disappear (extinguish) altogether.

In summary, we can change people's behavior most efficiently through the instrumental learning process. This requires that we know how to administer various types of rewards, and that we understand the consequences of these rewards. Since the organization has at its disposal a wide variety of rewards, it can have a powerful impact on the instrumental learning that takes place.

Learning from Role Models

There is one final aspect of the learning process that is very important for understanding how we come to know what behaviors are expected of us. When we join an organization, we are usually given a title of some sort, such as professor, secretary, research analyst, or administrative assistant. This title indicates the position we hold in the organization. Each position carries with it a number of duties, responsibilities, rules, regulations, and expected behavior patterns. The set of expected behaviors for a given position is called a *role*. The term *role* is used to reflect the fact that all individuals, regardless of their unique personal characteristics, are supposed to behave in a certain way if they occupy this specific position. A role, therefore, is impersonal.

One way to think about role expectations is that they specify the reinforcement contingencies that will apply for the person occupying that role; that is, they indicate what behaviors will be rewarded and what behaviors will not be rewarded. Sometimes these role expectations are very clear and can be easily communicated either verbally or in writing (e.g., a new security guard might be told, "You are to make sure that no one enters the building after 5 P.M. unless they have the proper written authorization."). Obviously, the clearer

FIGURE 2-5

Observing a model is often a very effective way to learn a new role.

the role the better. If expectations are explicit and agreed upon, people can see them, read them, verbalize them, and practice them. However, in many cases role requirements are not clearly specified. To the extent that this occurs, an individual will have to learn what behaviors are most appropriate for the role either by trial and error (i.e., via instrumental learning) or by observing the behavior of other individuals who occupy similar positions. These other individuals serve as *role models*. By observing these role models, we learn the prevailing reinforcement contingencies; we see what gets rewarded and what does not.

Several factors increase the effectiveness of the modeling process. First, the role model should be readily observable and attractive. It helps if the learner *wants* to be like the model. It is also important that the learner have the *capacity* to do what the model does, and that opportunities exist to try out what is learned from observing the model. Practice facilitates learning.

Finally, a crucial aspect of the modeling process is that the learner must receive some sort of feedback about the correctness or appropriateness of the behaviors learned from the role model. This feedback can be either direct or indirect. *Direct feedback* refers to the reinforcement or punishment that the *learner* receives when he or she tries out the behavior learned from the role model. For example, if you observe a person with more experience on the job engaging in a particular behavior (e.g., allowing someone who is recognized as a company employee to enter the building after 5 P.M., even though that individual does not have the required written authorization), you may try doing the same thing. If you are rewarded for that behavior (e.g., by the gratitude expressed by the employee you admit), the behavior is more likely to be repeated in the future. However, if you are punished (e.g., a supervisor observes you improperly admitting the employee and gives you a reprimand), the behavior is not likely to be repeated.

Indirect feedback, by contrast, refers to the rewards and punishments the *role model* is observed to receive as a consequence of engaging in the behavior. If the learner observes a role model being rewarded for a particular behavior, the learner is more likely to try out that same behavior. If, on the other hand, the learner observes the role model being punished for that behavior, the learner is less likely to try it out. Thus, we learn not only by observing the consequences of our own behavior, but also by observing the consequences of other people's behavior. The latter process is referred to as *vicarious learning* (Bandura, 1977).

Summary

The purpose of this chapter was to provide a general introduction to the causes of human behavior. If we know what causes behavior, we will be better able to realize both our limitations and our capabilities. We should have a better idea of what is changeable and how it is changeable. Let us review some of the most important points:

1. The human race is unique. While our genetic makeup may broadly influence our behavior, the most important contribution comes from what we learn.
2. The external environment is a very important determinant of behavior.

Many social scientists view personality traits as being less important than the environment, although this question is far from settled.

3. The individual has a great capacity for change. With increasing age it does become more difficult to change people's behavior, but this does not mean that older people are incapable of change. It often means that we cannot control many of the environmental aspects that would produce this change.

4. The major mechanism through which change occurs is learning. Learning involves the fairly permanent acquisition of new knowledge or skills.

5. Essential to the learning process are the consequences of behavior. Behavior that is followed by a reinforcer is more likely to be repeated in the future. Behavior that is followed by a punisher is less likely to be repeated.

6. The organization has control over a large number of reinforcers and punishers. Systems of financial reward, promotions, and informal praise by supervisors can all strongly affect the behavior of organization members.

7. Finally, learning can also occur by observing the behavior of others. The organization can facilitate learning by providing clear behavioral expectations and exemplary role models.

IMPLICATIONS FOR RESEARCH

In this chapter, we have argued that people in organizations are strongly influenced by their environment. This is especially true with regard to learning, and as we will see in later chapters, it is also true with regard to motivation and performance. However, we also noted that internal characteristics of people, especially their personality traits, attitudes, beliefs, and cognitions, also influence their behavior. This leads to the conclusion that in studying the behavior of people in organizations, we should examine characteristics of *both* the organizational environment and the people who make up the organization. Further, instead of focusing on these two types of factors separately, we should consider how environmental factors and the internal characteristics of people *interact* to influence their behavior (Schneider, 1983; Terborg, 1981).

At an operational level, therefore, it is important that we strive to develop high-quality measures of both relevant environmental characteristics and relevant characteristics of organizational members. Armed with these, we can begin to ask a number of research questions whose answers are likely to significantly advance our understanding of organizational behavior. Two examples of the types of questions that might be asked are suggested here.

One type of question that seems particularly interesting concerns the dynamic interplay between the person and the environment. The picture we have painted in this chapter is one of the environment influencing the individual. Yet there can be little doubt that individuals also influence and shape their environment. To take but one example, there is a good deal of evidence that our performance at work is strongly influenced both by the goals that have been set for us and by our acceptance of these goals (see Chapter 6). Yet the goals that are set are partly determined by our performance. If we perform very well, the goals are likely to be raised, and if we perform very poorly, they are likely to be lowered. The raised (or lowered) goals will influence our subsequent performance, which will in turn affect the level at which future goals are set, and so on. The point is that there is a dynamic interplay between environmental factors, person factors, and behavior that unfolds over time. At present we know very little about these dynamics. If we are to understand them better, a great deal more research will be needed.

A second type of research question that one might wish to pursue concerns people's perceptions of various organizational events. As we noted earlier in this chapter, our perceptions of the environment (e.g., of the prevailing reinforcement contingencies) strongly influence our behavior. We are likely to behave in accordance with our perceptions of a situation whether or not those perceptions are actually correct. Of course, it often happens that different people perceive the same situation in very different ways. If this is the case, however, can all of the different views be correct? And if they are not all correct, what are the environmental factors and internal characteristics that led to the incorrect views? Furthermore, what impact do these incorrect views have on behavior? Again, we currently have only a very general understanding of these phenomena (see Chapter 4). A great deal more research needs to be done if we want to understand them better.

IMPLICATIONS FOR PRACTICE

There are some important conclusions of practical value that should be strongly emphasized. The first point is that people are *changeable*. While increasing age may slightly decrease the ease with which change is brought about, it by no means should be seen as a serious limitation. We are always capable of learning new behavior.

The second point is that the *external environment makes an important contribution to what we learn and how we behave.* Most learning occurs as a function of the relationship between behaviors and their consequences. Thus, an organization can have a very powerful impact on the behavior of its participants. What is required is an understanding of what behaviors are desired and the type of consequences or social conditions that will increase the frequency of that behavior.

An example might help. Suppose you have an employee who continually fails to meet deadlines. The traditional view is to refer to internal states as the cause of that individual's behavior: "This employee must be either ornery or lazy." What we are suggesting is that you try out other interpretations. Look at the environment surrounding the individual. See if there are situational explanations for the person's behavior. Perhaps the employee fails to meet deadlines because of a work overload. Perhaps the task is too ambiguous. Perhaps the person's immediate boss also fails to meet deadlines. At issue here is our understanding of the ways in which individual employees are influenced by their environment. Many managers are not aware of the kinds of problems that may hinder an employee's effectiveness. This is especially true the more they are physically removed from actually viewing the employee at work.

If, in fact, you discover various situational explanations for the behavior, you can do something other than firing or punishing the person. Asking an employee to leave the organization is very expensive and time-consuming. A new person must be interviewed, selected, and trained, and the costs of these activities can range from about $2,000 for a retail clerk to about $70,000 for an account executive with a brokerage firm. Also, and this is important, if the cause of the poor performance was in fact situational, the new employee will soon have the same problem.

Since the organization has a large amount of control over environmental contingencies, you may be able to change the situation in such a way that the desired behaviors can be learned. Training can be used, tasks changed, and rewards administered. What was originally a problem with people becomes an organizational puzzle—a problem that may be solved through the learning process.

An article in *Industry Week* summarized this position well by stating "People don't cause problems for organizations. *Organizations* cause problems for people that get in the way of the organization's objectives. Until we realize this and change our focus from what's wrong with people to what's wrong with the organization, organizations won't be as effective as they can and must be and executives and managers won't be fully successful" (Ozley, 1979).

Discussion Questions

1. Is behavior caused by our environment or by internal mechanisms such as instincts, personality traits, and cognitions? What are the implications of your answer for social policy and organizational design?
2. Describe the learning process. What are the major elements involved?
3. What are the ways we learn in an organization? Are there ways to facilitate this process?

CASE: LEARNING ABOUT BOOZE

Through much of his college career and graduate school, Alan Daily was known as a conscientious and personable young man. He worked hard to get his master's degree in urban planning. Upon graduation he took a job with the Department of Housing and Urban Development as a technical analyst. He was excited about the job and looked forward to being involved with the policy issues focusing on urban housing.

Because of his rather easy social manner, Alan fit in on the job immediately. He made friends with everyone and was soon considered to be "one of the group." Most of his four or five professional peers had similar training and similar interests, so Alan enjoyed his interactions with them immensely. One of the times he liked best was the lunch break. Almost everyone went outside to one of the nearby restaurants to eat, and it was a good time to exchange ideas. Alan had been used to bringing a bag lunch in graduate school or eating at the university cafeteria, so eating out every day was a real treat.

Alan noticed that almost everyone had an alcoholic drink before lunch, sometimes two. At first he declined to have a drink, but eventually he decided to join in. He had had drinks before—plenty when he was in college—but drinking at lunch was new. However, he soon found that the drink seemed to make the lunch hour just a little bit more pleasant, and it didn't seem to disturb his effectiveness on the job. In fact, it seemed to relax him a little.

Over the next few years the newness of the job began to wear off. Alan was less excited about what he did—much of the job turned out to be paper pushing, and he felt that most decisions were being made based on political issues rather than technical knowledge. He began to look forward more and more to lunch and his two drinks beforehand. He also had a drink—sometimes two—before dinner. When he came home, he wanted to forget about the job, and alcohol seemed to help.

Before long, Alan knew he had a problem. He was drinking too much. He was ineffective most of the afternoon, and he found himself coming in late and then leaving early for lunch ("I'll go get a table."). He decided to seek out professional help.

One group in town was well known for its work with people with a drinking problem, so he signed up for a set of sessions designed to stop someone from drinking. At the first session, Alan was placed in a room that was very similar to a restaurant or tavern. There was a bar with other people, the lights were low, and there were plenty of tables and chairs. Alan was asked to order a drink and he did—a dry double martini on the rocks with lots of olives. The drink had a slightly funny taste, and after he finished it he felt violently ill. He ran to the nearest bathroom and threw up. Once again he was told to have a drink; again he threw up, and he was allowed to go home.

The sessions continued this way, and Alan soon found that the thought of a drink was very aversive. Every time he thought of alcohol he thought about being sick. His discussions with the medical director of the program confirmed his beliefs about what was happening—they were drugging his drinks to make him sick. He was told that in some cases of early alcohol dependency this sort of treatment could be effective. Alan was convinced. Just the thought of a bar and a drink made him ill. He started bringing his lunch to work and, although he missed the lively discussions at lunchtime, he felt he had learned a valuable lesson about himself.

Questions about the Case

1. What was the valuable lesson that Alan learned?
2. Would Alan have developed a drinking problem if he had been on some other type of job?
3. What was the cause of Alan's drinking problem? Was it Alan's personality or was it the job? Or was it his friends?
4. What was the process by which Alan gave up alcohol?
5. Do you think he will stay off the booze?

References

Arvey, R. D., & Ivancevich, J. M. (1980). Punishment in organizations: A review, propositions, and research suggestions. *Academy of Management Review, 5,* 123–132.

Bandura, A. (1977). *Social learning theory.* Englewoodd Cliffs, NJ: Prentice-Hall.

Barash, D. (1979). *The whisperings within: Evolution and the origins of human nature.* New York: Harper & Row.

Campbell, D. T. (1975). On the conflicts between biological and social evolution and between psychology and moral tradition. *American Psychologist, 30,* 1103–1126.

Darwin, C. A. (1859). *The origin of species.* London: J. Murray.

Darwin, C. A. (1871). *The descent of man.* London: J. Murray.

Epstein, S., & O'Brien, E. J. (1985). The person–situation debate in historical and current perspective. *Psychological Bulletin, 98,* 513–537.

Fiedler, F. E., Mitchell, T. R., & Triandis, H. C. (1971). The culture assimilator: An approach to cross-cultural training. *Journal of Applied Psychology, 55,* 95–103.

Funder, D. C., & Ozer, D. J. (1983). Behavior as a function of the situation. *Journal of Personality and Social Psychology, 44,* 107–112.

Gagné, R. M. (1984). Learning outcomes and their effects. *American Psychologist, 39,* 377–385.

Gardner, B. T., & Gardner, R. A. (1975). Evidence for sentence constituents in the early utterances of child and chimpanzee. *Journal of Experimental Psychology: General, 104,* 244–267.

Katz, R. L. (1974). Skills of an effective administrator. *Harvard Business Review, 52(5),* 90–102.

McDougall, W. (1908). *Social psychology.* New York: Putnam.

Mischel, W. (1968). *Personality and assessment.* New York: Wiley.

Mitchell, T. R., Dossett, D. L., & Fiedler, F. E. (1972). Cultural training: Validation evidence for the culture assimilator. *International Journal of Psychology, 7,* 97–104.

Ozley, L. M. (1979, August 20). Falling prey to a management fallacy. *Industry Week,* p. 59.

Piaget, J. (1970). Piaget's theory. In P. H. Mussen (Ed.), *Carmichael's manual of child psychology* (3rd ed.). New York: Wiley.

Sarason, I. G., Smith, R. E., & Diener, E. (1975). Personality research: Components of variance attributed to the person and the situation. *Journal of Personality and Social Psychology, 32,* 199–204.

Sarri, L. M., & Latham, G. P. (1982). Employee reaction to continuous and variable ratio reinforcement schedules involving a monetary incentive. *Journal of Applied Psychology, 67,* 506–508.

Schneider, B. (1983). Interactional psychology and organizational behavior. In L. L. Cummings & B. M. Staw (Eds.), *Research in organizational behavior,* (Vol. 5, pp. 1–31). Greenwich, CT: JAI Press.

Sims, H. P., Jr. (1980). Further thoughts on punishment in organizations. *Academy of Management Review, 5,* 133–138.

Terborg, J. R. (1981). Interactional psychology and research on human behavior in organizations. *Academy of Management Review, 6,* 569–576.

Watson, J. B. (1924). *Behaviorism.* New York: Norton.

Wilson, E. O. (1975). *Sociobiology: The new synthesis.* Cambridge, MA: Harvard University Press.

Wilson, E. O. (1978). *On human nature.* Cambridge, MA: Harvard University Press.

Woddruffe, C. (1984). The consistency of presented personality: Additional evidence from aggregation. *Journal of Personality, 52,* 307–317.

Chapter 3

Understanding Organizations

Key Terms to Watch for:

Organization Theory
Organization Structure
Horizontal Differentiation
Vertical Differentiation
Matrix Organizations
Scalar Chain of Command
Span of Control
Formalization
Bureaucracy
Centralization
Work Technology
Scientific Management
Industrial Engineering
Hawthorne Effect
Human Relations Movement
Autonomous Work Groups
Systems Theory
Congruence

Chapter Outline

*A formal organization is a system of coordinated activities
of a group of people working cooperatively toward a common goal
under authority and leadership.*
—W. G. SCOTT

I n the last chapter we examined a number of general assumptions about the nature of human beings. One conclusion we drew was that people are strongly influenced by their environment. The role of the environment in shaping people's behavior is at least as great as, if not greater than, the role of such internal factors as personality traits, attitudes, and cognitions. The purpose of the present chapter is to take a closer look at the environment. Specifically, we will examine the nature of organizations. Because organizations provide the context in which virtually all work behavior occurs, they can be viewed as a major element of the environment affecting work behavior. If we are to fully understand the factors influencing behavior at work, we must know something about the organizational environment in which that behavior occurs.

We will examine the nature of organizations from several different perspectives. Each of these perspectives focuses on a different facet of the organizational environment. These various facets include the formal structural features of organizations, their social characteristics, and the characteristics of the tasks people are asked to perform. After considering each of these facets individually, we will tie them together by presenting an open-systems view of organizations.

Before proceeding, it may be helpful to note that this chapter is not meant as a comprehensive overview of *organization theory*. Organization theory is the sister discipline of organizational behavior. It is distinguished from organizational behavior primarily by its focus. Whereas organizational behavior focuses on the behavior of individuals and small groups *within* organizations, organization theory focuses on the organization *as a whole*. As such, it is concerned not only with how the organization influences its members, but also with how the organization itself is influenced by factors operating in its own larger environment (e.g., market characteristics, available production technologies, regulatory constraints). These latter issues are quite interesting, but they go well beyond the scope of this book. Our intention in the present chapter, therefore, is to limit our discussion to those aspects of organizations and organization theory that are most relevant for understanding the behavior of people in organizations. Let us begin by considering the overall function of organizations.

WHY ORGANIZATIONS EXIST

Our society is an organizational society. The activities that surround our birth, education, work, leisure, spiritual growth, and death are all heavily regulated or influenced by an organizational environment. Probably the first question that should be addressed, therefore, is, why are organizations so pervasive? More fundamentally, why do organizations exist at all? How do they come to be? And why have they grown in size and number? The answers to most of these questions can be expressed in simple economic and rational terms. In most cases, people join forces and organize themselves in order to gain some sort of physical, personal, or economic advantage. Historically, the reasons for organizing have varied widely, from military might and safety, to affiliation, trade, and agricultural bounty. Regardless of the specific reasons, however, the underlying rationale is always the same. People organize because they believe that it is the most efficient way to reach their goals. Thus, organizations exist and are designed to facilitate goal attainment. Let us take a closer look at several implications of this statement.

Organization

When we use the term *organization,* a number of images come to mind. We often think of rules and regulations, standard operating procedures, people occupying positions of power and authority over others, multiple departments, and specialized jobs. At some level, all of these images ring true. One has only to walk into an organization to see these images spring to life.

Yet, there is a certain essence of organizations that all these images miss: Organizations are systems of coordinated *behavior.* Indeed, it can be argued that organizations *are* behavior. Rules, regulations, standard operating procedures, and all the other things we often think about when we use the term *organization* are simply mechanisms for coordinating behavior. It is the behavior itself that is the essence of an organization. Without people behaving, there would be no organization. Thus, rather than describing an organization as a *thing,* we might more accurately describe it as a *process.* An organization is the process of people behaving in a coordinated fashion (cf. Weick, 1979). Accordingly, when we speak of the organizational environment, we are in effect referring to the aggregate coordinated behavior of all the members of the organization.

It is also important to recognize that in the process of organizing, people voluntarily relinquish some of their individual flexibility and freedom. They do this in order to attain personal and organizational goals. To be organized is to be coordinated, and coordination is accomplished by allowing our behavior to be directed by others. If people do not allow their behavior to be directed by others and instead behave independently, doing whatever they feel like doing at the moment, coordination is impossible and the organization will cease to exist. Thus, the term *organization* implies a trade-off between personal independence and goal achievement. This trade-off is made by every member of the organization, even those who occupy the very top positions (e.g., Mizruchi, 1983).

Goals and Goal Setting

We stated previously that organizations exist to facilitate goal attainment. Actually, organizations facilitate the attainment of many goals. Some of these are the official goals of the organization: the broad, formal, publicly stated objectives that the organization seeks to achieve (e.g., designing scientific equipment for industry and education; offering inexpensive overnight package delivery services nationwide; providing shareholders with the highest possible return on investment). In addition, organizations serve to facilitate the attainment of many of the personal goals of their members (cf. Cummings, 1983; Schmidt & Kipnis, 1984). We all join organizations and continue to participate in them for a variety of reasons. These usually go well beyond wanting to achieve the formal goals of the organization. We may decide to join a particular organization because it allows us to meet certain personal financial goals (e.g., earn a high salary), because it satisfies our social needs (e.g., provides a lot of friendly interaction with other people), or because it offers us the opportunity to exercise skills that we could not exercise otherwise (e.g., where but in a hospital can an eye surgeon practice cornea implants?). From a behavioral standpoint, these personal goals are likely to be at least as important as the formal goals of the organization. Thus, organizations exist not only because they provide an effective way to achieve formal, organization-level goals, but also because they meet personal goals. If an organization were suddenly unable to meet the personal goals of its members, it would quickly lose those members; if it were unable to replace them, it would ultimately go out of existence.

In additon to motivating people to join and remain in organizations, goals also serve at least two other functions. First, as we discuss in more detail in Chapter 6, goals serve to guide behavior and stimulate effort on the job. Second, they serve as a standard of evaluation. Organizations are often judged in terms of the extent to which goals have been attained (cf. Gaertner & Ramnarayan, 1983). When goals are not attained, the overall effectiveness of the organization comes into question. In a similar fashion, the performance of individuals can be evaluated against goals (Drucker, 1954). Meeting or exceeding a goal is considered good performance, while failing to meet a goal is considered poor performance. Thus, goals cause people to join organizations and continue participating in them, they serve as a source of work motivation, and they provide a standard for assessing performance.

Management

Management involves the coordination of human and material resources toward the accomplishment of formal organizational goals. In every organization people perform a wide variety of jobs, and they need different physical and informational resources at different times to do these jobs. The responsibility for coordinating, regulating, and integrating all these activities so that overall goals are accomplished efficiently and on time falls largely to individuals called *managers*.

Let us look, for example, at the job of a manager of a freight-shipping company. In the process of moving freight from one place to another there are numerous operations. Packages must be taken in, some may need to be repacked, and they all must be shipped. Time schedules have to be established, and clerical help is needed to keep the records straight. Truck drivers are needed, as well as a maintenance staff to take care of the trucks. Phone operators, receptionists, filing clerks, and numerous other types of jobs need to be filled. Somehow, the manager has to keep track of all these operations and know what is being done, when, and by whom.

It should be obvious that in order to perform this job well, the manager must know the technical aspects of the work to be done. It is equally essential, however, that he or she also understand human behavior. Coordination is attained through people, and a firm knowledge of what motivates people's behavior in organizations is required. These two kinds of knowledge, technical and behavioral, are equally important to the success of both the individual manager and the organization as a whole.

Some Problems Facing Managers

Not so long ago most organizations were small. They involved simple divisions of labor, relatively few specializations, and lines of authority that were very clear. Resources and markets were close at hand, and methods of production were uncomplicated by today's standards. But times have changed. During the last 150 years organizations have become increasingly large and complex and have had to accommodate to scientific and technological advances that seem to come at an ever-accelerating rate. To be sure, these changes have had their benefits. But they have also caused a great many problems. Of particular interest here are the problems they have caused with regard to the management of people's behavior (cf. Scott & Hart, 1979; Scott, Mitchell, & Birnbaum, 1981). Let us consider just a few.

Complexity. Organizations have become more and more complex. With the development of different disciplines and areas of expertise (e.g., production, marketing, and research and development), we find increasing division of labor and specialization. We have more complicated units and problems. We have lots of different kinds of people doing many different kinds of jobs.

The heterogeneity caused by complexity puts stress on the two factors that hold organizations together: goals and management. With increased complexity, organizational participants develop very different orientations. As a consequence, the "purpose" or goal of the organization becomes more difficult to define. For example, the financial specialists in a large national hospital administration company may see the primary goal of their hospitals as maximizing profits. The medical staff in these hospitals, on the other hand, may be relatively unconcerned about profits and may instead view the humanitarian goal of providing health care services to the sick and dying as the primary objective. The result of these differing orientations and views is that complex organizations are frequently faced with internal conflict. These disagreements can cause significant problems in terms of decisions about how a particular organization should proceed. Without agreement about goals, it is hard to make decisions about the proper means to attain the goals.

Complexity also causes difficulty for management. Coordination and integration are much more difficult. Central to this problem is the issue of control and conformity. With different types of people holding different values and goals, it becomes increasingly difficult to encourage joint, agreed-upon action. Thus, in the hospital example above, the medical staff may persist in routinely ordering expensive diagnostic tests that the central administration has asked them to eliminate unless absolutely necessary. They may do this not out of spite or ignorance, but because they do not agree on the primacy of the administration's profit maximization goals. The point is that management is constantly being required to increase efficiency, and at the same time the task is becoming increasingly difficult to accomplish because of conflicting goals caused by organizational complexity.

Size. Another issue is simply the size of today's organizations. One hundred years ago organizations were much smaller. The average college enrolled fewer than 100 students and had ten faculty members, there were relatively few corporations with $5 million in annual sales, the total revenue of the federal government was less than the sales of *any* of the Fortune 500 companies in 1986, and there were few cities with populations exceeding the number of

FIGURE 3-1
The sheer size of
many organizations
has vastly
increased. Some
large universities
now graduate
almost 10,000
students a year.

employees currently working for GM, AT&T, or IBM (Leavitt, Dill, & Eyring, 1973).

With this increase in size have come problems. People no longer know what is being done in other parts of the company. They have less identification with the organization and its goal. And they do not know most of the people with whom they work. All of these factors make it much more difficult for the organization to motivate employees and to coordinate their ongoing activities.

Science and Technology. A final problem has to do with the fact that science and technology are playing an ever-increasing role in organizations. It used to be that the impact of science and technology was felt primarily on the technical side of organizations, especially in research and development laboratories and in production and manufacturing plants. Now, however, science and technology affect every conceivable aspect of organizational life. The flood of desk-top computers that appear even in the offices of senior management are but one example. Another is the use of behavioral science technology in employee selection, training, and performance evaluation. In some cases the technology is relatively easy to implement and use. But in many other cases, skilled professionals are needed to design and manage the technology. The need to employ people with such expertise further increases the complexity and diversity of the organization.

Beyond the dual question of complexity and diversity is the issue of change itself. New technologies imply new ways of doing things and new ways of thinking about the nature of one's work. While such changes may ultimately be beneficial for both the individual employee and the organization as a whole, people are frequently reluctant to give up their old habits and methods of work. Changing to new procedures and technologies can be threatening, especially if one does not fully understand the implications of the new technology for one's personal performance on the job. Thus, people often resist change, and sometimes even attempt to sabotage the new procedure or technology in an attempt to have it removed. Resistance to change thus represents another problem for managers who are trying to coordinate people's behavior and move the organization toward optimal efficiency.

In summary, modern organizations are faced with a number of problems, many of which have to do with their size, complexity, and the advance of technology. If organizations are to be run efficiently, managers must learn how to cope with these problems. Much of the content of this book is directed toward this issue.

STRUCTURAL CHARACTERISTICS OF ORGANIZATIONS

We turn now to consider the first of three major facets of the organizational environment—the formal structure of the organization. Mintzberg (1979) defines *organizational structure* as the sum total of the ways in which an organization divides its labor into distinct tasks and then achieves coordination among those tasks. The fact that one set of courses is taught in the business school and another (perhaps overlapping) set is taught in the psychology department is a formal structural feature of a university. That the business school and the psychology department each have their own separate budgets is another structural feature. So is the existence of a dean or vice president who oversees the teaching and research activity in both of these units. Other important structural features are the university's systems of pay, promotion, tenure, performance evaluation, and student admission. All these are aspects of the formal structure of the university organization. No two universities are likely to have exactly the same structure, but all will have *some* sort of structure. This is true of all organizations.

Elements of Structure

Let us examine several specific features of organizational structure. A great deal of research has been done on each of these features, and each has been shown to be related (sometimes in very complex ways) to organizational performance. Our purpose is not to discuss this research in any great detail. Rather, we simply wish to describe the various structural dimensions and suggest how they might influence the behavior of organizational members. A more thorough treatment of the research can be found in many excellent textbooks devoted exclusively to organization theory (see also Berger & Cummings, 1979; Porter & Lawler, 1965).

Horizontal Differentiation. Horizontal differentiation refers to the manner in which the various tasks done in an organization are divided up and grouped into units. There are numerous ways in which organizations may be horizontally differentiated. One way is on the basis of the function performed. Panel A of Figure 3-2 depicts an organization differentiated on the basis of function. In this example, all product research and development for the entire company is done in one division, all manufacturing activities are carried out in another

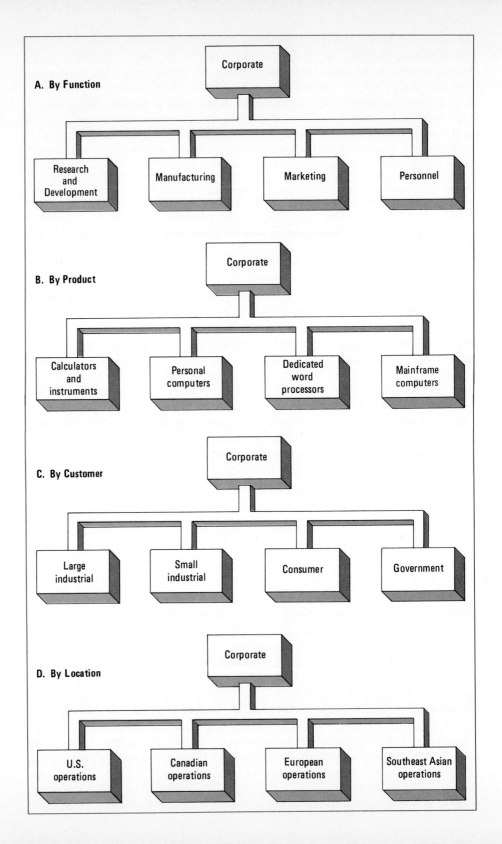

FIGURE 3-2
Examples of four different modes of horizontal differentiation.

A. By Function

Corporate

Research and Development | Manufacturing | Marketing | Personnel

B. By Product

Corporate

Calculators and instruments | Personal computers | Dedicated word processors | Mainframe computers

C. By Customer

Corporate

Large industrial | Small industrial | Consumer | Government

D. By Location

Corporate

U.S. operations | Canadian operations | European operations | Southeast Asian operations division, all product marketing is handled by a third division, and all personnel matters are handled in a fourth division. A second basis of differentiation is by product, as depicted in panel B of Figure 3-2. Here, each division is responsible for all the activities needed to develop, manufacture, and market, its own particular product. The implication, of course, is that the company will now have several *separate* R&D departments, manufacturing facilities, marketing departments, and perhaps even personnel departments. Another way organizations can be differentiated is by customer, as shown in panel C. Here again, each division must be able to perform all the tasks needed to manufacture and sell products to its particular customer group. As a final example, an organization may also be differentiated on the basis of geography. This is depicted in panel D.

Most organizations are differentiated on the basis of several of these criteria. For example, an organization might first differentiate on the basis of product, and within each product division differentiate on the basis of function. This is the way General Motors is structured. To take another example, consider the way in which the University of California is structured. The first level of differentiation is based on geography (e.g., UCLA, UC San Diego, UC Berkeley). In each geographic location one finds both academic and administrative units (differentiation on the basis of function). Within the academic units there are a variety of departments (differentiation by product), and within most of these departments one can find both graduate and undergraduate courses (differentiation by customer).

How an organization chooses to differentiate itself will strongly affect its ability to perform (Haimann, Scott, & Connor, 1982). This is partly because of the way differentiation affects the members of the organization. People tend to interact most often with those individuals in their own organizational grouping (e.g., division, department). Interactions outside these groupings do occur, but with much less frequency (e.g., neither author of this book has much interaction with faculty members in the art, chemistry, or foreign language departments of our universities). As a consequence, various organizational groupings often develop somewhat narrowly focused local orientations and solutions to larger organizational problems. The members of a manufacturing division, for example, may come to view cost containment as the best way for their company to achieve its overall financial performance objectives. Toward this end, they may strive to keep small inventories, use standard materials, schedule long production runs, and make as few equipment changes as possible. In contrast, those in the marketing division of the same company may see responsiveness to customer needs as the key to the organization's success. They may want the flexibility to meet special customer design requirements and offer quick delivery. Of course, if the marketing division were to get its way, the manufacturing division would have to keep larger inventories of nonstandard materials, schedule special production runs on very short notice, and reset their equipment more frequently than they would like. Clearly, there is the potential for a great deal of conflict between these two divisions with regard to the most appropriate way to achieve the overall goals of the organization.

Conflict of this nature is difficult to eliminate completely, but it can be substantially reduced when groups with highly interdependent jobs are put together in the same organizational unit. As they work together, they will naturally develop a common orientation to problem solutions, and much less conflict will occur. What we are saying is that the way in which an organization is differentiated (an aspect of the organization's structure) can strongly affect the degree of conflict (a behavior) that occurs among organizational members (Nadler, Hackman, & Lawler, 1979).

Vertical Differentiation. In addition to horizontal differentiation, organizations are also differentiated vertically. Vertical differentiation refers to the number of vertical levels of authority in the organization. It is essentially the degree to which *managerial activities* are divided up (Connor, 1984). In general, as organizations get larger they also develop more hierarchical layers. This makes sense: The more people employed in an organization, the more effort it takes to coordinate their behavior. The best way to distribute this effort among managers is to create additional hierarchical levels. However, even when the overall size of the organization is held constant, it is apparent that some organizations are more vertically differentiated than others. Those that have a large number of vertical layers for their size are called *tall* organizations, while those that have relatively few layers are called *flat* organizations.

The degree to which an organization is vertically differentiated can significantly affect the job satisfaction of organization members (Berger & Cummings, 1979). It was found in one study, for example, that the highest ranking managers in tall organizations were more satisfied with their jobs than were the highest ranking managers in flat organizations. However, the opposite was true for managers in lower level jobs. Lower level managers in flat organizations were more satisfied with their jobs than were those in tall organizations (El Salmi & Cummings, 1968). These differences in satisfaction seem to be related to the way power and control are distributed in tall versus flat organizations.

In most organizations, managerial activities are divided up following a strict *hierarchical* structure. That is, every manager in the authority structure is responsible to, and receives direction from, only one superior. This is called the *scalar chain of command*. A few organizations, however, deviate from this arrangement. They have what is called a *matrix structure*. In a matrix structure, the organization is simultaneously differentiated on the basis of *two* different criteria (e.g., function and product), and managers in this type of structure have *two* superiors. An example of a simple matrix structure is shown in Figure 3-3. In this example, the organization is simultaneously differentiated by function (across the top of the matrix) and by product (down the side). Thus, there is a different vice president in charge of each function and each product. Further, every manager inside the matrix has two bosses. The R&D manager for product A, for example, is responsible to both the vice president in charge of product A and the vice president in charge of R&D.

Matrix structures are used in order to capitalize on the advantages of both of the two simpler forms of differentiation on which they are based. However, they are very difficult to manage. It is vital to the success of a matrix organization that each pair of individuals with authority over a position in the matrix (i.e., the vice presidents in our example) have *equal* power. Further, it

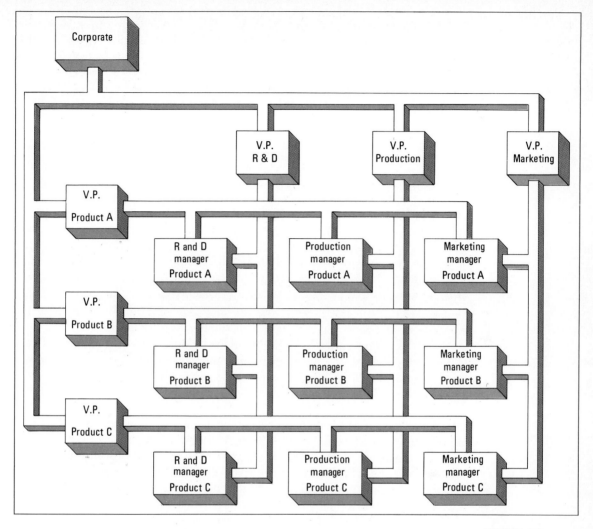

FIGURE 3-3
An example of a
matrix organiza-
tion.

is essential that they work in close cooperation with one another. No matter how closely they cooperate, however, it is inevitable that these two individuals will sometimes make conflicting demands on the manager inside the matrix. The manager inside the matrix must therefore be very skillful in dealing with the conflicting demands of two different bosses. Because of the conflicts they must deal with, the role of the matrix managers can be very stressful and anxiety-provoking (Davis & Lawrence, 1977; Lawrence, Kolodny, & Davis, 1977).

Span of Control. Closely related to the concepts of horizontal and vertical differentiation is the idea of span of control. Span of control refers to the *number of subordinates* that are supervised by any one manager. The average span of control in an organization is the average number of subordinates supervised by managers. Span of control is necessarily related to the degree of vertical differentiation in an organization. If the overall size of the organization is held constant, reducing the degree of vertical differentiation (i.e., the number of management layers) can be accomplished only by increasing the average span of control in the organization. Conversely, if one wants to reduce the average span of control, this can be done only by increasing vertical differentiation.

There are many factors that determine the optimal span of control for any one manager or supervisor. These include the complexity of the subordinates' tasks, the degree to which those tasks are similar to one another, and the degree to which they are interdependent (Bell, 1967; Udell, 1967). If the subordinates' tasks are complex, vary widely from one subordinate to the next, and are highly interdependent, the manager will need to spend a good deal of time and energy supervising and coordinating their work. In this type of situation, only a relatively small span of control is possible. On the other hand, if the subordinates' tasks are fairly simple, all subordinates perform the same type of task, and those tasks are essentially independent of one another, much less time and effort is needed (per subordinate) for supervision and coordination. This means that a larger span of control is feasible. In general, the optimal span of control for foremen and other first-line supervisors tends to be large (e.g., 20 to 30), while the optimal span of control for middle- and upper-level managers tends to be much smaller (e.g., 4 to 8).

Span of control can affect the behavior of organization members in two different ways. First, if a manager has too many subordinates, that is, a larger span of control than is optimal given the nature of the subordinates' tasks, he or she will not be able to cope successfully with the job. Subordinates will be inadequately supervised, and their performance is likely to decrease as a consequence. The job is simply too much for any one person to handle. A manager in this situation is likely to feel a substantial amount of stress, and unless the span of control is decreased, there is a high probability that he or she will quit the job. Second, if the span of control is too small, the manager has the opportunity to supervise subordinates too closely. Too much supervision can cause just as many problems as too little, since subordinates are likely to chafe at having someone constantly looking over their shoulders. Managers therefore need to exercise some restraint in this situation.

Formalization. Formalization is the degree to which there exist in an organization clearly specified rules and regulations that govern the work-related behavior of organization members, and the extent to which there is a reliance on formal, written communications that follow the hierarchical chain of command. Highly formalized organizations typically have thick manuals of standard operating procedures and detailed job descriptions that specify exactly what tasks various individuals are expected to perform. Furthermore, highly formalized organizations generally require an extensive amount of paperwork, in the form of memos, frequent reports, and the completion of standardized forms. A highly formalized organization is what Weber (1947) called a *bureaucracy*. In contrast, an organization that is not highly formalized operates with many fewer rules and regulations, has only very general job descriptions, and usually requires much less paperwork. In addition, organizations that are not highly formalized are much more likely to encourage direct lateral communications among individuals in different organizational divisions. Communication "through channels" (i.e., via the formal chain of command) is less insisted upon. Notice that formalization is not an all-or-none phenomenon. It is a continuum. Organizations exhibit different *degrees* of formalization. The more formalized they are, the more closely they fit the classical ideal of a bureaucracy.

Formalization has both advantages and disadvantages for the organization. On the positive side, a primary benefit of formalization is that it serves to coordinate the behavior of the organization's members. If everyone follows a standard set of procedures, there is little ambiguity about who is doing what when, and it is possible to get highly interdependent tasks accomplished with a minimum of confusion. Formalization serves this function best when the same set of tasks are performed over and over again. Less formalized organizations must rely on ad hoc decision making in order to achieve the same degree of coordination, and a great deal of this can slow the organization's operation (Galbraith, 1977). A second benefit of formal rules and procedures is that they can serve as an objective standard against which performance may be judged. For example, if in a machine shop there is a clearly stated rule that rework (i.e., correcting problems found in previously completed jobs) takes precedence over all other work and should be done immediately, compliance with the rule can be objectively assessed. But there is a negative side to this. Formalization tends to focus attention on the rules and procedures to the exclusion of the overall goals that they are intended to serve (Reimann, 1973). Thus, an employee may decide to follow the rules rigidly, even when doing so is not in the organization's best interest (e.g., a rush job for a special customer is stopped in order to do a small piece of rework on a job of much less importance). Such problems are not as likely to occur in less formalized organizations.

Centralization. The final structural feature we wish to mention concerns the locus of decision-making authority in organizations. If all or most of the important decisions that need to be made in order to keep an organization running smoothly are made by a few individuals at the top levels of the authority hierarchy, the organization is said to be highly *centralized*. By contrast, if decision-making authority is delegated to lower levels of the organization, so that the individuals who will actually have to implement the decisions become more directly involved in the decision-making process, the organization is said to be highly *decentralized*. Like formalization, centralization is a continuum. Organizations vary in the degree of centralization they exhibit.

There are many pros and cons for both centralized and decentralized decision structures. Some of these have to do with decision quality, which is likely to depend on both the perspective and the expertise of decision makers at various organizational levels. For example, it can be argued that in a decentralized decision structure the individuals who are actually making the decisions are likely to have greater technical expertise, in the sense that they are more familiar with the details of the problems they face. On the other hand, they may lack the experience and overall organizational perspective possessed by those in higher level positions. The organization's ability to respond rapidly to change is also an important consideration. In general, decisions can be made more quickly in decentralized decision structures, thus making decentralized organizations somewhat more responsive to changing environmental conditions.

Finally, it is also important to note that the degree to which an organization is centralized or decentralized can also affect the job satisfaction of organization members, particularly those at lower levels of the organization (Berger & Cummings, 1979). Individuals occupying lower level managerial positions, for example, tend to be significantly more satisfied with their jobs in decentralized organizations than in centralized organizations. In this respect, decentralized organizations have much in common with flat organizations—both are more satisfying to individuals who occupy lower level positions. The increased control and responsibility that accrue to lower level positions in both flat organizations and decentralized organizations seems to have a positive impact on the way people feel about their jobs.

Contingency Approaches to Organizational Design

In the foregoing discussion our purpose was to describe a number of important structural features of the organizational environment and to suggest how those features are likely to affect the attitudes and behavior of organization members. By now it should be clear that people who design organizations have a great many decisions to make regarding such questions as how much vertical and horizontal differentiation there should be, the average span of control managers should be given, and the degree to which the organization should be formalized and centralized. In answering these questions, organization designers need to take into account the likely impact of these various structural features on the members of the organization. In addition, they need to consider the relationship between these structural features and (1) the nature of the work done by the organization, and (2) the organization's own environment.

Technology and Structure. Think for a moment about the work that is done in a nursing home. What are the fundamental differences between this work and the work that is done in an insurance company? What are the differences between the work of a company that manufactures automobiles and one that refines gasoline? And what are the characteristics that distinguish the work of a real estate firm from that of an airline company? There are, of course, many differences. Some of these organizations offer a wide variety of services (e.g., the nursing home), while others offer only a few (e.g., the airline). In some cases there is a great deal of assembly-line work (e.g., the auto manufacturer), while in others there is no tangible product to be assembled (e.g., the insurance company). And while some of these organizations create original products and services for their clients, others act primarily as intermediaries between different client groups (e.g., the real estate firm). The various characteristics of the work that is done in an organization are collectively referred to as its *work technology*. One goal that modern organization theorists have sought to achieve is to identify the contingent relationships between critical dimensions of work technology on the one hand, and formal organizational structure on the other. That is, they have sought to identify the structural features that seem to be most beneficial for an organization (in terms of performance), given the organization's work technology.

The work of Charles Perrow (1967) provides one example of this type of research. Perrow examined two major dimensions of technology: the degree of variability in the tasks performed, and the degree to which the technology is analyzable. Variability refers to the number of exceptional cases. For example, a company that produces many custom-made products would have a large number of exceptional cases, while a company involved in mass production would have very few exceptions. The analyzability dimension refers to the degree to which the task and technology can be broken down into smaller components. The combination of these two dimensions, variability and analyzability, defines four basic technology types: routine, nonroutine, craft, and engineering. These are depicted in Figure 3-4.

An example of a routine technology is that used in a highly mechanized mass-production industry such as automobile manufacturing. Tasks are broken down and well specified, and there are few exceptional cases. An example of a nonroutine technology is the psychiatric care provided in a mental hospital. Every psychiatrist has his or her own approach, and each problem is unique. Craft industries are self-explanatory. The individual makes the whole product, and does so in pretty much the same way each time. Thus, there are few exceptions. Engineering technologies are those in which the task is analyzable, but a larger number of exceptional cases exists. For example, an architectural design firm may have many different types of contracts (and hence many exceptional cases), but the same basic principles of physics and design apply for all of them (i.e., each case is analyzable).

The argument made by Perrow is that if we classify organizations according to their technology, we should be able to predict the structure of those firms that are most effective. Some data exist to support this hypothesis (Fry, 1982). Magnusen (1973), for example, classified fourteen medium-sized manufactur-

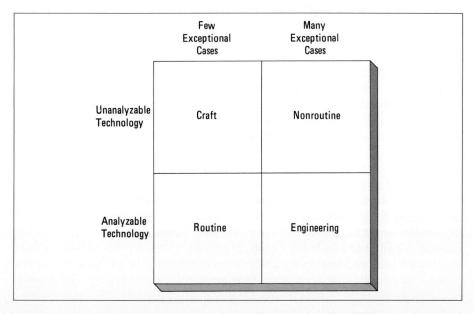

FIGURE 3-4
Perrow's (1967) two-dimensional framework for describing work technologies.

ing firms according to Perrow's system, and then looked at their organizational structure, goals, and processes. His results supported Perrow's analysis. He found that companies dealing with many exceptional cases needed more flexibility, greater decentralization, and less hierarchical control in order to be successful. Also, the less analyzable the task, the less control and close supervision were possible. Thus, while in highly routine situations a bureaucratic organizational structure might be appropriate, a more flexible structure is needed in a nonroutine setting.

Another well-known study examining the relationship between technology and structure was conducted by Joan Woodward (1965) in England. She was interested only in industrial firms, and she classified them into three types:

1. *Process production.* Continuous manufacturing industries with highly standardized goods. Production is done in anticipation of demand with long production runs and large lot sizes. Labor costs are low.
2. *Unit or small-batch production.* This is job-order manufacturing of customized products. Production is done according to demand in small runs and lots. Labor costs are high.
3. *Large-batch production.* A technology somewhere between the two above. There is some custom manufacturing and some manufacturing in anticipation of demand. Medium-sized lots and runs are the rule.

In analyzing firms using these different types of technologies, Woodward found many differences in structure. For example, much of the decision making was done by high-level policy committees in process industries. The chief executive acted as a committee chairperson rather than a unilateral decision maker. The complex mechanical technology of the process industries also demanded the greatest number of managerial levels, while unit manufacturing had the least. Therefore, the unit manufacturers had rather flat organizations with large spans of control, while process industries had tall organizations with narrow spans of control. The ratio of management to nonmanagement personnel was 1:8 in process industries and 1:23 in unit industries.

While Woodward's analysis is narrower in scope than Perrow's, there are some striking similarities. Both theorists believe that the degree to which the task can be broken down into component parts is an important determinant of organizational structure and process. Also important is the degree to which tasks are predictable. In Perrow's case the concern was with the number of exceptional cases, while Woodward focused on reactions to anticipated demand. Thus, predictability and analyzability are important aspects of both approaches.

Environment and Structure. In addition to indentifying the contingent relationships between structure and work technology, organizational theorists have sought to identify the structural features that are most beneficial for organizations in different kinds of *environments*. Burns and Stalker (1961), for example, attempted to classify organizations in terms of their ability to deal with uncertainty and instability in their environment. They studied a number of manufacturing firms that were moving into a new, highly changeable industry (electronics). Those organizations that had a bureaucratic managerial system with rigidly prescribed tasks and hierarchical arrangements were called "mechanistic organizations." Those that were flexible with more horizontal communication and decentralized decision-making power were called "organic organizations." The data gathered by Burns and Stalker strongly suggested that organic organizations were more likely to survive and perform well in this changing and unpredictable environment. Note that neither organizational form is viewed as inherently good or bad. Rather, effectiveness is seen as dependent upon an organizational design that fits the environment within which the company must operate.

Finally, research by Lawrence and Lorsch (1967) also attempted to describe the proper match between the organization and its environment. These authors directly compared organizations in turbulent (changing, unpredictable) environments with those in stable (static, predictable) environments. They found that effective organizations in highly turbulent environments used greater horizontal differentiation than did effective organizations in stable environments. Thus, the more changing and unpredictable the environment, the more horizontally differentiated the structure should be in order to allow effective coping with external pressures and demands.

In summary, the formal structure of an organization can have a significant impact not only on the attitudes and behavior of organization members, but also on the effectiveness of the organization as a whole. An organization is most likely to be successful when it is structured in a way that is best suited to its work technology and environment. With some work technologies and in some environments, high levels of formalization, hierarchical control, and centralization are most appropriate. With other technologies and environments, less formalization, hierarchical control, and centralization are needed. The structure of an organization should be viewed both as a major aspect of the environment affecting organization members, and as a variable that itself is affected by its own larger environment and work technology.

TASKS IN ORGANIZATIONS

It is evident from the preceding discussion that in order to understand the functioning of organizations, we need to know something about the basic characteristics of the work being done. As we have seen, work technology is one factor that dictates the type of formal structure an organization should have. Beyond influencing structure, however, the inherent nature of the tasks being performed in an organization also has a strong, *direct* effect on the attitudes and behavior of organizational members. Consequently, in addition to the structural characteristics of organizations, task characteristics must be considered as a second major element of the organizational environment.

Most of the tasks people perform in organizations can be done in a variety of ways. Consider, for example, the task of providing word-processing support to managers in a large insurance company. There are several ways this task can be accomplished. One possibility is to give every secretary in the company a word processor. The task of word processing would thus be combined with other tasks (e.g., filing, handling appointments, answering telephone calls) as part of each secretary's overall job. Alternatively, the word-processing task might be isolated, so that it is done by only one person in each department. This person's sole responsibility would be word processing, and he or she would handle all of the word-processing needs of the entire department. A third possibility is to centralize the word-processing function for the whole company. In this case all word processing would be done in a central location outside the departments, with little direct contact between the individuals doing the word processing and the managers they serve. These three alternatives for organizing the word-processing task are likely to have widely different effects. They are likely to differ not only with respect to efficiency and cost-effectiveness, but also in terms of how the individuals doing the word processing react to their jobs.

Let's take a second example. In a home appliance manufacturing firm the work of assembling dishwashers can be done in two fundamentally different ways. One way is to use the familiar assembly line. In an assembly line the various components of the assembly process are divided into a series of small steps, and each step is assigned to a different person on the line. Thus, one person installs the hot- and cold-water valves, another puts in the waste-water pump, a third mounts the dish-rack brackets, someone else attaches the door trim, and so on. Twenty to thirty people may be involved in the assembly of a single dishwasher, each one performing only his or her own specialized job. In contrast, a rather different approach to the assembly task is to organize these same twenty to thirty people into two-person work teams, and have each team assemble an entire dishwasher from beginning to end. In this arrangement, each employee would be able to perform all of the various steps of the assembly process, and each would be responsible for the overall functioning of an entire machine, not just one part of it. Again, how the task is designed is highly likely to affect both the overall efficiency of the organization and the way the assemblers react to their jobs.

Efficiency and Task Design

The concern with efficiency and cost-effectiveness in the design of work tasks has had a long history. One of the early pioneers in this area was Frederick W. Taylor. Taylor (1911) was an engineer who was employed in the production area of several large organizations, including Bethlehem Steel. He developed what he called the principles of *scientific management.* A central tenet of his approach was that there is one best way to do every job. He believed that by intensively studying work methods and procedures, the most efficient way to do a job could be determined exactly. This includes determining where employees should sit or stand, how their bodies should be oriented, where their tools should be placed, the order in which activities should be completed, and so on. Once these have been determined, the job should be done in precisely that way on every occasion—the ultimate in standardization.

As an example of his approach, Taylor cites the case of the pig-iron handlers at Bethlehem Steel. Pig iron is the crude iron that is poured from a blast furnace into various shaped molds for storage and shipping. In 1898 Bethlehem Steel had five furnaces producing pig iron, each pig weighing about 92 pounds. The company employed a gang of 75 men to handle these pigs. The work was done by the men with no implements other than their hands.

They had to stoop down, pick up a pig from the ground, walk several yards, and then place the pig onto a railroad car. These men were considered good pig-iron handlers, and they worked just about as fast and efficiently as pig-iron handlers anywhere else at the time. On average, they loaded 12.5 long tons (28,000 pounds) of pig iron per man per day. However, after carefully studying the "science" of handling pig iron, Taylor discovered that with proper rest periods a first-class pig-iron handler ought to be able to handle between 47.1 and 48 long tons per day. That is a rate nearly four times what was currently being done! He therefore arranged to have the work of the pig-iron handlers paced very carefully. Rather than being left on their own to decide when to work and when to rest, the handlers were told by a supervisor exactly when to pick up a pig and walk, when to sit down and rest, when to get up again, when to rest, and so on, following a scientifically designed work schedule. This happened all day long, day in and day out, with the result that all of the pig iron was eventually handled at the rate of 47.5 long tons per man per day. The pig-iron handlers did not object to this increased work load, in part because it enabled them to earn a higher rate of pay.

From such modest beginnings grew the discipline of *industrial engineering*. The primary focus of industrial engineers is the scientific design of work by means of very precise time and motion studies (e.g., Konz, 1983; Niebel, 1982). Almost every conceivable type of task and work situation has been studied. There have been studies concerned with the design of hand tools and work stations, and with the flow of parts and materials between work stations. There have been studies focusing on the work done in manufacturing plants, in large department stores, and in the back offices of banks and insurance companies. There have even been studies to determine the most efficient arrangement of equipment and furniture in dental offices! From all this research a number of design principles have emerged. These principles dictate job specialization, the decoupling of tasks, and the performance of all identical operations at the same point in time. Highly specialized jobs are expected to increase both the quality and quantity of work output, in part because the specialist becomes much more practiced and efficient at the particular task he or she performs. In addition, because specialization usually implies the need for a simpler and more narrow range of skills, training costs are reduced.

It is important to recognize the assumptions that underlie this approach to task design. First, it is assumed that there is one best way to do any job. Second, it is assumed that the best way to do a job can be discovered only by careful scientific study. The implication, of course, is that it is the expert industrial engineer, not the individual employee, who is in the best position to say how a particular job should be done. Third, it is assumed that people are motivated primarily by financial incentives, and that they will perform the (new and improved) specialized tasks as long as they are adequately paid. This assumption is perhaps best stated by Konz (1983), who writes:

> From the individual viewpoint, specialized work may be repetitive and monotonous. It has been difficult to recruit workers for monotonous jobs—if they have low pay. If the job has high pay, many workers can be found whether the job is monotonous or not. [p. 230]

As we will see, these three assumptions are overly simplistic.

Without a doubt, the attention that industrial engineers have given to the design of work systems has greatly improved the efficiency of organizations. However, as Konz (1983) suggests, this increased efficiency sometimes has negative side effects. The specialized jobs that result from a scientific analysis of task efficiency are often narrow and unexciting. The individual employee is required to exercise only a fraction of the skills he or she may have, and to perform only a small portion of the work needed to complete a product. Moreover, when taken by themselves, these specialized jobs often seem relatively unimportant. How would you feel, for example, if you took a summer job in a home appliance manufacturing plant? Would you be proud to explain to your friends that you worked on an assembly line attaching intake hoses no. 1 and no. 2 on every dishwasher the plant produced? Probably not. But what if the job required you to assemble the entire machine, check its operation, and then stamp your name on the serial-number plate in the back? From a technical point of view, this might not be a very efficient system; however, it is much more likely that you would feel some pride in your work and be motivated to do a good job at it.

A substantial amount of research concerned with the motivational implications of task design has been conducted in recent years (e.g., Griffin, 1982). This research will be reviewed in greater detail in Chapter 6. We wish to note here only the main conclusion from this research, which is that the work motivation and job satisfaction of some people are indeed strongly affected by the manner in which their jobs are designed. Some (although not all) people desire more stimulating jobs. Jobs that require the use of a variety of skills, that involve the completion of a whole product, and that provide feedback about performance effectiveness are much more likely to generate high levels of motivation and satisfaction in these individuals than are jobs that do not have such characteristics.

The implications of this are twofold. First, contrary to the assumptions of traditional industrial engineering, there usually is not one best way to design a job. There may be one best way to maximize efficiency, but this is not necessarily the best way to maximize employee motivation. The best way to design a job depends largely on what is meant by "best." A second and closely related implication is that financial incentives are not the only factor that motivates employees. The characteristics of the work being done can in many cases also have important motivating properties, and these must be taken into consideration.

One other point is worth mentioning. Researchers concerned with the motivational aspects of job design have often encouraged employees to participate directly in the design of their jobs, under the assumption that it is the *employee* who knows best what is motivating and what is not. For example, it is standard practice within the General Foods Corporation to give office employees a major role in incorporating new office automation technologies into their jobs (Smith, 1984). The efficiency engineer is considered only one source of expertise regarding how a job should be designed. The job incumbent also has expert information, especially with regard to issues of motivation.

Thus, the goals of efficiency and employee motivation are sometimes at odds with one another. Extreme job specialization can increase efficiency, but it will often reduce employee motivation. Eliminating specialization might increase motivation, but efficiency will suffer. Neither situation is desirable. An organization cannot succeed with a highly efficient work system if employees have no motivation to perform well. Nor can it succeed with highly motivated employees if those employees work in inefficient ways. The challenge, then, is to find the middle ground between these two extremes. Tasks in organizations need to be designed so that the work is done in a reasonably efficient manner and employees still find their jobs interesting and enjoyable. If this can be achieved, it is likely that whatever inefficiency lingers in the work system will be more than offset by high levels of employee motivation, thereby leading to better overall organizational performance.

THE SOCIAL ASPECT OF ORGANIZATIONS

So far we have examined two major elements of the organizational environment: (1) the structural characteristics of the organization, and (2) the characteristics of the tasks that organizational members are asked to perform. As we have seen, both of these components are important because both can have a significant impact on the job attitudes and work behavior of organization members. We now turn to the third and final major element of the organizational environment, the social aspect of organizations.

Working in an organization means working with other people, and the people we work with can strongly influence our behavior. This is true even of our peers, who hold no formal power or authority over us. Peer groups establish and reinforce norms of behavior that can influence how much effort we put into our jobs, whether or not we show up on time in the morning, our willingness to work overtime, and even the way we dress. These effects seem obvious to most people today, but the fact of the matter is that this aspect of the organizational environment has not always been given the attention it deserves. For example, 100 years ago organization theorists either ignored the social aspect of organizations altogether, or assumed that problems associated with social influence processes would disappear when more rational approaches to organization and task design were employed (cf. Locke, 1982). It was not until the second quarter of this century that organization theorists began to appreciate fully the impact of the informal work group on employee attitudes and behavior, and not until the third quarter that serious suggestions were made about how to put social influence processes to positive use. The research that began this period of enlightenment was done just before and during the Great Depression at the Hawthorne plant of the Western Electric Company in Chicago.

The Hawthorne Studies

The research done at the Hawthorne plant was reported by Mayo (1933) and Roethlisberger and Dickson (1939). The initial purpose of this research was to examine the effect of lighting conditions, rest periods, methods of payment, and other such factors on the productivity of factory workers. The research thus started out very much in the tradition of Taylor's scientific management studies. In the first phase of this research, a small group of women were moved into a separate testing room and studied while they were making telephone assemblies. As they were working, the researchers would change the amount of illumination and observe the resultant change, if any, in productivity.

The results seemed quite puzzling to the investigators. It appeared that no matter what type of change occurred, productivity was either maintained or increased. They found that as they increased the illumination, productivity went up. Even when they reached a point at which the illumination by objective standards was too bright, productivity increases continued. Moreover, when they decreased the illumination, productivity still went up! Obviously, there was something other than the level of illumination that was influencing the work habits of the women.

A second experiment was conducted with another set of women, this time focusing on changes in the timing and frequency of rest periods. Again, the results were the same. Increases in productivity seemed to occur independently of the actual changes being made. In order to better understand what was going on, the investigators decided to ask these women a number of questions about why they were working harder. The results were of major significance. The women reported six factors, in the following order of importance:

1. Smallness of the group
2. Type of supervision
3. Earnings
4. Novelty of the situation
5. Interest in the experiment
6. Attention received in the test room

The last three of these factors contribute to a methodological artifact that has come to be known as the *Hawthorne effect.* More specifically, the women seemed to increase their productivity partly because they knew they were in a research study. Research conducted today is usually carefully controlled to avoid the criticism that the results are due to the Hawthorne effect—that people worked harder simply because of increased attention and the novelty of the research situation, and because increased productivity seemed to be what the researcher wanted (Adair, 1984).

It is also evident from the answers given by these women that by putting together this separate small work team, the investigators had changed some variables that they had not realized were important. The size of the work group had decreased, and apparently supervision was more flexible and tolerant in the small experimental group. These facts led the investigators to conclude that motivation and productivity on the job are influenced by more than just simple economic principles. Other, more social factors must also be involved.

One final phase of the Hawthorne research was called the bank-wiring-room experiment. Here, fourteen men wired telephone switchboards (called banks), which required both individual and team effort. This phase differed from the other studies mentioned above in several significant ways. First, no experimental changes were made. The men were put in a separate room and observed while working, but nothing else was changed. Second, the conditions were designed to be as similar as possible to the ongoing wiring department's regular work conditions.

The results were dramatically different from the previous findings. Productivity did *not* increase; in fact, it slightly decreased. It is difficult to specify exactly why the results differed, because there were a number of ways in which this study was methodologically different from the other (e.g., the sex of the participants, the fact that no changes were implemented, and that little special attention was given to the participants). However, observational data and interviews provided some insights into what was happening.

One major finding was that the work group set an informal norm for what was a satisfactory day's work. While the time and motion specialists had determined that 2 1/2 banks could be done, the group decided that 2 banks was about right. Thus, employee and management expectations differed by 20 percent. A related result was that the group put pressure on its members to adhere to this norm—to avoid exceeding it or falling short. Those who fell below the norm were called "chiselers" and those who exceeded it were called "speed kings" or "rate-busters." This latter group was often subjected to social and physical pressure to slow down. When they didn't respond, they were occasionally "binged" on the arm by the other group members.

All these studies led to a number of important conclusions:

1. The organization is more than just a collection of individuals. It is a social system in which people have friends and enemies as well as hopes, fears, and desires.
2. The level of productivity is affected not only by management standards, but also by social norms set by the group.
3. Noneconomic rewards are often as important as economic ones. One's friends and interpersonal relationships are an important part of the job.
4. Employees do not always respond as individuals acting alone. Groups often make decisions, even though they might not be recognized as part of the formal organization.

These insights challenged the basic assumptions of scientific management, and gave rise to a new trend in management philosophy that came to be known as the *human relations movement*. The human relations movement explicitly recognized the existence of an informal social structure within organizations. This social structure, consisting largely of peer groups and supervisor-subordinate relations, evolves its own set of norms and values, and can have a substantial impact on the behavior of individual group members. The reason for this is simple. People generally value these informal groups, and they will do what is necessary to maintain them, which includes adhering to their norms of behavior.

The human relations movement thus urged management to pay attention to the social aspect of organizations. Those at the forefront of this movement argued that employees should be treated considerately, that they should be allowed to exercise some degree of self-determination on the job, and that management should strive to foster cohesive work units and friendly employee-management relations (Locke, 1976).

Since the days of the Hawthorne studies, there has been a great deal of interest in developing ways to put the energy and influence of the informal peer group to work for the good of the organization. Left on their own, peer groups sometimes have a positive effect (e.g., when the group norm is high performance) and sometimes have a negative effect (e.g., when the group norm is low performance). The question is, what can be done to increase the probability that their effect will be positive?

One suggestion that is gradually gaining wider recognition is to reorient the formal structure of the organization to make use of *autonomous work groups* (Emery & Thorsrud, 1976; Trist & Bamford, 1951). Autonomous work groups are relatively small groups of employees (generally less than 20) who work together as a team. The group is given the responsibility for performing all the various tasks required to produce either a complete product or major component of the product (e.g., an automobile engine). While performance goals are usually assigned by the organization, it is the group's responsibility to decide how best to achieve those goals. This means that the group is given the authority for making all day-to-day operating decisions. The group decides who will perform which specific tasks on a given day, the order in which tasks will be done, the schedule of job rotation and work breaks, and how to resolve special problems that arise. They are responsible for maintaining their own equipment, ordering materials and supplies, and inspecting the quality of their product. They are often even responsible for deciding group membership, that is, who can and who cannot belong to the group. Finally, the members of the group are rewarded for their group's performance. Typically between 10 and 30 percent of their pay comes from a bonus that is contingent upon the overall performance of the group. The amount of the bonus is usually shared equally among the group member (Fotilas, 1981).

The advantages of autonomous work groups have been demonstrated in a number of studies. One well-known study examined the productivity of English coal mines, comparing those mines that used autonomous work groups with those that did not (Trist, Higgin, Murray, & Pollock, 1963). There are three primary jobs that need to be done in a coal mine. One is to extract the coal from the mine face, the second is to transport the coal away from the face and out of the mine, and the third involves supportive and preparatory activities, such as installing roof supports and moving equipment forward as the miners cut deeper and deeper into the face. Each of these jobs consists of a variety of more specific tasks. At the turn of the century this work went rather slowly. Much of it was done by hand, and the mining crews worked on many small faces simultaneously. The subsequent introduction of new cutting and conveyor machinery greatly speeded up this work. Moreover, it became possible to work a single, very long face of the coal seam all at one time. This long face is known as a longwall. Working a longwall involved distributing from forty to fifty miners along the entire length of the wall. Each miner had a highly specialized task to perform, and each earned a different rate of pay depending on the particular skills needed for his task. Because the length of a longwall was so great, relatively little face-to-face interaction among the miners was possible. This meant that there was no way they could coordinate their own activities. So, supervisory staff were added to provide the necessary coordination. The responsibility for deciding what each miner should do at any given moment was thus handed over to a mining supervisor. The longwall method of mining treated each miner as an individual whose job was simply to follow orders.

Not every mining operation strictly adhered to the longwall method, however. Some made use of the same equipment, but instead of a longwall, they worked several shorter faces. In order to do this, the mining crews were divided into smaller groups, with each group given considerable autonomy for the work at its own face. Since the face was relatively short, a great deal of interaction was possible among the miners, thereby eliminating the need for supervisory staff to provide coordination. The miners thus made their own decisions about what to do, when to do it, and how to handle special problems encountered at the face. Of necessity, the jobs of these miners were less specialized, with a greater opportunity for task variety. Also, the miners' pay was partly contingent upon their groups' performance.

From the standpoint of pure technical efficiency, the longwall method of coal mining is clearly superior to the method of mining short faces using autonomous work groups. However, Trist et al. (1963) found that those mining operations employing autonomous work groups had higher levels of performance. They extracted more coal from the face, were better able to meet production schedules, had fewer accidents, and had less absenteeism.

More recent evidence from other industries also supports the benefits of autonomous work groups. Both Saab and Volvo, for example, have built automobile manufacturing facilities organized around fifteen- to twenty-person autonomous work groups (Gyllenhammar, 1977). Each work group is responsible for producing a major automotive component. These plants have cost substantially more to build than traditional assembly-line plants, but the improved productivity that has resulted has more than offset the initial start-up costs. Similar productivity improvements were reported when a General Foods manufacturing facility in Topeka, Kansas, was structured around autonomous work groups (Walton, 1972). Finally, in their recent book, *A Passion for Excellence*, Peters and Austin (1985) tell of a company that installed a sophisticated computer system for production scheduling and inventory control, only to find that this technological "fix" made things worse. Supervisors began to focus more on the needs of the computer system than on the needs of the customer, with the result that quality deteriorated and production schedules were missed. The company subsequently scrapped the computer system and switched to a customer-oriented work-team method of organization. Within 6 months the company experienced a dramatic turnaround in performance. Employee productivity doubled, and on-time delivery rates rose from less than 60 percent to over 90 percent.

An autonomous work group approach to organizing is not *the* answer to all organizational problems. Autonomous work groups may not be appropriate for some situations (Alber & Blumberg, 1981), and they have not always yielded the full range of benefits that have been hoped for (e.g., Goodman, 1979). Nevertheless, the point still remains that the group of individuals one works with must be taken into consideration as a significant element of the organizational environment. Whether or not this group becomes the central focus of

Changing the Organization for Changing Times

Two years ago, when the bottom fell out of the oil-field equipment business, Ray Gorcyca was confronted with both a challenge and a rare opportunity. As manufacturing vice president of the Houston-based McEvoy Div. of Smith International Inc., he knew that business as usual would be the wrong response—on both counts.

Today, things are anything but "usual" for the Texas builder of high-tech oil-well valves. Business volume is still well below optimum levels. But a new plant that had been virtually mothballed shortly after its completion is now back in production. Many of the firm's laid-off employees have been recalled. And the division is showing new competitive vigor.

To the returning workers, especially, the metamorphosis seemed startling. In their absence, the McEvoy Div. had undergone a dramatic change in its culture, management organization, job structure, and manufacturing operations. For one thing, a flattening out of the management structure had eliminated the position of foreman. And production employees now are organized into unsupervised manufacturing cells of three to five workers each. "The people in the office and shop almost universally love the idea of working without a boss looking over their shoulder all the time," says Mr. Gorcyca (pronounced "Gor-sic-ah"). "They never had been made to feel important before." . . .

FRESH START

A series of unprecedented developments propelled Mr. Gorcyca and his boss—Division President George Helland—to undertake the sweeping overhaul. In 1981, at a time when the oil-field equipment market was still booming, the division lost a major order to a Japanese competitor—the first time that had happened. . . .

The next big surprise occurred in 1982. Oil-drilling activity slowed to a standstill and the division's order rate dropped by 80% in a three-month period. This was a double blow since McEvoy had just completed a new plant in Temple, Tex., 60 miles north of Austin. . . .

The Temple plant never got into full production. And, by yearend, it was virtually shut down for lack of business.

Meanwhile, employment at McEvoy's other plant—in Tyler, Tex.—had also plummeted, from 235 people in 1981 to 100 in November 1982. . . .

BEHIND THE TIMES

Mr. Gorcyca's investigation of practices elsewhere had confirmed suspicions that the division's methods weren't up to date. In the shop, machines were set up along traditional lines—all boring mills in one department, lathes in another. And a single part, it was discovered, traveled 1.08 miles through 111 processing steps.

Workers had never been asked for their ideas. Scrap was costly, partly because workers had no idea of the value of the material. . . . And managers at times had turned down rush jobs rather than interrupt production on tools with long setup times.

Over a period of two years Mr. Gorcyca, other manufacturing managers, and Thomas Eastland, personnel director, developed—and began to implement—a combination human-relations and manufacturing plant overhaul. It included . . . relocating all 60 major tools at Tyler to fit the manufacturing-cell approach. (Instead of a lathe department, drill department, and milling department, the machines are arranged in family-of-product clusters which can produce related parts. The body-manufacturing cell, for example, includes all the tools needed to produce valve bodies.)

McEvoy call it "enterprise manufacturing." And enterprising workers have a chance to increase their earnings by learning to operate several machines; they receive a 7% increase for each new machine they master. The pay differential extends through four grades to "master machinist"—a worker who can operate any machine in the shop. All workers are now on salary and occasionally sit in on management staff meetings.

In addition to restructuring jobs in the shop, the management organization was flattened out so that no one has more than ten people reporting to him. . . . A version of quality circles—called "McEvoy Action Teams"—was adopted. And, to reinforce the new corporate culture, status symbols were eliminated, including reserved parking spaces for managers.

the organization's design, it can still have a powerful impact on the attitudes and behavior of organizational members. We will have a great deal more to say about the impact of work groups throughout this book (see especially Chapters 8 to 10).

PUTTING IT ALL TOGETHER:
AN OPEN SYSTEMS-THEORY PERSPECTIVE

*In one way or another, we are forced to deal with complexities,
with "wholes" or "systems" in all fields of knowledge.*
—LUDWIG VON BERTALANFFY

So far in this chapter we have examined organizations from several different points of view. We have discussed a number of characteristics of the formal structure of organizations, we have talked about the tasks that organization members are asked to perform, and we have discussed the social aspect of organizations and the impact of the informal work group. Each of these aspects is important, but taken individually they do not provide an adequate picture of what an organization really *is*. For an organization is not simply the sum of these various parts. It is more. It is the *interaction* among them. It is the way they function as a unified system that really defines what an organization is all about. Earlier in this chapter we stated that organizations are systems of coordinated behavior—that organizations *are* behavior. Organizations are not formal structures. They are not tasks and jobs. They are not peer groups and informal social relationships. They are not even people. They are behavior, and this behavior is the result of the interactions among people, formal structures, tasks, and informal social relationships. Thus, the way these various parts interact, or fit together, is of critical importance. This focus on the interplay among the component parts of organizations is a *systems theory* perspective (Katz & Kahn, 1978).

Open Systems Theory

A *system* is any set of interrelated elements. The term *interrelated* implies that a change in one element has a direct effect on one or more of the other elements. Thus, we speak of weather systems, economic systems, heating and cooling systems, and the autonomic nervous system. All have interrelated elements. There are two general types of systems, open systems and closed systems. *Open systems* interact with their environment. *Closed systems* do not. As living human beings we are open systems. We interact with our environment. We take in from our environment (among other things) food, air, and information, and give to the environment heat, waste products, and noise. We are affected by the environment, and in turn we have an effect upon the environment.

Organizations are also open systems. They interact with their environment, although on a somewhat different scale. Consider, for example, a university. A university is strongly affected by its environment. It is affected by the amount of money that is available (e.g., from alumni, tuition, and the state legislature), by the number and type of students in the region, by legal restrictions placed on it by governmental agencies, and by advances in knowledge. It also has an effect on the environment. Most obviously, it produces a lot of college graduates. In addition, it also produces research, entertainment (e.g, Saturday afternoon football games), frustration in the local community (e.g., because of traffic congestion in the vicinity of the stadium on Saturday afternoons), and garbage. Those factors in the environment that influence the organization are termed *inputs* into the organizational system, while the effects the organization has on the environment are called *outputs*. The organization as a system is said to take in inputs, transform them, and produce outputs. Thus, the university takes in new students, money, faculty, books, and computers. It then transforms these resources and produces graduates, research grants, new knowledge, win-loss records, and pollution.

Several features of this open systems view of organizations merit further consideration. First, it should be emphasized that the inputs into an organizational system include many things we might not normally think of when asked to name the "raw materials" the organization transforms. As suggested above, the inputs into a university include not only students, but also money, legal restrictions, and books. Similarly, steel is not the only important input into an organization that manufactures automobiles. Union agreements, technological advancements in robotics, and investment capital are also important inputs.

Second, the outputs of an organizational system also go well beyond what we think of as an organization's "products." A university produces not only graduates and new knowledge (the two stated goals of most universities), but also a scholarly reputation, more work for the local traffic-control authorities, and perhaps frustration among the faculty. In a similar fashion, the automobile manufacturing firm produces not only cars, but also customer loyalty, varying levels of employee satisfaction, and sometimes angry dealerships. In this regard, particularly high or low rates of absenteeism and turnover, union organizing, and changes in productivity should be thought of as outputs from the organizational system.

Finally, as open systems, organizations also receive feedback regarding the acceptability of their output. This feedback allows them to correct errors and change the type of outputs they produce. Thus, when a university discovers that its engineers are unable to compete in the marketplace against graduates from other institutions, it can make changes to improve the quality of its engineering programs. And when the automobile manufacturer learns of an unusually high absenteeism rate in one of its plants, action can be taken to correct the problem.

The Congruence Model

An elaboration of the basic open-systems concept that is particularly useful for understanding organizations is the congruence model developed by Nadler and Tushman (1980). This model is presented in Figure 3-5. An important feature of the congruence model is that it expands upon the process by which inputs are transformed into outputs. As can be seen in the figure, this model incorporates the three major elements of organizations we have covered in this chapter: (1) the formal structural features of the organization, (2) the characteristics of the particular tasks being performed, and (3) the informal social relationships that exist among work-group members. To these is added a fourth critical element, the characteristics of the people performing the tasks

FIGURE 3-5
The congruence
model of organiza-
tions. (*Adapted
from Nadler &
Tushman, 1980.*)

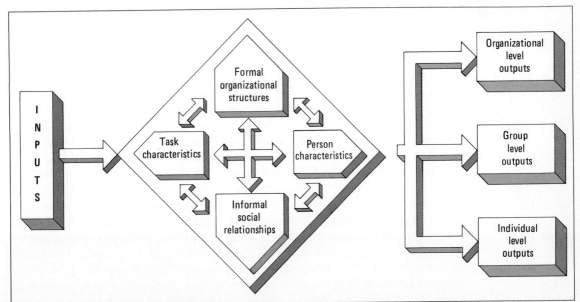

in question. Nadler and Tushman propose that the outputs from an organization are the direct result of the way these four elements relate to each other. When they fit together well, a state of congruence is said to exist, and desirable outputs can be expected. However, when they do not fit together well, a state of incongruence exists, and undesirable outputs can be expected.

A few examples may help. Let us consider first the relationship between the characteristics of the tasks being performed and the people performing them. Suppose we have a job involving a narrow set of highly specialized tasks that require relatively little skill to perform (e.g., a typical assembly-line job). In addition, suppose we have an employee who has little formal education, few marketable skills, and nothing in the way of career aspirations. In some sense, there is a fit between the job and the employee. The job demands relatively little of the employee, and the employee is unlikely to require much from the job. Now, what do you think would happen if we asked a second employee, a college graduate with high career aspirations, to do the same work? It seems likely that the college graduate would quickly become bored with the job and quit. The reason, of course, is that there is a poor fit between the individual and the job. A poor fit would also exist if we had asked the first employee to perform a very complex, highly skilled job. In this case the employee would probably not perform at a satisfactory level and would become quite frustrated at his or her lack of success. Thus, the congruence model predicts that when there is a poor fit between the person and the tasks he or she is asked to perform, the result is likely to be poor performance, low job satisfaction, and high turnover. Said differently, poor performance, low job satisfaction, and high turnover are organizational outputs that result from a lack of fit between organizational elements.

Let us take a second example, this time focusing on the relationship between person characteristics and the formal structural features of the organization. Suppose our college graduate with high career aspirations also has a very high need for autonomy. More than most, she likes to be independent and do things her own way. Suppose further that we place her in an organization that has a low degree of formalization (i.e., there are relatively few rules, regulations, and standard operating procedures) and a very decentralized authority structure (recall that Burns & Stalker [1961] refer to this as an "organic" type of organization). It would appear that our college graduate's high need for autonomy fits well with this organic structure. Thus, we would expect her to do well in this organization. Someone with a low need for autonomy might not fit as well. Conversely, our college graduate would not fit well in a highly bureaucratic organization; she would be expected to perform poorly and eventually leave. Again, the outcomes for the organization, good and bad, are the result of the degree of fit between organizational elements.

As a final example, let us consider a relationship that does not directly involve person characteristics. Turn back to page 44 and review Figure 3-2, which depicts four different modes of horizontal differentiation. Imagine that we have an organization that operates in an extremely volatile environment in which product life cycles are very short. In this type of situation, products must be designed, put into production, and marketed very quickly. Even short delays can mean substantial losses in market share. The task of getting products to market quickly demands a high degree of coordination between the design engineers, the manufacturing personnel, and the marketing staff. This level of coordination is most likely to occur when the organization is horizontally differentiated by product group, as in panel B of Figure 3-2. Differentiating by product creates some functional redundancy (i.e., multiple subunits performing the same function), but it also brings together those people who need to work in close coordination with one another. Hence, there would be a good fit between this aspect of the formal structure of the organization and the coordination requirements of the task. On the basis of this fit we would expect the organization to perform well, at least as far as getting its products to market in a timely manner. If, on the other hand, the organization were differentiated on the basis of function, as in panel A of Figure 3-2, the various groups involved with the product would probably be too widely separated for closely coordinated work. In this case, the formal structure would not fit very well with the nature of the task. Consequently, we would predict that the organization would experience many unnecessary delays in getting its products out.

Thus, it can be seen that the congruence model extends the basic contingency notion discussed earlier in this chapter in connection with the formal structure of organizations. Given the nature of the tasks to be performed, some formal structures, people, and informal social relationships will fit better than others. Similarly, given the nature of an organization's formal structure, some people, tasks, and informal social relationships will fit better than others. For every pair of organizational elements, it is theoretically possible to specify what is required for a good fit and what would constitute a bad fit (e.g., Brousseau, 1983; Randolf & Dess, 1984; Van de Ven & Drazin, 1985). The good fits are expected to result in favorable organizational outcomes, and the poor fits in unfavorable outcomes.

One final point made by the congruence model should be noted. The outputs from the organization are not all at the same level of analysis. Some outputs are at a very global level and relate to the organization as a whole. These organizational-level outputs include such things as overall productivity levels (e.g., market share, annual sales volume), organization-wide absenteeism and turnover rates, and perceptions of the organization developed by clients and members of the general public. Other outputs are at the level of the work group. Some examples include group productivity, the development of conflict and bad feelings between groups, and strong feelings of loyalty and cohesiveness within groups. Finally, there are also individual-level outputs, such as individual-level performance, job satisfaction, feelings of stress and anxiety, and the propensity to be absent from work. All these outputs result from the degree to which various elements of the organizational system fit one another to form a congruent whole.

Summary

This chapter was meant to provide a general framework for understanding organizations. Organizations are the context in which all work behavior occurs. In order to understand work behavior fully, some knowledge of this context is essential. The following major points were made in the chapter:

1. Organizations exist to facilitate goal attainment. They help to achieve both the broad goals that define the "purpose" or "mission" of the organization (e.g., educating students, making money, providing public transportation), as well as the personal goals of each organizational member (e.g., earning a living, having fun, doing something challenging).

2. A major component of the organizational environment is the formal structure of the organization. Important aspects of organizational structure are the type and degree of horizontal and vertical differentiation, the average span of control, and the degree of formalization and centralization. Each of these structural features has a demonstrable impact upon the members of the organization.

3. Task characteristics make up a second major component of the organizational environment. A natural tension seems to exist between designing tasks to optimize efficiency and designing them to optimize motivation.

4. The third important element of the organizational environment is the network of informal social relationships that exist. Informal work-group norms can have a significant influence upon many aspects of an individual's work behavior.

5. The most complete view of organizations is provided by open systems theory. An open systems perspective focuses on the interaction among the various elements of the organization, as well as on the interaction between the organization and its own larger environment.

IMPLICATIONS FOR RESEARCH

We have argued in this chapter that organizations can best be thought of as open systems. Organizational effectiveness, group performance, and the behavior of individual members of the organization can all be seen as products of the interaction among organizational elements. This perspective has several important implications for research in organizations.

One obvious implication is that our research must focus closely on the manner in which various organizational elements interact with one another, and examine how this interaction is related to organizational outcomes. Because it is so easy, we are often tempted to look at only a single aspect of an organization (e.g., the degree of centralization in its authority structure) and try to relate this one aspect to some output variable (e.g., productivity). If organizations really are open systems, however, this type of research strategy will not get us very far. A better approach would be to ask more complex questions such as, what will be the effect on productivity if a highly centralized organization is populated with individuals who have a high need for autonomy and control? or, if a task requires a high degree of coordination among groups of individuals, but there exists a great deal of intergroup hostility and conflict, what sort of organizational structure will be most helpful for getting the task accomplished? The former question involves an interaction between two organizational elements (formal organizational structures and person characteristics), while the latter involves a three-way interaction (task characteristics, informal group relations, and formal organizational structures). Only by examining these more complex questions can the systemic nature of organizations be studied.

A second research implication is that we need to learn how to measure each of the various elements of organizations in terms that are relevant for assessing their fit with every one of the other elements. We need to know, for example, how to measure formal organizational structures in ways that are useful not only for assessing their fit with the tasks being performed, but also for assessing their fit with the needs of individual organizational members and the characteristics of the informal group relationships that exist. It seems apparent that dimensions important for assessing the structure-task fit are likely to be quite different from those needed to assess the structure-person and structure-group fits. Some research along these lines has already been conducted, but a good deal more is needed.

A final implication for research is that organizational phenomena need to be studied at multiple levels of analysis (cf. Mossholder & Bedeian, 1983; Rousseau, 1985). As is suggested by the congruence model, organizations produce outputs at three different levels: organizational, group, and individual. There is something unique about each one of these levels. Outcomes at any one level cannot always be predicted from outcomes at the other levels. This is well illustrated by the professional basketball team that has many individual superstars but that nevertheless has a poor win/loss record because the individual players do not play well together as a team. How well the team plays as a whole (a group-level phenomenon) cannot in this case be predicted from how well the team members play as individuals (an individual-level phenomenon). Nor would we predict that many of the team members are superstars, knowing only the team's win/loss record. The point is that individual-, group-, and organizational-level outcomes are often very different from one another. We need to pay attention to, and get separate measures of, all three of these levels if we want a complete picture of the effect of various interactions among organizational elements.

IMPLICATIONS FOR PRACTICE

There are two important practical implications to be drawn from this chapter. The first one is that *there is no one best way to design an organization.* Standard formulas such as "centralize the decision process" and "simplify jobs to maximize efficiency" just do not work all of the time. Rather, organizational effectiveness comes from (1) maintaining the proper fit among organizational elements, and (2) maintaining the fit between the organization and its own larger environment. Thus, a centralized decision process will be beneficial only if it fits the other elements of the organization and only if it is appropriate given the characteristics of the external environment. If there is a poor match in either area, a centralized decision process could actually harm the organization. Similarly, under some circumstances designing jobs to be simple and technically efficient can be a benefit. However, under other conditions the same job characteristics will lead to less than optimal performance. Therefore, the question is not *whether* particular design elements should be used, but *when* and *under what conditions* they should be used.

The second important implication is that *what is effective today may not be effective tomorrow.* Jobs change, employees change, and so do organizational environments. New technologies replace old ones, new markets suddenly open up, and new competitors appear on the scene. Managers need to be constantly on the lookout for these changes, and they need to be aware of how such changes affect the organization. When new employees are hired to replace those who have retired, it is important to determine whether the new employees fit their jobs in the same way the old ones did. And, if the external environment suddenly becomes turbulent and unpredictable, it is important to reevaluate the appropriateness of the old modes of decision making.

So, not only is it hard to define the one best way to organize, it is apparent that any *specific* best way in a *specific* situation may lose its effectiveness over time. The implication for managers is to stay flexible and constantly monitor the fit among organizational elements and between the organization and its environment. Signs of discontent, such as grievances, turnover, and absenteeism, will occur when poor fits exist. They are indications of a poor match between organizational elements. The best approach is to try to understand where the poor fit exists and make the appropriate modifications. As we proceed through the text, the meaning of the term "appropriate" will become more clear.

Discussion Questions

1. What is an organization? How do terms such as *management* and *goals* fit into this definition?
2. What were the important substantive and methodological findings of the Hawthorne studies? What do these findings tell us about human nature?
3. What aspects of the organization are likely to be easiest to control? Does this suggest anything about managerial behavior?

CASE: STARTING A NEW DIVISION

After working 10 years for a large ($500 million sales) multidivision, multiproduct firm, you have been assigned the task of starting up a new division to produce and distribute recreational equipment. This is a new line of business for your company, so the management recognizes the need to provide you with enough independence and authority to get geared up and start operating effectively. To underscore this need and their support for you, while also making clear that the full responsibility for the success of this new venture is yours, the management has indicated that you will be designated as president of the recreational equipment division.

One of the first tasks that you will be concerned with is organizing your division for action. The parent company will help you staff your operation from its present managerial ranks and will help recruit any additional managerial or sales personnel you may need. But before you start considering the structural possibilities or the relationships between your managers and departments, you make the following assessments of your new organization's situation:

Because of the type of equipment that you plan to produce, the demand is likely to be very inelastic, that is, slight changes in your products' prices will have little effect on sales volume. Therefore, it will be relatively easy for you to secure distributors. In fact, one distributor has been willing to agree to a 3-year sales contract for your equipment. The rationale underlying this position is that since no other firm produces similar equipment, there will be little competition for sales. Additionally, consumers are likely to perceive your equipment as being of a unique quality, so that viable alternatives will be unavailable. Besides, patent protection for your type of product is virtually guaranteed.

In relation to production, you doubt that there will be many problems. On the one hand, your production process includes readily available materials, and there are many possible suppliers. Thus, it may be possible for you to contract with your suppliers for a 3-year period at a constant price. Also the production equipment required will necessitate little negotiation on your part, since such equipment is usually in stock and the cost is reasonable.

The current market for the type of labor that is needed can be characterized as open. Recent graduations from local trade schools have left the market with many available craftsmen. Additionally, it is unlikely that a union will enter the picture with this type of personnel. Recent attempts by the local AFL-CIO organizer to unionize recreational-equipment workers have been met with opposition. But even if unionization occurs, it is unlikely that there would be much disruption in the industry, since this particular branch of the AFL-CIO has not been excessively aggressive in other industries.

Another significant factor for your operations relates to government regulation. Up to this point the government has been fairly flexible with the industry, and it is likely that that position will be maintained. Governmental regulation has been increasing in all industries, but at this stage, regulation of the recreational-equipment industry is considered to be still inappropriate by most legislators. Consumer advocates seem to be less concerned with the social, economic, or political impact of the industry, thus little public scrutiny is likely. The public attitude is unlikely to be reflected in future financing of the operations, since strong financial backing has already been secured.

A final area of possible concern is future technological change. In the past the recreational-equipment industry has been characterized by frequent product improvements and new-product introductions. Your products, however, are unlikely to be subject to this volatility. Your products will employ the most current technology and materials, and the industry is expected to stabilize. The industry has innovated on the magnitude of about fifty new changes per year for the last decade; indications at a recent trade show, however, signal a change rate of around ten innovations or less per year for the foreseeable future.

Source: ©1976 by Bourgeois, Hughes, & Wartick, by permission. From L. J. Bourgeois, D. W. McAllister, & T. R. Mitchell (1978). The effects of different organizational environments upon individual decisions about organizational design. *Academy of Management Journal,* 21, 503–513.

Questions about the Case

1. Would you describe the environment as stable or turbulent? Is it risky or predictable? Can you control what is going on?
2. How much change is there likely to be? How certain are you about what the future will look like?
3. To what extent do you think procedures should be written down and clearly specified? Should there be a policy manual containing the rules?

4. What about communication processes? Should everything be kept in writing? Should people communicate mainly through the chain of command?
5. Will you encourage people to be able to handle a variety of tasks, or should all employees have a fairly distinct and clearly specified job of their own?

References

Adair, J. (1984). The Hawthorne effect: A reconsideration of the methodological artifact. *Journal of Applied Psychology, 69,* 334–345.

Alber, A., & Blumberg, M. (1981, Jan.–Feb.). Team vs. individual approaches to job enrichment programs. *Personnel, 63,* 63–75.

Bell, G. D. (1967). Determinants of span of control. *American Journal of Sociology, 73,* 90–101.

Berger, C. J. , & Cummings, L. L. (1979). Organizational structure, attitudes, and behaviors. In B. M. Staw (Ed.), *Research in Organizational Behavior* (Vol. 1, pp. 169–208). Greenwich, CT: JAI Press.

Brousseau, K. R. (1983). Toward a dynamic model of job-person relationships: Findings, research questions, and implications for work system design. *Academy of Management Review, 8,* 33–45.

Burns, T., & Stalker, G. M. (1961). *The management of innovation.* London: Tavistock.

Connor, P. E. (1984). *Organization structure and design.* Chicago: Science Research Associates.

Cummings, L. L. (1983). The logic of management. *Academy of Management Review, 8,* 532–538.

Davis, S. M., & Lawrence, P. R. (1977). *Matrix.* Reading, MA: Addison-Wesley.

Drucker, P. F. (1954). *The practice of management.* NY: Harper & Row.

El Salmi, A. M., & Cummings, L. L. (1968). Managers' perceptions of needs and need satisfaction as a function of interactions among organizational variables. *Personnel Psychology, 21,* 465–477.

Emery, F. E., & Thorsrud, E. (1976). *Democracy at work.* Leiden, The Netherlands: Martinus Nijhoff.

Fotilas, P. N. (1981, July). Semi-autonomous work groups: An alternative in organizing production work. *Management Review,* 50–54.

Fry, L. W. (1982). Technology-structure research: Three critical issues. *Academy of Management Journal, 25,* 532–552.

Gaertner, G. H., & Ramnarayan, S. (1983). Organizational effectiveness: An alternative perspective. *Academy of Management Review, 8,* 97–107.

Galbraith, J. R. (1977). *Organization design.* Reading, MA: Addison-Wesley.

Goodman, P. S. (1979). *Assessing organizational change: The Rushton quality of work experiment.* NY: Wiley.

Griffin, R. W. (1982). *Task design: An integrative approach.* Glenview, IL: Scott, Foresman.

Gyllenhammar, P. G. (1977). How Volvo adapts work to people. *Harvard Business Review, 55(4),* 102–113.

Haimann, T., Scott, W. G., & Connor, P. E. (1982). *Managing the modern organization* (4th ed.). Boston: Houghton Mifflin.

Katz, D., & Kahn, R. L. (1978). *The social psychology of organizations* (2d ed.). NY: Wiley.

Konz, S. (1983). *Work design: Industrial ergonomic* (2d ed.). Columbus, OH: Grid Publishing.

Lawrence, P. R., Kolodny, H. F., & Davis, S. M. (1977, Summer). The human side of matrix. *Organizational Dynamics,* 43–61.

Lawrence, P. R., & Lorsch, J. W. (1967). *Organization and environment: Managing differentiation and integration.* Boston: Harvard Business School, Division of Research.

Leavitt, H. J., Dill, W. R., & Eyring, H. B. (1973). *The organizational world.* NY: Harcourt, Brace.

Locke, E. A. (1976). The nature and cause of job satisfaction. In M. D. Dunnette (Ed.), *Handbook of industrial and organizational psychology* (pp. 1297–1349). Chicago: Rand McNally.

Locke, E. A. (1982). The ideas of Frederick W. Taylor: An evaluation. *Academy of Management Review, 7,* 14–24.

Magnusen, K. O. (1973). *Perspectives on organizational design and development.* (Research paper No. 21). NY: Columbia University Graduate School of Business.

Mayo, E. (1933). *The human problems of an industrial civilization.* NY: Macmillan.

Mintzberg, H. (1979). *The structuring of organizations.* Englewood Cliffs, NJ: Prentice-Hall.

Mizruchi, M. S. (1983). Who controls whom? An examination of the relation between management and boards of directors in large American corporations. *Academy of Management Review, 8,* 426–435.

Mossholder, K. W., & Bedeian, A. G. (1983). Cross-level inferences and organizational research: Perspectives on interpretation and application. *Academy of Management Review, 8,* 547–558.

Nadler, D. A., Hackman, J. R., & Lawler, E. E. III. (1979). *Managing organizational behavior.* Boston: Little, Brown.

Nadler, D. A., & Tushman, M. L. (1980, Autumn). A model for diagnosing organizational behavior: Applying a congruence perspective. *Organizational Dynamics,* 35–51.

Niebel, B. W. (1982). *Motion and time study* (7th ed.). Homewood, IL: Irwin.

Perrow, C. (1967). A framework for the comparative analysis of organizations. *American Sociological Review, 32,* 194–208.

Peters, T. J., & Austin, N. K. (1985). *A passion for excellence.* NY: Random House.

Porter, L. W., & Lawler, E. E. III. (1965). Properties of organization structure in relation to job attitudes and job behavior. *Psychological Bulletin, 64,* 23–51.

Randolph, W. A., & Dess, G. G. (1984). The congruence perspective of organization design: A conceptual model and multivariate research approach. *Academy of Management Review, 9,* 114–127.

Reimann, B. C. (1973). On the dimensions of bureaucratic structure: An empirical reappraisal. *Administrative Science Quarterly, 18,* 462–467.

Roethlisberger, F. J., & Dickson, W. V. (1939). *Management and the worker.* Cambridge, MA: Harvard University Press.

Rousseau, D. M. (1985). Issues of level in organizational research: Multi-level and cross-level perspectives. In L. L. Cummings & B. M. Staw (Eds.), *Research in organizational behavior* (Vol. 7, pp. 1–37). Greenwich, CT: JAI Press.

Schmidt, S. M., & Kipnis, D. (1984). Managers' pursuit of individual and organizational goals. *Human Relations, 37,* 781–794.

Scott, W. G., & Hart, D. K. (1979). *Organizational America.* Boston: Houghton Mifflin.

Scott, W. G., Mitchell, T. R., & Birnbaum, P. (1981). *Organization theory: A structural and behavioral analysis.* Homewood, IL: Irwin-Dorsey.

Smith, P. (1984, November). How work design teams introduced new technology to General Food offices. *Management Review,* 38–41.

Taylor, F. W. (1911). *The principles of scientific management.* NY: Harper & Brothers.

Trist, E. L., & Bamford, K. W. (1951). Some social and psychological consequences of the longwall method of coal-getting. *Human Relations, 4,* 3–38.

Trist, E. L., Higgin, G. W., Murray, H., & Pollock, A. B. (1963). *Organizational choice: Capabilities of groups at the coal face under changing technologies*. London: Tavistock.

Udell, J. G. (1967). An empirical test of hypotheses relating to span of control. *Administrative Science Quarterly, 12,* 420–439.

Van de Ven, A. H., & Drazin, R. (1985). The concept of fit in contingency theory. In L. L. Cummings & B. M. Staw (Eds.), *Research in organizational behavior* (Vol. 7, pp. 333–365). Greenwich, CT: JAI Press.

Walton, R. E. (1972). How to counter alienation in the plant. *Harvard Business Review, 50(6),* 70–81.

Weber, M. (1947). *The theory of social and economic organization* (A. M. Henderson & T. Parsons, Trans.). New York: Oxford University Press.

Weick, K. E. (1979). *The social psychology of organizing* (2d ed.). Reading, MA: Addison-Wesley.

Woodward, J. (1965). *Industrial organization: Theory and practice*. London: Oxford University Press.

Part Two

Individual Characteristics

The second part of the book discusses the individual in more detail. The material presented in Chapter 2, "Understanding People," provides the framework for this section. The focus is on those basic human processes and characteristics that the individual brings to the organizational setting.

Chapter 4, "Perception and Personality," begins with a definition of perception. The way in which perception affects our behavior is then described. Much of what we perceive is actually a biased interpretation of the real world (e.g., we hear what we want to hear). These biases often influence important organizational decisions (e.g., selection, evaluation), and some examples of how to remedy these problems are discussed.

The personality section of Chapter 4 defines personality and discusses in detail the controversy over whether personality is stable and enduring or more transitory in nature. We conclude that personality is indeed one cause of people's behavior. However, it is important to recognize that the situation and environment are just as important. The implications of this point are explored in some depth.

Chapter 5, "Attitudes," emphasizes the central role that attitudes play in organizational behavior. People have attitudes about nearly everything. We define attitudes and discuss how they develop and change. Much of the discussion focuses on job attitudes and what can be done to ensure that people are satisfied with their work environment. A number of suggestions are presented.

Chapter 6, "Motivation," might be described as the heart of the book. While perceptions have to do with how we process information, and attitudes relate to how we evaluate it, motivation focuses on what we *do* about it. If we know what motivates people, *and if the causes of motivation are under our control*, we can have a direct impact on people's behavior.

The chapter is organized around a single overall model of motivation. Broadly speaking, this model divides the topic of motivation into two separate questions: (1) What activates us or gets us aroused? and (2) What determines what we intend to do about it? For both of these questions, internal as well as external factors are examined. For example, theories that deal with internal causes of arousal focus on needs, with need-deprivation being a primary mechanism that goads the individual to action. Goal-setting theory, equity theory, expectancy theory, and reinforcement theory are all discussed in terms of what they tell us about the factors that affect people's intentions to behave in particular ways.

Finally, in Chapter 7, "Job Stress," we

examine a special kind of reaction that people often have to their work environment. A stress reaction has both physiological and psychological components. Job stress is a widespread phenomenon, and it results in many consequences that are harmful to both the individual and the organization. Both interpersonal and organizational factors that contribute to stress on the job are discussed. We also examine situational and personality factors that moderate the impact of various stressors, as well as strategies for reducing and preventing job stress.

By the time you reach the end of Part 2 you should have a better understanding of what people bring to the organizational setting, as well as some of the basic processes that regulate their behavior—perception, personality, attitudes, motivation, and job stress.

Chapter 4

Perception and Personality

One man's justice is another's injustice;
One man's beauty another's ugliness;
One man's wisdom another's folly.
—RALPH WALDO EMERSON

77

One of the most common observations of any manager or person working in an organizational setting is that people are different. They differ in physical characteristics such as size, weight, age, and sex. They differ in background characteristics such as training and education. And they differ in personality traits such as extroversion and aggressiveness. The major consequences of such differences are twofold. First, people need to be treated as individuals. Different types of people will want different kinds of organizational rewards and will probably work best in different kinds of settings. Second, every individual will not see things in the same way. There will be differences of opinion and evaluation on almost every topic.

In order to understand why people behave the way they do in organizational settings, we must understand what makes them unique. People have different reactions to similar situations, and the explanations given for such divergence frequently involve underlying psychological processes. Two such processes are *perception* and *personality*. Both of these contribute to the internal causes of behavior discussed in Chapter 2, "Understanding People." Perceptions are the result of cognitive processes that shape the way we think about the world. Personality reflects our genetic heritage and our early environment. While we've pointed out that personality is not the only determinant of behavior, there can be little doubt that it is an important contributing factor. In this chapter we will examine these two processes in light of their relationship to organizational behavior.

PERSON PERCEPTION: FORMING IMPRESSIONS OF OTHERS

Almost everyone spends a part of each day interacting with other people. Usually these interactions progress smoothly, and as a consequence most of our relationships with others are harmonious and pleasant. Maintaining these relationships requires a great deal of knowledge about social behavior. We are constantly making judgments about other people's thoughts, needs, and emotions, and we do this rather automatically. These judgments are based on a wealth of information that is constantly bombarding our senses. The process by which we interpret this sensory information and come to an understanding of the people around us is called *person perception*. This process is critical for both individual and organizational effectiveness.

Consider the following examples. Listed below are a number of situations in which the accurate perception and evaluation of other people's feelings and intentions could influence the success of an organization.

1. Evaluating a job candidate based on a short personal interview
2. Making decisions about how to proceed in a labor-management bargaining session
3. Evaluating an employee's performance for the purpose of making salary and promotional decisions
4. Encountering someone new from the "front office"
5. The initial exchange between a sales representative and a prospective customer

As several of these examples suggest, we sometimes make important judgments about other people based only on very short interactions and first impressions. In forming these first impressions, we often use rather simple types of information about the other person. Our first impressions are also affected by our own habits and beliefs, and by characteristics of the situation in which they are formed. Let us take a closer look at each of these factors.

The Person Perceived

In an interpersonal situation, one's evaluation of and behavior toward another person are partly influenced by the characteristics of that person. These characteristics fall under three headings: physical, social, and historical.

Some of the more important *physical* factors are gestures, posture, facial expression, and pigmentation. An example of how gestures can influence our judgments occurred in the early 1970s when Vice President Rockefeller raised his middle finger to a group of hecklers at a political rally. Since few Americans had a close personal relationship with Rockefeller, they had to form their impressions of him based upon his public behavior. For many people, this gesture represented a vulgar public display that negatively influenced their evaluations.

One's posture also is important. People often attribute laziness or lack of motivation to someone who slouches. Similarly, in face-to-face interactions posture influences our judgments of how interested the other person is in who we are and what we have to say (Harrigan & Rosenthal, 1983). In foreign countries, an individual's importance is sometimes judged according to how tall he or she stands in relation to others. For example, a Thai who is interacting with another Thai of higher status will try not to have his or her head be higher than that of the other, even when the other is physically shorter. Facial expressions and features may similarly influence our feelings about others. Smiling is related to positive attitudes, for example, and people with eyes that are small and close together are often judged to be shifty or dishonest. Finally, in some cultures darker skin pigmentation may be associated with negative attributes. Research in the United States has shown that many Caucasians see darkness as related to hostility, dishonesty, unfriendliness, shyness, and other negative attributes, while blondness and light skin are most frequently associated with heroes and positive characteristics (Brigham, 1971).

The *social* characteristics that appear to be most important are voice qualities and appearance. In many cases one's education, place of residence, and status can be inferred from one's manner of speech. It is also clear that one's clothes and grooming are used by others in their evaluation. Students who come to class dressed in very "preppie" clothes leave a distinctly different impression from those who always wear old jeans and a T-shirt. And police officers who wear traditional uniforms are often perceived more positively than those who wear civilian clothes (Mauro, 1984).

The *historical* factors or attributes that have a large effect on our evaluation of others include sex, age, occupation, religion, and race. For example, research has shown that racial background is often more important than occupation, religion, or nationality in determining whether an individual will

FIGURE 4-1
Clothing can strongly influence the way we perceive others.

be accepted into an American's social group (Triandis & Triandis, 1965). People from other countries tend to emphasize other characteristics such as religion (Greeks) or occupation (Germans) as most important.

To summarize, a wide variety of cues influence our evaluation of others. Some of these cues may give us accurate information and some may not. The particular way in which these cues are used is partially dependent upon one's culture and values. That is, the characteristics of the perceiver are also important for understanding how first impressions are formed.

The Perceiver

In general, there are two sets of variables related to the perceiver that are important in understanding perceptions of others. First, the perceiver's own social and personality characteristics make a difference. In one study mentioned previously, people who were more secure, more independent, and had a high tolerance for ambiguity were more accepting of others who were different from themselves. Also, people who were high on a scale reflecting social sophistication or breadth of perspective were more accepting than those who had low scores on this scale (Triandis & Triandis, 1965). The implications for employee selection and placement in multinational organizations are clear:

Choose people to work overseas who are independent, have a high tolerance for ambiguity, and are accepting of others.

The second important set of variables involves the complexity with which we characteristically describe others. Some individuals use rather simple physical labels to describe people (e.g., tall, dark, and handsome), while others use personality traits that are always consistent, and are dependent upon only one central trait (e.g., sly, tricky, and untrustworthy). In contrast, some people characteristically use very complex descriptions that include a wide variety of both positive and negative traits (e.g., friendliness, aggressiveness, honesty, and slyness). This last constellation of traits reflects a more complex mode of perceiving than that which uses either traits that are all very similar or physical attributes. Research shows that people who characteristically use very complex modes of perceiving tend to be more accurate in their perceptions than those who characteristically use very simple modes (Schneider, Hastorf, & Ellsworth, 1979). Further, research in the area of leadership has shown that the complexity with which leaders perceive their coworkers is significantly related to group performance in some situations (Fiedler, 1978). We will discuss this research in Chapter 14, "Leadership."

The Situation

The final set of circumstances related to one's perceptions of others is the situation in which one finds oneself. This is particularly true when first impressions are being formed. Since there are few behavioral cues, one must often rely on situational variables such as the place of meeting (a bar or the executive lunchroom), who is accompanying the target person (a respected colleague or a disliked subordinate), and the occasion for the meeting (an office party or a long-range planning session).

We are constantly meeting new people and forming impressions of them. These evaluations are often influenced by rather unreliable factors such as appearance and dress, and by our own personality. The interesting point is that even though these impressions may be inaccurate, the process by which they are formed is fairly consistent. Of course, first impressions change over time. As we observe more and more of a person's behavior, a somewhat different perceptual process begins to operate.

PERCEIVING THE CAUSES OF BEHAVIOR

Once we have the opportunity to interact with someone and to observe his or her behavior, we begin to form a richer picture of what that individual is really like. We make inferences about the person's motives, personality, feelings, and attitudes. While we can never know for sure what other people are thinking, the observation of their behavior is usually a more reliable cue than their dress or the way they comb their hair.

This inference process—the attempt to assess and evaluate people accurately based upon their behavior—is called the *attribution process*. An attribution is simply an inference about the causes of someone's behavior. From our observations we make inferences about internal states (like anxiety or joy),

De moro relato.

inferences about enduring personality traits, and inferences about the environment in which we observe the behavior (e.g., busy, calm). The study of the attribution process has been one of the most active areas of research in social psychology over the last 20 years, and it has produced a number of findings that are important for understanding people's behavior in organizational settings.

Theorizing about attributions began with the work of Fritz Heider (1958), who was interested in how people make judgments about causal relationships in their environment. Heider believed that people have a natural tendency to see events in terms of causal relationships, and that this process is relevant for how we treat other people. For events that involve nonliving objects, we usually see the causal relationships simply in terms of physical laws. Rocks fall because of gravity, tides change because of the position of the moon, and automobiles run because of certain chemical and mechanical principles. For events involving people, on the other hand, the situation is a bit more complex. People have personalities, intentions, motives, and goals. These have to be factored into any causal attribution. Thus, for example, when we see someone fall on the sidewalk we usually do not attribute the fall solely to gravity. Sure, gravity played a part, but we might also wonder whether the person is naturally clumsy, was momentarily distracted, or is having a medical emergency. The accuracy of our attribution could have life-or-death consequences.

The study of the attribution process has shown that people are remarkably consistent in how they evaluate others. The first and perhaps most important judgment that we make is one of internal or external causation. Is the person acting from free will, or is he or she being forced by the situation to engage in the action? If an employee leaves a job, is it because she did not work hard or was not smart enough (internal attributions), or because the boss was difficult to work with or the job was boring (external attributions)? If a subordinate is late with a financial report, is it because of laziness (internal) or overwork (external)? Our subsequent behavior toward the individuals involved in these examples will differ dramatically depending upon whether an internal or an external explanation is accepted.

In deciding whether an action is internally or externally caused, we make use of three important principles: the covariance principle, the discounting principle, and the augmentation principle. In addition, when it comes to job performance, we not only want to know whether the performance was due to internal or external causes, we also want to know whether those causes are stable over time. If the causes are stable, similar performance can be expected in the future. We will consider each of these issues in turn.

The Covariance Principle

The covariance principle states that we attribute an action to the one factor with which it most strongly covaries (Kelley, 1967). This principle is perhaps best explained by example. Consider a student who fails a final exam. We might wonder why the student failed. Was it because the student did not work hard or is not very smart? These are internal attributions. Or was it because the professor is a poor lecturer or the test was unfair (e.g., it did not cover the assigned material)? These are external attributions. In order to decide which type of attribution is most appropriate, we need to consider three kinds of information: (1) distinctiveness information, (2) consensus information, and (3) consistency information.

Distinctiveness information concerns whether this individual has failed the final exam in other courses or just this one. In other words, how distinctive or different was failing this particular exam? If the student got low grades on most other finals, we are more likely to make an internal attribution than if the student got A's on the other finals and an F in this course only.

Consensus information concerns whether most students in the class had trouble with the final, or whether this student was the only one with a low grade. If consensus is high (i.e., most other students did fail) we would expect an external attribution, and we would expect the reverse if consensus is low.

Finally, *consistency information* concerns whether our student has consistently failed past exams in this class. If the student failed the final exam but got an A on the midterm, we are more likely to think that failing the final was externally caused.

The combination of these three types of information, distinctiveness, consensus, and consistency, usually forms a pattern that allows us to make a fairly confident attribution. If failing the final exam is distinctive (the student did well on the final in other courses), if there is a high degree of consensus (many other students also failed this final), and if the failure is not consistent with this student's past performance (the student got an A on the midterm), an external attribution seems most appropriate. This is because the behavior covaries strongly with the situation. When the situation is changed (final exams in other courses or past exams in this course), we see a change in the student's performance. By contrast, when the student is changed (how other students did), we see no change in performance. On the other hand, if failing the final is not distinctive (the student also failed the final in other courses), if there is a low degree of consensus (no other students failed), and if the failure is quite consistent with this student's past performance (the student also failed the midterm), an internal attribution seems most appropriate. In this case the behavior covaries strongly with the person. When the student is changed (how other students did) we see a change in performance. By contrast, when the situation is changed (finals in other courses, and past exams in this course) we see no change in performance. These two patterns of information and the attributions they lead to are summarized in Figure 4-2.

The Discounting and Augmentation Principles

A second principle that we make use of when trying to decide whether an internal or external attribution is most appropriate is the *discounting principle*. The discounting principle states that our confidence in an internal attribution for behavior is lowered, or discounted, whenever plausible external explanations are also present (Kelley, 1971). For example, suppose two students perform very well on an exam. They get the top two grades in the class. It is apparent that both students studied very hard. The question is, why did they put out so much effort? In talking with these students you find that both are quite interested in the course. Thus, one plausible explanation for their high

FIGURE 4-2
The patterns of
distinctiveness,
consensus, and
consistency infor-
mation that would
lead to either an
internal or external
attribution for fail-
ing a final exam.

Covariance Information			
Distinctiveness	Consensus	Consistency	Most Probable Attribution
This student failed the final exam in other courses. (low distinctiveness)	All other students got a good grade on the final exam in this course. (low consensus)	This student also failed the midterm exam in this course. (high consistency)	INTERNAL
This student got a good grade on the final in other courses. (high distinctiveness)	All other students also got a low grade on the final in this course. (high consensus)	This student got a good grade on the midterm exam in this course. (low consistency)	EXTERNAL

level of performance is their interest in the material. This is an internal attribution. However, you also learn from someone else that one of these two students is in danger of losing an athletic scholarship if she does not improve her academic record. Thus, for this student you have a second plausible explanation, namely, that she tried to do well on the exam so that she would not lose her scholarship. This is an external attribution. According to the discounting principle, we will be less confident in attributing the high performance to intrinsic interest in the course material for the student with the scholarship. When there are no obvious external factors that could cause a behavior, we can be very confident in an internal attribution. But when plausible external explanations do exist, our confidence in an internal attribution goes down.

The reverse of the discounting principle is the *augmentation principle*. The augmentation principle states that our confidence in an internal attribution for behavior is raised, or augmented, whenever external circumstances would normally lead to the *opposite* behavior (Kelley, 1971). For example, suppose a series of debates are set up in class in which students are assigned different points of view on particular issues. You know you are to be graded on how well you criticize your opponent's presentation. If after a series of these debates you are asked whether all your classmates are normally as critical of others as they sound, you would probably reply negatively. It is likely that they are being critical because the situation demands it. But what about a student who fails to point out any of the shortcomings of an opponent's presentation? What would you think of this person? You would probably infer that he or she is particularly reluctant to criticize others. In other words, a behavior that differs from what the situation demands will probably result in more extreme and confident attributions about the person's internal traits and states than will an action that complies with those demands. There is substantial research evidence indicating that we do indeed make frequent use of the augmentation, discounting, and covariance principles when making causal attributions (Kelley & Michela, 1980).

Stable and Unstable Causes of Performance

In addition to knowing whether a behavior is internally or externally caused, it is also helpful to know whether the cause is stable or unstable (Weiner et al., 1971). As we suggested earlier, stable causes can usually be counted on to produce the same behavior again, whereas unstable causes cannot. Furthermore, when the behavior is attributed to an internal characteristic of a person, the stability of this characteristic can affect how we evaluate that individual. *why internal only.*

it is his characteristic.

For example, imagine that a new salesperson in the insurance business brings in a contract from a large corporation worth over $1 million to your company. You are this person's supervisor, and you want to determine why this happened. Your first task is to decide whether the success was due to internal or external causes. Using any available distinctiveness, consensus, and consistency information would help in this regard. For example, if this was a hard account to get (others had failed before), you would probably make an internal attribution. If, on the other hand, you knew this particular corporation was highly interested in what your company had to offer and that it was just a matter of time before they signed a contract, you might make an external attribution.

Your second task is to decide whether the cause is stable or unstable. If you decided that this salesperson was the cause of the good performance, you would want to know if it was due to his or her natural selling ability (a stable trait) or just superhard work—exerting an extreme amount of effort—to get this particular contract (an unstable cause—the amount of effort someone puts into a job can change overnight). If the behavior is seen as externally caused, is it because the task is easy (again, a stable characteristic) or is it due to luck (another unstable characteristic)? Figure 4-3 summarizes these possible

why is selling ability internal.

why is easy stable.

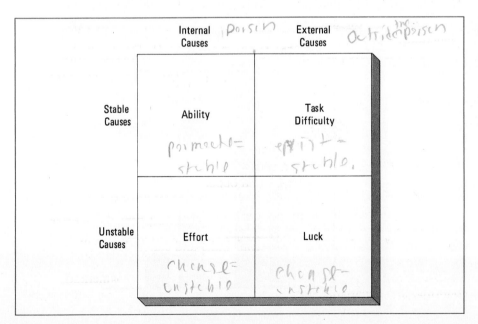

interpretations. If after examining all the available information you conclude that the salesperson's natural selling ability was the primary cause of his or her success, it seems reasonable to expect that he or she will continue to do well in the future. On the other hand, if you conclude that the salesperson's superhard work was the main cause, future success is more uncertain. It will occur only as long as he or she continues to exert extremely high effort. Similarly, if the salesperson's success seemed to occur primarily because the task was easy, success in the future can be expected as long as the task does not become more difficult. But if this success was only a stroke of good luck, future success cannot be predicted. It may or may not occur, depending on how lucky the salesperson is.

Thus, as perceivers we take the stability of the attributed cause of performance into account because it helps us predict *future* performance. In addition, however, the stability of the attributed cause can also affect the way we evaluate the *present* performance. This is well illustrated in a study by Knowlton and Mitchell (1980). They conducted a laboratory experiment in which subjects supervised three individuals who were working on a clerical task. There were four treatment conditions in this experiment. In one condition, one of the three workers performed substantially better than the other two, seemingly because of an unusually high level of ability. In a second condition, this worker appeared to perform better than the others because of a high level of effort. In the third condition, this worker performed substantially worse than the other two, this time because of low ability. In the final condition, this worker performed worse than the others because of low effort. After completing the supervisory part of their task, the subjects were asked to evaluate the performance of all three workers. Of primary interest were the ratings given to the one worker who performed either better or worse than the other two. The authors hypothesized that when performance was attributed to effort the subjects would rate this worker more positively in the above average

FIGURE 4-4
In comparison to ability attributions, effort attributions were hypothesized to lead to higher positive and lower negative performance ratings. (*Adapted from Knowlton & Mitchell, 1980.*)

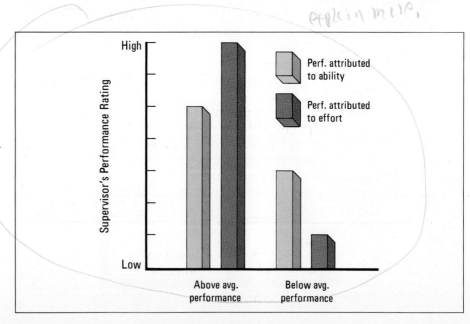

performance condition and more negatively in the below average condition than when performance was attributed to ability. These predictions are shown in Figure 4-4. The results from the study strongly supported this hypothesis. The subjects' performance ratings were more extreme when effort was seen as a cause of the worker's performance. This study demonstrates that our evaluations of other people's performance are influenced by the type of performance attributions we make.

SYSTEMATIC ERRORS IN PERCEPTION

The importance of perception cannot be overstated. It shapes what we see, how we evaluate what we see, and the way we behave. This is true for our observations of both objects and people. There are, however, a number of systematic errors that we often make because of the perceptual process. These errors can strongly influence our behavior in organizational settings. The most significant of these systematic errors are described below.

Attribution Errors

There are two important attribution errors that we frequently make, and both are relevant for understanding the performance-evaluation process. The first of these is the *actor-observer error*. The essence of this error is that people tend to attribute their own behavior to external environmental factors, while attributing the behavior of others to internal dispositional causes (Jones & Nisbett, 1972). When asked why we do something, we, as actors, frequently point to the demands of the situation that led to our action. However, when asked to explain the behavior of others, we, as observers, usually say such things as, "that's the way that person is." While numerous explanations for this phenomenon are available, perhaps the most reasonable one is that as actors we focus on the environment and have access to how the environment affects our thinking. As observers we tend to focus on the other person, not the environment, and we do not have direct access to how the environment influences other people's thinking.

The second error is the *self-serving bias*. There is much evidence that we tend to make internal attributions for the good things that happen to us and external attributions for the negative things. We succeed because of talent and hard work, but fail because of environmental circumstances. This type of bias serves to protect and enhance our self-esteem (Larson, 1977; Miller, 1976).

We can see the operation of both of these errors when a supervisor makes an attribution for a subordinate's performance. Here, the supervisor is an observer and the subordinate is an actor. When subordinates perform poorly, supervisors tend to use internal attributions for the failure, while subordinates are more likely to give external explanations. The actor-observer error clearly operates. A self-serving bias also operates, since if the supervisor blames the subordinate, the inference is that poor supervision is not part of the problem.

On the other hand, when a subordinate performs well, the supervisor is likely to be much more willing to take partial credit, saying, "Oh yes, that employee did work very hard on the report, but the fine performance was partly due to my making sure that he was not distracted by other less-important activities." In short, both of these biases are likely to lead to different and opposing views of the causes of both good and poor performance, and conflict and hard feelings are the likely result.

Finally, we want to point out that these biases cause problems in organizational settings not only because they distort perceptions, but also because they severely limit options for managerial responsiveness. In particular, if supervisors perceive poor subordinate performance as being due to something internal to the subordinate, they will use "internal solutions" to correct the performance. This means reprimanding the subordinate, seeking ways to improve the subordinate's motivation, or in extreme cases, firing the subordinate and searching for someone else who is better qualified to do the work. All these responses may be inappropriate if the subordinate's poor performance is actually caused by some aspect of the situation (e.g., not enough direction and guidance from the supervisor). In general, supervisors (and subordinates, for that matter) do not appreciate the extent to which behavior is influenced by the environment (cf. Ross, 1977). This means that they also do not appreciate the extent to which changing the environment will improve poor performance. We will have more to say about this topic in Chapter 16, "The Line Manager's Impact on Employee Performance."

Stereotyping

We are frequently confronted with situations in which we know very little about a person except one prominent characteristic, such as age, race, or occupation. Yet, given just this one bit of information, we have a tendency to want to categorize the person in such a way that we can attribute to him or her a whole set of additional characteristics. This categorization process is called *stereotyping,* and it serves the function of reducing the complexity of our interpersonal world. Instead of dealing with people in terms of their unique individuality, we frequently deal with them as representatives of a class, group, or category.

In some cases this process is helpful. Stereotyping reduces ambiguity and enables one to classify people quickly and easily. However, in other situations it may provide too simplistic an evaluation and lead to errors of judgment.

The interesting point is that there is a certain amount of consensus among people as to what attributes are most descriptive of a given group. For example, in one study 100 Princeton students were asked to indicate which attributes from a list of eighty-four were most applicable to ten national groups (Karlins, Coffman, & Walters, 1969). If traits were assigned at random, one would expect about 6 percent of the students to pick any given characteristic for any given group. However, for almost every ethnic group at least three traits were selected by over 20 percent of the students, and at least one attribute by over 50 percent of the students. For example, Americans were seen as materialistic (67 percent), English persons as conservative (53 percent), and Germans as industrious (59 percent). Thus, there appears to be some agreement about the attributes that belong with a given classification.

Some researchers argue that the reason for this consensus is that there may be a kernel of truth in the stereotype. They suggest that people make judgments of other groups by comparing them to their own group. If Germans on the average are seen as slightly more industrious than Americans, that characteristic will become part of the stereotype, even though the average difference may be very small.

A good example is the stereotype that people have about older workers. One study showed that older people were *perceived* as harder to change, less creative, more cautious, and having less physical capacity, even when their performance records were as good as those of younger employees (Rosen & Jerdee, 1976). The results indicate that a stereotype for older employees exists in many organizations. On the other hand, another study actually examined the decision-making styles of managers of different ages and found that, in fact, older managers *were* somewhat less risky (more cautious) than younger managers (Vroom & Pahl, 1971). So, at least on the risky-cautious dimension, there may be a kernel of truth in the stereotype about older workers.

The problem occurs when stereotypes influence judgments about individuals. More specifically, any particular individual may or may not become more conservative or cautious with advancing age. To base any sort of personnel decision (e.g., hiring, promotion) for an individual on the stereotype of a group is probably unjust, definitely poor management, and may well be illegal.

In recent years there have been a number of studies that have investigated the effects of stereotyping in the workplace. Particular emphasis has been placed on the organizational implications of stereotypes with regard to sex, race, and age. The research strategy employed typically asks people to look at films, read dossiers, or engage in a managerial simulation in which some personnel decision is to be made about the people involved (e.g., hire, evaluate, assign to jobs). For example, one study had people engage in a managerial simulation in which a number of decisions about hiring and placement were involved. Some of the dossiers were prepared with male names while others were prepared with female names. The substantive content of the dossiers, however, was exactly the same. The results showed that sex stereotypes can affect hiring and placement decisions (Terborg & Ilgen, 1975). Other studies have used a similar strategy to show the effect of age and race stereotypes on personnel decisions.

The findings from all these studies are clear. Females, minority-group members, and older employees are often the victims of negative stereotypes. Women, for example, are offered lower salaries, assigned more routine jobs, and expected to be followers rather than leaders. Older employees are given less challenging jobs.

The reaction against these stereotypes has become increasingly apparent. Women, for example, have formed a number of groups designed to bring pressure against employers who discriminate against them. Working Women-National Association of Office Workers has a membership of over 10,000 and is growing rapidly. Their activities include advertisements, demonstrations, political pressure, and various types of group meetings to spread information and gain support. In 1980, for example, the Working Women group in Cleveland bestowed its Pettiest Office Procedure Award on the *Cleveland Press*, where women clerical help were expected to make the morning "coffee run" for the editorial staff. After publicly acknowledging receipt of the award, the paper stopped the practice.

Besides these types of pressure and political tactics, legal actions are also on the rise. Sex and racial discrimination cases for bias in hiring, promotion, and firing have been in the courts for years (e.g., AT&T's $50 million settlement in 1973 for sex and racial discrimination). Also increasing are cases in which age discrimination is the allegation. Since 1967, when the Age Discrimination in Employment Act was passed, companies such as Eastern Airlines, Chemetron, Atlantic Container Lines, and Textron have been losing age discrimination cases. Standard Oil Company paid over $2 million on such a case, Pan Am over $900,000, and $250,000 was lost by the Hartford Fire Insurance Company. Suits have also been brought against Consolidated Edison, TWA, and NBC. The point is obvious. Companies must do everything they can to remove stereotypes and bias in all phases of the evaluation process.

Halo Effects

Another cause of bias in evaluating others is the halo effect. This refers to the process in which one's impression (either favorable or unfavorable) of a person in one area tends to influence one's judgment about other areas. Halo effects can be explained by attribution theory. We mentioned previously that people tend to attribute personality traits to others on the basis of the behavior they observe. These attributions tend to be overly consistent. For example, if we believe a person is an extrovert on the job, we also tend to assume he or she is an extrovert off the job, has been an extrovert for a long time, and will continue to be that way in the future (i.e., a stable internal attribution). Thus, we generalize what we think about someone to other settings and times on the basis of our limited observations.

People also use what might be called "implicit personality theories" (Wegner & Vallacher, 1977). We believe that certain personality traits go with other personality traits. Extroverts are warm, jolly, and generous, while introverts are cold, serious, and miserly. We use limited information to form an overall picture of the individual. Not only do we generalize people's specific traits, we tend to generalize our overall impressions of them.

In organizations, halo effects may have a serious impact on performance ratings (Bernardin & Beatty, 1984). In most cases a supervisor only observes a small sample of an employee's actual behavior. If for some reason the supervisor samples an area in which the employee does well (e.g., in meetings or on an interpersonal skill level), the supervisor may judge the individual's performance to be excellent in other areas about which he or she has little information. The reverse is also true—if you mess up once or in one area, your boss may think you are making mistakes elsewhere. The result of this latter bias is that many employees may be more concerned with not making a noticeable mistake than with striving for excellent performance.

Projection

Over the years the term *projection* has assumed a number of different meanings. Its original usage suggested that people relieve feelings of guilt by projecting blame onto someone else. More recently the term has come to mean any situation in which we attribute to others the same characteristics and feelings that we ourselves have. There is evidence that we are especially likely to attribute to others those characteristics we feel represent negative aspects of our own personality (Holmes, 1981). For example, some research shows that people high on traits such as stinginess, obstinacy, and disorderliness see others in a similar light.

This process serves an important role in allowing us to maintain a positive self-concept. We can justify our own aggressiveness, pettiness, or greed by saying that others are the same (or worse). These types of misperceptions are critical for a number of organizational situations. We frequently make inferences about the causes of people's behavior based on what we would do in the same situation. If we want a raise, we think others want the same thing. If we constantly butter up our own boss, we are suspicious of the motives of our subordinates. What we are saying is that our attributions of others are often based upon what we would do under similar circumstances. If we see someone behave in a particular way (e.g., asking for a raise), we assume that the motivation for the behavior is similar to what we would feel if we behaved in the same way (e.g., he or she needs the money and feels that a raise is deserved).

In many instances these attributions are incorrect. Perhaps the subordinate wants the raise because of the status attached to getting more money. Or perhaps the subordinate butters up the boss because he or she actually likes the boss. Like stereotypes and halo effects, projection can lead to systematic biases that can affect numerous organizational decisions such as hiring, firing, rewarding, and making job assignments.

Selective Perception

Such are promises, all lies and jest.
Still a man hears what he wants to hear
and disregards the rest.
—SIMON AND GARFUNKEL

A final perceptual process that leads to inaccuracies is called *selective perception*. Selective perception results from the fact that our current needs and past experience partly determine what we attend to and what we perceive. The more ambiguous the situation, the more we rely on these internal cues.

In a good research example of the selective perception process, twenty-three executives read a long (10,000 words) and complex case study about a steel company. Six of these executives were from sales departments, five were from production, four were from accounting, and eight were from various other departments (e.g., research and development, public relations). Each executive was asked to name what he or she thought was the *one most significant problem* that the new president of the steel company should deal with first. The results are reported in Figure 4-5. As you can see, the executives tended to see problems in the areas of major interest to themselves. Accountants and sales executives were concerned with financial sales problems. Production people were anxious about clarifying various organizational and production issues. Two executives in public and industrial relations saw human relations as the problem. These results are indicative of a more general

Department	Total Number of Executives	Number Who Mentioned		
		Sales	"Clarify Organization"	Human Relations
Sales	6	5	1	0
Production	5	1	4	0
Accounting	4	3	0	0
Miscellaneous	8	1	3	3
Totals	23	10	8	3

pattern, namely, that people attended to those aspects of the situation that are directly relevant to their own goals and concerns.

At a somewhat broader level, selective perception has a major impact on communication and decision processes. We hear what we want to hear and screen out other information. We overestimate the importance of past trends or circumstances. We simplify complex relations to fit our preconceived ideas.

In summary, we make many perceptual mistakes. To overcome these problems we must consciously develop "checking" mechanisms to aid us in situations in which these errors are most dangerous. We must attempt to use only accurate, observable, reliable information about others. We should become more aware of our own biases and learn to truly *take the role of the other*. It is hoped that through these various means we can reduce the inaccuracies and inequities that occur because of perceptual errors.

PERSONALITY

*Men acquire a particular quality
by constantly acting in a particular manner.*
—ARISTOTLE

Everyone has perceptual biases. And many of the factors that contribute to biased perceptions affect all of us in pretty much the same way. Yet it is also true that some of us are more susceptible to certain kinds of biases than others. Some of us will see a situation and respond to it in one way, while others will see and respond to the same situation in very different ways. For example, some students may get very anxious just before the final exam in a particular course, while others will not. Similarly, some managers will show great concern for the feelings of a subordinate when criticizing his or her performance. Other managers will show less concern. What is more, these differences often seem quite systematic. Some students *frequently* get anxious in testing situations, and some managers *frequently* show concern for the feelings of their subordinates.

We often explain these systematic differences among people in terms of their unique personalities. *Personality* can be defined as those characteristics of a person that account for consistent patterns of behavior (Pervin, 1984). Two aspects of this definition are important to note. First, personality is defined with reference to behavior. We can find out about someone's personality only by observing his or her behavior. This is just as true for the professional clinical psychologist as it is for the rest of us. The only difference is perhaps that the clinical psychologist has been trained to pay special attention to certain kinds of behavior. Second, personality is defined in terms of the consistency of behavior. If a student usually does not get anxious before exams, but does get very anxious just before the final exam in one particular course (i.e., in attribution theory terms the observed anxiety is a highly distinctive, low consistency event), we are not likely to view test anxiety as being a part of this student's basic personality makeup. Instead, the current anxiety is probably due to some unusual aspect of the situation. Only if the student is consistently anxious before many different types of exams are we likely to view test anxiety as part of his or her personality.

The notion of consistency in behavior has been hotly debated during the past 20 years. We alluded to this debate in Chapter 2, "Understanding People." Without some degree of behavioral consistency, the concept of personality is meaningless. In the following sections we will expand our discussion of the consistency controversy, focusing on two different aspects of consistency: cross-situational consistency and consistency over time. Both are relevant for understanding the degree to which organizations can influence the behavior of their members. In addition, we will also briefly discuss the origins and dynamics of personality and several aspects of personality that are particularly relevant for understanding people's behavior in organizational settings.

Cross-Situational Consistency

As we mentioned in Chapter 2, during the late 1960s and early 1970s several prominent researchers began to question the usefulness of the concept of personality. At issue was the notion of cross-situational consistency. Is behavior really consistent from one situation to the next? Reviews of the research literature at the time seemed to indicate that it was quite difficult to predict people's behavior from existing personality tests, and there was much evidence that people do in fact behave very differently across settings and circumstances (Mischel, 1968, 1973). If so, why bother with the concept of personality? Why not abandon the traditional study of personality and behavioral consistency, and instead focus on behavioral inconsistency?

Let us take an example. According to the Boy Scout creed, each scout should possess a series of laudable personality traits (e.g., loyalty, honesty, trustworthiness). the research on these traits is very interesting. Nearly 60 years ago it was shown that honesty and trustworthiness are highly dependent upon the situation. Almost everyone is honest under certain circumstances and dishonest under others (Hartshorne & May, 1928). Based on this kind of evidence, it was argued that we should pay attention to the circumstances that cause such variability in behavior, rather than focusing on behavioral consistency.

This debate has lost some of its vigor in recent years, but it is by no means over (e.g., Epstein & O'Brien, 1985; Pervin, 1985). And perhaps it never will be. The reason is that there is evidence for *both* consistency and inconsistency in behavior. Some students do get very anxious in testing situations, but they usually do not get anxious before *every* test. And some managers are very considerate of their subordinates' feelings, but they do not necessarily behave considerately *every* time they interact with their subordinates. Thus, consistency might best be viewed as a "more-or-less" phenomenon. Students are more-or-less test-anxious, and managers are more-or-less considerate of their subordinates' feelings. The more consistently the behavior occurs across situations, the more that behavior seems to reflect an underlying personality characteristic. But it is extremely unlikely that anyone will be perfectly consistent 100 percent of the time.

Focusing on the *degree* of consistency, rather than on absolute consistency or inconsistency, leads to an important question: What determines how consistently a person will behave across situations? The answer lies in both the person and the situation. Let us first consider the situation.

In most situations, there are cues that suggest how we should behave. They indicate what behavior is expected. Recall that the set of expected behaviors in a situation is often referred to as a *role.* Sometimes roles are very clear. Other times they are not. Furthermore, sometimes there are strong incentives for engaging in the expected role behaviors, while at other times incentives are absent. And sometimes, the required role behavior is rather simple. Everyone has the skill to do it. Other times the behavior is complex and requires training and practice. When the role requirements of a situation are so clear that anyone in that situation would know exactly what they were supposed to do, when there are powerful incentives for engaging in the role behaviors, and when the role behaviors are rather simple so that everyone *can* perform them, we say that the situational demands are very *strong* (Mischel, 1977). A good example of a strong situation is a meeting at which a company president is giving a speech to the company's top 100 managers. One is likely to find few individual differences in "talkativeness" in this situation. Everyone will probably sit quietly and listen. On the other hand, when the role requirements of a situation are ambiguous, when there are no clear incentives for engaging in the role behaviors, and when the role behaviors require some degree of effort and skill, we say that the situational demands are very *weak.* A good example of a weak situation is when a subordinate is seen coming to work in "questionable" attire (i.e., clothes that are somewhat inappropriate for his or her job). Will this subordinate be given feedback about his or her appearance? The expectations for when and how to give subordinates this type of feedback are seldom clear, there are likely to be incentives both for and against giving the feedback, and giving the feedback effectively will undoubtedly require some measure of interpersonal skill. Thus, we would expect to see large individual differences among managers in (1) whether or not they give any feedback at all, and (2) how they handle the situation if they do decide to give feedback (Larson, 1984).

When situational demands are strong, most people will behave in the same way. Personality will not play much part in determining their behavior. Moreover, when moving from one strong situation to another, where each situation has its own particular set of demands, little behavioral consistency will be observed. People will behave in whatever way is demanded by the situation at the time. However, when the situational demands are weak, people will behave in many different ways. Because strong external forces are absent, people will respond to weak situations in their own individual ways—

ways that reflect their unique underlying personalities. Further, when moving from one weak situation to another, we can expect to find a great deal of behavioral consistency. In each situation, people will behave in ways that are characteristic of their own individual personalities. The strength of the situation, therefore, is an important factor determining whether or not personality will influence behavior and thus whether or not behavioral consistency will be observed. Personality will play a much larger part in determining behavior in weak situations than in strong situations.

The second major factor determining whether or not behavioral consistency will be observed lies in the person. Some people are more attuned to situational demands than others (Snyder, 1979; Snyder & Campbell, 1982). Some people pay very close attention to what is expected in a situation and behave accordingly. Even in weak situations, these individuals spend a great deal of time and energy trying to determine what behaviors are most appropriate. They make very subtle distinctions among situations, and closely monitor their own behavior in order to make sure that it fits with the situational requirements. These people are called *high self-monitors*. Other people, by contrast, pay little attention to what is expected in the situation. They seem oblivious to all but the strongest external demands. They make only very rough distinctions among situations, ignoring most of the subtleties that exist. Their behavior is guided largely by internal cues and predisposition. Thus, these individuals do not closely monitor whether their behavior fits the requirements of the situation and are consequently called *low self-monitors*. Because high self-monitors are responsive to even slight differences in situational demands, their behavior should be rather inconsistent from one situation to the next. They will change their behavior to fit the particular demands of the situation. Low self-monitors, on the other hand, should behave quite consistently from one situation to another, since they are not very responsive to situational demands.

The relationship between situational strength, self-monitoring, and coss-situational consistency in behavior is depicted in Figure 4-6. As can be seen, the strength of the situational demands and the extent to which individuals are high or low self-monitors should interact to determine the degree of behavioral consistency. The greatest degree of consistency should be found in the behavior of low self-monitors across a set of weak situations. These situations make few behavioral demands, and the demands that are made are largely ignored by the individual. Here, the individual's personality will have a very large influence on his or her behavior. The least amount of consistency should be found in the behavior of high self-monitors across a set of strong situations. These situations make very explicit (and usually different) behavioral demands that are closely attened to by the individual. The high self-monitor will adjust his or her behavior to fit the situation. Personality will have very little influence. In the remaining two conditions there should be an intermediate degree of behavioral consistency. Both personality and the situation are likely to influence the behavior of high self-monitors in weak situations and low self-monitors in strong situations.

The implications of these concepts for organizations is very important. They indicate that organizations *can* often have a moderate-to-high degree of control and influence over the behavior of their members. If "strong" organi-

FIGURE 4-6
Cross-situational
consistency in be-
havior depends on
both the person
and the situations
involved.

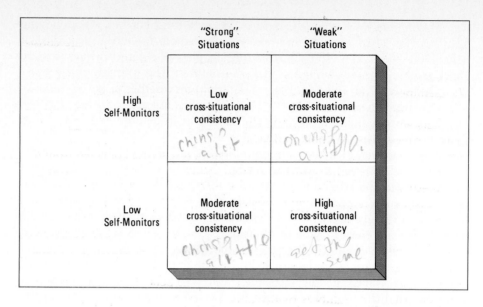

zational situations can be created by making work-role expectations clear, by providing incentives for ngaging in the expected role behaviors, and by making sure that the individual has the skills needed to perform the required behaviors, organizations can have a significant impact on the behavior and performance of their members. This will be true even for low self-monitors, as long as the work situation is truly a strong one. On the other hand, organizational control and influence become more problematic in weak situations. In weak situations, only high self-monitors can be counted on to perceive the few behavioral cues that do exist and to adjust their behavior appropriately. Low self-monitors may or may not engage in the appropriate behaviors, depending on other aspects of their personality (e.g., their need for achievement, interpersonal style). Consequently, in weak situations the organization is likely to get the behaviors and performance it desires only to the extent that the individuals in those situations either (1) are high self-monitors (in which case organizational control is still possible), or (2) have the appropriate personality traits or other personal characteristics needed for the job (in which case self-control will operate, but in the direction desired by the organization).

To summarize, cross-situational consistency in behavior probably does exist, but it depends on both the nature of the situations involved and the nature of the person. This means that personality *can* make a difference in organizations, but more so in some situations than in others. The personality of organizational members will become most critical to the success of the organization when roles and norms of behavior cannot be clearly communicated, when few (or conflicting) incentives exist for engaging in the desired role behavior, and when the role behavior requires some degree of effort and skill to perform. Under these circumstances, it becomes very important to *select* the right type of person for the job (i.e., someone with the appropriate personal characteristics). We discuss the process of employee selection in Chapter 15.

An issue that is closely related to cross-situational consistency is the consistency of behavior *over time*. The question here is essentially whether or not personality is stable over relatively long intervals. If it is not, then once again the usefulness of the concept of personality must be questioned.

Unlike the controversy that surrounds cross-situational consistency, researchers are in general agreement that people exhibit a moderate degree of temporal consistency in their behavior, even over rather long periods. For example, Conley (1984) found that personality test scores collected from 600 people in the 1930s and 1950s correlated positively (between $r = 0.25$ and $r = 0.40$) with scores collected between 1979 and 1981. These correlations are statistically significant and indicate a moderately positive relationship between the earlier and later scores: The higher the earlier scores were, the higher the later scores tended to be. The level of temporal consistency reflected in these correlations is particularly impressive considering the length of time covered.

Of course, a *moderate* degree of consistency in personality over time does not mean that personality is rigidly fixed. Systematic changes in personality can and do occur. An excellent example of this can be seen in the results of an ambitious study done at AT&T (Bray, 1982). This study, known as the Management Progress Study, was designed to assess the personality and individual difference factors that contribute to success as a manager. As part of this study, personality and other individual difference variables were measured for 266 new managers from six Bell System telephone companies between the years 1956 and 1960. The same measures were taken again 8 years later, and again 12 years after that. Thus, the study spanned a total of 20 years. Over the course of time, a clear pattern of change was observed on several of the assessed personality dimensions. Of particular note was the fact that the managers' need for autonomy and independence rose steadily over time, as did their leadership motivation. Their ambition, on the other hand, decreased. The increase in need for autonomy is illustrated in Figure 4-7. Over the course of 20 years, these managers became more oriented toward independently controlling and influencing what was happening in their immediate work environment (greater autonomy and leadership) and less oriented toward advancing upward in the organization (ambition).

Over time, then, personality seems both to change and to remain the same. Impossible, you say? Not really. Consider the following scenario. Two new employees are hired, and their personalities are assessed. One is found to have a high level of ambition and desire to move up in the company, while the other is found to have only an intermediate level of ambition. Consistent with the findings reported by Bray (1982), the ambition of both employees decreases over time: Twenty years later the employee who previously had a high level of ambition now has a moderate level, and the one who previously had only moderate ambition no has a rather low level. The personalities of both employees changed, but relative to each other they have remained the same. On an absolute scale, one still has a higher level of ambition than the other.

The implication of these findings for organizations is that over the course of

FIGURE 4-7
Managers' need
for autonomy rose
significantly over
the course of 20
years. (*Based on
data presented by
Bray, 1982.*)

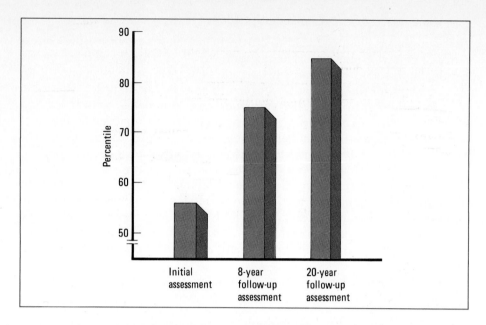

a career, employees may require very different sorts of rewards in order to remain interested in their jobs and motivated to perform well. The promise of a promotion may be just what is needed to motivate young managers to high levels of performance. The same promise made to older managers may be less effective. Older managers may be more highly motivated by increased autonomy and authority over matters of importance to their immediate work group (e.g., control over budgets or staffing). To maximize the performance of all employees, then, the organization needs to be flexible. It needs to establish incentives and reward systems, as well as other aspects of formal organizational structure, that take individual differences in personality into account.

The Origins and Dynamics of Personality

The evidence just presented suggests that there is good reason to conclude that personality does exist, that it exhibits some degree of both change and stability over time, and that it can strongly influence our behavior in at least some types of situations. The next logical question is, how does personality develop and what are its dynamics? The answer to this two-part question is extremely complex, and a full treatment is well beyond the scope of this book. We will therefore cover this topic only briefly here.

The Origins of Personality. Most theorists agree that *heredity* plays some role in personality development. What they do not agree on is *how great* a role it plays. The arguments back and forth on this point have been most heated with respect to intelligence, with some researchers claiming that intelligence is affected only slightly (if at all) by heredity, and others claiming that it is 75 to 80 percent inherited (e.g., Jensen, 1969). While it is likely that heredity does play some role, the latter position is probably an extreme overstatement of its effect.[1]

A second factor that contributes to personality development is the family and social setting during *early childhood*. It is here that a child learns many of the behavior patterns that will last a lifetime. Most theorists view environmental influences and learning during the formative years as essential to personality development.

Finally, as one moves into adulthood, so-called anchorage groups, or primary reference groups, help to mold one's personality (cf. Newcomb, 1943). These groups can often be found in the workplace, but may also arise out of social and recreational activities. They are called anchorage or reference groups because they provide a point of reference, helping to define the meaning of the roles one plays and one's position in society. It seems likely that the personality changes Bray (1982) observed among the managers participating in the Management Progress Study at AT&T were due in part to changing reference groups.

The Dynamics of Personality. There are many different views on the fundamental nature of personality and the process of personality change. Some personality theorists take a *psychodynamic* perspective. According to this view, personality can best be understood in terms of a complex interplay of motives, drives, needs, and conflicts, some of which we may not be fully aware of. Psychodynamic theorists view personality change as a process of discovering these underlying motives, needs, and drives, and working through the conflicts. Other theorists are more *phenomenological* in their approach. According to a phenomenological perspective, what really matters is how the individual experiences both the self and the world. If personality is to change, these perceptions must somehow be changed. Finally, some theorists take a *social learning theory* perspective. This perspective states that personality is really nothing more than a set of fundamental cognitions and beliefs that we have about the world around us. Social learning theory emphasizes that these beliefs are shaped by experience and that personality change occurs by the common mechanisms of learning (see Chapter 2, "Understanding People").

Each of these various approaches to understanding personality has something unique to offer, and over the years each has enjoyed a degree of popularity. The psychodynamic perspective was most prominent during the first half of this century, and the phenomenological perspective rose to popularity during the 1960s. Today social learning theory seems to be most widely accepted, at least in the academic world (Pervin, 1984). The social learning theory perspective is also the one that is most interesting from an organizational point of view, since it allows for the possibility that the organization can affect not only the behavior of its members, but also their

---

[1]It is interesting to note that very few psychologists treat intelligence as an aspect of personality, even though it clearly fits the definition of personality given earlier. Like other aspects of personality, intelligence is a characteristics of people that accounts for consistent patterns of behavior. One psychologist who does treat intelligence as a personality characteristic is Byrne (1974).

personalities. For example, social learning theory predicts that someone who works in a highly bureaucratic organization for many years may eventually develop a distinct "bureaucratic" personality! It also predicts that when people are put into positions of leadership, they may come to develop a strong leadership motivation. This is yet another way to interpret the Management Progress Study results reported by Bray (1982). Although no one really knows whether organizations can actually have this effect, it is a distinct possibility and one that can be tested with careful research.

PERSONALITY AND BEHAVIOR IN ORGANIZATIONS

So far we have talked rather broadly about personality and its impact on behavior. In this final section we will briefly discuss several specific aspects of personality that are especially relevant for understanding the behavior of people in organizations. Before proceeding, however, the concept of *personality trait dimension* should be introduced.

In our previous discussion we used as an example students who get very anxious just before exams. We suggested that although these students may not get anxious before *every single* exam they take, they get anxious regularly enough for us to conclude that test anxiety is a distinct feature of their personality. It is important to recognize, however, that test anxiety is not a discrete, all-or-none characteristic (i.e., one that people either have or do not have). Instead, it is something that we all have *more or less of*. Some of us are extremely test-anxious, others are moderately test-anxious, some are only slightly test-anxious, and a few are not test-anxious at all. Thus, when thinking about test anxiety, it is perhaps most accurate to think of a test-anxiety *dimension*. At one end of this dimension are those who get extremely anxious before exams, while at the other end are those who seldom get anxious. Using an accurate measure of test anxiety as a personality trait (e.g., Mandler & Sarason, 1952), we could discover exactly where on this dimension each of us falls. Combining this knowledge with information about self-monitoring and the strength of the demands in the testing situation, we could predict who is most likely to behave in an anxious manner before the final exam in a particular course.

In general, any personality characteristic on which people differ can be similarly represented as a personality trait dimension. And it is possible, at least in theory, to measure where a person falls on each one of these dimensions. A number of different strategies can be used to measure trait dimensions, but by far the most common method is to use some form of questionnaire. For example, several items from a questionnaire used to measure the self-monitoring dimension are listed in Figure 4-8. In all, there are 25 items in this questionnaire. Those who get a high score are considered to be high self-monitors and are expected to pay very close attention to their own behavior and to what is appropriate for the situation. Those who get low scores are considered to be low self-monitors and are expected to pay much less attention to the way their behavior fits situational demands.

There are many questionnaires like the self-monitoring scale that focus on a

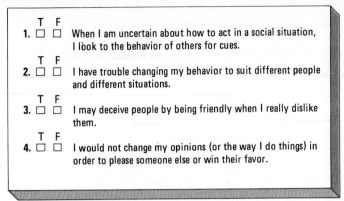

FIGURE 4-8

High self-monitors report that statements 1 and 3 are generally true as applied to them, and that statements 2 and 4 are generally not true. (*Items taken from the Self-Monitoring Scale: Snyder, 1974.*)

Figure content:

	T	F	
1.	☐	☐	When I am uncertain about how to act in a social situation, I look to the behavior of others for cues.
2.	☐	☐	I have trouble changing my behavior to suit different people and different situations.
3.	☐	☐	I may deceive people by being friendly when I really dislike them.
4.	☐	☐	I would not change my opinions (or the way I do things) in order to please someone else or win their favor.

single personality dimension. These questionnaires tend to be relatively short (e.g., ten to thirty items) and easy to administer. There are also a few questionnaires that are substantially longer (e.g., over 500 items) and that measure from fifteen to twenty personality trait dimensions simultaneously. Regardless of their length or the number of trait dimensions measured, however, one must be *very cautious* in using personality questionnaires. None of them provides a perfectly accurate measure of the trait dimensions they are intended to assess, and in a few cases the questionnaires are not valid at all. One reason is that people do not always answer these questionnaires in a frank and candid manner. It should also be noted that there are both legal and ethical restrictions that govern the use of these questionnaires. Thus, *a trained professional should always be consulted whenever it seems desirable to use a questionnaire to assess personality trait dimensions.*

Several personality trait dimensions that are useful for understanding behavior in an organizational context are discussed in the sections that follow. These include trait dimensions related to psychological need strength, cognitive style, interpersonal style, and Type A and Type B behavior patterns. Throughout the book, we will make reference to these and other trait dimensions whenever research indicates that they are important factors determining specific types of organizational behavior.

Psychological Need Strength

Personality trait dimensions related to the strength of various psychological needs have received a great deal of attention in the research literature. The most important among these from an organizational point of view are the need for achievement, the need for power, and the need for affiliation. The *need for achievement* is essentially a need to do a job well—to succeed at a task simply for the sake of success. The *need for power* is the need to influence and control the behavior of others. The *need for affiliation* is the need to interact with and be psychologically close to others.

People differ widely in the strength of these three needs. Some people have very strong needs in all three areas, some have strong needs in one or two areas

101

but weak needs in the others, and some people have relatively weak needs in all three areas. The pattern of needs people possess can significantly affect their behavior in a variety of organizational settings, as well as their likelihood of succeeding at certain kinds of jobs. For example, people with a high need for achievement show a distinct preference for work assignments that involve challenging tasks and clear feedback about how well they are performing (McClelland, 1985). This preference is not nearly as strong among individuals with a low need for achievement. But a high need for achievement does not always guarantee success in an organization, especially when success is defined as moving up through the managerial ranks. There is some evidence that successful managers in large hierarchical organizations require a combination of a high need for power and a low need for affiliation. A high need for achievement is less important (McClelland & Boyatzis, 1982).

The concept of need strength is a central element in several theories of motivation. According to these theories, people are motivated to engage in behaviors that satisfy their basic needs. Thus, one is likely to work hard and perform well on a job only when good performance is related in some fashion to the satisfaction of basic needs. Individual differences in performance can, by this account, be explained in terms of individual differences in need strength. This is an important concept and one that we will discuss in much greater detail in Chapter 6, "Motivation." For now we wish to note only that (1) the strength of various psychological needs is an important aspect of personality, (2) people show large individual differences in need strength, and (3) psychological need strength is systematically related to behavior.

Cognitive Style

There are several personality trait dimensions that reflect stable individual differences in cognitive style, that is, the way in which people think about and perceive the world (Goldstein & Blackman, 1978). We will discuss four of these cognitive style dimensions here: internal-external locus of control, risk taking, dogmatism, and cognitive complexity.

Internal-External Locus of Control. This dimension refers to individual differences in how much control people typically perceive they have over what happens both to them and in the world around them. At one end of this dimension are people who have an *internal locus of control.* These people see what happens to them as being caused largely by their own actions. Consequently, they believe that they can exert a substantial amount of control over the events that occur in their lives. At the other end of this dimension are people who have an *external locus of control.* These people see what happens to them as being largely due to luck, chance, or fate. Thus, they feel that they have little control over the events in their lives.

In general, "internals" tend to be more satisfied on the job when they are working under a participative management system. "Externals," on the other hand, seem to prefer working under a directive style of management (Mitchell, Smyser, & Weed, 1975). A consistent pattern also emerges when examining the behavior of internal and external managers. In comparison to external managers, internal managers tend to be more considerate of the feelings and welfare of their subordinates, more rewarding and less punitive, and often less directive. The latter characteristic is of potential importance for predicting managerial effectiveness in organizations that *do not* have a high degree of formalization (see Chapter 3).

Finally, internals seem to adjust better. They tend to be more involved in their jobs, show greater satisfaction, cope better with stress, and rise to leadership positions more frequently than externals (Anderson, 1977; Lefcourt, Martin, & Saleh, 1984). Clearly, an internal locus of control is associated with a wide variety of beneficial organizational responses.

Risk Taking. There has also been research examining the tendency of people to take risks, both individually and within group settings. Evidence suggests that there are individual differences on this dimension, and that this characteristic is systematically related to various aspects of group interaction and decision making.

For example, a study by Brown and McCollough (1976) used a questionnaire assessment of riskiness to assign forty-five bank managers to high-, medium-, or low-risk-taking teams. These teams were asked to make various simulated business decisions, and it was clearly demonstrated that the high-risk group took greater risks than the low-risk group.

In general, high-risk takers seem to spend less time making decisions and use less information. One study substantiated these findings with seventy-nine line managers from a large manufacturing firm (Taylor & Dunnette, 1974). These managers worked on simulated personnel decisions involving the choice of which individual to hire. High-risk takers took less time to make their choice and used fewer bits of information than did low-risk takers. Decision accuracy, however, was the same for both groups.

Dogmatism. At one end of this cognitive-style dimension are those people who are highly dogmatic. These individuals tend to be very closed-minded and inflexible in their approach to the world. At the other end are people who are very open-minded and flexible. Individual differences in dogmatism have been studied in relation to decision making, leadership, group process, and interpersonal adjustment. In the area of decision making, for example, highly dogmatic individuals tend to behave much like high-risk takers. They do not search as thoroughly as others do for decision-relevant information, and they tend to make their decisions rather quickly. Furthermore, they are usually quite confident in the accuracy of their decisions, even when those decisions are obviously incorrect.

Research also suggests that individuals varying in dogmatism react differently to people displaying different leadership styles. For example, one study found that a directive leadership style was more likely to be *preferred* by subordinates who were high on the dogmatism dimension than by those who were low. On the other hand, across four different types of tasks it was found that *performance* was highest when individuals low in dogmatism worked with a leader who was directive but who also showed respect for his or her subordinates and concern for their welfare (Weed, Mitchell, & Moffitt, 1976).

How Executives Think

The people at the top put their pants or skirts on just like you and me, right? Sure, they may draw down those fancy salaries, but for what? For politicking their way up the ladder and then taking the heat on all those big decisions, right? Okay, so some may be a little smarter than the average Joe, but when it comes down to it, they don't think any differently from you and me, right?

Wrong, on every count but the pants and skirts, about which there isn't good research. After years of studying the subject, certain path-breaking behavioral scientists have concluded that there is indeed something distinctive about the workings of the executive mind. While the researchers don't agree on all the particulars, their findings overlap enough to suggest rough consensus on what it is that those high-priced noggins do differently. A near-genius IQ by itself doesn't guarantee superior managerial thinking.

The expert who has probably toiled longest in this particular vineyard is Elliott Jaques, the director of the Institute of Organization and Social Studies at England's Brunel University. To call Jaques a polymath rather understates his qualifications: he holds a Ph.D. in social relations—sociology, psychology, and anthropology—from Harvard and an M.D. from Johns Hopkins; trained as a psychoanalyst, he is a Founder Fellow of the Royal College of Psychiatry; more to the point here, he conducted what may be the longest-running research project ever done on a corporation—a study of Glacier Metal Co., a British metals engineering outfit, that lasted from 1948 until the late 1970s. These days Jaques is working with clients that range from the U.S. Army to an Australian mining company.

At the heart of Jaques' findings is a concept he calls the time frame of the individual. His research indicates that individuals vary radically in terms of the time periods they can think out, organize, and work through. It taxes some folks to figure out what they have to do today, and in what order. Others—namely executive types—can see a long way, identifying the steps necessary for some move that will take years to complete, envisioning the consequences of each step, and then taking the measures to set the juggernaut in motion.

Over a lifetime a person typically becomes capable of handling progressively longer time frames. This development isn't smoothly incremental, though—it's discontinuous, occurring in spurts that carry the individual from a one-day time frame to a three-month time frame, and thence, after a decent interval at each stage, to one-year, two-year, five-year, ten-year, and 20-year time frames. The statistical distribution of people capable of the different time frames is also discontinuous: most of the population is never capable of more than a three-month time span; a smaller group is capable of envisioning an entire year, and so on; only one individual out of several million, Jaques estimates, is ever capable of a 20-year time frame. Though loath to speculate on the time frames of people he hasn't tested, Jaques does note that Konosuke Matsushita has laid down a 250-year plan for the giant Japanese company that bears his name.

What makes this stuff dynamite in a corporate context is Jaques' additional finding that there is a sort of natural structure to organizations engaged in work, wherein most jobs can be classified according to the time frame required of the incumbent. An unskilled shop-floor worker can almost always get by with no more than a one-day time horizon. A person holding down the lowest level managerial job, if he's to be any good at it, must be capable of at least a three-month time frame.

Jaques' research shows that the best organizations, in terms of morale and productivity, are those whose structure follows what might be called the natural hierarchy: one-day time frame workers report to a foreman who can organize at least the next three months; he follows the dictates of a manager who can plan a year or longer; he reports to a general manager with a two-year time frame; he answers to a vice president capable of charting strategy over five years. Atop it all sits a chief executive who can cast his mind forward to encompass the next ten or more years. In common parlance this ability, much sought after in executives, is called vision. For a rough handle on where you fit, think about the most distant deadline you feel comfortable with.

Jaques believes that time frame is the best indicator of the broader mental capabilities that psychologists call cognitive power. Cognitive power is not IQ—it reflects not raw brainpower but how someone's perception and thinking are organized, how they operate. Jaques concludes that an individual capable of thinking out a year ahead has one level of

Cognitive Complexity. This final cognitive-style dimension refers to the extent to which an individual views the world in relatively complex ways and apprehends subtle distinctions among events that on the surface seem to be the same. In assessing this dimension we might ask, for example, to what extent an individual is able to break a task down into its component parts, see the underlying similarities to and differences from other tasks, and generally view the situation in a complex fashion. People who are high in cognitive complexity tend to search for and process more information when making a decision, entertain more alternative solutions, and use more complex decision strategies than people who are low in complexity.

Interpersonal Style

As in cognitive style, there are a number of personality trait dimensions that reflect stable individual differences in interpersonal style, that is, the way people respond to the individuals with whom they interact. For example, there are measures of the extent to which people are empathetic, sociable, and insightful about the motives of others. Those who score high on these dimensions tend to do well in social settings, are warmly accepted by coworkers, and tend to interact more with others. There is also evidence that these differences may be related to leadership effectiveness, although the relationships are rather complex. Socially distant leaders, for example, tend to be rather directive in the way they deal with subordinates. Under some circumstances, directive behavior can lead to high group performance. In other situations, however, it can actually make things worse (House & Mitchell, 1974).

One interpersonal style dimension that stands out as being especially relevant to behavior in large bureaucratic organizations is *authoritarianism*. At one end of this dimension are those who believe that it is correct and just to have large status and power differences among people in organizations, and that centralized decision making is the proper way for organizations to function. These individuals are called *authoritarians*. At the other end of this dimension are the *egalitarians*—those who would prefer to see fewer status and power differences among people, and who view decentralized decision making as a more legitimate way for organizations to operate. In contrast to egalitarians, authoritarians are more likely to emerge as leaders when the situation calls for an autocratic and demanding style. They tend to be aggressive and prefer punishment as a way of motivating others. On the other

105

hand, when in a subordinate role, authoritarians readily conform to rules and regulations and are more likely to obey even unreasonable demands made by authority figures (Byrne, 1974). Thus, in a hierarchical organization, authoritarian managers can be expected to behave in one way toward their subordinates (autocratic) and in quite a different way toward their superiors (submissive).

Type A and Type B Behavior Patterns

As you might have guessed by now, the various personality trait dimensions discussed previously are not always independent of one another. Sometimes they are correlated; that is, sometimes people who are at one end of one particular dimension are also at the same end of several other, related dimensions. This correlation is exemplified in the personality of those who exhibit what is called the Type A behavior pattern. Type A individuals are distinguished by three characteristics. First, they have a very high need for achievement. They continually strive to be the best at whatever they are doing at the moment. Second, they are frequently very aggressive toward others. Normal performance situations are often construed as competitions or even as combat among opposing parties. Finally, Type A individuals have an exaggerated sense of time urgency. They constantly try to do more and more in less and less time. These three personality traits, high need for achievement, aggressiveness, and time urgency, fit the common stereotype of the hard-driving executive. Individuals with just the opposite set of traits (i.e., low achievement motivation, low aggressiveness, and little sense of time urgency) have what is called the Type B pattern. Of course, the Type A and Type B patterns represent two extreme situations. Most of us are somewhere between the two. At the same time, however, most of us tend to be closer to one extreme than the other.

Research indicates that Type A and Type B individuals do indeed exhibit the correlated pattern of personality characteristics just described (Yarnold, 1982). Furthermore, these characteristics are clearly related to organizational outcomes. In general, Type A individuals work harder, faster, and longer than Type B individuals; they more often hold positions of leadership; and they tend to achieve higher levels of organizational success (Sales, 1969). In one study of 91 employed women, for example, it was found that Type A women achieved a higher occupational level and held more demanding jobs than Type B women (Kelly & Houston, 1985).

However, research also indicates that the success of the Type A individual comes at a price. Type A individuals report being under significantly more stress and tension in their jobs than do Type B individuals. Furthermore, it has been shown that in comparison to Type B individuals, those who are Type A are much more likely to develop premature coronary heart disease. This is true for both men and women (e.g., Haynes, Feinleib, & Kannel, 1980). Not only is coronary heart disease an obvious negative outcome for the individual employee, it also has negative consequences for the organization. It means higher costs for medical insurance, employees who are away from work for medical reasons, and perhaps the loss of employees due to early, medically induced retirement, or death. Thus, while a Type A behavior pattern does have benefits in terms of success for both the individual and the organization, it also has costs.

107

Chapter 4:
Perception and
Personality

Summary

The following points summarize the major issues discussed in the chapter:

1. People vary widely in their needs, intentions, and behavior. Two reasons for these individual differences are the perceptual process and the development of a distinctive personality.
2. Perceiving people requires complex inferences about their internal states. First impressions are dominated by the physical and biographical characteristics of the person perceived, the personality of the perceiver, and situational constraints.
3. More intense interactions produce attributions about the observed person's personality. Decisions about the internal or external causes of behavior are based in part upon information regarding behavioral distinctiveness, consensus, and consistency.
4. The perceptual process can result in a number of systematic errors of judgment. People use stereotypes, generalize their impressions (halo), project their feelings onto others, make incorrect attributions, and selectively screen out what they do not want to see or hear.
5. *Personality traits* are defined as characteristics of people that account for consistent patterns of behavior. Personality is shaped both by genetic factors (heredity) and by experience, especially during the formative years.
6. Personality is likely to have a much stronger influence on behavior in some situations than in others. Personality is most likely to influence behavior when situational demands are weak and when the individual is a low self-monitor.
7. Some of the personality-trait dimensions that are most relevant for behavior in organizations pertain to psychological need strength, cognitive and interpersonal style, and the Type A and Type B behavior patterns.

IMPLICATIONS FOR RESEARCH

In this chapter we have argued that personality can influence behavior in organizations, but that the extent of its influence will depend greatly on both the situation and the person. Specifically, we suggested that when the demands of the situation are weak and the individual in question is a low self-monitor, personality can be expected to be a major determinant of behavior. However, when the demands of the situation are strong, or the individual is a high self-monitor, personality is likely to play a much smaller role in determining behavior.

We believe that the concept of situational strength is an important one. However, it has only recently been introduced into the organizational-behavior literature (Weiss & Adler, 1984), and a number of questions need to be answered before this concept can be put to full use in research. For example, what is the proper definition of a "situation?" As Weiss and Adler (1984) note, a situation is not the same as a job or a task. Jobs are clusters of tasks, and tasks are done *in* situations. A task may be a part of the situation, but the situation goes beyond the task itself. How does one define the physical and temporal boundaries of a "situation"? Do other people count as part of the situation? And if situational boundaries can be specified, how do we decide which ones are most relevant for organizational effectiveness? Other questions that are pertinent here concern the measurement of role clarity, incentive strength, and effort requirements (cf. Weiss & Adler, 1984). This is an area in which a good deal of conceptual and empirical groundwork still needs to be done.

The concept of self-monitoring is also relatively new in the organizational literature. It was first developed in social psychology and has for the most part been used to explain aspects of *interpersonal* behavior. Existing measures of the self-monitoring dimension are consistent with this interpersonal focus. They do not include items measuring self-monitoring in work and organizational settings. It is likely that measures of self-monitoring in the interpersonal domain will be inadequate for assessing self-monitoring activities relevant to work settings. New, organizationally relevant measures will be needed. Here again, much groundwork research lies ahead before the self-monitoring concept can be put to use in other areas of organizational research.

Personality has not been a "hot topic" in organizational research during the last 2 decades. This is partly because many researchers have accepted (perhaps prematurely) Mischel's (1968, 1973) initial argument that behavior is simply too inconsistent from one situation to the next for the concept of personality to be meaningful. It is also due to the fact that until now, researchers have had only very modest success in using personality measures to predict behavior in organizational settings. However, it may be time to take a second, closer look at the role that personality plays in determining organizational behavior. It seems unlikely that personality will ever become *the* predominant variable explaining all, or even most, behavior in organizations. But if we start taking account of factors such as situational strength and self-monitoring tendencies, it is quite possible that new organizational circumstances can be discovered in which personality does play a vital role. This would seem to be an important direction for future research.

IMPLICATIONS FOR PRACTICE

The discussion of perception and personality in this chapter points to two major issues with relevant implications for practice. First, people vary widely in their needs, characteristics, and skills. Each individual is unique, based upon physiological, psychological, and social development. The logical inference that follows from this fact is that organizations must be prepared both to deal with and to utilize this individualism.

What we are saying is that greater *flexibility* in organizational design, interpersonal interactions, and individual evaluations is necessary for organizational effectiveness. This point will reappear elsewhere in the book (e.g., in Chapter 6, "Motivation," and Chapter 15, "Formal Systems for Managing Employee Performance"). We will elaborate on some specific mechanisms to encourage flexibility. It is sufficient at this point simply to emphasize the fact that in order to gain the maximum commitment and motivation from an organization's human resources, we must systematically recognize and capitalize on the individual's unique capabilities.

The second point that stands out concerns the number and kind of perceptual errors we make, especially in our interpersonal judgments. We tend to use simple classification mechanisms, make attributions that are too broad in scope, use our own personality as a basis for inferring the causes of other people's behavior, and systematically select information (in or out) based upon our own particular needs, wants, and biases. From a perspective of what is right, what is legal, and what is most effective, these errors need to be corrected. Correction involves several activities. The first is an explicit recognition of the problems. Training courses, for example, are available that help managers recognize and remove rating errors (such as halo) from their evaluation judgments. We can also encourage the use of more factual and reliable information. Past performance records can be easily stored and retrieved by computers. Performance appraisal instruments can be designed to include a greater emphasis on observable behavior rather than inferred traits. Also, using multiple judges who are relatively indepedent can help to correct biases. Through active recognition of the problems and the systematic implementation of training and "checking" mechanisms, the impact of these perceptual biases can be reduced.

A number of companies such as Wells Fargo and Hewlett-Packard have introduced such programs. Their programs have included group meetings and training sessions to counter race and sex bias. James Motter, the senior vice president for personnel at Wells Fargo, notes that his company has "an employee population that is more aware of its rights than it has ever been before." He goes on to say that through proper training, personnel decisions can be made more equitable and fair, and that the consequence will be fewer lawsuits ("Coping with Lawsuits," 1979).

Another strategy is to attempt to remove any formal administrative bias that may exist in the system. Job descriptions should be written carefully, testing procedures can be tailor-made for specific jobs, personnel files can often be made available to employees, and so on. As additional insurance, many companies are putting everything in writing. Gerald Orlick, personnel director for Fisher Scientific Co. of Pittsburgh said, "In 1970 we didn't have either a personnel manual or an affirmative action manual." Now they have both ("Coping with Lawsuits," 1979).

The section of the chapter dealing with personality seems to be particularly relevant for current organizational practices. We used to believe that almost all behavior was determined by deeply ingrained personality characteristics. It is now evident, however, that this is not the case. Changes in the environment frequently produce changes in behavior. Only some of the time is personality a significant determinant of behavior.

This new conceptualization of the role of personality has caused changes in numerous personnel practices. Personality tests need to show clear relationships to performance on the job or they can be legally challenged as discriminatory selection or evaluation devices. Performance evaluations have shifted their emphasis from personality traits to observable and countable behavior. And in general there is recognition of the idea that maximum effectiveness comes from the proper match of people (personality) with the environment (job). The increased understanding of the important causal role of the situation has produced better techniques of job analysis and research on situational characteristics.

The best example of this more restricted utilization of personality tests combined with an increased emphasis on the environment can be seen in the growth of assessment centers (Bray, 1982). These centers use multiple sources of data combining such things as personality tests, work simulations, and group exercises. The simulations and exercises are tailored to the specific jobs for which the candidates are being considered, and the personality scores, while helpful, are only one of several types of predictors. We will discuss assessment centers, more fully later in the book, but it is important to mention here that there are now about 2000 corporate-run assessment centers and that many major companies such as AT&T and Massachusetts Mutual Life Insurance have found them extremely helpful in predicting on-the-job performance.

Discussion Questions

1. Are stereotypes a good or a bad thing? What is their effect on various organizational decision processes?
2. How can attributions lead you to make inaccurate judgments about others? Are there remedies for these problems?
3. What is the actor-observer error? Discuss. Think about your explanations of your own behavior and your explanations of other people's behavior. Do they differ? If so, why? How can we resolve this problem?
4. How stable and persistent are personality traits? What are the implications of the new way of looking at personality for organizational behavior?

CASE: THE SELECTION INTERVIEW

Corine Watson was tired. She had already conducted four interviews that afternoon and she had one more to go. One of the vice presidents in marketing was in need of a new administrative assistant—someone who could schedule activities, manage the production of important annual reports, keep track of budgets, and generally keep the marketing division running smoothly. The vice president wanted someone with experience, demonstrated secretarial and administrative skills, and the proper "attitude." Corine's job was to screen a number of people and send over the names of a couple of candidates.

This last interview was with a young man named Ed Baker. Corine looked through his resumé. Ed had received an undergraduate degree in education from the University of Wisconsin (Corine's alma mater). He had taken some business classes while at the university and some additional courses at a nearby business college. These latter courses dealt with typing and other secretarial skills. His record was above average. Ed had also worked summers as a supervisor in a foundry near Madison. His resumé indicated that he was single and enjoyed the outdoors, and his picture was attractive. Corine asked him to come into her office.

Corine started the interview by noting that Ed had gone to the University of Wisconsin and that she had too. She asked how he liked it. Ed responded very positively about his experience there. They soon discovered that they had taken courses from a few of the same professors and had some acquaintances in common. Ed belonged to the same fraternity as the man Corine had married, and although Ed graduated 8 years later, there were still some fun and interesting memories to discuss.

The interview then shifted to more specific, job-related questions. Corine explained what was to be expected of the administrative assistant and asked Ed why he thought he could handle the job. He responded that his experience in the foundry would help on the management and administrative side, and that his ability to get along easily with others would help on the interpersonal side. He elaborated on some of these issues and seemed enthusiastic about the job.

After discussing the specifics of the job—salary, chances for movement, raises, supplementary compensation in the form of vacation, health care, insurance, and so on—Corine started to wind up the interview. As Ed was getting up to leave, he noted a photograph of a mountainous area on the wall. He commented that it was a lovely picture and asked if Corine had taken it. She replied that she had—she loved hiking and photography and that picture was of an area she had visited the previous summer Ed mentioned that he had visited the same place a couple of years ago and had enjoyed it as well. After a few minutes discussing the joy of hiking and other outdoor activities, Ed left and Corine sat down to write her evaluation.

She felt very positive about Ed. He was friendly and seemed bright and capable. She sent his name along with the name of a woman she had interviewed over to the vice president. She was pleased to hear a few weeks later that Ed had been hired for the job.

Questions about the Case

1. Do you think Ed will do well on this job? Why or Why not?
2. Do you think that Corine's evaluations were biased in any unfair way? Did she do anything illegal?
3. What sort of chages would you suggest in the interview process?

References

Anderson, C. R. (1977). Locus of control, coping behaviors and performance in stress settings: A longitudinal study. *Journal of Applied Psychology, 62,* 446–451.

Bernardin, J. H., & Beatty, R. W. (1984). *Performance appraisal: Assessing human behavior at work.* Boston: Kent.

Bray, D. W. (1982). The assessment center and the study of lives. *American Psychologist, 37,* 180–189.

Brigham, J. C. (1971). Ethnic stereotypes. *Psychological Bulletin, 76,* 15–38.

Brown, S. L., & McCollough, W. A. (1976). Choice dilemma as a predictor of group risk behavior. *Decision Sciences, 7,* 868–872.

Byrne, D. (1974). *An introduction to personality* (2d ed.). Englewood Cliffs, NJ: Prentice-Hall.

Conley, J. J. (1984). Longitudinal consistency of adult personality: Self-reported psychological characteristics across 45 years. *Journal of Personality and Social Psychology, 47,* 1325–1333.

Coping with employee lawsuits. (1979, August 27). *Business Week,* p. 66.

Dearborn, D. C., & Simon, H. A. (1958). Selective perception: A note on the departmental identification of executives. *Sociometry, 21,* 140–144.

Epstein, S., & O'Brien, E. J. (1985). The person-situation debate in historical and current perspective. *Psychological Bulletin, 98,* 513–537.

Fiedler, F. E. (1978). The contingency model and the dynamics of the leadership process. In L. Berkowitz (Ed.), *Advances in Experimental Social Psychology* (Vol. 11, pp. 59–112). NY: Academic Press.

Goldstein, K. M., & Blackman, S. (1978). *Cognitive style: Five approaches and relevant research.* NY: Wiley.

Harrigan, J. A., & Rosenthal, R. (1983). Physicians' head and body positions as determinants of perceived rapport. *Journal of Applied Social Psychology, 13,* 496–509.

Hartshorne, H., & May, M. A. (1928). *Studies in the nature of character: Vol. 1. Studies in deceit.* NY: MacMillan.

Haynes, S. G., Feinleib, M., & Kannel, W. B. (1980). The relationship of psycho-social factors to coronary heart disease in the Framingham Study: III. Eight-year incidence of coronary heart disease. *American Journal of Epidemiology, 111,* 37–58.

Heider, F. (1958). *The psychology of interpersonal relations.* NY: Wiley.

Holmes, D. S. (1981). Existence of classical projection and the stress-reducing function of attribution projection: A reply to Sherwood. *Psychological Bulletin, 90,* 460–466.

House, R. J., & Mitchell, T. R. (1974). Path-goal theory of leadership. *Journal of Contemporary Business, 3*(4), 81–97.

Jensen, A. R. (1969). How much can we boost IQ and scholastic achievement? *Harvard Educational Review, 39* 1–123.

Jones, E. E., & Nisbett, R. E. (1972). The actor and observer: Divergent perceptions of the causes of behavior. In E. E. Jones, D. E. Kanouse, H. H. Kelley, R. E. Nisbett, S. Valins, & B. Weiner (Eds.), *Attribution: Perceiving the causes of behavior.* Morristown, NJ: General Learning Press.

Karlins, M., Coffman, T. L., & Walters, G. (1969). On the fading of social stereotypes: Studies in three generations of college students. *Journal of Personality and Social Psychology, 13,* 1–16.

Kelley, H. H. (1967). Attribution theory in social psychology. In D. Levine (Ed.), *Nebraska symposium on motivation* (Vol. 15, pp. 192–238). Lincoln, NB: University of Nebraska Press.

Kelley, H. H. (1971). *Attribution in social interaction.* Morristown, NJ: General Learning Press.

Kelley, H. H., & Michela, J. L. (1980). Attribution theory and research. In M. R. Rosenzweig & L. W. Porter (Eds.), *Annual Review of Psychology* (Vol. 31, pp. 457–501). Palo Alto, CA: Annual Reviews.

Kelly, K. E., & Houston, B. K. (1985). Type A behavior in employed women: Relation to work, marital, and leisure variables, social support, stress, tension, and health. *Journal of Personality and Social Psychology, 48,* 1067–1079.

Knowlton, W. A., Jr., & Mitchell, T. R. (1980). Effects of causal attributions on supervisor's evaluation of subordinate performance. *Journal of Applied Psychology, 65,* 459–466.

Larson, J. R., Jr. (1977). Evidence for a self-serving bias in the attribution of causality. *Journal of Personality, 45,* 430–441.

Larson, J. R., Jr. (1984). The performance feedback process: A preliminary model. *Organizational Behavior and Human Performance, 33,* 42–76.

Lefcourt, H. M., Martin, R. A., & Saleh, W. E. (1984). Locus of control and social support: Interactive moderators of stress. *Journal of Personality and Social Psychology, 47,* 378–389.

Mandler, G., & Sarason, S. B. (1952). A study of anxiety and learning. *Journal of Abnormal and Social Psychology, 47,* 166–173.

Mauro, R. (1984). The constable's new clothes: Effects of uniforms on perceptions and problems of police officers. *Journal of Applied Social Psychology, 14,* 42–56.

McClelland, D. C. (1985). *Human motivation.* Glenview, IL: Scott, Foresman.

McClelland, D. C., & Boyatzis, R. E. (1982). The leadership motive pattern and long term success in management. *Journal of Applied Psychology, 67,* 737–743.

Miller, D. T. (1976). Ego-involvement and attributions for success and failure. *Journal of Personality and Social Psychology, 34,* 901–906.

Mischel, W. (1968). *Personality Assessment.* NY: Wiley.

Mischel, W. (1973). Toward a cognitive social learning reconceptualization of personality. *Psychological Review, 80,* 252–283.

Mischel, W. (1977). The interaction of person and situation. In D. Magnusson & N. S. Endler (Eds.), *Personality at the crossroads: Current issues in interactional psychology.* Hillsdale, NJ: Erlbaum.

Mitchell, T. R., Smyser, C. M., & Weed, S. E. (1975). Locus of control: Supervision and work satisfaction. *Academy of Management Journal, 18,* 623–630.

Newcomb, T. M. (1943). *Personality and social change.* NY: Dryden.

Pervin, L. A. (1984). *Personality* (4th ed.). NY: Wiley.

Pervin, L. A. (1985). Personality: Current controversies, issues, and directions. In M. R. Rosenzweig, & L. W. Porter (Eds.), *Annual Review of Psychology* (Vol. 36. pp. 83–114). Palo Alto, CA: Annual Reviews.

Rosen, B., & Jerdee, T. H. (1976). The influence of age stereotypes on managerial decisions. *Journal of Applied Psychology, 61,* 428–432.

Ross, L. (1977). The intuitive psychologist and his shortcomings: Distortions in the attribution process. In L. Berkowitz (Ed., *Advances in Experimental Social Psychology* (Vol. 10, pp. 174–220). NY: Academic Press.

Sales, S. M. (1969). Organizational roles as a risk factor in coronary heart disease. *Administrative Science Quarterly, 14,* 325–337.

Schneider, D. J., Hastorf, A. H., & Ellsworth, P. C. (1979). *Person perception* (2d ed.). Reading, MA: Addison-Wesley.

Snyder, M. (1974). Self-monitoring of expressive behavior. *Journal of Personality and Social Psychology, 30,* 526–537.

Snyder, M. (1979). Self-monitoring processes. In L. Berkowitz (Ed.), *Advances in Experimental Social Psychology* (Vol. 12, pp. 85–128). NY: Academic Press.

Snyder, M., & Campbell, M. H. (1982). Self-monitoring: The self in action. In J. Suls (Ed.), *Psychological perspectives on the self* (pp. 185–207). Hillsdale, NJ: Erlbaum.

Taylor, R. N., & Dunnette, M. D. (1974). Influence of dogmatism, risk taking propensity, and intelligence on decision making strategies for a sample of industrial managers. *Journal of Applied Psychology, 59,* 420–423.

Terborg, J. R., & Ilgen, D. R. (1975). A theoretical approach to sex discrimination in traditionally masculine occupations. *Organizational Behavior and Human Performance, 13,* 352–376.

Triandis, H. C., & Triandis, L. M. (1965). Some studies of social distance. In I. Steiner & M. Fishbein (Eds.), *Current studies in social psychology.* NY: Holt.

Vroom, V. H., & Pahl, B. (1971). Relationship between age and risk taking among managers. *Journal of Applied Psychology, 55,* 399–405.

Weed, S. E., Mitchell, T. R., & Moffitt, W. (1976). Leadership style, subordinate personality, and task types as predictors of performance and satisfaction with supervision. *Journal of Applied Psychology, 61,* 58–66.

Wegner, D. M., & Vallacher, R. R. (1977). *Implicit psychology: An introduction to social cognition.* NY: Oxford University Press.

Weiner, B., Frieze, I., Kukla, A., Reed, L., Rest, B., & Rosenbaum, R. M. (1971). *Perceiving the causes of success and failure.* Morristown, NJ: General Learning Press.

Weiss, H. M., & Adler, S. (1984). Personality and organizational behavior. In B. M. Staw & L. L. Cummings (Eds.), *Research in organizational behavior* (Vol. 6, pp. 1–50). Greenwich, CT: JAI Press.

Yarnold, P. R. (1982). "Groundwork" research in the coronary-prone behavior pattern. (Ms. 2410) *JSAS Catalog of Selected Documents in Psychology, 12,* 4.

Chapter 5

Attitudes

Middle managers suffer from low morale, a new study suggests. A poll of 1,500 managers by the American Management Association finds that only 33% trust top officials. Disaffection with corporate leaders is greatest among those aged 51 to 55.
—THE WALL STREET JOURNAL (1/3/84)

What do the words *morale, trust,* and *disaffection* have in common? Each of these is used in the quotation above, and in that context they paint a not-so-rosy picture. The answer is that they all reflect an underlying *attitude*. In this particular case, it is the attitude of middle managers toward top management, and that attitude is decidedly negative.

Attitudes abound in organizations. One has only to keep one's eyes and ears open to see and hear people express their attitudes toward a whole array of things. People have attitudes about their jobs, about the company they work for, about their boss, about their coworkers, about the amount of money they earn, about the way they are treated by management, and even about the physical surroundings in which they work. What is more, these attitudes affect their behavior. We would not be surprised to learn, for example, that a person who enjoys his or her work plans to continue in the same job in the foreseeable future. Nor would we be surprised to learn that someone who dislikes the work plans to quit.

In this chapter we will examine the concept of attitude and its relevance for understanding the behavior of people in organizations. The first section of the chapter begins with a definition of what an attitude is and how it differs from other, related concepts. We then discuss the functional importance of attitudes, as well as how attitudes are formed. The latter discussion relies heavily on the notions of *instrumental* and *associative learning* introduced in Chapter 2. We also examine several ways to measure attitudes.

Next we examine the dynamics of attitude change. In particular, we focus on the way in which both beliefs and behavior influence attitudes. One conclusion we draw is that while attitudes influence behavior, behavior also influences attitudes.

A closely related topic is that of persuasion. *Persuasion* is an intentional attempt to change the attitudes of others by means of written, spoken, or filmed messages. Sometimes persuasion is successful in changing attitudes, and sometimes it is not. We will examine the reasons why in some detail.

Finally, in the last section of the chapter we give special attention to several attitudes that are very important in the world of work, namely, job satisfaction, organizational commitment, and job involvement. A great deal of research has been done on these topics, especially job satisfaction. We will discuss the factors that influence job satisfaction, as well as the relationship between job satisfaction and such variables as absenteeism, turnover, and productivity.

BACKGROUND

Broadly speaking, an *attitude* can be defined as *any affective reaction to a person, object, idea, or activity.* It might also be thought of as a judgment about where a person, object, idea, or activity falls on a liked-disliked continuum (cf. McGuire, 1985). Thus, an attitude can be either positive or negative. The more the attitude object is liked, the more positive one's attitude toward it. The more it is disliked, the more negative one's attitude.

To help get a better idea of what an attitude is, we should distinguish it from other well-known, but different, concepts. First, an attitude is not a fact. An attitude is an evaluative statement. It is how one feels about something. *Facts,* on the other hand, are statements about the existing state of nature. Telling someone that you like the UCLA basketball team is an expression of your attitude. Telling someone that the UCLA team won more college basketball championships from 1965 to 1980 than any other team is a fact. The facts may be related to the attitude, but they are different things.

Second, attitudes are different from *beliefs*. Beliefs are typically defined as statements about the relationships between objects, concepts, and events. "I like my job" is an attitude. "My job pays well" or "I have a smart supervisor on my job" are beliefs. These beliefs describe the relationship between one's job and other aspects of the work setting. Sometimes a belief may be a fact, but in other cases it may not. For example, the statement "I will get promoted if I stay on this job for another year" is a belief, but not necessarily a fact. Most attitude theorists see attitudes as influenced by beliefs. If we know all the beliefs that a person has about a job (e.g., it is interesting, pays well, involves long hours), we should be able to infer his or her attitude. Many attitude measurement techniques follow this procedure.

Attitudes are also different from *values*. As we use the term here, values are a special type of belief. They are abstract ideals about how one ought or ought not behave (Rokeach, 1968). They are not tied to any particular person, object, or situation. Rather, they are one's beliefs about *ideal* modes of conduct and *ideal* life goals. Rationality, honesty, loyalty, and fairness are examples of ideal modes of conduct, while security, happiness, equality, and freedom are examples of ideal life goals. Thus, our attitude about the treatment of various minority groups may be strongly influenced by the extent to which we hold fairness and equality as basic values.

Finally, attitudes are different from *personality*. Recall that personality refers to those characteristics of people that account for consistent patterns of behavior. Attitudes can also lead to consistencies in behavior. The difference is that personality is much more stable than attitudes. While personality can and does change, it changes much more slowly and over a much longer period of time than do attitudes. Personality traits may require 10 to 20 years to change, and even then the change is likely to be only moderate. An attitude, on the other hand, can change almost instantly. For example, if you discover that a friend at work has done something intentionally to embarrass you in front of your boss, your attitude toward that friend is likely to change rather quickly. We should note, however, that although attitudes are conceptually distinct from personality, sometimes attitudes and personality are systematically related. An individual with an authoritarian personality, for example, is more likely to hold conservative than liberal political attitudes (Byrne, 1974).

An attitude, then, is a fairly specific evaluative feeling. The relationship between attitudes and the other concepts just discussed can be seen in the model shown in Figure 5-1. As the model indicates, our attitudes are influenced by a number of factors, including our beliefs, values, and personalities. They are also influenced by our past behavior. We will elaborate on this point later in the chapter. Finally, attitudes are an important determinant of future intentions and behavior. We will discuss the link between attitudes and future behavior in the next section.

The Importance of Attitudes

Attitudes serve a number of functions and are important for a variety of reasons. From a personal perspective, attitudes provide a knowledge base that

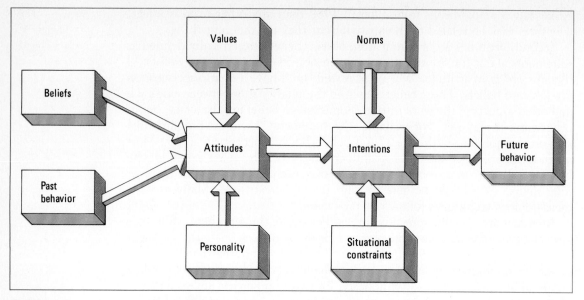

FIGURE 5-1
A model depicting
the relationship
between attitudes
and other related
concepts.

facilitates our interaction with others and with the world around us. For example, our attitudes about various social issues (e.g., abortion, gun control) help us form our opinions about political candidates. Also, as we come into contact with other people, we quickly learn whether their attitudes are similar to, or different from, our own. In many cases this mutual assessment of attitude similarity determines the extent to which future interaction will occur.

Attitudes are also used as social indicators. During presidential campaigns we are constantly bombarded with attitude surveys about the major candidates. These surveys usually start appearing more than two years before the election actually takes place. In a similar vein, the marketing departments of most large companies constantly monitor our attitudes toward their products. National surveys of job satisfaction provide information about the general well-being of the workforce. What is your attitude about this? and How do you feel about that? have become common questions in almost every aspect of our personal and organizational lives (Henry, 1984).

Given the proliferation of attitude surveys and their frequent use as social indicators, it is important to ask whether or not they really work. Do they really predict who we will vote for, whether we will purchase a particular product, and whether we will act on our job satisfaction or dissatisfaction? More fundamentally, do attitudes really influence our behavior? The answer is a qualified yes.

Perhaps the most famous research on this topic was conducted by Richard LaPiere (1934). From 1930 to 1932, LaPiere and a Chinese couple traveled around the United States by car. Of the 251 establishments they approached for services, food, or lodging, only one refused to serve them. LaPiere later sent out a questionnaire to each of these establishments to discover their attitude toward Orientals and their willingness to serve them. Of the reurned questionnaires, 95 percent of the respondents said *they would refuse service to*

Chinese. Clearly there was a discrepancy between the reported attitude of these establishments and their actual behavior.

The results caused an uproar among social psychologists, and numerous explanations were cited for LaPiere's findings. New theories were proposed, attitude was redefined, and rigorous procedures were developed. Out of all this activity came a clearer understanding of two important issues.

First, the more specific the attitude measured, the more likely it is to be related to behavior (Fishbein & Ajzen, 1975). The measure LaPiere used simply asked about Chinese people in general—not about the well-dressed, highly educated young couple who actually appeared at the desk. If you want to know whether an individual is going to join a particular union, your prediction will be better if you measure his or her attitude toward that specific union rather than toward unions in general. This principle was nicely demonstrated in a study that assessed people's attitudes and beliefs about unleaded gasoline and air pollution (Herberlein & Black, 1976). The attitudes of 303 people were assessed using four different types of attitude measures varying in specificity. It was found that the more specific attitude measures (i.e., those focusing on attitudes about purchasing leaded and unleaded gasoline under very specific circumstances) were better able to predict actual gasoline purchases than were the less specific measure (i.e., those assessing global attitudes about the environment and air pollution). These results are shown in Figure 5-2.

Second, as Figure 5-1 indicates, situational variables and norms often intervene between our attitude and our behavior. For example, an innkeeper might be opposed in principle to serving a minority group member, but be compelled by legal constraints to provide service. Similarly, it is easy to imagine a situation in which an employee wants to join a union but coworkers do not. In this case, even though the person's attitude favors joining a union,

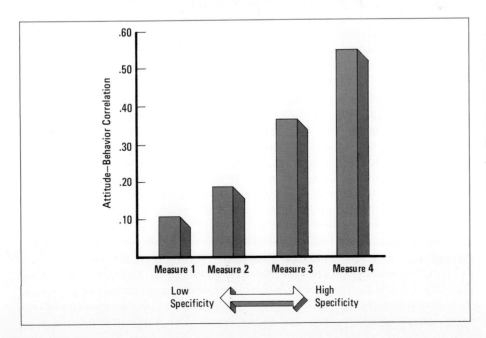

FIGURE 5-2
The more specific the attitude measure, the more strongly it was related to actual gasoline purchasing behavior. (*Based on data presented by Heberlein & Black, 1976.*)

the social pressure or norm against unions may deter action (cf. Youngblood, DeNisis, Molleston, & Mobley, 1984).

Thus attitudes *are* related to behavior. They indicate a personal predisposition to respond in a particular way. However, other forces can outweigh or counteract this predisposition. Sometimes the situation or social norms prohibit us from behaving in ways that are consistent with our attitudes. The important point is that if these other external forces *did not* exist, the individual probably *would* behave in accordance with his or her attitude. Therefore, if we can help to form or change a person's attitude, we can usually influence his or her behavior.

Attitude Formation and Development

In Chapter 2, "Understanding People," we discussed the ways in which learning takes place in organizations. We pointed out that attitudes are among the many things that people learn. Attitudes can be learned through two distinct processes. The first is *associative learning*. Recall that associative learning occurs whenever a neutral stimulus is systematically paired with another stimulus that by itself elicits a strong reaction. The strong reaction could be an intense feeling of either liking or disliking. After a number of pairings, the previously neutral stimulus will come to elicit the same strong feeling, and a new attitude is born.

Attitudes can also be learned through the process of *instrumental learning*. Recall that instrumental learning occurs whenever an individual's behavior is followed by some event that either increases or decreases the probability that that behavior will be repeated in the future. In the case of attitudes, the focal behavior is the expression of either positive or negative sentiments regarding some person, object, idea, or activity. For example, imagine that you have a summer job with the local power company. You work with a road crew that repairs and replaces aging power lines and worn-out line equipment. During your first week on the job you eat lunch each day by the side of the road with the other five members of the crew. Almost from the start you notice that one of the main topics of conversation is the way management treats its employees. The other crew members constantly grouse about the lousy way they are treated, about how management has taken advantage of the union, and about how poor management decisions have left the company unable to keep up with the rising power needs of the region. One day, just to get in on the conversation, you comment that the company's summer job program seemed to be one example of smart thinking on the part of management (after all, that is how you got *your* job!). Quite suddenly the conversation stops, and everyone seems to be staring at you. Then, one by one, each of the crew members begins to fire counterexamples at you, and someone shouts out, "What does a wet-behind-the-ears college kid know, anyway?" Everyone laughs—everyone but you. You feel pretty bad and are glad when the lunch break is over so that you can get out of this awkward situation.

Later in the week you are again on your lunch break, and again the rest of the crew is discussing how they are getting a raw deal from management. Once more you try to get in on the conversation, this time by asking whether the union can do something to make things better. The response you get now is very different from what you got before. The group seems pleased that you asked the question, and they take some time to explain to you the history of labor–managment negotiations in the company. Whereas the response of the work crew to your first comment about the summer jobs program clearly had the effect of punishing you for expressing a promanagement sentiment, they now are rewarding you for asking a question that could be construed as slightly prolabor. They are rewarding you with their positive reactions and with the serious attention they are giving to your question. And you are likely to feel good about that. So, over the course of the summer you gradually make more and more prolabor comments, and each time you are reinforced by the group's favorable reaction. Not only that, but you actually come to *feel* more prolabor; that is, as a consequence of the pattern of social reinforcement given by the group, you begin to develop a positive attitude toward labor and a negative attitude toward management.

Thus, the associative and instrumental learning processes are two important ways in which attitudes are formed. These processes can play a part in the development of attitudes about almost anything. Of course, there are many things that most of us do not have strong attitudes about one way or the other (e.g., Kwakiutl Indian art). This is usually true, however, only when we don't know much about them and have had little or no experience with them (cf. Sandelands & Larson, 1985; Smith & Swinyard, 1983). As our knowledge of and experience with various people, objects, ideas, and activities increase, our attitudes are quickly formed. Thus we *do* have attitudes toward most things that we frequently encounter in our everyday lives, both inside and outside the workplace.

Attitude Measurement

The most common and frequently used attitude measures are questionnaires that ask the respondent either to rate his or her feelings about the attitude object directly, or to indicate his or her beliefs about the attitude object. If, for example, you want to know how favorable your employees are toward a particular union, you might use a set of bipolar adjective scales to assess their attitudes. Some examples are shown in Figure 5-3. Alternatively, you could generate a number of belief statements, and have your employees indicate whether or not they feel those statements are true for the union in question. Several examples of such statements are given in Figure 5-4.

People's responses to these two types of questionnaire items should give you a fairly good assessment of their attitude. We should hasten to point out,

---

This Particular Union Is . . .

Pleasant : ____ : ____ : ____ : ____ : ____ : ____ : ____ : Unpleasant
     + 3   + 2   + 1   0   − 1   − 2   − 3

Good : ____ : ____ : ____ : ____ : ____ : ____ : ____ : Bad
     + 3   + 2   + 1   0   − 1   − 2   − 3

Beneficial : ____ : ____ : ____ : ____ : ____ : ____ : ____ : Harmful
     + 3   + 2   + 1   0   − 1   − 2   − 3

FIGURE 5-3
Attitudes can be measured by using bipolar adjectives.

FIGURE 5-4
Attitudes can also
be measured by
using belief state-
ments.

1.	T ? F	This particular union protects the rights of workers.
2.	T ? F	This particular union will bring about better wages.
3.	T ? F	This particular union increases conflict and tension in the workplace.
4.	T ? F	This particular union suppresses individual freedom.

however, that there are rigorous procedures for the development and scoring of such instruments (e.g., Fishbein & Ajzen, 1975). One should either use a standard questionnaire or consult an expert to obtain a valid measure of attitudes.

Job Attitudes: Measuring Morale

There are numerous job-related attitudes that have interested social scientists. The one most frequently researched, however, is that dealing with the individual's overall feeling toward his or her job. This attitude is typically called morale or job satisfaction, and specific methods have been developed to measure it.

The job satisfaction questionnaire that is most well known is the Job Descriptive Index (JDI), developed by Pat Smith and her coworkers (Smith, Kendall, & Hulin, 1969). This questionnaire presents the respondent with a series of adjectives for each of five aspects of the job (work conditions, pay, promotions, supervision, and coworkers). The employee places a "Y," "N," or "?" next to each adjective to indicate whether or not it is descriptive of that particular job aspect. Some sample items from this scale are presented in Figure 5-5.

The positive features of the JDI are worth mentioning. First, it generates a satisfaction score for five job areas as well as an overall score. This information can help the investigator in using the JDI as a diagnostic device. He or she can determine the specific areas with which people are more or less satisfied. Another strong point is the scale's ease of administration. It is not necessary to develop a new scale for each job. There are also extensive normative data available for the JDI. Thousands of employees have filled out this scale in many different types of organizations across the country. It is possible, therefore, not only to make comparisons between jobs in the same organization, but also to compare different organizations on the same job. For example, how does employee satisfaction with pay at firm A compare with pay satisfaction at firm B?

A second job satisfaction questionnaire that is frequently used was developed by Porter and Lawler (1968). Their method (called the Need Fulfillment Questionnaire) also gathers information about different job aspects. Employees are asked to what degree a certain job characteristic exists in their present position (e.g., supervision), and how much they think there ideally should be. They also rate the importance of that characteristic. A difference score between what there is now and what there should be is weighted by the importance score. Two or three questions are included for each job aspect. This questionnaire yields an overall score as well as a score for each aspect.

The JDI is typically employed for lower-level, routine jobs, while the Porter

Work on Present Job

Think of your present work. What is it like most of the time? In the blank beside each word given below, write

_Y_ for "Yes" if it describes your work

_N_ for "No" if it does NOT describe it

_?_ if you cannot describe

_____ routine

_____ satisfying

_____ good

_____ too much to do

Supervision on Present Job

Think of the kind of supervision that you can get on your job. How well does each of the following words describe this supervision? In the blank beside each word below, put

_Y_ if it describes the supervision you get on your job

_N_ if it does NOT describe it

_?_ if you cannot decide

_____ impolite

_____ praises good work

_____ influential

_____ doesn't supervise enough

Present Pay

Think of the pay you get now. How well does each of the following words describe your present pay? In the blank beside each word, put

_Y_ if it describes your pay

_N_ if it does NOT describe it

_?_ if you cannot decide

_____ Income adequate for normal expenses

_____ insecure

_____ less than I deserve

_____ well paid

Coworkers on Your Present Job

Think of the majority of the people that you work with now or the people you meet in connection with your work. How well does each of the following words describe these people? In the blank beside each word below, put

_Y_ if it describes the people you work with

_N_ if it does NOT describe them

_?_ if you cannot decide

_____ boring

_____ responsible

_____ intelligent

_____ talk too much

Opportunities for Promotion

Think of the opportunities for promotion that you have now. How well does each of the following words describe these? In the blank beside each word, put

_Y_ for "Yes" if it describes your opportunities for promotion

_N_ for "No" if it does NOT describe them

_?_ if you cannot decide

_____ promotion on ability

_____ dead-end job

_____ unfair promotion policy

_____ regular promotions

Your Job in General

Think of your job in general. All in all, what is it like most of the time? In the blank beside each word below, write

_Y_ for "Yes" if it describes your job.

_N_ for "No" if it does NOT describe it.

_?_ if you can't decide

_____ superior

_____ makes me content

_____ rotten

FIGURE 5-5 Sample items from the revised Job Descriptive Index. (*The JDI is copyrighted by Bowling Green State University. The complete forms, scoring key, instructions, and norms can be obtained from Dr. Patricia C. Smith, Department of Psychology, Bowling Green State University, Bowling Green, OH 43403.*)

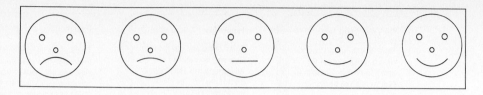

and Lawler questionnaire is frequently used for managers. Both measures assume that the respondent can read. For illiterate or marginally literate employees there is a scale called the Faces Scale (Kunin, 1955), which presents five faces similar to those pictured in Figure 5-6. The employee is asked to circle the face that best represents his or her feelings about the job.

While there are a number of other good attitude measures available, these three are representative of those most frequently used today.

ATTITUDE ORGANIZATION AND DYNAMICS

*Isn't it because you're free to choose the one that you love
that you love the one you choose like you do?*
—CASHMAN AND WEST

At the beginning of the chapter we state that attitudes are related in a systematic way to a number of other things, including beliefs, values, personality, and past behavior. A major thrust of contemporary research on attitudes in both social psychology and organizational behavior has been to clarify these relationships. Of particular interest are the relationships between attitudes and beliefs and between attitudes and past behavior. From the point of view of organizations, these relationships are especially important to understand because they tell us something about the way employees' attitudes are likely to change when their work-related beliefs or behaviors change.

The Effect of Beliefs on Attitudes

Fritz Heider (1946) was one of the first investigators to suggest a general theory of attitude organization (called *balance theory*). Heider's model was very simple. He was interested in the relationship between (1) a person's attitude toward an object or concept (e.g., my attitude toward management), (2) that same person's beliefs about *someone else's* attitude toward the object or concept (e.g., my beliefs about *my supervisor's* attitude toward management), and (3) that person's attitude toward the other individual (e.g., my attitude toward my supervisor). Heider was interested mostly in the area of interpersonal attraction, and he suggested that we like people who we believe like the same things we like. When this situation does not exist (e.g., when we believe that a friend likes something we dislike, or that an enemy is attracted to something we do like), we feel uncomfortable and are motivated to change one of our attitudes. In other words, we try to maintain some degree of *consistency* or *balance* among our attitudes.

This type of consistency model has been developed for other issues besides interpersonal attraction. Complex attitude structures have been analyzed that contain links between beliefs about multiple persons and attitude objects. The strength of the links has also been quantified so that the *degree* of attitude change can be predicted. As a basic model, Heider's theory has been very helpful. It points out that we tend to hold consistent attitudes, and that when they become inconsistent we are motivated to change them.

The Effect of Behavior on Attitudes

Although Heider's balance theory has been useful, it is limited in two respects. First, it is somewhat simplistic, and second, it fails to consider behavior. In an attempt to deal with these two problems, Leon Festinger (1957) developed the theory of cognitive dissonance. According to Festinger, two cognitive elements are dissonant if the *opposite* of one follows from the other. These cognitive elements can be more than just attitudes and beliefs. They can also be observations of one's own behavior. Thus a belief, such as "union X is ineffective in protecting worker rights," coupled with the act of participating in union X organizing activities, would be expected to arouse feelings of discomfort (dissonance), and would motivate the individual to change either the behavior or the beliefs.

Two qualifications should be noted here. First, Festinger argues that we must look at the overall *proportion* of dissonant elements to consonant elements in order to predict changes in behavior or attitudes. We must examine the overall cognitive structure to see how much dissonance exists. Thus one dissonant belief in the midst of many consonant ones will probably not generate enough psychological discomfort to produce change. Second, Festinger argues that these cognitions must be weighted by their importance. Therefore, sometimes even when only a few elements are dissonant, their importance may be high enough to motivate attitude change.

How does one reduce dissonance? Festinger suggests three major strategies. First, one can reduce the importance of the dissonant elements. Second, one can add more consonant elements. Third, one can change the dissonant elements. Let us say, for example, that you work in an advertising firm that accepts an account for a pharmaceutical product you believe might be harmful to people's health (including your own, perhaps). You thus have a negative attitude toward the product. You must help market the product (behavior), but you are uncomfortable doing so. One strategy to reduce this dissonance would be to say to yourself, "Well, any drug we take probably does a little harm," thereby reducing the importance of the dissonant element. You might, on the other hand, try to find out more about the positive effects of the product in an attempt to outweigh the dissonant element. Finally, you might put in a request to be transferred off this particular account. A number of applications of dissonance theory are especially related to decision-making issues, three of which are discussed below.

Postdecisional Dissonance. Decision making produces dissonance. Whenever we are forced to choose one alternative from a set of possible courses of action, we must usually forgo the good aspects of the unchosen alternatives and live with whatever bad aspects there may be of the selected alternative.

Imagine, for example, that after graduation you are offered a job at two different firms, A and B. Both jobs are attractive, but of course you can only accept one. The choice is tough, but you end up accepting the offer made by firm A. Now that you have made your choice, you must reconcile the fact that you have rejected a job that in fact had many attractive qualities (job B). Dissonance theory predicts that several things will happen. First, there may be a brief stage of regret in which the unchosen alternative (job B) becomes *more* attractive. This period lasts only a brief time, however, after which dissonance begins to operate (i.e., you begin to justify to yourself mentally the choice you have made). Dissonance theory predicts that you will *bolster* your positive attraction toward firm A and gradually become more negative toward firm B.

Research results confirm these predictions. For example, in a classic study reported by Brehm (1956), college women were asked to evaluate the attractiveness of a set of similarly priced consumer products (e.g., a toaster, a silk-screen print). Afterward, as payment for participating in the study, each subject was given a choice between two of these products to keep for herself. After making a selection, all of the products were evaluated a second time. Of interest here is the manner in which the attractiveness of the two "choice" products changed over time. The attractiveness ratings are shown in Figure 5-7. As you would expect, before the choice was made the product that was eventually chosen was seen as more attractive than the product that was eventually rejected. What is interesting is that this difference was even larger *after* the choice was made. After the choice, and before the products were actually used, the rejected product became significantly less attractive, while the chosen product became slightly more attractive. This occurred even when the subjects had no additional information about the products. Thus the subjects' initial attitudes (first attractiveness rating) affected their behavior (choice), which in turn affected their subsequent attitudes (second attractiveness rating).

Two points about postdecisional dissonance should be emphasized. First,

FIGURE 5-7
After making a decision, the rejected alternative became even less attractive. (*Based on data presented by Brehm, 1956.*)

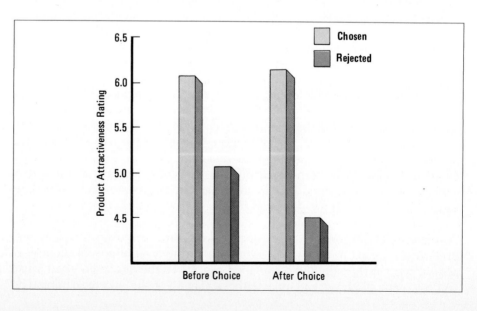

note that we are talking about attitude change that occurs *after* the behavior (choice). In other words, the behavior is the cause of the attitude rather than the reverse. One of the major contributions of dissonance theory has been its focus on the fact that people often behave first and change their attitude in line with the behavior.

Note also that once dissonance has occurred and new attitudes are formed, our new attitudes will then influence later choices. That is, behavior causes attitudes, which in turn cause behavior. When our choices are repetitive and between alternatives that are initially close in attractiveness, we will continue to reject and devalue the unchosen alternative. This phenomenon has great importance in organizational settings. A decision alternative that at one time was rejected may at some later date turn out to be just the course of action needed to maximize the organization's payoffs. Because of the dissonance process, however, this alternative may become increasingly devalued. Consequently, it is more likely to be rejected again in the future, even when it is objectively the best alternative.

Disconfirmed Expectancies. Another situation that occurs frequently in organizations is one in which some sort of expectation is disconfirmed, that is, turns out to be incorrect. For example, suppose you decide that the route to success for your company is to buy out a number of small competitors, and you spend a substantial amount of the company's resources doing this. Six months later, however, performance and productivity are down, you have little in the way of a financial cushion, and the company is in trouble. An outsider might easily believe that the decision and subsequent drop in productivity are related.

Your position as the decision maker is likely to be one of acute dissonance. You might attempt to reduce the dissonance in a variety of ways. For example, you might argue that the cause of the slump is really something other than the purchase of the small firms. Or, you may come to believe that the basic decision was all right, even though the expectation was incorrect. Different positive outcomes may be emphasized ("Well, we're not making more money, but we are reaching a wider audience and we're better known."). Rather than recognize and admit that a poor choice was made, you may actually become more committed to the mistake.

An excellent study by Staw (1976) illustrates this point (it was appropriately entitled "Knee Deep in the Big Muddy"). A simulation was run in which business students played the role of corporate executives in a financially troubled company. There were four different variations of the simulation. In one variation, the students were told to imagine that the date was 1967 and that they had to make a decision about which of the company's two largest divisions (consumer products or industrial products) should be given a $10 million infusion of additional R&D Funds. After making this decision, the students were presented with a financial report dated 1972—a 5-year update. They learned that following their decision the company's performance improved. In a second variation of the simulation, the students made the same 1967 decision but learned that following their decision the company's performance worsened. In the third variation, the students did not themselves make the 1967 decision. Instead they read about the decision that another "executive" had made. These students then also got the 1972 financial report, and they learned that the company's performance subsequently improved. Finally, the fourth variation was similar to the third, except that the 1972 report indicated that following the 1967 decision the company's performance worsened. Thus half of the students in the study made the initial 1967 decision themselves (i.e., they were personally responsible for the decision), while the other half read about a decision that someone else had made (i.e., they were not personally responsible for the decision). And half of each of these two groups discovered that the 1967 decision was followed by improved company performance (i.e., the decision maker's expectations about the effect of the decision were confirmed), while the other half discovered that it was followed by worsened company performance (i.e., expectations were disconfirmed). All of the students were then asked to make a further allocation of funds to the two divisions. The dependent variable in the study was the amount of money allocated to the same division that had been given the $10 million in 1967.

Suppose *you* had been in this study. What would you have done? Specifically, suppose you had learned that *your* 1967 decision was followed by worsening company performance? How would you have felt, and how much additional money would you have allocated to the same division the second time arond? Disonance theory makes a very clear prediction. It predicts that after having your expectations disconfirmed, you will experience cognitive dissonance (e.g., "I generally think of myself as a pretty good decision maker, yet here is a decision that didn't turn out too well."). One way you can reduce this dissonance is to convince yourself that the original decision was actually not such a bad idea (e.g., "Things might have been even worse had the other division been chosen."). But if you do convince yourself of this, dissonance theory predicts that you are likely to allocate even *more* money to the same division in the future! By committing additional resources, you can hope to overcome your "setback" and thereby demonstrate the ultimate rationality of

FIGURE 5-8
Students allocated significantly more additional funding to the same division when they were personally responsible for a decision that was followed by worsened company performance. (*Based on data presented by Staw, 1976.*)

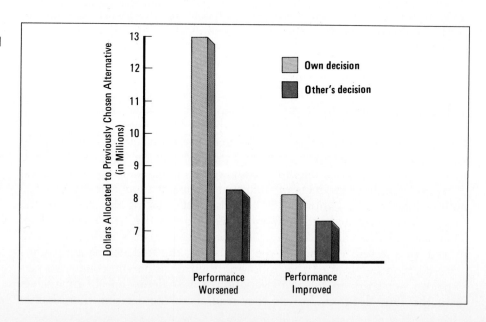

your original decision (Staw, 1981). As you can see in Figure 5-8, this is exactly what Staw (1976) found. When the original 1967 decision was followed by worsened company performance, and the students had made the 1967 decision themselves, they allocated substantially more additional money to the same division than did students in any of the other three conditions. When the 1967 decision was not made by the students themselves, or when it was followed by improved company performance, no dissonance occurred and lower levels of subsequent funding were allocated.

The ramifications of this study are important. It suggests that people change their attitudes and values to justify their behavior. For the decision-making process, it means that time and effort is spent in justifying a choice already made rather than objectively determining a better course of action. Instead of learning from our mistakes and correcting our errors, we may often compound our errors and make more serious mistakes.

Attitude-Discrepant Behavior. This third area of application is perhaps the most interesting, as well as the most controversial, topic in dissonance theory. Frequently we are asked to do things that we find unpleasant. Tough decisions must be made about allocating resources, hiring, firing, and so on. When we behave in ways that are discrepant with our underlying attitudes, we usually experience dissonance. The critical questions are (1) how much pressure is needed to produce the attitude-discrepant behavior? and (2) what are the implications for attitude change?

The predictions that dissonance theory makes can be seen in Figure 5-9. This figure indicates how an individual is likely to respond, both behaviorally and attitudinally, to varying degrees of pressure to engage in an activity that

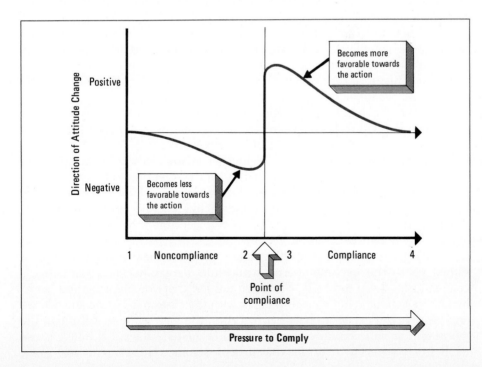

FIGURE 5-9
Positive attitude change is most likely to occur when there is just barely enough pressure to gain compliance (point 3). Negative attitude change is most likely to occur when the maximum pressure that still does not lead to compliance is applied (point 2).

he or she would really rather not do. The best way to understand this figure is to work through an example. Therefore, let us imagine that you want to have a particular subordinate handle a customer complaint (usually a fairly unpleasant task). We'll call this subordinate Pat. Suppose we start out with a situation of minimal pressure to comply—point 1 in Figure 5-9. For example, you might mention the customer's complaint in your weekly staff meeting with your subordinates and ask if there is anyone who wants to handle it. You hope that Pat will raise her hand, but since handling complaints is something that Pat does not like to do, she probably will not volunteer. And, since you did not put any pressure on her, Pat's attitude toward handling customer complaints is not likely to change.

Now, let us increase the pressure to point 2 in Figure 5-9. You run into Pat in the hall, casually mention to her that a complaint has been received, and ask her if she would mind handling it. Since your phrasing is that of a request, Pat still has the option of turning you down. Let us say that she does in fact decline. By turning you down, Pat has successfully avoided doing something that she prefers not to do. On the other hand, she has run the risk of incurring other negative consequences later on (e.g., will turning you down affect the ratings you give her on her annual performance review?). This cannot have been an easy choice for Pat, and she is likely to experience some degree of dissonance because of it (e.g., "I'm not the kind of person who goes around looking for trouble from my boss."). One way to reduce this dissonance is for Pat to change her attitude somewhat, becoming even more negative about handling customer complaints than before (e.g., "I never turn down a request from my boss unless I *really hate* the task.") Thus, negative attitudes are likely to become even more negative when pressure is put on a person to engage in attitude-discrepant behavior, but that pressure is insufficient to actually gain compliance.

Let us now move to point 3 in Figure 5-9. Again you approach Pat about handling the complaint, and again you state it as a request. But this time you phrase it in a way that subtly adds just a little bit more pressure, and she complies. This, too, cannot have been an easy decision for Pat. Yes, she had avoided the negative consequences that might accrue from turning you down, but now she is committed to doing a task that she doesn't like to do. Thus, once again Pat will feel some degree of dissonance (e.g., "I'm not the kind of person who agrees to do things I don't really want to do."). As before, this dissonance can be reduced by changing her attitude toward the task. This time, however, the attitude change will be in the direction of becoming more *positive* (or at least less negative) toward the task (e.g., "How bad can it really be, anyway?"). Thus, negative attitudes are likely to become more positive when *just enough* pressure is put on a person to get him or her to engage in the attitude-discrepant behavior.

Finally, let us consider point 4 in Figure 5-9. Here the pressure to comply is turned up to the maximum. You stride into Pat's office and state that a complaint has been received. Then you tell Pat that you are assigning her to handle it. You hand her a piece of paper with the customer's name and address and say that you expect to hear her report on the matter the first thing in the morning. Pat will certainly comply. But her attitude toward the task is not likely to change. The reason is that little dissonance will be generated (e.g.,

"What else could I do? My boss gave me a direct order."). There is little need to justify her behavior by distorting her attitudes. Your direct order is justification enough. Thus, negative attitudes are unlikely to change when a high level of pressure is put on a person to engage in attitude-discrepant behavior.

Research generally supports the predictions made by this model (Chialdini, Petty, & Cacioppo, 1981). Attitudes are most likely to change when the pressure to comply is at an intermediate level, and thus the person still feels some freedom to comply or not comply. The greater the amount of freedom, the more powerful the effect of the dissonance. As the poet Milton once said, "He who overcomes by force hath overcome but half his foe." If someone has no choice but to comply, the underlying attitude will remain unchanged.

This finding is of crucial importance for the execution of decisions and leadership. Obviously a manager does not want to have to constantly increase the pressure on subordinates in order to obtain their compliance. It is unpleasant to have to push and threaten. Managers prefer situations in which their subordinates come to enjoy what they are doing. The implication of the model discussed here is that it is perhaps better to start out with a little too much pressure (point 4) and then work back to less pressure (point 3) than to do the reverse. If too little pressure is exerted, the subordinate will not comply and will come to dislike the task even more (and will then require more pressure the next time to obtain compliance).

PERSUASION AS A STRATEGY FOR ATTITUDE CHANGE

As we have seen, attitudes are affected by both external contingencies of reinforcement and the internal dynamics of cognitive consistency. One implication of the latter point is that under the right conditions, attitudes can change as a consequence of one's behavior (e.g., making a decision, or engaging in an attitude-discrepant behavior). In addition, experience tells us that attitudes can also be changed through the process of persuasion. *Persuasion* is an intentional attempt to change attitudes by means of written, spoken, or filmed messages. We run into persuasive advertising everywhere: on the radio and television, in newspapers and magazines, inside buses and subways, and even on product packaging. Our families and friends are constantly trying to change our minds about one thing or another. And in the organizations in which we work, we encounter attempts at persuasion on a daily basis. In this section we will take a closer look at the persuasion process and at some of the factors that influence whether or not our attitudes are changed by persuasive messages.

A Model of Attitude Change Through Persuasion

When one person tries to change another person's attitude through persuasion, a number of factors are involved. Figure 5-10 presents a model that lists these factors. First, the personal characteristics of the communicator may influence how much change occurs: Is the person believable? Second, the way in which the message is presented may make a difference: Is the message biased

FIGURE 5-10
A model of the
factors involved in
the persuasion
process.

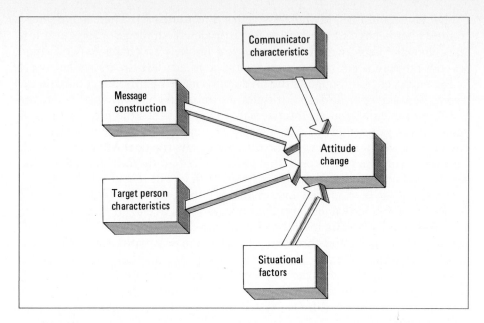

or poorly organized? Third, the characteristics of the target person are important. Is he or she paying attention? And finally, some situational variables may help to increase change: Is there a supporting audience surrounding the target person? The research on all these factors is extensive, and the findings are summarized below.

Communicator Characteristics. There are a number of communicator characteristics that influence the likelihood of attitude change *independently of the message*. The first, and perhaps the most important, is the expertise or prestige of the communicator. If the communicator is seen as well qualified in the area, more change will occur. Thus, if exactly the same message is delivered by two different communicators, one of high prestige and one of low prestige, greater attitude change will result from the message delivered by the high prestige communicator (Mills & Harvey, 1972).

A second characteristic of the communicator that is important is whether he or she is perceived as biased. The target is likely to question whether the communicator has something to gain or lose in the issue. The more bias thought to exist, the less attitude change there will be. The advertisements on TV that refer to an "independent study" done by a "team of experts" are trying to make you believe you are hearing an unbiased report from a very prestigious source.

Finally, people that we like and identify with are more persuasive than those we dislike or are unfamiliar with. The reason football players and movie stars advertise spark plugs and beef stew is not that they are expert mechanics or cooks. It is because these people are attractive and liked. This phenomenon is quite consistent with the previously discussed balance model suggested by Heider (1946). We like products that are liked by people for whom we have positive feelings.

The Communicator. There are several ways in which the message itself can be constructed to influence the chances of attitude change. One issue is the degree to which an extreme stand should be taken. Should we try the hard sell or the soft sell? Research results seem to suggest that if the topic is fairly unimportant to the target, an extreme position taken by the communicator can produce large amounts of change. However, if the issue is of great importance (e.g., job assignments, politics, religion), an extreme position will be rejected and very little, if any, change will occur. In this type of situation a more moderate appeal is likely to be successful. This makes sense when you

Mark Waters was a chain smoker. Wonder who'll get his office?

Too bad about Mark. Kept hearing the same thing everyone does about lung cancer. But, like so many people, he kept right on smoking cigarettes. Must have thought, "been smoking all my life... what good'll it do to stop now?" Fact is, once you've stopped smoking, no matter how long you've smoked, the body begins to reverse the damage done by cigarettes, provided cancer or emphysema have not developed. Next time you reach for a cigarette, think of Mark. Then think of your office—and your home.

American Cancer Society

FIGURE 5-11
Sometimes fear arousal can be effective as a technique to change attitudes.

realize that attitudes are embedded in a complex framework of other beliefs, attitudes, and values. If the topic is unimportant, it is likely not to be bolstered by many beliefs and important values. It should therefore be relatively easy to create change without producing discomfort. However, if the attitude is firmly supported by many important beliefs and values, trying to change it means that many deeply held values may also need to be changed. The person is far more likely to reject an extreme communication under these circumstances.

A second issue is whether the communicator should present a one-sided or two-sided argument. Should you recognize the strong points of your competitor? Most of the research says yes. A two-sided argument is generally seen as less biased and therefore more persuasive, especially for intelligent audiences.

A third and highly controversial issue is the use of fear appeals. Does it help to tell people of all the terrible consequences that may occur if they do not change their attitudes and behavior? For example, suppose you have the job of designing an antismoking campaign directed toward your company's employees. Which do you think would be more effective: a campaign that mentions all the details about lung cancer, or one that depicts the smokers as rather socially inept (e.g., bad breath, nervous)? Research results show that fear appeals can be effective, especially when the target can do something to reduce the fear immediately. Studies on automobile safety, atom-bomb testing, fallout shelters, and tooth decay all show that fear appeals can change attitudes and behavior if the person can do something about the problem. However, when there is little that someone can do to relieve the fear and anxiety, the appeal to fear will be less effective (Dembroski, Lasater, & Ramirez, 1978; Mewborn & Rogers, 1979).

Characteristics of the Target. Perhaps the most important characteristic of the target is his or her commitment to the old attitude. Has the person taken any action or made any public statements about where he or she stands? If so, the person's attitude is less likely to change (Salancik, 1977). Also, the more central the attitude is to other attitudes and values, the less change is possible. Firmly held attitudes to which we are verbally and behaviorally committed are hard to change.

It also appears that people who are generally more self-confident and have high self-esteem are less susceptible to persuasion (Zellner, 1970). Apparently, people with high self-esteem believe their attitudes are more correct and justified than those with low self-esteem. People with high self-esteem may be more likely not to care about what attractive movie stars or athletes have to say.

Situational Factors. There are a number of situational variables separate from the communicator, message, and target factors that may affect how much attitude change occurs. One often heard homily that seems to be true is that "forewarned is forearmed." If people know that someone else is going to try to change their attitude on a subject, they are better able to resist the persuasion attempt. One plausible reason for this is that they have the opportunity to think through their position beforehand. They can construct counterarguments and strengthen the defense of their own position. All this activity tends to reduce the amount of change that occurs.

Another situational factor concerns the support of people around you. Is everyone in favor of what the communicator says? Are they nodding their heads in agreement and miling? Are they paying attention? If the target believes that the group is favorable toward the communicator, more change should occur, especially if these people are important to the target.

In summary, there are many ways to change people's attitudes. A liked or respected communicator giving a two-sided, unbiased argument is probably most effective. The uncommitted, low-confidence individual is most likely to change. And social support for the communicator's position is likely to result in high levels of attitude change. At first blush it sounds quite easy—we ought to be able to change people's attitudes whenever we want. Our everyday experience, however, tells us that this is not true, and the following section briefly documents why.

Media-Based Persuasion Campaigns

If so much is known about changing attitudes, why are companies unable to sell their products easily, and why do political candidates find it so hard to get elected to office? Why is it that most studies of political and advertising campaigns show that very few people actually change their attitudes as a result of these persuasion attempts?

Research on why people often are not influenced by media-based persuasion campaigns shows that both personal and situational factors are involved. With regard to personal variables, the target frequently rejects either the expertise or the attractiveness of the communicator. President Ford, in the closing days of the 1976 campaign, had Joe Garagiola (a sports announcer) travel around with him, and in fact Garagiola introduced the President when he made his last-minute appeal to the voters on election eve. If you were not already a Ford supporter, an easy way to reject this appeal would be to say, "What does Joe Garagiola know about politics? Nothing!" The rest of the message would then have little impact.

People also occasionally distort a message. They hear what they want to hear (remember our discussion of selective perception in Chapter 4). The target may not perceive that the communicator is advocating as much change as he or she really is. Furthermore, people are selective about the communicators they expose themselves to in the first place. If, for example, you know that there is an upcoming television show discussing the negative effects of smoking, and you are a heavy smoker, you are less likely to view that show than if you do not smoke.

Situational variables are also important. Most attitude-change appeals of a political or advertising nature occur in social settings in which the communicator does not have the target's full attention. The appearance of an advertisement on television, for example, is often used as a time to get a snack or talk with friends. In addition, most people live and interact with others who are generally similar to themselves in attitudes. Therefore, there is likely to be substantial social support for arguments that refute the communicator's position if the target is initially against that stand.

All of this supports much of what we already know: It is very hard to change people's attitudes and behavior by means of media-based persuasion campaigns, especially on important topics. Individual, one-on-one discussions are likely to be much more effective as a persuasion strategy. Of course, a one-on-one approach requires much more time and energy on the part of the communicator, and large audiences are almost impossible to reach. Thus, there are trade-offs that must be considered when choosing between media-based and more personally oriented approaches to persuasion.

What implications does all this have for organizations? Organizations regularly try to influence the attitudes of their members in order to get them to engage in particular types of behavior. Frequently they try to do this through some sort of media campaign. Campaigns designed to change employee attitudes toward quality (zero defects), service, productivity, and safety can be found in almost any large industrial or service organization. These campaigns consist of orchestrated attempts to influence attitudes through articles printed in internal company newspapers, signs and posters put up in prominent places, and lapel buttons, hats, and T-shirts given to employees to wear. Slogans promoting the desired attitude can be found on bumper-stickers, jackets, key chains, coffee cups, and ball-point pens. The company president may speak before large gatherings of employees, and sometimes slick, professionally made films are shown throughout the company to promote desired attitudes. All of this effort may have some impact, but in most cases the impact will be relatively small. Employee attitudes are in general much more strongly influenced by the attitudes of those in their work groups, and by other aspects of their job and their immediate work environment. Thus, if an organization wishes to achieve a significant change in employee attitudes toward quality, safety, service, or any other job-related activity, more than just a media-based persuasion campaign will usually be needed. The media-based campaign will not be useless, but it will not be sufficient either. In the next section we discuss some of the factors that have a much stronger influence on job-related attitudes.

ATTITUDES AND THE WORLD OF WORK

As we have stated throughout this chapter, we all have many different job-related attitudes. We have attitudes about our supervisor, our pay, the organization in general, safety programs, our specific job, and so on. Even though people engage in many different types of jobs, they all have evaluative feelings about these jobs. Job satisfaction, as a summary attitude about one's job, is a good reflection of these feelings and has been an important aspect of organizational research for more than 60 years. Over 3000 studies have been done on the topic.

There are two reasons why it is important to understand job satisfaction and the factors that affect it. First, from the organization's point of view, satisfaction can influence a number of important job behaviors, including tardiness, absenteeism, and turnover. These behaviors can have serious consequences for the overall effectiveness of the organization and its ability to survive. Second, we should also try to understand the nature and causes of job satisfaction simply because satisfaction is an important job outcome for the individual employee. Recall that in Chapter 3 we suggested that one very useful way to think about organizations is in terms of open systems theory. According to an open systems view, the interaction among people, formal organizational structures, tasks, and informal social relationships produces a series of outputs at the individual, group, and organizational levels of analysis. Job satisfaction is one important individual-level output. Thus, we should strive to understand the factors that affect job satisfaction both because satisfaction is a system output that is of importance to individuals, and because it is one factor that can affect other group- and organizational-level outputs.

Trends in Job Satisfaction

The Hawthorne studies discussed in Chapter 3 first highlighted the importance of employee attitudes. As a result of the attention they received while being observed, the employees in these studies reported a more positive attitude about what they did on the job. They felt the organization was interested in them, and they liked it. Their social and work activities changed, and their performance increased. These initial studies prompted the researchers to investigate further the attitudes of all the employees in the company, and an extensive program of interviewing was commenced. From these data, management gained an insight into the employees' attitudes about work conditions, rate-busters, supervisors, and many other issues that affected their behavior on the job and their overall job satisfaction.

As it became obvious that job attitudes were important, more interest and concern were demonstrated by management, and more and more research was done. The result of much of this work has been a growing concern that people are disenchanted with their jobs, have negative and distrusting attitudes about management, and show little commitment to the organization (*Work in America*, 1973). One summary of Gallup surveys showed that 15 to 20 percent of the workforce are not satisfied with their jobs, and when unemployed persons are included (5 to 10 percent), up to one-quarter of our country's population may have negative attitudes about the workplace (U.S. Department of Labor, 1974). Surveys of both managerial and lower-level employees show the same results (Smith, Scott, & Hulin, 1977; Cooper, Morgan, Foley, & Kaplan, 1979). What is especially clear is that the most dissatisfied are minorities, women, the poorly educated, the very young, and those in low-status occupations. What is also evident is that while satisfaction with wages and supervision has gotten better, satisfaction with issues like "concern for employees," "fairness," or "respect" has gotten worse.

Causes of Job Satisfaction

If we want to know how to increase job satisfaction, we have to know what causes it or is associated with it. There is a considerable body of research that deals with both the causes and the consequences of job satisfaction (Locke, 1976). We will briefly summarize this literature in the following two sections.

Opinions about Employee Attitude Surveys

Attitude surveys appear to be one of the "bread and butter" activities among industrial/organizational psychologists. To better understand the perception of the consumer toward attitude surveys, LOMA* conducted a survey of Human Resources (H.R.) executives representing 375 life and property/casualty insurance companies. (Only a psychologist, of course, would conduct a survey on conducting surveys.)

EXPERIENCE WITH EMPLOYEE ATTITUDE SURVEYS

Approximately one-half the respondents reported that their companies had conducted at least one employee attitude survey during the last ten years; however, only a small percent (16%) conduct attitude surveys on a regular basis. Of those that do conduct surveys on a regular basis, the majority administer surveys on a two- or three-year cycle. The use of attitude surveys appears to be related to company size. Generally, the larger a company's home office population is, the more likely it is to: (1) have conducted a survey during the last ten years; (2) conduct a survey on a regular basis; and (3) plan on conducting a survey in the next five years. . . .

ATTITUDES TOWARD ATTITUDE SURVEYS

Human Resources executives were asked to express their agreement with 12 statements about attitude surveys. Responses were made on a 4-point agreement scale. [The table below] shows the statements and the percent of agreement with each. The findings show overwhelming agreement among executives that attitude surveys are not only a good employee relations tool, but can be useful toward solving productivity and communication problems. Although H.R. executives strongly extol the virtues of assessing employees' opinions, attitude surveys are not seen as a panacea. Approximately one-half point to alleged faults of the surveys—that they are difficult to interpret and tend to be overly focused on negative issues. . . .

*Life Office Management Association (LOMA) is an Atlanta based international center for management research and education among insurance companies.

Opinions about Employee Attitude Surveys

Opinion	Agree	Disagree
1. Employees appreciate the opportunity to express their opinions and attitudes in an employee attitude survey.	98%	2%
2. Assessing employee attitudes is a waste of time.	5	95
3. Management should consider employee opinions and attitudes when formulating or changing company policies and practices.	98	2
4. Assessing employee opinions and attitudes is a good step toward developing methods to increase productivity.	93	7
5. Employee attitude surveys create more problems than they solve.	13	87
6. Employee attitude surveys can help management identify causes of labor problems (e.g., turnover, absenteeism).	94	6
7. Employee attitude surveys are too expensive and time-consuming.	21	79
8. Employee attitude surveys are useful, even in companies that have good communication channels.	90	10
9. Attitude survey results are difficult to interpret.	51	49
10. Employee attitude surveys raise expectations on issues that management may not want or be able to address.	81	19
11. Conducting an attitude survey can be useful, even when a company has undergone a recent change.	88	12
12. Employee attitude surveys tend to focus more on the negative, rather than the positive, aspects of an organization.	59	41

Note: For reporting purposes, "strongly agree" and "agree" were combined, as were "strongly disagree" and "disagree."

Opinions about employee attitude surveys, particularly regarding their negative aspects, appear to be moderated by experience with attitude surveys. H.R. executives from companies which have not conducted a survey in the last 10 years are more likely to feel that attitude surveys: (1) create more problems than they solve; (2) are too expensive and time-consuming; and (3) tend to be overly focused on negative issues.

CONCLUSIONS
Assessment of employee attitudes is highly endorsed by H.R. executives (not a complete surprise considering the source). In spite of such high praise, only a small percent of insurance companies regularly conduct attitude surveys. Two possible explanations for this apparent inconsistency are that H.R. executives do not have the clout to push a survey through management or that they are doing an ineffective job convincing management of attitude survey benefits.

H.R. executives often encounter some initial skepticism and resistance when making employee attitude survey proposals to top management. Attitude surveys tend to carry several stigmas, the most prominent being difficulty in interpreting the results and an inordinate focus on negative issues. Also, upper management often thinks it already knows all it needs to know, or is afraid to find out what it doesn't. . . .

Source: Neiner, A. G. (1985). *The Industrial Organizational Psychologist, 22* (3), 44–47. Reprinted by permission.

Supervision. In general, considerate supervisory behavior seems to correlate positively with job satisfaction. A number of studies show, first, that changes in supervision lead to changes in satisfaction, and second, that a considerate style of behavior is positively related to satisfaction (Bass, 1981). Two precautionary comments should be made, however. First, most of the evidence for the above relationships, and for many that follow, is correlational and therefore does not imply causality. It is plausible that having satisfied workers causes a supervisor to be considerate rather than the reverse. Second, since the relationships are generally moderate (correlations of $r = .20$ to $r = .40$), there are numerous cases in which consideration does not lead to improved satisfaction. There just happen to be more cases in which it does (at least for the situations that have been empirically investigated).

Another important aspect of supervision is the degree to which subordinates may participate in decisions that affect their work. In general, participation is related to positive attitudes about the job (Locke & Schweiger, 1979). However, there are some limiting conditions. The decisions should be about topics with which the employees are familiar and have some expertise (for example, the work place). The participation should be real—that is, the information offered by the employees should actually be part of the decision process. And finally, too much participation may be related to negative attitudes. To some extent employees want and need direction, and they do not want to be inundated with all of the organization's problems.

The nature of the supervision that employees get is in part a function of the degree of formalization in the organization. Recall from Chapter 3 that a highly formalized organization is one in which there are many rules and regulations that govern the behavior of employees, and in which there is a heavy reliance on formal, written communications that follow a strict hierarchical chain of command. The more formalized an organization, the more closely it fits the classic ideal of a bureaucracy. And research evidence indicates that employees in organizations that have bureaucratic characteristics are often dissatisfied (e.g., Snizek & Bullard, 1983).

A good example of a highly formalized organization is AT&T. Telephone operators working for AT&T have to work under extremely close and controlling bureaucratic supervision. They are subjected to daily work-load and performance measures, the speed with which they handle calls is closely monitored, evaluators constantly plug into conversations to assess the quality of service, and there are very stringent lateness and absenteeism regulations. What is more, when they have to go to the bathroom, operators have to raise their hands, get put on a list, and wait maybe 15 to 20 minutes for their turn! No wonder telephone operators are often dissatisfied with their jobs (e.g., "The Dissatisfaction at AT&T," 1979).

Job Challenge. A number of factors that are positively related to job satisfaction can be placed under the heading of job challenge. Included here are such things as variety on the job, creativity, difficulty of goals, and the use of one's own skills. People seem to be more satisfied with their job when it demands something from them. Such challenge may have other benefits as well. People tend to be more committed to the job and are more involved with their work when they are challenged by what they do.

The opposite of challenge is boredom. Numerous studies show that boredom can lead to high levels of dissatisfaction, and may eventually result in absenteeism and turnover. Challenge, or the lack of it, can have both attitudinal and economic impacts.

Job Clarity. Another set of factors that seems to be important for job satisfaction involves the degree to which the job is clear rather than ambiguous. Up to a point, people like to have a clear, unambiguous work environment. Studies of factors like job clarity and specificity show positive relationships with job satisfaction.

Two related factors are role clarity and feedback. When one's job responsibilities are fairly clear (role clarity), job satisfaction seems to be higher than when these responsibilities are ambiguous. People also like to know how they are doing (feedback). Giving accurate and frequent feedback can increase job satisfaction. In general, what all of these variables suggest is that reducing uncertainty and ambiguity seems to increase job satisfaction.

Job Content. Both the standardization and specialization of work tasks have tremendously increased productivity throughout the world. But the relationship with satisfaction appears to be curvilinear. A moderae amount of these variables can lead to high satisfaction, but too much or too little can lead to low satisfaction. When the job is neither specialized nor standardized, an employee has difficulty knowing what or how to do the job. At the other extreme are situations in which the work is highly repetitive and boring. The relationship between specialization, standardization, and satisfaction is shown in Figure 5-12. Although the point of inflection in this curve may differ for different types of people or jobs, it is clear that the extreme ends of the continuum are related to low morale.

Two possible corrections for the problem of too much specialization are job-rotation and job-enlargement programs. In these programs employees are able either to expand the number of tasks they are doing or to rotate to different tasks. We discuss these strategies more fully in the next chapter. The impor-

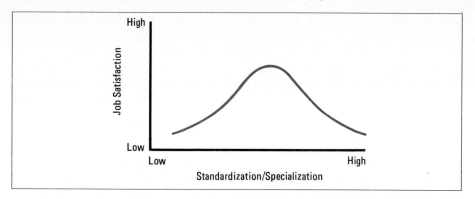

FIGURE 5-12
The highest levels
of satisfaction are
associated with in-
termediate levels
of standardization
and specialization.

tant point to make here is that one must first ascertain the current location of employees on the curve.

Traditional Incentives. Promotional opportunities and wages have tradi-tionally been used by organizations to foster job satisfaction. In the case of promotions, it does appear that employees are more satisfied with situations in which this opportunity is likely than those in which it is not. The relationship is weak, however, and this is probably due to the fact that promotions are a relatively infrequent experience. There are numerous other factors present every day (e.g., supervision, the job content) that are more highly related to job attitudes.

The research on the effect of wages on satisfaction and productivity is vast. In general, people are more satisfied with high wages than low wages. How-ever, the strength of the relationship is moderated by other variables. An important factor is one's reference group (Lawler, 1981). People seem to be satisfied when their wages are equal to or a little higher than those received by others who are doing a similar job. No matter what the actual dollar amount, when the pay compares favorably, the employee is satisfied. Satisfaction with wages, therefore, seems to be a joint function of the absolute amount and a comparison with others.

Social Cues. Finally, there is a small but growing body of research indicating that job satisfaction may also be significantly affected by the satisfaction of coworkers and others in the work environment who might act as role models. For example, in a laboratory study Weiss and Nowicki (1981) had college-student subjects watch a training film in order to learn how to perform an assembly task. In addition to learning about the task procedures, however, the subjects also learned about the task attitude of one of the two role models in the film. In one experimental condition one of the models was overheard expressing a positive attitude toward the task (e.g., "You know, I'm really enjoying this."), while in a second condition the same model was overheard expressing a negative attitude (e.g., "This is boring."). After viewing the training film the subjects performed the assembly task themselves and com-pleted an attitude questionnaire. It was found that subjects had a more favorable attitude toward the task when the model in the film expressed a positive task attitude than when the model expressed a negative attitude. Subsequent research has shown that similar effects can occur in real organizations when factory supervisors are the role models (Griffin, 1983).

These results are quite interesting, and they point to yet another mechanism by which job attitudes can be formed—social modeling. The implication for organizations is obvious. If an organization wants to help ensure that new employees develop favorable attitudes toward their work and toward the company in general, the employees should be put in work groups with others who already have the desired attitudes. Quite independent of any social reinforcement that may occur, the new employees will quickly learn the attitudes modeled by the rest of the group. If the group reinforces the expression of the favorable attitudes, those attitudes will be learned (via instrumental learning) even faster.

Consequences of Job Satisfaction

Although it is easy to justify the study of job satisfaction from the point of view of the individual employee, from the organization's point of view we must be able to demonstrate that job satisfaction is indeed related to one or more important organizational outcomes. Therefore, we now consider the relationship between job satisfaction and turnover, absenteeism, health, and productivity.

Turnover. One would expect the relationship between job satisfaction and turnover to be negative: the greater the satisfaction, the lower the turnover. In general, research results support this hypothesis. It appears, however, that the strength of this relationship is partly dependent on the degree to which alternative employment opportunities exist (Jackofsky & Peters, 1983). There are always going to be some people who leave because of dissatisfaction and some who leave because they have to (e.g., they move, there is a family crisis). In times of full employment when numerous job opportunities are available, we would expect the percentage of those who leave because of low satisfaction to be greater than when times are hard. Accordingly, the relationship between turnover and satisfaction should be stronger during full employment, and indeed this is what is reported in the literature.

Absences. The relationship between absenteeism and satisfaction is also predicted to be negative: the higher the satisfaction, the fewer the absences. Although generally supportive, the results are far from conclusive (correlations ranging from $r = -.14$ to $r = -.38$). Again, the issue is clearer if one considers a third variable. Many long-term periods of absence are experienced by old faithful members of the organization, and these people are probably not dissatisfied. One study in a metal-fabrication factory pointed out this problem (Kerr, Koppelmeier, & Sullivan, 1951). Job satisfaction was correlated $r = .51$ with total absenteeism for twenty-nine departments. This figure suggests that satisfied departments had *greater* absenteeism. However, when *unexcused* absences were correlated with satisfaction, the coefficient was $r = -.44$; that is, high satisfaction was related to low absenteeism. As we would expect, people who choose to stay at home and lose their pay are less satisfied than those who have good attendance.

Health. While the studies in this area are fewer in number and poorer in methodological rigor, the findings are consistent and significant. They overwhelmingly suggest that both physical and mental health are increased by working on a satisfying job. Reports of fatigue, headaches, and ill health are lower for satisfied employees, as are measures of cholesterol and heart disease (Matteson & Ivancevich, 1979). In fact, a number of studies suggest that life expectency is higher for satisfied workers! The same is true for studies of mental health: Less anxiety and tension are found in satisfied employees (Kornhauser, 1965). The data clearly suggest a causal relationship between job satisfaction and other psychological and physical factors related to one's health.

The negative health outcomes associated with job dissatisfaction have implications for both the individual and the organization. (We made a similar point in Chapter 4 in connection with the Type A and Type B behavior patterns.) The implications for the individual are self-evident. The implications for the organization are in terms of lost work time due to employee sickness, greater costs for medical insurance, and the costs associated with premature, medically induced employee turnover (e.g., early retirement). By one estimate, for example, organizations in the United State lose upward of $20 million a year in employee work time due solely to drug- and alcohol-related problems, both of which can be caused and/or exacerbated by job dissatisfaction (Reitz, 1981). Numbers of this magnitude are not inconsequential.

Productivity. For many years it was assumed that a happy ship was a productive ship. The way to obtain higher levels of efficiency and productivity was through morale. However, a number of thorough and rather devastating reviews have shown little support for this hypothesis. The average correlation between job satisfaction and productivity is about $r = .17$ (Iaffaldano & Muchinsky, 1985). Thus, satisfaction and productivity are not strongly related to one another. Some authors have even argued that what little relationship does exist could be attributed to the reverse relationship: Productivity causes satisfaction (e.g. Porter & Lawler, 1968).

If you think about the general model of attitudes presented in Figure 5-1, and the various factors that can influence job satisfaction as discussed in the previous section, the lack of a strong relationship between job satisfaction and performance is really not all that surprising. For the most part, people are satisfied with their jobs when they get out of them the things that they like. People are attracted to jobs for various reasons (e.g., the working conditions, the friendships, the supervision). They may find that all these things can be obtained without extra effort, which is indeed the case in many organizations. It is true that some rewards may be lost, such as a bonus or a promotion, but in many instances these incentives are not of utmost importance. Furthermore, other incentives that are important (e.g., salaries, vacation days) are often not related to effort or performance. It should not be surprising, therefore, that overall job satisfaction is only slightly related to productivity.

To summarize, a variety of things lead to high satisfaction. Some of these variables are related to the people with whom one works (e.g., one's supervisor and coworkers), and some are related to the payoffs that occur (e.g., pay, promotions). An increase in satisfaction can have positive benefits for both the individual and the organization, including better physical and mental health and lower absenteeism and turnover. While individual productivity may not be increased, these other factors are sufficiently important to make job satisfaction a major variable of interest from both an individual and an organizational point of view.

Organizational Commitment and Job Involvement

Before ending the chapter, we would like to discuss briefly two additional job attitudes that have begun to receive substantial attention in the research literature. These two attitudes are referred to as organizational commitment and job involvement.

Organizational Commitment. There is a good deal of confusion in the research literature regarding the meaning of the concept "organizational commitment." Terms such as loyalty, identification with the organization, and acceptance of organizational goals have all been used to define commitment (e.g., Morrow, 1983). While these terms are not necessarily wrong, they are needlessly vague and ambiguous. It seems much more useful and precise to define organizational commitment as one's attitude toward *continued participation* in the organization. Thus, whereas job satisfaction is an attitude toward the job itself (e.g., "I like this job."), organizational commitment is an attitude toward one's own future behavior vis-à-vis the organization (e.g., "I would like to continue working for this company."). Organizational commitment is therefore a future-oriented attitude. One implication of this future orientation is that organizational commitment should be more closely related to *actual* future participation than other job-related attitudes that are not future-oriented. Research evidence bears this out. For example, in comparison with job satisfaction, organizational commitment has been shown to be a better predictor of employee turnover (Mowday, Porter, & Steers, 1982).

Organizational commitment is related to various personal characteristics (such as a high need for achievement), to certain job characteristics (such as degree of responsibility), and to job experience. Those employees with high commitment tend to have a greater desire to remain in the organization and have better attendance than those with low commitment. They also have a greater desire to reach company goals and adhere to company policies (Steers, 1977).

Job Involvement. Like organizational commitment, there has also been confusion in the research literature about the meaning of the concept "job involvement." Indeed, some authors have used the terms *organizational commitment* and *job involvement* interchangeably (cf. Morrow, 1983). There is good reason to keep these concepts separate, however. As we stated previously *organizational commitment* refers to one's attitude toward continued participation in the organization. *Job involvement,* on the other hand, focuses more on the degree to which the employee is *personally invested* in his or her work and the extent to which work is a *central* part of his or her life (cf. Lodahl & Kejner, 1965). One implication of being highly involved in one's work is that one is likely to put much more time and energy into the job. Assuming that investments of time and energy lead to higher levels of performance, job involvement, unlike job satisfaction and organizational commitment, should be significantly related to employee performance (Jewel, 1985).

As was the case with commitment, various personal characteristics, such as age, belief in the Protestant ethic, and high need for growth, all result in high job involvement. Job factors such as autonomy, task variety, and participation in decision making also lead to job involvement. The consequences of involvement are lower turnover, less tardiness, and more hours worked (Rabinowitz & Hall, 1977).

Finally, it is important to note that while there may be some degree of correlation between job satisfaction, organizational commitment, and job involvement, this correlation is not necessarily very high. It is probably true that high levels of organizational commitment and job involvement require at least a moderately high level of job satisfaction. However, just because one is satisfied with a job does not necessarily mean that one will be either highly involved in it or favorably disposed toward working in the organization in the future. For example, you might be quite satisfied with your current summer job as a lifeguard because it allows you to be out in the sun and not work too hard. Yet, you may not view this job as a very central part of your life (low job involvement), and next summer you may plan to seek alternative employment that is more relevant to your future career (low organizational commitment). Thus, job satisfaction, organizational commitment, and job involvement should be viewed as three conceptually distinct, although related, job attitudes.

Summary

The material on attitudes presented at length in this chapter serves as an important underpinning for much of the material discussed in Chapter 17, "Change in Organizations." The major points about attitudes are listed below:

1. Attitudes are a predisposition to respond in a favorable or an unfavorable way. They are learned, evaluative feelings about the people, objects, concepts, and activities that exist in the world around us.
2. Attitudes are firmly embedded in our psychological makeup. They are related to personality and values, and they reflect a summary of our beliefs about a topic. If measured with enough specificity, and if other factors such as social norms are taken into account, attitudes can be powerful predictors of our behavior.
3. Most measures of attitudes use our beliefs about a topic as a reflection of our underlying attitude. For attitudes about the job, some of the most important beliefs concern factors related to supervision, the work environment, and traditional incentives such as pay and promotions.
4. Most people try to maintain a consistent and unified pattern of beliefs, values, attitudes, and behaviors. When elements of this structure are found

to be inconsistent, the individual is motivated to eliminate this inconsistency. Thus, by changing one attitude, other attitudes and behavior can be modified.

5. Dissonance theory points out that by changing one's behavior, one's attitudes can be changed. This principle has been used to explain why we often stick with bad decisions, and come to like tasks that we initially felt were unpleasant.

6. In order to be effective in changing attitudes about people, issues, or products, persuasion attempts should involve (1) a high-status, expert, or well-liked communicator, (2) a fair, unbiased message, and (3) a receptive and attentive audience that is (4) not pressured or bothered by outside factors.

7. Job satisfaction is the most important and frequently studied job attitude. The main causes of high job satisfaction are considerate supervision and coworkers, a challenging and unambiguous job, and adequate pay and traditional incentives.

8. The consequences of having satisfied employees are better physical and mental health, lower absenteeism, and lower turnover. However, high satisfaction does not necessarily result in high productivity.

9. Two other important job attitudes are organizational commitment and job involvement. As with job satisfaction, these also are related to organizational-level outcomes such as absenteeism and turnover.

IMPLICATIONS FOR RESEARCH

Although a great deal of research has already been done in the area of job attitudes, there are a number of significant issues that have yet to be resolved. One set of questions concerns the relationship between overall job satisfaction and the more specific attitudes that contribute to job satisfaction.

As we stated earlier, one of the most frequently used measures of job satisfaction is the Job Descriptive Index (JDI) (Smith, Kendell, & Hulin, 1969). This measure asks the respondent to report his or her attitude toward five different facets of the job (working conditions, pay, promotions, supervision, and coworkers). An overall job satisfaction score is computed by summing these more specific scores. This procedure raises two questions. First, do the five job facets that are assessed actually represent the total set of job components important for determining overall job satisfaction? It seems likely that, at least for some jobs, other important job characteristics also exist and should be taken into consideration. More research is needed to identify systematically all of the various job factors that may be related to overall job satisfaction.

Second, are the five job characteristics really equal in terms of their contribution to overall job satisfaction? By defining the overall job satisfaction score as a simple sum of the component attitude scores, the JDI implicitly assumes that the component attitudes are of equal importance. This assumption is not made by the Need Fulfillment Questionnaire (Porter & Lawler, 1968), which asks the respondent to indicate how important each job facet is, and then includes these importance ratings in the computation of the total job satisfaction score. It is possible to obtain very different job satisfaction scores using these two questionnaires if respondents give different weights to different job facets. Although asking respondents to rate the importance of each job facet intuitively seems more appropriate, there is no clear evidence one way or the other regarding which approach is best. Thus, research is needed to determine not only the factors that are necessary for measuring overall job satisfaction, but also the relative importance of these factors.

Another set of questions that needs to be answered concerns the relationships between job satisfaction, organizational commitment, and job involvement. We argued previously that these should be viewed as three conceptually distinct, although related, job attitudes. However, the specific nature of their interrelationship is not well understood. We suggested that job satisfaction is likely to be a prerequisite for both organizational commitment and job involvement, but this needs to be verified with empirical research. Further, it would be useful to know whether the factors that influence job satisfaction also affect organizational commitment and job involvement, and whether there are variables that affect commitment and involvement that do not affect satisfaction. An additional question is whether satisfaction, commitment, and involvement are all equally easy (or difficult) to change. They probably are not, although relatively little empirical evidence is presently available on this point.

Finally, it would be interesting to know whether or not there are stable individual differences in job satisfaction, commitment, and/or involvement (cf. Staw, 1984). It may be, for example, that no matter what the job is, some people are consistently more satisfied with their work than others. These people may have a tendency to focus on the positive features of their jobs, all but ignoring any negative aspects that may exist. Others may dwell on the problems and difficulties in a job, paying relatively little attention to the job's positive aspects. One implication of such individual differences, if they exist, is that job satisfaction may be more difficult to change than our current models suggest. Improving the conditions of work and the quality of supervision, for example, might do little to improve the overall job satisfaction of some employees, since there are always likely to be other negative aspects of the job to complain about (e.g., incompetent coworkers, lousy pay). This is an area in which we might reap substantial benefit from some good empirical research.

IMPLICATIONS FOR PRACTICE

It is essential that we recognize the pervasiveness of our attitudes and their importance. We have attitudes about many topics that are related to our behavior in organizations. We have attitudes about safety programs, minority groups, and unions, and, of course, there is our overall job satisfaction. These attitudes are firmly embedded in a complex psychological structure of beliefs, other attitudes, and values. Since these attitudes are related to our behavior (e.g., Do we wear a safety helmet? Do we discriminate against women? Do we participate in a work slowdown?), the crucial question becomes the method and means by which these attitudes can be influenced and changed.

Two major conclusions can be drawn from this chapter. First, since attitudes are based in part upon beliefs, it is possible for two people to hold exactly the same attitude, *but for very different reasons.* Two people may dislike a safety program with equal intensity, but one may feel that way because he or she believes the program is a bother and takes up time, while the other may believe that the program will not work. These individuals' belief structures are a product of their own learning experiences.

Therefore, to be effective in changing attitudes you should first have some idea of what people think. If you want to change attitudes by changing beliefs, you must identify the important beliefs before trying to change things. If, for example, there is a high level of absenteeism, you cannot automatically assume that low pay or lazy employees are the causes. It might be poor supervision or a boring job. You must find out the problem first, then try to change the appropriate beliefs and attitudes.

A second conclusion, generated by dissonance theory, is that in some situations the best way to change attitudes is to work directly on behavior. For many years people said that forced racial integration in the areas of housing, jobs, schools, and services would not work. They contended that people's attitudes had to be changed first. However, legislation was passed and enforced, and all indications are that attitudes have, in fact, come into line with behavior. It is never pleasant to pressure people into doing something they do not want to do, but if this pressure is (1) not too extreme, (2) maintains the individual's freedom of choice, and (3) is explained in a reasonable, rational manner, it can be an effective way to change both attitudes and behavior.

Finally, our review of the job-satisfaction literature points out a very important fact: Job satisfaction does not necessarily lead to high productivity. A happy ship is not necessarily a productive one. This should not be too surprising. Job satisfaction is caused by multiple factors, only some of which should logically increase effort and performance.

Although job satisfaction may not directly affect productivity, it does have indirect effects. People are healthier, are present on the job more often, and stay with the company longer if they are satisfied. These outcomes can have a substantial effect on other costs such as health benefits, selection and training costs, and retirement costs. Changing job satisfaction in a positive direction can thus benefit any organization.

And it *can* be changed. Obviously, when physical discomforts are at issue, they can be removed, or when ambiguity or misperceptions seem the problem, more accurate or detailed information can be provided. Participation and involvement in meaningful decisions can increase satisfaction. Realistic job previews can clarify expectations and facilitate adjustment to new jobs. Techniques that involve role playing in which employees attempt to see organizational life from the point of view of someone else (e.g., their supervisor, an upper-level manager), can also be helpful. Finally, many types of job redesign can change attitudes.

Finally, attitude surveys can help an organization in numerous ways. They allow people to say how they feel without threat of punishment (most surveys are anonymous). A manager can track data over time to see where problems are, when they occur, and how attitudes respond to the implementation of various programs. Attitude surveys are thus a tool that managers can use to understand better the behavior of the people in their organization.

Discussion Questions

1. How are attitudes different from other familiar concepts such as facts, beliefs, and values?
2. How are attitudes related to each other and to behavior? Do changes in attitude cause changes in behavior? Is the reverse true?
3. It has been reported to you (as personnel manager) that morale is low. It is your job to correct the situation. What would you do?

CASE: MORALE AND MALAISE

Gerry Buckland heard the alarm but he didn't move. He didn't even turn it off. The thought of facing another day on the line was just too much. "Maybe I'll call in sick," he thought. But then he dismissed that idea—he'd skipped 2 days last week. If he was absent any more, he might lose the job.

Just then Janet, his wife, walked in. "Come on, Gerry, it's a lovely day, get up and have some breakfast before you leave for work. I hate to see you miss breakfast."

Gerry exploded: "What the hell difference does breakfast make?" he asked. "Breakfast has nothing to do with it. I just don't want to go to work. I hate it down there. Every day it's the same thing. You get there, change your clothes, say hi to your buddies, and then the bell rings. For most of the day I stand at the same spot using the same drill doing the same thing—attaching doors to the cab of a truck—big deal. I feel like a robot."

"Oh come on, Gerry, let's not get into that again," replied Janet. "I know you don't like it sometimes, but think of the positive things. The pay is good and you've got some seniority after 13 years. Pretty soon you might get a shot at the supervisor's job. Besides, you've got plenty of friends there."

"The friends and the money don't count a thing," responded Gerry. "It's the work itself. It's so boring and repetitious—the same thing day after day. It's noisy, dirty, and you can't talk to anybody except at break time. I'm spending one-third of my life sleeping and one-third doing something I despise. That doesn't leave much, does it? I've had it. I'm going to look for another job."

"Well," Janet mused, "I'm certainly not going to tell you what to do. It's your life and your job. If you hate it so much, you probably ought to look around for something else. But don't forget that Christmas is next month and we'll need some money for the kids. Also, Danny has to have braces put on his teeth—why don't you wait until the new year?"

Janet left the room as Gerry sat up. "She is probably right," he thought. "We do need the money and now is a particularly bad time to be short. I guess I'll just have to put up with it a little while longer."

Questions about the Case

1. What do you think was the major cause of Gerry's dissatisfaction?
2. Could the job be improved in such a way that his attitude would change? What would you suggest?
3. Do you think Gerry will ever leave the job? What sorts of pressures besides the economic ones would keep him where he is?

References

Bass, B. M. (1981). *Stogdill's handbook of leadership: A survey of theory and research* (Rev. ed.). NY: Free Press.

Brehm, J. W. (1956). Post-decision changes in the desirability of alternatives. *Journal of Abnormal and Social Psychology, 52,* 384–389.

Byrne, D. (1974). *An introduction to personality* (2d ed.). Englewood Cliffs, NJ: Prentice-Hall.

Chialdini, R. B., Petty, R. E., & Cacioppo, J. T. (1981). Attitude and attitude change. In M. R. Rosenzweig & L. W. Porter (Eds.), *Annual Review of psychology* (Vol. 32, pp. 357–404). Palo Alto, CA: Annual Review.

Cooper, M. R., Morgan, B. S., Foley, P. M., & Kaplan, L. B. (1979, Jan.–Feb). Changing employees' values: Deepening discontent. *Harvard Business Review,* 117–125.

Dembroski, T. M., Lasater, T. M., & Ramirez, A. (1978). Communicator similarity, fear-arousing communication, and compliance with health care recommendations. *Journal of Applied Social Psychology, 8,* 254–269.

Festinger, L. (1957). *A theory of cognitive dissonance.* Evanston, IL: Row, Peterson.

Fishbein, M., & Ajzen, I. (1975). *Belief, attitude, intention, and behavior: An introduction to theory and research.* Reading, MA: Addison-Wesley.

Griffin, R. W. (1983). Objective and social sources of information in task redesign: A field experiment. *Administrative Science Quarterly, 28,* 184–200.

Heberlein, T. A., & Black, J. S. (1976). Attitude specificity and the prediction of behavior in a field setting. *Journal of Personality and Social Psychology, 33,* 474–479.

Heider, F. (1946). Attitudes and cognitive organization. *Journal of Psychology, 21,* 107–112.

Henry, J. D. (1984). Syndicated public opinion polls: Some thoughts for consideration. *Journal of Advertising Research, 24(5),* I-5–I-8.

Iaffaldano, M. T., & Muchinsky, P. M. (1985). Job satisfaction and job performance: A meta-analysis. *Psychological Bulletin, 97,* 251–273.

Jackofsky, E. F., & Peters, L. H. (1983). The hypothesized effect of ability in the turnover process. *Academy of Management Review, 8,* 46–49.

Jewel, L. N. (1985). *Contemporary industrial/organizational psychology.* St. Paul, MN: West.

Kerr, W. A., Koppelmeier, G., & Sullivan, J. J. (1951). Absenteeism, turnover, and morale in a metals fabrication factory. *Occupational Psychology, 25,* 50–55.

Kornhauser, A. W. (1965). *Mental health of the industrial worker: A Detroit study.* NY: Wiley.

Kunin, T. (1955). The construction of a new type of attitude measure. *Personnel Psychology, 8,* 65–78.

LaPiere, R. T. (1934). Attitudes versus action. *Social Forces, 13,* 230–237.

Lawler, E. E. III. (1981). *Pay and organization development.* Reading, MA: Addison-Wesley.

Locke, E. A. (1976). The nature and cause of job satisfaction. In M. D. Dunnette (Ed.), *Handbook of industrial and organizational psychology* (pp. 1297–1349). Chicago: Rand McNally.

Locke, E. A., & Schweiger, D. M. (1979). Participation in decision making: One more look. In B. M. Staw (Ed.), *Research in Organizational Behavior* (Vol. 1, pp. 265–339). Greenwich, CT: JAI Press.

Lodahl, T. M., & Kejner, M. (1965). The definition and measurement of job involvement. *Journal of Applied Psychology, 49,* 24–33.

Matteson, M. T., & Ivancevich, J. M. (1979). Organizational stressors and heart disease: A research model. *Academy of Management Review, 4,* 347–357.

McGuire, W. J. (1985). Attitudes and attitude change. In G. Lindzey & E. Aronson (Eds.), *Handbook of Social Psychology* (3d ed., Vol. 2, pp. 233–346). NY: Random House.

Mewborn, C. R., & Rogers, R. W. (1979). Effects of threatening and reassuring components of fear appeals on physiological and verbal measures of emotion and attitudes. *Journal of Experimental Social Psychology, 15,* 242–253.

Mills, J., & Harvey, J. (1972). Opinion changes as a function of when information about the communicator is received and whether he is attractive or expert. *Journal of Personality and Social Psychology, 21,* 52–55.

Morrow, P. C. (1983). Concept redundancy in organization research: The case of work commitment. *Academy of Management Review, 8,* 486–500.

Mowday, R. T., Porter, L. W., & Steers, R. M. (1982). *Employee–Organization Linkages.* NY: Academic.

Porter, L. W., & Lawler, E. E. III. (1968) *Managerial attitudes and performance.* Homewood, IL: Irwin.

Rabinowitz, S., & Hall, D. T. (1977). Organizational research on job involvement. *Psychological Bulletin, 84,* 265–288.

Reitz, H. J. (1981). *Behavior in Organizations* (Rev. ed.). Homewood, IL: Irwin.

Rokeach, M. (1968). *Beliefs, attitudes, and values.* San Francisco: Jossey-Bass.

Salancik, G. R. (1977). Commitment and the control of organizational behavior and belief. In B. M. Staw & G. R. Salancik (Eds.) *New directions in organizational behavior,* (pp. 1–54). Chicago: St. Clair.

Sandelands, L. E., & Larson, J. R., Jr. (1985). When measurement causes task attitudes: A note from the laboratory. *Journal of Applied Psychology, 70,* 116–121.

Smith, J. F., Scott, K. D., & Hulin, C. L. (1977). Trends in job related attitudes. *Academy of Management Journal, 20,* 454–460.

Smith, P. C., Kendall, L. M., & Hulin, C. L. (1969). *The measurement of satisfaction in work and retirement.* Chicago: Rand McNally.

Smith, R. E., & Swinyard, W. R. (1983). Attitude-behavior consistency: The impact of product trial versus advertising. *Journal of Marketing Research, 20,* 257–267.

Snizek, W. E., & Bullard, J. H. (1983). Perception of bureaucracy and changing job satisfaction. *Organizational Behavior and Human Performance, 32,* 275–287.

Staw, B. M. (1976). Knee deep in the big muddy: A study of escalating commitment to a chosen course of action. *Organizational Behavior and Human Performance, 16,* 27–44.

Staw, B. M. (1981). The escalation of commitment: A review and analysis. *Academy of Management Review, 6,* 577–587.

Staw, B. M. (1984). Organizational behavior: A review and reformulation of the field's outcome variables. In M. R. Rosenzweig & L. W. Porter (Eds.), *Annual Review of Psychology* (Vol. 35, pp. 627–666). Palo Alto, CA: Annual Reviews.

Steers, R. M. (1977). Antecedents and outcomes of organizational commitment. *Administrative Science Quarterly, 22,* 46–56.

The dissatisfaction at AT&T. (1979, June 25). *Business Week,* p. 91.

U.S. Department of Labor. (1974). *Job satisfaction: Is there a trend?* (Manpower Research Monograph No. 30). Washington D.C.

Weiss, H. M., & Nowicki, C. E. (1981). Social influence on task satisfaction: Model competence and observer field dependence. *Organizational Behavior and Human Performance, 27,* 345–366.

Work in America: Report of a special taskforce to the secretary of HEW. (1973). Cambridge, MA: M.I.T. Press.

Youngblood, S. A., DeNisi, A. S., Molleston, J. L., & Mobley, W. H. (1984). The impact of work environment, instrumentality beliefs, perceived labor union image, and subjective norms on union voting intentions. *Academy of Management Journal, 27,* 579–590.

Zellner, M. (1970). Self-esteem, reception, and influenceability. *Journal of Personality and Social Psychology, 15,* 87–93.

Chapter 6

Motivation

*The hope and not the fact of advancement
is the spur of industry.*
—ROBERT SOUTHEY

As we observe people at work, we are frequently struck by their different work habits. Some people are always on time, put in a good day's work, and stay late. Others are less punctual and tend to get through the day with a minimal amount of effort. It has been estimated that a firm's best employee may often be two to three times as productive as its worst. Part of this difference may stem from personal styles, and part from the attitudes the employees bring to the task. The tendency, however, is to attribute some of the differences between these two extremes to skill. That is, we say that the employee with poor performance just doesn't have the ability. But frequently there is something more than that. There often seems to be a willfulness about the difference. The employee with excellent performance seems to *want* to do well, while performance may seem irrelevant to the marginal employee. In this instance, we usually refer to motivation. We say that one individual is more motivated or driven than the other.

Thus, motivation is partly inferred from performance. In behavioral terms, motivation can be thought of as the effort one exerts. In psychological terms, it is often felt as wanting or intending to do well. In this chapter we present an overall motivational model, discuss the theories that have made important contributions to our understanding of motivation, and evaluate some applications of the principles suggested by these theories.

A MODEL OF MOTIVATION AND PERFORMANCE

Figure 6-1 presents the model that forms the foundation for the rest of this chapter. While some of the terms presented in the model are familiar, others are new and need to be defined. We will proceed with a step-by-step explanation of the model, giving formal definitions as well as examples of its components.

Our first task is to define what we mean by *motivation*. Many nonacademic persons describe motivation as the degree to which an individual *wants* and

FIGURE 6-1
A motivation-performance model. Note that motivation includes the arousal and intended choice parts of the model. Performance is defined as behavior aggregated over time, people, or settings, and judged against some standard or criterion of excellence.

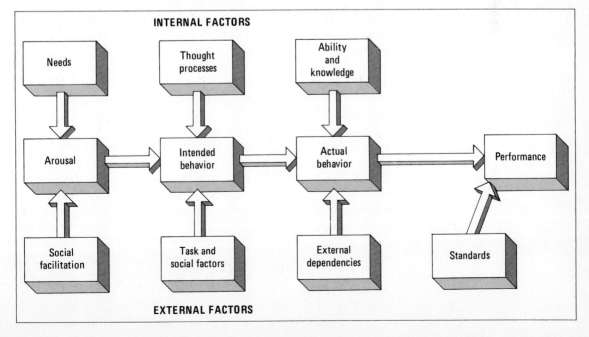

INTERNAL FACTORS

Needs → Arousal

Thought processes → Intended behavior

Ability and knowledge → Actual behavior

Performance

Social facilitation

Task and social factors

External dependencies

Standards

EXTERNAL FACTORS

tries hard to do well at a particular task or job. A more technical definition of motivation is that it is *the psychological process that causes the arousal, direction, and persistence of behavior.* Many social scientists add both a voluntary component and a goal-directed emphasis to this definition. Thus, *motivation* refers to those psychological processes that cause the arousal, direction, and persistence of voluntary actions that are goal directed.

While there is some disagreement among researchers about the importance of different aspects of this definition (e.g., whether arousal or direction is more important), there is consensus about several underlying properties of motivation. First, motivation is an *individual* phenomenon. Each individual is viewed as unique, and *all* of the major motivational theories allow in one way or another for this uniqueness to be demonstrated (e.g., different people have different needs, expectations, values, attitudes, reinforcement histories, goals, and so on).

Second, motivation is usually considered to be *intentional.* That is, motivation is to a large extent under the individual's control. Most behaviors thought to be influenced by motivation (such as effort on the job) are typically viewed as actions that the individual has voluntarily chosen to engage in.

Third, motivation is multifaceted. The two facets of greatest theoretical importance are the *arousal* (activation, energizing) and *direction* (intended choice) of behavior. The arousal question focuses on what gets people activated. What are the circumstances that arouse people so they want to do well? Intended choice deals with the pressures on the individual to engage in one specific behavior as opposed to another. These distinctions are reflected in much of the writing on motivation. *Persistence* is of somewhat less theoretical importance, partially because the maintenance of behavior (once it is started and directed) can be simply defined as the reaffirmation of the initial choice of action.

The fourth point is that motivational theories predict *behavior.* Motivation is concerned with action and with the internal and external forces that influence an individual's choice of action. Note that motivation is not the behavior itself, and it is not performance. The behavior is an observable action—that which is chosen. In some cases, the chosen action will be a good reflection of both the antecedent (motivation) and the consequence (performance). But the motivational processes, the actual behavior, and performance are all different things, and confusion of the three has frequently caused problems in analysis, interpretation, and application.

This last point is especially important for the structure of the rest of the chapter. While the definition and appraisal of performance are key parts of our overall model, they are distinctly different from motivation. In the present chapter, therefore, we only briefly discuss performance as it is relevant to our understanding of motivation. We provide a more detailed discussion of performance appraisal in Chapter 15, "Formal Systems for Managing Employee Performance."

Causes of Arousal

Now, let us consider the model shown in Figure 6-1 in a sequential and comprehensive fashion. Our starting point in the motivational process is *arousal*—those mechanisms that get us "up" or energized. Traditionally, need deficiencies have been seen as one of the major causes of arousal. That is, people have categories of things that they desire, want, or must have. When we feel that we are not getting as much of these things as we want or believe we should be getting, we become aroused. The consequences of this arousal is that we try to reduce the discrepancy between what we are getting and what we want.

From a management perspective, employee needs are simply those things that employees want. Thus, rewards and incentives will influence motivation to the extent that they are related to what employees need, and hence to the arousal function.

It is important to point out that arousal can be caused by mechanisms other than needs. We can classify needs as *internal* causes of arousal in the sense that we focus on processes going on inside the person. A focus on *external* factors influencing arousal, on the other hand, has led to research on the concept of social facilitation. *Social facilitation* refers to the fact that the presence of other people can sometimes cause arousal and thereby facilitate performance. Physiological research has shown that one's heart rate and galvanic skin response, two indicators of arousal, are both raised by the presence of others (compared to doing the same job alone). The reason we are aroused can be attributed to our desire to "look good," or our fear of "looking bad." In other words, having other people around can make us more self-conscious, thereby increasing our effort to do well.

Causes of Intentions

Social scientists studying the causes of intended behavior have also focused on both internal and external factors. Those who have been interested in internal factors have concentrated on the thought processes that determine intentions. Three major theoretical orientations have evolved.

First, some theories assume that people are fairly rational decision makers who try to maximize their rewards. They suggest that people evaluate alternative courses of action in terms of the probability that each alternative will lead to valued rewards. The second body of research focuses on the idea that goals and one's commitment to them are important determinants of intentions. People aspire to accomplish both short- and long-term objectives, and these objectives, or goals, determine the specific behaviors in which they engage. The third research area concentrates on social comparison processes, and is based on the idea of fairness or equity. These theories suggest that people analyze what they are putting into a job (e.g., time, effort) and what they are getting back (e.g., money, praise) and behave accordingly.

Note that these three different approaches emphasize quite different aspects of human nature. Maximizing satisfaction, goal aspiration, and maintenance of equity are very different ways of looking at the psychology of choosing actions.

One group of theories with an external focus examines the social factors affecting intended behavior. Most of the studies of social factors in one way or another are concerned with how other people communicate to us how we should behave. Coworkers, group norms, and role models all influence our behavior.

Another theoretical orientation concerned with external factors focuses on the properties of the job itself. These theories suggest that people want to work hard on jobs that are interesting, stimulating, rewarding, confidence building, and so on. Theories of job enlargement and job enrichment have evolved from this school of thought.

The final research tradition focusing on external factors is concerned with reward systems. The frequency of reinforcement and the magnitude or objective value of the reinforcement (e.g., the amount of money) are viewed as important factors in predicting behavior.

We have now arrived at the point in the motivation process at which people want to do well. They are highly motivated—they intend to try hard to do those things that they believe will lead to good performance. Is this enough? Is this all we need? The answer, of course, is *no*. The link between motivation (intended behavior) and actual behavior is influenced by both internal and external factors.

Causes of Behavior

The internal factors that combine with behavioral intentions to influence actual behavior are ability and job knowledge. Careful employee selection and training are mechanisms both for ensuring high levels of ability and for enhancing job knowledge.

The external factors that influence behavior are called *behavioral dependencies*. The kinds of behavioral dependencies that are most important fall into three classes: social, technological, and environmental. Social dependencies have to do with the other members of one's work group. The more we have to coordinate and communicate with others, the greater the impact those others will have on our behavior. Technological dependencies are impersonal—they may involve machinery, or they can be administrative (e.g., work flow, material deliveries). Environmental dependencies include the weather, noise, a clean work space, and room to do what needs to be done. For example, it is hard to concentrate in a noisy room.

In short, behavior is caused not only by motivation, but also by ability, knowledge, and external dependencies. The more our work depends upon others and upon technology, the less important the role of motivation will be. Also, the more it depends on skill, the less important motivation will be. Thus, behavior is determined by a complex set of factors that vary in their relative contribution across jobs and tasks.

Causes of Performance

Performance refers to the *results* of behavior as judged against some criterion or standard of excellence. Thus, when we speak of performance, we usually think in terms of a good-bad dimension.

The degree to which performance reflects behavior varies in a number of ways:

1. Performance may reflect the same behavior aggregated over time (e.g., a batting average).
2. Performance may reflect different behaviors aggregated to a "higher level" of conceptualization (e.g., attendance).
3. Performance may reflect outcomes that are not closely linked to specific actions (e.g., sales).
4. Performance may be defined in general terms that reflect global traits rather than specific behaviors (e.g., assertiveness, outgoingness).
5. Performance may be defined as the result of group rather than individual behavior (e.g., baseball games won, number of innovations produced by a research and development division).

Note that the assessment of performance often involves an *aggregation* of behavioral results. In work organizations, numerous examples come to mind: monthly attendance, traffic citations per day or week, packages delivered per day, and so on. Note also that aggregation can be either over the same behavior over time, or over different behaviors (getting up, driving to work) that are strung together to form a larger behavioral unit (e.g., attendance).

Performance can also have a greater or lesser focus on behavior. A performance outcome such as sales may be composed of a whole set of behaviors (e.g., making calls, reading literature about the product line) and may be partially dependent on the behavior of other people. For example, a sale is not made without a buyer. Other performance measures are more directly related to behavior, such as the number of customers served in a grocery check-out stand.

Another performance definition issue is the degree to which the criteria or standards are easily translated into behavioral terms. In some organizations, performance evaluations consist of personal checklists based on subjective evaluations. An employee might be rated on how assertive, committed, and organized she or he is. One problem with this type of performance evaluation is that these terms mean different things to different people—both raters and ratees.

Finally, performance may reflect a team product. Many supervisors are evaluated based on their unit's performance, and it is often difficult to tease out individual contributions.

Several summary points should be made about these definitional issues. First, the criterion used by an organization to define performance is often determined by the task itself. For example, jobs in which people are highly interdependent almost by definition require a group performance criterion. Second, criteria are often selected because they are easy to measure. It is easier to measure sales volume than it is to monitor calls made, preliminary spadework done, or product knowledge. The more removed the performance criterion is from well-specified, individually controlled behavior, the more difficult it is to know (1) whether motivation or something else is the major contributor to performance, and (2) how to motivate the person in such a way that his or her performance will increase.

We can now begin our review of research and practice in the field of motivatin. In the preceding section we differentiated three major concepts: arousal, intention to behave in a particular way, and actual behavior. Research has examined both internal and external contributors to each of these. For each concept, we review the theories that focus on the internal and external factors, and we provide a section that describes practical applications of these theories. At the end of the discussion of both theory and practice for each of the three concepts, we provide a brief review.

Theories of Arousal: Internal Focus

By far, the most frequently cited cause of arousal is need deprivation. There are theories dealing with individual needs and theories dealing with groups or systems of needs. We first review work on individual needs and then turn our attention to need systems.

Individual Needs: Competence. A number of writers have presented evidence for what is called a need for competence (White, 1959). Humans and other animals show a desire to master their environment, and this mastery is pleasurable independent of outside rewards. This motive is aroused whenever we are faced with new, challenging situations, and it dissipates after repeated mastery of the task. The implications for job design are that challenging jobs are motivating in and of themselves, and that if enough variability is present, the competence motive may be maintained.

Individual Needs: The Achievement Motive. Perhaps the most thoroughly researched individual motive is the need for achievement (nAch). David McClelland (1961; 1985) is most closely connected with this work, and he has developed a rather comprehensive theory of achievement motivation.

The behavioral characteristics of high and low achievers are as follows: In comparison to those with a low nAch, those with a high nAch tend to prefer moderate risk, immediate feedback, and a sense of accomplishment. Because of this interest in accomplishment, the high achiever frequently becomes deeply involved with a task and may be seen as "task oriented." High need-achievement managers are characterized by candor, openness, sensitivity, and receptivity. They tend to use a participative leadership style and find meaning in their work. Low need-achievement managers, on the other hand, see work as less central and are more secretive and insensitive than those with high need for achievement.

One question that can be asked is how does a person come to have a high need for achievement? McClelland suggests that child-rearing practices are very important: Children who are fairly independent but have parents who provide clear expectations and feedback (preferably physical rewards such as hugging) develop into high achievers. But McClelland also believes that adults are changeable and can acquire greater nAch, and some of his more applied work deals with the idea of changing and developing nAch (e.g., McClelland, 1978).

Individual Needs: Power. Research on the need for power has experienced something of a revival during the past 15 years (Kipnis, 1976). This revival is also evident in the nonacademic press. A number of recent popular books have been published that advocate the use of power to get ahead in organizations. This literature argues that one needs to be assertive and "go for it" to be successful. While these prescriptions are not scientifically based, they do have some descriptive information suggesting that people who desire power frequently get it and are successful because of it.

There has been extensive research on the sorts of power used most frequently in organizations, and on the effects of power use (see Chapter 13, "Power and Politics"). The view that power is a *need* has been most prominently presented by McClelland and Burnham (1976). Power-oriented managers are characterized by a preference for influencing others over being liked by them, but this need is tempered by social norms of restraint and goal commitment; that is, people with high need for power are successful only if that need is accompanied by a commitment to organizational goals.

In summary, a number of individual motives combine to affect people's behavior. In general, these motives can be viewed as personality traits; that is, they all have the earmarks of personality traits as discussed in Chapter 4. They tend to be consistent over moderately long periods of time and over settings, they are often hard to change, and they may be learned at an early age. The problem has been to show how these motives are interrelated. Is there a systematic relationship among these motives, or do they all vary independently? It is this question to which we turn next.

Motive Systems: Maslow's Hierarchy of Needs. The first major attempt to classify needs relevant to organizational behavior was that of Abraham Maslow (1954). His formulation suggests that we have a *prepotency* of needs; that is, some needs are assumed to be more important (potent) than others, and those that are the most important must be satisfied before the other needs can serve as motivators. He postulated that there are five needs categories. These are presented in Figure 6-2.

There are a number of specific elements of this theory that need elaboration. First, Maslow argues that this category system holds for most normal, healthy people. However, it is not necessarily applicable to everyone. Second, while the idea of prepotency is important, it is not entirely rigid. More specifically, while Maslow argued that belonging needs must generally be fulfilled before esteem needs begin to operate as motivators, he did *not* argue that the belonging needs have to be *100 percent* fulfilled. The general idea is that the greater the fulfillment of a particular need, the less it serves as a motivator, and the more the next higher level need becomes activated as a motivator.

A final point is that in our society the physiological and safety needs play a relatively minor role for most people. Only the severely deprived and handicapped are dominated by these lower order needs. The implication for organi-

FIGURE 6-2
Maslow's hier-
archy of needs.

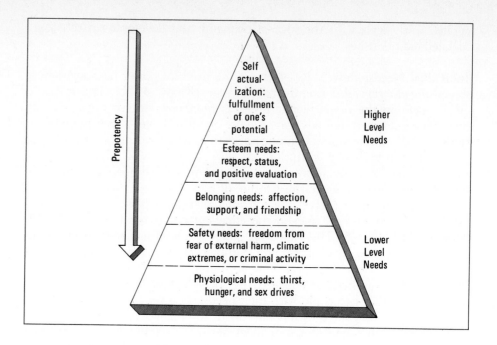

zation theorists is that higher order needs should be better motivators than lower order ones. This fact seems to be supported by surveys that ask employees about what motivates them on the job.

Unfortunately, the empirical research that specifically tests Maslow's theory has shown only limited support for some aspects of his formulation (Wahba & Bridwell, 1973). In particular, the hierarchical ordering proposed by Maslow is perhaps more specific and less flexible than what really exists. Employees do seem to have rather broad categories of higher and lower order needs. Managers, for example, seem to prefer self-actualization and esteem motivators to belonging and safety rewards. But there is very little evidence to support the specific five-category system.

The prepotency idea has also been criticized. It is not clear that the fulfillment of one need automatically means that the next higher order need is activated as a motivator. Also, it has been shown that deficient needs are not necessarily the most important ones. Thus, some of the specific dynamics of the theory have received minimal support.

But the impact of this theory should not be dismissed. Maslow's theory was the first clear statement that management should recognize the importance of higher order needs. His work began to shift the attention of organization theorists from the more traditional lower order motivators (pay, promotion, hours of work) to higher order motivators (autonomy, responsibility, challenge). This was an important contribution to management thought.

A second contribution of Maslow's theory is its emphasis on individual differences. People will be at different levels of the hierarchy at different times. Managers must be aware of individual differences in reward preferences. What will motivate one subordinate will not work with another. Different people want different things, and managers must be sensitive to these needs if they want their employees to be highly motivated.

Practical Applications of Need Theory

As we mentioned in our review of individual needs, achievement motivation theory is probably the most thoroughly developed. Not surprisingly, it has also received the most attention in practical applications.

McClelland (1978) has developed a comprehensive training program designed to increase achievement motivation. In a series of studies he has used this training program to demonstrate that (1) nAch contributes to success, and (2) it can be learned. The training program consists of people learning about the theory and engaging in exercises to help them develop and practice achievement behavior. With a number of groups of entrepreneurs, McClelland has demonstrated that taking his training program can result in greater performance and better firm survival rates, as well as more active participation by the entrepreneurs in new economic ventures.

Beyond their implications for training, the various need theories point out that different employees have different needs. One implication is that organizations should provide more *flexibility* in work schedules, reward systems, and other personnel functions. A review of current practice suggests that this flexibility is on the increase.

In order to create more flexible work schedules, some organizations have introduced *flexitime*. Flexitime is a schedule which demands that all employees be in the office during a set of "core" hours (e.g., from 10 A.M. to 2 P.M.), but allows them flexibility in determining when the rest of their time should be put in. One recent study of ten Western European countries showed that 60 percent of the organizations surveyed had adopted the use of flexible working hours (Zippo, 1982a). The research on flexible hours suggests that employees are generally more satisfied with their job as a result of the flexibility. And since higher satisfaction leads to less absenteeism and turnover, there is a definite impact on the organization's costs. Furthermore, under some limited circumstances, flexible working hours may result in greater productivity (Ralston, Anthony,& Gustafson, 1985).

There are other flexibility ideas that, while less popular, are also being tried. Home-based work, part-time employment, and job sharing are all being tried here and in Europe. Such programs have reduced layoffs (in one case only 75 out of the 200 jobs that were planned to be cut were actually lost) and increased flexibility for those who want it (Zippo, 1982b).

Beside flexibility in work arrangements, need theory suggests that organizations should also provide new and more varied benefits that better match people's varied needs. We are also seeing more of this type of flexibility in today's organizations. A survey by the Bureau of Labor Statistics found that almost 100 percent of the organizations in this country offer paid vacations, 99 percent offer paid holidays, 97 percent have health insurance, 96 percent have life insurance, and 87 percent have pension benefits. Beyond these basics, there are a host of new and more exotic benefits. For example, many companies are becoming sensitive to the needs of working women. At Southern

New England Telephone, for example, mothers with young infants have flexitime, part-time work, and home work options available. Also, the National Employer-Supported Child Care Project reports that 240 employers sponsor child-care facilities, a 100 percent increase since 1978. A texas insurance company provides a baby-sitting allowance, and Polaroid pays up to 85 percent of its employees' day-care costs (Foegen, 1982a, 1982b).

The point, we think, is clear. Companies are beginning to be more flexible in how benefits are administered, as well as in providing more benefits. Benefits already average about 37 percent of payrolls, and that figure will probably increase. The average amounts to $2.96 per payroll hour or $6084 per year, per employee (Foegen, 1982b). Recognition of this need for flexibility and variability should be helpful for increasing the match between individual employees' needs and organizational rewards. Having a good match should increase people's desire to do a good job.

Theories of Arousal: External Focus

As we shall see throughout this chapter, the focus on external factors is generally less well developed than the focus on internal factors; that is, both theory and practice are more recent and less extensive. The major external factor contributing to arousal is the presence of other people, and the process involved is called *social facilitation.*

Social facilitation is really the result of two closely related processes. First, there is evidence that the mere *presence* of other people raises arousal. People's physiological reactions demonstrate such arousal. In terms of their behavior, those who are aroused in this manner typically employ well-practiced (dominant) responses; that is, they tend to do what they know best.

Second, people are often concerned that others who are present and can observe their performance may be evaluating them. It is presumed that all of us want to look good in the eyes of others, and that "evaluation apprehension" causes arousal. This desire to look good, or fear of looking bad, should therefore increase one's desire to do well. Thus, social facilitation theory suggests that employees (1) are aroused by the presence of others, (2) wish to be evaluated favorably by them, and (3) are therefore motivated to perform well or to do whatever they can to project a favorable image (Ferris, Beehr, & Gilmore, 1978).

Practical Applications of Social Facilitation

The first element of the social facilitation process, the influence of the mere presence of others, has been demonstrated in a number of research projects. In practical situations, however, the utilization of this phenomenon has been sporadic. One application is seen in the attempts of sports teams to "fill the house." Interviews with athletes after big games invariably reveal that the big crowd got them "pumped up."

The evaluation apprehension part of the process has been more widely recognized and implemented. The notions of close supervision and personal responsibility both go hand in hand with this idea. For example, one study with hourly workers (White, Mitchell, & Bell, 1977) showed that those who put their name on their work performed significantly better, felt more anxiety about being evaluated, and felt more performance pressured than did those who did not put their name on their work (even though their pay was the same). Many companies now make employees personally responsible for adjusting, maintaining, and repairing their own equipment.

Of course, the question we are left with is, if individual needs are potentially satisfiable (through flexible and varied rewards), and people are "up" (through the presence of others and evaluation apprehension), why don't they work hard, or why isn't their performance better? To answer this question we must first recall that arousal is only part of the motivation process. We also have to want to behave (i.e., intend to behave) in an appropriate way, that is, in a way that will lead to greater performance.

THEORY AND PRACTICE: INTENTIONS

During the past 25 years the largest amount of motivation research has taken place in the area of intended choice theories. As we did for arousal theories, we will cover theories that include both internal and external factors as causes of the intended choice of behavior.

Theories of Intended Choice: Internal Focus

The major theories with an internal focus are expectancy theory, goal-setting theory, and equity theory. All three focus to some extent on perceptions of outcomes that are a result of one's behavior. In terms of quantity of research, expectancy theory and goal-setting theory have been studied most frequently, and they will be reviewed first.

Expectancy Theory. One approach to understanding intended choice suggests simply that people try to maximize their payoffs (Vroom, 1964). More specifically, expectancy theory states that people look at their various choice alternatives (e.g., coming to work versus not coming to work) and choose the one alternative that they believe is most likely to lead to the rewards they want most. If they believe that staying home is likely to lead to more good things than going to work, they are likely to stay home.

There are a number of important elements in this type of analysis. First, it is the *subjective anticipation* (expectation) of what will occur that influences choice. It is our estimate of the future that is important. A second point is that the theory includes two major factors: (1) the expectation that some set of outcomes will occur, and (2) the value (anticipated satisfaction) of each of those outcomes. These two factors are called *expectancies* and *valences*, respectively. Third, the theory is designed to predict the *force* on the individual to choose a particular behavior; that is, the theory predicts intention rather than action. However, writers using this approach often assume that intention is directly translated into action, and therefore the theory is frequently used to predict actual behavior.

Researchers usually assess expectancies and valences through a questionnaire or interview. For each outcome, the expectancy score is multiplied by the valence score, and these products are summed across all outcomes for a particular behavioral alternative in order to yield that alternative's *expected value* (EV). This EV roughly represents the expected payoff or return for that behavioral alternative. For example, one could measure an employee's subjective expectation of how likely it is that each of several outcomes (e.g., getting a pay raise, getting tired, having one's spouse get angry) will result from regularly working late at the office versus leaving every day promptly at 5 P.M. If these estimates are multiplied by the valence of each outcome (note: valences can be either positive or negative), an EV can be computed for each behavior (i.e., an EV for staying late and an EV for leaving at 5 P.M.). The theory predicts that the employee will choose the behavior with the highest EV.

The research on this model is extensive (Connolly, 1976). Over seventy studies have been done, and a number of comprehensive reviews of this literature are available. In general, expectancy models do an excellent job of predicting occupational choice and job satisfaction, and a fair job of predicting job effort. One review of the occupational choice literature reported on sixteen different studies using expectancy or expected-value-like models (Mitchell, 1983). Every single study provided strong, significant support for the theory. In some cases, the model was able to predict actual job choice with 80 to 90 percent accuracy.

In summary, expectancy theory has generated considerable research, and most of the results have been supportive. In general, people intend to work hard when they think that working hard is likely to lead to desirable outcomes (or avoid undesirable ones—see Figure 6-3).

One final point should be made, however. Expectancy theory is a *normative* model—it predicts how people *should* think—as opposed to a *descriptive* model, which describes how people *actually do* think. Thus, according to the expected value approach, people should (1) know all the alternatives, (2) know all the possible outcomes of each alternative, (3) know all the action-outcome relationships, and (4) know how they feel about these outcomes. Further, they should use a rather complex formula to come up with an estimate of the best choice of action. It is obvious that people do not have all the information just described, nor do they use a complex formula in determining their actions. Thus, the expected value model should be seen as a general approximation of people's behavior. It points out several factors of importance

FIGURE 6-3
What sort of expectations are being created here?

(i.e., expectancies and valences), and it suggests ways in which these variables alone and in combination influence behavior. In that perspective it has made a valuable contribution to the field.

Goal-Setting Theory. Another major contribution to our understanding of motivation is that of Edwin Locke (1978). He argues that employees have certain goals they set for themselves, and that an organization can have a strong influence on the work behavior of its employees by influencing their goals. More specifically, goal-setting theory states that hard goals yield better performance than easy ones, as long as they are accepted by the employee (Erez & Ziden, 1984). One might also expect that employee participation in the goal-setting process would increase its effectiveness, since participation should increase acceptance, that is, increase the degree to which the employee adopts the goal as a personal target to strive for. Finally, the more specific and well defined the goal, the greater its impact on motivation. According to the theory, nonspecific goals such as "do your best" are ineffective.

There are now available a number of reviews of the empirical work on goal-setting theory, and the findings are very clear on some issues (Locke, Shaw, Saari, & Latham, 1981; Locke & Latham, 1984). First, almost every study that has tested the question has shown that situations with goals lead to higher performance than situations without goals. Second, most of the research has clearly supported the idea that specific, difficult goals lead to better performance than easy or nonspecific goals.

However, there are still some areas of goal-setting theory that are surrounded by controversy. For example, the effects of participation in the goal-setting process are not clear. A number of studies have shown that participative goal setting leads to higher satisfaction than situations in which goals are simply assigned by someone else (e.g., one's boss). However, the effects of participation on performance are more ambiguous. Several authors suggest that participation may increase the difficulty of the set goals (e.g., Latham, Mitchell, & Dossett, 1978). If so, performance might also be higher due to a goal difficulty effect. In studies in which the difficulty level of the goal is held constant, either there are no differences in performance between the assigned goal and participative goal groups, or performance is actually better in the assigned group. These findings suggest that assigned goal setting can serve an important motivational function, especially if the assigned goals are difficult but attainable.

Another set of studies has questioned the goal-setting theory proposition that other factors such as rewards, knowledge of results, and social pressures influence motivation only insofar as they influence goals. A number of studies have shown that rewards (e.g., bonuses) do have an independent motivating effect on behavior, as does social pressure. Also, goals combined with feedback are generally more effective than goals alone. Taken together, however, these studies suggest that goal setting combined with incentive systems, accurate performance appraisals, and feedback may be one of the best ways to increase and maintain high levels of motivation to perform well (Locke & Latham, 1983).

In summary, the research evidence demonstrates rather convincingly that goals are a major source of work motivation. Goal setting is currently one of the most frequently tested theories in the field of organizational behavior, and despite the caveats we have noted, it has received considerable support.

Equity Theory. There is also a large body of literature that suggests a more economic-like analysis as an underlying dynamic of intended behavior. This literature indicates that individuals have an internal balance sheet they use in order to figure out what to do. The theory predicts that the individual will choose a behavioral alternative for which a *fair exchange* exists. The three major components of this theory are listed below:

Outcomes: Any stimulus or event that contributes to need gratification.

Inputs: Any cost incurred while trying to attain an outcome (e.g., effort, fatigue, anxiety).

Comparison level: Any standard used to assess the "fairness" of a particular exchange. In organizational settings, the comparison level is often what exists for one's coworkers.

Equity theory suggests that we look at our inputs (e.g., how hard we are working) and the outcome we receive (e.g., pay), and we compare these to the inputs and outcomes of other people doing a similar job. If a state of equity exists—that is, if there is little difference when this comparison is made—the individual will be comfortable with the situation and no change is predicted to occur. However, if one's *inputs* are seen as too great relative to one's outcomes when compared to others, a state of *underreward inequity* is experienced. People find this state dissatisfying and are motivated to change it by restoring equity. To do this they can (1) reduce their inputs, (2) try to increase their outcomes, or (3) change their comparison level. If, on the other hand, *outcomes* are too great when compared to inputs, a state of *overreward inequity* exists. In this situation, people can restore equity by (1) increasing their inputs (e.g., working harder), (2) decreasing their outcomes (e.g., accepting less pay), or (3) changing their comparison level.

Note that the idea of comparing the overall favorability of behavior is similar to expectancy theory. However, the notion of subjective probability is not included in the equity theory analysis, while the idea of cost or input invested is made more explicit here than in the expectancy approach.

The research on equity theory has been reviewed a number of times; both underreward and overreward inequity have been found to produce some interesting results (Goodman, 1977; Carrell & Dittrich, 1978). When people experience underreward inequity under salaried conditions, they generally decrease their effort, thereby reducing both the quality and quantity of their work. When they experience overreward inequity under salaried conditions (i.e., get paid more than others for doing the same job), the quality and quantity of their work goes up. Under a straight incentive plan (e.g., piece rate), however, the results are somewhat different. People experiencing underreward inequity are likely to decrease the quality of their output in order to increase quantity, while those perceiving overreward inequity generally attempt to increase the quality (which requires more effort) without increasing quantity. Notice that in the latter case, to increase the quantity of output under a piece-rate system would simply increase one's pay, thereby exacerbating the inequity. Thus, changes in both quality and quantity of output can be predicted from the equity theory approach.

We should point out that relative to expectancy theory and goal-setting theory, very little research on equity theory has appeared during the last few years. A number of comprehensive literature reviews point out some of the problems very clearly (Goodman, 1977; Vecchio, 1982). First, very little is known about how people select a "comparison other." Second, it is very hard to define inputs and outcomes objectively. Third, there is little known about how inputs and outcomes are combined. And finally, it is hard to know how these factors change over time.

In summary, the emphasis of equity theory is different from that of goal-setting or expectancy theory. Equity theory suggests that people choose a level of effort on the job that they think is fair or equitable. There is not the same emphasis on maximizing rewards as there is in expectancy theory. The expectancy theory model predicts that an individual will choose that work level that is perceived to bring the highest payoff, while equity theory predicts the choice of that level of effort perceived to produce the fairest level of reward.

Practical Applications of Intended Choice Theories: Internal Focus

Each of the three theories described has obvious implications for practice. For each theory we will summarize these implications and attempt to give one or two practical examples of how these principles are applied in today's organizations.

Expectancy Theory. There are three main implications for management practice that are readily inferred from expectancy ideas. First, it is the anticipation of reward that is important. People make choices based upon what they think they will get in the future, not on what they have gotten in the past. Second, rewards need to be closely and clearly tied to those behaviors that are seen as desirable by the organization. If attendance, punctuality, and working hard are important, they should be rewarded explicitly, publicly, and frequently. Finally, since different people value different rewards, there should be some attempt to match organizational outcomes (rewards) with the particular desires of the individual employee.

Some of these implications are similar to those arising from need theories. The valence component of expectancy theory reflects the idea that the attractiveness of various job outcomes is important, and that this attractiveness may vary with people and types of outcomes. Our earlier review of current organizational practices that emphasize flexibility and new types of compensation highlighted the application of these ideas.

The probability, or expectancy, part of the theory also has important implications. In order to increase the expectancy that organizationally desired behaviors (e.g., working hard) will indeed be followed by valued outcomes, organizations must (1) clearly describe what is wanted, (2) give positive and negative feedback that clarifies what is appropriate and what is not, and (3) have reward systems tied to these behaviors (e.g., merit pay). The notion of feedback is crucial for clarifying expectancies. But in order to give appropriate feedback, managers must be clear on what it is they expect their employees to do. This requires a thorough job description and an objective appraisal system (see Chapter 15, "Formal Systems for Managing Employee Performance").

Beside specific performance feedback, people also like information about why things are going on around them, and about topics that may relate to organizational policies or managerial decision making. Such information can also clarify expectancies. Some companies have implemented special systems designed to provide this type of information. For example, Sandia National Laboratories has a company-wide program called "Feedback," which is designed to increase employee knowledge and understanding of company policies and activities. Employees are encouraged to submit questions (they can sign the form or remain anonymous) concerning issues of benefits, personal treatment, managerial policy, or any other topic of interest, and the company gets a response back to the employee in 10 days. Sandia reports that the system has been used frequently and that the main issues inquired about are (1) administration (e.g., practices and policies), (2) personnel (e.g., compensation, equal opportunity), and (3) the work environment (e.g., safety, plant engineering). The company reports that numerous queries have led to changes in practice, and that the employees like and appreciate the system (Zippo, 1982c).

Goal Setting. The principles generated from goal-setting theory are, at first glance, fairly straightforward: Set specific, difficult goals, and get acceptance and commitment to them. These ideas rest at the foundation of a large number of strategies for performance appraisal and management by objectives (MBO) that are widely in use.

FIGURE 6-4
Goal setting increased the loading performance of truck drivers. (*Based on data presented by Latham & Baldes, 1975.*)

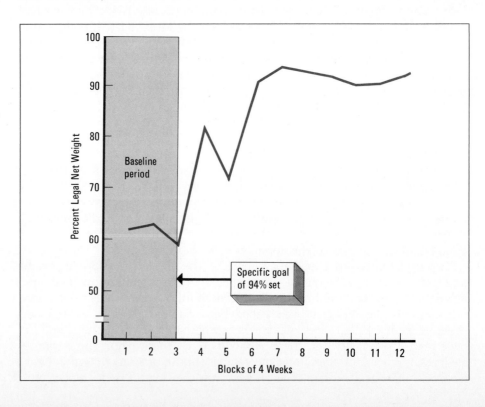

FIGURE 6-5
Truck drivers'
performance was
helped by the
setting of specific
goals.

One researcher (Gary Latham) has utilized the goal-setting principles in a whole series of applications with Weyerhaeuser Company. Secretaries, re-search scientists, tree planters, beaver trappers, and truck drivers have all been included. For example, in one application a goal-setting program was intro-duced for the drivers of thirty-six logging trucks (Latham & Baldes, 1975). For 3 months before the goal-setting program started, the average net weight of the loaded trucks had been at about 60 percent of their maximum legal net weight. It was decided to set a specific, difficult goal of 94 percent of the maximum legal net weight. Within 3 months the average net weight rose to over 90 percent and stayed there for the next 6 months (at which point, the researchers terminated their data collection effort). These results are shown in Figure 6-4.

This increase in performance saved the company hundreds of thousands of dollars. It is especially impressive because the employees were paid hourly, they were company employees as opposed to independent entrepreneurs, and they were members of a union. In other words, there was no additional financial incentive for productivity improvement, and they felt fairly secure as company employees and union members.

One final point should be emphasized. Setting goals is often a difficult practice for managers to learn. There are now a number of training programs available that help managers implement the goal-setting process. For example, one of these programs has been developed by Locke and Latham. In it, managers are given an introduction to the idea of goal setting, and specific examples are provided. Films are used that show goal-setting sessions. The major points emphasized by the films are (1) the participative give-and-take nature of goal setting; (2) the level of specificity and difficulty of the goals; (3) the ways in which interruptions in schedules, interdependencies, or changes in plans are to be handled; and (4) the process of giving feedback on goal attainment or the lack of it. After viewing the films, the managers engage in a role-playing exercise. It has been demonstrated that using such training can significantly increase the effectiveness of managerial goal setting, and has had subsequent positive effects on performance (Locke & Latham, 1983).

Equity Theory. For equity theory, two major implications are important. First, organizations must strive to reward people equitably. When people feel they are not being treated fairly, they may be dissatisfied, reduce their effort, and/or leave the job. An equally important implication is that employees see rewards in a *relative* rather than an absolute fashion. It is not how much one is getting that is important, it is how much one is getting *compared to other people who have the same type of job.* It is the social or interpersonal comparison that is important, not the absolute amount of compensation.

These implications are directly relevant to some of the notions we have already discussed: objective appraisal, frequent feedback, tying desirable rewards to desired behavior, treating each person as an individual, and so on. Not surprisingly, interventions designed to reduce inequity can reduce turnover and absenteeism, and increase job satisfaction (Telly, French, & Scott, 1971).

One final implication of equity theory that has been given some attention is the idea of making pay scales (or actual salaries) public. The rationale behind this idea is that people are often inaccurate in their estimates of how much their coworkers make, and these inaccuracies can be a major source of feelings of inequity. A number of companies have tried this strategy, with mixed success. It seems that public disclosure of salaries works well only when an objective and fair appraisal and reward system is in place. When pay is based on subjective judgments, who you know, and personality traits, disclosing pay scales simply increases the problem.

Summary of Intended Choice Models: Internal Focus

Let us review the three choice models with an internal focus before moving on to the next section. There are several important differences and similarities among these three approaches that should be noted. The most striking difference is in the underlying motivational mechanism postulated to cause an individual to behave in a certain way. There is (1) the intention to reach a goal (goal-setting theory), (2) the expectations of maximum payoff (expectancy theory), and (3) the desire for fairness (equity theory). The major similarity is that all three approaches define motivation as an individual, intentional process. Also, all three focus on relatively current information processing. In this respect, the arousal and choice models seem to be headed in a similar direction. Finally, two of the models view motivation as directly influenced by outcomes (expectancy and equity theory), while goal-setting theory sees outcomes as indirectly influencing motivation through goal difficulty level.

These theories tell us a lot about motivation, and most people agree that they all have an element of truth in them. Empirical research combining various parts of these strategies (e.g., goal setting and reward flexibility) has generally shown that goal-setting ideas can be combined with expectancy and equity ideas. However, in order to use what we have learned from these approaches, one must be able to set specific goals, tie rewards to individual behavior, and treat people fairly and equitably. The ability to do this depends on the presence of a number of social, task, and situational conditions. Unfortunately, these conditions are often absent.

For example, one major problem is that many jobs involve considerable interdependence. People must frequently work with others in order for the job to be accomplished successfully. This interdependence often makes it difficult to specify or identify individual contributions. To the extent that we cannot accurately assess individual behavioral contributions, there will be trouble with individual goal setting and reward administration. Group goals and group rewards will have to be used.

A second important factor is observability. Individual feedback and reward administration both depend on knowing exactly what employees are doing. In many cases, people work alone or in relatively isolated situations (e.g., within enclosed offices, on the road). To the extent that there is poor information about what people actually do, there will be difficulty with implementation.

A third problem has to do with change. In certain situations, jobs and people change fairly rapidly. The changes in jobs may be due to changes in technology, and the changes in people may be due to turnover. Note again that motivation emphasizes an individualized behavioral approach. Changes in jobs and people mean that there will be different behaviors to observe and different rewards to administer. However, continued high performance will be ensured only if the changes in people and jobs are well matched. (Recall that a similar point was made in Chapter 3 when we discussed the congruence model, pp. 65–67.)

Finally, heterogeneity in jobs and people causes difficulty as well. Each different job requires a different set of behaviors, and therefore should ideally have a different reward system. But this ideal is seldom realized. Implementing motivational principles usually involves compromise. In many cases, for appraisal or administrative purposes, people or jobs are lumped together (e.g., over time, jobs, or settings). When this aggregation occurs, it becomes more and more difficult to set individual goals and/or provide individual rewards and feedback. In short, when managers deviate from an individual, behavioral conceptualization of motivation, they will probably reduce the effectiveness of the organization's motivational program, as well as their ability to measure its impact.

What we are saying, then, is that for many jobs the traditional intended choice models of motivation may be inappropriate or hard to apply. Some jobs require working in teams. Performance on some tasks may be hard to specify and measure. Close supervision may not be possible on all jobs. Ambiguity and change may be inherent in some tasks. The question thus becomes one of determining what factors control motivation in these circumstances. What prompts people to want to work hard in teams or under conditions of change or ambiguity? Research on this question has focused on (1) the objective reward system, (2) the task, and (3) the social context factors that influence motivation. It is these issues that we turn to next.

The theories that emphasize external factors can be divided into three groups: (1) those that emphasize rewards (e.g., operant conditioning), (2) those that emphasize the task (e.g., job enrichment), and (3) those that emphasize social interactions (e.g., social norms). We will review each of these approaches and examples of their applications.

Reinforcement Theory. One of the dominant influences in the field of psychology has been behaviorism. The two major components of the theory are the ideas of reinforcement and environmental determinism. Reinforcement was discussed in some detail in Chapter 2. Recall that a reinforcer is defined as any event following a behavior that *increases* the probability that that behavior will be repeated. Reinforcement can occur either by introducing a desirable stimulus (e.g., complimenting an employee for his or her good work) or by removing an undesirable stimulus (e.g., fixing a drafty window in the employee's office). In the former case we are talking about positive reinforcement, and in the latter case, negative reinforcement. Any event following a behavior that *decreases* the probability that that behavior will be repeated (e.g., a verbal reprimand) is called a *punisher*. (In reviewing these distinctions, you may wish to refer back to Figure 2-4 on page 27.) Once we discover what events serve as reinforcers and punishers for a particular behavior (e.g., coming to work), we can manipulate the frequency of the behavior by manipulating these events.

Two types of empirical research using this approach are available. The first simply introduces some system of reinforcement and then compares the behavior of people who are reinforced with that of people who are not reinforced. Studies that have used this method have provided strong support for the hypothesis that reinforcement improves performance (e.g., Luthans, Paul, & Baker, 1981).

The second type of study compares different types of *reinforcement schedules*, that is, the relative frequency with which a reinforcer is given. The three types of schedules most often studied are the *continuous schedule* (a reinforcer is provided after *every* incidence of the desired behavior), the *fixed ratio schedule* (a reinforcer is provided, for example, on every third incidence of the desired behavior), and the *variable ratio schedule* a reinforcer is provided *on the average* every third incidence of the behavior). The results from this type of research are highly confusing. The findings are difficult to summarize primarily because each of the studies finds somewhat different things. However, it is safe to conclude from these studies that (1) there is relatively little difference in performance between the various types of schedules, and (2) there is a big difference in performance between using a schedule and not using one (Babb & Kopp, 1978; Davis & Luthans, 1980).

Job Design, Enlargement, and Enrichment. It has been known for a long time that the properties of the tasks that people work on can influence their motivation and performance. One of the earliest attempts to design tasks systematically with performance in mind was carried out by Frederick W. Taylor. Recall that we introduced Taylor's "scientific management" ideas in

Chapter 3. Taylor was among the first to argue that the methods of science could be used to design jobs and train people to attain maximum output. While Taylor himself espoused the rather broad ideal of management and workers involved in a cooperative effort to increase productivity, his followers were more restrictive in their application of his ideas. They concentrated on two main issues: (1) determining the one best way to do the job, and (2) using incentive pay to ensure compliance with the prescribed work methods.

Emphasis on finding the "one best way" to do a job led to what are called *time and motion* studies. These studies are designed to do the following:

1. Find the best way for people to move, stand and physically perform a task.
2. Break complex jobs down into easily repeatable, learnable tasks.
3. Arrange tools and equipment in a manner that minimizes effort and lost time.
4. Construct the work environment in such a way that noise, ventilation, and other support facilities do not reduce effectiveness.
5. Design special tools for specific jobs, such as conveyors and other machines to reduce unnecessary actions.
6. Eliminate all activities that are fatigue-producing or that are unrelated to the task at hand.

The efficiency of the assembly lines in many modern manufacturing organizations is living testament to the success of time and motion studies. However, these studies have not brought forth all of the benefits originally hoped for by Taylor. Training costs continue to be very high because of high turnover, high wages are needed to keep people on these jobs, and people are bored with repetitive work.

Beginning in the late 1950s and early 1960s, recognition of these problems stimulated interest in finding alternative ways to design jobs. Gradually, more and more research has been directed toward solving the human problems associated with work. The solutions proposed for some of these problems fall into two main categories: job enlargement and job enrichment. Under the heading of *job enlargement* are job design changes that involve the *horizontal expansion* of the job (widening the scope of the job). Job enlargement usually leaves the employee with the same level of autonomy and responsibility, but expands the variety of tasks he or she is asked to perform. *Job enrichment,* on the other hand, also tries to increase the employee's autonomy and responsibility.

The name most readily associated with job enlargement is that of Frederick Herzberg (1979). While there is some disagreement in academic circles about the validity of certain specific aspects of his theory, there is little doubt about his impact on the general idea of job enlargement. Four major ways to enlarge jobs have generally been discussed:

1. *Challenging the employee.* Ask employees to work up to their potential. This must be accompanied by changes in the job itself.
2. *Replacing difficult, repetitive, and boring tasks by machines when possible.* This leaves the employee wit the more interesting aspects of the job.
3. *Assigning more tasks or more operations to the job.* This will result in less monotony and more variety.

4. *Using job rotation.* This allows the employee to learn new skills and to engage in a variety of tasks.

In general, the available evidence supports the use of such techniques, and we will discuss some examples in our applications section. However, there is often a more recognizable impact of job enlargement on employee satisfaction than on productivity. While increased satisfaction should reduce turnover and absenteeism, it may be that more inclusive changes are needed to improve productivity; that is, job enlargement may not go far enough. Job enrichment may be needed.

Job enrichment entails both the horizontal and vertical restructuring of jobs in an effort to increase the meaningfulness and satisfaction of work. It involves more than just an expanded job with more varied tasks. It involves the creation of a new job with greater responsibility and autonomy (the vertical component). New skills and abilities can be used, and the job is upgraded. Below are listed some principles of vertical job loading:

1. *There is less direct control of the employee.* The emphasis is placed on results. The employee has discretion in choosing how best to achieve those results.
2. *Personal accountability is increased.* The individual is responsible for his or her activities.
3. *Whenever possible, complete units of work are assigned.* The individual performs a whole, meaningful task (e.g., assembling a whole product) rather than one or two fragmented parts of the task.
4. *One has greater freedom on the job and greater access to information.* The employee understands why activities are being done by those around him or her.
5. *Upgrading the skills and development of each employee is emphasized.* New and challenging tasks are frequently assigned. These may include tasks previously done by one's supervisor (e.g., scheduling the work to be done).

Job enrichment is more comprehensive than job enlargement. The employee has more responsibility and discretion. There is feedback about performance, communication is two-way, and there is some attempt at having an individual do a whole job from beginning to end. Through these practices, it is hoped that motivation, performance, and satisfaction will increase.

A fairly specific theory of job enrichment called the "job characteristics model" has been developed by Hackman and Oldham (1980). They suggest that certain core job dimensions have an impact on a number of psychological states, which in turn relate to attitudes and behavior on the job. Figure 6-6 presents their theory.

There are some important implications of this theory. First, changing only one job characteristic may have a minor impact on eventual behavior. Second, changing the job will change behavior only by changing the critical psychological states. Third, the theory will vary in effectiveness, depending upon individual needs. It would be expected to work better for people who highly value autonomy, growth, and responsibility.

Research data show that the effects of job enrichment on satisfaction tend to be stronger than its effects on productivity, although some productivity increases do occur (Roberts & Glick, 1981). Moreover, in cases in which

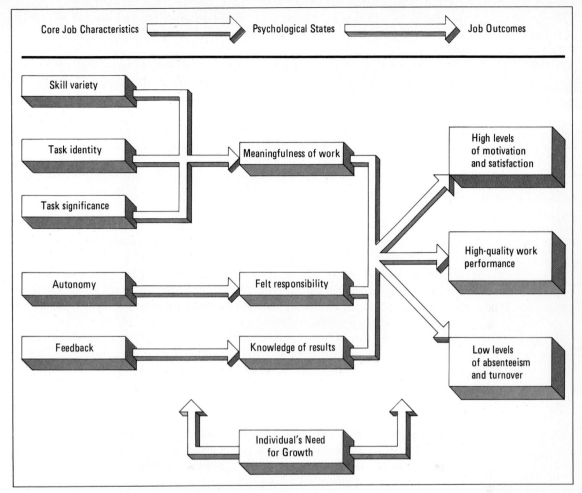

Core Job Characteristics ➡ Psychological States ➡ Job Outcomes

- Skill variety
- Task identity
- Task significance
→ Meaningfulness of work

- Autonomy → Felt responsibility

- Feedback → Knowledge of results

Individual's Need for Growth

- High levels of motivation and satisfaction
- High-quality work performance
- Low levels of absenteeism and turnover

FIGURE 6-6
Hackman and Oldham's job characteristics model of job enrichment. (*Adapted from Hackman & Oldham, 1980.*)

enrichment is combined with a technique such as goal setting, both high satisfaction and productivity are readily attined (Steers & Mowday, 1977).

Social Factors. The third and last category of external theories focuses on the social conditions that can affect the intended choice of behavior. For example, some researchers have found that one's reactions to a task may be as much a function of what one's coworkers say about the tasks as they are of the actual task properties themselves (White & Mitchell, 1979). These studies consistently show that individuals who have coworkers who like the task say that their job is significantly more enriched than those who have coworkers who dislike the task (even though, objectively, the job is the same). Thus, coworkers' impressions can have a powerful effect on one's evaluation of and satisfaction with a job.

Social factors have also been shown to affect performance. For example, studies conducted over 30 years ago examined the impact of coworkers who asked the subjects either to slow down or to speed up their effort on a task. The results consistently showed that these coworker requests produced a large difference in performance in cohesive work groups, but had little or no effect in noncohesive work groups (Schachter, Ellerston, McBride, & Gregory, 1951).

Social norms provide yet another example of a social factor that can influence an intended choice of behavior. Ever since the classic Hawthorne studies, social scientists have been keenly aware of the fact that norms for productivity can be powerful predictors of actual productivity. The empirical research clearly shows that when a whole group expects a coworker either to work hard or to slack off, the person usually conforms to this pressure. This should be especially true the more important the group's opinion is to the individual and the more the group members have to work together (i.e., are dependent on one another). We will have much more to say about the impact of group norms in Chapter 9, "Roles, Norms, and Status."

One final stream of research that emphasizes a slightly different set of variables is the social learning approach. One of the cornerstones of social learning theory is that individuals often model the behavior of salient and important people with whom they interact. Modeling is seen as both a learning proces and a regulating process; that is, people learn new behaviors from models, and, in addition, they use models as guides for what is called for or expected in various situations.

Research on the effects of role models has been supportive of these ideas. For example, studies have shown that a high effort model results in higher productivity than a low effort model, and that high competence models have a positive influence on task satisfaction (Weiss & Knight, 1980). Thus, another way to increase motivation through social factors is to provide hard-working models (Rakestraw & Weiss, 1981).

A summary of the literature dealing with task and social context variables leads to a rather important conclusion. To the extent that the tasks people work on are (1) done in groups, (2) difficult to observe, (3) done without feedback, or (4) performed under conditions of change or ambiguity, approaches to motivation such as equity theory, expectancy theory, goal-setting theory, or reinforcement theory may be either hard to apply or simply inappropriate. Under these circumstances, we may be better able to instill high motivation through task or social mechanisms such as job enrichment, social norms, or role models. The key point is that we need to *diagnose* the situation—figure out which set of procedures is most applicable under the existing sets of conditions.

Applications of Theories of Intended Choice: External Focus

There are good examples of the application of principles generated from the reinforcement, task design, and social factors approaches. However, the "cleanness" of these applications is often questionable; that is, the applications frequently incorporate principles from more than just one approach. We will point out these potential alternative explanations throughout our discussions.

Reinforcement Approaches. There are three principles of application derived from reinforcement theory: (1) rewards should be closely tied to behavior, (2) reward administration should be frequent and consistent, and (3) people are motivated by outcomes.

An excellent example of the application of reinforcement principles can be found in the work of Komaki, Waddell, and Pearce (1977) in a grocery store. The employees of interest in the study were two male clerks. An observer noted the performance of each clerk on three behaviors during four 15-minute periods each day. Scores were generated that represented (1) the percentage of time the clerk was in the store and available, (2) the percentage of time customers were assisted within 5 seconds, and (3) the percentage of shelves and counters that were filled to at least 50 percent of capacity. A baseline of 3 weeks' data was gathered before reinforcement was introduced. The store owner then agreed to give time off with pay each week as a reward for good performance. Over the next 7–9 weeks, the average performance increased from 53 to 86 percent for the first behavior, from 35 to 87 percent for the second behavior, and 57 to 86 percent for the third behavior. Figure 6-7 summarizes these results.

Some industrial applications of reinforcement techniques have also attempted to examine the relative effectiveness of different types of reinforcement schedules. For example, Latham (1974) did a study with tree planters employed by the Weyerhaeuser Company. The job of the tree planters was to place new seedlings in those areas in which tree harvesting had already taken place. The seedlings were packed in small test-tube-like biodegradable containers. The planters would take a large sack of seedlings and walk through an area, first making a hole in the ground, then placing a seedling in it. The behavior that was to be reinforced was the number of bags of trees planted, and four different reinforcement schedules were established.

The planters in one group received a $2 bonus for each bag of trees planted

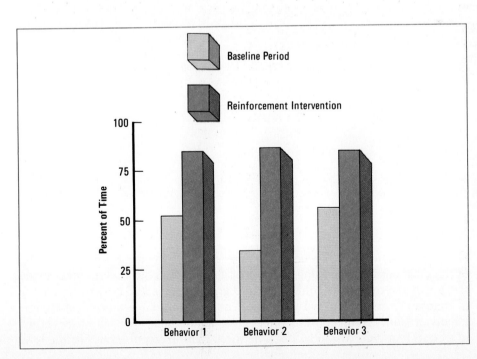

FIGURE 6-7
Results of a reinforcement theory intervention. *Note:* Behavior 1 = availability, behavior 2 = customer assistance, and behavior 3 = filling stock shelves. (*Based on data presented by Komaki, Waddell, & Pearce, 1977.*)

A Million-Dollar Incentive Plan

Two and half years ago, the 325 employees who manufactured paper egg cartons at a Diamond International plant in Palmer, Mass., faced a cloudy future. Styrofoam containers were creating stiff competition, the recession was biting into profits, and with the American economy worsening, workers were suffering a bad case of unemployment jitters. Recalls Daniel Boyle, personnel director of the Diamond plant: "Relations between labor and management were strained at best."

Then, Boyle, 35, devised a system of productivity incentives called the 100 Club. The results exceeded his wildest expectations. Today productivity at the plant is up 16.5%, and quality-related errors are down 40%. As of last year, worker grievances had decreased 72% and lost time due to industrial accidents 43.7%. The turnaround has meant more than $1 million in gross financial benefits for the parent company, a New York–based conglomerate that had 1982 sales of $781 million.

The Palmer plant's formula for success is disarmingly simple. Employees are allocated points in recognition of above-average performance. Any employee who works a full year without having an industrial accident is awarded 20 points; 100% attendance is worth 25 points. Every year, on the anniversary of the program's Feb. 2, 1981, launching date, points are totaled up, and a record is sent to the individual's home. Upon reaching 100 points, the worker gets a light blue nylon jacket emblazoned with the company logo and a patch signifying membership in the 100 Club. Every one of the plant's employees has now earned a jacket.

Those who accumulate more than 100 points can receive additional gifts. With 500 points, employees can choose such items as a blender, Corning Ware, a wall clock or a pine cribbage board. Pointing out that none of the prizes is beyond the purchasing power of the workers, Diamond's management stresses that the real value is as a sign of appreciation from the company. "For too long, the people who have got the majority of attention have been those who cause problems," says Boyle. "The program's primary focus is the recognition of good employees."

That philosophy has in turn instilled an unprecedented sense of good will and optimism among Diamond's workers. According to a survey conducted before the program started, 65% of the plant's work force felt management did not treat them respectfully, 56% approached their work pessimistically, and 79% thought they were not being rewarded for a job well done. When the survey was repeated earlier this year, 86% of the employees said that management considers them important or very important, 81% felt that their work was recognized, and 79% reported that their work and product were of much greater concern to them.

Not surprisingly, labor relations have also improved. Even though employees were due a 58 cents-an-hour wage hike this July, to an average of $8.53 an hour, they have agreed to forgo it because of concerns about competition. Labor leaders credit the 100 Club with keeping the company afloat and fostering a new atmosphere of cooperation with management. "Things have been tough," says Henry Sarrette, president of the local union. "But at least we are now in it together." Says Boyle: "I'm a little tired of all those Japanese success stories. What we've done here shows you can have American success stories as well." As a sign of the success, the 100 Club has been phased in at Diamond's three other fiber product plants in Mississippi, California and New York.

(continuous schedule). A second group received a $4 bonus for planting a bag of trees *and* correctly guessing the toss of a coin (the coin toss in effect made this a variable-ratio-2 schedule). A third group received $8 for planting a bag of trees and correctly guessing two coin tosses (a variable-ratio-4 schedule). Finally, a fourth group continued receiving their regular wage and thus served as a control or comparison group. The three reinforcement groups in the long run should theoretically receive the same amount of money: $2 every time, $4 half of the time, or $8 one-fourth of the time. These groups showed an average increase in productivity of about 14 percent, while there was no change for the control group. From both a cost-benefit analysis and productivity-increase perspective, the continuous schedule did best (a 33 percent increase in productivity and a savings of $4.14 per bag of trees).

Changes in the Task. Unlike most other theories of work motivation, the task design and job enrichment literature consists almost exclusively of studies of actual job changes in real work organizations. In some ways, this emphasis on the "real world" is a blessing. There are many examples to discuss. It is also a problem, however, in that very few of the research projects are neat or tidy; that is, most of these studies include some enrichment variables, some social variables, some reward variables, and so on, and it is very hard to tease out the specifics of what seems to work best and when. Given this caveat we will examine several types of changes that have been made and consider their cost-effectiveness.

One review of 53 different job enrichment projects revealed the variety of changes that are being tried (Alber & Blumberg, 1981). Ford Motor Company, for example, has a program that includes both participation in decision making and changes in job content. The job-related changes are that employees (1) watch for and correct quality problems, (2) are allowed and expected to do simple equipment repair jobs, (3) have more flexibility to work on different tasks, (4) clean and oil equipment, and (5) are given authority to use any machine for which they are technically certified (Tavernier, 1981).

The employee participation aspect of the program includes the use of problem-solving groups, participative decision making, and the encouragement of active planning and directing on the part of employees. Ford has reported a number of successes with these work content and personal involvement changes. The Ford plant in Indianapolis found that the reject rate for parts processed through its valve clustering machine was reduced by 37 percent. At the Dearborn Engine plant, employees corrected a serious scrap problem caused by broken timing belts on cylinder-head milling machines. Considering that one broken belt incident could cost up to $25,000 in damaged parts, tooling, and production, this was a considerable savings.

The Alber and Blumberg (1981) review cited previously summarizes both the costs and benefits of this type of job change program. Overall, both costs and benefits are high. Cost factors include training, changing floor space, duplication of tools and equipment, hiring of outside consultants, and changes in reward systems. On the benefit side there is often less turnover and absenteeism (average reduction is about 16 percent), higher quality (average reduction in rejects, complaints, and recycled work is about 20 percent), and better resource use (average reduction in machine breakdown and forced labor idle time and average increase in output is about 13 percent). Also, workforce reductions have resulted in an average of $4500 in savings per month. One additional thing is clear. Almost all reports of projects that have been well managed according to sound job-enrichment principles indicate that most (although not all) people are more satisfied with their job, and that they generally welcome the changes.

Social Factors. Our final set of applications is concerned with how an organization can get employees to influence other employees to try hard to do a good job. The major way to do this is through the social factors approach: Get people to agree on what should be done, have it well known, and have the group enforce it.

To some extent, some of the job-enrichment projects include these ideas. Programs that emphasize a team approach and participation are especially likely to have an impact on productivity norms. For example, Motorola instituted a trial participation project with twelve hundred of its employees. Their groups discussed a variety of problems having to do with quality, delivery, safety, inventory, and costs. The groups recommended solutions, and shared in the savings that were generated by their suggestions. Motorola reported not only that specific ideas increased output 25 percent, but also that "spinoffs" resulted from the participation program. Employees became more willing to fill in for absent coworkers, they openly brought forth problems, and most important, they self-policed their groups with respect to work habits, lunch breaks, and rest periods (Scott, 1981). Thus, some aspects of enrichment programs have resulted in social norms being established and enforced by the group.

Summary of Theories of Intention

Let us take stock of where we are. The presence of arousal sets the stage for intending to behave in a particular way. Need deficiencies, along with evaluation apprehension brought about by the presence of others, are the major causes of arousal. Intentions themselves are influenced by what people see as the outcomes of their actions, their goals, and their sense of what is equitable or fair treatment. Thus, through the use of goal-setting programs coupled with contingent and public reward systems based on fair and just appraisals, we can influence these intentions. They can also be influenced by enriched jobs and group norms.

At this point we have an employee who *wants to work hard and behave appropriately.* We have, in other words, what is traditionally called a *motivated* employee. One final task, then, is to discuss what we need to do to translate motivation into behavior, and subsequently, into performance.

MOTIVATION, BEHAVIOR, AND PERFORMANCE

As we discussed earlier in the chapter, motivation does not guarantee good performance. First, motivation needs to be translated into behavior, and a number of factors must be present for this to occur. The person must have (1) the ability, (2) the appropriate knowledge, and (3) the technology (e.g., machines, information, supplies, parts) to do the job. All of these factors can be just as important as motivation in determining behavior (Blumberg & Pringle, 1982).

Second, behavior is not the same thing as performance. Performance refers to the results of one's behavior. And to the extent that performance is measured by results that are not closely tied to observable behavior (e.g., sales, "on time" record, customer complaints), it will be hard to tell the extent to which motivation plays a role. We will discuss performance, its definition, and its measurement more fully in Chapter 15.

Finally, having the ability, the knowledge, and the motivation is not enough. Various task, social, situational, and administrative factors may constrain or modify behavior. In some settings more variance in behavior may be controlled by these factors than by either ability or effort. The implication is that organizations must do a thorough job analysis *before* they worry about issues of selection (i.e., selecting people with high levels of ability) or motivation. In order for ability and effort to have their maximum effect on behavior, these social and situational factors must be taken into account so that machines, schedules, and the task environment facilitate rather than hinder highly motivated employees.

Summary

In this chapter we have introduced many new terms, some important distinctions, and a variety of theoretical and practical ideas and interventions. The major points may be summarized as follows:

1. *Motivation* is the intention to engage in a specific action. It encompasses the idea of arousal, and it is not the same thing as either behavior or performance. Arousal, intention, behavior, and performance are all separate concepts.
2. Traditional theories of arousal focus on need deficiencies. Having varied reward systems and matching individual rewards to individual employees are important.
3. Arousal is also caused by the presence of others (via social facilitation and evaluation apprehension). The presence of a supervisor and a sense of personal responsibility can both heighten arousal.
4. Traditional theories of intention focus on cognitive processes. Expectancy theory, goal-setting theory, and equity theory emphasize the ideas that people should be given explicit goals to strive for, rewarded frequently for appropriate behavior, given clear expectations, and treated fairly.
5. Theories of intentions that focus on external factors deal with the job and the social setting. Jobs that are enlarged and enriched have positive motivational properties in the form of autonomy, variety, feedback, significance, and so on. Social factors such as group norms and role models can also help.
6. The motivation to do well is not enough to ensure good performance. One must have the ability to do well, as well as an environment that supports and enhances one's capacity to translate motivation into good performance.

IMPLICATIONS FOR RESEARCH

Throughout this chapter we have noted a number of specific areas in which additional research is needed. Our purpose here, therefore, will be to discuss the broader implications of the model we have outlined for further research on motivation.

To start with, the model presented here distinguishes among several important constructs. There are clear differences among arousal, intention (these two in summary are called motivation), behavior, and performance. Unfortunately, these terms are often used interchangeably in both theory and practice. If our knowledge is to continue to increase in this area, we must clearly discriminate among these terms and among their various causes and consequences.

Another important distinction made by the model is between the internal and external causes of arousal, intention, and behavior. For most of the last 50 years research on motivation has focused more on the internal factors than the external ones. However, with the increasing recognition that the environment has an important impact on our behavior, and with the recognition that in many jobs people work in teams, are highly dependent on technology, and are not directly observable, it has become clear that we need a shift in focus. More research is needed on how the environment—social, administrative, and technological—influences motivation, behavior, and performance.

We also need to know more about how to combine the various theories. As we have shown, needs, expectations, group pressures, goals, rewards, role models, fear of evaluation, equity, ability, and experience all can influence behavior. Future research must address two major questions. First, how do these various factors combine? Do they complement or contradict one another? For example, it is not clear that one can be concerned with maximizing rewards and maintaining equity at the same time. On the other hand, goal setting and providing social support may be complementary over a wide range of settings. Second, rather than asking which theory of motivation is best, we should be asking under what circumstances and with what kinds of people a given theory (or combination of approaches) works best.

This latter point is slowly being recognized in the literature. For example, a paper by William Miller (1981) described how he implemented four or five different motivational strategies in each of three different organizations. The strategies included reinforcement approaches, need-theory approaches, participation, and group support. Quantitative and qualitative performance data were collected, and relative comparisons were made. While some strategies did better than others overall, the most striking conclusion was that "none of the theories or techniques is applicable to all individuals or all circumstances" and that "diversity is the rule, not the exception" (p. 52). We need to know more about these contingencies if our knowledge about motivation is to continue to grow.

IMPLICATIONS FOR PRACTICE

One conclusion you should have drawn from this chapter is that there are no easy answers. On the other hand, you ought to have gotten a better idea of what sorts of questions you should be asking. The task for the future manager is to have on hand diagnostic models—sets of questions, ordered in priority and sequence—to use when confronted with performance problems. Given our analysis, we suggest that the sequence eventually traces *backward* through our model. The steps would be roughly as follows:

1. *Define performance.* The organization first has to decide how it wants to define *good performance* and *poor performance*.
2. *Assess performance.* After performance is defined, we must have an accurate and reliable way to assess it. Unless performance can be adequately defined and reliability measured, there is no sense in proceeding further.
3. *Determine the extent to which specific behaviors contribute to performance.* If performance is defined as an aggregated result (e.g., number of bottles of beer produced per month), we may find that the best predictor of that performance is something other than behavior—for example, the amount of time a piece of machinery is working correctly. Performance may often be more closely related to the quality of maintenance or to the age and sophistication of the machines than to the behavior of the operators. Changing the people (e.g., through selection or training) or trying to affect motivation (e.g., through recognition or fringe benefits) may have only a minor impact on performance relative to changing the technology. The key word here is *relative*. We must determine the extent to which behavior is important *relative to other factors*.
4. *Determine what factors influence behavior.* If behavior is important (and in many cases it is), we come to the most crucial diagnostic question: Is behavior controlled by ability, knowledge, motivation, or some external dependency? Rough estimates of these factors will tell us how to proceed.
5. *Determine the importance of external behavioral dependencies.* No matter to what extent ability, knowledge, and motivation are important, if there are important external dependencies, we need to work on them. These dependencies (on people, policies, and machines) are factors that *limit* performance, and they are things that the organization usually has a good deal of control over.
6. *Determine the relative importance of ability and knowledge.* For a great percentage of the jobs people do, ability and knowledge are as important as, or more important than, motivation. If ability is a major factor, systems of selection and training will need to be emphasized. If knowledge is a major factor, training and experience should receive the greatest emphasis.
7. *Select an appropriate motivational strategy.* If after going through all the steps listed above motivation is still judged to be important, a number of additional questions need to be asked. For example, can we observe the behavior directly? Do we have the flexibility to administer different rewards? Can behavior be described in terms of goals? Does the reward system match the extent to which people are dependent on one another (i.e., individual versus group rewards)? In short, we need to know whether we should focus on external factors (i.e., the task) or internal factors (i.e., needs) or both. Once we know this, we can select an appropriate motivational strategy using the concepts outlined in this chapter.

1. How is behavior different from performance? What difference does it make?
2. How would you apply the ideas inherent in social facilitation and evaluation apprehension?
3. How would you apply expectancy, equity, and goal-setting notions? List two or three principles that you would use from each approach.
4. What are the relationships among ability, motivation, and job knowledge? How do these factors contribute to behavior and performance?
5. If you are confronted with a performance problem, what questions would you ask and in what order?

CASE: PUSHING PAPER CAN BE FUN

A large metropolitan city government was putting on a number of seminars for managers of various departments throughout the city. At one of these sessions the topic to be discussed was motivation—how we can get public servants motivated to do a good job. The plight of a police captain became the central focus of the discussion.

"I've got a real problem with my officers. They come on the force as young, inexperienced rookies, and we send them out on the street, either in cars or on a beat. They seem to like the contact they have with the public, the action involved in crime prevention, and the apprehension of criminals. They also like helping people out at fires, accidents, and other emergencies.

"The problem occurs when they get back to the station. They hate to do the paperwork, and because they dislike it, the job is frequently put off or done inadequately. This lack of attention hurts us later on when we get to court. We need clear, factual reports. They must be highly detailed and unambiguous. As soon as one part of a report is shown to be inadequate or incorrect, the rest of the report is suspect. Poor reporting probably causes us to lose more cases than any other factor.

"I just don't know how to motivate them to do a better job. We're in a budget crunch and I have absolutely no financial rewards at my disposal. In fact, we'll probably have to lay some people off in the near future. It's hard for me to make the job interesting and challenging because it isn't—it's boring, routine paperwork, and there isn't much you can do about it.

"Finally, I can't say to them that their promotions will hinge on the excellence of their paperwork. First of all, they know it's not true. If their performance is adequate, most are more likely to get promoted just by staying on the force a certain number of years than for some specific outstanding act. Second, they were trained to do the job they do out in the streets, not to fill out forms. All through their career it is the arrests and interventions that get noticed.

"Some people have suggested a number of things like using conviction records as a performance criterion. However, we know that's not fair—too many other things are involved. Bad paperwork increases the chance that you lose in court, but good paperwork doesn't necessarily mean you'll win. We tried setting up team competitions based upon the excellence of the reports, but the guys caught on to that pretty quickly. No one was getting any type of reward for winning the competition, and they figured why should they bust a gut when there was no payoff.

"I just don't know what to do."

Questions about the Case

1. What is the behavior that the captain wants to motivate?
2. What are the characteristics of the situation that cause problems for motivational systems?

3. Do you think he has tried everything he can do?

4. What would you suggest he do? Think of some specific strategies that might help.

References

Alber, A., & Blumberg, M. (1981, Jan.–Feb.). A team versus individual approach to job enrichment programs. *Personnel, 58,* 63–75.

Babb, H. W., & Kopp, D. G. (1978). Applications of behavior modification in organizations: A review and critique. *Academy of Management Review, 3,* 281–290.

Blumberg, M., & Pringle, C. D. (1982). The missing opportunity in organizational research: Some implications for a theory of work performance. *Academy of Management Review, 7,* 560–569.

Carrell, M. R., & Dittrich, J. E. (1978). Equity theory: The recent literature, methodological considerations, and new directions. *Academy of Management Review, 3,* 202–210.

Connolly, T. (1976). Some conceptual and methodological issues in expectancy models of work performance motivation. *Academy of Management Review, 1,* 37–47.

Davis, T. R. V., & Luthans, F. (1980). A social learning approach to organization behavior. *Academy of Management Review, 5,* 281–290.

Erez, M., & Ziden, I. (1984). Effect of goal acceptance on the relationship of goal difficulty to performance. *Journal of Applied Psychology, 69,* 69–78.

Ferris, G. R., Beehr, T. A., & Gilmore, D. C. (1978). Social facilitation: A review and alternative conceptual model. *Academy of Management Review, 3,* 338–347.

Foegen, J. H. (1982a, May–June). The creative flowering of employee benefits. *Business Horizons, 25,* 9–13.

Foegen, J. H. (1982b, October 18). Fringe benefits are being diversified, too. *Industry Week,* 74–75.

Goodman, P. S. (1977). Social comparison processes in organizations. In B. M. Staw and G. R. Salancik (Eds.), *New Directions in Organizational Behavior* (pp. 92–132). Chicago: St. Clair Press.

Hackman, J. R., & Oldham, G. R. (1980). *Work redesign.* Reading, MA: Addison-Wesley.

Herzberg, F. (1979, Winter). Motivation and innovation: Who are the workers serving? *California Management Review, 22,* 60–70.

Kipnis, D. (1976). *The powerholders.* Chicago: University of Chicago Press.

Komaki, J., Waddell, W. M., & Pearce, M. G. (1977). The applied behavioral analysis approach and individual employees: Improving performance in two small businesses. *Organizational Behavior and Human Performance, 19,* 337–352.

Latham, G. P. (1974, October). *The effect of various schedules of reinforcement on the productivity of tree planters.* Paper presented at the annual meeting of the American Psychological Association, New Orleans.

Latham, G. P., & Baldes, J. J. (1975). The practical significance of Locke's theory of goal setting. *Journal of Applied Psychology, 60,* 122–124.

Latham, G. P., Mitchell, T. R., & Dossett, D. L. (1978). The importance of participative goal setting and anticipated reward on goal difficulty and job performance. *Journal of Applied Psychology, 63,* 163–171.

Locke, E. A. (1978). The ubiquity of the technique of goal setting in theories and approaches to employee motivation. *Academy of Management Review, 3,* 594–601.

Locke, E. A., & Latham, G. P. (1984). *Goal setting: A motivational technique that works.* Englewood Cliffs, NJ: Prentice-Hall.

Locke, E. A., & Latham, G. P. (1984). *Goal setting for individuals, groups and organizations.* Chicago: Science Research Associates.

Locke, E. A., Shaw, K. N., Saari, L. M., & Latham, G. P. (1981). Goal setting and task performance 1969–1980. *Psychological Bulletin, 90,* 125–152.

Luthans, F., Paul, R., & Baker, D. (1981). An experimental analysis of the impact of contingent reinforcement on salespersons' performance behavior. *Journal of Applied Psychology, 66,* 314–323.

Maslow, A. H. (1954). *Motivation and personality.* New York: Harper.

McClelland, D. C. (1961). *The achieving society.* Princeton, NJ: Van Nostrand.

McClelland, D. C. (1978). Managing motivation to expand human freedom. *American Psychologist, 33,* 201–210.

McClelland, D. C. (1985). *Human motivation.* Glenview, IL: Scott, Foresman.

McClelland, D. C., & Burnham, D. H. (1976, March–April). Power is the great motivator. *Harvard Business Review, 54,* 100–110.

Miller, W. B. (1981). Motivation techniques: Does one work best? *Management Review, 70(2),* 47–52.

Mitchell, T. R. (1979). Organizational behavior. *Annual Review of Psychology* (Vol. 30, pp. 243–281). Palo Alto, CA: Annual Reviews.

Mitchell, T. R. (1983). Expectancy-value models in organizational psychology. In N. Feather (Ed.), *Expectancy, incentive and action* (pp. 293–314). Hillsdale, NJ: Erlbaum.

Rakestraw, T. L., Jr., & Weiss, H. M. (1981). The interaction of social influences and task experience on goals, performance, and performance satisfaction. *Organizational Behavior and Human Performance, 27,* 326–344.

Ralston, D. A., Anthony, W. P., & Gustafson, D. J. (1985). Employees may love flexitime, but what does it do for the organization's productivity? *Journal of Applied Psychology, 70,* 272–279.

Roberts, K. H., & Glick, W. (1981). The job characteristics approach to task design: A critical review. *Journal of Applied Psychology, 66,* 193–217.

Schachter, S., Ellertson, N., McBride, D., & Gregory, P. (1951). An experimental study of cohesiveness and productivity. *Human Relations, 4,* 229–238.

Scott, W. B. (1981). Participative management at Motorola: The results. *Management Review, 70(7),* 26–28.

Steers, R., & Mowday, R. T. (1977). The motivational properties of tasks. *Academy of Management Review, 2,* 645–658.

Tavernier, G. (1981). Ford's employee involvement program. *Management Review, 70(6),* 15–20.

Telly, C. S., French, W. L., & Scott, W. G. (1971). The relationship of inequity to turnover among hourly workers. *Administrative Science Quarterly, 16,* 164–172.

Vecchio, R. P. (1982). Predicting worker performance in inequitable settings. *Academy of Management Review, 7,* 103–110.

Vroom, V. H. (1964). *Work and motiation.* New York: Wiley.

Wahba, M. A., & Bridwell, L. G. (1973). Maslow reconsidered: A review of research on the need hierarchy theory. *Proceedings of the Academy of Management,* 514–520.

Weiss, H. M., & Knight, P. A. (1980). The utility of humility: Self-esteem, information search and problem-solving efficiency. *Organizational Behavior and Human Performance, 25,* 216–223.

White, R. W. (1959). Motivation reconsidered: The concept of competence. *Psychological Review, 66,* 297–333.

White, S. E., & Mitchell, T. R. (1979). Job enrichment versus social cues: A comparison and competitive test. *Journal of Applied Psychology, 64,* 1–9.

White, S. E., Mitchell, T. R., & Bell, C. H. (1977). Goal setting, evaluation apprehension, and social cues as determinants of job performance and job satisfaction in a simulated organization. *Journal of Applied Psychology, 62,* 665–673.

Zippo, M. (1982a, July–August). Flexible benefits: Just the beginning. *Personnel,* 56–58.

Zippo, M. (1982b, March–April). Job sharing: A way to avoid layoffs? *Personnel,* 58–60.

Zippo, M. (1982c, March–April). Management responds to employee questions. *Personnel,* 60–63.

Chapter 7

Job Stress

It's not the large things that send a man to the madhouse. No it's the continuing series of small tragedies that send a man to the madhouse. Not the death of his love, but a shoelace that snaps with no time left.
—CHARLES BUKOWSKI

Did you ever stop to think when you picked up the phone to make a call on Mother's Day what it would be like to be an operator for the phone company? The operator (let us call him Gary) sits in a room with about forty other operators with a headset on, facing a computer console. At the beginning of each shift he fits his earpiece tightly into place and plugs into the computer. The console displays over eighty lighted buttons, and the calls start to pour in. As soon as a call is completed, the computer automatically sends another call to Gary's open line. The computer records the time it took to complete the last call and notes the time of the new call and the incoming number. When the call is put through, the computer records the phone number called and the type of billing. If a mistake is made by Gary, it is recorded. The time to complete the call is figured into his average working time per call (AWT). This process continues at an average rate of 23.5 seconds per call, 7.5 hours per working day—over one thousand calls during his shift (Forslund, 1981).

Various guidelines and measures control how Gary performs. For example, there is an expected time per call. Each operator is closely monitored, and the AWT and an error rate are computed. If Gary wants to go to the rest room, he must display a "special"—a red plastic octagon resembling a stop sign on top of his console. Gary also knows that he has to display it early (in anticipation of his bodily demands as it were), because he may have to wait up to 40 minutes before he can leave. Time away from the console is also recorded. When the pressure of the job gets too intense, Gary pops a big green pill supplied by the company—a powerful analgesic laced with caffeine. He takes three or four of these a day.

What are the long-term effects of such a job? What does it do to Gary's psychological and physical health? What does it do to an organization's turnover and absenteeism rate? How would you like such a job? There are many jobs like Gary's that are stressful and fast-paced, involving high demands, little control, and constant pressure. The purpose of this chapter is to discuss the topic of stress, which some authors have described as epidemic. We will define it, describe its causes and consequences, and suggest some ways to reduce it.

PREVALENCE OF STRESS

"No issue in the psychology of health is of greater interest and importance than whether and how stress influences adaptational outcomes such as well-being, social functioning, and somatic health" (Lazarus, DeLongis, Folkman, and Gruen, 1985, p. 770).

These are strong words. Yet there seems to be massive evidence to back them up. According to the American Academy of Family Physicians, about two-thirds of the visits to family physicians are the result of stress-related symptoms. The three most frequently prescribed medications in this country are an ulcer medication, a hypertension drug, and a tranquilizer ("Stress," 1983). Stress is now known to be a contributor to coronary heart disease, lung ailments, cancer, accidental injuries, cirrhosis of the liver, and suicide—six of the leading causes of death in the United States (Beehr & Bhagat, 1985). As we shall see, stress can be caused by a variety of things and can have a host of consequences, many of which are related to people's behavior in organizations.

Costs of Stress

The financial impact of stress-related problems has been estimated at 75 to 90 billion dollars annually (Ivancevich & Matteson, 1980). These figures are based on data from industry, health groups, and the government, and are probably conservative. Ivancevich and Matteson (1980) suggest that the costs approach 10 percent of the gross national product of the United States.

The economic cost of peptic ulcers and cardiovascular disease alone is about 50 billion dollars annually in the United States (Moser, 1977). Albrecht (1979) has estimated that for a moderate-sized organization with 2000 employees, stress-related factors amount to a cost of 5.9 percent of sales, which could easily be greater than profit figures. At any given point in time, 15 percent of the general population reports stress severe enough to require treatment of some kind. When one averages the cost per employee, it is more than $750 a year for each person working in the United States ("Stress," 1983).

Cost Factors

Where does the money go? Some of the cost factors are more obvious than others. For the employee there are the direct costs of medical treatment, the loss of earnings, and various intervention costs (e.g., stress-reduction training). Less direct costs that affect both the employee and the employer are losses in productivity, replacement costs, sick leave, insurance premiums, early retirement, lost clients or customers, theft, and sabotage. To this list one should also add the potential costs of accidents (e.g., health disability, legal costs, and liability suits).

When considering the costs of stress, one must take into account such factors as (1) prevention, (2) diagnosis, (3) treatment, (4) continuing care, and (5) rehabilitation. Additionally, from the organization's perspective, one should also include replacement costs, productivity losses, lost clients, and legal liabilities. The exact cost of these factors is exceptionally hard to assess accurately. Thus, the estimates given above may be conservative. But one thing is sure: Stress pervades our lives. As Dr. Joel Elkes, director of behavior medicine at the University of Louisville said, "Our mode of life itself, the way we live, is emerging as today's principal cause of illness" ("Stress," 1983, p. 48).

Public Response

There is a high level of public interest in the topic of stress. A past president of the Institute of Medicine (part of the National Academy of Science) has noted that no aspect of health and disease elicits more interest among government leaders than the relationship between stress and health ("Research on Stress," 1981). The popularity of the topic among the general public is attested to by the frequency of books and articles appearing in the lay press dealing with stress and its management. In fact, public beliefs about the importance of stress as a cause of disease may surpass what the scientific community has been able to demonstrate. For example, in a study of beliefs about the causes of heart attacks, the causes most frequently cited were stress, worry, nervous tension, and pressure. Fifty-one percent of the people polled failed to mention any of the three major risk factors: cigarette smoking, blood pressure, and serum cholesterol. However, despite these public beliefs and the real costs of stress, stress research remains a relatively low priority in the scientific community. The Institute of Medicine has estimated that the total support for stress-related research in a variety of disciplines amounted to no more than 35 million dollars in 1980 ("Research on Stress," 1981).

Two major explanations have been offered for this lack of commitment by the scientific community. First, researching the topic of stress is inherently complex and far more difficult than studying, for example, the effects of a noxious chemical in the work place. A toxic chemical such as carbon monoxide can be measured independently of employees' perception of it, and it affects all employees regardless of personality type or social support. The same is not true of stress.

A second reason for the lack of commitment to stress research is that the problem is interdisciplinary by nature, and there is relatively little interdisciplinary research conducted in most of science. Adaptation to stress occurs at all levels of organization, from the cellular and organic level, to the level of the whole organism (behavior), to the level of groups of organisms (organizations). It thus spans the content areas of the biological sciences, the behavioral sciences, and the social sciences. An adequate understanding of the consequences of stress requires the input of all of these sciences. Several authors have decried the lack of interdisciplinary research as a major stumbling block to our understanding of stress (e.g., Schuler, 1980; Cooper & Marshall, 1976).

CONCEPTUALIZING STRESS

Stress is clearly important, but exactly what is it and what do we do about it? In the following section we concentrate on the definition of stress, its measurement, and the ways it has been studied.

History

The word *stress* comes from the Latin *stringere*, which means "to draw tight" (Skeat, 1958). It has been used for centuries in English literature. However, its conceptual meaning that relates to today's usage probably started with discoveries a century ago. Claude Bernard, a French physiologist, recognized that environmental changes often disrupt organisms, and that stability or balance in the organic system is important. In the 1920s an American physiologist used the term *homeostasis* to describe this balance, and in his later work he used the word *stress* to mean an upset or collapse of this balance (Cannon, 1935).

However, the person most identified with the current usage of the term stress is Dr. Hans Selye, an endocrinologist who did his work at the University of Montreal. In a series of studies he found that external agents such as x-rays, extreme temperatures, and noxious stimuli could bring about tissue damage after extensive exposure. He began to use the word *stress* to refer to the general breakdown of the body in response to the wear and tear of modern life. In his volume entitled *Stress* (Selye, 1950), he suggested that there are environmental agents called *stressors,* and that the response or internal condition of the organism when faced with stressors is stress.

Selye also described what is known as the *general adaptation syndrome.* It consists of three stages:

1. The *alarm stage* is the body's reaction to a threat in the environment. The alarm is sounded, and almost every major organ in the body responds to make ready for "flight-or-fight." In many cases this stage is short-lived, as when you are startled by a car backfiring.
2. The *resistance stage* occurs when the stressor is more persistent and results in physiological or mental changes. The person adapts to the stressor, and the symptoms usually disappear.
3. The *exhaustion stage* takes place when physical and psychological resources are overcome. Prolonged exposure to stressors may eventually overcome one's adaptive capacity and may result in many physical manifestations such as fatigue, disease, disability, and even death. During the exhaustion stage, the adverse consequences of stress become apparent in terms of both productivity and physical and mental well-being.

A key point recognized by Selye is that there is a distinction between the stressor and the fact of being stressed. Not all external events are reacted to in the same manner by all people. A second insight is that it is the prolonged exposure to a stressor that brings about dysfunctional consequences. And finally, he recognized that both physical and social factors can be stressors.

Current Definitions

In the last 20 years there have been hundreds of books and research articles written on the topic of stress. One of the most thorough treatments of the subject was presented by McGrath (1970). He sees stress as a process involving four distinct stages. First, the environment, either social or physical, puts some amount of *objective demand* on the individual. This demand is sometimes called the input, load, stressor level, or force. The next step is the reception stage, in which the individual perceives, recognizes, appraises, and accepts this demand level. This is often called the *subjective demand* or strain. The third stage is the individual's *response* to the subjective demand. This response may involve physiological, psychological, and behavioral systems. Finally, there are the *consequences* of the response, both for the individual and the environment (see Figure 7-1).

Note that there are a number of factors that intervene in each of these

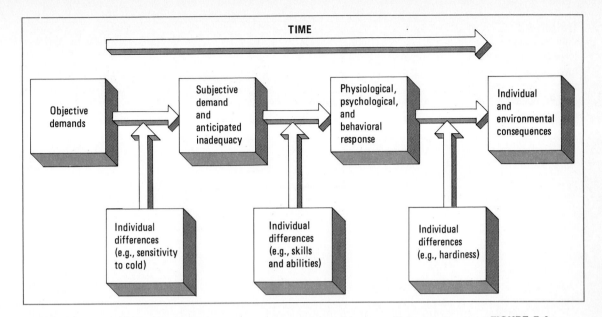

TIME

Objective demands → Subjective demand and anticipated inadequacy → Physiological, psychological, and behavioral response → Individual and environmental consequences

Individual differences (e.g., sensitivity to cold)

Individual differences (e.g., skills and abilities)

Individual differences (e.g., hardiness)

FIGURE 7-1
A definition of stress. (*Adapted from McGrath, 1970.*)

stages. Attributes of the person influence the extent to which objective demand is felt as subjective demand. Some of us are more sensitive than others to the same objective level of noise, cold, rejection, insult, and so on. Second, given some subjective demand, there are attributes of the individual such as skills, experience, and preferences that influence his or her response. Some people walk away from insults, while others trade insult for insult. And some who walk away are deeply affected, while others easily shrug them off. Finally, both the *evaluation* of the consequences and personal characteristics such as hardiness (to be defined later) affect the response-consequence link.

This complex definition of the stress process raises a number of key points. Stress is clearly seen as a *relationship* between the person and the environment. Also important is the notion that these events occur over time. For McGrath (1970), stress occurs when there is a substantial imbalance between the demands of the environment and the response *capability* of the person. This notion includes the idea that the person at some point *anticipates* that he or she may not be able to cope adequately with the imbalance. That is, for stress to occur, the person must recognize the possibility of not being able to adapt (Lazarus, 1966). This assumes that adaptation is important to the person.

Finally, we should note that McGrath (1970) also recognized the fact that one can be faced with two different kinds of imbalance: overload and underload. Overload is what we usually think of when we think about stress—the demand is too great for us to respond. However, underload can also cause an imbalance, and thus can be threatening. Figure 7-2 depicts this relationship.

More recent formulations of stress by authors such as Beehr and Bhagat (1985) and Sethi and Schuler (1984) include most of these ideas plus some new ones. For example, Beehr and Bhagat (1985) emphasize that it is the *uncertainty* of being able to cope combined with the *duration* of the demand and the *importance* of the issue that results in stress. They also point out that the crucial issue in determining both underload and overload is the *person-*

FIGURE 7-2
Both very high
(overload) and very
low (underload)
stressor levels can
lead to negative
consequences.

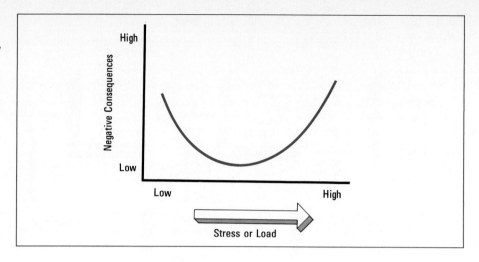

environment fit. This fit might include the match between the person's needs and the rewards available. It could also entail the fit between the demands of the job and the skills and abilities of the employee (French, Caplan, & Harrison, 1982). Over the long run, mismatches in important areas result in strain and stress and eventually have debilitating consequences.

A Definition of Stress

As can be seen from the preceding review, stress is a complex construct. In order to capture the richness of this construct, we describe stress using the following main points:

1. Stress is multifaceted. There are multiple causes of multiple psychological and physiological states, and there are multiple outcomes. Thus, we will try to understand stress by examining its component parts (demands, reactions, and consequences).

2. Stress involves both physiological and psychological states. However, the causal link between these two can go both ways. That is, psychological states can both cause and be caused by physiological states (e.g., anxiety can cause headaches; ulcers can cause depression).

3. The stress process is one that evolves and develops over time. There are both short-term and long-term events that take place in the environment, and there are both short-term and long-term reactions to these events. Most people agree that it is only when strain states occur (i.e., long-term reactions) that the debilitating effects of stress begin to appear.

4. This conceptualization of the stress process allows us to look at the different forms of relationships that exist between environmental (external) variables, short-term states, strain states, and consequences. There are essentially two phases in the process: (1) an environment-stress (i.e., short-term states and strain states) phase, and (2) a stress-consequence phase.

There are numerous ways in which stress has been measured. McGrath (1970) presents a long list of measures and the research that used them. Figure 7-3 summarizes the major categories used to classify these measures. In a later section of this chapter we discuss a whole array of causes of stress, and in another section, peoples' *reactions* to these stressors. In both of these sections we present examples of measures that are currently being used to assess physiological, psychological, and behavioral indicators of stress.

One final point about the measurement of stress concerns the context in which the research has gone on. Studies have been done in both field and laboratory settings. In real-world settings, there have been studies of people in combat, military training, extreme environmental conditions, isolation, natural disasters, custody or internment, evaluative (appraisal) contexts, and impoverished social conditions (e.g., poverty, slum background). Studies in the laboratory have involved physical stressors (shock, injections, threat of pain, drugs, deprivation, distraction, and restricted environments), social-psychological stressors (evaluation, failure, negative reinforcement, conflict, and ambiguity), and task stressors (involving high risk, complexity, time pressure, speed demands, or work that is dull or repetitive).

The wide variety of research approaches that have been taken point out not

---

Physiological Measures

Self reports: e.g., personality tests or checklists asking about somatic symptoms such as lack of sleep, diarrhea

Observations: e.g., signs of perspiration or measurement of physiological processes such as galvanic skin response, blood pressure, and pulse rate

Chemical traces: e.g., epinephrine, corticosteroids, serotonin, acetylcholine, or dopamine found in one's urine, saliva, and blood

Records: e.g., medical records of physical ailments and symptoms such as ulcers or cancer

Psychological Measures

Self reports: e.g., personality tests or checklists assessing psychological symptoms such as anxiety and fear

Observations of psychological upset: e.g., disorientation, anger, or stuttering

Projective tests: e.g., the Rorschach or TAT, in which people react to inkblots or write stories about pictures

Records: e.g., psychiatric records indicating neurotic or psychotic symptoms

Behavior Measures

Self reports: e.g., questionnaires and interviews about performance, satisfaction, uncertainty, conflict, and ambiguity

Observations: e.g., of the quality, quantity, and speed of success or performance, as well as activities such as communication

Records: e.g., of absenteeism and tardiness, and performance evaluations

FIGURE 7-3
Measures of stress.

only that there are numerous ways to induce stress, but also that the complex approach to the problem we suggested previously probably makes the most sense. While there are some general categories of stressors, reactions, and consequences, we cannot limit stress to any simple definition that fits all people and all contexts. We turn now to a review of major stressors people encounter on the job.

ENVIRONMENTAL AND INTERPERSONAL STRESSORS

The list of potential and actual stressors is quite extensive. In an attempt to organize the literature on this topic, we have categorized stressors in some fairly arbitrary ways, starting with a review of the factors related to one's specific job and progressing to a broader perspective that looks at the whole organization as well as one's life outside the organization.

Task Stressors

Hackman (1970) reviewed the important factors about one's job that induce stress. He differentiated between information-related items (e.g., information, expectations, ambiguity, uncertainty) and other aspects of the task. We cover the former items in the next section under the heading "Role Factors." The other aspects of the task mentioned by Hackman include:

1. *Issues dealing with time.* Are requirements sequenced appropriately, and is enough time allocated to do each part of a task well? Both the rate of presentation and the required rate of response are important.
2. *Properties of the task stimulus.* How much complexity and ambiguity is there *inherent* in the task itself? Are there multiple ways to accomplish the job? Are there multiple solutions?
3. *Danger.* Is the task potentially dangerous or threatening psychologically or physically? Can one get hurt on the job? How physically demanding is the job?

Hackman's (1970) review of the literature indicates that both extremes of the first two dimensions are causes of stress. That is, extremely high or low time demands and extremely high or low task complexity have been shown to cause stress. However, while extremely high levels of threat or danger do cause stress, extremely low levels do not.

A more recent review by Shaw and Riskind (1983) examined a whole series of studies that looked at job characteristics and both psychological and physiological measures of stress. Their review confirmed a number of the propositions suggested previously by Hackman (1970). For example, using health data as criteria (e.g., hypertension, ulcers, cirrhosis, suicides, accidents, and health visits), the major predictors of stress were (1) *low* levels of processing information, (2) performance of manual labor, (3) being in an unpleasant physical environment, (4) *low* levels of decision making, and (5) hazardous job situations.

Another recent study dealt with the timing of job demand. Eden (1982) investigated the stress induced by critical job events (CJE). He defined a CJE as "a time bounded peak of performance demand made on the individual as an integral part of his job" (p. 315). In his study he measured a variety of psychological and physiological indices of stress before, during, and after two CJEs for nursing students (their first patient-care assignment and their comprehensive exam). The results showed a consistent pattern of rising and falling anxiety, systolic blood pressure, pulse rate, and serum uric acid.

Finally, one of the most frequently studied time-related variables is shift work. A recent review of the literature (Hood & Milazzo, 1984) shows that the major negative effects of shift work are fatigue, gastritis, and the use of alcohol, tobacco, caffeine, and other drugs. Shift work also seems to be disruptive of family and social relations when the employee has no control over the shift schedule. On the plus side, in many jobs shift work is less hectic than other types of work, and the employee often has more autonomy and better relations with coworkers. Thus, while there are some negative aspects of shift work, there are some positive ones as well.

Role Factors

We discuss the concepts of role ambiguity, role overload, and role conflict in greater detail in a later chapter. Here we wish only to point out how these variables are related to stress. A working definition of a *role* is that it is a set of expectations that others have with respect to a particular job or position. Roles are impersonal and aggregated (made up of the expectations of numerous others). When these expectations are unclear, *role ambiguity* exists. A typical statement expressing role ambiguity is, "I don't know exactly what my boss expects of me." When expectations are too numerous, *role overload* exists. A statement expressing role overload is, "I simply have more work to do than can possibly be done in an ordinary day." Finally, when the expectations of others are in disagreement, we have *role conflict*. A statement expressing role conflict is, "I get caught in the middle between my supervisors and my subordinates."

These three role problems have been shown to be consistent predictors of both psychological and physiological stress. They have been linked to heart disease, high blood pressure, elevated cholesterol, obesity, tension, job dissatisfaction, depression, and anxiety (Ivancevich & Matteson, 1980; Cooke & Rousseau, 1984).

Interpersonal Relations

How we get along with our coworkers also seems to be a major factor in producing stress. For example, French and Caplan (1973) demonstrated that low trust, low support, low interest and large power differences often cause stress. Steiner (1970) reports a study demonstrating that disagreements and conflict are producers of stress. Thus, getting along well with others seems to be an important way to reduce stress.

Career Issues

There appear to be certain times or events in one's career when stress can become particularly acute. For example, when one reaches a certain level in an organization, one often becomes responsible for the work of others (e.g., when one becomes a supervisor or manager). French and Caplan (1973) found that responsibility for people in clerical, managerial, and technical/professional positions produces heavier smoking, higher blood pressure, and elevated cholesterol.

Also important in career development is the so-called midlife crisis. There is a time when employees must reconcile their actual success with their expected success. Such a situation often results in stress (Blau, 1978), as does changing careers in midlife.

Finally, there is considerable evidence that not being "on track," that is, not getting promotions when expected, or not developing or learning as much as one had hoped, can also be a significant cause of stress (Ivancevich & Matteson, 1980).

Group Process

Some of the variables related to group process have already been discussed. For example, unclear expectations and interpersonal conflict can both lead to stress. Two other variables that should be mentioned are group cohesiveness and intergroup conflict.

Group cohesiveness refers to the extent to which group members like one another and are attracted to the group. When cohesiveness is low, there is often low morale, less communication, more conflict, feelings of isolation, and role ambiguity. Many of these variables are in turn related to stress.

Intergroup conflict can also create stress. To the extent that groups compete for scarce resources or disagree about how things should be done, there is usually tension, competition, and political activity. These activities can be

The Workaholic Boss: An 18-Hour-a-Day Menace

The biggest problem with trying to manage stress in organizations is that we try to do just that, manage it, instead of getting rid of the people who are causing all the stress in the first place. It really is pointless to recommend relaxation response periods, deep breathing exercises and other "stress-reduction" techniques when the carriers of the malady are breathing fire just around the corner.

I'm talking about the so called workaholic manager—a contradiction in terms, because if you're a workaholic, you can't be a manager. A workaholic placed in a management position, and that's usually where he ends up, is one of the most divisive forces roaming the corridors of the industrialized world.

Just think about the contradictions involved. Where a manager must set priorities, the workaholic must do everything. (This also occurs on a temporary basis for start-up entrepreneurs. Within a short time, they usually learn to do only what is important.)

A manager must be patient in gaining the commitment of others, in order to multiply his efforts. The workaholic has little or no patience with others and works unending hours to make up for their perceived lack of commitment. This creates the self-fulfilling prophecy of only being able to rely on his own work.

Where a manager negotiates objectives and time frames for accomplishment, the workaholic sets arbitrary deadlines and then applies follow-up pressure to assure compliance. He often is rewarded with malevolent obedience, usually with shoddy results.

I wish the following example were not true. While attending a three-day management meeting at a resort hotel, a junior staff member approached his boss during an after-dinner cocktail party. His objetive was to see if he could ride back on the plane with the boss on the following day and discuss his next six-months support plans. Repeated previous attempts to get a meeting date had failed. The ever cheerful high-energy boss said that he already had an in-flight meeting scheduled but, "No problem, let's step into the next room and go over the plans right now." And so at 12:45 a.m. the subordinate did his best to make an orderly presentation of the plans and objectives of his department for the next six months.

Any manager who behaves like that is an "18-hour-a-day-menace," who carries stress wherever he goes.

He arrives early and leaves late. He sends a message that this is the standard of behavior expected. Since most people can't follow his leadership, he breeds resentment and antagonism.

The lunch at the desk and scheduling of every working hour further cut off conversation, commitment and contributions of others.

There is no doubt, of course, that companies need dedicated employees who put in long hours and love attention to detail. It just has to be remembered that this is not necessarily the type of person you want to be in charge of gaining the quality commitment of others. The biggest, strongest worker has not historically made the best foreman, even though that was often the promotion policy.

How about finding some nice staff projects for your workaholics, so they can immerse themselves in the incredible detail they love?

Direct their high energy levels to tasks, not the management of people.

Just stop and think about all the workaholic "war stories" you have heard. Think about the running through airports, about the two meetings going on at once, about the lines waiting outside of "executive" offices trying to get on the schedule, about the blizzard of phone messages generated around these so-called managers. Many organizations and people are resilient enough to succeed in spite of this type of direction. But survival should not be the standard of performance.

So do what you can to reduce the stress level in your organization to reasonable operational levels. Do it by keeping the workaholic out of the management function. Control and concentrate energy into the most compact and narrow areas possible in order to do the most important things best and to reward the best people with the business leadership they deserve. Come and go at reasonable hours. Families all throughout your organization will be forever grateful. Don't confuse high energy levels with the brainpower necessary to produce results.

If you are a manager think about your effect on others. They are the ones who must produce the results that you are judged on. Are you a workaholic in a management position? Are you reading this at 5:30 a.m. or midnight? Have two or three people sent you this article? Have 10 people sent it to you?

Source: J. Falvey. (1982, May 10). Manager's journal. *The Wall Street Journal.* Reprinted by permission.

distracting, time-consuming, and emotionally involving. And again, they often result in stress.

Organizational Characteristics

There has been less research on this topic than on other causes of stress. Ivancevich and Matteson (1980) suggest that an organization's climate may be a cause of stress, as may some structural variables. For example, Ivancevich and Donnelley (1975) demonstrated that a flat organizational structure results in less stress and higher satisfaction for sales persons than a tall organizational structure.

Physical Environment

There are clearly some physical factors in the environment that cause stress. The amount of light, noise, and temperature can all be related to psychological and physiological measures of stress. Air pollution is also known to be a potential hazard, and various occupations (e.g., mining, pulp and paper making, chemical manufacturing) potentially expose people to airborne chemical pollutants that can cause both stress and illness. It is also true that working with new technologies such as computer consoles can sometimes have deleterious effects on individuals (remember our telephone operator). Brod (1984) suggests that boring data-entry jobs and the use of video display terminals can cause stress, and Forslund (1981) reports that compared to clerical workers, phone operators have more emotional problems, drink more alcohol, are more depressed, and use more drugs.

Occupation

A number of studies have compared occupations in terms of their stress levels. For example, Colligan, Smith, and Hurrell (1977) looked at mental health admissions for 130 occupations. Among the high-stress jobs they identified were secretary, office manager, laborer, and waiter and waitress. Among the low-stress jobs were package wrapper, freight handler, and university professor. Other studies have shown that air traffic controllers have high stress, as do lawyers, physicians, and insurance agents.

The problem with this type of data, of course, is that occupations really represent groupings of jobs. Thus, while there may be average differences in stress levels for different occupations, there is probably a lot of variance within an occupation. A university professor teaching at a small Midwestern private liberal arts college is likely to have a very different type of job from a professor at a large Eastern state university, who in turn has a different job from a professor teaching at an urban junior college. So, while the occupational data are helpful in terms of the "big picture," they are not as helpful in making predictions for specific jobs.

Nonwork Factors

Stress is not caused simply by work-related factors. Much of our stress comes from our life outside our job, and yet the two can combine and influence each other. For example, shift work can influence family relations, and family problems can influence attentiveness and satisfaction at work.

Probably the best known measure of general life stress was developed by Holmes and Rahe (1967), and is called *the social readjustment rating scale*. These researchers developed a list of forty-three life events and ordered them in terms of their level of severity (mostly based on the amount of *change* required to cope with the event). Each event is assigned a value from 10 to 100. One simply checks off which things have happened during the previous year, and then adds up the score. The death of a spouse is given 100 points, while divorce is worth 73, separation 65, major illness 53, being fired 47, retirement 45, pregnancy 40, entering a new line of work 36, promotion 29, in-law troubles 29, moving 20, vacation 13, traffic ticket 11, and so on. Note that some of these events are positive and some are negative, and that some involve work while others do not. Holmes and Rahe (1967) suggest that a score of 150 to 300 implies about a 50 percent chance of a major health breakdown in the next 2 years. A score of 300 raises the odds to 80 percent.

Since the original publication of the social readjustment rating scale, a great deal more research has been done on it. There is now some evidence that negative life events carry more weight than positive ones, and that uncontrollable events (remember uncertainty) are more important than controllable ones (e.g., Stern, McCants, & Pettine, 1982). Nonetheless, this measure has been consistently shown to be a good predictor of stress.

But note that the focus of this measure is on *major life events* that cause *change*. Lazarus and his colleagues (Lazarus, DeLongis, Folkman, & Gruen, 1985) have suggested a quite different approach. They use what is called the hassles scale to assess ongoing daily hassles as opposed to major life changes. They measure hassles in eight categories: (1) household (e.g., preparing meals), (2) health (e.g., taking medication), (3) time pressure (e.g., too many things to do), (4) inner concerns (e.g., loneliness), (5) environment (e.g., noise), (6) finances (e.g., debts), (7) work (e.g., dissatisfaction), and (8) future security (e.g., retirement). These are ongoing worries and not necessarily issues of major life change.

Using this measure, Lazarus et al. (1985) found that these hassles are significantly related to indices of psychological symptoms and dysfunction. The results from two separate analyses are presented in Figure 7-5. These authors argue that their hassles scale is more strongly related to stress symptoms than are measures of major life changes. However, the implications of both research streams are clear: Daily hassles *and* major life events are significantly related to stress. Stress at work and at home is measured in both scales, and they seem to be related to one another.

PERSONAL AND SITUATIONAL MODERATORS

As we mentioned in our discussion of Figure 7-1, some people more readily perceive and react to the external environment than others, and some are better able to cope with the same objective stressors than others. A number of personal characteristics and situational variables have been shown to predict

FIGURE 7-5
Daily hassles and
psychological
symptoms. (*Based
on data presented
by Lazarus et al.,
1985.*)

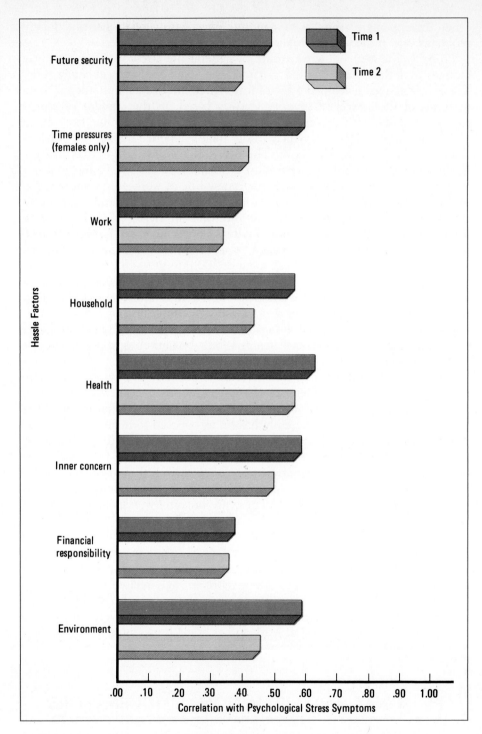

who is most likely to experience stress and who is not. A brief review of these characteristics is given below (Rosenzweig, 1985).

Type A and Type B Behaviors

We discussed this variable at some length in our review of personality in Chapter 4. People with a Type A behavior pattern tend to be competitive, hard driving, aggressive, impatient with people and situations that hinder accomplishments, achievement oriented, and continually under time pressure (Friedman & Rosenman, 1974). They often react to stressors with hostility and anger. Type A people also seem to be the major sufferers of the prolonged effects of stress—heart disease, alcoholism, and other medical and behavioral problems (Diamond, 1982).

Type B individuals tend to respond differently to stress. They are more relaxed and are not as easily irritated. However, this does not mean they are necessarily apathetic, lazy, or lacking in ambition (although Type A individuals may see them this way). The Type B person seems to have natural or learned immunities to the impact of stressors, just as some people have immunities to bacterial invaders. Although substantial evidence indicates that Type A individuals are much more likely to suffer heart attacks than those classified as Type B, recent results suggest that Type A heart attack victims can be trained to change their behavior enough to reduce significantly the probability of a second attack (Matthews, 1982).

Hot Reactors

Another way to distinguish individual responses to stressors, suggested by Eliot and Breo (1984), focuses on physiological processes rather than behavior patterns:

> Our basic hypothesis is that "hot reacting"—extreme cardiovascular reactions to standardized stress tests—indicates how people handle stress physiologically in everyday life. Some people experience alarm and vigilance so strongly that when they are under stress their bodies produce large amounts of stress chemicals, which in turn cause great changes in the cardiovascular system, including remarkable rises in blood pressure (p. 38).

These researchers indicate that about 20 percent of healthy people who feel stressed are hot reactors. The frightening aspect of this finding is that people are not aware of their automatic physiological responses to stress. Type A behavior is observable and potentially changeable. Hot reacting may be a subtle, silent killer.

Because Type B people do have coronary heart disease and heart attacks, it seems reasonable to suppose that some Type B individuals may be hot reactors and some Type A people may not be. The obvious high-risk condition is a combination of a Type A behavior pattern and a hot-reacting physiology. It should also be noted that blood pressure can increase for two reasons: (1) the heart increases the output of blood (the fight-or-flight response), and (2) the blood vessels severely constrict when under stress (alarm or vigilance). Thus, the ultimate in risk is a Type A person who is a *combination* hot reactor, that is, he or she pumps more blood against more resistance. Such people go through life behaving like "drag racers with their brakes on" (Eliot & Breo, 1984).

Hardiness

A third approach to understanding individual differences focuses on hardiness—psychological characteristics that buffer the reactions of people to potentially stressful conditions or events (Maddi & Kobasa, 1984). Stress-resistant people have the following psychological strengths (Pines, 1984):

1. *Challenge.* They are open to change and welcome it as a challenge rather than a threat.
2. *Commitment.* They get deeply involved in whatever they are doing, finding it interesting and important—the opposite of alienation.
3. *Control.* They have a sense of control over events.

In a long-term study of Illinois Bell executives during the breakup of AT&T, it was found that those who rated high on hardiness remained healthier than others. All of the employees experienced essentially the same traumatic events during the changeover from a heavily regulated business environment to a competitive industry. There were many changes and day-to-day uncertainties for everyone. Those who rated high in psychological hardiness seemed to take the breakup in stride, and even felt exhilarated by the opportunities. They reported half as many physical or mental difficulties as those who rated low in hardiness. The latter group had many more problems. "Their symptoms—which could be the precursors of illness—included high blood pressure, obesity, insomnia, inability to concentrate, impaired sexual performance, irritability, suspicion of others, and the obsessive need to go over their work because they were worried about it" (Pines, 1984, p. 40).

The hardiness scores were also combined with measures of the Type A and Type B behavior patterns. "The executives who became the sickest were those who were high in Type A behavior and low in hardiness" (Pines, 1984, p. 41). On the other hand, hardiness served to ameliorate the negative consequences of being a Type A person in a stressful situation. Coping ability seemed to be enhanced by drive and persistence. Preliminary evidence seems to indicate that hardiness can be increased to some degree by making people aware of the importance of attitudes, and by teaching them how to reconstruct situations mentally.

Cognitive Complexity

This is another variable we touched on in Chapter 4. It has to do with the amount and kinds of information people use in making decisions. Cognitively complex individuals are multidimensional. They see situations from different perspectives simultaneously. They are able to keep several variables in mind, cope with conflicting information, and discern complex relationships. They think in terms of systems and contingencies, while remaining flexible and sensitive to changing conditions. These characteristics are often used to describe highly effective managers. Unfortunately, these attributes may be dangerous to executive health. As Streufert reports:

The startling news is that a person's very competence may lead to illness. There is a growing amount of evidence that an executive with this style of decision making faces a greater risk than others of heart attacks and other circulatory diseases. When compared with less-multidimensional executives, the [more-] multidimensionals show higher levels of physiological strain when challenged in work situations. For example, in our laboratory we measured blood pressure, heart rate, and other physiological indices of strain while representative samples of two groups made decisions on typical management problems in competition with one another. On average, the more-multidimensional executive had elevations in blood pressure, heart rate, and physiological arousal that were at times 83 percent higher than the increases for other executives (1983, p. 8).

Additional supporting evidence was obtained by comparing matched samples from the general population. Heart attack victims rated much higher on multidimensionality than did others.

Social Support

Several studies have shown that social support is an important moderator of people's reactions to stressors. For example, Cobb (1976) found that social support obtained from supervisors, coworkers, friends, and relatives could alleviate a number of psychological distress symptoms such as depression, anxiety, and dissatisfaction. One study found that men who lost their jobs had an increased incidence of physical and mental ill health in comparison with employees who continued working, but that anxiety and depression were higher only in the laid-off men who had less than average social support. Another study of 100 men who lost their jobs after a permanent plant shutdown found that employees who were well supported socially had significantly less physical and mental ill health than those who lacked social support. Incidentally, it was found that rural subjects had more social support than urban subjects ("Research on Stress," 1981).

In yet another study of men affected by a plant closure, it was found that plasma cholesterol and urate levels increased, but only in those with low social support (Caplan, Cobb, French, Harrison, & Pinneau 1975). The same authors reported that escapist drinking may increase from stress, but only in those with inadequate social support, and that men with high social support from others in the work environment show less physiological response to stressors in terms of serum cortisol and glucose, blood pressure, number of cigarettes smoked, and the rate of quitting smoking. Finally, marital status has been found in a number of studies to correlate with incidence of various stress-related diseases, as well as mortality rate, and this has been hypothesized to be related to differential social support. However, how marital status relates more specifically to occupational stress has not been as well studied. One investigation found that in married couples in which the husbands were employed as engineers or accountants, a measure of husband-wife compatibility correlated with measures of stress management (Burke, Firth, & McGrattan, 1974).

Control

A final variable of importance is the amount of control the person feels he or she has over the stressor. In general, the more perceived control one has, the lower the impact of the stressor. For example, Pittner, Houston, and Spiridigliozzi (1983) demonstrated that when faced with uncontrollable electric shock, Type A subjects had greater pulse rates and higher blood pressure than Type B subjects. Thus, being a Type A, hot-reacting person, with high complexity, low hardiness, and low social support, would seem to make an individual more susceptible to stress, especially when he or she has little control over the stressor.

REACTIONS TO STRESSORS

At this point we have defined stress and listed the major stressors identified by current research. We have also suggested some of the psychological and physiological ways in which people react to stress. In this section we describe more specifically the physiological reaction that seems to occur and the related psychological states. We also suggest the reasons these variables result in the consequences we have described. At the end of this section we present a comprehensive model that summarizes most of what has been said so far.

The Chemistry of Stress

Over the last 20 years researchers have discovered that stress clearly results in chemical changes in the brain. Figure 7-6 describes this process. Particularly sensitive to emotional strains are the *neurotransmitters*, which act as messengers between nerve cells. The most frequently studied neurotransmitters have been serotonin, epinephrine (previously called adrenaline), norepinephrine, acetylcholine, and dopamine. Prolonged stress seems to reduce epinephrine and norepinephrine levels, while acute stress often results in an initial increase in epinephrine and morphine-like chemicals (the body's natural pain killers) called *endorphins* ("Stress," 1983).

Scientists at the Salk Institute have synthesized the remarkable chemical that triggers the body's stress reactions, called the *corticotropin releasing factor* (CRF). This chemical is produced by the hypothalamus. Knowledge of the chemical properties of CRF may help scientists to discover a way to block the body's reaction to stress.

These physiological changes are related to other physiological indicators such as the electroencephalogram (EEG), which is a recording of brain waves, heart and pulse rates, blood pressure, body temperature, and the presence of sugar, carbon dioxide, and corticosteroids in the blood. Many of these chemicals are related to high blood pressure, coronary heart disease, gastric distress, and immunological dysfunction leading to infections, asthma, some cancers, and various somatic pain syndromes such as chronic headaches and low back pain.

In the psychological realm, these processes result in depression, anxiety disorders, and perhaps schizophrenia, as well as behavioral consequences such as smoking, alcohol and substance abuse, and accident proneness.

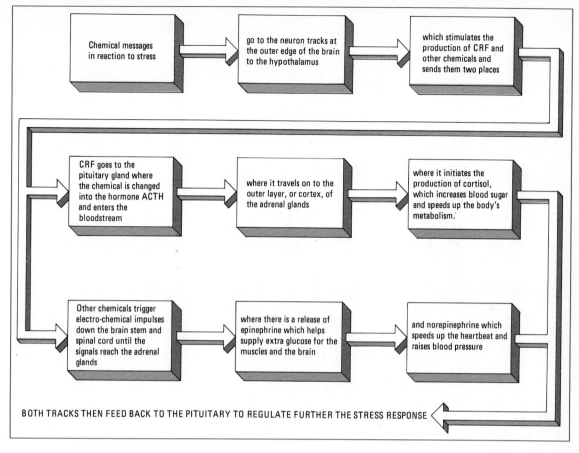

Chemical messages in reaction to stress → go to the neuron tracks at the outer edge of the brain to the hypothalamus → which stimulates the production of CRF and other chemicals and sends them two places

CRF goes to the pituitary gland where the chemical is changed into the hormone ACTH and enters the bloodstream → where it travels on to the outer layer, or cortex, of the adrenal glands → where it initiates the production of cortisol, which increases blood sugar and speeds up the body's metabolism.

Other chemicals trigger electro-chemical impulses down the brain stem and spinal cord until the signals reach the adrenal glands → where there is a release of epinephrine which helps supply extra glucose for the muscles and the brain → and norepinephrine which speeds up the heartbeat and raises blood pressure

BOTH TRACKS THEN FEED BACK TO THE PITUITARY TO REGULATE FURTHER THE STRESS RESPONSE ←

FIGURE 7-6
Physiological reactions to stress.

An Overall Summary of Stress

All of the preceding leads us to the comprehensive model presented in Figure 7-7. Here, our list of stressors is divided into three main categories: organizational, working conditions, and life conditions. These stressors are related over time to short-term and long-term psychological and physiological states. These states have both organizational and individual consequences, and all of these relationships are moderated by individual difference variables. Clearly, this is a complex process. However, it is important to recognize that while we do know a lot about stress, we still have a lot more to learn.

THE MANAGEMENT OF STRESS

We have documented quite thoroughly what stress is, what causes it, and how in the long run it may have negative consequences for both the individual and the organization. The important question at this juncture is, what can be done about it? That is, what can an organization do to reduce the problem?

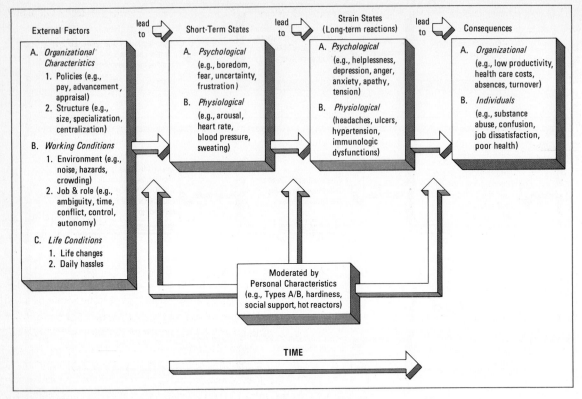

FIGURE 7-7
An overall model
of stress.

Recognizing Stress

First, managers should be well informed about what to look for. There are both individual and organizational indicators of stress. At the individual level we would expect to see:

1. *More "nervousness."* The employee may seem distracted or have difficulty concentrating. The manager may notice this in conversations, in written documents, or simply by observing the person at work.
2. *An increased rate of tardiness or absenteeism.* The employee may be late to work more than usual, miss appointments, or miss deadlines.
3. *Interpersonal difficulties.* There may be more conflict, more arguments, and lack of collaboration or cooperation.
4. *Decrease in performance.* There may be more careless mistakes, such as forgetting various steps to be done or people to be contacted, or the person may reveal an inability to make decisions.
5. *Evidence of substance abuse.* The person may be smoking more, drinking more coffee, or taking longer lunches and smell of alcohol.

We should emphasize that the manager should be looking for a *pattern* of behavior. That is, just one symptom may not be indicative of any long-term or serious problem. But continual difficulties in a number of areas may indicate a more pervasive and potentially damaging stress reaction.

At the organizational level, many of the variables are the same. One simply looks at broader indicators:

1. Absenteeism, tardiness, and turnover may be high in particular units.
2. Job accidents or violations of safety regulations may indicate that people are both pressured and distracted.
3. Performance in general may fall off. Both quantity and quality should be monitored.
4. Other indicators may appear as hostile actions. There may be increases in grievances, theft, and sabotage.

Again, some of these problems when occurring in isolation may not be due to stress. However, if a long-term pattern begins to emerge, stress may be a likely cause of at least part of the problem. The next three sections discuss some ways to cope with on-the-job stress. One approach is to treat the symptoms, a second is to change the person, and a third is to remove the stressor.

Treating the Symptoms

There are three main strategies for dealing with stress symptoms. The first is through the direct use of *medication*. High blood pressure can be reduced through the use of medication, as can anxiety. Sleep problems and depression can also be treated chemically. As mentioned previously, tranquilizers, along with blood pressure and ulcer medicines, are three of the most frequently prescribed medications in this country.

A second and slightly different way of dealing with the symptoms of stress is through *behavior therapy*. Behaviorists look at a symptom (e.g., tardiness) and work on ways to decrease its rate through reinforcement schedules. In some cases these reinforcement schedules are self-imposed, while under other circumstances they are organizationally imposed. Such techniques have been applied successfully for a variety of problems such as anxiety, depression, social skill difficulties, alcoholism, obesity, smoking, and absenteeism.

Finally, there are several *physical* ways to deal with stress symptoms that involve neither therapy nor drugs. Some people find massage to be relaxing, while others use a hot tub, jacuzzi, or sauna. The important point to recognize about the "treating the symptom" approach is that the cause of the problem is not removed, and the person is not changed in any fundamental way.

Changing the Person

A second broad class of stress management techniques involves teaching the person new skills and abilities to help him or her respond differently to stressors. There are now numerous techniques available that are designed to help people change either the way they think about a stressor or the way they react to it. Most of these techniques are designed to change people's physiological reactions to stressors, and some have become very popular.

Biofeedback. Biofeedback involves the use of medical technology to help individuals to monitor and eventually control their physiological processes. Muscle tension, skin surface temperature, blood pressure, and heart rate can all be brought under voluntary control using this method. For example, in order to learn how to control muscle tension better, an employee might be given biofeedback therapy involving the use of an electromyograph (EMG), a machine that measures muscle tension and relaxation. The person can observe the objective changes in muscle tension, and can work to eliminate thoughts or feelings that produce tension and promote those that produce relaxation (Fuller, 1978). Tension headaches and lower back pain are two symptoms that can often be helped through this process.

Relaxation Training. There are a variety of techniques that are designed to help people relax and cope with stress that do not involve technology. Yoga and other forms of meditation involve concentrating on a single word, object, phrase, or idea while seated in a comfortable position. This technique is often combined with various deep breathing exercises that slow down the heart and help one to relax. The underlying idea is that you cannot be tense and relaxed at the same time.

Research using these approaches has shown some promise. For example, Roskies, Spevack, Sukis, Cohen, and Gilman (1978) demonstrated that relaxation training significantly reduced the cholesterol and blood pressure of twelve professionals and executives classified as Type A. These results are important because they were not confounded by changes in diet or exercise.

Other relaxation techniques focus on cognitive processes. Again, the key idea is that your emotions are caused largely by your thoughts. Some therapists suggest visualization techniques (e.g., imagine you are on the beach in the sun) or cognitive restructuring. The latter involves changing what you *think* when you are asked to "do just one more thing before you go home." One analyzes one's spontaneous thoughts (e.g., "I can't do this . . . I don't have time . . . It has to be done") and replaces them with new and less stressful thoughts (e.g., "Everything will get done . . . there are other things that are more important . . . I can say 'no' and nothing terrible will happen").

Interpersonal Strategies. These techniques focus on interpersonal problems. Team building, sensitivity training, and assertiveness training are all designed to help people cope with interpersonal difficulties. Some of these strategies are discussed more fully in Chapter 17, "Change in Organizations."

The other important factor that can help is social support. One can actively increase one's "network" of friends. Having people to talk to helps. By sharing and talking about problems we often find that (1) others have them too—we are not alone, (2) the problems do not seem so bad after all, and (3) people often have good ideas about how to deal with them.

Physical Changes. The last set of factors that the person can change has to do with physical changes. People can reduce their weight, exercise, get more sleep, and generally increase their physical well-being. "Many physicians believe that the single most important indicator of health is cardiovascular endurance, and that is what regular exercise can develop, particularly activities such as jogging, bicycling and swimming" (Ivancevich & Matteson, 1980, p. 220). Ismail and Trachtman (1973) suggest that regular exercise increases blood circulation to the brain and increases the availability of glucose, which results in better oxygen utilization and improved mental functioning.

So, there are lots of things that an individual can do to help reduce his or her reaction to stressors. An important factor that we have not addressed, however, is what an organization can do to help reduce stress in the workplace. It is this question to which we turn next.

Organizational Methods for Reducing Stress

Brief, Schuler, and Van Sell (1981) document in some detail six main ways in which the organization can be involved in the management of stress.

Structure. Variables related to organizational structure that appear important for stress management are centralization (e.g., the amount of participation in decision making), formal policies for performance evaluation, review, transfer, and promotion (e.g., frequency, who does it, evaluation versus development focus), and methods and directions of communications (e.g., directives versus discussions, open-door policies). In general, the more participation, the more one is likely to be satisfied with one's job. (The participation literature will be reviewed in Chapter 12, "Group Decision Making.") Also, clear and honest communications about how one is to be evaluated, one's chances for promotion, and how job assignments are made seem to reduce stress. In general, such strategies reduce ambiguity and uncertainty while increasing the person's sense of satisfaction and involvement.

Roles. As we mentioned, role overload, role ambiguity, and role conflict are major stress producers. In order to correct these problems, individuals can meet in groups to discuss their expectations for particular jobs. At such a meeting, people can say (1) what they think is expected of them, (2) what they expect of others, and (3) what they think others think that they expect of them. Exchanging such information, coupled with an action plan, can significantly reduce role problems.

Interpersonal Relationships. Probably the three biggest problems in interpersonal relationships in organizations are differences in goals, poor communication, and interpersonal insensitivity. The first two are fairly easy to work on. Management systems can be used to clarify and specify goals—when goals seem to be in conflict, the organization can make changes. Poor communication can be dealt with through various training programs. Especially important is contingent reward communication—giving people strokes when they deserve them (Schuler, 1976). Helping groups to be more cohesive and have less conflict often involves training as well. However, selecting the right people in the first place is also important.

Change. Since stress is often related to organizational or personal change (remember the social readjustment rating scale), one important way the organization can help manage stress is through its handling of the change process. Takeovers, reorganizations, and the introduction of new control systems, new regulations, and even new managers are all potentially stressful events. A number of factors can help to reduce the stressfulness of these events. First, open and frank discussion beforehand helps people to understand *and* contribute to the change process. Second, when change is occurring, management should keep lines of communication open, solicit input, be sensitive to complaints, keep track of peoples' reactions, and generally monitor the change. Finally, once the new changes are in place, communication, organization structure, and personnel practices should all be set up to reinforce and support the new system (Hackman & Suttle, 1977).

Job Stressors. Some jobs are stressful primarily because of the technology used or the nature of the tasks performed. In many cases it may be possible to reduce the stressfulness of the job through job redesign. We discussed job design issues in Chapter 6. For example, variety, feedback, autonomy, and a sense of meaningfulness all help to increase job satisfaction and motivation. These same factors may also be instrumental in reducing job stress.

Stress may also arise on the job because there is too little time to complete all that needs to be done. Sometimes this problem can be solved by better time management. One technique available for improving one's time management skills involves keeping a daily diary that documents what one actually does—with whom, regarding what, for how long, in what setting, and using what sort of communication. Such a diary is shown in Figure 7-8. To make use of the diary, one looks for "time robbers," such as meetings that wander off

FIGURE 7-8
Daily diary for recording time management.

DAILY DIARY FOR EACH MAJOR INCIDENT

INCIDENT: PLANNED   YES_____   NO_____   COULD BE DELEGATED: YES_____   NO_____

LOCATION		TIME	
My office	_____	Start	_____
Subordinate's office	_____	Finish	_____
Superior's office	_____	Duration	_____
Meeting room	_____	On time?	_____
Other	_____		
Proper place?	_____		

WHO INVOLVED		ACTIVITY	
Group: Composition	_____	Meeting	_____
Boss	_____	Phone	_____
Subordinate	_____	Social	_____
Other internal	_____	Reading	_____
External	_____	Writing	_____
Alone	_____	Thinking	_____
Right people there?	_____	Appropriate mode?	_____

CONTENT		FUNCTION	
Personnel	_____	Plan	_____
Public relations	_____	Organize	_____
Production	_____	Staffing	_____
Marketing	_____	Directing	_____
Accounting/finance	_____	Reporting	_____
Stay on track	_____	Budget	_____
		Complete goal?	_____

target, people who are late, too many phone calls, trivial issues that should be delegated to others, and so on. Such an analysis can be very useful in helping one to manage one's time more effectively and thereby reduce stress.

Physical Environment. Two main areas of the environment can be controlled by management. First, aversive conditions (noise, pollutants, glare, heat) need to be controlled. If that is impossible, people must be given work breaks or other ways to reduce prolonged exposure. Also included in this category are basic safety practices.

The second category is really the flip side of the first. Is it a nice place to work, is there music, is the lunch facility adequate, is there an exercise facility, are there windows and plants, is there art work on the wall? One factor mentioned by Levering, Moskowitz, and Katz (1984) in *The 100 Best Companies to Work For in America* was that the employees *liked the environment.* It was a pleasant place to work.

General Organization Strategies. Given all the preceding techniques, the choices confronting an organization are numerous. Several authors have suggested that there are multiple levels of health care management (Collins, 1982) and that different levels involve different types of programs (Kiefhaber & Goldbeck, 1984). These levels are summarized in Figure 7-9. A *disease orientation* focuses on detection and control. A more *wholistic approach* attempts to be proactive—information is given and self-help programs are available. The *systems approach* includes corporate policies to change the environment.

In summary, there are numerous individually and organizationally initiated actions that can be taken to reduce stress. Unfortunately, most stress management programs in applied settings make use of more than one technique. It is therefore often difficult to measure precisely which techniques have the most benefit. Also, since stress is composed of both physiological and psychological states that develop over time and result in a wide variety of consequences, it is often hard to track down exactly what influences what. Yet, we know a lot more about stress and stress management than we did 20 years ago, and this progress should continue.

Summary

This has been a fairly comprehensive review of a complex phenomenon—on-the-job stress. The main points are as follows:

1. Stress is widespread and costly, and results in many consequences that are harmful to the individual and the organization.
2. Stress is a reaction to a stressor. It is a relationship that reflects an imbalance between the demands on a person and his or her perceived ability to cope.
3. There are numerous symptoms of stress that can be measured. Stress shows up as changes in our physiological and psychological processes, as well as in our behavior.
4. Stress is caused by a variety of stressors. A large group of these have to do with the job (e.g., task variety, autonomy, feedback, importance) and the

FIGURE 7-9
Organization well-
ness programs.

Level	Health Care Management Strategy	Examples
Disease orientation	Detection of disease	Hypertension screening Glaucoma testing Blood testing Diabetes screening Cancer detection: Breast self-exam Periodic physical exams Weight control
	Control of disease	Hypertension control Alcohol/substance abuse

Wholistic approach	Assessment of high-risk behaviors	Computerized health risk—
		  self-administered questionnaires
		Health fairs
		Information dissemination
		  about health risks

	Risk-reduction programs	Information dissemination:
		  Seminars
		  Food/menu labeling
		Behavior modification
		Self-help manuals
		Incentives

Systems approach	Corporate policies	Smoking restrictions Flexitime Quiet rooms
	Management styles	Wellness programs Environmental facilitation of health behavior

expectations surrounding the job (role ambiguity, role overload, and role conflict).

5. Another group of stressors is interpersonal in nature. The cohesiveness of the group, the level of friendship, and conflict are all related to stress.
6. Organizational and environmental factors also influence stress. The climate in the organization as well as the physical aspects of the work setting (e.g., noise, temperature, danger, pollution) are good examples.
7. The impact of these stressors on any individual is moderated by both situational factors (e.g., social support) and personality variables (e.g., type A and B behavior patterns, hot reacting, hardiness, and cognitive complexity).
8. The chemistry of how the body reacts to what is perceived as a threat (an imbalance of demand and perceived ability to cope) is very complex and only now is beginning to be understood.
9. The ways to reduce stress can be grouped into three main categories: those that treat symptoms (e.g., drugs), those that teach the individual new skills (e.g., biofeedback, relaxation, cognitive strategies), and those that

change the work environment (e.g., reduction of danger, provision of exercise facilities).

10. Organizations are becoming more concerned about stress prevention and are likely to continue to be concerned in the future.

IMPLICATIONS FOR RESEARCH

Research on stress is incredibly difficult to conduct. First, there are a variety of ethical issues related to how the research is done. If stress only develops over the long run, and if it has such potentially damaging consequences, we certainly cannot experimentally introduce it in any systematic way. Thus, we are limited either to using animals or to studying the phenomenon as it naturally occurs. The former presents ethical problems regarding the treatment of animals, as well as questions about generalizing to humans. The latter causes problems too; when you study a phenomenon such as stress in a naturally occurring environment, it is extremely difficult to tease out what causes what.

Although the research will be difficult to do, there are clearly some areas that need further work. Substantial amounts of money are now being spent on research that links stress with the body's immune system (Maier & Laudenslanger, 1985). This research has identified certain types of white cells that can attack antigens (invader or cancerous cells), and recent studies show that some types of stress may repress the production or activity of these cells. More work is needed to clarify these relationships.

There is also a substantial amount of work to be done in classifying types of stressors, types of reactions, and types of people who are more or less susceptible to stress. This research will require large samples, will involve the gathering of massive amounts of psychological and physiological data, and will need to be done over time. It will also probably require an interdisciplinary focus. For all of these reasons it will be expensive, time-consuming, and difficult research to conduct. But it *should* be done.

Finally, at a somewhat more refined level, we need to look at some theoretical issues more closely. We need to know more about levels of stressors—when they become noxious and when they can be helpful (remember the curvilinear relationship shown in Figure 7-2). Second, we need to know more about the length of time it takes for various stressors (at high levels) to result in a stress response, and how that stress response results in psychological and physiological symptoms. And last, but not least, we must have a better idea of what sorts of treatments are most effective for different kinds of stress. This is a substantial agenda for research.

IMPLICATIONS FOR PRACTICE

There are two obvious implications of the information we have presented that are important for organizations. First, stress is pervasive, and it is a potential killer. It has become part of our everyday existence—and it seems to be getting worse. Second, organizations will clearly have to take a proactive stance to deal with the problem. We need to focus not just on how to reduce stress symptoms, but on how to reduce stressors to a level at which they no longer result in deleterious outcomes.

Some companies are already doing this. About one out of five Fortune 500 companies has started some sort of program to manage stress. Although most of these programs are for top executives, there is an increasing tendency to make the programs available for everyone. These programs range from the commonplace alcoholism program, to exercise facilities, meditation classes, and company-sponsored biofeedback training. At the Equitable Life Assurance Society in Manhattan, stressed employees participated in an in-house biofeedback program and reduced their average visits to company medical clinics from about twenty five to five per year ("Stress," 1983). The company reportedly saved $5.52 in medical costs for every dollar spent on the biofeedback program.

At New York Telephone, a program involving regular health and heart checkups, as well as meditation lessons for those with stress-related symptoms, helped to cut the corporate hypertension rate for 18 percent (near the average for the United States) to half that amount. New York Telephone estimates its savings at $130,000 in reduced absenteeism alone ("Stress," 1983).

According to Kiefhaber and Goldbeck (1984), such programs are on the rise. There are two key issues from a practical point of view that concern the organizational implementation of such programs. First, there is the question of "fit." As we mentioned in our theoretical section, stress is often the result of a misfit between the individual and the job. Organizations need to do a better job of screening and classifying people, and of analyzing jobs. The obvious hoped-for outcome is an optimal match between the work environment and the employee.

The second issue has to do with the relative costs and benefits of various health maintenance and stress-reduction programs. The issues here are more complex, in part because many of the costs to the employee are not easily measured (e.g., the psychological costs of chronic pain or a reduced quality of life). However, it is our belief that organizations should engage in these programs if not for their obvious benefit to the organization as a whole (and in the long run, they probably will be beneficial), then for the clear benefits that are likely to accrue to their employees as individuals.

Discussion Questions

1. What factors in your college or university environment would you classify as stressors? Could they be changed? How?
2. Do you know when you are under stress? How does your body react—what are the symptoms you display?
3. Have you ever tried relaxation techniques, biofeedback, or any of the other individual coping procedures? Did they help?
4. Do you believe that an organization should be concerned about the stress level of its employees? Should stress-management programs be introduced even if they are not cost-effective?

Julie woke up when Jenny's alarm went off at 6:00 A.M. She knew she didn't have to get up for a while, and she resented waking earlier than she had to. But with three teenagers and a husband needing to use the shower and have breakfast as well as herself, she knew that it was a necessity that someone get up early. The morning rush was on—get up, jog, eat, shower, dress, and get herself as well as everyone else off to work or school. It was a race from 6:00 until 8:15 when the kids left for school, and then a race to make it to work by 9:00.

Julie was usually a little late. She was a manpower analyst for the labor department, and her commute, while only 20 minutes, required crossing two bridges. If either one was up, or had just been up, she was bound to be late. Today they were both up, and she was angry. She had to meet with her subordinates at 9:30, and she wanted some time to prepare for the meeting. "Oh well, I'll just wing it," she thought.

Their main project at the moment was to evaluate the effectiveness of five new manpower training programs for minorities. The project was a disaster from the start. She had not been given enough money to do an appropriate evaluation. She had too few participants and no control group. All they could do was interview the participants and track their employment record over a 3-month period following the training.

The meeting at 9:30 highlighted some of the problems. First, a number of the participants had dropped out before completing the training. From a cost/benefit perspective, such people should be included in any analysis. However, from a scientific perspective, it is difficult to say whether a program works or not if some of the people haven't completed it. Second, some of the participants who had completed the training had left the city or could not be found for follow-up interviews. The whole morning was consumed by discussions about what to do—with little resolution. Meanwhile, the office next door was being renovated, and the noise was bothersome.

The afternoon was not much better. Her boss made it clear in an early afternoon meeting that there was substantial political pressure to do a good evaluation and have positive results. Julie told her boss about the problems discussed earlier in the day with her scientific colleagues, but her boss was adamant. "This is a big political football, and we are counting on you to carry it."

Upon returning to her office, she still had to deal with the mail and a number of phone messages that required immediate attention. Plus, she had some personal calls to make (the cleaning crew was needed before the party on Friday, the car needed to be scheduled for its 10,000-mile service, and John—her 16-year-old—needed to see the dentist). She had a headache and took two aspirin.

Before she knew it, it was 5:30 and she was back in the car; only one bridge was up on the way home. She beat her husband home, so she grabbed some frozen dinners, popped them into the microwave, and had a glass of wine. They had a quick dinner and two of the kids left immediately to visit friends. She and her husband went their separate ways as well: He had a meeting of the church council, and Julie was involved in the political campaign of a friend at work who was running for the school board.

At about 10:30 everyone arrived home and collapsed in the living room. They watched the evening news and went up to bed—exhausted. As Julie started to fall asleep, she remembered that she had forgotten to do the laundry and to pick up the food for Friday night. She got up, took a sleeping pill, and went back to bed.

Questions about the Case

1. Do you think this is a typical day? What are some of the stressors that occurred throughout the day?

2. How did Julie react to the stressors? Are there other things she could have done?
3. How could her environment have been changed to make things less stressful? What do you think will happen if she keeps working at this pace?

References

Albrecht, K. (1979). *Stress and the manager.* Englewood Cliffs, NJ: Prentice-Hall.

Beehr, T. A., & Bhagat, R. S. (1985). *Human stress and cognition in organizations.* New York: Wiley.

Blau, B. (1978, August). Understanding mid-career stress. *Management Review, 67,* 57–62.

Brief, A. P., Schuler, R. S., & Van Sell, M. (1981). *Managing job stress.* Boston: Little, Brown.

Brod, C. (1984). *Technostress: The human cost of the computer revolution.* Reading, MA: Addison-Wesley.

Burke, R. J., Firth, J., & McGrattan, C. (1974). Husband-wife compatibility and the management of stress. *Journal of Social Psychology, 94,* 243–251.

Cannon, W. B. (1935). Stresses and strains of homeostasis. *American Journal of Medical Science, 189,* 1–14.

Caplan, R. D., Cobb, S., French, J. R. P., Jr., Harrison, R. V., & Pinneau, S. R., Jr. (1975). *Job demands and worker health.* [HEW Publication No. (NIOSH) 75-160]. Washington, DC: Department of Health, Education, and Welfare.

Cobb, S. (1976). Social support as a moderator of life stress. *Psychosomatic Medicine, 38,* 300–314.

Colligan, M. J., Smith, M. J., & Hurrell, J. J. (1977). Occupational incidence rates of mental health disorders. *Journal of Human Stress, 3,* 34–39.

Collins, G. H. (1982). Managing the health of the employee. *Journal of Occupational Medicine, 24,* 15–17.

Cooke, R. A., & Rousseau, D. M. (1983). Relationship of life events and personal orientations to symptoms of stress. *Journal of Applied Psychology, 68,* 446–458.

Cooke, R. A., & Rousseau, D. M. (1984). Stress and strain from family roles and work role expectations. *Journal of Applied Psychology, 69,* 252–260.

Cooper, C. L., & Marshall, J. (1976). Occupational sources of stress: A review of the literature relating to coronary heart disease and mental health. *Journal of Occupational Psychology, 49,* 11–28.

Diamond, E. L. (1982). The role of anger and hostility in essential hypertension and coronary heart disease. *Psychological Bulletin, 92,* 410–433.

Eden, D. (1982). Critical job events, acute stress, and strain: A multiple interrupted time series. *Organizational Behavior and Human Performance, 30,* 312–319.

Eliot, S. R., & Breo, D. L. (1984). *Is it worth dying for?* New York: Bantam Books.

Forslund, S. (1981, September 30 to October 6). Dial O for tension. *The Seattle Weekly,* pp. 17–19.

French, J. R. P., Jr., & Caplan, R. D. (1973). Organizational stress and individual strain. In A. J. Marrow (Ed.), *The failure of success.* New York: AMACOM. pp. 30–66.

French, J. R. P., Jr., Caplan, R. D., & Harrison, R. V. (1982). *The mechanisms of job stress and strain.* London: Wiley.

Friedman, M., & Rosenman, R. H. (1974). *Type A behavior and your heart.* New York: Knopf.

Fuller, G. D. (1978). Current states of biofeedback in clinical practice. *American Psychologist, 33,* 39–48.

Hackman, J. R. (1970). Tasks and task performance in research on stress. In J. E.

McGrath (Ed.), *Social and psychological factors in stress.* New York: Holt, Rinehart & Winston. 202–237.

Hackman, J. R., & Suttle, J. L. (Eds.). (1977). *Improving life at work.* Santa Monica, CA: Goodyear.

Holmes, T. H., & Rahe, R. H. (1967). The social readjustment rating scale. *Journal of Psychosomatic Medicine, 11,* 213–218.

Hood, J. C., & Milazzo, N. (1984, December). Shiftwork, stress and well-being. *Personnel Administrator,* pp. 95–105.

Ismail, A. H., & Trachtman, L. E. (1973). Jogging and imagination. *Psychology Today, 6,* 79–82.

Ivancevich, J. M., & Donnelly, J. H., Jr. (1975). Relation of organizational structure to job satisfaction, anxiety-stress and performance. *Administrative Science Quarterly, 20,* 272–280.

Ivancevich, J. M., & Matteson, M. T. (1980). *Stress and Work: A managerial perspective.* Glenview, IL: Scott Foresman.

Kiefhaber, A. K., & Goldbeck, W. B. (1984). Background papers: Work site wellness. In *Proceedings of Prospect for a Healthier America: Achieving the Nation's Health Promotion Objectives.* Washington, DC: USDHHS/Public Health Service.

Lazarus, R. S. (1966). *Psychological stress and the aging process.* New York: McGraw-Hill.

Lazarus, R. S., De Longis, A., Folkman, S., & Gruen, R. (1985). Stress and adaptational outcomes. *American Psychologist, 40,* 770–779.

Levering, R., Moskowitz, M., & Katz, M. (1984). *The 100 best companies to work for in America.* Reading, MA: Addison-Wesley.

Maddi, S. R., & Kobasa, S. C. (1984). *The hardy executive: Health under stress.* Homewood, IL: Dow Jones-Irwin.

Maier, S. F., & Laudenslanger, M. (1985, August). Stress and health: Exploring the links. *Psychology Today,* pp. 44–49.

Matthews, K. A. (1982). Psychological perspectives on Type A behavior patterns. *Psychological Bulletin, 91,* 293–323.

McGrath, J. E. (1970). *Social and psychological factors in stress.* New York: Holt, Rinehart & Winston.

Moser, M. (1977, August). Hypertension: A major controllable public health problem—industry can help. *Occupational Health Nursing,* 19–26.

Pines, M. (1984, July/August). Ma Bell and the Hardy boys. *Across the Board,* pp. 37–42.

Pittner, M. S., Houston, B. K., & Spiridigliozzi, G. (1983). Control over stress, Type A behavior pattern and response to stress. *Journal of Personality and Social Psychology, 44,* 627–637.

Research on stress and human health: Report of a study. (1981). National Academy of Science. Washington, DC: National Academy Press.

Rosenzweig, J. (1985). *Technological change, stress and burnout.* (Working Paper). Seattle, WA: University of Washington.

Roskies, E., Spevack, M., Sukis, A., Cohen, C., & Gilman, S. (1978). Changing the coronary prone (Type A) behavior pattern in a nonclinical population. *Journal of Behavioral Medicine, 1,* 201–216.

Schuler, R. S. (1976). Participatory supervision and subordinate authoritarianism: A path goal theory reconciliation. *Administration Science Quarterly, 21,* 320–325.

Schuler, R. S. (1980). Definition and conceptualization of stress in organizations. *Organizational Behavior and Human Performance, 25,* 184–215.

Selye, H. (1950). *Stress.* Montreal: Acta.

Sethi, A. S., & Schuler, R. S. (1984). *Handbook of organizational stress coping strategies.* Cambridge, MA: Ballinger.

Shaw, J. B., & Riskind, J. H. (1983). Predicting job stress using data from the P.A.Q. *Journal of Applied Psychology, 68,* 253–261.

Skeat, W. W. (1958). *A concise etymological dictionary of the English language.* Oxford: Oxford Press. 1958.

Steiner, I. D. (1970). Strategies for controlling stress in interpersonal situations. In J. E. McGrath (Ed.), *Social and psychological factors in stress* (pp. 140–158). New York: Holt, Rinehart & Winston.

Stern, G. S., McCants, T. R., & Pettine, P. W. (1982). Stress and illness: Controllable and uncontrollable life events' relative contributions. *Personality and Social Psychology Bulletin, 8,* 140–145.

Stress: Can we cope? (1983, June 6). *Time,* 48–54.

Streufert, S. (1983, October). The stress of excellence. *Across The Board,* pp. 8–16.

Part Three

Social Processes

Given that we know something about what people perceive, what their attitudes are, what motivates them, and how they respond to stress, managing them seems like it should be easy. But, alas, this is not the case. The reason is that organizations are social entities. When we work in organizations, we do not work alone; we work with other people. And as we noted in Chapter 6, the people we work with can strongly influence our behavior. Thus, employees may perceive that working hard will get them more money, and money may be a very important reward to them, but this does not necessarily mean they will actually work hard or perform well. There may be social pressure to keep production down, or the coordinating aspects of interpersonal interaction may misdirect or spoil their efforts. Such social processes can have a dramatic effect upon people's behavior. The three chapters in this part of the book are devoted to examining these social processes.

Chapter 8, "Group Dynamics," provides an overview of small-group behavior. A definition of the "small group" and how it develops is provided. We discuss in some detail how people behave differently in a group setting than they would if they were alone. We present a model of group interaction that suggests that behavior in the group is caused by three major factors: (1) per-

sonal characteristics of the group members (e.g., attitudes, personality), (2) situational characteristics (e.g., space, type of task, group size), and (3) group structure (e.g., communication patterns, roles, status differences). Since much of the literature on personal characteristics was discussed in Part 2, this topic receives relatively little attention here. The major focus is on how situational factors and group structure affect group process, and eventually, satisfaction and productivity.

Chapter 9, "Roles, Norms, and Status," discusses the social processes that clarify the organizational environment for the individual. Roles are the total set of expectations that others have about how someone in a particular organizational position should behave. These external expectations are often the primary determinant of what we do—even when they run counter to our own desires.

Norms deal with a slightly different topic. They are defined as expectations about how *everyone* within a group should behave (as opposed to roles, which focus on specific positions). There are norms about how you should dress, where you should eat, whom you should talk to, and so on. There are ways in which groups enforce these norms, and violating them often causes the individual to experience considerable stress.

The existence of status hierarchies further clarifies one's position with respect to others. A recognition of who has high or low status can also give one a good idea of what the group values and scorns.

The topic of Chapter 10 is communication. Patterns of communication in organizations are discussed, and a model of the communication process is presented. This model includes the sender, the message, and the recipient. Each of these three factors is discussed in terms of how more effective communication—that is, agreement about the meaning of a message—can be attained.

In short, while Part 2 focused on the individual, Part 3 focuses on the social setting. A knowledge of both is essential to understand the behavior of people in organizations.

Chapter 8

Group Dynamics

Key Terms to Watch For:

Small Group
Formal Group
Informal Group
Social Facilitation
Social Loafing
Brainstorming
Quality Circles
Attitude Polarization
Territoriality
Personal Space
Reciprocal Interdependence
Sequential Interdependence
Pooled Interdependence
Reward Differential
Congruence
Conformity
Leader Emergence
Group Cohesiveness

Chapter Outline

When many are got together, you can be guided by him whose counsel is wisest. If a man is alone he is less full of resource and his wit is weaker.
—HOMER

Experience tells us that people in organizations spend a large percentage of time interacting with one another. Much of this interaction takes place in small groups. The purpose of this chapter is to describe what goes on in these groups and to suggest how what goes on can influence performance. More

223

specifically, we will describe (1) how people working in groups behave differently from people alone, (2) why people join groups, (3) how groups develop, and (4) the factors that influence the manner in which a work group actually carries out its task. This knowledge can help both individuals and organizations function more effectively.

WHAT IS A SMALL GROUP?

A *small group* can be defined as a set of two or more individuals who interact with one another in such a manner that each person influences and is influenced by each other person (Shaw, 1981). Small groups often have from three to eight members, although they may have as many as fifteen to twenty. By convention, however, we generally do not consider groups with more than about twenty members as *small* groups. The reason for this is that the frequent, *face-to-face interaction* and *mutual influence* that is characteristic of small groups is much less likely to occur when there are more than about twenty people involved.

The small groups that are most important for understanding the behavior of people in organizations usually exist over a relatively long period of time. They meet on a more-or-less regular basis, usually in the same general location. And while individual members of the group may come and go, the group itself endures. Further, the members of these small groups show a commonality of interest. This commonality is usually expressed in terms of goals upon which there is mutual agreement. These goals bind them together. Indeed, group members usually think and speak of the group as a single entity (e.g., "We did this" or "We think that") rather than as a collection of individuals. To facilitate the actual process of goal accomplishment, a differentiation of roles and functions usually occurs in a small group. One person might take the role of the leader, another the comic, another the organizer. Finally, a small group has some amount of self-sufficiency that enables it to adapt to changing conditions in its environment.

Given this description, it is easy to see why other collections of people do not qualify as a small group. The people riding on a bus, waiting in line for football tickets, or attending a play do not comprise small groups. Either they lack a common goal, they do not interact, they are too numerous, or they show no differentiation of roles. Similarly, the U.S. House of Representatives is not a small group (although the U.S. Supreme Court is). The local chapter of the Teamsters Union is not a small group, nor are six people sitting together in a room taking a civil service exam. Finally, the students in a large introductory management course would not qualify as a small group (but those in a small seminar probably would qualify).

Formal and Informal Groups

Within organizations there are all sorts of small groups. Perhaps the most important distinction among them is whether they are formal or informal. *Formal groups* are usually prescribed by the organization. People are assigned to specific positions in these groups. Formal groups often appear as part of the organization chart. The most common formal groups are task groups and committees. A task group might consist of a supervisor and his or her immediate subordinates. Examples include research teams, commando units, highway crews, and boards of directors. Committees usually are formed for some specific purpose and usually, but not always, are temporary. As anyone working in an organization knows, there can be committees for just about anything. When the committee's work is done, the group is disbanded.

Informal groups also exist. You will recall that the Hawthorne studies first pointed out the importance of such groups for organizational effectiveness. People join together because of common interests, friendship, or other social needs. Informal groups seldom appear anywhere on the organization chart, yet they do exist. The members of an informal group may eat together, go to and from work together, play cards or golf together, and/or take their coffee breaks together. They have their unwritten rules and norms about appropriate behavior and responsibilities. They know who belongs to the group and who is an outsider. The effective functioning of both formal and informal groups is important for the organization.

INDIVIDUALS AND GROUPS

One obvious question that needs to be asked is, why should organizations be concerned with groups at all? Why not simply have people work by themselves and have managers coordinate their efforts? From a theoretical perspective, the question boils down to understanding how group work processes differ from those of individuals working alone. From a practical perspective, the question is whether groups are *more effective* than individuals. The answers to these questions have important policy implications. They should tell us, for example, whether it is better to use committees as opposed to single individuals for particular decision-making tasks, and whether it is advantageous to use a team approach as opposed to an assembly line for production tasks.

Research investigating these questions has examined the work process and performance of individuals and groups working on comparable tasks. In general, the findings indicate that whether groups or individuals are more effective depends both on the task and on a number of personal and situational factors. In this section we begin to introduce this research by discussing some of the ways in which groups can affect their individual members.

Social Facilitation

Groups can influence individuals in a variety of ways. For example, by its *mere presence,* a group can sometimes facilitate an individual's performance. This process, discussed previously in Chapter 6, is known as *social facilitation.* The earliest research on social facilitation was reported by Triplett (1897). He collected data on the results of bicycle races from the official records of the Racing Board of the League of American Wheelmen. Of interest were the results for races in which cyclists rode individually over a given course trying to beat an established time, compared to races that involved direct head-to-head competition. He found that the winning times in the head-to-head competitions were significantly faster than the winning times in races against the clock. Since the primary difference between the two types of races was the presence of other cyclists on the course, the results seem to be due to social facilitation.

Subsequent research has strongly supported Triplett's conclusions (e.g., Zajonc, 1965; Markus, 1978). With one major exception, the presence of others does seem to improve performance. Furthermore, there does not have to be direct competition between individuals for social facilitation to occur. It can occur even when the other people present in the situation are simply bystanders. The one major exception to the general social facilitation rule has to do with tasks that are unfamiliar or not well learned. The presence of other people tends to facilitate performance only when the task has been well learned. When the task has not been well learned, the opposite occurs: The presence of other people worsens performance.

Part of the explanation for this phenomenon is that having other people around increases one's concern about being evaluated. This concern arouses us to perform well, so that we will both look good and please others. As long as the task is well learned, the arousal will lead to better performance. However, when the task is new and unfamiliar, the arousal resulting from our concern with evaluation can actually cause us to make mistakes. Thus, performing in a group situation can cause arousal, and under some circumstances this arousal can be helpful.

Inhibiting Participation and Effort

Groups can also have effects that run counter to social facilitation. For example, they can cause strong imbalances in participation. If five people work individually on a problem and we aggregate their work, each person's contribution is roughly 20 percent. If we observe a group, however, a very different picture emerges. No matter what size the small group may be, the interaction is usually dominated by a small percentage of the group members. For example, in groups of four or five, two people may often speak 70 to 80 percent of the time. This results in differential rather than equal participation of the group members. If the heavy contributors are bright, competent members, effectiveness will be the result. However, talkative people are not always the most effective, and this differential weighting can cause problems in group functioning.

A related phenomenon is called *social loafing*. It appears that when people work in groups in which *their individual contributions cannot be assessed*, they work *less hard* than they would if they were working alone (Latané, Williams, & Harkins, 1979a, 1979b). This phenomenon was first demonstrated long ago in a classic study by Ringmann (summarized in Moede, 1927). Ringmann had workers pull as hard as they could on a rope in groups of two, three, and eight. Connected to the rope was a meter that measured the force of their pull. Ringmann carefully compared the force of the pull of the various sized groups. He found, of course, that as the size of the group went up, more overall force was exerted. However, he also found that as the size of the group went up, the *average force per person* went down! These data are presented in Figure 8-1. As you can see, when a two-person group pulled on the rope, the individual group

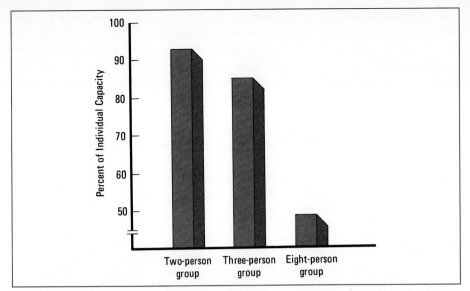

FIGURE 8-1
As the size of the group increased, the average effort expended per person decreased. (*Based on data summarized in Moede, 1927.*)

members pulled at approximately 93 percent of their individual capacity. When a three-person group pulled, the group members pulled at 85 percent of their individual capacity. And when an eight-person group pulled, the group members pulled at a level that was only 49 percent of their individual capacity. These results give new life to the old saw, "Many hands make light the work."

Latané et al. (1979b) speculate that social loafing may have contributed to the decline in productivity in this country in recent years. There seems to be an increasing emphasis in our country on collective work situations in large organizations. In these settings, people may feel less responsible for the group product, may see little relationship between their individual effort and organizational sanctions, and may be tempted to become "free riders." Note, however, that this is likely to happen only when individual contributions cannot be monitored, and therefore little evaluation apprehension is present. The ability to assess the separate contributions of individual group members is critical for determining whether social loafing or social facilitation will occur.

Problem Solving

A somewhat different question is whether a group can generate more and better ideas than can the same number of individuals acting alone. We have already mentioned that not everyone in the group is necessarily heard, and that certain people often dominate the discussion. Also, there is a tendency for group members to evaluate suggestions as they arise, and this process may inhibit a free flow of ideas. Thus, there is some evidence that groups inhibit free exchange, spontaneity, and creativity (McGrath, 1984).

On the other hand, we all know that sometimes an idea generated by someone else can trigger a novel idea in our own thinking. The trick is to develop a technique that will overcome the prohibitions to spontaneity (e.g., domination by a few persons, early criticism) and to increase the opportunity for creativity.

One procedure that was designed with this specific goal in mind is called *brainstorming*. Brainstorming is a technique that attempts to create an environment in which ideas can be generated without criticism and individuals can use the ideas of other group members to stimulate their own thinking. All evaluation of ideas is supposed to be withheld until the idea-generation phase has been completed. We will discuss the effectiveness of brainstorming in more detail in Chapter 12, "Group Decision Making."

In recent years it has become quite fashionable in industry to use small groups to solve significant company problems. Perhaps the most well-known example of this is the current boom in quality circles. *Quality circles* are small groups of employees from the same work area that meet regularly (e.g., once a week for an hour) to solve problems affecting their area. The members of the quality circle are usually volunteers. They receive training in problem solving, statistical quality control, and group process. The quality circle's job is to identify problems and recommend solutions to management. The problems that quality circles typically deal with range from quality improvement and productivity enhancement to employee involvement (Lawler & Mohrman, 1985). Lawler and Mohrman (1985) estimate that 90 percent of the Fortune 500 companies now have quality circle programs.

One example of a solution generated by a quality circle was reported by Westinghouse Electric Corporation's Defense and Electronic Systems Center in Baltimore. They had found, over the years, that their vendors were overshipping merchandise to them in the hope that sending more would increase sales. An idea generated by one of their quality circles was to charge the vendors for the shipping expenses incurred when the overshipped merchandise was returned. Implementing this idea saved the company an estimated $36,000 a year ("Quality Circles," 1980).

Attitude Polarization

A final effect that groups can have on their individual members is known as *attitude polarization*. After participating in a group discussion about some issue, the attitudes and opinions of the group members often shift to become more extreme than they were before the discussion started (Lamm & Myers, 1978). The shift, however, is always in the same direction as the group members' prediscussion opinions. That is, if before a discussion most of the members of a group are somewhat opposed to an idea, afterward they will be even more opposed. Similarly, if most of the members are somewhat in favor of the idea beforehand, afterward they will be even more in favor of it. Thus, group discussions often have the effect of *polarizing* the attitudes of group members, moving them away from the neutral position and toward the endpoints (poles) of the attitude continuum.

A number of explanations have been offered for this effect (cf. Shaw, 1981). One that seems particularly plausible has to do with the number and type of persuasive arguments that are likely to arise in the group discussion. If most of the group members are moderately in favor of an idea before a discussion, there is a good chance that more arguments will be raised in favor of the idea than against it. This does not necessarily mean that there *actually are* more reasons for favoring the idea, just that more reasons in favor of the idea are likely to be aired in the group discussion. The opposite would be true if most of the group members were moderately against the idea beforehand—it would be likely that more arguments against the idea would be raised. In either case, the polarization effect is hypothesized to result simply from hearing a majority of persuasive arguments supporting the position the group members were leaning toward in the first place (cf. Bordley, 1983).

The implications of this phenomenon for organizations are clear. When small groups are used to make important decisions, there is a danger that there will be a systematic bias in the way arguments are brought up in group discussions. Specifically, arguments that support the group's initial prediscussion position may predominate, to the exclusion of arguments that do not support that position. This leaves open the real possibility that (1) important issues relevant to the decision will be overlooked, (2) the discussion will bolster faulty prediscussion attitudes and opinions, and (3) the resultant decision will be of a lower quality than it might otherwise have been. This is another issue that we will consider in more detail in Chapter 12, "Group Decision Making."

AN OVERVIEW OF GROUP VARIABLES

A frame of reference for thinking about the functioning of small groups is presented in Figure 8-2. The variables listed in this figure represent most of the significant factors that need to be taken into consideration in order to understand small-group behavior fully. As the figure suggests, group behavior and

FIGURE 8-2
An open-systems-theory model of small-group behavior.

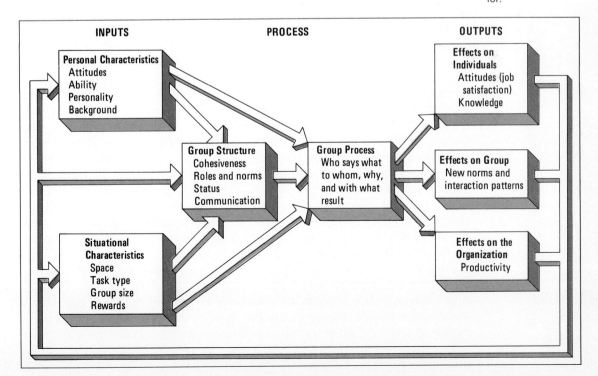

functioning constitute a complex phenomenon. It is important to recognize, however, that part of this complexity arises from the fact that small groups are *open systems.* Recall from our discussion of open-systems theory in Chapter 3 that open systems are affected by *input* variables and that they in turn have an effect upon *output* variables. In the case of small groups, there are three classes of input variables that are important to consider. First, there are the personal characteristics of the group members, which include their abilities, attitudes, personality, and other background factors. Second, there are the characteristics of the situation in which the group operates, including physical space constraints, the type of task being performed, the size of the group, and organizational reward structures. Finally, there are the structural features of the group itself. These include the cohesiveness of the group, role and status relationships, norms, and communication patterns. These three classes of variables (personal, situational, and group) influence the group interaction process, that is, who says what to whom with what effect. The group interaction process, in turn, affects the individual members of the group (e.g., by changing their attitudes and knowledge), the group itself (e.g., by fostering the development of new norms and patterns of communication), and the organization as a whole (e.g., through productivity changes). Finally, as in any open system, these outputs serve as inputs that can affect group process in the future.

Thus, both organizations and small groups are open systems. In a sense, an organization can be thought of as a system of systems. Small groups are simply sets of open systems that function within the larger organizational system. Indeed, if we also include individuals as open systems, organizations are really systems of systems of systems! There is a clear hierarchical relationship among these three levels of systems, and when we speak of system inputs and outputs we must be careful to specify the level of analysis we are talking about.

Group Formation

Earlier in this chapter we stated that small groups in organizations can be either formal or informal. Formal groups are created by the organization with the specific intention of achieving some desired organizational goal. Informal groups, on the other hand, are not created by the organization. Instead, they form almost spontaneously without any help from (and sometimes in spite of) the organization. Regardless of whether groups are formal or informal, however, individuals frequently *want* to join them. They willingly volunteer to work in formal groups, and they naturally come together to form informal groups. This raises an important question: Why do people want to join groups? What benefits do they get out of small groups that make them so attractive? Several benefits can be identified.

First, people join groups because of the need to affiliate with others. Just being with other people can fulfill a desire for social interaction. Second, groups can provide a source of information about oneself and about the outside world. Other people can serve as an important source of comparison, enabling us to evaluate our skills and abilities and to assess the accuracy of our attitudes and opinions. Third, groups serve as a source of rewards. Being on the job, on the bowling team, a member of a special task force, or a member of a committee can bring rewards of friendship, recognition, status, and financial benefit. Fourth, being in a group allows us to accomplish goals that would be difficult to accomplish alone. It is hard to play bridge by oneself or to run a business without any employees. People thus join together and jointly contribute their resources in order to accomplish personal goals. Finally, we often join groups because we are asked or directed to do so by our boss. In this situation, the group is formed out of compliance.

Group Development

Once a group has been formed, there is an initial period of *group development* that takes place. During this period the group members seek to clarify their place in the group. An individual's position in the group may vary on a number of dimensions, all of which need to be sorted out. People soon find out who the high-status and powerful members of the group are. They learn who demands deference and who should defer. They quickly learn who they like. Personal attraction greatly influences later group interaction. The communication patterns also get clarified. To some extent, the communication pattern will be determined by situational variables, such as the group's size and the physical location of group members. However, attraction and status differences will also affect who talks to whom.

The early life of a group is thus characterized by a great deal of flux. However, after a while things begin to settle down. People begin to know where they fit and what is expected, and interactions become more stable and predictable.

This developmental stage can be of great importance to later group performance for two major reasons. First, it establishes the pattern of interaction for subsequent group meetings. As we shall see, the communication, attraction, and status structures of a group greatly influence group process and problem-solving abilities. Second, this early development process makes later interaction easier. Little time will be wasted on group development issues. Occasional reaffirmations of position will occur, but in general the group will be able to devote most of its resources to the task at hand. This is especially true if the development process has gone well—when the people involved are relatively certain of their positions and responsibilities in the group.

Once the development stage is over and a stable group exists, we can examine how different situational factors, personal characteristics of the group members, and group structures (e.g., communication and influence patterns) affect the group's interaction process and outputs. The remainder of the chapter focuses on these topics.

SITUATIONAL VARIABLES AFFECTING GROUPS

There are a number of situational variables that can have an effect upon the output of a group. These include territorial factors (e.g., spatial arrangements), the characteristics of the task, and organizational control systems. As the model in Figure 8-2 suggests, these situational variables have their impact on group outputs by means of their effects on both group structure and group process. From an organizational point of view, it is important to pay attention to these variables, because organizations usually have at least some degree of control over them. Thus, by changing the characteristics of the situation in which a small group operates, an organization can dramatically influence that group's outputs.

Territorial Factors

One type of situational variable that can strongly influence group structure and process has to do with territoriality and physical space. Think of the classes you have been in where there are no assigned seats but where you usually sit in the same place every day. How would you feel if you came in and someone was in the seat you typically occupy? You would probably resent the intrusion. You might even ask the person to move from "your" seat. Also, think about the different seating arrangements in classrooms. In some classrooms you sit in a horseshoe-type arrangement, which allows you to see both the professor and your classmates. In other classrooms there are fixed rows of seats and the professor stands up in front. This latter arrangement only allows you to see the professor. It is a much more impersonal setting. As we shall see, these factors can have a significant effect on the group interaction.

Territoriality. It is a common observation that individuals and groups often come to feel that they own or have rights to certain objects or space. These objects may be chairs, desks, offices, buildings, or neighborhoods. This feeling is distinguished from actual ownership in that the people involved have no legal right to these objects or territories. The territory is simply used or occupied by them, and they act as if they own it.

This orientation can affect group functioning. If, for some reason, people are not allowed to maintain their territorial integrity, conflict can occur (cf. Whyte, 1943). If a group member takes your favorite seat or makes it clear that he or she covets your office, bad feelings will be the result. There is often resentment of an "intruder" or "newcomer" who comes uninvited into the office. Research clearly demonstrates that people will take action to defend "their" territory when it is threatened and will seek to regain it when it is lost (e.g., Sommer, 1969).

Personal Space. Personal space differs from territoriality in that it refers to our bodies. We carry our personal space around with us; it is that area around the individual that is felt to be private—a space that others should not enter. It does not have firm physical referents as is characteristic of territoriality. The boundaries of our personal space may vary according to the situation.

People resent intrusion into their personal space. Negative feelings are the result, and people will seek to reestablish the distance at which they feel most comfortable. If this alternative is not available, conflict and poor interpersonal relationships often result.

The interesting point is that there are both appropriate and inappropriate distances for various types of interpersonal interactions. Close friends stand nearer than acquaintances or strangers. People of similar ages or status interact more closely with one another than with people who are older or of higher status. There are even cultural and subcultural differences in personal space. For example, in some cultures (e.g., Latin America, Greece, the Middle East) people prefer to stand much closer when having a conversation than many Americans are typically comfortable with (Sommer, 1969).

In summary, people try to establish a comfortable distance for each type of interpersonal exchange. When this distance is violated, discomfort and anxiety are often produced.

Spatial Arrangements. One implication of these feelings of territoriality and personal space is that the spatial arrangements established for a group interaction can strongly influence the quality of that interaction. Where we sit, whom we sit next to, the closeness of the seats, and their orientation all affect group process (Davis, 1984).

Look at the different arrangements diagrammed in Figure 8-3. People who want to cooperate tend to prefer a side-by-side arrangement, and people who are working fairly independently prefer a distant opposite or end-to-end arrangement. Competing people prefer a face-to-face or corner-to-corner arrangement. Empirical research shows that arrangements that place a physical object such as a desk or table between individuals, or in which individuals are physically far apart, result in less interaction overall, and are characterized by less friendly and more formal exchanges (McCaskey, 1979). Two studies particularly relevant for students found that faculty members who placed their desks between themselves and a visiting student were older, of higher status (academic rank), and were rated less positively by students than faculty who used a less formal interaction arrangement (Becker, Gield, & Foggatt, 1983; Zweigenhaft, 1976).

There have also been surveys of the frequency of various office arrangements used in American businesses. In one study by Preston and Quesada (1978), for example, almost 70 percent of the offices were arranged in one of two patterns. The first, called "the throne," is shown in the left-hand panel of Figure 8-4. These offices had the desk placed between the occupant's seat and the other places to sit. People with this type of office were seen as having a

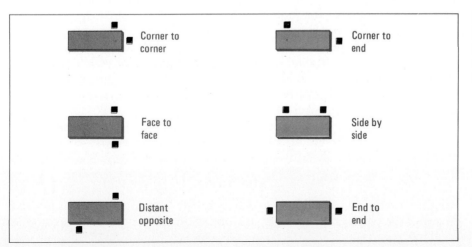

FIGURE 8-3
Possible seating arrangements around a rectangular table.

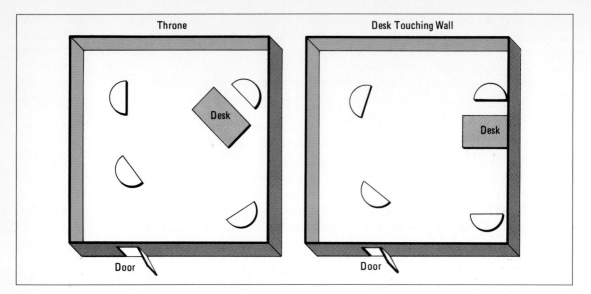

FIGURE 8-4
Typical furniture
arrangements in
American offices.

high need for structure and a desire to control the communication process. The second arrangement had the desk touching a wall (see Figure 8-4). This arrangement allows more informal interaction and is more personal in its tone.

We should also point out that there has been a recent resurgence of "open design" offices. In these situations there are many windows, aisles designed for ease of movement, and partitions (but not walls) between work spaces (see Figure 8-5). Interestingly, research on employee reactions to these arrangements has not been very positive. One study, for example, clearly showed that an organization's transition to an open-design office arrangement resulted in lower satisfaction, less motivation, and lower concentration (Oldham & Brass, 1979).

These results suggest strongly that the quantity, quality, and pattern of interpersonal interactions can be manipulated simply by controlling the environment in which the interactions take place. The manager who wishes to maintain distance and assert his or her status can use props and seating arrangements to do so. If a more informal exchange is desired, he or she can move around to the other side of the desk or perhaps sit corner to corner. A leader's position in the group can be accentuated or played down according to where he or she sits at the table. [We might also note that people who sit at the head of a table are more likely to participate actively in group discussions and to emerge as a leader of the group when the group does not already have an established leader (Baker, 1984; Strodtbeck & Hook, 1961).] It is thus clear that one may influence group interactions simply by changing the physical arrangements and orientations among group members.

The Task

Another situational variable that can strongly affect group structure and process is the type of task the group is working on. A task can be thought of as

FIGURE 8-5
Open offices pro-
vide access and
freedom of move-
ment but also
violate some peo-
ple's need for
privacy and per-
sonal space.

making certain *demands* on the group. If the task is to be performed successfully, these demands must be met.

A good example of a task demand is the degree of interaction that is
required among group members. Some tasks demand a very high degree of
group interaction. This is the case, for instance, when a research team is
assigned to discovering cheaper ways to manufacture the chemicals that a
company produces. The performance of the group (i.e., the number of cost-
saving manufacturing methods discovered) will be highly dependent on the
quality of the interaction among the group members, especially with regard to
exchanging information and stimulating one another's creativity. This type of
situation is referred to as one of *reciprocal interdependence*. Reciprocal interdependence always requires a high degree of group interaction.

There are other tasks that demand much less interaction among the group
members. Consider, for example, a group of three people who manufacture
handmade leather handbags. One person stains and cuts the leather, another
stitches the leather pieces together, and the third applies a coat of protective
oil to the finished bags and then packages them in specially designed boxes.
Here there is *sequential interdependence* among the group members, and only a
small amount of interaction is required in order to ensure that their efforts are
properly coordinated (i.e., so that no one is either overworked or idle for any
length of time). Note that whenever a task involves sequential interdependence, the group's performance (e.g., the number of handbags made) will
depend to a large extent upon the speed of the *slowest* group member.

235

Private Office? That's Not Japanese Style

LOS ANGELES—When Toshiaki Yamamoto was sent here to be general manager of the regional office of NKK America—the Japanese steel giant—the biggest adjustment he had to make wasn't to freeway driving or smog. It was to working in a private office, shut off from his staff by walls and doors—the traditional barriers of executive America.

The dramatic contrast between Japanese and American management styles perhaps shows up most clearly in the way executive offices are designed.

In Japan, up to 50 members of a department will be arranged in one big room, with each desk—including that of the section supervisor—cheek-by-jowl with the next. The department head or general manager gets to sit apart, usually on a raised dais against one window, but he remains on display, his every action or conversation observable by everyone else in the room.

Privacy is virtually unknown in the Japanese workplace. If a staffer has a telephone argument with a client or a spouse, his colleagues know about it immediately. If a sales rep is about to close a deal, his success or failure will be instantly monitored by all the other reps in the office.

By contrast, the American system seems excessively individualistic and lonely to the Japanese posted here.

IN A CORNER

"I am uncomfortable being cut off from my staff," explains Yamamoto, ensconced in a small, tasteful office. "If I want to have a conversation I either have to call one of them into this office or go out and find them. In the Japanese system, they would be seated next to me all day long."

In the year that Ryosuke Zakoh has been general manager of Fuji Bank's Los Angeles office, he has refused to sit in his private office. Instead, he has installed himself in a corner of the office's main room. Zakoh is getting ready to move his office, but the plans show him stationed with an open desk, with a private office reserved strictly for receiving guests. "Privacy may be preferable," Zakoh says, "but our system is better for convenience and communication in smaller spaces."

Yamamoto believes the different office designs also reflect different management philosophies. In Japan, workers have poorly defined job titles; the emphasis is on teamwork and group performance. In America, however, white collar workers are more territorial, with clearly defined specialties or "turf" never to be trespassed on by other workers.

"We try to bring up our people as generalists, often moving them from job to job at one level before promoting them. You emphasize specialties," Yamamoto says. "You might say the way to the top for us is a spiral, while you try to walk up the ladder."

IDLE CHATTER

Yamamoto admits that the arena-like Japanese office design encourages gossip and idle chatter, but he thinks whatever is lost in wasted time is made up for in added efficiency through a team approach and improved morale. "It may look like we are wasting our time," Yamamoto comments, "but by sitting so close together, the staff is more likely to help each other."

According to Dr. Gordon Berger, director of the East Asian studies center at the University of Southern California, the Japanese learn to live in an unprivate world from birth.

"Space is always at a premium. Even in their homes, the Japanese live close to one another, separated only by a thin wall," says Berger. "The Japanese have to learn how to find ways of being alone without being shut off physically from one another."

Not all Japanese who have been exposed to the American office system think the Japanese plan is superior, however. Seiichi Noto, manager for engineering and technology at NKK here, says he prefers having a private office and secretary, because "psychologically, it makes me feel more free from my boss."

But Hitoshi Watanabe, an NKK marketing specialists, says that the "touching desk" system allows the Japanese to apply a "group task force" system to business problems. "The Japanese tend to make friends of their colleagues at the office. That is part of the reason the Japanese task force system is so successful," said Watanabe.

"By being so close together all day," says Berger, "when the assistant general manager proposes a plan, it has the backing of everyone under him. At some point they all have to put their stamp of ap-

Finally, there are some tasks that demand no group interaction at all. The task performed by a group of telephone operators is a good example. The performance of the group (e.g., the total number of calls handled per day) is simply the sum of performance of the individual group members. This type of situation is referred to as one of *pooled interdependence.* Not only is group interaction not required when there is pooled interdependence among the group members, but if too much interaction does occur it could conceivably lower performance (by distracting group members from their work).

Thus, some tasks demand more group interaction than others. Unless the required level of group interaction occurs, performance will suffer. Moreover, achieving the required level of interaction has predictable consequences for subsequent group structure and process. For example, when the task demands a high degree of group interaction (e.g., reciprocal interdependence), and this demand is met, close, cohesive intragroup relationships and strong group norms are likely to develop. In contrast, when the task demands little or no interaction among group members (e.g., pooled interdependence), such interaction is less likely to occur, and the group is less likely to develop close intragroup relationships and strong group norms.

McGrath's Task Typology. The level of required group interaction is only one type of demand that a task can make on group members; there are many others. Attempts to classify tasks according to the demands they place on a group has resulted in a number of *task typologies.* These typologies organize tasks into clusters, so that all of the tasks within each cluster are similar with respect to certain demands. One example of a task typology is that proposed by McGrath (1984). This typology is presented in Figure 8-6. It divides tasks into four basic types according to what the group is expected to do. These four basic types are represented as quadrants in the figure. Each quadrant is further subdivided into two more specific task types.

Quadrant I, "Generate," is divided into tasks that require the generation of plans of action and those that require the generation of creative ideas (e.g., solutions to a problem). Quadrant II, "Choose," is composed of problem-solving and decision-making tasks. The primary distinction between these two is that problem-solving tasks are ones for which there is an objectively correct answer (e.g., the fastest way to ship freight between Seattle and Chicago), while decision-making tasks are ones for which there is no objectively correct solution. In the latter case the "correct" solution is simply the preference of the group majority (e.g., whether to order a bottle of red or white wine with dinner). The group's task is thus to discover their collective preference.

237

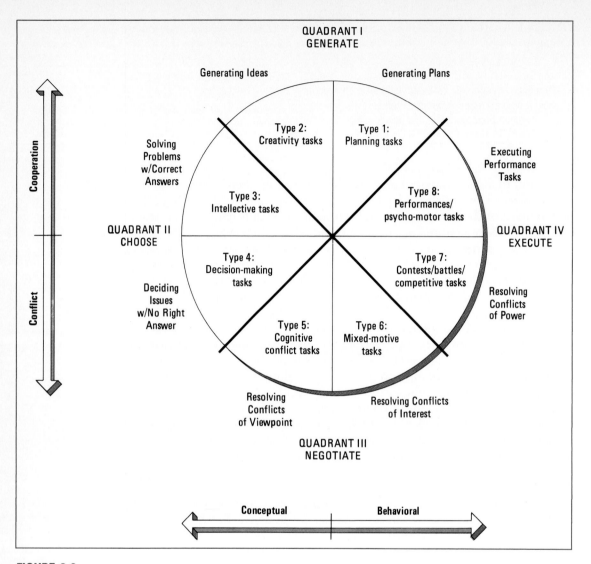

QUADRANT I
GENERATE

Generating Ideas   Generating Plans

Cooperation

Conflict

Solving
Problems
w/Correct
Answers

Type 2:
Creativity tasks

Type 1:
Planning tasks

Executing
Performance
Tasks

Type 3:
Intellective tasks

Type 8:
Performances/
psycho-motor tasks

QUADRANT II
CHOOSE

QUADRANT IV
EXECUTE

Type 4:
Decision-making
tasks

Type 7:
Contests/battles/
competitive tasks

Deciding
Issues
w/No Right
Answer

Type 5:
Cognitive
conflict tasks

Type 6:
Mixed-motive
tasks

Resolving
Conflicts
of Power

Resolving
Conflicts
of Viewpoint

Resolving Conflicts
of Interest

QUADRANT III
NEGOTIATE

Conceptual   Behavioral

FIGURE 8-6
McGrath's typology
of group tasks.
(*Source: McGrath,
1984.*)

Quadrant III, "Negotiate," is divided into cognitive conflict tasks (e.g., resolving conflicting points of view regarding the best way to reinvest company profits) and mixed-motive tasks (i.e., what to do when the payoffs of the various courses of action are different for different group members). The distinction between cognitive conflict tasks and mixed-motive tasks is that in the former case the various possible courses of action being considered by the group would affect all group members in essentially the same way, whereas in the latter case different courses of action would affect different group members in very different ways. Note also that as McGrath uses the terms, cognitive conflict tasks (quadrant III) involve a fundamental disagreement among group members regarding how they interpret and/or weight various pieces of information relevant to a group decision, whereas decision-making tasks (quadrant II) do not. Finally, quadrant IV, "Execute," is divided into competitive tasks and performance tasks. In both cases the focus is on overt physical behavior. The primary distinction here is that in competitive tasks the group is in competition with some other group and performance is interpreted in terms of winning and losing (e.g., a football game), whereas in performance tasks the group is trying to achieve some objective standard of excellence (e.g., zero defects).

Note that some of these task types, especially those on the left-hand side of Figure 8-6, emphasize conceptual skills (generating ideas, choosing, resolving conflicting points of view), while others focus on physical behavior (generating plans of action, executing). Further, the four task types on the bottom of the figure imply some level of conflict, either within or between groups, whereas those on the top generally require cooperation. Thus, these different task types are likely to make different demands on the group with respect to cooperation and conflict and with respect to behavioral versus conceptual skills.

In short, the task itself can strongly affect the pattern of behavior observed in a group. Independent of the particular characteristics of the group members, some tasks naturally lead to group conflict and others lead to group cooperation. Still others lead to the development of cliques, coalitions, and particular patterns of power and status. These factors all need to be taken into consideration when trying to understand the causes of behavior in a small group.

Reward Structure

A final type of situational variable that can strongly affect group structure and process is the manner in which group members are rewarded by the organization. In some organizations one's rewards are tied explicitly to one's own personal output (piece-rate systems, for example) while in others, salaries or bonuses may be partially tied to group efforts (e.g., athletic teams). Still other organizations establish systems in which a fixed amount of money must be divided among employees so that what one person stands to gain another may lose (academic salaries and raises are often drawn from a "fixed pot"). Under some circumstances these various reward structures can have a beneficial effect on both group process and group performance. Under other circumstances, however, they can have a detrimental effect. The key is whether or not the reward structure is *congruent* with, or matches, the demands of the task. (Recall that the notion of congruence was first introduced in our discussion of open-systems theory in Chapter 3.)

As we suggested previously, some tasks demand a high degree of group interaction and cooperative effort (e.g., when there is a high level of reciprocal interdependence), while others demand very little (e.g., when there is only pooled interdependence). When a high degree of cooperation is demanded by the task, the organization can encourage cooperative behavior by establishing a reward structure with a *low reward differential*. A low reward differential implies that all group members are paid the same or nearly the same. Moreover, their pay should be based upon overall group performance, so that when the group does well all of the group members are rewarded, and when the group does poorly no one is rewarded. If the organization does this, the reward structure will be congruent with the interaction demands of the task, and the result will be more cooperation among group members and higher group performance.

On the other hand, if the organization's reward structure involves *high reward differential,* the result is likely to be *less* cooperation among group members and *lower* group performance. An example of a high differential reward structure is one in which the most efficient group member is paid, for example, twice as much as the least efficient member, and their pay is drawn from the same, fixed pool of dollars. This reward structure is more likely to foster competition than cooperation, and thus would clearly not be congruent with the task.

It is important to emphasize here that what matters is the degree of *congruence* between the reward structure and the task, not simply whether the reward structure involves a high or low reward differential. This can be illustrated by considering a task involving pooled interdependence (e.g., the work of telephone operators). In such a task there is no demand for group interaction or cooperation, since group performance is really just the sum of the individual group members' performance. In this situation a higher level of performance is likely to be achieved when the reward structure involves a *high* reward differential, with individual group members rewarded differently based on their own individual performance. If the reward structure were instead to involve a low reward differential, with all the group members rewarded exactly the same regardless of their performance, there would be little reason for individual group members to excel, and lower overall group performance would result.

The relationship between task demands for group interaction and cooperation on the one hand, and reward differential on the other, is presented in Figure 8-7. As the figure suggests, when reward differential is congruent with task demands, higher performance is likely. However, when reward differential is not congruent with task demands, lower performance is likely. This relationship is strongly supported by research results. For example, in one

FIGURE 8-7
Group performance is likely to be higher when the level of reward differential is congruent with task demands for interaction and cooperation.

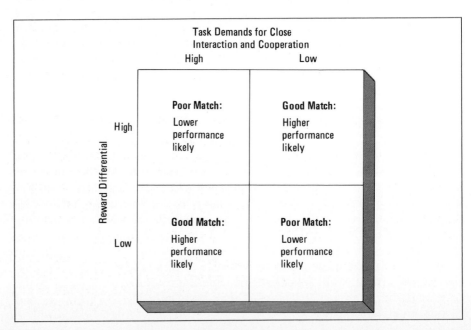

review of the research literature, the results of 20 out of 24 studies were found to be consistent with this model (Miller & Hamblin, 1963).

The implications of these findings are important. Organizations should be careful to match their reward structure with the degree of interaction and cooperation demanded by the task. To introduce what is traditionally called a competitive system (high-differential rewards) when employees are dependent upon each other may very well decrease performance instead of increase it. And to make sure that everyone gets the same compensation on a task on which employees work and contribute independently may hinder effectiveness.

We recently did some research of our own on this issue. We contacted a number of different types of professional sports teams (baseball, basketball, football) and inquired about the use of individual incentive clauses in the players' contracts. In sports like football, in which task demands for closely coordinated effort are extremely high, there were fewer individual incentives, while in sports like baseball, in which task demands for closely coordinated effort are less extreme, there were more individual incentives. Not only were the teams practicing these principles, they readily verbalized them as policy. The Seattle Seahawks (football) organization clearly downplays individual incentives in favor of team or unit (e.g., offense/defense/special teams) rewards. The appropriate matching of rewards with task demands can have an important impact on motivation.

THE IMPACT OF GROUP COMPOSITION

We now turn to a second broad class of variables that can affect small-group structure and process. As indicated in Figure 8-2, in addition to situational variables, behavior in small groups can also be significantly influenced by the personal characteristics of the group members. These include member abilities, attitudes, personality characteristics, and biographical background variables (e.g., age, sex, race, and tenure in the group). In this section we will briefly examine the way in which some of these characteristics influence small-group functioning. In addition, we will examine how group functioning is influenced by the size and cohesiveness of the group.

Member Characteristics

A large number of studies have examined the manner in which the personal characteristics of group members affect behavior in small-group settings. Several consistent relationships have been found. For example, there is evidence that conformity to group norms is more likely when group members are young, low in general intelligence, and/or high in authoritarianism. Conformity to group norms has also been shown to be greater among females than males, although this is more likely to reflect a cultural difference in sex roles than an inherent difference between men and women (cf. Shaw, 1981). Another group process variable that has been studied in relation to group member characteristics is leader emergence. Research indicates that individuals who are high in dominance, assertiveness, and empathy, and who are more emotionally stable, are more likely to emerge as informal group leaders (Bass, 1981; Shaw, 1981). Leader emergence is also influenced by the possession of specialized task-relevant abilities. Those with abilities that are crucial for accomplishing the group's task tend to become more active in the group, make more contributions to the group's performance, and have more influence in important task-related decisions. This greater overall participation in the group causes these individuals to emerge as informal group leaders (cf. Hollander, 1985; Stein & Heller, 1979).

Conformity and leader emergence are not the only group-process variables that have been studied in relation to group-member characteristics. Others that have been studied include group cohesiveness, competitiveness, communication patterns, and emotional expressiveness. It is important to note, however, that the magnitude of relationships observed between member characteristics and these various process variables has in general been quite small. This is perhaps not too surprising, given our discussion of the determinents of behavior in Chapter 4, "Perception and Personality." As we argued there, most behavior is determined by the *interaction* of personal factors and situational factors. This means that in order to comprehend fully the causes of behavior, whether that behavior occurs alone or in the context of a group, we must take the characteristics of the situation into account.

One obvious aspect of the situation that needs to be considered is the nature of the task being performed by the group. As we stated earlier, task characteristics by themselves can significantly influence group behavior. It is also true, however, that group behavior can be affected by the interaction of task characteristics and group-member characteristics. For example, Sistrunk and McDavid (1971) conducted a study examining the relationship between gender and conformity in groups performing several different types of tasks. They found that on traditionally "male-oriented" tasks (e.g., identifying hand tools), females conformed more to group pressure than did males, while on traditionally "female-oriented" tasks (e.g., identifying types of needlework) males conformed more to group pressure than did females. These results can be seen in Figure 8-8. These researchers were better able to predict conformity in small groups by taking into account the *interaction* between gender and task type than by focusing on either gender or task type alone. We might also note that the results of this study suggest that it is the group members' general familiarity with the task, rather than their sex per se, that influences conformity. Group members were most likely to conform to group pressure when they were relatively unfamiliar with the task (i.e., males working on a "female-oriented" task, or females working on a "male-oriented" task). When they switched to a task they were more familiar with, and thus were more confident about the correctness of their answers, their conformity went down—regardless of their sex.

Member Compatibility

When trying to understand the causes of behavior, it is always useful to consider the ways in which individual characteristics and task characteristics interact. In addition, however, when it is the causes of *group* behavior we are trying to understand, other important interactions need to be taken into

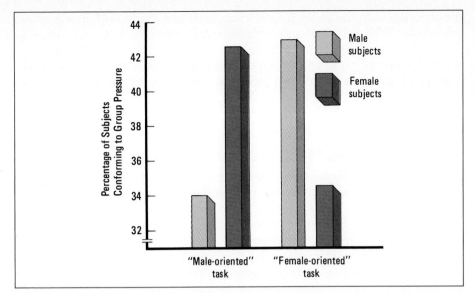

account. Some of these have to do with the personality traits of the *other group members*. The central question is, are the personalities of the various group members *compatible?*

To illustrate the concept of group-member compatibility, consider for a moment the simple situation of a two-person work team. Let us suppose that one of the two team members has a very dominant type of personality. If we were to choose someone else to work with this individual, we might prefer to select someone who has a very submissive personality. That is, there is a sense in which the dominant style of one team member would be compatible with the submissive style of the other. The dominant individual would undoubtedly take charge and become the leader of the team, and would be the person primarily responsible for the team's decisions and overall performance. These two individuals would probably get along quite well with one another. Of course, whether or not they perform well would be heavily dependent upon the judgment and skill of the dominant member. If we assume, however, that the dominant member does have the requisite skills for the task, it is reasonable to expect that the work team will perform successfully.

Compare this situation to one in which *both* group members have a very dominant personality style. In this case, the two personality styles, although similar, would be incompatible. We might expect there to be a substantial amount of conflict in this situation, especially when the task is ambiguous. This conflict is likely to lead to poor performance. Poor performance might also be expected when two submissive personalities are placed together in the same two-person work team. In this case, however, poor performance is likely to occur not because of conflict, but because of a lack of leadership, since neither member will be anxious to assume the leadership role.

Although there are some exceptions, the research literature in this area generally supports these predictions (Shaw, 1981). When group members have compatible personality traits they seem to behave more cooperatively, the atmosphere in the group is more congenial, and the group functions more effectively. When, on the other hand, group members have incompatible personality traits, they tend to behave less cooperatively, the atmosphere in the group is more tense, and the group functions less effectively. These results have been found in two-person groups as well as in larger groups, and for dominance as well as other personality traits (e.g., authoritarianism, dependence, assertiveness, and need for affiliation).

Group Homogeneity and Heterogeneity

Beyond personality traits, there are other group-member characteristics that can interact to influence group behavior and performance. These include the abilities possessed by group members, their sex and racial background, and the distribution of age and tenure in the group. It is difficult to speak of any of these variables in terms of compatibility, at least in the way we do when talking about personality compatibility. Instead, the focus is usually on the degree to which the group is *homogeneous or heterogeneous* on these characteristics. If all or nearly all of the group members possess the same set of skills and abilities, they are all members of the same race or sex, and/or they are all of approximately the same age or tenure in the group, we say that the group is homogeneous on these variables. Alternatively, if the group is composed of members who possess widely different skills and abilities, some are male and some are female, they come from several different racial or ethnic backgrounds, and/or they vary widely in age or tenure, we say that the group is heterogeneous on these variables.

Research suggests that it is advantageous for a small group to be heterogeneous on certain of these variables and homogeneous on others. The results are perhaps clearest with regard to ability. Ability heterogeneity is usually an advantage for a group. Other things being equal, groups composed of members with a wide variety of complementary skills and abilities perform better than groups in which all the group members possess essentially the same set of skills (Shaw, 1981).

With regard to the racial and sexual composition of the group, the research results are more mixed. One benefit of racial and/or sexual heterogeneity in a group seems to be the integration of new minority group members (Kanter, 1977a, 1977b). When the group is already racially or sexually heterogeneous, new minority group members (e.g., blacks, women) will often be more readily accepted by the rest of the group than when the group is predominantly of one race or sex. With regard to performance, on the other hand, many studies suggest that the racial and sexual composition of the group makes little difference. This is only a tentative conclusion, however, since there are also studies that have found racial and/or sexual heterogeneity to be a disadvantage, with heterogeneous groups performing more poorly than homogeneous groups. As suggested previously, such results are likely to be a reflection of fundamental cultural norms rather than anything about race or sex per se. One implication of this is that as cultural norms related to race and sex change, the impact of racial and sexual heterogeneity in small groups will also change.

Finally, there appears to be some benefit to age and tenure homogeneity within small groups, at least with regard to turnover. In one study, for example, turnover was examined in the top management groups of thirty-one Fortune 500 companies between the years of 1976 and 1980 (Wagner, Pfeffer, & O'Reilly, 1984). Some of the companies studied were Chrysler, Dow Chemical, Exxon, Weyerhaeuser, and Xerox. Not surprisingly, turnover in the top management teams was higher in companies that were performing poorly than in those that were performing well. However, it was also found that turnover was higher in those management groups that were more heterogeneous in terms of age and tenure. Independent of company performance, the greater the variability in the age and tenure of the top management team, the higher the rate of turnover. It is important to emphasize that these results apply only to *small* groups. With large groups (e.g., large departments or divisions within an organization), certain forms of age and tenure heterogeneity are related to *lower* rates of turnover (McCain, O'Reilly, & Pfeffer, 1983; Pfeffer, 1983).

Group Size

Managers are often faced with the job of setting up special task forces, committees, project teams, and other small groups to carry out particular functions. Many of the research findings discussed so far can be helpful in deciding exactly how to form these groups. For example, a group is likely to be more effective if its members have a heterogeneous set of complementary skills, if their personalities are compatible, if they are rewarded in a manner consistent with the demands of the task, and so on. In addition, one other important factor that should be considered is the size of the group. Size can influence the way in which the group members interact, their satisfaction with the group, and the group's overall productivity. Furthermore, unlike some other factors, the size of the group is usually very easy for managers to control.

Size and Interaction. Perhaps the most well-known research on small-group interaction has been done by Robert Bales. His interaction process analysis (Bales & Cohen, 1979) is one of the most reliable observation systems that has been developed. Observations are made about who says what to whom, and each act is placed in one of twelve categories (e.g., gives information; shows tension). In one study using this observation system, the interactions of groups ranging in size from two to seven members were investigated (Bales & Borgatta, 1956). The experiment was carried out in a laboratory with subjects working on a human-relations problem. The findings from this study indicate that very small groups show more tension, agreement, and asking for opinion, whereas larger groups show more tension release and giving of suggestions and information. The authors argue that in very small groups an emphasis is placed on everyone getting along well together and people having time to develop their ideas and arguments. In larger groups, on the other hand, getting along is not as strongly emphasized. Also, group-member behavior becomes more directive in larger groups, in part because the greater number of people involved means that any given individual's talking time is reduced. Finally, there is evidence that groups with an even number of members behave differently from groups with an odd number of members. The even-numbered groups have greater difficulty in obtaining a majority, and there is more tension, antagonism, and disagreement.

Size and Satisfaction. A study by Slater (1958) replicated the findings described above, and extended the research to include member satisfaction. Subjects were again placed in groups of two to seven members working on a human-relations case. Their interaction was recorded, and afterward they filled out a questionnaire that included questions about their feelings toward the size of the group.

Besides replicating Bales' results, Slater found an interesting relationship between group size and satisfaction. For this task, participants were most satisfied when working in a group of five. This numerical result is probably task specific, making generalizations problematic. The *reasons* subjects gave for choosing five, however, do seem to be more general. Slater reports that smaller groups were tense and nondirect, while larger groups failed to provide enough time for everyone to speak. He summarizes the results by stating that very small groups provide physical freedom with psychological restrictions, while large groups are physically restricting but psychologically less tense.

Slater's finding of dissatisfaction with large task groups in the laboratory is consistent with the results from field research conducted in industrial organizations. As work groups grow larger and larger, members often become increasingly dissatisfied with them. This dissatisfaction can result in significant costs for the organization in terms of higher rates of both absenteeism and turnover (Baumgartel & Sobol, 1959; Cleland, 1955). Thus, there are clear advantages to keeping work groups relatively small.

Size and Productivity. The relationship between group size and group performance is heavily dependent upon the nature of the task on which the group is working. For tasks involving pooled interdependence between group members, in which group performance is simply the sum of the members' individual performances, there is a strong positive relationship between group size and performance. Thus, for example, the time it takes to clean the cabin of a jumbo jet between flights is directly related to the size of the maintenance crew. As the size of the crew goes up, the job can be done more quickly. On the other hand, for tasks involving reciprocal interdependence between group members, in which group performance is heavily dependent upon the quality of the group's interaction (e.g., an industrial research team), the addition of new group members will become increasingly *less* beneficial. With each new person the added increment of new skills and knowledge decreases, while the difficulty of coordinating the group's efforts increases. At some point the coordination problems will begin to outweigh the gains in skill and knowledge until further increases in group size may actually worsen performance (cf. Yetton & Bottger, 1983). Here again, the characteristics of the task being performed must be taken into consideration.

Group Cohesiveness

The final group composition factor to be discussed is called *group cohesiveness*. Group cohesiveness can be defined as the degree to which group members are attracted to the group (cf. Cartwright, 1968). A highly cohesive group is one in which all of the members have a very positive attitude toward the group and are strongly attracted to it. A noncohesive group is one in which the members do not have a positive attitude toward the group and/or are not attracted to it. Note that cohesiveness is a group-level variable. It refers to the *overall pattern* of attraction of *all* the group members. It does not refer to the attraction of individual group members. Thus, a group as a whole might be highly cohesive, and yet there may still be one or two individual members who are not strongly attracted to it.

Group cohesiveness holds a special place among the variables considered in this section. Unlike the other group composition variables that have been discussed (member characteristics, member compatibility, group homogeneity, and group size), group cohesiveness both influences group functioning and is itself influenced by group functioning. Thus, it is important to examine not only the effects that cohesiveness can have on group process and performance, but also the factors that influence the development of group cohesiveness. We will focus on the development issue first.

Antecedents of Group Cohesiveness. Several variables can affect the development of group cohesiveness. By now you have probably guessed that one of these is the type of task being performed. In general, tasks that foster a high degree of interaction among group members are also the ones most likely to generate group cohesiveness. As we have seen previously, tasks involving reciprocal interdependence fit this category. Thus, other things being equal, we can expect reciprocal interdependence to generate more group cohesiveness than pooled interdependence. Similarly, the way in which the task is physically arranged can also affect interaction and cohesiveness. Tasks that are arranged so that group members all work in close physical proximity (e.g., in the same small room) will generate more cohesiveness than tasks that are not arranged in this way (e.g., when group members work on different floors or in different buildings). The reason is that working in close physical proximity to other group members facilitates interaction, even when interaction is not technically required by the task. This increased interaction leads to higher group cohesiveness.

A second factor that can affect the development of group cohesiveness is the group's history of success at the task. In general, groups that are successful at their task become more cohesive, while groups that are not successful become less cohesive (e.g., Blanchard, Weigel, & Cook, 1975). Note that the direction of causality here is performance-causes-cohesiveness. Thus, when performance is artificially manipulated in a laboratory setting—some groups are randomly told they are performing well, while other groups are told they are performing poorly—the "high performance" groups become more cohesive than the "low performance" groups. (The reverse causal relationship, cohesiveness-causes-performance, also holds, and will be discussed shortly.)

Some characteristics of the group also lead to group cohesiveness. For example, when the group members have a common goal, there is higher cohesiveness than when the group members have different goals. The common goal provides a focus around which attraction to the group can develop. Similarly, groups that engage in participative decision making are generally more cohesive than those that do not. Being able to influence the group's decision process seems to increase attraction to the group.

A final contribution to group cohesiveness is the personal characteristics of the group members. In our discussion of attitude theories in Chapter 5, one idea that frequently appeared was that people like other people who like the same things they do. That is, people are attracted to those individuals and groups who are similar to them. Empirical results suggest that similarities in race, background, education, attitudes, and values all lead to greater group cohesiveness. For example, one study examined the relationship between attitude similarity and cohesiveness in a set of newly formed task groups (Terborg, Castore, & DeNinno, 1976). The groups worked on a series of six projects over the course of 3 months. Group member attitudes on a wide variety of issues were assessed at the beginning of the 3-month period, and cohesiveness was measured after the completion of each of the six projects. It was found that over time groups whose members initially held similar attitudes became more cohesive than did groups whose members initially held dissimilar attitudes. This occurred even though the attitudes involved were not directly related to the tasks being performed.

To summarize, the factors contributing to the development of high group cohesiveness include group interaction, group success, shared goals, and group-member similarity. Once developed, high cohesiveness in a group can influence future group process and performance, as we will now discuss.

Consequences of Group Cohesiveness. One consequence of high group cohesiveness is that the group members are likely to spend more time communicating with one another. Further, their communication will generally be more free and unrestrained than is the case in noncohesive groups. Thus, both the quality and quantity of group interaction is increased by high group cohesiveness.

A second consequence of high group cohesiveness is that the group is likely to exert a strong influence on the behavior of individual group members. Group members are more likely to comply with group norms, and are more likely to yield to pressure from the group, when the group is highly cohesive. Only in those cases in which the individual feels it is extremely important to maintain independence will the expected compliance with group norms fail to occur.

Another consequence of high group cohesiveness is that group members are likely to have a high level of job satisfaction. This makes sense. As we discussed in Chapter 5, many measures of job satisfaction include at least one component focusing on the respondent's relationship with coworkers. If the other components of job satisfaction are held constant, greater attraction to the group (i.e., coworkers) should result in higher job satisfaction.

Finally, high group cohesiveness also has implications for performance, although the relationship is somewhat complex. As we stated previously, group members will usually be more willing to comply with group norms and yield to group pressure when the group is highly cohesive than when it is not. This means that in cohesive groups, members will usually be more willing to maintain whatever performance norm the group sets for itself. If high performance is the norm, each individual member of the group can be expected to try his or her hardest for high performance. If low performance is the norm (e.g., doing the least amount of work possible without getting hassled by superiors), each individual member can be expected to restrict his or her output to low performance. (Recall from Chapter 3 that this is exactly what occurred in the bank-wiring-room experiment in the Hawthorne studies.) In contrast, in noncohesive groups, members will be less motivated to behave in accordance with whatever performance norms exist. They will be less motivated to strive for high performance when high performance is the norm and less motivated to maintain low performance when low performance is the norm. In summary, cohesive groups should perform better than noncohesive groups when high performance is the norm, while noncohesive groups should perform better than cohesive groups when low performance is the norm.

These predictions were tested in two classic laboratory experiments (Berkowitz, 1954; Schachter, Ellertson, McBride, & Gregory, 1951). Both experiments used the same general procedure. Three-person work groups were set up to perform an assembly-line type of task. The three members of each group performed their individual parts of the overall task in separate rooms. The cohesiveness of the group and the type of performance pressure placed on the group members were experimentally manipulated. Group cohesiveness was manipulated by varying the degree to which the group members perceived themselves to be similar to one another (recall that perceived similarity is a variable that fosters the development of group cohesiveness). Some groups were led to believe that they were very similar to one another (high-cohesiveness condition), while others were led to believe that they were quite dissimilar (low-cohesiveness condition).

As they worked on the task, the group members received a series of handwritten notes allegedly coming from the other two members of the group (but actually written by the experimenter). Within each of the two cohesiveness conditions, some groups received notes urging them to work faster, while others received notes urging them to work more slowly. Thus, there were four conditions in the experiments: high-cohesive groups in which faster performance was urged, high-cohesive groups in which slower performance was urged, low-cohesive groups in which faster performance was urged, and low-cohesive groups in which slower performance was urged. The dependent variable was always the actual productivity of the individual group members. The results from one of the two studies are summarized in Figure 8-9.

As can be seen, the results are consistent with the predictions stated previously. Members seemed to be more willing to comply with the performance requests in the high-cohesive groups than in the low-cohesive groups. When they were urged to work faster, members of the high-cohesive groups worked faster than the members of the low-cohesive groups, and when they were urged to work more slowly, members of the high-cohesive groups worked slower than members of the low-cohesive groups. Thus, group cohesiveness can either improve or worsen performance, depending on whether the group norm is to strive for high performance or low performance.

FIGURE 8-9
In comparison to low-cohesive groups, members of high-cohesive groups worked faster when urged to work more quickly, and worked slower when urged to work more slowly. (*Based on data presented by Berkowitz, 1954.*)

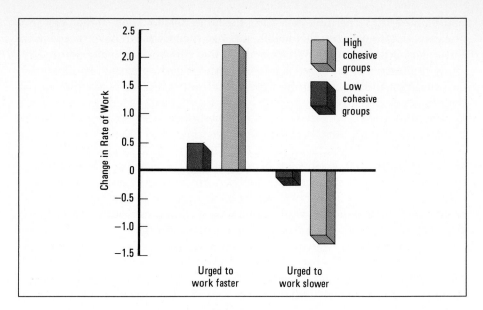

Summary

The purpose of this chapter was to introduce the dynamics of group behavior. A systems framework was used, and a portion of the chapter was devoted to reviewing the input factors that influence group process and output. The complexity of small group behavior is by now surely apparent. By recognizing this complexity, and taking it into account, organizations can do a better job of designing formal groups and can more effectively manage informal groups. The end result will be greater overall productivity for the organization and greater satisfaction for the group members.

Some of the major points from the chapter are listed below:

1. A small group consists of a few people (less than twenty) who interact over a fairly long period of time. They have common goals but often have different roles and responsibilities.
2. When people work in group settings they behave differently than when they work alone. They often become aroused by the mere presence of others. Sometimes they work harder and sometimes they work less hard, depending on both the group and the task. They can be more creative, and their attitudes can become more extreme.
3. An overall systems analysis of groups suggests three classes of input variables: personal characteristics, situational characteristics, and group structure. These inputs affect group interaction as well as group outputs (e.g., job satisfaction and productivity).
4. People join groups for a variety of reasons: To fulfill affiliative needs, to obtain information, to obtain rewards, and to accomplish goals.
5. Groups go through a distinct development phase. This stage clarifies the status, influence, and communication patterns that later affect group process and output.

6. Situational characteristics play an important role in structuring group interaction and performance. The physical placement of chairs and desks, the type of task, and the reward system all affect process and output.

7. Group composition can also significantly influence group process and performance. Important aspects of group composition include member characteristics, member compatibility, group homogeneity, and group size.

8. Finally, group cohesiveness is also important. Similar, interdependent, successful group members with common goals tend to develop a high level of group cohesiveness. Whether this increases or decreases group effectiveness depends on the norms of the group.

IMPLICATIONS FOR RESEARCH

A review of the research on small group behavior reveals an uneven distribution of scientific effort in several substantive and methodological areas. Perhaps the most glaring deficiency is in the area of group tasks. Our understanding of group tasks, in comparison to other variables, is rather limited. The reason has to do with the way social scientists who study small group behavior usually go about their business. What generally happens is that a researcher, interested in testing certain choice predictions from a pet theory, designs a neat study and devises a clever task that is uniquely suited to the particular subject population, variables, and conditions under investigation. Alternatively, the researcher might seek out existing groups that are already working on such a task. In either case, the chosen task is not likely to be very representative of the thousands of tasks that exist in organizations. Added to this is the fact that different researchers frequently use different tasks, and that even the same researcher will often use different tasks for different studies. The end result is a hodgepodge of research results, none of which are totally comparable with the others.

Two major problems occur as a function of this lack of comparability. First, as we have noted repeatedly throughout this chapter, the type of task the group is asked to perform strongly influences group process and output. This means that different tasks will lead to systematic variations in results across studies. Thus, what is found for one task may not hold when someone else tries to replicate the study using the same group variables and a slightly different task. This might not be a problem if we understood all of the important ways in which the tasks employed were similar and different, but we seldom do. Consequently, the generalizability of results is severely limited.

The second problem is that tasks usually have multiple performance criteria, and different types of criteria are appropriate for different types of tasks. Creativity of solutions, for example, might be appropriate for some types of tasks (e.g., solution-generation tasks—see McGrath's task type 2, Figure 8-6) but inappropriate for others (e.g., problem-solving tasks for which there is one objectively correct answer—see McGrath's task type 3). How then do you compare performance on such tasks? Again, the lack of comparability means that generalization is difficult.

Thus, the overall problem is that small group researchers have used tasks as a vehicle for studying groups, without giving much thought to studying the similarities and differences among the tasks themselves. To be sure, some work in this area has been done. McGrath's (1984) task typology presented earlier in this chapter is an example (see also Wood, 1986). But McGrath is only one of a small number of researchers working in this area. Furthermore, while his typology is one of the best currently available, it is by no means complete or without limitations. Much more research is needed in this area. Given the strong influence that task characteristics can have on group functioning, large advances in our understanding of group behavior can be made by improving what we know about the relationships among group tasks. This would seem to be a promising area for further research.

IMPLICATIONS FOR PRACTICE

Many people in organizations believe that groups can do a better job than people working alone. The research simply does not support such a sweeping generalization. Groups may sometimes take more risks than individuals, they may take a longer time to solve a problem, they may loaf, and they may sometimes intentionally restrict output. On the other hand, certain types of complex, interdependent tasks *are* better handled through group interaction. What is important to recognize is that groups work differently from people working alone. To maximize their effeciveness demands a complex match of people, situations, and jobs to be done. This is not an impossible task, and many of the following chapters will explicitly point out how this matching can be facilitated.

The important point to recognize here is that organizations *can* have a significant impact on how a group carries out its task. The physical environment (e.g., tables, chairs) can be manipulated, as can the size of the group or the way in which rewards are distributed. These variables can increase or decrease the formality, cooperativeness, and freedom of information exchange that results. One thing to remember is that the places in which people meet represent territory, and people form strong preferences and attachments to places and settings. A manager should actively decide (1) where a meeting should take place, (2) who should be there, and (3) where participants should sit. One good example is discussed by McCaskey (1979). He describes a manager who, just before beginning a tough negotiation at another manager's office, came early and sat in the biggest chair, which was obviously the preferred space of his adversary. He reports that the other manager was so upset by this event that he did not pay full attention to the discussion and consequently failed to press home the negotiation to his advantage.

McCaskey also points out how managers can arrange the offices of key subordinates to encourage or discourage interaction. Conference rooms with formal and informal arrangements are both available. In fact, space can be used as a means of recognition and motivation. John Dean, while a member of President Nixon's staff, noticed that the office arrangement in the White House was clearly a reflection of the degree to which someone had the President's ear (Dean, 1976).

Various strategies can also be used to manipulate the group composition and process. The organization can construct a group with similar or dissimilar people, with independent or interdependent activities, with public or private recognition or evaluation, with structured or unstructured regulations, and so on. These variables can increase or decrease the amount of influence or attraction among group members. Thus, to a much greater extent than is typically recognized, the organization can construct and change the ways in which a group will go about doing its job.

Another point that needs elaboration is the fact that highly cohesive groups, in which everyone likes one another and is committed to the group, are not necessarily a good thing. Some of the propositions generated from the human-relations movement and its current proponents have been over-simplified. Many managers may believe that having highly cohesive groups will be the answer to increased performance and productivity—"If everyone likes one another, communicates openly, and is committed to the goal, we are bound to be effective." Well, it just is not necessarily so. Who gets into the group, the match between their skills and the task, and the problem-solving process are equally important factors in group performance.

Too much cohesiveness and homogeneity can be stifling. It is comfortable for everyone to like one another, agree on important issues, and generally be supportive. However, it often leads to an oversimplified decision process. We will discuss this issue more fully in our chapter on group decision making (Chapter 12).

In summary, groups in organizations provide both positive and negative outcomes. They may sometimes be inefficient information generators, and various elements of individual initiative or responsibility may suffer. On the other hand, because of task complexities people frequently must interact in groups in order to understand and deal successfully with broad problems. The question is thus not groups versus no groups, but rather, when are groups most effective, and how can they be used to best advantage?

Discussion Questions

1. What are the differences in an individual's behavior when working as a member of a group versus working alone? When does it seem particularly useful to form groups?
2. Discuss the various territorial variables that seem to affect group process. How could you manipulate these variables to increase or decrease intimacy?
3. What makes a group highly cohesive? When is this type of group desirable and undesirable?

CASE: THE DRILL TEAM

Bobby wasn't sure why he had volunteered or why he had been chosen, but it sounded like it might be fun. He had been in the Marines 3 years, and when they asked for volunteers for a special drill unit that would put on exhibitions, he signed up. Their first performance was tomorrow in front of a large crowd, and thinking back about it Bobby was sure they were ready. They would do a dynamite job.

But it hadn't been easy. He hadn't a clue what to expect when he showed up the first day, but the captain in charge quickly clarified things. First, all of the men were separated into a special barracks. They ate together, practiced together, and partied together. Bobby was surprised to see that almost all of the men chosen seemed to be people he would like as friends. They were the same age, had similar interests, and liked the same things he did. He actually enjoyed their company. They had lots to talk about and had fun together.

He also liked the special treatment. They all had special uniforms and were given special privileges. They had a song they sang when they were practicing, and before every meal they all stood and chanted a short hymn:

> They work us hard
> No time to rest
> But the 473rd
> Is the goddamn best.

The pressure to do well was intense. You didn't want to let your buddies down. They practiced on a special field where visitors and VIPs would watch. And every time anyone made a mistake it meant 10 extra minutes of drill. However, when they got it right the whole unit got some extra leave time. He had to admit it—the captain was tough but he was fair. And now, after 12 weeks they were ready—a well-practiced, disciplined, cohesive unit. He was excited.

Questions about the Case

1. List some things the captain did that helped make the drill team cohesive.
2. Why do you think Bobby liked the other members of the unit?
3. Do you think the team will be bothered by the crowd?
4. Under what sort of circumstances are the leaders who form such groups likely to be effective?

References

Baker, P. M. (1984). Seeing is believing: Visibility and participation in small groups. *Environment & Behavior, 16,* 159–184.

Bales, R. F., & Borgatta, E. F. (1956). Size of group as a factor in the interaction profile. In A. P. Hare, E. F. Borgatta, & R. F. Bales (Eds.), *Small groups.* New York: Knopf.

Bales, R. F., & Cohen, S. P. (1979). *SYMLOG: A system for multiple level observation of groups.* New York: Free Press.

Bass, B. M. (1981). *Stogdill's handbook of leadership: A survey of theory and research* (rev. and expanded ed.). New York: Free Press.

Baumgartel, H., & Sobol, R. (1959). Background and organizational factors in absenteeism. *Personnel Psychology, 12,* 431–443.

Becker, F. D., Gield, B., & Foggatt, C. C. (1983). Seating position and impression formation in an office setting. *Journal of Environmental Psychology, 3,* 253–261.

Berkowitz, L. (1954). Group standards, cohesiveness, and productivity. *Human Relations, 7,* 509–519.

Blanchard, F. A., Weigel, R. H., & Cook, S. W. (1975). The effect of relative competence of group members upon interpersonal attraction in cooperating interracial groups. *Journal of Personality and Social Psychology, 32,* 519–530.

Bordley, R. F. (1983). A Bayesian model of group polarization. *Organizational Behavior and Human Performance, 32,* 262–274.

Cartwright, D. (1968). The nature of group cohesiveness. In D. Cartwright & A.

Zander (Eds.), *Group dynamics: Research and theory* (3d ed.). New York: Harper & Row.

Cleland, S. (1955). *Influence of plant size on industrial relations.* Princeton, NJ: Princeton University Press.

Davis, T. R. V. (1984). The influence of the physical environment in offices. *Academy of Management Review, 9,* 271–283.

Dean, J. W. (1976). *Blind ambition: The White House years.* New York: Simon & Schuster.

Hollander, E. P. (1985). Leadership and power. In G. Lindzey & E. Aronson (Eds.), *The handbook of social psychology* (3d ed., Vol. 2, pp. 485–537). NY: Random House.

Kanter, R. M. (1977a). Some effects of proportions on group life: Skewed sex ratios and responses to token women. *American Journal of Sociology, 82,* 965–990.

Kanter, R. M. (1977b). *Men and women of the corporation.* New York: Basic Books.

Lamm, H., & Myers, D. G. (1978). Group induced polarization of attitudes and behavior. In L. Berkowitz (Ed.), *Advances in experimental social psychology* (Vol. 11, pp. 145–195). New York: Academic Press.

Latané, B., Williams, K., & Harkins, S. (1979a). Many hands make light the work: The causes and consequences of social loafing. *Journal of Personality and Social Psychology, 37,* 822–832.

Latané, B., Williams, K., & Harkins, S. (1979b, October). Social loafing. *Psychology Today,* p. 104.

Lawler, E. E. III, & Mohrman, S. A. (1985, Jan.-Feb.). Quality circles after the fad. *Harvard Business Review, 63,* 64–71.

Markus, H. (1978). The effect of mere presence on social facilitation: An unobtrusive test. *Journal of Experimental Social Psychology, 14,* 389–397.

McCain, B. E., O'Reilly, C., & Pfeffer, J. (1983). The effect of departmental demography on turnover: The case of a university. *Academy of Management Journal, 26,* 626–641.

McCaskey, M. B. (1979, November-December). The hidden messages managers send. *Harvard Business Review, 57,* 135–148.

McGrath, J. E. (1984). *Groups: Interaction and performance.* Englewood Cliffs, NJ: Prentice-Hall.

Miller, L., & Hamblin, R. (1963). Interdependence, differential rewarding and productivity. *American Sociological Review, 28,* 768–778.

Moede, W. (1927). Die Richtlinien der Leistungs-Psychologie. *Industrielle Psychotechnik, 4,* 193–207.

Oldham, G. R., & Brass, D. J. (1979). Employee reactions to an open-plan office: A naturally occurring quasi-experiment. *Administrative Science Quarterly, 24,* 267–284.

Pfeffer, J. (1983). Organization demography. In L. L. Cummings & B. M. Staw (Eds.), *Research in organizational behavior* (Vol. 5, pp. 299–357). Greenwich, CT: JAI Press.

Preston, P., & Quesada, A. (1978). What does your office "say" about you? In P. J. Frost, V. W. Mitchell, & W. R. Nord (Eds.), *Organizational reality* (pp. 110–114). Santa Monica, CA: Goodyear.

Quality circles become contagious (1980, April 14). *Industry Week,* p. 99 ff.

Schachter, S., Ellertson, N., McBride, D., & Gregory, D. (1951). An experimental study of cohesiveness and productivity. *Human Relations, 4,* 229–238.

Shaw, M. E. (1981). *Group dynamics.: The psychology of small group behavior* (3d ed.). New York: McGraw-Hill.

Sistrunk, F., & McDavid, J. W. (1971). Sex variable in conformity behavior. *Journal of Personality and Social Psychology, 17,* 200–207.

Slater, P. E. (1958). Contrasting correlates of group size. *Sociometry, 21,* 129–139.

Sommer, R. (1969). *Personal space: The behavioral basis of design.* Englewood Cliffs, NJ: Prentice-Hall.

Stein, R. T., & Heller, T. (1979). An empirical analysis of the correlations between leadership status and participation rates reported in the literature. *Journal of Personality and Social Psychology, 37,* 1993–2002.

Strodtbeck, F. L., & Hook,, L. H. (1961). The social dimensions of a twelve man jury team. *Sociometry, 24,* 397–415.

Terborg, J. R., Castore, C., & DeNinno, J. A. (1976). A longitudinal field investigation of the impact of group composition on group performance and cohesion. *Journal of Personality and Social Psychology, 34,* 782–790.

Triplett, N. (1897). The dynamogenic factors in pacemaking and competition. *American Journal of Psychology, 9,* 507–533.

Wagner, W. G., Pfeffer, J., & O'Reilly, C. (1984). Organizational demography and turnover in top management groups. *Administrative Science Quarterly, 29,* 74–92.

Whyte, W. F. (1943). *Street corner society.* Chicago: University of Chicago Press.

Wood, R. E. (1986). Task complexity: Definition of the construct. *Organizational Behavior and Human Decision Processes, 37,* 60–82.

Yetton, P., & Bottger, P. (1983). The relationships among group size, member ability, social decision scheme, and performance. *Organizational Behavior and Human Performance, 32,* 145–159.

Zajonc, R. B. (1965). Social facilitation. *Science, 149,* 269–274.

Zweigenhaft, R. L. (1976). Personal space in the faculty office: Desk placement and the student-faculty interaction. *Journal of Applied Psychology, 61,* 529–532.

Chapter 9

Roles, Norms, and Status

All the world's a stage,
And all the men and women merely players.
They have their exits and their entrances;
And one man in his time plays many parts.
—WILLIAM SHAKESPEARE

In Chapter 2, "Understanding People," we introduced the idea that much of our behavior in organizational settings is learned behavior. Part of what we learn are the specialized technical skills that are needed for the job. Often these are acquired in formal training programs. Beyond technical skills, however, we also learn a great deal about the way in which the organization around us operates, and about what types of behavior are appropriate and inappropriate. This information can be just as important as technical skills for ensuring our success on the job. However, it is hardly ever acquired in formal training programs. Instead, this type of information is usually learned informally through experience. By both observing and interacting with the organizational environment, we learn what is expected and what gets rewarded. We learn the ropes, if you like. To understand better what we mean by the phrase "learning the ropes," consider the following story about a typical employee's first experience with a new job.

Jim Hanson had recently received his B.A. degree from a big Midwestern school of business. Shortly before graduating he interviewed for a number of jobs. He was interested in the field of marketing, and was happy to receive a job offer from a large corporation that produces computer software. He eagerly accepted the job and reported for work.

The first day on the job was rather routine. Jim, along with other new employees, was given a brief, 2-hour orientation. They learned the history of the company, its size, its locations throughout the world, and heard some general statements about how management hoped that everyone would feel as if they were part of one big happy family. Along with this orientation came a number of forms and pamphlets. These materials provided important information about insurance and health care benefits, recreational opportunities, and general organizational policies. In addition, they were each given a neatly bound organization handbook that explained most of the important rules and regulations.

After this meeting everyone went their separate ways, and Jim was off to meet the people in the marketing department. The department's administrative assistant showed Jim around. He was introduced to everyone (twelve people), shown his desk, and given some materials to look over. This latter information was meant to help Jim understand what was currently going on in the department and the kind of work that he would be doing. He was encouraged to ask questions and get acquainted with everyone on a leisurely basis.

Over the next few weeks, Jim was fairly cautious. He observed what went on, and he listened to what was said. He made a couple of mistakes, and he was corrected. He asked questions about things he did not understand, and after a short time he began to feel like part of the group.

What exactly did Jim observe? The following is a list of things that anyone new to a job might notice during the first few weeks of work:

1. The types of tasks one is expected to do and one's particular areas of responsibility.
2. The quantity and quality of the work that is expected.
3. How people behave in positions similar to one's own.
4. The degree to which people obey the rules and regulations of the organization (e.g., Do people come to work on time?).
5. How others dress—formally or informally.
6. How hard people work.
7. Who talks to whom—who talks and who listens.
8. One's relationship with one's boss: What does he or she want? How is he or she treated by others?

Concept	Behavioral Focus	Key Relationships
Role	Job	Horizontal and vertical
Norm	Subgroup: same level	Horizontal
Status	Subgroup: all levels	Vertical

FIGURE 9-1
A summary of role, norm, and status concepts.

This list is not inclusive. There are other things that would undoubtedly be noticed. The important point is that we can systematically classify this list as a function of *what* is being learned.

First, items 1 through 3 deal with specific things Jim must learn about his job. They clarify expectations about how someone in his particular position should behave. He must learn what to do, how to do it, whom to talk to, how much to do, and the general responsibilities that accompany his position. This set of expectations, rules, and regulations for a particular position is called one's *role* in the organization.

Second, items 4 through 6 focus on the appropriate or expected behavior *for the work group as a whole,* not for a specific position. Jim can thus learn the "informal" rules and expectations of his peers. These expectations are called group *norms.* Their focus is on the lateral, or horizontal, interactions within a group.

Finally, items 7 and 8 focus on behavior that occurs with respect to people above and below one in both the *formal* and the *informal* organizational hierarchy. Jim can learn to whom he should defer and how to interact with people who are his immediate superiors and subordinates. These expectations are often discussed under the heading of *status differences.*

In summary, Jim probably learned a lot in those first few days. He undoubtedly began to understand the scope of his job—his role. He also probably began to understand the behaviors generally expected in his group—the norms—and the complex vertical relationships inherent in any organization—the status hierarchy. Figure 9-1 summarizes these relationships. The rest of this chapter discusses roles, norms, and status in more detail.

ROLE RELATIONSHIPS

As we have suggested, the set of *expected* behaviors for a particular position is called a *role.* In our example, Jim's knowledge about how to do the job, whom he should work with, and the kinds of interactions that are expected of him are all part of his role. These expectations come with the *position* and are not part of Jim's personal characteristics. The role expectations would be the same for anyone filling that position.

But let us continue with Jim's story a little further. After work, Jim catches a bus to get home. There are a number of women who get on the bus at the same time as Jim, but there are too few seats for everyone. Jim decides to stand. When he gets home his wife is fixing dinner and the children are outside playing. Since there are a few hours of daylight left, Jim quickly mows the backyard before eating. After playing with the children for a while and talking to his wife, Jim leaves with a couple of his buddies to go bowling. Jim belongs to a bowling league and is the captain of his team. This means that he has to be there every week. He feels responsible for choosing who will bowl in what position and for motivating his teammates. He loves it. After a few laughs, a few beers, and some good sport, Jim returns home and goes to bed.

The point of this example is that we all fill numerous roles. There are certain expectations that come along with being a man, husband, father, and bowling-team leader. Generally, men are expected to let women sit down on the bus. In some families, husbands are expected to mow the lawn and wives to cook dinner. And leaders are expected to organize and motivate team members. While sex-role stereotypes are gradually breaking down, and in a few cases even reversing, this does not negate the existence of these roles. It simply means that the expected behaviors that accompany them are changing.

We all have many roles to fill. Our primary concern here, however, is with *work roles*, that is, roles directly related to our behavior on the job. Several characteristics of these roles should be emphasized. First, work roles are *impersonal*. They apply to *anyone* occupying a given position. Second, they are related to *task behavior*. An organizational role is that set of expected behaviors that goes with a particular job. If you like, it is an informal behavioral job description. Third, work roles can be fairly difficult to pin down exactly. The problem is in defining who determines what is expected. Is it the role occupant's perceptions of what others expect? Or should we ask other group members what they expect of someone in a particular job and then use some sort of average to define the role? What the role occupant actually does—that is, how he or she behaves—could also be used. What we perceive as our role, what others perceive as our role, and what we actually do may all be very different from one another (cf. Berger-Gross & Kraut, 1984). This makes it difficult to define what the "real" role is. Finally, roles are learned quickly and can result in major changes in both attitude and behavior. Much of what we *think* and *do* is determined by our roles.

A classic example of just how pervasive the effect of organizational roles can be was provided by Lieberman (1956). He gave a questionnaire to over 2,000 rank-and-file employees in two appliance manufacturing plants in order to determine their attitudes toward management. After a year he returned and discovered that twenty-three of these employees had subsequently been promoted to the role of foreman, and thirty-five had subsequently been elected to the role of union steward. Lieberman readministered the attitude questionnaire to these fifty-eight people and compared their attitudes before and after the role changes. The main findings from this study are summarized in Figure 9-2. Before any of the role changes, these employees had fairly similar attitudes toward management. After the changes, however, the foremen became more positive toward management, while the union stewards became more negative. Thus, for example, after being promoted, the foremen were more likely to endorse the principle of incentive pay, while the union stewards were more likely to endorse seniority as a basis for wage payments. Although several weaknesses in Lieberman's study have been noted by other researchers (e.g., Cook & Campbell, 1976), his results strongly suggest that work roles can indeed affect not only behavior, but attitudes as well.

Lieberman's (1956) study illustrates one other important point. The role of the first-line supervisor is one of the most difficult roles to hold in an

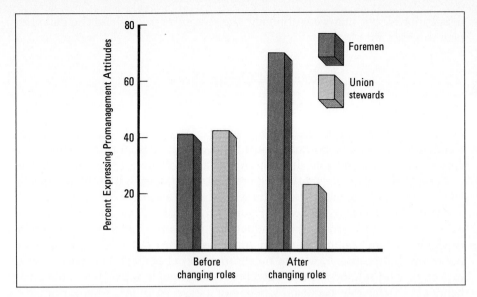

FIGURE 9-2
After changing roles, employees who became foremen expressed more positive attitudes toward management, while employees who became union stewards expressed more negative attitudes toward management. (*Based on data presented by Lieberman, 1956.*)

organization. The supervisor who has risen through the ranks was at one time probably a union member and a friend to many of his or her coworkers. However, after being promoted, the supervisor is likely to find that the expectations of his or her superiors about attitudes and support for the company directly conflict with many of the feelings and attitudes of the people below. The managers above are likely to be interested in efficiency, performance, and cost, while the employees below will be concerned about wages, security, and comfort. Management is likely to see labor contracts and work rules as restrictive, while the employees see them as protection against arbitrary and capricious actions. Managers expect loyalty and commitment, while subordinates want recognition. The first-line supervisor is caught right in the middle. Some of the conflicting demands and expectations that confront the first-line supervisor are listed below (Sasser & Leonard, 1980):

1. The supervisor may not be privy to management policy but is expected to carry out directives.
2. The supervisor is no longer a member of the workforce but must depend heavily on the workers.
3. The supervisor is the first level of management but has little real authority.
4. The supervisor is expected to maintain high morale but is forced to spend lots of time involved in record keeping and "putting out fires."
5. The supervisor is asked to have commitment to management but is often in a dead-end job.
6. The supervisor's age, training, and education are often more similar to those of the subgroup he or she supervises than to the group with whom he or she is supposed to identify.

Thus, first-line supervisors clearly have a tough job to perform. Middle management must make sure that these built-in conflicts and ambiguities do not overwhelm the supervisor. We will discuss some of these issues in more detail shortly, but first we will review the research on roles and the part they play in group interaction.

Roles and Group Process

Work roles have been the focus of a vast amount of organizational research. A large portion of this research concerns itself with the ways in which work roles are learned, change, and affect group behavior and performance (e.g., Katz & Kahn, 1978). Three important concepts have evolved from this research: role episode, role set, and role differentiation. Each of these is discussed below.

Perhaps the most frequently used concept for understanding the process by which work roles are learned and change is the *role episode.* The components of a role episode are diagrammed in Figure 9-3. A role episode begins with the expectations that a group of individuals hold for a particular position. These expectations are communicated in some fashion to the role occupant (the person in that position), who in turn forms a set of perceptions about what is expected. The role occupant's perceptions then guide his or her subsequent behavior. If the role occupant's behavior (stage 4) differs widely from the group's expectations (stage 1), additional communication about expectations occurs in an effort to correct the role occupant's behavior. This process continues either until the actual behavior of the role occupant changes to conform to the expectations of the group, or until the expectations of the group change.

Note that stages 1 and 3 are essentially cognitive or perceptual in nature. They have to do with what people think *should* be done. On the other hand, stages 2 and 4 consist of observable behavior—what is communicated and what is *actually* done. Data can be gathered about all four stages, and comparisons between and among the stages can yield some important insights about job stress and morale. We return to these points in the next section.

A second important concept for understanding work roles is that of the *role set.* The role set refers to the group (set) of individuals who hold *and communicate* expectations regarding how a role occupant should behave. These are the individuals referred to in stages 1 and 2 of the role-episode model. In most cases the role set consists of people who interact frequently with the role occupant and discuss important matters with him or her. They are often peers and supervisors in the role occupant's immediate work group, but they may

FIGURE 9-3
The role episode.

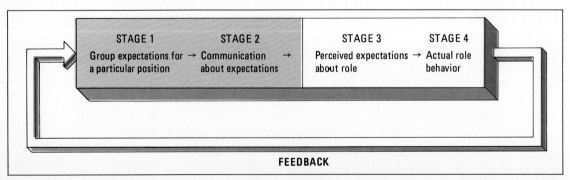

STAGE 1	STAGE 2	STAGE 3	STAGE 4
Group expectations for a particular position	→ Communication about expectations	→ Perceived expectations about role	→ Actual role behavior

FEEDBACK

also be subordinates, individuals from other work units in the organization, and even individuals who are not part of the organization at all (e.g., important customers, or agents of governmental regulatory bodies). All of these people may qualify as members of the role set for a given position if they (1) have expectations for how the role occupant should behave, and (2) make their expectations known to him or her. Finally, it should be emphasized that the role set is identified with the position, not the occupant. Thus, the role set can remain the same even though the role occupant may change.

The role set concept is useful in several ways. The size and diversity of the role set, for example, can tell us much about the patterns of communication that exist in an organization. Further, role occupants are likely to have clearer role perceptions (stage 3 in the model) when the role set is small than when it is large. The reason is that as the size of the role set increases, the opportunity for conflicting expectations among the role set members also increases. Finally, small role sets are often associated with the development of cliques and isolated groups within the larger organizational unit.

A final concept, and one that has been especially useful in understanding the *formal* role structure of work groups, is called *role differentiation*. Role differentiation refers to the extent to which distinctly different types of functions are performed by different (as opposed to the same) group members. For example, in many task groups several different roles can be identified. One role might focus on procedures. A person performing this role might be concerned with such issues as time schedules, agendas, and deadlines. Another role might have to do with information. Here, the role may call for clarifying problems and for acquiring and disseminating information necessary to solve those problems. Yet another role might focus on providing emotional support for the group. A person performing this role would be concerned with maintaining harmonious interpersonal relations among the group members. Other roles could also be identified. Although it is possible for a single person to perform all of these roles (e.g., the group leader), this generally does not happen. Instead, the roles usually get divided up. For example, a group member who is highly active in performing task-oriented roles generally is not the person who is most active in performing the emotional support role (McGrath, 1984). To the extent that the various informal roles performed in a group are performed by *different* group members, a high degree of role differentiation is said to exist.

Thus, an understanding of roles tells us much more than just how people learn about what they are supposed to do in their particular position. Roles also help us understand the ongoing interaction and communication process in organizations. Further, they help us see how the various contributions of different members fit together like the pieces of a puzzle to produce a smoothly running, effective unit.

Role Problems

In addition to telling us about the effective functioning of organizations, roles also help us understand many of the problems that exist in organizations. Three such problems are discussed below: role conflict, role ambiguity, and role overload.

Role Conflict. Role conflict occurs whenever two or more role expectations are *incompatible* (Katz & Kahn, 1978). Incompatibility means that any attempt by the role occupant to comply with one expectation makes compliance with other expectations difficult or impossible.

There are four different types of role conflict. The difference among these four types is simply the source of the incompatible expectations. The first type is known as *intrasender role conflict.* This occurs whenever a single member of the role set sends two or more incompatible expectations. An example might be when your boss says, "I don't care how you get it done, just get it done this afternoon. And don't break any rules in the process!" Another example is, "Give this project your top priority, but don't neglect any of your other responsibilities while you are working on it."

A second type of role conflict is called *intersender role conflict.* This type occurs whenever two or more members of the role set send incompatible expectations. As we indicated above, the job of a first-line supervisor is full of intersender role conflict. Management often sends the first-line supervisor role expectations (e.g., increase productivity) that are incompatible with the role expectations sent by subordinates (e.g., give us more time off). Another situation in which there is a high incidence of intersender role conflict is a matrix organization (Davis & Lawrence, 1977). Recall from Chapter 3, "Understanding Organizations," that a matrix structure is one in which the organization is simultaneously differentiated on the basis of *two* different criteria (e.g., by function and by product) and that managers in this type of structure have *two* bosses (e.g., one representing the function and one representing the product). These managers frequently encounter incompatible expectations from their two bosses (e.g., the product boss expects the manager to allocate resources in a way that is beneficial for the product, although not necessarily for the function as a whole, while the function boss wants the manager to allocate resources in a way that is beneficial to the function as a whole, although this may hurt some individual products).

Yet another type of conflict is called *interrole conflict.* This occurs whenever two or more roles held by the same person make incompatible demands. Consider, for example, the head of the marketing department who must meet with the heads of the other departments to discuss how certain monies will be distributed. As a member of the management team, this individual will want to do what is best for the whole organization, but as the head of marketing he or she will want that department to receive extra benefits. These two goals may not be compatible.

Another good example of interrole conflict is often experienced by working women. The traditional role of homemaker, mother, and housewife is being accepted by fewer and fewer women. Half of the workforce in the United States today is composed of women. The problem is that men often expect women to hold full-time jobs *and* be full-time mothers, wives, and homemakers. Indeed, research suggests that women actually do assume a larger share of household duties than men in families in which both spouses work full time. Only when the husband provides a great deal of support and help in handling family affairs does this interrole conflict get reduced (Terborg, 1977).

A final type of role conflict is called *person-role conflict.* This refers to the conflict that occurs whenever the role occupant's personal attitudes or values are incompatible with role expectations. For example, suppose you see a fellow student cheat on an exam. Your personal values may tell you to report the incident, but your role as a friend and a student may inhibit you. The Watergate affair was filled with examples of person-role conflicts, and it is interesting to note how different people resolved them. Some left the government, some looked the other way, some actively joined in the cover-up, some pleaded ignorance, and some went to the prosecutor.

In summary, there are a number of different ways in which conflict can occur in work roles. Given all of these possibilities, it seems highly unlikely that any work role can be completely conflict-free. If this is the case, it is important to ask what impact role conflict has. What are the consequences of role conflict?

The research on this point is fairly clear. A recent review of fifty-nine independent studies found that role conflict has its strongest effect on satisfaction with coworkers and supervisors, satisfaction with pay, job involvement, and commitment (Fisher & Gitelson, 1983). In comparison to those who experience low levels of role conflict, those who experience relatively high role conflict tend to be less satisfied with coworkers and supervisors (two groups who are likely to be sources of role conflict), often feel underpaid, are frequently less personally invested in their work, and tend to be less committed to their organization. Role conflict also has an effect on performance and actual turnover, although these effects are fairly weak. Compared to those who experience low role conflict, those who experience high role conflict tend to perform more poorly and have a higher rate of turnover. It thus seems fairly safe to say that role conflict can be a serious problem for organizations.

Role Ambiguity. *Role ambiguity* simply means that the role occupant is uncertain about what he or she is supposed to do (Katz & Kahn, 1978). Role ambiguity can exist either because the role occupant is unsure of the goals to be achieved in the position, or because he or she is unsure of how to achieve those goals. Uncertainty about goals sometimes occurs when an organization creates a new job just to accommodate a promising young employee. If a new job is created primarily for the purpose of rewarding (and thus retaining) an extremely capable person, there is a good chance that neither the employee nor the organization will have a very clear idea about what the ultimate goals of the job are. And, even when the goals are clear, there may still be considerable ambiguity about how best to achieve them. How, for example, does one go about achieving the goal of improving the efficiency of a company's personnel department? Both of these types of role ambiguity (ambiguity about goals and ambiguity about the means to achieve goals) seem more likely to occur in middle- and upper-level management positions than in lower-level positions.

The role-episode model presented in Figure 9-3 suggests that the root source of role ambiguity is in the role set. It occurs when the members of the role set either do not themselves have very clear expectations for the position, or do not effectively communicate their expectations. Note here the distinction between role ambiguity and role conflict. Role ambiguity occurs when expectations communicated by the role set are not clear, whereas role conflict occurs when expectations communicated by the role set are clear but incompatible.

Like role conflict, role ambiguity has been shown to have important negative consequences for both the role occupant and the organization as a whole (Fisher & Gitelson, 1983). In general, higher levels of role ambiguity can lead to lower satisfaction, lower job involvement, and lower commitment to the organization. There is also evidence that high levels of role ambiguity can lead to lower performance. This latter finding is consistent with the results from the goal-setting literature discussed in Chapter 6, "Motivation." Recall that the performance of individuals tends to be significantly higher when specific (as opposed to "do your best") goals are set (Locke, Shaw, Saari, & Latham, 1981). One reason for this is that specific goals reduce role ambiguity.

Given that negative effects can result from both role ambiguity and role conflict, we might wonder which problem is more serious. The answer depends on the level of the position we are talking about (Schuler, 1975). Role conflict seems to be a more serious problem at lower levels of the organization, while role ambiguity causes more difficulties at higher levels. The explanation for this is that at higher levels managers can use their power and influence to reduce conflict by changing rules, regulations, structural variables, or responsibilities. These upper-level jobs may continue, however, to be ambiguous or hard to define. At lower levels the jobs may be better defined and less ambiguous, but role conflict may be more extreme. Moreover, the lower-level employee is less likely to have the resources to remove the conflict.

Role Overload. There is one additional role concept that deserves our attention—role overload. *Role overload* occurs when the expectations and demands of a role exceed the role occupant's ability to respond. Overload frequently appears in situations that are also ambiguous. Because expectations are unclear, more and more demands are made of the individual.

The human-resources director within a personnel department might serve as a good example. This individual is often seen as an expert on human problems and is frequently asked to serve as an organizational troubleshooter. There are few explicit demands in this role except to help people out when they have difficulties. What frequently happens is that all employees think they have access to this person's time and expertise. They have no idea who else is demanding the director's time, so they go to him or her and say, "We have a managerial problem with our group in Peoria" or "How can we keep the union out of our Albany plant?" or "Turnover is high for our production groups—can you help us solve the problem?" The number of projects the director may get involved in can quickly get out of hand. Yet it is hard to say *no*, simply because few clear regulations exist as to how the director's time should be spent. It can be a very frustrating experience.

Research on role overload has produced findings similar to those for role conflict and ambiguity. In general, overload creates dissatisfaction, fatigue, and tension. Further, role overload has also been shown to be related to medical symptoms not unlike those observed among people exhibiting the Type A behavior pattern. In one study of government employees, for example, role overload was measured both objectively and subjectively (i.e., by self-report questionnaire). Both types of measures indicated that employees who experienced a high level of role overload also had higher heart rates and higher levels of serum cholesterol than did employees who experienced less role overload (Caplan, 1972). Although these findings are only correlational, they do suggest the possibility that some organizational role problems can produce serious health effects.

The problems created by role ambiguity, conflict, and overload are serious. The impact on both individuals and organizations is immense. Several remedies for these problems are described in the following section.

Remedies for Role Problems

Given the potential problems that role conflict, role ambiguity, and role overload can cause, it is important to consider what an organization can do to reduce these effects. Essentially, there are three alternatives: (1) change the job, (2) train the person, or (3) select the "right" type of person in the first place. We will discuss each of these options.

Changing the Job. The goal here is to reduce ambiguity, conflict, or overload through structural changes. Interdependencies can be reduced, and lines of authority can be modified. More explicit job descriptions can be supplied. A number of studies have shown that these techniques can successfully reduce ambiguity and conflict (cf. Goode, 1960).

The real problem with this alternative is that many jobs have ambiguity or conflict inherently built into them. For example, a portion of the role-theory literature focuses on what are known as boundary-spanning positions. These are jobs that require employees to deal with organizations or organizational units outside of the one in which they are employed. The procurement of resources, public relations, and marketing are activities that often demand such positions.

One might predict that people occupying boundary-spanning positions would experience a high degree of role conflict, and in general, research results support this hypothesis (Fisher & Gitelson, 1983). However, these types of positions are important and necessary for the functioning of the organization. Getting rid of them is simply not a viable option.

The same argument could be made for other types of positions. Roles that demand creativity are often unstructured. The position of university professor is one example, as are positions in marketing and in research and development in business organizations. Although ambiguity abounds in these jobs, it is not feasible to change or eliminate them. If we cannot change these jobs, we must explore other means of resolving the problem.

Training. A second alternative is to train people to adjust to their roles. One training technique that can be effective is role playing. *Role playing* involves the following steps: (1) a group of people read a script or case about some situation, (2) they are each assigned to play the role of one of the persons in the case, (3) the case is actually played out, and (4) the participants in the exercise, along with the trainer, discuss and evaluate how they behaved in the role play.

The purpose of role playing as a method of dealing with role problems is twofold. First, it acquaints the individual with situations that he or she may actually face in an organizational setting. If the player has just been hired or promoted, it can serve as a useful job preview. Having knowledge about areas of conflict and ambiguity before events occur can help people adjust to and deal with those problems. Second, it gives people practice in developing skills to cope with ambiguity and conflict. Thus, one can actually learn how to become more proficient at the role.

Selection. Beyond training, there is evidence that some types of people are just better able to deal with conflict and ambiguity than others. For example, people who have a high need to achieve have difficulty in ambiguous situations (McClelland, 1985), while extroverts do not. There are personality measures available to assess these types of characteristics. If management knows that a job has built-in conflicts and ambiguities, it should try to select someone who can cope with these demands.

In closing this section, we would like to state two conclusions. First, organizations should be aware of role ambiguity, conflict, and overload as potential causes of such problems as low morale and decreased productivity. These negative outcomes are all too frequently attributed simply to the personality characteristics of the job holders. What role theory says is that the way in which the job is defined is also a crucial determinant of morale and effectiveness. The second conclusion is that organizations can assess these problems and can seek out methods to remedy them. Through proper job analysis, job design, training, and selection, problems such as role ambiguity, conflict, and overload can become manageable issues.

NORMS

If you observe any work group for even a short period of time, you will quickly begin to notice certain regularities in the behavior of the group members. They may all come to work a little early each morning so that they have a few minutes to chat before starting their daily routine; they may take the same length coffee break at almost exactly the same time each morning and afternoon; they may produce close to the same amount of work each day; and they may all leave work a few minutes early. You may also notice regularities in the way they dress, how they interact, and the way they go about their jobs. If you ask them why they behave the way they do, they may say, "That's the way things are done around here" or "All of us expect to leave a little early."

These regularities in group behavior are termed *social norms*. Norms reflect shared group expectations about appropriate behavior. Just as roles define what is appropriate for a particular job, norms define acceptable behavior for the work unit as a whole. Roles *differentiate* group members. They specify how group members should behave *differently* from one another. Norms, on the other hand, tend to *integrate* the group. They indicate how group members should behave *the same*. In this section we will discuss the characteristics of norms and the important function they serve in group interaction.

FIGURE 9-4
Learning the norms
on a new job is
very important for
success.

Properties and Characteristics of Norms

Implicit in the definition of norms just given are two important characteristics. First, norms involve relatively clear beliefs about what behaviors are appropriate. These beliefs are usually clear enough that they can be articulated by the group members (e.g., "No one here breaks his neck for the company."). Second, there is a certain degree of agreement among group members about these beliefs. If there were no agreement, and instead the group members had very different ideas about what behaviors were appropriate, we would be forced to conclude that no coherent norms existed.

Beyond these two characteristics, several other properties of norms can be identified. The first is that norms generally have an "oughtness" about them. That is, they describe how one "should" behave. As such, they are sometimes closely linked to basic values held by the group members (e.g., groups will usually develop informal norms for distributing work among themselves based on the values of equity and fairness). Second, norms are generally more obvious and more easily recognized for behaviors that are important to the group. In a bank, for example, norms about the appropriate way to dress are often much more apparent among groups whose jobs bring them in contact with the bank's customers (e.g., tellers, loan officers) than among those who work in the "back office" (e.g., in the bank's data processing center). Third, norms are enforced by the group. Many of the behaviors expected on the job are monitored and enforced by the organization. For norms, however, it is the group members who must regulate the behavior. Fourth, there is variability in both the degree to which norms are shared and the degree to which behavior that deviates from the norm is acceptable.

269

The Structure of Norms

The last characteristic listed above, that is, variability in both the degree to which norms are shared and the degree to which deviant behavior is acceptable, warrants further discussion. To help with this discussion, it is useful to consider a more detailed example. The following narrative was written by the first author and describes an early job experience.

> During college I worked in the summer for the department of motor vehicles in a big city. We painted the lines on the streets. There were a number of crews, and each crew consisted of three or four men. We came to work at 8:15 A.M. (punched a time clock) and left at 4:45 P.M. Like a good, eager new employee I was there the first day at 8:00 A.M., and I was ready to paint lines at 8:15 A.M. Well, it turned out we had to spend a little time loading up the truck, getting our work orders, changing our clothes, and generally fooling around until about 9:00 A.M., when it was appropriate for the trucks to leave the yard. Few left before. Once we were in the truck there was a regular stop at the nearby drugstore for doughnuts and coffee, and by the time we actually started painting it was usually 10:00 A.M. Lunch (formally 30 minutes) usually lasted from 12:00 noon to 1:00 P.M., and we began to pick up our cones and clear the streets by 3:00 P.M. to 3:30 P.M. We were always back in the yard by 4:00 P.M. The next 45 minutes were spent "reporting," changing clothes, and cleaning up. My overall estimate was that on the average we worked about a 4-hour day.

There are numerous examples of social norms in this story. But let us examine just two: the amount of time spent on the street painting lines, and the time the crew left the yard. Suppose we gave the members of each painting crew a questionnaire that they were sure would never be seen by management. In this questionnaire we include the following two items:

1. How acceptable would it be to you if your crew spent the following amounts of time on the street actually painting lines?
   _____ One hour
   _____ Two hours
   _____ Three hours
   _____ Four hours
   _____ Five hours
   _____ Six hours
   _____ Seven hours
   _____ Eight hours
2. How acceptable would it be to you if your crew left the yard in the morning at the following times?
   _____ 8:15
   _____ 8:30
   _____ 8:45
   _____ 9:00
   _____ 9:15
   _____ 9:30
   _____ 9:45

Let us say that the acceptability of each alternative for both questions is rated on a -10 to $+10$ scale, in which -10 means very unacceptable, $+10$ means very acceptable, and 0 means indifference (i.e., no strong feelings one way or the other). If we plotted the average of the responses given by all of the members of the various crews, we might get results something like those presented in Figure 9-5.

Two aspects of these hypothetical results are important to note. The first is that there is some *variability* in the norms. While 4 hours' work and a 9 A.M. departure time are most desirable, other behaviors are still acceptable. You could be on the street anywhere from about 3 1/2 to 5 hours without much comment. You could also leave the yard a half hour earlier or later. However, beyond these limits, other crews might begin talking to you about it: "Leaving a little early these days, aren't you?" or "What's your big hurry to get out on the street?"

The second point to note is the relative importance of different norms as illustrated by the different *heights* of the curves. These hypothetical data indicate that the total number of hours spent on the street is more important than the time the truck leaves the yard. If a truck leaves early and comes back early, it might be alright. However, if a truck leaves early and comes back *late*, that crew is likely to be in for some social criticism: "Trying to make us look bad?" or "What did you do, paint the whole northeast part of the city?"

This method of analyzing group norms has actually been used in research (e.g., Jackson, 1965, 1966). It reveals the *structure* of social norms. Specifically, it can tell us something about (1) what the group views as the *most* appropriate behavior, (2) what the acceptable range of behavior is, (3) how important the issue is overall, and (4) the degree of agreement or consensus that exists among group members.

How Norms Develop

Norms often develop slowly and over a rather long period of time, although some norms can come about very quickly. Feldman (1984) suggests that norms develop in one or more of the following four ways. The first way is through

FIGURE 9-5
Diagrams of two hypothetical norms.

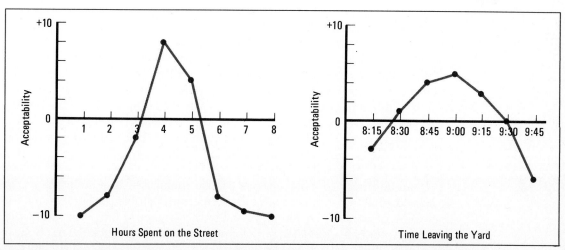

explicit statements made by members of the group. For example, the supervisor of the street-painting crew may set rather strict norms about drinking during the lunch break because of the potential for both poor performance (wobbly lines in the afternoon) and serious accidents (getting hit by a car in traffic).

Norms may also arise out of critical events in the group's history. For example, the members of a painting crew may informally agree among themselves to drop one of their members off at his house on the way back to the yard one afternoon so that he can make the first inning of a baseball game. If a crew member talks about this plan with people from other crews, and the painting department supervisor subsequently finds out, a strong norm for keeping such behavior secret may develop ("Loose lips sink ships!").

A third way in which norms may develop is by what Feldman (1984) calls *primacy*. Primacy simply means that the first pattern of behavior that occurs in the group often becomes the norm. If on its first trip out a newly formed painting crew stops at a nearby store for doughnuts and coffee, the morning "doughnut run" could quickly become a norm. Had the crew decided to stop somewhere else that first morning, or had they not stopped at all, very different norms might have evolved.

Finally, norms may also carry over from past situations. For example, if our painting crew is transferred to the vehicle maintenance department, where they work inside all day rather than out on the street, they may still arrange for a morning "doughnut run." The old norm may persist even though it is now more difficult (or at least less convenient) to enact.

Why Norms Are Enforced

As we suggested previously, it is the group that enforces norms, not the organization. It seems rather unlikely, however, that a group will enforce a norm unless that norm is somehow useful to the members. Feldman (1984) lists four different ways in which norms can be useful to a group. First, norms can facilitate the group's survival. Certainly the norm of no drinking during the lunch break has survival value for the members of the street-painting crew. Not leaving the yard too early in the morning, and getting back "on time," also have survival value, in the sense that they help the group avoid harassment from the members of other painting crews.

Norms can also be useful, and are thus more likely to be enforced, if they simplify or make more predictable the behavior that occurs in the group. For instance, the painting crew may develop a regular rotation of jobs, so that each day a different crew member is responsible for a different task (driving the truck, operating the paint sprayer, setting the cones). When such a rotation is enforced as a norm, the crew does not have to spend time each day negotiating among themselves about who will do what. They know before they arrive for work what job they will be doing.

Yet another way in which norms can be useful is if they help the group avoid embarrassing or uncomfortable interpersonal problems. For example, if one of the crew members has a physically handicapped child, the rest of the crew may informally develop a norm of not discussing topics related to physical disabilities, birth defects, or perhaps even the athletic accomplishments of their own children. They are also likely to refrain from telling jokes that poke fun at physically disabled individuals. The reason for these norms is to avoid upsetting or embarrassing their colleague.

Finally, norms can also be of use, and are thus enforced, if they express a central value of the group and/or clarify what is distinctive about the group. For example, a particular painting crew may establish a norm of being the first to leave the yard in the morning and the last to return in the afternoon if doing so helps the members to reinforce their self-image as the hardest working crew in the department. As long as this norm is not widely deviant from the norms of the department as a whole (i.e., this crew never leaves *too much* before the others in the morning or returns *too much* later), this norm is likely to continue being enforced by this group.

How Norms Are Enforced

The functions that are served by a norm help to explain *why* a group would try to enforce it, but they do not clarify *how* it is enforced. In general, norms are both learned by new group members, and enforced for the group as a whole, through the processes of instrumental and vicarious learning. Recall from Chapter 2, "Understanding People," that *instrumental learning* occurs whenever an individual's behavior is followed by some event that either increases or decreases the probability that that behavior will be repeated. Events that increase the probability that a behavior will be repeated are called *reinforcers,* while events that decrease the probability that a behavior will be repeated are called *punishers. Vicarious learning,* on the other hand, occurs whenever we observe *someone else* being reinforced or punished. Thus, norms are learned and enforced both by the consequences of the group members' own behavior and by observing the consequences of other people's behavior.

Groups have a variety of ways they can reward their fellow members for adhering to norms. First, they can praise you—tell you that you are doing a good job. Second, they can include you in various social activities and functions. Third, they can pass the word along to others about how well you're performing. This latter point suggests that group acceptance not only can be a powerful emotional reward, it also can help with respect to such tangible outcomes as who gets a bonus or who gets promoted.

Groups also have a variety of ways they can punish their members for deviating from group norms. Punishment can take the form of a look, a snide comment, or an angry denunciation. An individual can be ostracized or left alone by the group. A person can be made a social outcast. In some settings the individual may actually be subject to physical abuse. (Remember the Hawthorne studies in which group members hit rate-busters on the arm.)

Research on the enforcement of group norms has mostly focused on the consequences of deviating from the group. The pressure to go along with the group can be intense, and most people comply. (Otherwise we couldn't say that a norm existed.) But what about the individuals who do not go along? What happens to them?

The first thing that often happens is that the group tries to convince the deviant of the error in his or her behavior. They will try to change the person's opinion about the issue through increased communications (Emerson, 1954;

Schachter, 1951). The interactions will be more frequent, more direct, and more explicit as time goes on. The clearer the norm, the more important the norm, the more cohesive the group—the greater the pressure. Eventually the deviant must change the behavior or be rejected by the group.

If rejection does occur, a number of interesting things may take place. The deviant is likely to become isolated interpersonally from the other group members. However, the rest of the group may still need the deviant in order to complete its task successfully. If the deviant cannot be replaced, some sort of agreed-upon truce will develop in which the deviant is tolerated but is still excluded from most group activity and interpersonal interactions. All that stops is the harassment.

Coch and French (1948) described a classic example of a new employee's reaction to group norms about productivity. They reported the productivity of a woman who was hired as a presser in a garment factory. Figure 9-6 shows her productivity level over her first 40 days on the job. For the first few days she approached and then passed the standard production output of about fifty units per hour (the norm). Social pressure was then brought to bear by the other pressers she worked with to make her slow down, which she did. However, after 20 days the group was split up, and the woman worked alone thereafter. Almost immediately her efficiency rating increased by over 70 percent. Thus, the group norm seemed to be responsible for artificially restricting the group members' productivity.

We will have more to say about the process of learning group norms when we discuss the topic of *Socialization* in Chapter 16.

Conformity to Norms

While groups do take action to enforce their norms, it is important to recognize that group members often conform to the group majority even

FIGURE 9-6
Group norms seemed to reduce substantially the amount of productivity that was possible. When the group was split up, productivity rose dramatically. (*Based on data presented by Coch & French, 1948.*)

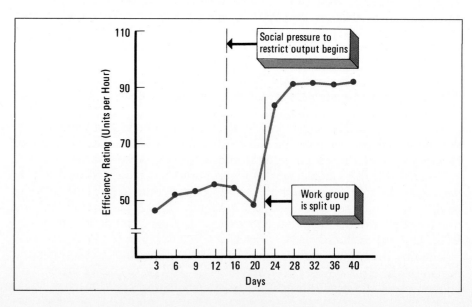

without such pressure. Perhaps the best known and most dramatic demonstration of this was presented by Solomon Asch (1955). Asch conducted a series of experiments in which small groups of people sat around a table and made a series of judgments about visual stimuli such as those depicted in Figure 9-7. The task was to state which of the comparison lines is closest in length to the standard. Not all members of these groups were actually subjects, however. In fact, in each group there was only one true subject. All of the other members were really (and unknown to the subject) confederates of the experimenter, who had previously been instructed to give incorrect answers on certain occasions.

In one such study, for example, groups were presented with fifty problems, each involving a slightly different stimulus set (a standard and three comparison figures). For each problem, the group members simply announced, one at a time, their judgments about which comparison figure was most similar to the standard. It was arranged that the true subject always gave his or her answer last. On 38 of the problems, the confederates all gave the correct answer. Not surprisingly, so did the true subjects. On the remaining 12 problems, however, the confederates all gave the same *wrong* answer (e.g., for the stimuli in Figure 9-7, the confederates might all have been instructed to say that C was the answer, even though A is obviously correct). The research question asked was what percentage of the time on these twelve trials would subjects deny the evidence of their own vision and conform to the group majority by giving the same, obviously incorrect answer.

The results were quite remarkable. Although the subjects rarely made errors on any of the thirty-eight problems for which the rest of the group gave the correct answer, on the twelve problems for which the group unanimously gave an incorrect answer, the subjects gave the *same incorrect answer* 32 percent of the time! Given the accuracy of the subjects' performance on the other thirty-eight problems, it seems highly unlikely that the results for these twelve problems reflect honest errors of judgment. Instead, the subjects probably knew that the answers being given by the rest of the group were incorrect. Nevertheless, they felt compelled to conform to the majority opinion. These

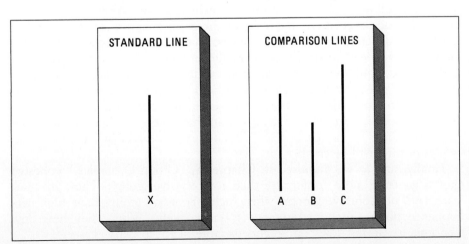

FIGURE 9-7
Stimuli similar to those used by Asch (1955). Confederates might be instructed in advance to make the false statement that *C* is closest in length to the standard line.

results have been confirmed in many later studies (e.g., Cialdini, 1985) and indicate that people do frequently conform to the behavior of a group majority even when there is no overt pressure from the group to do so.

There are a number of factors that can affect how much conformity occurs in a group situation. These include task characteristics, characteristics of the group, and characteristics of the individual group member whose behavior is in question. We will briefly review these here.

Task Characteristics. When the behavior in question is task related (e.g., making judgments about stimuli, painting lines on the street), a critical variable that can significantly influence conformity to group norms is the ambiguity of the task. Asch (1955) demonstrated that conformity can occur with unambiguous tasks. However, research has shown that the level of conformity will be even higher when the task is ambiguous (Shaw, 1981). Thus, for example, when an individual is given an ambiguous performance goal (e.g., "Do your best"), he or she is more likely to conform to informal group performance norms than when he or she is given a very specific performance goal. Similarly, when the means to achieve a goal are ambiguous, conformity to group norms regarding procedures is more likely. Finally, for problem-solving tasks, conformity is more likely when the problem has no real "correct" solution (e.g., when a corporate board tries to decide which of several charities should be given a contribution).

Characteristics of the Group. One result found by both Asch (1955) and others is that the unanimity of the group is strongly related to how much conformity occurs. Specifically, individuals tend to conform less to the group consensus when this consensus is not held by all the members. All it takes is one other person to disagree with the group and conformity drops significantly.

The size of the group also affects conformity. In general, as the size of the group increases, conformity to group norms will increase. However, there are two limitations that should be noted. First, it is important that all of the members of the group majority be perceived as behaving thoughtfully, independently, and of their own accord (Wilder, 1977). If it appears that they are all blindly following the lead of one individual, greater conformity will not occur. Second, even if the members of the group majority are perceived as behaving independently, it is still the case that larger and larger increases in group size will lead to smaller and smaller *increases* in conformity (Latané, 1981). Thus, conformity to a unanimous group majority is likely to be higher in groups of five than in groups of three, and higher still in groups of seven. However, the increase in conformity observed when moving from groups of five to groups of seven will be smaller than that observed when moving from groups of three to groups of five. The increase observed when moving to groups of nine will be smaller yet.

Finally, and as we discussed in Chapter 8, "Group Dynamics," cohesive groups generate more conformity than noncohesive groups. Thus, in comparison to noncohesive groups, when highly cohesive groups have high performance norms, high performance is more likely. When they have low performance norms, low performance is more likely.

It is important to point out that most of the research cited here deals with behavioral conformity, not necessarily attitude change. There is a difference between *outward compliance* and *private acceptance*. In both cases the individual conforms, but in the former case only the public behavior is changed, not the underlying perceptions or attitudes about that behavior. In the case of private acceptance, the individual comes to believe that what he or she did was in fact the correct course of action. Both behavior and attitudes are modified. Most groups would probably prefer acceptance but may settle for compliance.

Individual Group Member Characteristics. Research on the kinds of people who are most likely to conform is limited. One well-known study by Crutchfield (1955) correlated a variety of personality test scores with the amount of conformity displayed in an Asch-type experimental setting. Negative correlations were reported between conformity and intelligence, tolerance, and ego-strength scores. Brighter, more tolerant people with a strong self-concept or ego tend to conform less than those who are low on these dimensions. Also reported was a positive relationship between a measure of authoritarianism, or rigidity, and conformity.

Conformity Outcomes. Finally, it is important to consider the consequences of conformity for the group as a whole, the group members as individuals, and the organization. Note that conformity often has a negative connotation. No one wants to be labeled a "conformist." Yet, the fact of the matter is that we are all conformists to some extent. We all conform to the informal norms of the groups to which we belong. This conformity, in and of itself, is neither good nor bad. It is the consequences of conformity that define any particular act as good or bad.

As we stated earlier, the reason that groups have norms at all and are motivated to enforce them is that norms are in some way useful to the group's functioning and survival. Thus, to the extent that individual members conform to group norms, the continued functioning and survival of the group is facilitated. From the group's perspective, this is a clear benefit.

Conformity can also have benefits for the individual group members. Conformity to group norms means that the members of the group all behave in a more-or-less similar manner. As we discussed in Chapter 8, similarity among group members can lead to increased cohesiveness in the group. This applies just as much to behavioral similarity as it does to attitudinal similarity and personality similarity. In Chapter 8 we also discussed the fact that group cohesiveness is closely tied to one element of job satisfaction—satisfaction with coworkers. Thus, if we link together the concepts of conformity, behavioral similarity, group cohesiveness, and job satisfaction, we might predict that employees will have somewhat higher job satisfaction when the members of their group all conform to important group norms than when such conformity does not exist. The one case in which job satisfaction is likely to be negatively affected is when an employee personally experiences extreme pressure from the group to conform.

Finally, from the organization's point of view, conformity to group norms can be both good and bad—it all depends on what the norm is. If the norm is in the direction of high performance, or facilitates the attainment of desired organizational goals (e.g., not drinking during the lunch break), conformity is desirable. On the other hand, if the norm is in the direction of lower performance, or inhibits the attainment of desired organizational goals (e.g., stopping work 45 minutes before the official quitting time), then conformity will be undesirable.

Deviating from Group Norms

Given that groups actively try to enforce their norms, and that compliance with norms can often be beneficial both for the group as a whole and for individual group members, why do people sometimes deviate from the norm? Why do they sometimes fail to go along with the group majority? The research in this area is rather complex, and a thorough review is beyond the scope of this book (see Archer, 1985). However, two points are worth mentioning.

The first is that we sometimes deviate from a group norm because that norm conflicts with the norms of other important groups that we either belong to or identify with. These other groups are called *reference groups*. Thus, for example, an accountant employed in a hospital may choose not to go along with a group norm dictating that certain insured patients be charged additional fees for services not actually rendered in order to recoup losses incurred from delinquent, low-income, uninsured patients. The accountant may view this norm as a direct violation of his or her professional standards. The accounting profession, in this case, serves as an important reference group, and its norms are in direct conflict with the norms operating in the hospital. The dilemma generated by this conflict is identical to that which occurs when interrole conflict exists. The accountant cannot conform to one norm (either the hospital's or the profession's) without deviating from the other. To the extent that an individual strongly identifies with the reference group and endorses its norms, those norms can be expected to prevail whenever they come in conflict with the norms of other groups to which the individual belongs. Note that it is just this sort of norm conflict that leads to whistle-blowing—going to the authorities with information about corporate or governmental violations of law or regulation (cf. Westin, 1981).

The second point that should be mentioned is that groups do sometimes tolerate deviant behavior on the part of certain group members (although usually not when the deviance takes the form of whistle-blowing!). The degree to which the group tolerates someone who deviates from group norms appears to be tied to that individual's past record of performance and conformity. Research indicates that individuals who have in the past displayed competence and have conformed to group norms can subsequently deviate from these norms in order to initiate change or move the group in a new direction (Hollander, 1985). It is argued that the competent, conforming individual builds up *idiosyncrasy credits* with his or her fellow group members. They come to trust this person's judgments, and believe that he or she has the group's interests at heart. When this happens, the individual may initiate change without great fear of rejection or refusal. (The concept of idiosyncrasy credit is discussed in more detail in Chapter 14, "Leadership.")

Before concluding this section there is one other concept that we would like to introduce briefly. That concept is organizational culture. *Organizational culture,* also called *corporate culture,* refers to the pattern of values and norms that is shared by the *entire organization,* not just by the members of isolated work groups (cf. Schein, 1985). Like norms that operate within small groups, the norms that define the culture of an entire organization describe the ways in which all of the organization's members *ought* to behave. Some organizations have a very "strong" culture, meaning simply that there exists in the organization a set of clearly defined and well-developed norms of behavior that is shared by a majority of its members. Other organizations seem to have a very "weak" culture, meaning that widely shared norms of behavior do not exist.

The book *In Search of Excellence,* by Peters and Waterman (1982), is replete with examples of organizational culture. The phrases "a bias for action," "close to the customer," "autonomy and entrepreneurship," and "MBWA—management by wandering around" all express norms of behavior that seem to exist in many of the "excellent companies" they studied. These norms transcend the boundaries of the individual work units in these organizations. They saturate the organization as a whole. Everywhere Peters and Waterman looked, they were able to find examples of people doing rather than planning, interacting with customers and being responsive to their needs, trying out new ideas and procedures, and wandering around in ways that stimulated an informal exchange of ideas and information.

Having a "strong" culture does not necessarily imply that an organization will perform well, however. It means only that the organization-wide norms of behavior are clear. Thus, organizations with strong cultures might be characterized as "high energy," "entrepreneurial," "autocratic," "sleepy," or "reluctant decision makers." Each of these terms summarizes the essential nature of a set of specific norms of behavior that is widely accepted and practiced in the organizations to which the term applies.

The way in which an organization's culture influences its performance depends a great deal on the environment in which that organization operates. A "sleepy" organization, for example, in which the norms foster careful study, slow and deliberate decision making, and a general lack of initiative, may do well in stable, mature, or heavily regulated market environments. The same company in a fast-paced, volatile market may fail miserably. Organizational success is therefore dependent, in part at least, on the match, or congruence, between the culture of the organization and the larger environment in which it operates.

Thus, in a number of respects organizational culture functions in a manner analogous to the way norms operate at the small-group level. Perhaps the biggest difference is in the difficulty of managing organizational culture. In the small group, norms are enforced through face-to-face interaction. Further, when it becomes necessary to change the norms, all of the group members are physically present to reinforce whatever new norms are developed. This process is infinitely more difficult when applied to the organization as a whole. It is one thing for a supervisor or manager to try to influence the norms of behavior that arise among the members of his or her immediate work group. It is quite another for a chief executive to try to influence the organization-wide norms of 300,000 people working in eight countries on three continents!

STATUS

The social animal does not merely seek to dominate his fellows;
he succeeds. And succeeding, he achieves a status in the eyes
of the other. That status will be permanent;
and oddly enough satisfying as a rule to all parties.
—ROBERT ARDREY

A final facet of group structure that influences expectations about appropriate behavior is called status. *Status* refers to an individual's rank, worth, or prestige within some group, organizational, or social setting. It is determined by the group itself. If a person has attributes or possessions that are valued by the group, he or she will have high status. Those people without these attributes or possessions have low status.

Three things should be noted about this definition. First, status is determined by criteria set by the group. These criteria are generally agreed upon by the group members as being of value. Thus, if the group values some attribute you possess (e.g., age, an M.B.A. the title of "manager"), you will have a higher status in that group than if they do not value that attribute. Second, status is an aggregate or overall estimate of worth. It is typically based on more than just one dimension or attribute. Third, and most important, status serves as a device for ranking people, for putting them in some order in relation to one another.

Status thus tells us about the *hierarchical structure* of groups. It is easily observed that almost every group or organization has some sort of either informal or formal hierarchical ordering. Once we discover this ordering, we know to whom we must defer, and who in turn should defer to us. Thus, status provides *vertical differentiation*. Just as roles differentiate jobs, status provides differentiations up and down the hierarchy. It is one more way to reduce ambiguity and clarify what is expected of us.

The Characteristics of Status

We noted previously that roles and norms occur both inside and outside the organizational context. So does status. At the broadest level of analysis is what we call *social status*. This term refers to our rank in society as a whole. Numerous variables determine this rank, such as age, wisdom, wealth, family relationships, occupation, and personality. Social status is a composite of all those attributes valued by society at large.

If we divide people into groups on the basis of their social status, we get a set of *social classes*. People in the "upper" classes are generally higher than people in the "lower" classes on such status-relevant dimensions as education, occupation, income, and social background. One can find very distinct differences in expected and actual behavior for these groups in areas such as child rearing, social relationships, and on-the-job behavior. Also, informal rules exist about how people from one class should behave toward people from another class. In a fairly mobile society such as the United States, in which social status levels can be changed relatively easily and are not so clearly recognized by attributes such as titles or dress, these rules are not very specific. However, in societies in which social status is more obvious and clear, as in India, there are quite specific behavioral expectations across status levels. This is true for many of the societies in Asia.

Besides societal level status differences, status differences are also found within the world of work. Here, two status related concepts are important. One is called occupational prestige, and the other, organizational status.

Occupational prestige refers to the relative status of one's occupation. Occupational prestige is clearly not the same thing as social status, since it refers only to a single variable. However, it is a very powerful determinant of one's overall social status. In general, there is a moderately high degree of agreement about which occupations are high in prestige and which ones are low. For example, Figure 9-8 provides a list of thirty occupations ranked by their prestige within the United States. Prestige rankings such as this tend to remain rather stable over long periods of time.

If you think about your last interaction with a physician (ranked no. 2 in the list), you may begin to realize the degree to which occupational prestige influences your interactions. Part of the reason physicians have such a high prestige ranking is that they know an awful lot more than most of us about something that is very important to us all—our health. As a consequence, we tend to show a great deal of deference to them. Our interactions with physicians tend to be stiff and formal (much more so than they would be with, say, a taxi driver—ranked twenty-seventh in the list), and we allow them to initiate most of the verbal exchange. They ask the questions and we answer, not the other way around. On the surface, this seems like a reasonable way to proceed in order to arrive at a diagnosis. However, how many times have you

Rank	Occupation	Rank	Occupation
1	U.S. Supreme Court Justice	16	Insurance agent
2	Physician	17	Manager of a small store in a city
3	Nuclear physicist	18	Mail carrier
4	State governor	19	Plumber
5	Lawyer	20	Automobile mechanic
6	Architect	21	Machine operator in a factory
7	Psychologist	22	Truck driver
8	Priest	23	Clerk in a store
9	Banker	24	Restaurant cook
10	Accountant for a large business	25	Filling station attendant
11	Building contractor	26	Coal miner
12	Electrician	27	Taxi driver
13	Farm owner and operator	28	Janitor
14	Member of police force	29	Garbage collector
15	Reporter on a daily newspaper	30	Shoeshiner

FIGURE 9-8
Thirty jobs ranked in order of occupational prestige. (*Based on data presented by Hodge, Siegel, & Rossi, 1964.*)

wanted to ask a question about a symptom that the physician did not mention, but you were reluctant to speak up? And how many times have you sought a second opinion about a physician's diagnosis? Casual observation would indicate that most of us are more likely to seek a second opinion when an automobile mechanic (ranked no. 20) suggests a cure for a sputtering, coughing automobile engine than when a physician suggests a cure for our own sputtering and coughing. The point is, the formality of the interactions we have with other people, our willingness to take advice, and our reluctance to ask questions can all be influenced by the relative prestige of the person's occupation.

An interesting question raised by the data presented in Figure 9-8 is, why do people choose the occupation they do? If occupations can be ordered in terms of prestige, why don't we find large numbers of people crowded into those occupations with the highest prestige? More generally, what factors determine who will get into the prestigious occupations and who will not? A massive study conducted by Christopher Jencks (1979) provides an answer. He found that the single most important factor determining the prestige of the occupation people go into is family background. This includes father's occupation and income, parents' education, and race. Next comes test scores in school, followed by personality characteristics. The data suggest that family background accounts for about 50 percent of the variation in occupational prestige.

These data say something important about our society. They clearly suggest that characteristics over which one has no control (family background) often determine one's potential for success. (Note that occupational prestige and economic success are highly correlated.) This means that even in a relatively open society such as the United States, strong forces are at work that can make social change very difficult (Yankelovich, 1979).

The other status-related concept that is important within the world of work is called organizational status. *Organizational status* refers to the informal differentiation that occurs within an organization. Like the broader concept of social status, organizational status also reflects a combination of many factors. It usually reflects not only one's formal position in the organizational hierarchy, but also such factors as one's tenure in the organization, one's professional affiliation (occupational prestige), and even one's performance. In a university, for example, there may be five full professors in the physics department. They all have the same formal rank but not necessarily the same status. A professor who has outside grant support gets excellent teaching ratings, and gets along well with the dean is likely to have higher status than a professor who is lacking in these characteristics. As we shall discuss, these differences in status have important implications for a number of aspects of group interaction and organizational effectiveness.

To summarize, status refers to one's rank as determined by a group. One has a status level in every organizational setting. This status helps to clarify how one should behave toward others and how they should behave in return. It is based on socially valued attributes such as birth, personality, achievements, possessions, and/or formal position or rank. We defer to people with higher status because we respect them, fear them, idolize them, want favors from them, or want to be like them. Whatever the reason, status helps us structure our interactions with others.

In most group settings, status differences are easily recognized, even in very short periods of time. The recognition of status differences within a group is facilitated by the presence of status symbols. Once status differences are recognized by group members, predictable differences in group process follow. These topics are briefly discussed in the following section.

Status Symbols. As the name suggests, status symbols are objects or labels that denote one's status level in the group or organization. For example, certain types of apparel indicate position and status, such as a judge's robes, a nun's habit, a doctor's white coat, or a monarch's crown. Some organizations, such as the military, require their members to wear uniforms that are systematically marked to clearly distinguish different levels of status.

Titles, such as doctor, senator, professor, captain, and vice president, can also serve as indicators of status. Note that the titles just listed are generally familiar to us all, and as a consequence they accord the bearer relatively high status in almost any group he or she enters. However, there are many other titles that are not generally familiar and hence symbolize status only in very specific organizational contexts. For example, in some organizations the title of director (e.g., of product development) implies a senior-level, high-status position. In other organizations, the same title refers to a middle-management position that carries much less status. Also, titles that convey high status in one organizational context may actually reduce one's status in other contexts. For example, in most academic institutions having a Ph.D. increases one's

FIGURE 9-9
The judge's robe and elevated seat suggest high status.

status. Thus, faculty and administrators who have earned this degree often go by the title of "doctor." It is not uncommon, however, for those who have earned a Ph.D. and who work in business *not* to use this title. This is particularly true outside technical R&D units. The reason is that such an advanced degree is often not valued by the rest of the organization. Indeed, there is a danger that if the title is used, the individual will be prejudged as putting on airs, or as being too theoretical, not practical minded, or too "ivory tower."

Finally, material possessions can also convey status. These might include the type of car one drives and the quality of one's clothes, house, or attaché case. In large business organizations the size and location of one's office, the view, the rug on the floor, and whether or not one has a personal secretary can all be symbols of status. An organization can either accentuate or play down status differences among its members by the way it chooses to distribute such perquisites.

Status and Group Interaction. Research on status differences has found a number of ways in which status can influence group process (Shaw, 1981). People with higher status tend to take more initiative in a group. They are more likely to start a conversation or exchange. These same people will frequently make policy statements or generalizations without providing data or information to back them up. They usually talk more, are more likely to act as the group's representative, and have the greatest number of connections within the group. Overall, they seem to have more influence and power.

There is, however, one problem with this line of research. This problem is inherent in the definition of status itself. Because a person's status is based on a combination of factors, it is often difficult to determine exactly what actually *causes* these differences in behavior. Is it the position, the personality, or the expertise of the high-status person that counts? Thus, although we know that status has an impact on a wide variety of activities, it is sometimes hard to identify exactly what aspects of status are related to specific behaviors.

Status Change. Throughout our lives our status changes numerous times. Some of the obvious occasions of status change include graduation from college, passing a state licensing exam, getting a promotion, getting new job responsibilities, and even retiring. These changes can sometimes cause serious problems. A change in status often implies that one is expected to behave in new ways. The old norms and reference groups must be left behind. New things must be learned. However, exactly *what* must be changed or learned is often ambiguous. One's future relationships with others may also be unclear. To the extent that a status change is surrounded by ambiguity, the change itself is more difficult to make.

In many societies major changes in status (e.g., puberty, marriage) are accompanied by rites or religious ceremonies. These activities serve both to mark the event and to provide information about the expected behavior in the new position. These rites are meant to make the status transition easier and to clarify expectations.

Similar sorts of procedures are often found in large organizations. There are certain expected career steps and a general timetable for taking them. In many cases the change is highlighted by some sort of new training, recognition, raise in salary, and/or change in physical location. In many respects, the more clearly defined the transition points are, the easier those transitions are to make.

Situations that do not have explicit passage events are often anxiety-producing. For example, in graduate school, students are often treated as students yet told they are colleagues. When do they become professionals? Is it after their "general" exams or after they get their Ph.D.? Since many students take their first job before they finish their Ph.D., they are often filling an assistant-professor position before they are "officially" in the club. Their colleagues and students at the new job may treat them appropriately, but every time they return to their old institution to work on their Ph.D., the relationships are unclear. For these reasons, many academics report that getting their Ph.D. was anticlimactic, and that the transition was difficult to make.

The implication is that there are ways to reduce the stresses of status change. Previews of what is to come, training in new skills, and ceremonies to mark the occasion all help the transition. They reduce uncertainty and ease adjustment.

Status Incongruence

Nothing is more annoying than a low man
raised to a high position.
—CLAUDIAN

A final area of concern has to do with what is called *status incongruence*. This state exists either when someone is high on a few valued dimensions but low on others, or when one's characteristics seem inappropriate for the particular position one holds. One of the best illustrations of status incongruence is the college student who works as a laborer during the summer. Most of the student's fellow employees will be older and have more experience but less formal education. In some cases this can be a very uncomfortable situation for the college student. Unless he or she is able to play down the educational attributes, the student is likely to be labeled a "smart guy" or the "college kid." It may be very difficult to gain full acceptance.

This type of problem often occurs with respect to decisions about selection, placement, and promotions in organizations. If almost everyone in a particular management area has a certain advanced degree (e.g., an M.B.A.), is it feasible to hire someone to be the department head who only has a B.A.? What kinds of problems would this create?

Research on status incongruence relies heavily on equity theory and balance theory to explain the results (e.g., Adams, 1953). People feel first of all that it is not fair for someone who does not have all the other qualifications to have a high-status position. It is not equitable. Alternatively, status incongruence can be thought of as creating a type of cognitive imbalance. When there are incongruent characteristics for group members to deal with, psychological tension is created, and this state is unpleasant and dissatisfying.

Older Worker Versus Young Boss

After 20 years of cooking, cleaning and kids, a middle-aged woman gets a job and finds herself working for a woman 10 or more years her junior. How does she feel?

"It's a double whammy," says 45-year-old Joanna Henderson, who helped organize a seminar at Boston's Simmons College on the subject after she was hired by a younger woman. "The stigma is more intense if your boss is both younger and a woman."

The phenomenon of older women working for younger women is the latest of a series of social upheavals unsettling corporate psyches. While older women long have accepted the inevitability of working for younger men in a largely male domain, and even older men know that aggressive younger men may surpass them, other pairings meet greater resistance. Many white workers still resent taking orders from blacks and many men chafe at working for women.

But experts say the conflict between older women and their younger women bosses can be especially intense.

The older woman generally has entered the workforce late after raising a family, or has been stuck for years in a dead-end, traditionally female job—secretary, nurse or teacher. So she often resents younger managers, who have advantages she generally was denied—a business school education, specialized training and fewer barriers to the corporate fast track.

Meanwhile, the younger women managers harbor their own resentments toward their older colleagues. And because this situation was once so rare, younger women managers have few role models who have handled such conflicts.

Today more than 1.3 million women under age 35 hold managerial or administrative posts, up from only 322,000 a dozen years ago. Meanwhile, more than half the women over age 45 also work. "Your first reaction" to having a younger woman boss, says Eileen Bergquist, a 39-year-old Wheaton College career counselor, "is 'what the heck does this kid know?'"

When Ms. Henderson, the seminar organizer, abandoned her career as a sociology teacher for a job with Data Resources Inc., a McGraw-Hill Inc. market-research subsidary, one of her first bosses was Marnie Hoyle, a 31-year-old marketing manager with a master's degree in business. Ms. Hoyle admits she was dubious about hiring the older woman and even though she did eventually, the two "tread lightly" with each other.

"MBAs have a horror of being over 25 and not a vice president, so they look with pity at anyone older." Ms. Hoyle says. She wonders if discomfort caused by the age difference eventually led to Ms. Henderson's transfer a year later. Ms. Henderson concedes that the year under Ms. Hoyle "wasn't easy."

Older women workers admit that they are sometimes deferential with colleagues and maternal with superiors. "I freaked out when I started working for younger people," says a 46-year-old software specialist at Data General Corp. "You sort of want to pick up after them and wipe their noses."

But such an attitude infuriates younger women managers, raised on the feminism of the 1970s. "I don't respond to a mother, because I've got one and that was plenty," says Lori King, a Boston University career counselor, who supervises women 10 and 20 years older.

And those older women haven't been easy to manage, she concedes. She claims they resist her directives and become dismayed when she treats them as employees instead of sisters. "They say, 'I expected something different from a woman,'" she says, and accuse her of being "pro-male" in making assignments and doling out criticism.

Younger women managers also run into conflicts with long-time women employees who may feel they know better how things should be done. Bosses grow annoyed when their older secretaries "come in and tell you perhaps your letter needs to be revised or they don't like the word you used," says Jayne Hurley Morgan, a 30-year-old Air Force contracting officer.

And as relative pioneers in the business world, younger managers can feel insecure and easily threatened by veteran corporate women who may have a better idea of its culture and politics, all "the soft stuff they don't teach you in business school," says Betty Lou Marple, a Harvard University dean

All of this suggests that status incongruence is uncomfortable and may lead to motivational and behavioral problems. The two obvious solutions are either to (1) select or promote only those people whose characteristics are all congruent with the job, or (2) change the group's values about what is congruent and what leads to high status. Unfortunately, neither solution is terribly attractive. The first is not acceptable because it would seriously limit mobility, while the second is hard to accomplish. It is not easy to change people's values. Perhaps the best we can hope to do is make people aware of when they are entering incongruous situations and the types of problems they are likely to face.

Summary

There are a number of specific points from the chapter that bear repeating:

1. Roles deal with the appropriate behavior for a specific job. They are behavioral job descriptions.
2. Roles suffer from incidents of conflict, ambiguity, and overload. All three problems are related to negative organizational outcomes.
3. Norms serve as general behavioral expectations for all group members. There are both pressures and sanctions to enforce norms.
4. Violation of norms can lead to breakdowns in communication and the isolation of group members.
5. People are often motivated to go along with the group majority even when there is no outward pressure to do so.
6. Status refers to an individual's rank based upon those attributes valued by the group. It is concerned with clarifying vertical relationships.
7. Status is quickly and easily recognized. There are many cues and symbols denoting status in organizations.
8. Status change and incongruence can cause uncertainty and ambiguity. Low morale, high tension, and high stress may be the result.

Besides these particular points, there are several broader themes that should also be emphasized. First, and probably most important, roles, norms, and status all serve to reduce ambiguity in social settings. In general, people like to live in a fairly predictable world, and these are social mechanisms to help us do that. Roles, norms, and status are useful for reducing uncertainty, which results in lower tension and anxiety.

A second point about roles, norms, and status is that they are all *socially* determined. It is group consensus or agreement that characterizes all three concepts. This again shows the impact of external factors on an individual's behavior. Thus, what at first appears to be a person problem may ultimately turn out to be a group problem.

A final theme concerns the generality of the role, norm, and status concepts. Throughout the chapter we have stated that all three concepts apply both inside and outside the work environment. They exist in our social groups, family, church, recreational groups, and political groups. Almost every organizational context can be viewed in terms of roles, norms, and status.

IMPLICATIONS FOR RESEARCH

In this chapter we discussed the various ways in which roles, norms, and status can influence the behavior of people in organizations. We also suggested several mechanisms by which two of these variables, roles and status, can be managed. An organization can manage status differences among its members, for example, by the manner in which it distributes status symbols. It can enhance someone's status by giving him or her a prestigious title, a desirable office, a personal secretary, and/or other valued perquisites. Doing so will have the effect of increasing that individual's informal power and influence over others. Conversely, the organization can diminish someone's status by removing these symbols. A manager who suddenly finds him- or herself without a personal secretary has lost more than just an administrative convenience.

The key to managing roles is the role set—that group of individuals who have and communicate expectations about how a particular role occupant should behave. One member of the role set who is likely to be particularly important is the role occupant's immediate supervisor (cf. Graen, 1976). An organization will be much more successful in managing a role occupant's behavior when the supervisor communicates clear and mutually compatible expectations to the role occupant and when these expectations are consistent with those communicated by other members of the role set. The role occupant's behavior becomes more difficult to manage when members of the role set send ambiguous or contradictory expectations or when a large proportion of the role set is from outside the organization (e.g., customers).

In contrast to roles and status, we have not indicated how an organization might go about managing norms. The reason for this omission is that relatively little systematic research has been done in this area. Research on norms has tended to focus on the way they affect behavior and on the ways they are enforced by the group. Relatively little work has been done on how norms are influenced by factors *outside* the work group.

We often think of norms as developing independently of the formal organization and as being beyond its control. To some extent this may be true. Certainly the group itself is largely responsible for norm enforcement. However, it also seems plausible that, at least in some cases, there may be systematic things an organization can do to (1) facilitate the development of group norms that are consistent with broader organizational goals, (2) change norms that are inconsistent with those goals, and (3) ensure the continued existence of norms that do facilitate the attainment of organizational goals. Research needs to be done to examine these possibilities. The growing body of work concerned with the management of organizational culture may be a guide here (e.g., Deal & Kennedy, 1982; Schein, 1985).

Similarly, it seems likely that there may be organizational factors that affect the structure of norms. To take but one example, consider an organization that gradually becomes more and more formalized, saddling its members with an increasing number of rules, regulations, standard operating procedures, and so forth. In becoming more formalized, the organization gradually assumes control of more and more group member behavior, leaving less and less to be controlled by the group itself. In a sense, the increased formalization of the organization dilutes the group's influence over its members. Does this affect in any fundamental way the structural characteristics of the group's norms? Perhaps. One possibility is that the strength of the group's norms (as indicated by the height of the curve when the norms are plotted, as in Figure 9-5) will be diminished. That is, increased formalization may tend to reduce the strength of group norms—and the group's ability to enforce them—even for norms not directly related to the areas of formalization.

What is needed is more research to determine the factors outside of the group that can significantly influence the development and structure of group norms. If these factors can be systematically cataloged, we will be in a much better position to make recommendations in the future for how an organization might go about managing not only roles and status, but also norms.

IMPLICATIONS FOR PRACTICE

There are two main implications for organizational practice to be drawn from this chapter. First, once one comes to see the importance of roles, norms, and status, one can develop diagnostic techniques to assess problems in these areas. Questionnaires can be developed to assess expectations. Data gathered through the use of these questionnaires can provide information about the ambiguity of roles and the extent of conflicting demands or overload. Observing groups in action as well as actively interviewing group members can provide information about work norms. Simple observations can tell a lot about status differences within a company. Mound (1968), for example, points out how the types and number of titles that exist in an organization are reflective of status issues. He suggests that one should be wary of status inflation (too many vice presidents) or the reverse (little formal recognition). The military services, for example, have been heavily criticized for being top-heavy. Mound also discusses the status implications of offices, their size, furnishings (type of desk, carpet), and location, and other perquisites such as a good parking space, a personal secretary, and access to the executive washroom. All these factors can be observed and measured. These data can help to pinpoint areas of uncertainty, ambiguity, status incongruence, and so on.

The second point is dependent upon the first. Once we ascertain where problems exist, we can begin to devise mechanisms that will remedy the problem. Various types of structural changes can be made that will clarify roles and norms. Sasser and Leonard (1980), for example, suggest a series of things management can do to help first-level supervisors. Included in their recommendations are the following:

1. *Increase the use of delegation.* Give first-line supervisors more responsibility for issues to which they can make a contribution (e.g., recommendations about job design).
2. *Increase power.* Provide first-line supervisors with the levers (rewards and punishments) to have some influence on motivation.
3. *Increase experience.* Find out what first-line supervisors actually do. Go observe them at work.
4. *Increase information.* Make sure that first-line supervisors know the reasons for actions and management's priorities.
5. *Increase education and training.* Keep the first-line supervisors current in new developments in technology.
6. *Increase input.* Ask for first-line supervisors' participation on issues of importance to them and in areas in which they can reasonably contribute to the decision.

These strategies should reduce the conflict, ambiguity, and uncertainty in their role.

Other techniques, such as job previews and simulations, can help people learn roles and norms quickly in a new occupation or following a change in jobs. Training programs can be devised both to mark the event of change and to clarify situations to be faced in the future. For example, *Business Week* described a program called "Inroads," a nonprofit organization designed to select, sponsor, and support bright minority students ("Ghetto to Management," 1980). These students are given tutoring, counseling, and summer internships with local corporations. The purpose of the program is to "help talented minority students overcome the lack of business-oriented role models in their home environment" and to help them "learn how to play the game." To date, the program has been quite successful. These strategies plus better selection and placement systems can help people to face new jobs and to match the right person with the right job.

Discussion Questions

1. Describe your first experience in a college class. How did you learn what was expected of you? Did roles, norms, and status differences influence your behavior?
2. Describe the various types of role conflict and ambiguity that can occur. How do these factors help or hinder effectiveness?
3. What people do you think have high status? What attributes or characteristics do you use to make these judgments?

CASE: CROSS-CULTURAL ENCOUNTER

Jason Mahler was in charge of a new agricultural assistance program in Thailand. The purpose of the program was to get Thai farmers to utilize new seed and new planting and harvesting technology. With the proper use of such technology and a great deal of hard work, Mahler was convinced that yields could easily be doubled.

One of the first areas the program was instituted in was northeast Thailand, near Khon Kean. The person in charge of this region was Jim Hikler, an ex-AID official from Nebraska. Jim had a lot of practical farming experience, and Mahler was sure he could do the job.

However, after the program had been running a few months, disturbing signals were received by Mahler in his Bangkok office. The reports from Hikler were very discouraging. The people were not pleased to see him, they were reluctant to use the new techniques, and the outlook for the harvest was bleak. Mahler decided to have Hikler come to Bangkok to discuss the problem.

When Hikler arrived, it was clear that he was frustrated. He told Mahler that he had the equipment, tools, and seed that he needed. However, he had absolutely no idea how to get people to use them. He had expected everyone in the village to welcome him enthusiastically and to try out his new techniques eagerly. Instead, he received polite but passive acceptance.

Mahler said some unflattering things about the work habits of the villagers and then inquired about who the village leader was. Hikler told him it was a man named Preecha Thumrunakul. Mahler suggested that Preecha be put in charge of motivating people and gaining acceptance. This seemed like a good idea, so Jim returned to Khon Kean determined to get some action.

Jim arrived back at Khon Kean in the early evening and promptly went to Preecha's home and asked him to come outside. Some of the villagers, guessing that something was up, began to gather around. Preecha, who was in the middle of dinner, finally appeared after a couple of minutes. He bowed politely and inquired about Jim's health. Jim dismissed these formalities and told him the following:

"Preecha, I have just returned from Bangkok. My boss is very discouraged by our lack of progress and believes that the village could do better. To some extent he feels that you are to blame for this failure, and he wants to see some changes. So, from now on I want you to convince your people to use our supplies and machines, and I'm holding you responsible. If the crop is down this year, it will be your fault." Preecha smiled and said he would do what he could. He went back inside and the crowd dispersed.

Jim went home and fired off a report to Mahler. He was sure that things would start to move in the right direction now. However, during the next few days he noticed very little change. At the end of the month he was forced to send another discouraging report to Mahler: "Very little progress at this end. Suggest we terminate project."

Questions about the Case

1. Discuss the roles played by the three main people in the case. Were they clear and unambiguous? How could things have been changed?
2. Do you think Jim Hikler understood the norms of the Thai villagers? Where do you think he made mistakes?
3. What was Preecha's status? Do you think that Jim treated him correctly?
4. How would you have handled this situation—right from the start?

References

Adams, S. (1953). Status congruence as a variable in small group performance. *Social Forces, 32,* 16–22.

Archer, D. (1985). Social deviance. In G. Lindzey & E. Aronson (Eds.), *The handbook of social psychology* (3d ed., Vol. 2, pp. 743–804). New York: Random House.

Asch, S. E. (1955). Studies of independence and conformity: A minority of one against unanimous majority. *Psychological Monographs, 20*(Whole No. 416).

Berger-Gross, V., & Kraut, A. I. (1984). "Great expectations": A no-conflict explanation of role conflict. *Journal of Applied Psychology, 69,* 261–271.

Caplan, R. D. (1972). Organizational stress and individual strain: A socio-psychological study of risk factors in coronary heart disease among administrators, engineers, and scientists (Doctoral dissertation, University of Michigan, 1971). *Dissertation Abstracts International, 32,* 6706b–6707b (University Microfilms No. 72-14822).

Cialdini, R. B. (1985). *Influence: Science and practice.* Glenview, IL: Scott, Foresman.

Coch, L., & French, J. R. P., Jr. (1948). Overcoming resistance to change. *Human Relations, 1,* 512–532.

Cook, T. D., & Campbell, D. T. (1976). The design and conduct of quasi-experiments and true experiments in field settings. In M. D. Dunnette (Ed.), *Handbook of industrial and organizational psychology* (pp. 223–326). Chicago: Rand McNally.

Crutchfield, R. S. (1955). Conformity and character. *American Psychologist, 10,* 191–198.

Davis, S. M., & Lawrence, P. R. (1977). *Matrix.* Reading, MA: Addison-Wesley.

Deal, T. E., & Kennedy, A. (1982). *Corporate culture.* Reading MA: Addison-Wesley.

Emerson, R. (1954). Deviation and rejection: An experimental replication. *American Sociological Review, 19,* 688–693.

Feldman, D. C. (1984). The development and enforcement of group norms. *Academy of Management Review, 9,* 47–53.

Fisher, C. D., & Gitelson, R. (1983). A meta-analysis of the correlates of role conflict and ambiguity. *Journal of Applied Psychology, 68,* 320–333.

Ghetto to management: A tough training plan. (1980, June 2). *Business Week,* p. 54.

Goode, W. J. (1960). Norm commitment and conformity to role-status obligations. *American Journal of Sociology, 66,* 246–258.

Graen, G. (1976). Role-making processes within complex organizations. In M. D. Dunnette (Ed.), *Handbook of industrial and organizational psychology* (pp. 1201–1245). Chicago: Rand McNally.

Hodge, R. W., Siegel, P. M., & Rossi, P. H. (1964). Occupational prestige in the United States, 1925–1963. *American Journal of Sociology, 70,* 286–302.

Hollander, E. P. (1985). Leadership and power. In G. Lindzey & E. Aronson (Eds.), *The handbook of social psychology* (3d ed., Vol. 2, pp. 485–537). New York: Random House.

Jackson, J. (1965). Structural characteristics of norms. In I. D. Steiner & M. Fishbein (Eds.), *Current studies in social psychology.* New York: Holt.

Jackson, J. (1966). A conceptual and measurement model for norms and roles. *Pacific Sociological Review, 9,* 35–47.

Jencks, C. (1979). *Who gets ahead: The determinants of economic success in America.* New York: Basic Books.

Katz, D., & Kahn, R. L. (1978). *The social psychology of organizing* (2d ed.). New York: Wiley.

Latané, B. (1981). The psychology of social impact. *American Psychologist, 36,* 343–356.

Lieberman, S. (1956). The effects of changes in roles on the attitudes of role occupants. *Human Relations, 9,* 385–402.

Locke, E. A., Shaw, K. N., Saari, L. M., & Latham, G. P. (1981). Goal setting and task performance: 1969–1980. *Psychological Bulletin, 90,* 125–152.

McClelland, D. C. (1985). *Human motivation.* Glenview, IL: Scott, Foresman.

McGrath, J. E. (1984). *Groups: Interaction and performance.* Englewood Cliffs, NJ: Prentice-Hall.

Mound, M. C. (1968, Autumn). The concept of status as practiced in business organizations. *MSU Business Topics*, pp. 7–19.

Peters, T. J., & Waterman, R. H., Jr. (1982). *In search of excellence.* New York: Harper & Row.

Sasser, W. E., Jr., & Leonard, F. S. (1980, March–April). Let first-level supervisors do their job. *Harvard Business Review*, pp. 113–121.

Schachter, S. (1951). Deviation, rejection, and communication. *Journal of Abnormal and Social Psychology, 46,* 190–207.

Schein, E. H. (1985). *Organizational culture and leadership.* San Francisco: Jossey-Bass.

Schuler, R. S. (1975). Role perceptions, satisfaction, and performance: A partial reconciliation. *Journal of Applied Psychology, 60,* 683–687.

Shaw, M. E. (1981). *Group dynamics: The psychology of small group behavior* (3d ed.). New York: McGraw-Hill.

Terborg, J. R. (1977). Women in management: A research review. *Journal of Applied Psychology, 62,* 647–664.

Westin, A. (Ed.). (1981). *Whistleblowing: Loyalty and dissent in the corporation.* New York: McGraw-Hill.

Wilder, D. A. (1977). Perception of groups, size of opposition, and social influence. *Journal of Experimental Social Psychology, 13,* 253–268.

Yankelovich, D. (1979, July). Who gets ahead in America? *Psychology Today,* p. 28.

Chapter 10

Communication

It takes two to speak truth—
one to speak and another to hear.
—HENRY DAVID THOREAU

I f we could unobtrusively enter an organization and observe the activity of the people within, it is safe to say that a very large percentage of what we would see would involve some form of communication. We would probably see people discussing work-related problems and issues in their offices, in conference rooms, and in hallways. We would see managers giving directions to their subordinates, and subordinates giving information to their bosses. We might see people giving speeches, and we would certainly see people talking on telephones, dictating letters, reading reports, writing messages, and conversing around the office water cooler. All of these activities involve communication. Although there is some ambiguity about the precise meaning of this term (Dance, 1970), for our purposes *communication* can be defined simply as the process of sharing information, ideas, or attitudes, resulting in a degree of understanding between a sender and a receiver (cf. Lewis, 1980). This can come about through face-to-face interaction; telephone conversations; listening to formal presentations; reading reports, letters, and memos; or using a variety of electronic media.

Estimates of the amount of time managers spend communicating in organizations range from 70 to 80 percent (Lawler, Porter, & Tennenbaum, 1968; Mintzberg, 1973). Most organizational participants are engaged in communication most of the time. We are constantly involved in the absorption, evaluation, and distribution of ideas and information.

In a very real sense, communication is the lifeblood of the organization. Effective communication is essential, and is frequently cited as an important reason for major organizational triumphs. The opposite is also true. Ineffective communication can lead to disaster. Among other things, faulty communications have been cited as an important contributing factor to such events as (1) the Watergate affair, (2) the escalation of the war in Vietnam, (3) the Bay of Pigs fiasco, (4) the Chinese intervention in the Korean conflict, and (5) the "surprise" attack at Pearl Harbor (e.g., Janis & Mann, 1977). The January 1986 space shuttle disaster also appears to have been due in part to ineffective communication. Critical information that might have halted the fatal launch was available. However, it was never brought to the attention of the top NASA officials responsible for the launch decision.

Thus, communication involves more than just having the right information. That information must reach the right decision maker, be clearly understood and believed, and be weighted correctly. It is a highly complex process, and one that cannot be taken for granted.

THE MOTIVES FOR COMMUNICATING

People communicate in organizations for a wide variety of reasons. Sometimes we seek to give or get technical information or assistance. Other times we want to learn whether other people in our work group hold the same opinions we do. And sometimes we simply want to share our experience with others. The various motives for communicating with others can be understood from three different perspectives: the organization's perspective, the work group's perspective, and the individual's perspective. We examine each of these in some detail below.

Communication from the Organization's Perspective

One motivation for communicating in organizations is the successful performance of organizational tasks. In Chapter 8, "Group Dynamics," we introduced the concept of *task demands*. Tasks can be thought of as demanding certain behaviors of organization members. In order to complete these tasks successfully, the behavioral demands must be met. To the list of task demands we discussed in Chapter 8, we can now add communication. When tasks are extremely simple, routine, and predictable, and when they can be easily completed by a single individual, communication demands are relatively low (although never totally absent). As the tasks become more complex or unpredictable, the communication demands rise dramatically. And for very complex tasks, especially those that are nonroutine and/or involve a high degree of interdependence among a large number of people (e.g., designing a laser-guided weapons system), the communication demands are extremely high. These demands can be analyzed in terms of the *direction* of the flow of information.

Downward Communication. *Downward communication* refers to communication that originates at some higher level of the organizational hierarchy and is transmitted downward to one or more lower levels. The main motivation for downward communication is to guide and direct the behavior of those individuals at the lower organizational levels. Katz and Kahn (1978) identify the following five types of downward communication:

1. *Job instructions.* Directives stating what should be done and/or how to do it
2. *Job rationale.* Information designed to produce an understanding of the task and its relationship to other organizational tasks
3. *Procedures and practices.* Information about regulations, policies, and benefits
4. *Performance feedback.* Information about how well an individual, group, or organizational unit is performing
5. *Indoctrination of goals.* Information of an idealogical nature designed to inculcate a sense of mission

These various forms of downward communication can be found across all hierarchical levels of an organization, and they can be transmitted through any of a variety of media, including informal face-to-face interactions between supervisors and subordinates, staff meetings, formal presentations, written memos and letters, and even companywide newspapers and magazines.

Note that downward communication can sometimes skip many organizational levels. This is a common occurrence when the communication is about organizational policies. For example, a senior vice president for personnel might communicate information about personnel policies directly to the company's rank-and-file employees by means of a memo distributed with the monthly paychecks. In this instance the communication is received by those at the lowest levels of the organization without going through intermediate management levels.

Other types of downward communication, especially job instructions, tend not to skip organizational levels. Instead, they are more often transmitted down through the organization one level at a time. At each level the message is interpreted and filtered before it is retransmitted to the next lower level. In the process two things happen: (1) the content of the message tends to become increasingly more specific, and (2) it can get distorted.

The content of the communication gradually becomes more specific because the message is successively reinterpreted by a series of managers whose areas of responsibility are more and more narrowly defined. Thus, for example, a directive from top management to improve the financial performance of the organization may be interpreted by the director of marketing and sales as a need for greater sales volume. The general manager in charge of production, on the other hand, may interpret the same directive as a need for increased production efficiency. These two individuals are thus likely to retransmit the communication to their respective subordinates in terms of these more specific objectives. Their subordinates, in turn, will interpret these new, more specific communications in terms that are relevant for their own narrower areas of responsibility and then retransmit even more specific messages to the people below them. This process is clearly a functional one for the organization, since it will ultimately refine the general directive to a set of concrete behaviors (e.g., permitting members of the sales force to promise custom work and rush delivery; slowing production until warehouse inventories are reduced by 60 percent).

This refinement is achieved at the risk of distortion, however. For example, there is a danger that those in the marketing and sales division may come to view top management as being primarily interested in increasing sales volume, while those in the manufacturing division may come to believe that top management is primarily interested in more efficient production. Neither is really correct. These misperceptions can lead to interdivisional conflict if actions taken to improve sales volume interfere with production efficiency, or vice versa.

Upward Communication. *Upward communication* refers to communication that originates at lower levels of the organizational hierarchy and is transmitted upward to higher levels. The main motivation for upward communication is to provide higher organizational levels with information about what is going on down below. Upward communication is a critical feedback mechanism that can help those higher up assess the effectiveness of (1) their downward communications, and (2) the overall functioning of the organization below them (Glauser, 1984). Thus, a primary type of information the organization desires to have communicated upward is information concerning task performance. First-line supervisors may ask their employees to complete daily productivity reports. Middle managers may hold weekly or biweekly staff meetings in which they ask their subordinates to report on what they have accomplished and what work they are currently doing. And senior managers may pore over monthly, quarterly, and annual reports on the performance of whole divisions. In addition to these, other types of information that are communicated upward include information about work problems, recommended solutions, opinions about policies and procedures, grievances, and job attitudes (i.e., morale). With regard to the last item, it should be noted that whenever an organization uses a questionnaire or some other procedure to survey the job satisfaction of its employees, it is in essence creating a special mechanism for upward communication.

Although upward communication can be thought of as a companion to downward communication, it is generally more problematic. Not only is it subject to the same sorts of interpretation, filtering, and distortion as downward communication, people are often reluctant to communicate upward (cf. Jablin, 1979). One reason is that upward communication, especially about one's performance, can be threatening. How will that information be used? If you are not performing well, will it lead to reprimands or punishment? Or, if you are performing well, will it be used to raise work standards or in some other way increase the amount of effort you have to put into your job?

In addition, some of the problems associated with communicating upward can be attributed to the role and status differences inherent in any hierarchical organizational structure (Katz & Kahn, 1978). With regard to roles, the role of "manager" or "supervisor" generally requires that one direct and coordinate the work of subordinates. As a consequence, individuals occupying such a role are more likely to be in the habit of telling than of listening. Subordinates, in turn, become conditioned to do more listening than telling. Concerning status, and as suggested in Chapter 9, people may often be reluctant to initiate communications with anyone of higher organizational status. Thus, we might predict that as the status difference between supervisors and subordinates becomes greater, the amount of unsolicited upward communication will decrease. There is some research support for this prediction (e.g., Hage, 1974). Overall, then, organizations are more likely to have difficulties maintaining upward communication than downward communication.

Lateral Communication. *Lateral communication* (also known as *horizontal communication*) refers to communication between individuals at the same organizational level. From the organization's point of view, the main motivation for lateral communication is again task-related. Lateral communication provides the bulk of the *coordination* necessary for individuals who work on interdependent tasks. Thus, the flow of lateral communication often follows the flow of work. Individuals who are very close together *in the work flow* will tend to communicate much more frequently than those who are not close together (Landesberger, 1961). Note that this uneven distribution of lateral communication can occur even though the various individuals involved with the task may be equally close in terms of physical distance (e.g., their offices are all on the same floor of the building).

Lateral communication frequently takes place by means of informal face-to-face interaction, telephone conversations, short memos or notes, and work orders, requisition forms, and the like. However, for very complex tasks that involve a high degree of interdependence among large groups of people, these media will often not be sufficient to cope with the extremely high demand for lateral communication. Simply put, it may become physically impossible for everyone who needs to communicate to do so on an individual basis. Under such circumstances, the organization can create special mechanisms to facilitate the necessary lateral communication (Galbraith, 1977). These include special committees, teams, and task forces, as well as project or product managers. Liaisons and ombudsmen would also fall into this category. Some of these roles may be temporary, created to deal with a specific, short-term communication problem. Others may be more permanent. In either case, their main function is to facilitate lateral communication and thereby improve task coordination.

External Communication. External communication refers to communication that either originates inside the organizations and is transmitted outside (outward communication) or originates outside the organization and is transmitted inside (inward communication). The importance of external communication for the overall functioning of the organization is obvious. It is through various channels of external communication that the organization is able to assess and successfully interact with its environment. The organization communicates information about itself to the environment (e.g., about its products and services) and receives communications from the environment about such matters as market opportunities, product demand, materials availability, and customer satisfaction.

One type of external communication that is particularly relevant for understanding the behavior of people in organizations is the communication of behavioral expectations by external role-set members. Recall from the last chapter that a role set is that group of individuals who both have and communicate expectations concerning how a role occupant should behave. As previously discussed, the members of a given role set may not all be members of the organization. Some may be from outside. This is particularly true for those positions at the organization's boundaries (e.g., jobs in marketing and sales, purchasing, personnel recruiting, and public relations). Communications received by individuals in these positions from external role-set members can significantly affect the manner in which they perceive and carry out their roles (Adams, 1976). Thus, external communication can affect not only the organization's transactions with its environment, but the internal functioning of the organization as well.

Communication from the Group's Perspective

As we have seen, from the organization's perspective the primary motivation for communicating is task accomplishment. From the work group's perspective, by contrast, the primary motivation is the attainment of group goals. These goals may or may not overlap with the formal goals of the organization. The group attains its goals by exerting influence on group members to behave in particular ways. Oftentimes this process is synonymous with the enforcement of group norms, and as we saw in the last chapter, communication plays a large part in norm enforcement (see pages 273–274). When a group member deviates from an important norm, communication to that member increases dramatically in an effort to persuade him or her to change the deviant behavior. If the individual complies, verbal rewards may be communicated. If, on the other hand, the individual persists in the deviant behavior, communication from the rest of the work group may become increasingly punitive. If after all of this the individual continues to deviate from the norm, he or she may be rejected by the group, in which case all communication that is not essential for task performance may cease. Informally, this is known as getting the "silent treatment." In a very real sense, the individual is punished by the withholding of communication.

Communication from the Individual's Perspective

That work groups can use the simple ability to communicate with others as a reward for compliance with norms, and the loss of this ability as a punishment for deviance, suggests that the ability to communicate is something of value to the individual. That is, apart from the organization's concerns for task performance, and the work group's concerns for attaining group goals, there would appear to be motives for communicating that uniquely reflect the individual's perspective. Several distinct motives can be identified, and each is discussed in the sections that follow.

Exerting Influence. One motive for communicating that the individual has in common with both the group and the organization as a whole is influencing others in order to achieve a goal. Through the process of communication, an individual can try to persuade someone to change his or her beliefs, attitudes, or behavior in a way that helps the individual attain some personal objective. We might, for example, try to persuade a coworker to take over a part of our work load. We might try to persuade a subordinate to reschedule a meeting to a more convenient time. Or we might try to persuade our boss to give us a raise. Although persuasion is not the only way an individual can influence other people, it is one method that is very important in organizational settings.

It should be noted that any single act of communication may serve not only the individual's motive to exert influence, but also the group's and the organization's motives as well. This will happen, for example, when the personal objectives of the individual, the goals of the group, and the organization's objectives are all the same. This can also happen, however, when these three are *not* the same. For example, imagine you are the manager of one of four departments in the legal services division of a large Fortune 100 corporation. You learn that one of your brightest young attorneys has been asked to join a small prestigious law firm. This person is well liked by the other members of your staff, and she seems to be an informal leader of the group. At a convenient moment, you call her into your office and try to convince her to stay with the company. Your primary motive in doing this is to maintain your staff size, which is directly related to the amount of power you have in the division. You realize that because of severe budget cuts, there is a strong possibility you will not be able to replace anyone who leaves. Furthermore, in the last 18 months you have lost two other subordinates, both of whom were transferred to other departments. You feel that your organizational power is on the wane, and you do not want to see it eroded further. Thus, from your own perspective your communication is motivated by a personal objective—maintaining your power in the division. However, your communication also serves group and organizational goals. With regard to the group's goals, perhaps the most fundamental goal of any informal group is survival. The survival of a group is threatened whenever a member leaves the organization, especially when that member is an informal group leader. Thus, if you are successful in persuading your subordinate to stay, you will have helped to achieve an important group goal. With regard to organizational goals, if you can prevent a bright, talented individual from leaving the organization, you will have helped to maintain the overall quality of the organization's pool of human resources. This clearly has long-term benefits for the organization and its performance objectives.

Thus, a single communication episode can help to achieve goals at multiple levels of analysis. This can occur even if the individual is not aware of or does not care about these other goals. Of course, a communication motivated by an individual's desire to influence someone may also work against group and/or organizational goals. The point we are trying to make is simply that attempts to influence others through persuasive communications may often be motivated by personal objectives that are quite distinct from the objectives of the group or organization.

Reducing Uncertainty. A second motive that individuals have for communicating with others within their organization is to reduce uncertainty. When you first arrive at a new job you may be uncertain about what the appropriate norms of behavior are, what your role is to be, or who the high-status members of your work group are. Later on, you may be uncertain about how your pay raises stack up to what others get. Do you get more or less than others, and why? What do these differences mean? At other times you may wonder about the meaning of unusual, nonroutine events. Suppose you have suddenly been asked to document how much time you devote to each of the various projects you work on. Was this request made because your boss does not trust you or does not believe that you work hard enough? Or, suppose you are asked to represent your work group at a companywide conference? Is this a reward given only to valued subordinates, or is it an odious task that typically falls to lower-status individuals?

Uncertainties such as these crop up over and over again almost on a daily basis, and they can sometimes make people feel rather uncomfortable and anxious. One reason is that uncertainty can make it difficult for organization members to do their jobs and control what happens to them (cf. Larson & Mitchell, 1977). This is particularly true with regard to uncertainties about roles, norms, and status. Consequently, people are motivated to communicate with others in order to reduce these uncertainties.

To illustrate how sensitive people are to communications from others that help them clarify uncertainties even about seemingly objective aspects of their organizational environment, consider the following study by White and Mitchell (1979). In this study, forty-three undergraduate business students were paid to work on a task that involved compiling information about stock market prices. These students were led to believe they were doing this in order to help out a group of university professors. The task on which the students worked required them to look up stock prices from weekly American Stock Exchange quotations listed in the local newspaper. These prices had to be transferred to a special coding sheet. Next, they had to calculate and record the percentage price change from week to week. Finally, they had to graph the weekly price changes on specially prepared graph paper. The students worked on this task in groups of three, although each group member performed all parts of the task for all of his or her assigned stocks. Overall, each group spent 2 hours on the task. At the end of the 2 hours, the subjects filled out a questionnaire that asked about their perceptions of the task. The items in this questionnaire focused on such issues as the degree to which the task allowed them to exercise a variety of skills, gave them freedom to make their own decisions about how best to go about doing the work, and provided information about how well they were performing. A primary goal of this study was to determine whether the students' perceptions of these task characteristics would be influenced by communications they received from other group members.

Suppose *you* had been in this experiment. Do you think your perceptions of these variables would have been affected by communications from other members of your work group? Specifically, suppose one of the other group members made comments such as, "This is interesting. It's nice to finally use the skills I've developed in school." Do you think a comment of this sort would affect your perceptions of the degree of skill variety required by the task? Or, suppose the comment had been, "This isn't very interesting. It doesn't require any of the skills I've acquired in school." Would this affect your perceptions?

If you are like the students who participated in this study, your perceptions probably would be affected by such comments, for this is exactly what was found. As you have probably guessed by now, one of the students in each work group was actually an accomplice of the researchers. The accomplice was coached to communicate opinions to the other two group members stating either that the task seemed to involve a variety of skills, a high degree of autonomy, and a lot of feedback (positive task characteristics) or that it seemed to involve few skills and little autonomy or feedback (negative task characteristics). These two sets of communications had very different effects on the perceptions of the other group members. These effects are shown in Figure 10-1. Students who received positive task characteristic communications rated the task more favorably than did those who received negative task characteristic communications (panel A). Moreover, those who received the positive communications also reported being more satisfied with the task than did those who received the negative communications (panel B).

Thus, even when a task is as straightforward as the one used in this study, there are still sufficient areas of ambiguity and uncertainty to make people sensitive to the opinions communicated by others. As the study suggests, such communications can affect not only one's perceptions of the task, but also one's satisfaction with it.

Performance Feedback. People are also motivated to communicate with others in the organization in order to obtain feedback about their performance. They want to know how well they are performing and how their performance is judged by others. This is actually just another type of uncertainty that employees wish to clarify. However, it is sufficiently important that it deserves to be discussed separately.

Feedback is important because it facilitates goal attainment. It tells people

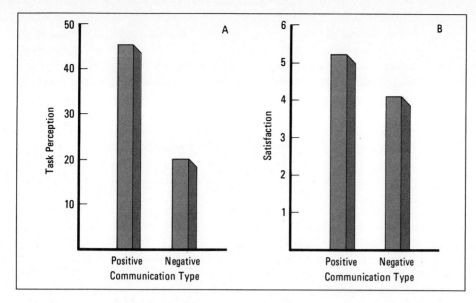

FIGURE 10-1
Positive commu-
nications about
task characteristics
led to more favor-
able task
perceptions and
higher satisfaction
with the task than
did negative com-
munications. Note
that higher num-
bers indicate more
favorable task per-
ceptions (panel A)
and higher satis-
faction (panel B).
(*Based on data
presented by
White & Mitchell,
1979.*)

how they are doing and thus whether or not they need to adjust their behavior
(e.g., work harder) in order to attain their goals. Feedback is therefore a
valuable resource for organization members, and as such it is actively sought
out by them (Ashford & Cummings, 1983; Hanser & Muchinsky, 1978). One
way people can seek feedback is by directly asking questions of others. (New
York City's mayor, Ed Koch, has actually made this strategy a campaign
theme. He has frequently been heard at campaign functions asking, "How am
I doing?") People can also seek feedback by monitoring the subtle meanings in
the unsolicited communications they receive or overhear. For example, an
employee may attend closely to the number of positive references made to his
or her work during staff meetings. Hearing ten positive comments may mean
something quite different from hearing only one or two.

If feedback is a resource that is actively sought by organization members,
what happens when feedback is not available? An answer to this question is
provided by the results of a study by Walsh, Ashford, and Hill (1985). They
had eighty-nine pharmaceutical sales representatives complete questionnaires
about feedback, anxiety, job satisfaction, and turnover intentions. They found
that when feedback from various sources (e.g., supervisors, coworkers, the
task itself) was unavailable, the representatives were more likely to be anxious,
have low job satisfaction, and express intentions of leaving their jobs. This
was particularly true when the representatives could not obtain feedback from
supervisors. Thus, feedback is an important resource, and when it is not
forthcoming, negative consequences occur. We will have more to say about
the importance of feedback from supervisors in Chapter 16, "The Line Manager's Impact on Employee Performance."

Affiliative Needs. Finally, people are also motivated to communicate with
others in order to fulfill their affiliative needs. Individuals generally prefer to
be with other people and share experiences with them, and this sharing is

accomplished through communication. All of us have experienced the strong effects of this motive at one time or another. For example, after you have spent all day Saturday working quietly by yourself in the library or in your room, you may want to go out and spend some time with friends or colleagues. You do not necessarily want to influence them, clarify uncertainties, or obtain performance feedback. You just want to talk and be with other people. It is simply a part of our human nature.

COMMUNICATION NETWORKS: WHO COMMUNICATES WITH WHOM

Thus far we have focused on the various motives that exist for communicating in organizational settings. These motives can be viewed from the perspective of the organization, the informal group, and the individual organization member. These motives all operate on a more-or-less continuous basis, and their joint effect accounts in large part for the pattern of communication that arises in an organization.

The overall pattern of communication in an organization is referred to as the organization's *communication network*. It is important to recognize that the communication network is not the same thing as the formal structure of the organization. An organization's communication network refers to who communicates with whom. The formal structure of the organization, on the other hand, refers to divisions of responsibility and lines of authority. These reveal only a small amount of information about the pattern of communication that exists. We know, for example, that people generally communicate more with other individuals within their own organizational unit than with those outside it, and that people generally communicate more with their own boss than with their boss's boss. Thus, by knowing the formal organizational structure and the relationship between the positions that two individuals hold (i.e., whether they are in the same organizational unit; whether one is the supervisor of the other), we may *sometimes* be able to get a general feeling for their likely level of communication (e.g., the vice president for marketing is more likely to communicate with the director of market research than with the director of college recruiting). However, the formal organizational structure will reveal little about *intraunit* communication networks, particularly among individuals at the same hierarchical level. For this information, some form of either direct or indirect observation is required.

Perhaps the easiest way to get a complete picture of an organization's communication network is to have the members of the organization fill out a questionnaire in which they report whom they usually talk to during the day. This questionnaire might ask them to list the names of those individuals they *initiate* communication with on a regular basis about important matters (e.g., in order to obtain information or assistance, or to give information or direction), as well as those they *receive* communication from on a regular basis about important matters (e.g., requests for information, assistance, or direction). Responses to this questionnaire could then be analyzed and represented in a diagram such as that shown in Figure 10-2, called a *sociogram*. This

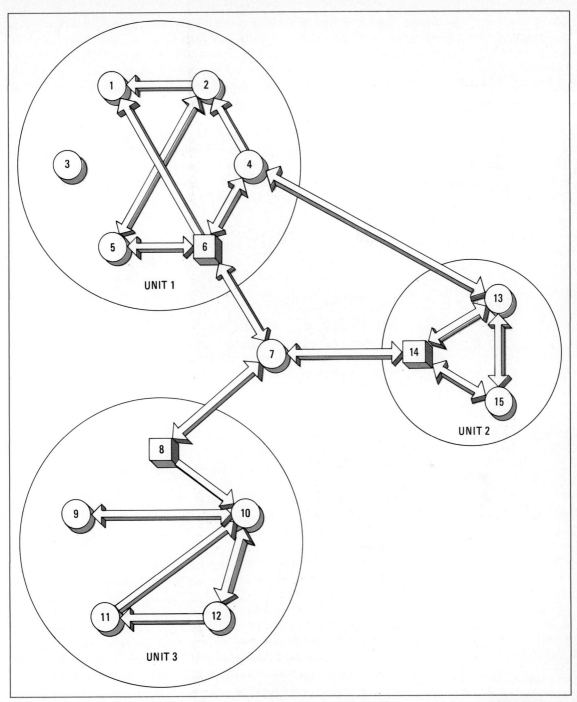

FIGURE 10-2
A hypothetical sociogram. The unit managers are identified by square boxes.

sociogram depicts a hypothetical pattern of communication among fifteen people from three different organizational units (e.g., research and development, manufacturing, and sales). Each organizational unit is indicated by one of the large circles. Within each circle, the unit manager is identified by a square box. The arrows indicate the pattern of communication. If an arrow has only one head, it means that the communication tends to be one-way (e.g., person 2 frequently initiates communication with person 1, but person 1 does not often initiate communication with person 2). If the arrow has two heads, it means that both individuals frequently initiate communication with one another. Also note that person 7 has a formal position in the organization that is outside all three groups. This might be a liaison position, in which the role of the occupant is to facilitate the exchange of information between the groups. Person 7 could also be the boss of the three unit managers.

Several aspects of this sociogram warrant discussion. First, note that there is much more communication within the units than between them. Second, the pattern of communication within each of the three units varies substantially. Within Unit 2, all three individuals both initiate and receive communication. This is not true for the other two units. Indeed, in Unit 1, one individual (person 3) seems neither to initiate nor receive much communication from anyone. This individual might be labeled an *isolate*. Third, the unit manager in each group seems to play a *gatekeeping role*. This is particularly true in Unit 3. All or most of the information coming into the group flows through the unit manager. The manager can thus control what information gets passed on to others and what does not. Finally, a rather peculiar situation exists in Unit 3. The unit manager seems to communicate very little with others in the group. Instead, it is person 10 who is at the center of the communication network in this unit. This would suggest that although person 8 is the formal unit manager, person 10 is the informal leader of the group. We will have more to say shortly about the relationship between leadership and one's centrality in the communication network.

Sociograms such as that shown in Figure 10-2 have been used to study communication networks in all sorts of organizations. One area in which they have been particularly useful is in studying the innovation process in research and development (R&D) laboratories. R&D laboratories often are not as highly formalized as other parts of an organization (i.e., fewer rules, regulations, and standard operating procedures), and the tasks performed there are inherently less structured. As a consequence, the informal communication network is likely to have an especially powerful impact on performance. In support of this, Keller and Holland (1983) have shown that high-performing scientists (i.e., those who produce more innovations) tend to be those who are more central in the communication network. Furthermore, a good deal of their communication is with individuals *outside* their immediate work group but still inside the organization (Pelz & Andrews, 1976). What is ambiguous, however, is the direction of causality in these findings. That is, it is not clear whether being more central in the communication network causes these scientists to be more productive, or whether being more productive causes them to become more central in the communication network. We suspect that a little of both may be occurring.

As noted previously, the formal structure of an organization has its primary influence on the amount of communication that occurs *between* (as opposed to within) organization units and across hierarchical levels. Consider, for example, the way in which an organization is horizontally differentiated. Had the fifteen people in Figure 10-2 been organized into four units instead of three, a differently shaped network would certainly have emerged.

The degree of decision centrality in the formal organization will also affect the shape of the communication network. In highly centralized organizations, in which most significant decisions are made by a few individuals at the top of the hierarchy, there is likely to be more upward and downward communication and less lateral communication between organizational units than in highly decentralized organizations (Burns & Stalker, 1961). More lateral communication between units is needed in decentralized organizations in order to bring together in one place the information needed to make a decision. In centralized organizations, this "bringing together" of information is taken care of by upward communication. The communication network shown in Figure 10-2 is more characteristic of highly centralized organizations than highly decentralized ones.

Within organizational units, task demands account for a good deal of the variation found among different communication networks. Besides the task, however, characteristics of both the informal work group and the physical environment also help to determine who talks with whom. One important group characteristic is the degree to which the group is cohesive (Shaw, 1981). Members of highly cohesive groups communicate much more with one another than do members of noncohesive groups. Referring once again to Figure 10-2, one might suspect that Unit 2 is a more cohesive group than either Unit 1 or Unit 3. The relative status of the group members also makes a difference. In general, more communications are both initiated and received by high-status group members than by low-status members (Barnlund & Harland, 1963). This suggests that person 10 in Figure 10-2 is possibly the highest status individual shown, while person 3 is the lowest status individual.

Finally, with regard to the physical environment, the simple physical proximity of group members can affect their communication with one another. For example, in their study of innovation in R&D laboratories, Keller and Holland (1983) found that individuals whose offices were located closer together were more likely to communicate with one another than those whose offices were located farther apart. Also, it has been shown that open-design offices (i.e., those with low, movable partitions rather than fixed walls) can actually *inhibit* some kinds of communication in comparison with traditional private offices (Becker, Gield, Gaylin, & Sayer, 1983). This is a rather intriguing finding, since one rationale for installing open-design offices in the first place has been to facilitate communication! (Open design offices were also discussed in Chapter 8 in connection with territorial factors affecting groups. See p. 234.) All of these factors—organizational structure, task demands, group characteristics, and the physical environment—combine to influence the shape of an organization's communication network.

Consequences of Communication Networks

The real importance of communication networks in organizations lies not in the factors that determine their shape, but rather in the consequences that they can have for group process and performance. Independent of the variables that give rise to a particular communication network, once that network is established, its shape can significantly influence not only the group's ability to perform a task well, but also the job satisfaction of group members and the emergence of informal group leaders. We will examine each of these consequences of communication networks here.

One method that has often been used to study the effects of communication networks is to create various shaped networks experimentally in a laboratory setting and compare their effects on performance, member satisfaction, or whatever other outcome variable is of interest. In most investigations of this nature, subjects are placed in adjacent cubicles and are allowed to communicate with each other only by means of written messages passed through specially designed slots in the cubicle walls (e.g., Bavalas, 1950). The shape of the communication network can be varied by opening some slots and closing others. The tasks the subjects are asked to perform range from simple mathematical or identification problems (e.g., determine which playing card all members of the group have in common when information about each member's hand can be communicated only one card at a time), to much more complex decision problems. Performance is typically measured by assessing the time it takes to solve the problem, the number of errors made, or the number of messages that are sent before a solution is reached. Satisfaction with the communication arrangement and with the group's performance is usually measured by questionnaire after the task is completed. Thus, if performance, satisfaction, or other similar variables change in a systematic fashion when the shape of the communication network is changed, it can be concluded that the shape of the network itself was the cause. Figure 10-3 shows some of the networks that have been most extensively studied.

The experimental research over the years has produced a number of important findings (Shaw, 1964, 1978, 1981). When the communication network has one position that is clearly more central than the others—that is, has relatively more channels of communication than other positions—the person occupying that central position tends to (1) receive more messages, (2) express more personal satisfaction with the task, (3) be chosen more frequently by the other group members as the group's leader, and (4) have more social influence than other group members. That individual is also usually the one who becomes responsible for processing most of the information and coming up with the final solution to the problem. The wheel and the Y are examples of networks in which one position is clearly more central than the rest (see Figure 10-3). These are thus referred to as *centralized networks*. Contrast these with networks such as the circle or comcon that do not have a central position. These latter structures are called *decentralized networks*.

The performance effectiveness of particular networks depends upon the difficulty of the task. For complex problems, a decentralized network produces a quicker solution time, fewer errors, and greater member satisfaction than a

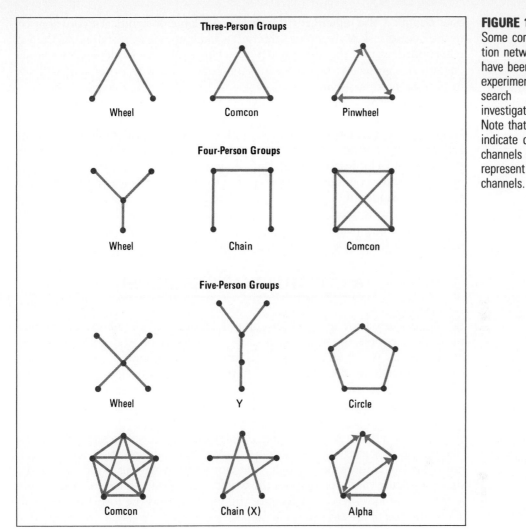

Three-Person Groups

Wheel   Comcon   Pinwheel

Four-Person Groups

Wheel   Chain   Comcon

Five-Person Groups

Wheel   Y   Circle

Comcon   Chain (X)   Alpha

FIGURE 10-3
Some communication networks that have been used in experimental research investigations. Note that arrows indicate one-way channels and lines represent two-way channels.

centralized structure. For rather simple problems, on the other hand, a centralized structure seems to be quicker and produce fewer errors.

These results point out a very crucial problem. They suggest that when a complex problem needs to be solved, a centralized communication network has serious drawbacks. First, the leader or person in the central position can become overloaded. He or she may have too much information to be able to function effectively. Second, a centralized network does not allow the other members to have as much input as in a decentralized network. Specific members are often isolated from the exchange, and satisfaction with the group seems to decrease.

This latter finding has implications for understanding why some types of jobs and formal organizational structures are inherently satisfying and others are inherently dissatisfying. To the extent that a job is narrowly defined and does not allow the incumbent to make a very large or significant contribution to the overall task of the group, that job is likely to be dissatisfying. As the job is expanded, so that the individual plays a larger role—as evidenced by a larger amount of significant, task-relevant communication with others—it is likely to become more satisfying.

Taken together, these results indicate that the pattern of communication that exists in a group is yet another variable that can influence individual-, group-, and organizational-level outcomes in rather predictable ways. More generally, by taking communication networks into consideration, we are better able to (1) describe what actually goes on in an organization, and (2) understand how communication is related to job performance and job satisfaction. We can identify those who are isolated in the organization, and we can determine who is overloaded with information. Blocks in the process can be located, and key people identified. These data can be extremely useful for helping to establish better communication.

A COMMUNICATION MODEL

Having discussed the motives for communicating and the nature of communication networks in organizations, we now focus on the communication process itself. As we stated at the beginning of the chapter, communication can be defined as the process of sharing information, ideas, or attitudes resulting in a degree of understanding between a sender and a receiver. Effective communication thus implies that the message has a similar meaning to both parties. Figure 10-4 presents a model that details the components of this process. The remainder of the chapter elaborates on these components.

Our initial concern will be *what is sent.* Verbal communication is more than just words: It is the tone of voice, the emphasis on various phrases, and the smile or gesture that accompanies the words. For written communication there is the type of letterhead, the form of the message, and the formality implied. Thus, the actual message sent encompasses a number of verbal and nonverbal cues.

The next issue we will discuss is the *mode,* or *medium,* of the message. Is it written or verbal? Why choose one or the other? Is one more effective than the other? We will briefly describe some research on this topic. The *flow of the message* is also of importance. Is it one-way or two-way? Is feedback involved?

FIGURE 10-4
The communication process.

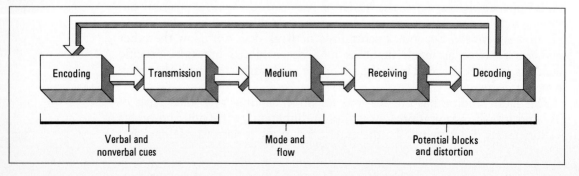

The final stage of the communication process involves the *reception of the message and its decoding*. Here we are concerned with the meaning ascribed to the message by its recipient. There are many reasons why this meaning may be very different from the one intended. The message may be distorted, the recipient may be hassled by other things, or the message itself may get changed through the transmission process. Each of these problems will be discussed.

Verbal and Nonverbal Communication

There's a language in her eye, her cheek, her lip,
Nay her foot speaks.
Her wanton spirits look out
At every joint and motive of her body.
—WILLIAM SHAKESPEARE

When one decides to communicate, some sort of verbal or written message must be sent. This message is usually composed of words. But far more information is conveyed than just the dictionary definitions of the words (Edinger & Patterson, 1983). The particular choice of words and the way in which they are put together are important sources of information. We may know, for example, that our boss uses certain terms only when he or she actually wanted something done yesterday. Thus, the phrase, "I really need this as soon as possible" may actually mean "I should have had this last week, and you had better get it to me pronto or there will be big trouble."

A number of vocal cues are also important. The speed, accent, loudness, and number of errors or breaks in the message provide us with additional information. People who are anxious tend to speak quickly and make a number of errors, while a more dominant, confident person will speak more slowly and loudly. Researchers have had people listen to tape-recorded messages in which the exact same words were spoken in different ways (e.g., they varied on dimensions such as breathiness, flatness, and loudness). The ratings of both the communicator and the communication vary widely as a function of the qualities of delivery (e.g., Addington, 1965).

A whole area of research has also evolved around the study of nonverbal cues in communication. The purpose of this research is to determine what information is sent by the communicator that is independent of, and different from, the verbal information. There are two main categories of nonverbal cues: physical cues and symbolic cues. Physical cues are all those characteristics of the individual's physical presentation (e.g., gestures, posture, facial expression) that might convey information. Symbolic cues are objects such as religious medals and school rings. These symbols tell the recipient something about the communicator that may strongly influence the interpretation of the message. By one estimate, these two categories of nonverbal cues account for about 55 percent of the meaning conveyed in our everyday communications with others (Mehrabian, 1968).

The information conveyed in physical nonverbal cues can be of two types: process and content. *Process information* refers to information that helps to structure the interaction between sender and receiver. For example, people will often raise their eyebrows, take a deep breath, or extend an arm in order to signal that they want you to stop talking so that they can say something.

You, on the other hand, may hold up your index finger to signal that you are not quite finished with what you have to say. Both sets of nonverbal cues help to regulate the conversation (i.e., who talks when).

Far more important, however, is the *content information* conveyed by physical cues. Physical cues can actually enhance or alter the meaning of a message. They may also provide one with information about the attitude of the sender. A communicator may convey a "superior attitude" by standing very erect, not smiling, and staring directly at the recipient. Or, if the communicator grimaces as he or she mentions a particular topic, you immediately learn something about his or her attitude toward that topic. Finally, physical cues are a good indication of the communicator's emotional state. Anger, anxiety, fear, despair, and joy are all readily interpreted from facial expressions, gestures, and tone of voice. These cues have a major impact on how a particular message is interpreted. Figure 10-5 summarizes some of the factors that can convey nonverbal information.

Imada and Hakel (1977) conducted an interesting study that demonstrates the power of nonverbal cues. These authors hypothesized that the nonverbal cues given off by a job applicant can significantly affect the ratings and decisions made by an interviewer. To test this hypothesis, they arranged to have a series of interviews conducted in which the interviewers (people who

FIGURE 10-5
Factors that can provide nonverbal information. (*Based on Argyle, 1972.*)

1. **Static features**

    a. *Distance*. The distance one stands from another person frequently conveys nonverbal messages. In some cultures distance is a sign of attraction, while in others it may reflect status or the intensity of the exchange.

    b. *Orientation*. People may orient themselves toward one another in various ways. Face-to-face, side-to-side, or even back-to-back orientations may convey specific information. For example, cooperating people are likely to sit side-by-side, while competitors frequently prefer to face one another.

    c. *Posture*. Posture can convey information about the degree of formality or relaxation in an exchange. Is the communicator slouching or sitting erect? Standing, or lying down? Having one's arms folded can sometimes convey anger. And whether one is leaning forward or backward in a chair can convey interest or disinterest.

    d. *Physical contact*. We can be touched, held, kissed, or embraced. Shaking hands, kissing, and patting on the back can all convey messages. In many cases they reflect an element of intimacy or feelings of attraction.

2. **Dynamic features**

    a. *Facial expressions*. The smile, frown, raised eyebrow, yawn, puckered lips, and sneer all convey information. These features are continually changing during an interaction and are constantly monitored by the recipient.

    b. *Gestures*. Some of the most frequently observed but least understood cues are hand movements. Most people have certain hand movements they regularly use when talking. While some gestures (e.g., a clenched fist) have universal meanings, most others seem to be individually learned and idiosyncratic.

    c. *Eye contact*. A major feature of social interaction is eye contact. It can convey emotions, as well as signals about when to talk or when to finish. The frequency of contact can suggest interest or boredom.

had some, but not extensive, training in interviewing) were given a standard list of questions to ask a potential job candidate. Twenty-four separate interviews were conducted. The interviewee (who was always the same person) answered the questions the same way in every interview. However, in half of the interviews she exhibited nonverbal cues suggesting "enthusiasm," such as greater eye contact, smiling, an attentive posture, smaller interpersonal distance, and a direct body orientation. In the other interviews, she exhibited nonverbal cues suggesting "aloofness," such as lack of eye contact, no smiling, a slouching posture, greater interpersonal distance, and an indirect body orientation.

The results were quite clear. The nonverbal cues used to suggest "enthusiasm" had the predicted effect. In those interviews the applicant was (1) liked more, (2) seen as having better qualifications, (3) seen as more competent and as having a higher likelihood of success, and (4) more likely to be recommended for hiring than in the interviews in which the applicant exhibited "aloof" cues. These results are shown in Figure 10-7.

Research suggests that people learn the meaning of many nonverbal cues very early in life (Burgoon, 1985). Some authors have even argued that the meaning conveyed by facial expressions and eye contact may be instinctive. In general, facial expressions, eye contact, and orientation convey information about the type of emotion a communicator is experiencing, while posture, gestures, and distance cues are more highly related to the intensity of the emotion or feeling.

Thus, whenever we communicate with someone, we are sending more information than is contained in the words. In order to understand communication fully and optimize its effectiveness, we must analyze both the verbal and nonverbal content of the message.

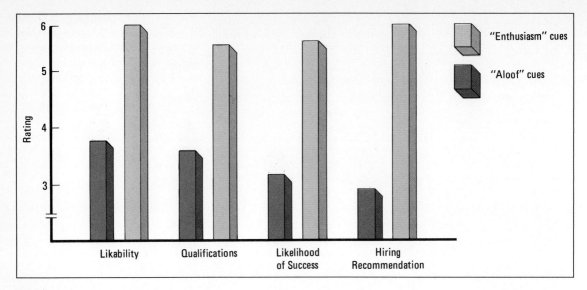

Rating

6
5
4
3

Likability | Qualifications | Likelihood of Success | Hiring Recommendation

"Enthusiasm" cues
"Aloof" cues

FIGURE 10-7
When the job applicant exhibited nonverbal cues conveying "enthusiasm," interviewers (1) liked her more, (2) rated her as having higher qualifications, (3) rated her as having a higher likelihood of success on the job, and (4) were more likely to recommend that she be hired. Note that higher numbers indicate more favorable ratings on each question. (*Based on data presented by Imada & Hakel, 1977.*)

The Choice of the Medium and the Flow of the Message

Once we decide to communicate, we must next decide whether to have a one-way or two-way communication process. Do you want feedback? Will it be helpful to allow for questions of clarification about the message? Using the phone or calling a meeting usually results in a two-way exchange of information. The most frequent medium chosen for one-way communication is the written message. Using one-way communication has both advantages and disadvantages (Leavitt, 1964). These are summarized in the sections that follow.

Formality. A one-way message can be phrased and presented more formally. It seems more official and businesslike. For example, military officers often come into a room, brief their subordinates, and leave. An official memo, on official stationery, can have a similar effect. It makes the message appear important.

Speed. One-way messages often take less time, especially when one is communicating with large numbers of people. There are occasions in which managers have to endure long meetings when a simple two-page document could have accomplished the same goal.

Simplification. When two-way communications occur, the process becomes much more complex. The recipient not only has to understand the sender, but the reverse is true as well. People's needs, feelings, and attitudes become involved. One-way messages avoid these complexities.

Organization. In many cases a formal, written document is more carefully planned than the things that are said in a meeting or in a personal exchange. One can be more thorough, orderly, and systematic with a written message.

Effectiveness. If we define effective communication as the agreement between the sender and the recipient on the meaning of the message, then a two-way process usually does a better job. Points can be clarified and corrections made. Sharing and discussing information may take more time, but it will probably result in better agreement about what was said.

Thus, while one-way communication has a number of advantages, it can have serious drawbacks in terms of agreement and comprehension. These considerations suggest that a one-way communication process will be appropriate only if the message to be communicated is rather simple and is not likely to be misunderstood. When the message is more complex, and thus there is a danger that disagreements and misunderstandings will arise, a two-way communication process will usually be more appropriate.

These ideas are clearly supported by empirical research. One study, for example, asked business supervisors to rate the effectiveness of (1) written, (2) oral, (3) written followed by oral, and (4) oral followed by written communication for different types of situations (Level, 1972). In general, the oral-followed-by-written technique came out best. Supervisors saw it as most effective for (1) calling for immediate action, (2) passing along a company directive or order, (3) communicating an important policy change, (4) reviewing work progress, (5) praising a noteworthy employee, and (6) promoting a safety campaign. The written-only technique was judged best for passing along information that (1) requires action in the future, or (2) is of a general nature. Note that the primary distinction between the oral-followed-by-written technique and the written-only technique is that the former involves an initial two-way communication process, while the latter does not.

It is important to point out that managers and supervisors not only *rate* two-way communication as being generally more effective in a wider variety of situations, they actually *engage* in much more two-way communication (cf. Mintzberg, 1973). For example, in a study of 577 civilian employees in a U.S. Navy agency, Klauss and Bass (1982) found that approximately 83 percent of the communications occurring in the agency involved one or more two-way media (i.e., individuals face-to-face, groups, and the telephone). Indeed, individual face-to-face interactions accounted for an average 55 percent of all the communications taking place. It is thus apparent that while one-way communication does have a place in organizations, two-way communication occurs much more frequently.

BLOCKS TO EFFECTIVE COMMUNICATION

Now that we better understand some of the elements of the communication process, we turn to one final and very important question. What factors prevent individual A from sending a message to individual B and having both of them agree about its meaning and importance? In other words, what are the blocks to effective communication?

The magnitude of this problem should be emphasized. We mentioned at the beginning of the chapter that up to 80 percent of an individual's time may be spent communicating. Yet studies show that sometimes as much as 50 percent of the information transmitted is interpreted incorrectly. The boss may think that he or she gave a formal order, but the subordinate sees it as a friendly suggestion. Or, a manager institutes a new safety plan and circulates a memo describing its implementation. Two weeks later the manager notices employees who are not wearing safety gear and inquires why they are not following the new regulations. "What new regulations?" is the response.

Understanding the reasons for poor communication is the first step toward improving communication effectiveness. Discussed below are three sets of problems: (1) the information never getting from A to B, (2) the message getting distorted by the sender or by someone transmitting the information, and (3) the recipient distorting what is received.

A Break in the Communication Link

One factor that frequently causes a breakdown in the communication process is the sheer size and complexity of large organizations. To get a message to another person can sometimes be terribly frustrating. Mail can get lost, phone messages can get thrown away, or the person might be out of town. People sometimes seem to play "telephone tag," leaving plenty of messages for one another, yet somehow never quite linking up.

Part of the reason that these problems exist at all has to do with the horizontal differentiation that takes place in organizations. As organizations grow in size, people get grouped into units that perform increasingly more specialized jobs. These units tend to become physically separated from one another, to the point that different units may be located in different buildings, cities, or states. As a result of the physical separation, many opportunities for informal, face-to-face interaction are lost, and greater reliance must be placed on formal meetings, telephone conversations, memos, and so forth. As we have seen, face-to-face interaction is a very important form of two-way communication, and its loss can occasionally lead to significant breakdowns in communication. Thus, organizational growth and differentiation are accompanied by a narrowing of communication channels and growing communication problems.

Communication problems are also related to the number of levels in the organizational hierarchy. When a communication travels from one organizational level to another, it often gets filtered and reinterpreted, with only the most relevant information being passed on to the next level. We made this point when we discussed upward and downward communication earlier in the chapter. The result can be that important bits of information are inadvertently dropped along the way. The more hierarchical levels a message must pass through, either upward or downward, the more filtering will be done, and the more likely it is that critical information will be lost.

Notice that when a message is sent either upward or downward in an organization, the filtering that takes place at intermediate hierarchical levels may be either intentional or unintentional. *Unintentional filtering* occurs when bits of information are deleted without the individual who is transmitting the message being aware of it. *Intentional filtering*, by contrast, occurs with the full knowledge of the transmitter. For example, you may discover a problem in your department that you feel should ultimately be brought to the attention of a vice president four levels above you. You tell your boss about the problem, and your boss reports it to her boss. But the message does not get any further than that because your boss's boss feels that the next person above would not be interested in the information. Or, maybe your boss's boss wanted to hoard the information and use it later for political purposes. In many respects, having information is synonymous with having power. Thus, one way to gather power is to gain access to vital sources of information that other people need.

Distortion by the Sender

Even when a communication sent by individual A successfully reaches individual B, it is still possible that the information will be distorted. As we suggested, some of this distortion may arise from filtering and interpretive processes as the message gets passed along by intermediate transmitters. In many cases, however, the communication is distorted by the senders themselves. There are two reasons for this.

First, in communicating information to other people we often present a sharper, more certain picture of the world than really exists (cf. Weick, 1979; Zajonc, 1960). The world around us is inherently uncertain and ambiguous. In an attempt to impose some sort of order on this ambiguity, thereby making our ideas more concrete and understandable, we often overemphasize salient pieces of information and underemphasize vagaries. This process is called *uncertainty absorption*. An example of this can be heard on the nightly news, when stock market analysts make comments such as, "The market was off sharply today in response to the President's new tax proposal." The implication is that the President's tax proposal caused the market's behavior. And indeed this may have been one important factor. However, on any given day hundreds of factors are likely to influence what happens on Wall Street. The analyst is undoubtedly aware of this, and his or her presidential attribution may have been intended solely to focus our attention on one of the many factors believed to be important. But, by simplifying the message in this manner, the analyst has probably caused many people to overvalue the role of the President and undervalue the role of other factors. In a similar fashion, we are guilty of uncertainty absbsorption when we tell the auto mechanic, "When I step on the accelerator, the car hesitates before picking up speed." Experience suggests that this is unlikely to be absolutely true. There may be a few times when, for unknown reasons, no hesitation occurs. But most of the time it does hesitate, and it is this salient feature of the situation that gets emphasized. The result is a clear, concise—and somewhat distorted—picture of what really occurs.

The second reason a sender may distort a communication is that he or she may be uncomfortable about the content of the message. We mentioned earlier that people are often reluctant to communicate information about their own performance upward to higher levels of the organization, especially when they know their performance has been less than what the organization desires. They may be justifiably concerned that that information will have negative consequences for them in the future. Thus, to the extent that it is possible, they may distort required performance reports, presenting themselves in as favorable a light as is feasible under the circumstances.

Also, managers and supervisors sometimes distort the negative performance feedback they communicate downward to subordinates (Fisher, 1979; Larson, 1986). It is often uncomfortable to criticize people, in part because of the angry reaction the criticism occasionally generates. Managers can lessen the probability that these negative reactions will occur by distorting their performance feedback, making it seem less negative than they really feel. The problem, of course, is that the subordinate may think there is nothing seriously wrong and that only slight changes in behavior are needed, when in fact he or she is on the verge of being fired if significant improvements do not occur immediately.

Distortion by the Recipient

The recipient of the communication is also a source of distortion, in the sense that the recipient can misinterpret the meaning of the message. There are many reasons why misinterpretation can occur. One has to do with language. Again as a consequence of the horizontal differentiation and specialization found in organizations, different organizational units often come to speak very different languages (Galbraith, 1977). They are likely to use technical terms that are specific to their own particular areas, and they may often develop their own unique jargon to refer to various procedures, pieces of equipment, activities, and so on. The use of specialized jargon can greatly facilitate communication *within* an organizational unit, since large volumes of information can be exchanged using relatively few words or symbols. However, jargon can be difficult for outsiders to understand, thus making communication *between* organizational units more problematic. Even when jargon is not involved, misinterpretation can still occur, because different organizational units may evolve somewhat different meanings for the same words. Consider, for example, the phrase "I need it as soon as possible." To a sender who works in a department in which task cycle times (i.e., the total time it takes to complete a task) are generally very short, and many separate tasks are completed in a single day (e.g., purchasing), this phrase may be equivalent to "I need it this afternoon." In contrast, to a recipient who works in a department in which task cycle times are very long, and where months may go by before a single task is completed (e.g., R&D), this phrase may be interpreted to mean "He needs it sometime this week." When the same words have different meanings for the sender and the receiver, misinterpretation is bound to occur.

A second reason why a recipient may misinterpret the meaning of a message has to do with selective perception (selective perception was discussed in some detail in Chapter 4). Often we are motivated to look for certain meanings in a communication, such as whether our boss thinks well or poorly of the work we are doing. Our attention may be drawn so strongly to subtle cues indicating our boss's evaluation that we all but miss the main points he or she wishes to communicate. As songwriters Simon and Garfunkel so aptly put it, "A man hears what he wants to hear and disregards the rest."

Yet another reason for misinterpretation has to do with expectations. For a variety of reasons, we may expect to see or hear certain types of messages. Such expectations can significantly influence the way we interpret the com-

In the cartoon, the blackboard shows:

$$\sqrt[n]{\frac{8032^4}{T^{\frac{n}{2}}} \cdot \frac{3n^7}{6 \cdot 7 P^{\frac{3}{2}} \cdot y}} = \text{A VERY LARGE NUMBER}$$

"I'm afraid that's not the way to bridge the communications gap between scientists and non-scientists."

munications we receive. This can be easily illustrated. Look at the four words listed below. Slowly pronounce each one.

M - A - C - B - E - T - H

M - A - C - T - A - V - I - S - H

M - A - C - D - O - N - A - L - D

M - A - C - H - I - N - E - R - Y

If you are like most people, you pronounced the last word *MacHinery* rather than *machinery* (Luthans, 1981). The first three words set up an expectation that influences one's interpretation of the last word. Only upon reconsideration does the error come to light.

Such expectations frequently influence the way we interpret all sorts of communications. Suppose, for example, that your boss is a rather grumpy person who never has anything pleasant to say to anyone. Over time you learn to expect a lot of criticism and little or no praise. Then one day he or she says to you, "Nice work." Your first inclination may be to interpret this as a sarcastic remark meaning "Boy, you have really screwed things up this time." It may take a while for you to realize that it was a genuine compliment. In general, the stronger the expectation and the more ambiguous the message, the more likely the message will be misinterpreted when the meaning the sender wishes to convey is not consistent with the recipient's prior expectations.

A related phenomenon is the perceived credibility of the sender. If the recipient does not perceive the sender as being a reliable source of information, he or she may discount the message or fail to perceive its importance. A

Communication at 35,000 Feet

. . . The large percentage of aircraft incidents and accidents attributed to "human error" has focused increasing attention upon the performance characteristics of the individual pilot. Traditionally, human factors specialists have channeled their research energies toward exploration of the pilot's job as a function of human perceptual and information-processing capabilities, and toward the important goal of designing equipment best suited to the characteristics of the human operator. As a direct result of the limitations and imperfections of individual humans, multi-pilot aircraft cockpits were designed to ensure needed redundancy. Yet, this system of redundancy has failed in many cases. It has failed too often because captains have not heeded the warnings of other crew members. It has failed because crew members who possessed adequate information have, for some reason, not provided it to others. Although individual pilot performance remains an important research topic, these occurrences suggest that more attention be placed upon crew performance and the factors which affect crew coordination.

COCKPIT COMMUNICATION

There is a feeling among human factors specialists, airline training departments, and social and personality psychologists that communication patterns exert significant influences on important performance-related factors. At the very least, communication patterns are crucial determinants of information transfer and crew coordination, but research has shown that they are also related to such factors as group cohesion, attitudes toward work, and complacency. That communications difficulties arise in the cockpit is not surprising in light of the fact that some large carriers employ thousands of pilots who, in many cases, have never met prior to flying a trip together. Thus, responsibilities that may be implicitly understood in crews that have flown together frequently, must be explicitly delineated in those that have not.

In a recent study, we took a more systematic look at cockpit communication patterns utilizing the data acquired in a NASA full-mission simulation study conducted by Ruffell Smith and NASA researchers. In that study, fully qualified B-747 crews flew a simulated, routine line segment from Washington to New York followed by a segment from New York to London in which a mechanical problem was introduced that necessitated an engine shutdown and diversion from the original flight plan. The simulation included all normal communications, air traffic control services, weather, closed runways at the only favorable diversion airport and, later, an inoperative autopilot which further increased pilot workload. The scenarios were constructed in such a way that good crew coordination, cockpit communications, decision making, and planning skills were required, but they were not complex enough to preclude an entirely safe operation given proper performance and coordination.

This study allowed the examination of flight crew performance in a controlled setting. Errors in performance were monitored and recorded. Eighteen volunteer line crews flew the scenario; marked variations in their behavior and performance were observed. Frequent problems were noted in areas related to communication, decision making, crew interaction, and integration. The presence or absence of strong leadership seemed to mediate the frequency and severity of the errors committed by the flight crews. . . .

Overall, there was a tendency for crews that did not perform as well to communicate less, but the type or quality of communication played a more important role. There was a negative correlation $(r = -0.51)$ between crew member observations about flight status and errors related to the operation of aircraft systems. In short, when more information was transferred about aspects of flight status, fewer errors appeared which were related to such problems as mishandling engine, hydraulic, and fuel systems, misreading and missetting instruments, failure to use ice protection, and so forth.

In a similar fashion, a negative relationship $(r = -0.61)$ was evident between aircraft systems errors and acknowledgements to information which had been provided. In crews in which commands, inquiries, and observations were frequently acknowledged, these types of errors were less apparent. Acknowledgements were also related to fewer errors overall $(r = -0.68)$. It would appear from these data that acknowledgements serve the important function of validating that a certain piece of information has, in fact, been transferred. These types of communication also serve as reinforcements to the input of other crew members. This relationship is entirely straightforward. When a person makes an attempt to communicate with someone who does not respond, the probability of further communication is reduced. Even the simplest response is more likely to elicit further input from others. . . .

In addition to the importance of communication style, the precision of communication plays a pivotal role. The ASRS [Aviation Safety Reporting System] data bank contains a number of incidents where each pilot thought he knew what the other meant or intended to do when, in reality, he did not. The following report to ASRS conveys the potential severity of this state of affairs:

> I was monitoring an autoland approach on a flight to Runway 22L at Newark in visual conditions when a GPWS [Ground Pullup Warning System] "pullup" warning occurred . . . the entire crew's attention was directed toward confirming configuration, position, speed, and sink rate, all of which were normal. I commanded, and simultaneously with the copilot, selected 50 degree flaps, considering that the landing flaps not selected mode was possibly the reason for what I considered to be "probably" a false warning due to a possible failed flap position switch. The FE [Flight Engineer] said something which I could not clearly grasp while the "pullup" was sounding. As the flaps extended to 50 degrees, the GPWS warning silenced. A normal auto landing occurred. Sounds simple and somewhat everyday—until during taxiing I was informed that the FE had inhibited the GPWS without being commanded to . . . he stated he asked me if I wanted it cancelled, but I did not reply so he assumed I did.

Source: H. C. Foushee (1982, November). The role of communications, socio-psychological, and personality factors in the maintenance of crew coordination, Aviation, Space, and Environmental Medicine, 1062–1066. Reprinted by permission.

casual comment made by a distrusted subordinate about an impending budget cut may be dismissed. The same casual comment made by one's boss is likely to be taken very seriously.

Finally, misinterpretation can occur simply as a function of information overload. A recipient may receive so many communications from so many different senders that less than full attention is given to some of them. A few communications may receive only a moment's thought before they are discarded. Under a heavy information-processing load, the recipient may fail to appreciate the importance of some of the messages received.

Some Remedies for Poor Communication

There are many barriers to effective communication. A message can be distorted by the sender, by other individuals who transmit it, and/or by the recipient. In some cases, messages may not get to the recipient at all. There are, however, a number of things that can be done at both the individual and organizational level to help overcome some of these communication problems.

At the individual level, communicators should always attempt to use language that is clear, concise, *and* appropriate to the situation. Think twice, go over the message one more time, and try to imagine the audience. Will the information be appropriate? Is the language clear and precise?

A communicator must also establish credibility. The message should be both understood and believed. One rule of thumb is to make sure that what is said can be factually validated or in some other way independently verified. Information has to be believed to have any impact.

Also, try to avoid the use of labels and unnecessary classifications and let the recipient receive as much factual information as possible. If an employee has failed to meet three deadlines in a row, it is better to state this fact than to describe the person as "lazy" or "irresponsible." This does not mean that attitudes, opinions, and feelings should be omitted, but simply that they should be labeled as such.

Finally, the communicator should actively seek out feedback in order to ensure that the intended meaning of the communication was perceived by the recipient. One way this can be accomplished is to ask the recipient to restate the communication in his or her own words. If the restatement does not jibe with the meaning that was intended, the message can be rephrased in clearer, more easily understood terms. Note that simply asking the recipient "Do you understand?" is not a very effective way to get feedback. A "yes" response indicates only that the recipient *thinks* he or she understands. It does not indicate that he or she *actually* understands.

There are also things that can be done at the organizational level to facilitate communication. Some of these have already been mentioned, such as establishing special liaison and intergrator roles to aid with lateral communication. The organization can also set up formal feedback channels to check on the effectiveness of downward communication. And computer technology can be added to increase the ease, speed, and accuracy with which information is transferred within the organization.

In addition to these measures, organizations can provide key employees with specialized training in communication skills. In large organizations, communication training is often done "in-house." In smaller organizations, employees may be sent "off-site" to firms that specialize in communication training. Communication training may also be included as part of a more comprehensive management or leadership training course, again offered either in-house or off-site. Communication training usually involves various types of role playing, and sometimes requires the simultaneous participation of those employees whose everyday interactions are critical to the operation of the organization. The training is intended to help their interpersonal exchanges by improving speaking, writing, and listening skills, and by getting them to understand the other person's point of view. Although this sort of training has not been effective in every case, managers often do report positive results (e.g., "Game Playing," 1979).

Summary

In this chapter we have attempted to define and describe the communication process. Blocks to effective communication have been discussed, and a number of remedies suggested. Some of the most important points made in the chapter are as follows:

1. Communication is important. It takes up much of our time and is often the cause of major organizational failures.
2. The motives for communicating are complex. They can be analyzed from the perspective of the organization, the work group, and the individual organizational member.

3. The pattern of communication that occurs in an organization is called a communication network. The shape of the network can affect not only group performance, but also member satisfaction and leader emergence.
4. The communication process involves a sender, a message, a channel or method of communication, and a recipient.
5. The message itself is composed of both verbal and nonverbal cues. The latter are in many cases as important as the written or spoken words.
6. There are many different ways and combinations of ways to send information. Two-way communication is generally more frequent and useful than one-way communication.
7. There are a number of ways in which effective communication can be disrupted or blocked. A message may not be received, may be distorted, or may be misinterpreted by the recipient.
8. A number of personal and organizational aids are available to help people communicate more effectively.

IMPLICATIONS FOR RESEARCH

The rapid technological advances of the past 10 years have made it increasingly feasible for organizations to use a new and exciting mode of communication—computer-mediated communication. Computer-mediated communication can take many forms, including electronic mail, computer bulletin boards, large-scale data transfer, and computer conferencing. From a purely technical standpoint, this new mode of communication holds great promise for organizations. Through computer-mediated communication, more people will be able to communicate with one another more cheaply than ever before. What is not yet known, however, is how this new communication technology will affect the basic structure and functioning of organizations. Several aspects of this problem have recently been discussed by Becker (1986) and Kiesler, Siegel, and McGuire (1984).

At a rather basic level, one set of issues concerns the regulation and effectiveness of computer-mediated communication. When we communicate interactively via computer, the communication may not be as easy as it is when we interact face-to-face. Two factors are likely to make computer-mediated communication more difficult. First, communicating via computer is likely to be slower, simply because we cannot type as quickly as we can speak. Second, and more important, information transmitted from one computer terminal to another contains no nonverbal cues. This may make regulation of the interaction (e.g., turn-taking) more awkward, as well as making the content of the communication more difficult to comprehend. As we discussed earlier in this chapter, nonverbal cues are important in both respects. Thus, individuals using this new technology may have to work harder in order to ensure that the meanings of their communications are understood by others, and even then, disagreements and misunderstandings may be more likely to occur.

A second set of issues has to do with the flow of communications throughout the organization. If all or most of the organization's employees are linked in a computer network, does the old (noncomputer-mediated) communication network change in any substantial way? Do information gatekeepers lose their influence? Do isolates become better integrated into the organization? Is interunit communication facilitated to the point that integrators and liaisons are no longer needed? And what about the flow of communication upward and downward in the organization? If employees have access to all levels of the organizational hierarchy via electronic mail, do formal distinctions among organizational levels begin to break down?

What about the effect of computer-mediated communication on group decision making? Kiesler et al. (1984) report that when decision-making groups interact via computer, group members participate more equally than when they interact face-to-face. One reason may be the absence of salient nonverbal cues indicating the relative status of the group members. High-status individuals, who often dominate the discussion in face-to-face interactions, are more difficult for other group members to identify, which may reduce the inhibitions of the otherwise low-status members. Of course, whether this is good or bad from the point of view of decision effectiveness all depends on which group members, those with high status or those with low status, possess important decision-relevant information.

Finally, there is a series of questions one can ask about the impact of computer-mediated communications on the structure of informal work groups. Electronic mail has the capacity for allowing people to do their work without having to come together in the same location. Indeed, there may not even be a need for them to work on the same schedule. How does such an arrangement affect the development of group norms? Do organization members even feel as if they are a part of a work group? And if not, what effect does this have on their job satisfaction and commitment to the organization?

These are only a few of the questions that can be asked about the impact of this new technology. There are many others. Computer-mediated communication is growing in importance as a tool used by organizations. What needs to be recognized is that this tool may change the organization itself. Computer-mediated communication will undoubtedly be an increasingly important factor for understanding organizational behavior in the future, and it is an area in which a great deal of empirical research needs to be done.

IMPLICATIONS FOR PRACTICE

We have already listed a number of ways in which poor communications can be made more effective. Using clear, appropriate language, establishing credibility, avoiding labels, and making use of training programs and communication courses all can increase the effectiveness of an individual's communication. But there are several additional issues that should be mentioned.

First, organizations seem to take communication for granted. People tend to *assume* that what they have said or written is received and understood. It is only when blunders occur that the extent to which poor communication exists is recognized. This need not be the case. Organizations can and should take a proactive role in analyzing their communication patterns. Isolated positions can be made less isolated. Overloaded positions can be relieved. Messages that have to travel through many levels or units can be checked on. And upward communication can be solicited. An analysis of the communication structure can remedy old problems *and* establish more effective patterns for the future.

Second, individuals should be made aware of both the complexity of the communication process and the alternatives that are available. There are a variety of ways that ambiguity can be decreased, labels avoided, and irrelevant information kept to a minimum. There are also things that can be done to make sure that the message is received by the appropriate persons. Think about who should receive a message—err in favor of keeping others informed. The more important the issue, the better it is to use multiple messages and multiple modes of communication (e.g., written and oral). Build in feedback loops if you can. When you know that an important face-to-face exchange will take place, you can do things that will help you to listen as well as communicate. You can make sure you will not be interrupted, you can find a quiet place and a quiet time for the interaction, and you can try to attend to the speaker's message without evaluating or prejudging the remarks beforehand.

Finally, individuals can learn about the nonverbal cues they transmit to others by watching a film (without sound) of themselves. This exercise dramatically points out how people use facial expressions and gestures to communicate, and how sometimes the words they speak differ substantially from the message they send. It is also possible to learn general principles about nonverbal cues that might be helpful in a variety of settings. For example, middle-class white Americans typically show respect and attention to a speaker by maintaining eye contact. On the other hand, in various Latin American and Eastern cultures it is a sign of respect to *avoid* maintaining eye contact. This type of knowledge can help one screen out irrelevant nonverbal cues sent by others and read accurately those cues that carry important information about others' "true" feelings.

The important point is that good communication is not just speaking or writing clearly or unambiguously. It is a matter of understanding the whole process. Good communication includes the accurate encoding and transmission of a message, *and* accurate interpretation by the recipient. Understanding all of the factors that can influence each of these stages is an important first step toward developing effective communications among people in organizations.

Discussion Questions

1. Why do we communicate with others? What is meant by effective communication?
2. What are some nonverbal cues that you pay attention to when interacting with others? Do you think these cues are more or less important than the substance of the message?
3. In your experience, what are the major blocks to effective communication? How would you remedy these?

CASE: ON BEING INFORMED
AND BEING WELL INFORMED

Atlantic Aircraft produces small pleasure and business airplanes. It is situated in the Northeast, and has recently been plagued by problems of turnover, absenteeism, and suspected sabotage. The president of the company, Craig Kaplan, called in his vice presidents and asked them what they thought the problem was. After much discussion they decided that the employees felt they were being overworked and underpaid, and it was agreed that some sort of bonus system should be tried. Peg Randolph, the director of personnel, was asked to develop and implement such a system.

It became obvious to Peg that to have a good bonus system one must first develop a good performance appraisal device. With this goal in mind, she interviewed a number of managers about how high and low performers actually behave on the job, and a behavioral checklist was developed that described the actions of good performers and poor performers. A bonus system was then aligned with scores on the checklist so that people who behaved appropriately would receive a bonus and those that did not would get nothing.

Before implementing the system, Peg called two meetings. First, she sat down with the vice presidents and explained what she had done. Copies of the appraisal form were distributed, reviewed, and discussed. The vice presidents seemed preoccupied with other problems, but in general the group was supportive. While not terribly enthusiastic or excited, the group told Peg to proceed with the program. The second meeting involved a group of middle managers and first-line supervisors. They were the people who would be asked to use the form. There was some grumbling and whispers, but not many overt objections. Several people suggested that one form did not cover all the types of jobs people did, but this point was not pressed. When Peg mentioned that the vice presidents were behind the idea, she was again given the green light to proceed.

A brief memo describing the bonus system was distributed to all employees, and the new system was implemented. Rating forms went out to all supervisory and managerial personnel asking that they rate each of their subordinates twice during the next 3 months and return the forms to her. She would handle the processing of the data and the distribution of the bonuses.

It was not long before Peg began to sense that something was wrong. Instead of getting positive reports about employee attitudes toward the bonus system, the opposite began to occur. Employees were angry that they were being watched and evaluated. They did not like the idea of their behavior being rated, especially on a form that they had never seen before and had no help in developing. The use of only one form seemed silly and oversimplified.

The data also presented problems. Only a small percentage of the rating forms were actually being turned in. And on those submitted, almost everyone was rated high. At this rate, everyone would end up getting a bonus. Peg was convinced that the rating instrument was scientifically sound. If used properly, people would get rewarded for doing a good job. However, somehow the process of implementation had been bungled. The support and enthusiasm she expected were not there. The whole system had to be scrubbed.

Questions about the Case

1. Do you think that Peg acted too hastily? What cues were there that should have alerted her to some possible difficulties?

2. Were the employees properly informed? Do you think the descriptive memo provided sufficient information?
3. How could the program have been implemented in such a way that it would have been accepted?

References

Adams, J. S. (1976). The structure and dynamics of behavior in organizational boundary roles. In M. D. Dunnette (Ed.), *Handbook of industrial and organizational pyschology* (pp. 1175–1199). Chicago: Rand McNally.

Addington, D. W. (1965). The relationship of selected vocal characteristics to personality perception. *Speech Monographs, 35,* 492–503.

Argyle, M. (1972). Nonverbal communication in human social interaction. In R. Hinde (Ed.), *Non-verbal communication.* NY: Cambridge University Press.

Ashford, S. J., & Cummings, L. L. (1983). Feedback as an individual resource: Personal strategies of creating information. *Organizational Behavior and Human Performance, 32,* 370–398.

Barnland, D. C., & Harland, C. (1963). Propinquity and prestige as determinants of communication networks. *Sociometry, 26,* 467–479.

Bavalas, A. (1950). Communication patterns in task oriented groups. *Journal of the Accoustical Society of America, 22,* 725–730.

Becker, F. D. (1986). Loosely coupled settings: A strategy for computer-aided work decentralization. In B. M. Staw & L. L. Cummings (Eds.), *Research in organizational behavior* (Vol. 8, pp. 199–231). Greenwich, CT: JAI Press.

Becker, F. D., Gield, B., Gaylin, K., & Sayer, S. (1983). Office design in a community college: Effect on work and communication patterns. *Environment and Behavior, 15,* 699–726.

Burgoon, J. K. (1985). Nonverbal signals. In M. K. Knapp & G. R. Miller (Eds.), *Handbook of interpersonal communication* (pp. 344–390). Beverly Hills, CA: Sage.

Burns, T., & Stalker, G. (1961). *The management of innovation.* London: Tavistock.

Dance, F. E. X. (1970). The "concept" of communication. *The Journal of Communication, 20,* 201–210.

Edinger, J. A., & Patterson, M. L. (1983). Nonverbal involvement and social control. *Psychological Bulletin, 93,* 30–56.

Fisher, C. D. (1979). Transmission of positive and negative feedback to subordinates: A laboratory investigation. *Journal of Applied Psychology, 64,* 533–540.

Galbraith, J. R. (1977). *Organization design.* Reading, MA: Addison-Wesley.

Game playing to help managers communicate. (1979, April 9). *Business Week,* p. 76.

Glauser, M. J. (1984). Upward information flow in organizations: Review and conceptual analysis. *Human Relations, 37,* 613–643.

Hage, J. (1974). *Communication and organizational control: Cybernetics in health and welfare settings.* New York: Wiley.

Hanser, L. M., & Muchinsky, P. M. (1978). Work as an information environment. *Organizational Behavior and Human Performance, 21,* 47–60.

Imada, A. S., & Hakel, M. D. (1977). Influence of nonverbal communication and rater proximity on impressions and decisions in simulated employment interviews. *Journal of Applied Psychology, 62,* 295–300.

Jablin, F. M. (1979). Superior-subordinate communication: The state of the art. *Psychological Bulletin, 86,* 1201–1222.

Janis, I. L., & Mann, L. (1977). *Decision making: A psychological analysis of conflict, choice, and commitment.* NY: Free Press.

Katz, D., & Kahn, R. L. (1978). *The social psychology of organizations* (2d ed.). New York: Wiley.

Keller, R. T., & Holland, W. E. (1983). Communicators and innovators in research and development organizations. *Academy of Management Journal, 26,* 742–749.

Kiesler, S., Siegel, J. & McGuire, T. W. (1984). Social psychological aspects of computer-mediated communication. *American Psychologist, 39,* 1123–1134.

Klauss, R., & Bass, B. M. (1982). *International communication in organizations.* New York: Academic Press.

Landesberger, H. (1961). The horizontal dimension of bureaucracy. *Administrative Science Quarterly, 6,* 299–332.

Larson, J. R., Jr., & Mitchell, T. R. (1977). Changes in behavior following changes in control over outcomes: A theory based on response to uncertainty. *JSAS Catalog of Selected Documents in Psychology, 7,* 5, No. 1141.

Larson, J. R., Jr. (1986). Supervisors' performance feedback to subordinates: The role of subordinate performance valence and outcome dependence. *Organizational Behavior and Human Decision Processes, 37,* 391–408.

Lawler, E. E., III, Porter, L. W., & Tennenbaum, A. (1968). Managers' attitudes toward interaction episodes. *Journal of Applied Psychology, 52,* 432–439.

Leavitt, H. (1964). *Managerial psychology.* Chicago: University of Chicago Press.

Level, D. A. (1972). Communication effectiveness: Method and situation. *Journal of Business Communication, 10,* 19–25.

Lewis, P. V. (1980). *Organizational communication: The essence of effective management* (2d ed.). Columbus, OH: Grid Publishing.

Luthans, F. (1981). *Organizational behavior* (3d ed.). NY: McGraw-Hill.

Mehrabian, A. (1968, September). Communication without words. *Psychology Today,* pp. 53–55.

Mintzberg, H. (1973). *The nature of managerial work.* NY: Harper & Row.

Pelz, D. C., & Andrews, F. M. (1976). *Scientists in organizations* (rev. ed.). Ann Arbor, MI: Institute for Social Research, University of Michigan.

Shaw, M.E. (1964). Communication networks. In L. Berkowitz (Ed.), *Advances in experimental social psychology* (Vol. 1, pp. 111–147). NY: Academic Press.

Shaw, M. E. (1978). Communication networks fourteen years later. In L. Berkowitz (Ed), *Group processes* (pp. 351–361). NY: Academic Press.

Shaw, M. E. (1981). *Group dynamics: The psychology of small group behavior* (3d ed.). NY: McGraw-Hill.

Walsh, J. P., Ashford, S. J., & Hill, T. E. (1985). Feedback obstruction: The influence of the information environment on employee turnover intentions. *Human Relations, 38,* 23–46.

Weick, K. E. (1979). *The social psychology of organizing* (2d ed.). Reading, MA: Addison-Wesley.

White, S. E., & Mitchell, T. R. (1979). Job enrichment versus social cues: A comparison and competitive test. *Journal of Applied Psychology, 64,* 1–9.

Zajonc, R. B. (1960). The process of cognitive tuning in communication. *Journal of Abnormal and Social Psychology, 61,* 159–167.

Part Four

Accomplishing Organizational Objectives

The purpose of any organization is to get things done. In order to accomplish goals and meet objectives, two basic kinds of activities need to occur: (1) decisions must be made about the actions that will be taken in pursuit of the goals and objectives, and (2) the behavior of other people must be influenced in the direction of carrying out those actions. The chapters in Part 4 deal with these two topics.

Individual decision making is the subject of Chapter 11. Here we discuss how people perceive problems, evaluate information, generate alternative solutions, and finally, make a choice. To a large extent, the type of decision strategy people use depends on the type of problem and the circumstances surrounding the problem.

After discussing individual decision making, in Chapter 12 we turn to group decision making. The central issues covered in this chapter are the degree to which participative (group) decision making should be used in organizations, and how to manage the group decision-making process.

The topic of Chapter 13, "Power and Politics," is influence. How does one get other people and groups to do what one wants them to do? By definition, each of us relinquishes a part of our freedom in order to join an organization. As a consequence, we may be asked to do many things by others, some of which may be unpleasant. In other words, we can be influenced. When this influence process takes place between individuals, it is called *social power*. When it occurs between groups, it is called *organizational politics*. Chapter 13 deals with both of these issues.

Influence is also the central topic of Chapter 14, "Leadership." Here, however, it is the influence of one individual, the leader, on the group that is of central concern. In this chapter we begin by defining leadership and discussing its fundamental nature. We then examine the question of what makes some leaders more effective than others. Early approaches to this question suggested that personality traits are the answer. Thus, according to this view, one has only to find out what personality traits effective leaders have in common, and then select people with those traits for leadership positions. Unfortunately, this notion is overly simplistic. Different situations seem to demand different types of leaders and leader behavior. In this chapter we examine in detail several contemporary theories that take the situation into account. These theories attempt to specify what sort of person is likely to be a good leader in a specific situation. These theories have important implications for organizational policies regarding personnel selection, training, placement, and promotion.

To summarize, Part 4 examines how people in organizations get things done. Decisions have to be made and people have to be influenced. If these two basic activities can be carried out successfully, the organization will be well on the road toward achieving its goals and objectives.

Chapter 11

Individual Decision Making

I am at war twixt will and will not.
—WILLIAM SHAKESPEARE

Decision making is central to the effectiveness of any group or institution. Some people view it as the heart of administrative action; others have even based their approach to management on an analysis of how and where decisions are made (e.g., Simon, 1957).

Because of the breadth of behavior covered by the term *decision making*, we must try to limit and clarify our focus for this chapter. Our concern is for decision making in the organizational context. We examine the process that leads up to and includes the choice of a course of action from among two or more alternatives. These alternative courses of action are meant to help achieve important group or organizational goals. Thus, organizational decision making can be defined as the process of choosing actions that are directed toward the resolution of significant group or organizational problems.

Finally, this process can be carried out either by individuals acting alone or by groups. This distinction is an important one. The processes involved and the decision-making theories and models that have been developed are different for individual and group decisions. In this chapter, we describe the processes, theories, and models used to explain individual decision making, with an emphasis on how the decision-making process can increase organizational effectiveness. In the next chapter we consider group decision making.

WHY STUDY DECISION MAKING?

Decision making is important for organizational effectiveness because of its central role in the overall process of directing and controlling the behavior of organizational members. Decisions are made that cover the setting of goals, strategic planning, organizational design, personnel actions, and individual and group actions. Besides its organizational effect, however, decision making also has an individual effect. The quality of a manager's decisions has a bearing on his or her professional success and sense of satisfaction. So, studying decision making is important from both an organizational and an individual perspective.

Another major reason for studying decisions is to enable us to make better quality decisions than we do presently. This point must be emphasized strongly, because the quality of our decisions is often much poorer than we realize. Some of the reasons for the poor quality have been discussed in earlier chapters. Selective perception tends to bias the information we use in making decisions, and our attitudes and values influence how we interpret that information. Drives for consistency lead to oversimplified interpretations. Our willingness to attribute positive outcomes to ourselves (e.g., taking credit for good decisions) and to attribute negative outcomes to forces outside our control makes us remember the results of decisions in a personally favorable light. All these forces degrade our decisions and, at the same time, limit our understanding of the decision-making problem.

Besides being unaware of our human limitations in the decision-making process, we are often unaware of methods that can be used to increase our

Se how is this a method.

333
Chapter 11:
Individual
Decision
Making

decision effectiveness. Very little training that emphasizes the actual decision-making process is available either inside or outside of organizations. In most cases experience is our guide, and while experience can be a good teacher, it can be misleading as well. In many cases we may learn the wrong way to do something, or we may learn information that is actually irrelevant for the quality of the decision.

In order to increase our effectiveness in decision making, we must first understand the decision-making process. Appreciating the complexity of this process is the focus of the next section.

THE DECISION-MAKING PROCESS

Decision making is more than just making a choice. It is also the actions and activities that precede the choice. It is a process—a series of distinct steps that lead up to and beyond the actual choice. Figure 11-1 presents a diagram of the process. *who + oher tems that follow.*

Decision Phases

Every organization has goals and objectives. They are part of the reason for organizing in the first place. These goals and objectives tell us where we are going and why. They are a general blueprint for organizational design and action, and they form the first phase in the decision process. *reached*

In many cases, however, our goals and objectives are not realized. Individuals, subgroups, units, and whole organizations often fall short of their targets. It is this discrepancy between what is observed and what is desired that provides the basis of the problem-recognition stage of decision making. Somehow things are not as they should be, and the person in charge must find out why and resolve the problem. *there is a problem leading to the gap we realize what we desire.*

Problem recognition really involves two activities. First, the manager or decision maker must be scanning and keeping track of what is going on. He or she must be alert to recognize discrepancies when they exist. Second, the decision maker must evaluate the discrepancy. Only if the discrepancy is deemed to be an important one will the next phase of the process be engaged.

Figure 11-1
The stages of
decision making.

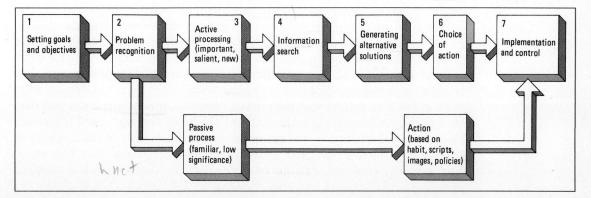

what

search for cause/
info.

3.

what kind
of values

why?

we don't
know what
the future
will bring.

If the problem is serious, or new, or important, the decision maker must actively try to find out *why* the problem occurred. This is known as the *information-search phase*. The decision maker must gather information about both causes of the problem and some possible ways to proceed to solve the problem. Past records can be used, interviews may be held, and opinions can be solicited. This phase takes time and ingenuity. Unfortunately, it is often the phase that is handled least well.

Once the information is gathered, it must be integrated, and alternative choices or courses of action must be explored. Typically, a large set of alternatives is narrowed down to a smaller set. This stage is known as the *alternative-generation phase*. Generating plausible solution alternatives requires experience, creativity, and the ability to integrate complex information and make judgments about the future. It can be very demanding intellectually.

Finally, there is the evaluation of alternatives—the *choice phase*. At this point the possible courses of action have all been laid out. They must now be compared to one another, and some decision about what is best must be made. In most cases, there are good and bad points about any alternative, and one must weigh these aspects carefully. Values play an important role in determining what are actually judged to be the good and bad aspects of each alternative. There is also uncertainty and ambiguity about the consequences of most actions. But a decision must be made. Somehow, one alternative must be selected.

The last phase of the process involves the implementation and evaluation of the decision. Did the discrepancy between what was desired and what was observed disappear? Did we solve the problem? If not, it is back to the drawing board. We cycle back to phase 2 and try again.

One can also see by looking at Figure 11-1 that in some cases a much more passive, or less analytic, process occurs. If a problem is a familiar one, or one for which there already exists a personal or organizational policy, much of the active processing described above never takes place. Also, when there is a problem that needs immediate attention one does not have the time to be reflective. In this type of a situation the decision maker often uses a subjective "feeling" or "gut reaction" to make a choice. Or the response may simply be based on habits or norms—"this is how we do things around here."

For a long time much of the research in decision making assumed that most managers use the more analytic process described first. The prevailing view was that managers make decisions rationally: They sit in their offices reviewing information, contemplating alternatives, and making choices.

However, more recent research has changed that view. The life of most managers is actually very unsystematic and often borders on chaos. The best description of this phenomenon was provided by Mintzberg (1975). He went out and watched what managers did—how they actually made decisions. His conclusions were revealing.

First, his data suggest that managers work at an unrelenting pace, and that most decisions are made quickly. Rather then being systematic and reflective, managers are unsystematic and action-oriented. In his study of chief executive officers, for example, over half of their activities lasted less than 9 minutes. Kotter (1982) confirms these conclusions, showing that the typical manager engages in hundreds of activities every day, and that almost all of an executive's verbal contacts are ad hoc. In other words, systematic planning and long-term, reflective, and rational decision making are hard to find.

A second finding of Mintzberg's research was that aggregated, systematically gathered and analyzed data are not weighed heavily by most managers. A variety of studies show that managers like "soft" information, information about gossip, hearsay, and speculation. These items are current and help them get a "feel" for a problem (cf. Kotter, 1982). Thus, both analytic and nonanalytic decisions are made. The question that needs to be answered, therefore, is *when* are decisions made analytically and *when* are they made nonanalytically?

A CONTINGENCY MODEL OF INDIVIDUAL DECISIONS

Mintzberg's work and related research generated some important conclusions. People seem to be unsystematic and nonanalytic most of the time. Different people use different strategies on the same problem. And different strategies are used by the same person when confronted with different problems. These conclusions dramatically change the task of the researcher. Rather than just looking for the one best decision-making strategy, we need to better understand why people use different decision strategies on different types of decisions. What is needed is a contingency model of individual decision-strategy selection (cf. Payne, 1982).

Beach and Mitchell (1978) have presented such a contingency model. They argue that the decision maker uses one of three general types of decision strategies: aided analytic, unaided analytic, and nonanalytic. The aided analytic strategy employs some sort of formal model or formula, or an aid such as a checklist. An unaided analytic strategy is one in which the decision maker is very systematic in his or her approach to the problem and perhaps follows some sort of model, but does it all in his or her head. Thinking of all the pros and cons for each alternative or trying to imagine the consequences of each action would fall in this category. Finally, there is the category of nonanalytic strategies. Here the decision maker chooses by habit or uses some simple rule of thumb ("nothing ventured, nothing gained" or "better safe than sorry") to make the choice.

Which strategy is selected depends on the personal characteristics of the decision maker and the demands of the task. Figure 11-2 lists some of the variables that are likely to be important. The underlying assumption of this model is that a person will choose that strategy that requires the least amount of time and effort to reach a satisfactory decision. The more analytic the strategy, the more time and effort required to use it.

Since aided analytic techniques take the most effort and analysis, the use of such techniques requires that (1) the individual have the personal characteristics necessary to employ them (e.g., knowledge, ability, and motivation), and (2) such techniques are demanded by the characteristics of the decision problem.

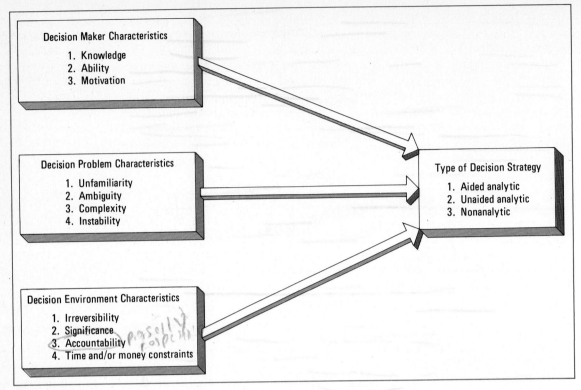

Decision Maker Characteristics
1. Knowledge
2. Ability
3. Motivation

Decision Problem Characteristics
1. Unfamiliarity
2. Ambiguity
3. Complexity
4. Instability

Decision Environment Characteristics
1. Irreversibility
2. Significance
3. Accountability
4. Time and/or money constraints

Type of Decision Strategy
1. Aided analytic
2. Unaided analytic
3. Nonanalytic

Figure 11-2
Factors that contribute to the choice of an analytic versus nonanalytic decision strategy. (*Adapted from Beach & Mitchell, 1978.*)

As you can see from Figure 11-2, the characteristics of the problem are divided into two groups: the decision problem itself and the decision environment. The model suggests that as the *decision problem* becomes less familiar and more ambiguous, complex, and unstable, the decision maker will use more time and analysis (more analytic strategies) to reduce the uncertainty caused by these factors. However, this process continues only up to a point. When the uncertainty due to these factors becomes too great, the decision maker is likely to return to a simpler rule. The reason is that when there is an extremely high degree of uncertainty in the decision problem, the potential gains of a more accurate analytic decision are small and are often far outweighed by the costs (i.e., time and effort) required to arrive at that decision.

The *decision environment* is composed of four factors. The model suggests that more analytic strategies will be selected when decisions are not reversible and very important, and when the decision maker is personally accountable. Also, analytic procedures are more likely to be used where there are no time or money constraints.

Research generally supports this model. For example, one set of studies confirms the underlying cost/benefit explanation for strategy selection (Christensen-Szalanski, 1978). People do seem to choose their decision strategy based upon considerations of costs (e.g., time and effort) and benefits (e.g., rewards for making a good decision).

Another series of three studies found support for the predicted effects of the

Figure 11-3
The pressure on American managers to make decisions quickly and accurately is very intense.

6

decision environment on the choice of a decision strategy (McAllister, Mitchell, & Beach, 1979). In the first two of these studies, managers worked on eight different cases (e.g., purchasing new machinery, marketing a product) under time and resource constraints. Each case could be solved using any of four decision strategies that varied in the amount of analysis required. Accompanying each case was information about the decision environment. Embedded in this information were three independent variables. Of interest were the strategies selected when the decision was significant as opposed to not significant, reversible as opposed to not reversible, and when the decision maker was accountable as opposed to not accountable. These three variables, each with two different conditions, yield eight possible combinations ($2 \times 2 \times 2$). Each manager worked eight problems representing the eight different combinations. The results showed that analytic strategies were se-

why more
or less?

7.

Figure 11-4
High degrees of
irreversibility,
accountability, and
significance in a
decision cause one
to use a more
analytic decision
strategy. (*Based on
data presented by
McAllister et al.,
1979.*)

lected when the problem was significant, the solution irreversible, and the decision maker accountable, and nonanalytic strategies were selected in the opposite conditions.

In the second study, people were actually hired to make some marketing decisions. They were provided with information about various products, and there were more or less analytic ways the information could be used to generate choices. Half of the people were accountable (they had to justify their answer before a group), and half were not. Half of the people were told they could reverse their judgments later on if necessary, and half were not. And half of the people were told their judgments were significant (the researchers would actually use them), and half were not. Again, this was done so that all eight combinations were represented.

The findings over both studies were consistent and were quite supportive of the model. The more significant the problem, the more responsible the decision maker, and the more irreversible the decision, the more analytic the procedure selected to make the decision. These findings are summarized in Figure 11-4. What this research demonstrates is that different strategies are used depending upon the decision problem and the person involved. In the next three sections of this chapter we will describe some of the more analytic and less analytic strategies in detail. But first we want to describe some decision examples that reflect the sorts of distinctions we are trying to make.

or cases   *decisions*

An Analytic Decision

Imagine that you are the personnel manager for a small hospital in the Southwest. You are in charge of all personnel activities, such as training, selection, placement, performance appraisal, handling of grievances, and public relations. Over the last year, it has come to your attention that there is some sort of problem in the pharmacy. The pharmacy employs a head phar-

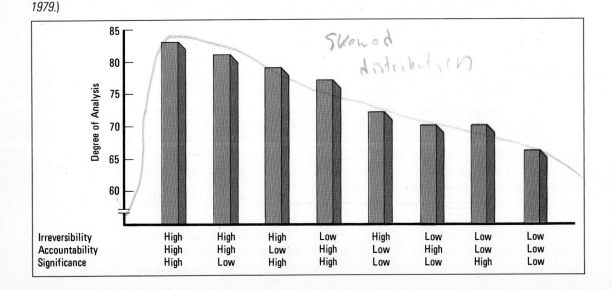

Skewed distribution

	High	High	High	Low	High	Low	Low	Low
Irreversibility	High	High	High	Low	High	Low	Low	Low
Accountability	High	High	Low	High	Low	High	Low	Low
Significance	High	Low	High	High	Low	Low	High	Low

macist and two assistants. A number of patients have complained about long waits to get their drugs, and the employees themselves have griped about being overworked. You note that absenteeism in the group has been higher than expected lately. You also find out from one of your colleagues in the accounting department that the 20 percent projected increase in prescription drugs sales for the year has not materialized. The demand should be there. The number of patients has increased, as has the number of prescriptions given by the physicians. Somewhere, something is wrong.

You attempt to find out the cause of the problem. You interview some of the patients, as well as the employees. You also look at past sales records. A number of causes are possible. Your people could be poorly trained or lazy. Perhaps increased paperwork and record-keeping responsibilities caused by new federal regulations are taking up their time. Perhaps certain crucial ingredients are in short supply or prescriptions are becoming more complex to make up.

After searching around for all this information, it becomes fairly obvious that the cause of the problem is that the staff is overworked. The employees are well qualified; however, due to the complexity of their job and increased demand, they need more help. An additional person is needed. You put an advertisement in the newspaper requesting applicants for the job.

In 2 weeks you have four people who want the job. You have five alternatives: hire one of the four people or hire no one. Each person represents a complex aggregate of skills, training, experience, and personal characteristics. After a while the choice is narrowed down to two people. Both have excellent training. One of the persons seems more friendly and outgoing, and it is your estimate that this characteristic will help in the group as well as with public relations. The other person, however, has more experience, having worked at another pharmacy for 5 years. This experience should help in dealing with the pressures of the job and with difficult problems that might arise.

In your final analysis you try to weigh the importance of experience, personality, and skills, and you decide to hire the person with more experience. You inform both candidates of your decision, and the hired employee starts to work the following month. After a 6-month period you note that sales are up, complaints are down, and absenteeism has decreased. You recognized the problem, discovered its cause, evaluated some alternatives, and made a choice which you followed up.

A More Passive Decision

Now imagine that you are the teacher of a large lecture class. The topic is organizational behavior, and there are 300 students in the class. It is one of two large introductory organizational behavior sections that are part of the undergraduate core curriculum.

You and the instructor of the other section have worked together to make the teaching of the class as similar as possible for both groups. After you give your first quiz a student comes to your office to discuss his grade. He tells you that he failed the quiz and that he is very distressed about it. He starts to tell you a whole set of reasons why he did not do well, but you cut him off by telling him that you have a policy for handling his problem. You and the other professor have agreed that all students can drop their lowest quiz grade. This opportunity to drop one score will allow students to avoid being penalized by chance circumstances, such as having two tests the same day, being sick, and so on. The student thanks you for the information and leaves.

Note that the decision process here was quite different. You cut off information gathering—in fact you did not really want to hear all the reasons for the poor performance. You simply applied a formal policy, and any other students with similar problems will be treated in the same way (you also decide to write yourself a note to announce the policy in class so that the students will know the rule). In this decision example, very little information gathering went on, there was no evaluation of alternatives, the decision was clear cut, and it took a minimum of time.

AIDED ANALYTIC DECISION PROCESSES

It should be clear by now that there are lots of ways to make decisions and that these strategies vary from very formal and highly analytic to simple rules or heuristics that provide a quick and ready-made solution. In the next three sections we describe some of the more popular aided analytic, unaided analytic, and nonanalytic strategies. We discuss their strengths and weaknesses and the situations for which they seem to be most appropriate. We also discuss many of the mistakes that people make when using these strategies, as well as potential remedies.

Beliefs and Values

Probabilities direct the conduct of the wise man.
—CICERO

The basic concepts that form the cornerstone of most aided and unaided analytic decision making are *beliefs* and *values*. Any item of information can be evaluated in light of two criteria: its truth and its importance. The truth of a piece of information is often a question of probability; that is, we try to estimate how probable it is that the piece of information is true. If we estimate that it has a high probability of being true, we say that we have a strong belief in it. If, on the other hand, we estimate that the piece of information has a low probability of being true, we say that we do not believe it. In addition to its truth, we also judge a piece of information by its importance and/or relevance. Information judged to be very important or relevant is highly valuable, while that judged to be unimportant or irrelevant is not valuable.

Let us return to our example in the hospital pharmacy. Our decision maker had to evaluate a number of possible causes of the problem at hand. Numerous alternatives (beliefs) were considered (e.g., that employees were overworked, lazy, or poorly trained), but the one deemed to be most probable was the overwork hypothesis. The remedy to the problem was to hire an additional person. The decision problem focused on the choice of this new employee.

Each applicant had a number of attributes, such as experience, training, and personal traits. Each attribute-person combination served as a belief for the decision maker. For example, "Person A is well trained" indicates a belief about person A. Somehow all these beliefs had to be combined to gain an overall impression of each person.

Two factors in this combination process are important. First, the decision maker will be more or less certain about the truth of various attributes. That is, the degree of confidence in each belief will vary. For example, one may feel absolutely certain that person A has had 4 years of experience but be only moderately confident in the belief that that person is rather shy and withdrawn. In classical decision theory terms, when we know that an item of information has a 1.00 probability of being true, we call it decision making under conditions of *certainty*. When we are sure that an item of information has a specific probability of less than 1.00 (e.g., when flipping a coin we know the probability of heads or tails is 0.50), we call it decision making under conditions of *risk*. When we are unsure of the probabilities, we call it decision making under conditions of uncertainty. Second, beliefs will vary in their importance. Perhaps the past history of this manager has suggested that experience is a more important determinant of good performance than an employee's personality. In this sense, experience is a more valuable characteristic than a pleasant personality (which is possessed by candidate B). Both the beliefs and their values are important for making the final choice.

Much of the research on individual decision making has focused on two major questions: (1) how do people *actually* form and combine their beliefs and values? and (2) how *should* they combine them? The first question is a descriptive one. It attempts to find out what people actually do. The second question is normative in nature. It seeks to show how people should make decisions. Both descriptive and normative models exist for the generation and evaluation phase of decision making, as well as for the choice phase. We will briefly review the most important of these models.

Processing Models

After we have searched for information, we begin the process of generating and evaluating alternatives. This activity requires us to integrate and combine many of our beliefs and our values. Decision theorists have developed a number of models to describe and help us be more effective in this information-processing activity.

Say, for example, that a small Midwestern college has recently decided to include a master of business administration (M.B.A.) program in its curriculum. The admissions office is swamped with applications. Fifty people want to get in, but there are only twenty positions. Each applicant has a large amount of information in his or her folder, but the three most important items are (1) college grade point average (GPA), (2) score on the business entrance examination (BE), and (3) a rating of excellence of the applicant's undergraduate institution (UI). Somehow the admissions director must combine this information, rate the candidates in terms of predicted success, and choose the top twenty. From a descriptive point of view, we want to know how this is actually done. From a normative point of view, we want to know how it ought to be done.

We can gather much of the descriptive information by watching what choices are made by the decision maker. After fifty people are ranked and twenty are selected, we can examine the dossiers of the chosen applicants and compare them to those of candidates that were not chosen. Various mathematical procedures can provide us with what is called the decision maker's "policy." This policy reflects the underlying rule combining information that was used.

Perhaps in looking over the data we find that everyone chosen had a high score on the business entrance exam, while those not chosen had a low score. Most (but not all) of the people chosen had high GPAs in college, while most of those rejected had low GPAs. Finally, a slight majority of those chosen went to an excellent undergraduate institution, while many of those rejected did not. These data suggest that the admissions officer weighed the BE score most heavily, the GPA score next, and the UI last. Mathematical models can provide actual numerical weights that reflect the magnitude of importance of each of these factors. One might find, for example, that BE was twice as important as GPA, which in turn was twice as important as UI. This policy might best be represented by the following formula:

$$PS = (4 \times BE) + (2 \times GPA) + UI$$

where PS = predicted success.

This information is descriptive in that it tells us how the admissions officer actually made the decisions. It is often very useful for feedback purposes. People are frequently unaware of how they weight information, and these procedures provide them with a mathematical model that reflects their decision process. They can then formalize the procedure by using the mathematical model instead of agonizing over each dossier. Or they can systematically change their decision procedure so that some new set of weights is used that they feel is more appropriate.

But often the decision maker wants more than just descriptive information. He or she may want to know how to make *better* decisions. The question of concern is how the three predictors (BE, GPA, and UI) *should* be combined to get the twenty best students. Fortunately, models exist to do this as well.

Let us say that the school admitted thirty students because it was felt that some might fail or drop out for various reasons. After two quarters in the M.B.A. program, each of the thirty students has a GPA that reflects how well he or she is actually doing. These scores can then be mathematically compared to the scores on the three predictors, and a model can be generated that indicates how the three predictors ought to be weighed. Perhaps college GPA turns out to be the best predictor, followed by BE and UI. The formula would be:

$$GPA_m = (4 \times GPA_c) + (2 \times BE) + UI$$

where GPA_m reflects the grades in the master's program, and GPA_c is the college GPA.

If the admissions officer feels that the GPA from two quarters in the M.B.A. program is a good criterion of excellence, this new policy model can be used to select the next class of incoming students.

Use of Processing Models. The types of models just described are being used with increasing frequency in organizations. The research conducted has included studies of people actually engaged in admissions tasks, as well as studies of investment counselors, bank loan officers, physicians making diagnoses, clinical psychologists, court judges setting bail, personnel staff in charge of selection and promotion, and many others. The characteristics of the task are very much the same: some stimulus (e.g., a person or a stock) has multiple characteristics (e.g., grades, symptoms, growth potential) that must be combined to form an overall evaluation. This evaluation is compared to similar stimulus objects, and some sort of rank order of alternatives is generated (Ebert & Mitchell, 1975).

The descriptive and normative policies that are used can be helpful in a number of ways. They can tell us how we actually combine information in comparison to how we should combine it. However, research has also pointed out some limitations in both the models and in humans. These limitations are briefly discussed below.

Criticisms of the Models. One major controversy that is still to be resolved concerns the basic psychological processes that people use in combining information. Some researchers argue that a weighted sum of information is the best representation, while others argue that a weighted average is more accurate. There is support for both sides of the issue (e.g., Anderson, 1970). While the models indicate that people can and do combine complex information to make overall assessments, just exactly how they do it is as yet unknown.

A second problem is that the models always fall short of an exact description or exact prediction. No matter how sophisticated the model, it never completely describes what the decision maker has done or should do. This is partly because humans are not computers—they make mistakes, change their minds, get tired, and forget things. But it also has to do with the mathematical characteristics of the models themselves. If it is possible to describe exactly what the decision maker does, we have not yet figured out how to do it (Slovic & Lichtenstein, 1971).

Finally, most models are static. That is, they represent a decision maker's policy for only one specific time. As we all know, people and situations change over time. Perhaps a new entrance exam for business students is developed, or perhaps everyone's college GPA rises so high (due to a general easing up on the part of professors) that GPA is no longer an effective predictor. The old model is obsolete. A new model is needed. This problem has prompted some attempt to analyze the process of revising evaluations, and a whole body of literature is developing on this topic (Beach, 1975).

Criticisms of People. The shortcomings of the models are important, but their contributions to our understanding of human information processing should not be overlooked. Perhaps their most important contribution has been to point out sources of human error. There are some ways in which people are just poor judges, and the models have helped us to identify these areas.

First, people are *inconsistent*. While the policy generated from a mathematical formula may represent the *overall process* by which information is combined, it does not represent any *specific instance* very well. People change around their weights and are influenced by extraneous factors. Second, people use *irrelevant information*. A number of studies have shown, for example, that evaluations are higher if the applicants (e.g., for a loan or promotion) have similar attitudes to the decision maker (Landy & Farr, 1983). Third, the overall policies are *hard to change*. People get set in their ways and tend to modify their weights less than new information that is available would suggest they should. And finally, people are *limited information processors*. They tend to use only a few cues or factors to make their judgments. Complex information is handled poorly, and the greater the distractions or time pressures, the simpler the policies people use (see Ebert & Mitchell, 1975, for a review).

What this suggests is that, in spite of their faults, the models can be helpful. They can provide an excellent feedback mechanism, and they can increase fairness and consistency. More complex information can be handled. Decision makers who have been trained in the use of such techniques can use the models as helpful tools to increase the effectiveness of their decisions.

Choice Models

Other decision models focus on the end point of the decision process: the actual choice between alternatives. The early literature on decision theory focused almost exclusively on this issue. The questions again are both descriptive and normative in nature: How is the choice actually made, and how should it be made?

One normative model that has served as the foundation for much of the work in this area is called the *expected-value model*. It is one of the most pervasive theoretical explanations of human behavior available today. It appears in one form or another in theories of attitudes, motivation, social power, and decision making. The basic idea is simple. The model suggests that in a choice situation a person will select the alternative that promises to bring the highest payoff (or highest expected value). This expected value is determined by two factors: (1) the probability that a particular action will lead to various outcomes, and (2) the value or importance of the outcomes. The model predicts that we will choose the alternative that is most likely to lead to the outcomes we value or desire most.

Notice that these two components are a direct representation of beliefs and values. The probabilities reflect our belief about the action-outcome relationship (does action X really lead to outcome Y?), and the values reflect our evaluations of the outcomes. According to the model:

$$EV = \sum_{i=1}^{n} \psi_i V_i$$

Figure 11-5
We make deci-
sions mainly as a
function of what
we believe to be
the likely conse-
quences.

The plain, unfiltered fact is that people who smoke cigarettes get lung cancer a lot more frequently than nonsmokers.
  And lung cancer can finish you. Before your time.

We'd rather have you stay alive and in good health. Because even if you do gain a few pounds, you'll have the time to take them off.
American Cancer Society

THIS SPACE CONTRIBUTED BY THE PUBLISHER AS A PUBLIC SERVICE

where EV = the expected value of a specific choice alternative

  ψ = the probability that a particular outcome will occur

  V = the value of that particular outcome

  n = the number of outcomes

To compute EV one multiplies the probability by the value for each outcome and then sums up the products. (The symbol

$$\sum_{i=1}^{n}$$

in the equation means "sum up.") The EV for each choice alternative is then

345

Figure 11-6
Payoff matrix for
purchasing
automobile
theft insurance.

	Outcomes	
Choices	Stolen	Not Stolen
Buy insurance	− $2050.00	− $50.00
Do not buy insurance	− $8000.00	0

compared to the *EV* for each other choice alternative. The model predicts that the alternative with the highest *EV* will be chosen.

Suppose, for example, that you have to decide whether to insure your company car against theft. You are told by your insurance agent that an automobile policy is available that will pay you 75 percent of the value of your $8000 car if it is stolen. The cost of the insurance is only $50 a year. However, you know the chances are only about one in a hundred that someone will steal your car. Should you buy the insurance? The payoff matrix is presented in Figure 11-6.

If the car is stolen and you have the insurance, you lose $8000 plus your $50 premium, but you are paid $6000 by the insurance company (a net loss of $2050). If you buy the insurance and nothing happens, you lose $50. If you do not buy the insurance and the car is stolen, you lose $8000. And, of course, if you do not buy the insurance and nothing happens, you neither gain nor lose. These figures represent the values of the four possible outcomes.

The choice of the two alternatives (to buy or not to buy) depends upon the chance that the car will be stolen. If it is very likely to be stolen, you should buy the insurance; if it is unlikely, you should not. But we already know these probabilities, so we can use them directly in the equation to determine the proper choice:

$$EV_{buy} = (\psi_1)(V_1) + (\psi_2)(V_2)$$
$$= (.01)(-2050) + (.99)(-50)$$
$$= -\$70$$

$$EV_{do\ not\ buy} = (\psi_1)(V_1) + (\psi_2)(V_2)$$
$$= (.01)(-8000) + (.99)(0)$$
$$= -\$80$$

where subscript 1 refers to the stolen outcome, and subscript 2 refers to the not-stolen outcome. In this particular case you should buy the insurance. Your expected loss is less if you purchase it than if you do not.

Note that from a normative point of view this model tells you how you ought to behave in the long run. Thus, over a period of years (which may include the occasional pilfering of your automobile), you would be wise to buy the insurance. You will come out ahead.

One of the most common uses of this general type of logic in management

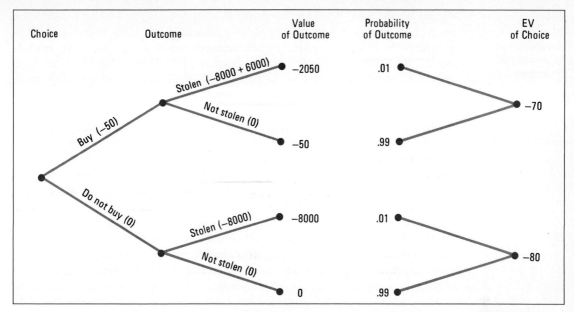

Choice	Outcome	Value of Outcome	Probability of Outcome	EV of Choice

Buy (−50)
Stolen (−8000 + 6000) −2050   .01
Not stolen (0) −50   .99   −70

Do not buy (0)
Stolen (−8000) −8000   .01
Not stolen (0) 0   .99   −80

Figure 11-7
A decision tree
analysis of
whether or not to
purchase
automobile
theft insurance.

practice is the decision tree. This technique requires the decision maker to represent graphically the available alternatives, the outcomes, the probabilities, and the values. Figure 11-7 presents a decision tree for the problem just discussed.

Using this technique forces people to think about the components of the decision problem. They uncover things they had not thought of, and they use probabilities in a manner that is much more systematic. A number of research papers have shown that the use of such models can be helpful in decisions about military matters, predicting the weather, choosing an occupation, making medical diagnoses, and making various investment and financial decisions (Beach, 1975). Therefore, as a model to shoot for, *EV* can be helpful. As a normative model, it is very powerful.

From a descriptive point of view, on the other hand, the model is fairly demanding. It suggests that people have exact information about actual probabilities and values, and that they combine this information in very specific ways (multiplying and adding). There is also an assumption that people will always choose to maximize their gains or payoff. As you might suspect, some of these assumptions are difficult to justify. Thus, just as for the information-processing models, the expected-value model in its original form is useful but imperfect as an explanation of how we normally make decisions.

Other Aided Analytic Models

Several models that are normative in nature have been developed to deal with more specific problems. For example, a "break even analysis" is designed to determine how many units of an item must be sold in order for cash inflow to equal cash outflow. Various inventory models are designed to keep down the costs of having too much inventory (purchase costs, carrying costs), as well as reducing the costs of not having enough inventory (ordering costs, out-of-stock costs). These models help to determine how many units of an item should be purchased and how to time these purchases. Similar models have also been developed for queuing problems—when cars, people, planes, or whatever must form a queue for service. For example, deciding how many check-out lines to make available in a grocery store is a queuing problem. Finally, there are various economic forecasting models designed to predict future demand, supply, and other related factors.

Many of these other aided analytic models come out of a very different tradition from behavioral decision theory. Operations management is a separate, distinct discipline that focuses on problems of scheduling, work layout and sequencing, queuing, assigning people to shifts and stations, and various other problems that are critical for the effective functioning of an organization. Also, many marketing models deal with issues such as forecasting demand, product distribution and delivery, and market segmentation. Accountants have developed complex models of how much information to sample, when to check further for errors as a result of cost variances, and so on. In short, there are lots of aided analytic models that are available in a variety of areas. A recent review by Rowe, Boulgardies and McGrath (1984) discusses some of these aids in more detail.

UNAIDED ANALYTIC DECISIONS

This category contains those decision-making strategies that involve an attempt to explore the dimensions of the problem without using any aids or tools. That is, the decision maker restricts processing to the confines of his or her mind. These are the decision strategies that have been studied most by psychologists using the normative models from the aided-analytic category as comparison models.

Subjective Expected Utility

One of the most critical problems with the expected-value model is its use of objective probabilities and values. The decision maker has to know what the probabilities are, and be able to place some objective monetary value on the outcomes. This requirement is extremely demanding and not very realistic.

Research indicates that subjective estimates of probabilities and subjective feelings of value (called *utility*) can replace the objective measures. In fact, in many cases, the subjective estimates are better predictors of behavior than the objective ones. People make decisions based more on what they feel is important than on some objective (external) measure of probability or value. Thus, the model switches from expected value to *subjective expected utility* (SEU).

The SEU model and its variants are fairly structured and demand sophisticated cognitive activities. Using these strategies, the decision maker attempts to think about all the outcomes that could result from the available choices, as well as the chances of those outcomes occurring, and then chooses the alternative that seems in some rough way to offer the best potential. Gray (1975) found that third-grade children choose arithmetic problems to solve by this strategy, and Tversky (1967), Shanteau and Anderson (1969), Shanteau (1974), Holmstrom and Beach (1973), and many others have found that adults frequently use something quite like it too. Research stemming from expectancy models (Mitchell, 1983), which are similar in form to the SEU model, reinforces the conclusion that people sometimes attempt such strategies.

It should be noted that the SEU model is compensatory in nature. This means that less of one aspect of an outcome can be compensated for by more of another aspect. This characteristic makes the SEU model quite cumbersome for the unaided decision maker, because each outcome must be evaluated separately for each of its aspects, and then the utility of each aspect must be summed to arrive at the outcome's overall utility.

Simon's Model

A well-known but less demanding strategy was suggested by Simon (1957). It is a noncompensatory strategy known as the "satisficing" model, in which the decision maker selects the *first* decision alternative that exceeds some *minimum aspiration level.* This strategy's procedure consists of comparing the various choice alternatives one at a time to some predetermined set of minimally acceptable criteria, then selecting the first alternative that is found to exceed those criteria, that is, the first alternative that is sufficient. Note that the decision rule is sufficiency rather than maximization or optimization. Related strategies have been proposed by Coombs (1964), Dawes (1964), and Einhorn (1970).

Similar yet simpler noncompensatory strategies are the elimination by aspects strategy (Tversky, 1972) and the lexicographic strategy (Tversky, 1969). When using the former, the decision maker selects one aspect of the decision alternatives, eliminates all alternatives that do not possess that aspect, then selects another aspect, eliminates alternatives, and so on, until only one alternative remains. When using the lexicographic strategy, the decision maker selects the most important aspect of the alternatives and eliminates all alternatives except the one that is superior to all the others on that aspect. If none are superior on that aspect, the decision maker moves to the next most important aspect, and so on. These kinds of strategies have the advantage of reducing information processing by restricting the decision maker's attention to only part of the available information about the alternatives, but they have the disadvantage of introducing possible irrationalities (Tversky, 1969).

Cost/Benefit Models

Another way of thinking about a problem without the use of technical aids involves a sort of cost/benefit analysis. In this case the person tries to look at the overall costs and benefits of some action and chooses the one with the greatest benefit or least cost. This is similar to the SEU model, but people who report using it generally do not report breaking down their estimates by probabilities and values. On the contrary, they seem to make a global estimate of the positive (benefit) and negative (cost) aspects of a choice and try to integrate that information for each alternative.

The one thing all these unaided analytic strategies have in common is that they require some degree of fairly sophisticated cognitive work. While this clearly happens some of the time, most of the time the process is much simpler.

NONANALYTIC STRATEGIES

This category contains fairly simple, preformulated rules that are applied by rote to decision tasks. They differ from aided- and unaided-analytic strategies in that relatively little information is procured or processed, little time is needed, and the rules do not require that the decision be decomposed or that multiple aspects be considered. It seems highly likely that most decisions are made using strategies from this nonanalytic category.

Scripts

Perhaps the most complex of the nonanalytic strategies involves the construction of mental movies, or "scripts" (Abelson, 1976), in which the decision maker imagines how things might be if this or that decision alternative were chosen and picks the alternative for which the script turns out best. The scripts can be simple and sketchy or elaborate and detailed, but the principle is the same for all of them—imagine how things would be if X or Y or Z were the chosen alternative, and choose the one for which the imagined result is best (Gioia & Poole, 1984).

In many cases the decision maker does not even go through the process of choosing among scripts. That is, the person knows the behavior sequences that are most appropriate for specific situations or problems. People have a relatively large repertoire of such scripts, and they can be readily described (Thomas & Griffin, 1983; Shrivastava & Mitroff, 1984). Such scripts provide an understanding of situations, and they serve as a guide to allow quick responses to familiar settings.

Policies

A somewhat different strategy is a policy. *Policies* can be either self-generated or externally generated. In either case their basic feature is that they are more like rules than scripts are. For example, our professor who simply dropped the lowest quiz grade was using a policy—a self-made one based on experience and perhaps expediency.

Of course, policies can also be externally imposed. For example, many organizations have policies as a result of union-management contracts. A manager dealing with an employee who is absent frequently may have a specific set of actions prescribed in a specific sequence for a specific time period. The first absence in a month may require a verbal reprimand, the second a written reprimand, and the third a docking of pay; the fourth might result in dismissal. Such policies often guide our decisions (Liden & Mitchell, 1982).

Simplistic Rules

Of a somewhat different nature are the informal and somewhat simplistic rules that people often use. Examples are "eeny, meeny, miney, mo . . .," flipping a coin, or basing the decision to go sailing on "red sky at night—sailors' delight; red sky in morning—sailors take warning." Such homiletic rules frequently are heard in organizational settings. Both "better safe than sorry" and "a bird in the hand is worth two in the bush" represent conservative strategies in contrast to the riskier "nothing ventured, nothing gained."

Many such rules are acquired to deal with specific tasks through experience, training, or instruction. Familiar examples of the latter are the lists of helpful hints included in the instruction booklets that accompany appliances, tools, cameras, or the like, or the "tips to homemakers" columns in newspapers.

More idiosyncratic rules might be such things as alternating daily between wearing a blue suit and a brown suit, or never going to a restaurant that one has visited recently. Not having the same kind of meat for dinner as one had for lunch is another example.

Convention

Other nonanalytic strategies involve compliance with convention. This may be conscious (explicit) or unconscious (implicit). We each know the rules of our culture and subculture, though we do not always know that we know them (Hall, 1969). Thus, for example, we may consciously elect to comply with the new conventions of nonsexist language by referring to someone as a "chairperson," while we may unconsciously comply with our culture's conventions of leaving a stool between ourselves and the next person at a café counter, or maintaining rather specific speaking distances between ourselves and others of different social status or sex.

Habit

Finally, the most nonanalytic strategy of all is habit. Habit is not to be scorned merely because it is the extreme example of the rote application of a rule. After all, it is efficient, and it may be the product of an earlier, more reasoned approach that has become mechanical in order to realize the economy of not having to go through the whole strategy selection process each time the task is encountered. Because the majority of our decisions are mundane and made repeatedly, habit is a valuable strategy. Moreover, neither habit nor any of the nonanalytic strategies is completely without analytic qualities—at least some analysis is necessary if the decision maker is to recognize that the habit is appropriate for the present decision situation. This is why habit and the other nonanalytic strategies are true strategies. They require at least a little processing prior to actually making the decision.

352

Part Four:
Accomplishing
Organizational
Objectives

IMAGE THEORY

To summarize what we have said so far, sometimes people make highly analytic decisions, but most of the time they use simple rules. The contingency model research (Beach & Mitchell, 1978) discussed earlier in the chapter is an attempt to describe the parameters and situations in which more analytic strategies are used. Recently, we have developed a new theory, called *image theory*, to describe what we believe is the process underlying the less analytic strategies (Mitchell, Rediker, & Beach, 1986).

While the motivation for formulating image theory derives from our earlier work, it also has roots in what has come to be called *control theory*. In psychology, the most notable example of control theory, at least until recently, was Miller, Galanter, and Pribram's *Plans and the Structure of Behavior* (1960). The thesis of control theory is that behavior is a complex process that is guided both by goals and by feedback about how well one is progressing toward those goals. Those who have read the Miller et al. book probably remember the TOTE system (test, operate, test, exit) as its main contribution. However, greater attention was given in the book to (1) *images*, which are private representations of the actor's self and his or her world, that (2) guide *plans*, that in turn (3) ultimately control behavior. The general idea is that the actor executes a plan in order to realize an image—to make reality conform to some favored state of affairs (in short, a goal). In image theory we have adopted the Miller et al. (1960) notion of images as goals (see also Boulding, 1956) and adapted it specifically to fit decision making. To keep our terms consistent with those of contingency theory, however, we use the term *strategy* to mean what Miller et al. meant by *plan*.

In addition to our own prior work and to control theory, image theory has roots in work on personal development (e.g., Levinson, Darrow, Klein, Levinson, & McKee, 1978), career development (e.g., Mihal, Sorce, & Comte, 1984; Rhodes & Doering, 1983), and philosophy (e.g., MacIntyre, 1981). All of this work has expanded the idea of images as guiding concepts in behavior. Here images are thought of both as one's recollection and reconstruction of one's past (where one has been) and as one's dreams and aspirations for the future (where one hopes to go). Most important, images constitute one's view of oneself, what one stands for, what one wants to be, what one wants and likes to do—in short, one's goals. As the philosopher Alasdair MacIntyre states, "There is no present which is not informed by some image of some future and an image of the future which always presents itself in the form of a *telos*—of a variety of ends or goals—toward which we are either moving or failing to move in the present" (1981, p. 200). Image theory is an attempt to represent the role of such images, or goals, and how such "moving or failing to move" is assessed in human decision making.

Finally, in addition to the three areas described thus far, image theory has roots in recent research on postdecisional commitment (see Chapter 5). Part of this research comes from organizational behavior (Staw, 1981; Northcraft & Wolf, 1984), and part comes from social psychology (Brockner & Rubin, 1986). The respective terms that are used are *commitment* and *entrapment*. Both refer to those cases in which one sticks with a course of action (and may invest even more effort, time, or money) even though it is failing to achieve the desired goal. That is, they refer to the tendency for decision makers (both organizations and individuals) to stay with the status quo beyond the point at which some neutral observer (particularly one operating on normative principles) would generally prescribe a change in course. According to image theory, the decision maker sticks with the status quo because of its embeddedness in his or her images, and because of a great resistance to changing these images. That is, image theory broadens the entrapment/commitment concept by regarding them as special cases of a more general tendency to stick with the status quo, whether status quo is a failing course of action or a successful one. The implication of this tendency for day-to-day decision making in organizations is of general importance, and it constitutes a major part of our theory.

In summary, decision makers have images of their past, present, and future, and some of these images contain goals, both those that have already been reached and those that have yet to be attained; indeed, it is the continuity of past and future goals that lends continuity to one's view of one's life. These images are central and important, and the goals provide both motivation and justification for action. Moreover, it is difficult for decision makers to make great changes in their images, with the result that they tend to favor "business as usual," the status quo. All of these ideas serve as the foundation for the following, more formal, presentation of image theory.

A Brief Summary of Image Theory

We begin with the assumption that decision makers process four informational representations, called *images,* that are the bases of decision making. The construction and coordination of these four images constitute the decision process. The images are:

1. The *self-image,* which is composed of policies that reflect the way one sees oneself, and the principles by which one tries to live one's life. These policies dictate the goals (events and states) to which the decision maker aspires, and they serve as the backdrop against which new goal-candidates (prospective goals) are compared and evaluated.
2. The *trajectory image* consists of one's view about where, ideally, one is going. It is the blueprint, however vague, for how one thinks the present should be, and how and when future events and states (goals) should be achieved. It includes the ends one thinks it appropriate to pursue in light of the self-image, and the landmarks one anticipates along one's idealized course. In short, it provides a chronological ordering of one's goals. These can be organizational as well as personal.
3. The *projected image* consists of the chronological ordering of the events and states that one anticipates will occur if the flow of current activities, the status quo, is not changed. It is called the projected image because it describes one's view of the anticipated future. One can anticipate, with some degree of certainty, what will happen if one maintains one's course, and one can anticipate what might happen if one changed that course. Clearly, a comparison between the trajectory image (the ideal) and the projected image (what is most probable given the status quo) provides

In Spite of Huge Losses, Procter & Gamble Tries Once More to Revive Pringle's Chips

Procter & Gamble Co. usually won't hesitate to kill a product that doesn't make the grade. But Pringle's potato chips, an engineering marvel that has produced losses nearly as great as the Edsel's, is one product P&G refuses to let die.

Pringle's is P&G sole entry in the potentially lucrative snack-food market. The company has been particularly patient in nursing the product along because it wants to learn as much as possible about what makes snack foods appeal to people and what doesn't.

CATCHING UP

Lately the company has been promoting a new line of what it calls "better-tasting" chips, supported by an advertising budget of about $8 million for this year, compared with $339,700 in 1980. Each of Pringle's three varieties comes in a bright red cannister. The campaign theme, "I've got the fever for the flavor of new Pringle's," follows several largely unsuccessful attempts to bring onetime users back to the fold.

So far, the new approach seems to be helping. In the first three months after the company began promoting the new line in May, Pringle's share of the $2 billion potato-chip market grew to 5.5% from 4.5%. An analyst predicts 1981 sales will approach $80 million, compared with about $65 million last year. But P&G still lags far behind PepsiCo Inc.'s Frito-Lay unit (maker of Ruffles and Lay's, with about 30% of the market) and Borden Inc. (maker of Wise and other brands, with about 15%). The rest of the market belongs to small, firmly entrenched regional chipmakers.

P&G introduced Pringle's in 1968 and began national distribution in 1975. The company has spent an estimated $300 million or more on development. So far, Pringle's losses exceed $200 million, according to Hercules A. Segalas, senior vice president of Drexel Burnham Lambert Inc. Ford Motor Co. lost $250 million or more in the three years it produced the Edsel. (A P&G spokesman says Pringle's is profitable now but declines to elaborate.)

Like Ford, P&G apparently got carried away with its own technological capabilities and lost sight of consumer needs. The concept behind Pringle's was to make a potato chip that would stay fresh longer, break less often and travel and store more conveniently than conventional potato chips.

TISSUE, TENNIS BALLS

The company used its know-how in food oils and paper products to devise a way to process potatoes into chips much as paper is made from wood pulp. According to Drexel Burnham's Mr. Segalas, P&G forms dehydrated potatoes into a potato tissue to be cut into chips of uniform size that are easily stacked. The chips are cooked in a vacuum and packaged in crush-resistant cannisters resembling tennis-ball cans.

The chips were an engineering achievement, and the novelty of the packaging attracted large numbers of consumers. At one point, the brand led in national market share, and Frito-Lay and other rivals rushed their own versions into test markets.

But Pringle's heyday ended within 18 months of the start of its national distribution. The consequence of Pringle's unusual shape was a bland, processed taste. Says Gordon Wade, a consumer-products consultant and former P&G brand manager: "Pringle's tasted more like a tennis ball than a potato chip."

THE SNACK BOWL

Pringle's also suffered from other negative consumer perceptions—some real, some imagined. To offset them, the company had to dig deep into its bag of marketing and technological tricks, frequently changing its advertising approach and even the product's formulation.

Some consumers, for example, didn't believe that P&G crammed as many chips into the Pringle's can as they were getting in bags of competing potato chips. The company responded with ads showing that a can of Pringle's would fill a snack bowl as full as a bag of chips. To fight consumer perception of Pringle's as too expensive, P&G ran ads arguing that fewer broken chips and prolonged freshness make Pringle's "a great value."

Other problems weren't so easily resolved. To many people, Pringle's represented everything plastic and unnatural about foods at a time when the country was becoming increasingly diet conscious and "natural" foods were in vogue. Sensing Pringle's vulnerability, competitors zeroed in.

GETTING THE HINT

Among the most damaging was a campaign developed by Jay's Foods Inc, a Chicago-based chip-maker. The ads called attention to preservatives and additives contained in Pringle's, while pointing out that Jay's chips contained only potatoes, corn oil and salt.

"We blew Pringle's out of the water," gloats Joseph Whelan, Jay's executive vice president and treasurer. Jay's says its ads were so successful that other regional chip-makers obtained permission to run them in their territories, substituting local brand names for that of Jay's. By 1977, P&G got the hint and began selling a reformulated Pringle's, without preservatives or artificial ingredients.

P&G believes its latest line of Pringle's—regular, light and rippled—has overcome most obstacles. A company spokesman says P&G finally "learned how to deliver delicious taste in Pringle's"—apparently by adjusting the salt and cooking oil. If consumers agree, industry analysts expect P&G to follow up, perhaps early next year, with other snack foods (probably including a taco and a corn chip). The company also is believed to be discussing with foreign companies possible arrangements to market Pringle's in Europe.

Source: D. Rotbart. (1981, October 7). *The Wall Street Journal*, p. 29f. Reprinted by permission of *The Wall Street Journal*, copyright © 1981 by Dow Jones & Company, Inc. All rights reserved.

information about whether one is likely to achieve one's personal goals or the organization's goals if one continues with the status quo.

4. The *action image* consists of the plans of action, or strategies, for reaching goals and reconciling discovered incongruities among the first three images. When the projected image (what is most probable) differs sufficiently from the trajectory image (the ideal), the decision maker is motivated to add a corrective strategy to the action image. That is, he or she will take specific concrete action to produce congruence between the trajectory and projected images—to attain the goals that are based on the trajectory image.

The construction and coordination of these images involves both *adoption decisions*—decisions about adopting or rejecting new or potential policies, goals, strategies, or tactics as components of the respective images—and *anticipation decisions*—decisions about whether the incongruity between the trajectory and projected images (and, by implication, between the self-image and projected image) is sufficient to warrant a change in behavior. These adoption and anticipation decisions can appear in two forms, which are called *optional change* and *nonoptional change* decisions. An *optional change decision* is one in which the status quo is one of the alternatives that is being evaluated. When one considers changing jobs, introducing a new product, or diversifying one's investment portfolio, the status quo is one of the alternatives that the new alternatives are compared to. Optional change decisions constitute most of the decisions that people make in organizations. On the other hand, there are occasions when because of environmental circumstances (e.g., new government regulations; a competitor introducing a new and clearly better product) the status quo ceases to be an option—it is no longer one of the alternatives that one can decide to select. These *nonoptional change decisions* occur less frequently than optional change decisions do. They force one into a new course of action because the old one ceases to be viable.

355

Adoption and anticipation decisions are made using either of two evaluative criteria. One of these is *lateral attractiveness,* which is the congruence or degree of 'fit' between a particular candidate for adoption and the existing policies, goals, strategies, or tactics that already constitute the images. The other criterion is *marginal attractiveness*—the degree to which an alternative appears to offer positive consequences over and above congruence alone.

To make decisions, we use one of two rules: (1) *sufficiency,* which means that the attractiveness of the alternative exceeds some variable threshold that is contingent upon the characteristics of both the decision maker and the circumstances in which the decision is made (similar to Simon's [1957] notion of satisficing), and (2) *maximization,* which means that among competing alternatives, the one alternative with the greatest fit and positive consequences (overall attractiveness) is selected.

There is one more concept, *doubt,* that plays an important role in all of this. Predicting one's future, either ideally or as a consequence of what one is doing, involves doubt about the accuracy of the predictions. Doubt arises from many sources (e.g., incongruences, low estimates of one's ability, complexity of the strategies, physical and situational barriers). Doubt has the effect of reducing the attractiveness of an alternative.

The preceding, together with collateral concepts that are not crucial here, combine to represent two general approaches to decision making, approaches that are available to the decision maker to use depending upon the circumstances (see Tversky & Kahneman, 1973). The first approach is *passive* and tends to be less analytic. Most passive decisions are of the adoption type and the optional change form—does one want to change from the status quo to some decidedly different course of action or to pursue some decidedly different goal? Such an approach often makes decisions look like nondecisions, because the status quo tends to win out. Research clearly shows that there is a strong bias to remain with the status quo unless the alternative is excessively attractive (e.g., Beach, Hope, Townes, & Campbell, 1982). The second approach is *active* and much more analytic. Active decisions tend to be about whether to change one's course of action because the current course is failing to produce progress toward one's goals, or about adoption of new constituents for the images when the status quo is no longer an option. The evaluative criterion for the passive approach tends to be congruence with existing policies, goals, strategies, and tactics (lateral attractiveness), and the sufficiency rule is most often employed. The criterion for the active approach tends to be the benefits that one anticipates from the potential change (marginal attractiveness), and a maximization rule is most often employed.

Figure 11-8 summarizes the main point of image theory. Briefly, decision makers have images that are composed of policies, goals, strategies, and tactics. These images are interrelated, and their congruence forms the underlying dynamic for how and why decisions are made. There are two *types* of decisions (adoption and anticipation), two *forms* of decisions (optional and nonoptional), two evaluative *criteria* (lateral and marginal attractiveness), two *decision rules* (sufficiency and maximization), and two approaches or *modes* of decision making (passive and active). In addition, doubt acts to discount the attractiveness of alternatives. While little research on image theory has been conducted as of the moment, we believe that our formulation is a major step

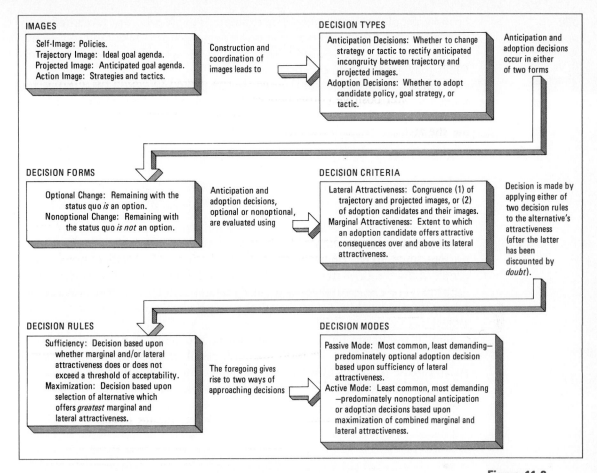

IMAGES		
Self-Image: Policies. Trajectory Image: Ideal goal agenda. Projected Image: Anticipated goal agenda. Action Image: Strategies and tactics.		

Construction and coordination of images leads to

DECISION TYPES

Anticipation Decisions: Whether to change strategy or tactic to rectify anticipated incongruity between trajectory and projected images.
Adoption Decisions: Whether to adopt candidate policy, goal strategy, or tactic.

Anticipation and adoption decisions occur in either of two forms

DECISION FORMS

Optional Change: Remaining with the status quo *is* an option.
Nonoptional Change: Remaining with the status quo *is not* an option.

Anticipation and adoption decisions, optional or nonoptional, are evaluated using

DECISION CRITERIA

Lateral Attractiveness: Congruence (1) of trajectory and projected images, or (2) of adoption candidates and their images.
Marginal Attractiveness: Extent to which an adoption candidate offers attractive consequences over and above its lateral attractiveness.

Decision is made by applying either of two decision rules to the alternative's attractiveness (after the latter has been discounted by *doubt*).

DECISION RULES

Sufficiency: Decision based upon whether marginal and/or lateral attractiveness does or does not exceed a threshold of acceptability.
Maximization: Decision based upon selection of alternative which offers *greatest* marginal and lateral attractiveness.

The foregoing gives rise to two ways of approaching decisions

DECISION MODES

Passive Mode: Most common, least demanding—predominately optional adoption decision based upon sufficiency of lateral attractiveness.
Active Mode: Least common, most demanding—predominately nonoptional anticipation or adoption decisions based upon maximization of combined marginal and lateral attractiveness.

Figure 11-8
A summary of image theory concepts.

forward in describing the less analytic processes that seem to dominate much of decision making.

COGNITIVE BIASES

In an earlier discussion of the analytic models we described several biases that often degrade the quality of decisions. There has also been research on various "natural" biases occurring in the less analytic processes. There are certain cognitive activities people naturally engage in that seem to lead to inappropriate strategy and/or alternative selection. The best overall summary of this work is a recent comprehensive review of individual decision making by Abelson and Levi (1985). We will briefly discuss some of these cognitive processes that seem to cause problems for unaided and nonanalytic decisions.

Frames

Kahneman and Tversky (1984) have described a number of situations in which the way in which a problem is presented can have a significant impact *rephrase*

on how people make choices. For example, people who are presented with problems framed in such a way that positive gains are at stake tend to be fairly conservative (risk averse), while they tend to be risk seeking toward problems when they are faced by potential losses.

To illustrate this, consider the two choices given in Figure 11-9. Choice 1 is framed in terms of gains, while choice 2 is framed in terms of losses. Notice that the expected values of both alternatives in each choice are equal. That is, for choice 1

$$A = (1.00 \times \$250) = \$250 = (.25 \times \$1000) + (.75 \times \$00) = B$$

and for choice 2

$$A = (1.00 \times \$-750) = \$-750 = (.75 \times \$-1000) + (.25 \times \$00) = B$$

The expected value model would predict indifference in both choices—just about as many people should choose alternative A as alternative B. However, the data given in the right-hand column in the figure clearly demonstrate that people do not follow the expected value model when faced with these two decisions. For choice 1 there is a clear preference for the certain alternative (alternative A), while for choice 2 there is a clear preference for the risky alternative (alternative B).

Similar results are found for more realistic problems. For example, a problem involving the use of a risky drug to save people from dying from an unusual Asian disease produces different results depending on whether the problem is framed in terms of potential lives saved (gains) or potential lives lost (losses). The implication is that how a problem is framed will influence the alternative selected, with risk aversion for gains and risk seeking for losses.

9.

Heuristics

Another area of research has focused on the general cognitive processes and implicit rules that people use in making judgments. These implicit rules,

Figure 11-9
An example that demonstrates how framing the question influences the answer. (*Based on data presented by Kahneman & Tversky, 1984.*)

Choice 1	
	Choice made by 150 people
Choose between	
A: A sure gain of $250	84%
B: A 25% chance to gain $1,000	16%
A 75% chance to gain nothing	

Choice 2	
	Choice made by 150 people
Choose between	
A: A sure loss of $750	13%
B: A 75% chance to lose $1,000	87%
A 25% chance to lose nothing	

called *heuristics,* are often helpful in that they can greatly simplify the overall decision-making process. However, they can also be impediments to decision accuracy. Nisbett and Ross (1980) have discussed such heuristics in great detail.

Availability. One implicit rule is the *availability heuristic.* This heuristic involves relying on easily remembered (available) instances of some event in order to estimate the general frequency with which that event occurs. For example, suppose that in the processs of making a marketing decision a manager needs a rough estimate of the percentage of Americans who own Japanese automobiles. Suppose further that she needs this estimate quickly and that there is no time to search for objective statistical information. In making this estimate it is highly likely that the manager will be influenced by the number of specific examples of this event she can think of. If she can easily think of many friends, relatives, and colleagues who own such cars, she is likely to greatly overestimate the true percentage. On the other hand, if she can think of no one who owns such a car, the percentage is likely to be greatly underestimated. Thus, judgments are affected by the availability of examples in memory.

Representativeness and Insensitivity to Base Rates. People also tend to have rather strong stereotypes about the way certain variables covary, and these stereotypes can significantly affect their judgments. Indeed, they can have such strong effects that other relevant information, such as base rates, is completely ignored. Kahneman and Tversky (1973) demonstrated this nicely in a study that began with subjects reading a description of a man named Jack whose hobbies (carpentry, sailing) and traits (conservative, careful) were somewhat more representative of engineers than of lawyers. After reading about Jack, the subjects were told that Jack's name had been drawn at random from a group consisting of seventy lawyers and thirty engineers. The 70/30 distribution is the base rate information. Since Jack's name was drawn at random from this group, the laws of chance predict that Jack is much more likely to be a lawyer than an engineer. Nevertheless, when asked whether they thought Jack was an engineer or a lawyer, most subjects guessed he was an engineer. Clearly, the traits and hobbies that were attributed to Jack seemed so strongly characteristic of engineers that this information dominated the judgment, even when the actuarial odds were better than 2 to 1 against this being the correct answer.

Probability Estimations. When people try to make subjective estimates of the probability of an event occurring they often make a number of systematic errors. First, they tend to overestimate the probability of positive instances of events, or successes, while underestimating negative instances, or failures (Einhorn & Hogarth, 1978). Also, people have a general tendency to overestimate the probability of two events occurring together (called a conjunctive probability). While probability estimation is more likely to be used in an analytic strategy (either aided or unaided), it is also part of the "doubt" concept discussed in connection with image theory.

Overload. One variable that can have a significant impact on how people process information is simply the amount of information to be processed. There are practical limits to what one can assimilate. When there is an overload of information, people are more prone to use the biases described previously. That is, they will use available information, categorize information according to stereotypes, base judgments on experience rather than base rates or objective probabilities, and generally try to simplify the problem.

Stress. A related variable is the amount of stress placed on the decision maker. Janis and Mann (1977) point out that conflict, importance, commitment, threat, and a variety of other factors can increase stress. The result is what they call *defensive avoidance*—prematurely aborting the search for information, distorting warning messages, selective memory and forgetting, and wishful thinking. All of these processes can degrade the accuracy and appropriateness of strategy selection.

Summary of Biases

By now it should be clear that human decision makers can make many errors in the decision process. In the analytic mode numerous problems can occur. First, there are errors of information gathering and processing. When we gather information, our needs, wants, desires, and past experience all bias the search process. After the information is in, there are additional limitations and errors in the way we treat it. We have limited capacities. Only a few items can be handled at a time. We have difficulty with information reflecting negative or nonlinear relationships. We are inconsistent in our uses of information, and we are slow to learn new relationships between the information at hand and important criteria or outcomes.

Second, errors can be made with regard to the final evaluation and choice of an alternative. Decision makers seldom consider all the alternatives or all the outcomes. We frequently evaluate alternatives sequentially rather than all at once. In some cases people will settle on the first acceptable alternative (satisficing) rather than choosing the best alternative (maximizing).

Third, our follow-up judgments are biased as well. Because we strive for consistency, we try to fit results into some existing consistent pattern. In many cases we bias what we remember so that we look good in retrospect. Hindsight biases lead us to say that things we thought were initially improbable were obvious all along.

What all of this indicates is that decision makers, even when they are trying to be rational, make plenty of errors. Most of the time they do not closely approximate the normative models. The press for action, the need to "feel" the situation, and the fact that almost all decisions are made under conditions of uncertainty, all lead to an inescapable conclusion: The use of highly rational and normative decision models is (1) not a very good description of what people *can* do, and (2) not a very good description of what they *actually* do.

When we look at the use of less analytic strategies, we also find that the decision maker is subject to biases. Subjective probability and frequency estimates are biased by the availability and salience of information. The way in which the problem is framed influences the kind and amount of risk we take. Problems are often too quickly stereotyped, which leads to the use of fairly simple rules, habits, or policies. And overload and stress reduce our capacities to make accurate judgments.

Thus, we all make mistakes and are prone to some pervasive tendencies to simplify things, see things in a consistent and favorable light, and use our experience as a foundation for judgment. Much of the time, this works pretty well. That is, most of us manage to make good decisions a large percentage of the time. However, we can often do better. Understanding and using decision aids when they are appropriate will help. Making people aware of their natural biases can help to reduce the effects of those biases. In some cases training can also help. We discuss some of these issues further in our sections on implications for research and practice.

Summary

Individual decision making is a pervasive and important process. Some of the major points discussed in the chapter are as follows:

1. Organizational decision making is the process of choosing actions that are directed toward the resolution of work-group or organizational problems. It often includes the phases of problem identification, information search, generation and evaluation of alternatives, and choice.
2. Beliefs and values are the major components of the last two decision phases, and analytic models are available that describe both how they are combined (descriptive) and how they should be combined (normative). The *EV* and *SEU* models are the most well-known normative models.
3. Processing information and combining it to make judgments are parts of the preliminary stage of the decision process. Analytic models using multiple regression are available to describe how people actually do this, as well as to aid them in their accuracy.
4. Human beings are less than perfect in their decision making. Their search techniques are not thorough, their processing of information is prone to error, and they often choose satisfactory alternatives rather than optimal ones. In short, they make numerous errors.
5. It is also true that managers infrequently use long-term, systematic, rationally planned decision procedures. Most of the time their decisions are based on haphazardly gathered information, most of which comes from personal interactions.
6. No one decision strategy is used all the time. People use more or less analytic strategies, depending upon their personal characteristics, the characteristics of the decision environment, and the characteristics of the decision problem itself.
7. Even when using less analytic strategies based on scripts, policies, images, rules, and so on, people's decisions are often degraded by cognitive biases and social pressures.

362

Part Four:
Accomplishing
Organizational
Objectives

IMPLICATIONS FOR RESEARCH

There are two main areas in which there are distinct needs for more research. First, we need to know a lot more about the nonanalytic processes of making decisions—when they are used, how they work, where we make mistakes, and how we can make good decisions using these strategies.

Our work on image theory has shown us that people in fact do some of the things we suggest. We have interviewed numerous business executives, entrepreneurs, and lower level employees about how they make their non-analytic decisions, and they report using a process similar to that outlined in the theory. We were particularly struck by one marketing executive whose office wall was filled with posters. When we inquired about them he told us they were posters that had been rejected for distribution. When we asked why, his answer was that "they didn't fit our image."

Also, the distinction between optional and nonoptional decisions seems to be an important one. In the optional mode the status quo has a powerful force behind it. Barbara Tuchman's book *The March of Folly* (1984) documents situations throughout history in which people have pursued a course of action way beyond a point at which most rational decision makers would have pulled out. These were, of course, major decisions made at the highest levels of government and business. However, we believe such decisions occur all the time for very mundane problems, and one type of research that needs to be conducted would have as its purpose to help us understand better why this process occurs and how it can be corrected before too much damage is done.

Finally, we need to do substantially more research on training people to (1) recognize errors and correct them, and (2) recognize accurately what type of problem they are facing and choose an appropriate strategy for that decision type. Some of this work is currently being done (e.g., Fischhoff & Bar-Hillel, 1984) but with mixed results. It is difficult research to conduct, especially without a good theoretical base from which to operate.

IMPLICATIONS FOR PRACTICE

There are several important areas of the decision-making process that can be handled more effectively than they are currently being handled. One point that needs to be strongly emphasized is that decision making is a long process involving many steps. It concerns more than just the choice phase or the action phase. All too often managers confuse action with decision making. They evaluate problems too quickly, they generate only readily available and well-practiced solutions, and they confuse symptoms with problems.

This behavior is understandable. There is immense pressure to act and to act quickly. However, every person making an important decision should ask him- or herself whether the preliminary phases of the decision process have been handled well: Have all information sources been tapped? Do we know the real cause of the problem? All the evidence indicates that better decisions are made when these preliminary decision phases are dealt with thoroughly and comprehensively.

A paper by E. R. Archer (1980) summarizes his own practical experience and the experience of others. He argues that we must teach people to do the following:

1. *Monitor the decision environment.* Keep track of internal and external factors that deviate from normal.
2. *Define the problem.* The essential details must be identified, including distasteful or negative aspects.
3. *Specify the objectives.* Make it clear where you want to end up.
4. *Engage in diagnostic activities.* Find out the cause of the problem.
5. *Develop alternatives.* Actively seek out different courses of action.
6. *Establish criteria.* Set up a criterion to judge the adequacy of the decision.
7. *Appraise and evaluate alternatives.* Compare alternatives to objectives and criteria.
8. *Make a choice.*
9. *Implement the choice.* Follow up on the decision.

However, even when people are made aware of the stages of decision making, they can still make mistakes. In some cases our information-processing capabilities are just not up to the complex mathematical computations required. We also make certain systematic judgment errors in combining and evaluating information.

There are two ways to help remedy these problems. First, people can be trained to recognize their fallibilities and the contexts in which errors are most likely to occur. This training can be coupled with instruction on the use of various models, formulas, and decision aids. If people know their limitations, and if they can learn to use an aid such as the expected-value formula or decision tree, they can compensate for their natural inaccuracies.

Another remedy is the use of computers. Many human errors are made either in the recollection of past events or the anticipation of future ones. Computers can store and accurately retrieve vast amounts of data. They can use complex formulas to estimate future events. They can help combine and process information of a complex nature. In short, training, decision aids, and computers can all help us overcome our human limitations and increase the effectiveness of our decision making.

Many companies are instituting formal systems and processes to increase the effectiveness of their decision making. One such process is known as "environmental scanning." Many corporations now hire people exclusively to keep track of new developments in a particular area. It is also increasingly common for a company to try to forecast the social and political environment in which it will operate.

One important factor in all of this is the use of on-line data bases. These are huge banks of information that can be stored, processed, and delivered electronically by the computer. These data include financial records, census data, market research studies, insurance actuarial tables, and so on. Companies such as LEXIS, PROMT, Enviroline, New York Times Information Bank, and Dow Jones News/Retrieval Service make this information available for $50 to $110 per hour, and many companies are using it. Companies are spending millions of dollars each year to maintain this service, and it is hoped that this expense will be justified by the attainment of better decision making (Kiechel, 1980).

However, before we become too dependent on technology, we must remember that this type of information and comprehensive treatment may not be applicable for many of the decisions that managers make. Thus, we also need better and simpler rules to help with the everyday nonanalytic decisions that are made quickly and with limited information. These decisions tend to dominate a manager's time, and they are the type of decision we know the least about. Our task for the future must be to increase the effectiveness of these nonanalytic decisions, along with the more rational, comprehensive decisions on which we have traditionally focused.

Discussion Questions

1. Who did you vote for (or who would you have voted for if you had voted) in the last presidential election? What did you believe the consequences would be of each candidate being President? Were these important and highly valued consequences? Does this sort of analysis help to explain your choice?
2. Think about your own strategies for making decisions. Do they vary as a function of the problem and the situation? What are the important factors that make you use one strategy rather than another?
3. Do you actually spend time gathering information and generating alternatives for most of your decisions? What do you do? Review your activities when you made some important decision recently.

CASE: THE VEHICLE OF CHOICE

Julie Beamon wanted to buy a new car. She knew the car was likely to be expensive, so she wanted to make a good decision. She went to the library and read up on ways to make important decisions. Armed with her insight and some decision aids, she felt she was ready to go.

First, she made some decisions that narrowed down her field of choice. The car had to be economical, easy to drive in traffic and to park, and cost less than $8000. The compacts and subcompacts seemed to be reasonable choices. Next Julie gathered information on all the domestic models that fit her criteria. She wanted to buy American because of her patriotism and because she didn't want to have the hassle of foreign-made parts and repair problems. She went to the library again and looked at *Consumer Reports* and other magazines that reviewed the cars on her list. All those cars that received unsafe ratings were crossed off until the list was down to five.

Once she had a small set of possibilities, she called the various dealerships and asked them to send out brochures and information about the different cars and the options available. Across the top of the page on which she had listed her five alternatives, she placed the options that were important to her (e.g., rear-window defogger, radio, whitewalls, automatic shift). In each cell of her matrix she placed the cost of the option, and she added all these items up to determine the cost of each alternative. Convinced that she was close to a decision, Julie went out to drive her top two cars and make a choice. Her expectations came crashing down around her. She thought both cars gave a rough ride, were sluggish, and were unattractive. After a whole day of looking at different models, she was totally frustrated. On the way home she heard an ad for the new Honda Civic, the "hottest car in town." The next day she visited her Honda dealer, drove the car, and liked it. Even though she knew it would cost over $1000 more than her other choices and that she would have to wait 6 months to get it, she put her money down and signed the papers. "What a relief," she said. "That's the last time I'll try to be scientific about making a decision."

Questions about the Case

1. Is this the type of decision for which analytic procedures can be used? What types of aids might help?
2. Did Julie have all the information she needed? What more could she have done?
3. Describe the steps in Julie's decision process. Was this a good way to proceed? How could she have done it differently?

References

Abelson, R. P. (1976). Script processing in attitude formation and decision-making. In J. S. Carroll and J. W. Payne (Eds.), *Cognition and social behavior*. New York: Erlbaum.

Abelson, R. P., & Levi, A. (1985). Decision-making and decision theory. In G. Lindzey & E. Aronson (Eds.), *Handbook of social psychology* (3d ed., vol. 1., pp. 231–309). Reading, MA: Addison-Wesley.

Anderson, N. H. (1970). Functional measurement and psychophysical theory. *Psychological Review, 77*, 152–170.

Archer, E. R. (1980, February). How to make a business decision: An analysis of theory and practice. *Management Review*, pp. 54–61.

Beach, B. H. (1975). Expert judgment about uncertainty: Bayesian decision making in realistic settings. *Organizational Behavior and Human Performance, 14*, 10–59.

Beach, L. R., Hope, A., Townes, B. D., & Campbell, F. L. (1982). The expectation-threshold model of reproductive decision making. *Population and Environment, 5*, 95–108.

Beach L. R., & Mitchell, T. R. (1978). A contingency model for the selection of decision strategies. *Academy of Management Review, 3*, 439–449.

Boulding, K. E. (1956). *The Image.* Ann Arbor: University of Michigan Press.

Brockner, J., Rubin, J. Z. (1986). *Entrapment in escalating conflicts: A social psychological analysis.* New York: Springer-Verlag.

Christensen-Szalanski, J. J. J. (1978). Problem-solving strategies: A selection mechanism, some implications, and some data. *Organizational Behavior and Human Performance, 22*, 307–323.

Coombs, C. H. (1964). *A theory of data.* New York: Wiley.

Dawes, R. M. (1964). Social selection based on multidimensional criteria. *Journal of Abnormal and Social Psychology, 68*, 104–109.

Ebert, R. J., & Mitchell, T. R. (1975). *Organizational decision processes.* New York: Crane, Russak.

Einhorn, H. J. (1970). The use of nonlinear, noncompensatory models in decision-making. *Psychological Bulletin, 73*, 221–230.

Einhorn, H. J., & Hogarth, R. M. (1978). Confidence in judgment: Persistence of the illusion of validity. *Psychological Review, 85*, 395–416.

Fischhoff, B., & Bar-Hillel, M. (1984). Focusing techniques: A shortcut to improving probability judgments. *Organizational Behavior and Human Performance, 34*, 175–194.

Gioia, D. A., & Poole, P. P. (1984). Scripts in organizational behavior. *Academy of Management Review, 9,* 449–459.

Gray, C. A. (1975). Factors in students' decisions to attempt academic tasks. *Organizational Behavior and Human Performance, 13,* 147–164.

Hall, E. T. (1969). *The hidden dimension,* New York: Anchor.

Holmstrom, V. L., & Beach, L. R. (1973). Subjective expected utility and career preferences. *Organizational Behavior and Human Performance, 10,* 201–207.

Janis, I. L., & Mann, L. (1977). *Decision making: A psychological analysis of conflict, choice and commitment.* New York: Free Press.

Kahneman, D., & Tversky, A. (1973). On the psychology of prediction. *Psychological Review, 80,* 251–273.

Kahneman, D., & Tversky, A. (1984). Choices, values, and frames. *American Psychologist, 39,* 341–350.

Kiechel, W. III (1980, May 5). Everything you always wanted to know may soon be on-line. *Fortune,* p. 226ff.

Kotter, J. P. (1982, November–December). What effective managers really do. *Harvard Business Review,* pp. 156–167.

Landy, F. J., & Farr, J. R. (1983). *The measurement of work performance.* New York: Academic.

Levinson, D. J., Darrow, C. N., Klein, E. B., Levinson, M. H., & McKee, B. (1978). *The seasons of a man's life.* New York: Knopf.

Liden, R. C., & Mitchell, T. R. (1982). Personal policy development as a response to ineffective performance. *Proceedings of the 1982 National Meetings of the American Institute for Decision Sciences, 1,* 395–397.

MacIntyre, A. (1981). *After virtue.* Notre Dame, IN: University of Notre Dame Press.

McAllister, D. W., Mitchell, T. R., & Beach, L. R. (1979). The contingency model for the selection of decision strategies: An empirical test of the effects of significance, accountability and reversibility. *Organizational Behavior and Human Performance, 24,* 228–244.

Mihal, W. L., Sorce, P.A., & Comte, T. E. (1984). A process model of individual career decision making. *Academy of Management Review, 9,* 95–103.

Miller, G. A., Galanter, E., & Pribram, K. H. (1960). *Plans and the structure of behavior.* New York: Holt, Rinehart and Winston.

Mintzberg, H. (1975, July–August). The manager's job: Folklore and fact. *Harvard Business Review,* pp. 49–61.

Mitchell, T. R. (1983). Expectancy-value models in organizational psychology. In N. Feather (Ed.), *Expectancy and actions: Expectancy value models in psychology* (pp. 293–312). Hillsdale, N.J.: Erlbaum.

Mitchell, T. R., Rediker, K. J., & Beach, L. R. (1986). Image theory and organizational decision making. In H. P. Sims, Jr. & D. A. Gioia (Eds.), *The thinking organization: Dynamics of organizational social cognition.* San Francisco: Jossey-Bass.

Nisbett, R. E., & Ross, L. (1980). *Human inference: Strategies and shortcomings of Social Judgment.* Englewood Cliffs, NJ: Prentice-Hall.

Northcraft, G. B., & Wolf, G. (1984). Dollars, sense and sunk costs: A life cycle model of research allocation decisions. *Academy of Management Review, 9,* 225–234.

Payne, J. W. (1982). Contingent decision behavior. *Psychological Bulletin, 92,* 382–402.

Rhodes, S. R., & Foering, M. (1983). An integrated model of career motivation. *Academy of Management Review, 8,* 631–639.

Rowe, A. J., Boulgardies, J. D., & McGrath, M. R. (1984). Managerial decision making. In J. E. Rosenzweig & F. E. Kast (Eds.), *Modules in management.* Chicago: Science Research Associates.

Shanteau, J. (1974). Component processes in risky decision making. *Journal of Experimental Psychology, 103,* 680–691.

Shanteau, J., & Anderson, N. H. (1969). Test of a conflict model for preference judgment. *Journal of Mathematical Psychology, 6,* 312–325.

Shrivastava, P., & Mitroff, I. I. (1984). Enhancing organizational research utilization: The role of decision makers' assumptions. *Academy of Management Review, 9,* 18–26.

Simon, H. A. (1957). *Models of man.* New York: Wiley.

Staw, B. M. (1981). The escalation of commitment to a course of action. *Academy of Management Review, 6,* 557–588.

Slovic, P., & Lichtenstein, S. (1971). Comparison of Bayesian and regression approaches to the study of information processing in judgment. *Organizational Behavior and Human Performance, 6,* 649–744.

Thomas J., & Griffin, R. (1983). The social information processing model of task design: A review of the literature. *Academy of Management Review, 8,* 672–682.

Tuchman, B. W. (1984). *The march of folly.* New York: Knopf.

Tversky, A. (1967). Additivity, utility and subjective probability. *Journal of Mathematical Psychology 4,* 175–202.

Tversky, A. (1969). Intransitivity of preferences. *Psychological Review, 76,* 31–48.

Tversky, A. (1972). Elimination by aspects: A theory of choice. *Psychological Review, 79,* 281–299.

Tversky, A., & Kahneman, D. (1973). Availability: A heuristic for judging frequency and probability. *Cognitive Psychology, 5,* 207–232.

Chapter 12

Group Decision Making

If participation is to be used as a tool for the furtherance of man's happiness and well-being, then it must be in a context which recognizes not only individual differences in knowledge and ability, but the primacy of reason over feelings in organizational decision making.
—E. A. LOCKE

G roup decision making is often criticized as frustrating and wasteful. Committees in particular have been lampooned by such sayings as: "A camel is a horse designed by committee" and "The possibility of avoiding a decision increases in proportion to the square of the number of members on the committee." However, more and more decisions are being made by groups, and it is therefore important to know what factors help groups make good decisions. In this chapter, we examine how group decision making is different from individual decision making, when it is preferable to individual decision making, and some ways in which we can increase its effectiveness.

The foundations for group decision making are similar in many ways to those for individual decision making. We are still dealing with beliefs and values. However, now we must figure out ways to combine the beliefs and values of several individuals. Thus, both the gathering of information and agreement about its content are important. Also, we are still dealing with the same decision process. That is, for analytic decisions we have problem identification, information search, alternative generation, and choice stages. But for group decision making we usually have more than one individual participating in some or all of these stages. For less analytic decisions, an image theory process occurs in groups. That is, under some circumstances, groups go with the status quo and use fittingness or congruence criteria for making decisions. Thus, many of the dimensions that were important for understanding individual decisions are also important for understanding group decisions. However, the process is much more complex due to the fact that we have multiple actors processing complex information often under public scrutiny.

BACKGROUND

A substantial amount of the research on group decision making focuses on the question of *participation:* Is group participation in decision making a good thing or not? By and large, this research contrasts the products of group decision making with those of individual decision making. In the first part of the chapter, we discuss this research and the conditions under which groups are most effective.

It is interesting to note, however, that while a great deal of attention has been paid to the critical preliminary decision of *whether* (or when) managers should use participation, very little research has been done on *how* they ought to proceed once the decision to use participation has been made. That is, how do you get people involved? How do you motivate them to be committed to making a good decision? The effectiveness of group decision making depends not only on the fact that participation has been used, but also on the *process* of participation. We review what is known in this area, even though much of the work on the process of participation is speculative in nature.

370

Part Four:
Accomplishing
Organizational
Objectives

A Decision Example

As a way of getting oriented to some of these issues, let us consider an example. Suppose you are the chairperson of a large management department in a state university. The dean of the business school informs you that the legislature has granted the school's request for three new academic positions, and your department will get one of them. Within your department there are five subareas: organizational behavior, operations systems, personnel, policy, and organization theory. A decision must be made about which subarea will get the new position. The problem that confronts you is how to make this decision. One possibility is that you could simply look at the existing teaching load in each area (i.e., the number of faculty in relation to the number of courses offered) and make a decision yourself. This strategy would not involve group decision making at all.

It is far more likely, however, that you would use some degree of participation. Perhaps you could hold a department meeting to get the faculty's input, and then go off and decide. Alternatively, you could let each group present a formal written proposal on why it should get the position. Or you could let the department vote on where the position should go. All these alternatives are feasible, and all have been used at one time or another in different departments.

In many cases, it is this preliminary decision about whether or not to use participation, and if so, how much, that captures our attention. And, indeed, the bulk of the research on participation has its focus here. However, a second issue, and one of equal importance for effectiveness, is how participation should take place. What sort of information do you need? Who will attend the group meetings? Will there be representatives from each subarea or will the department as a whole meet? Will you try to regulate both the structure and the process of the meetings? What sort of decision rules will be used? In short, group decision making involves not only a decision about the degree of participation that should be used, but also an understanding of group process.

One final point: Participation and the use of group decision making can be studied and discussed from a number of different perspectives. One important distinction is between the political and technical views. Participation as a political process involves issues dealing with the sharing of power and the rights of employees. In many European countries, both Eastern and Western, employees are formally included in the decision process *as a right* (cf. Dachler & Wilpert, 1978). We touch on some of these political issues in Chapter 13. In the present chapter we concentrate on the technical aspects of participation and group decision making. Yet we wish to point out now that in our current decision example there may be questions about *who* needs to be part of the selection process for political reasons, and that *how* the candidate is selected may have political overtones.

In order to understand better the parameters of our decision example, we need to consider a number of factors. We need to take into account the differences between individuals working in groups and individuals working alone. We need to know when and under what circumstances various amounts of participation should be used. And we need to know how to facilitate the *process* of actually making a group decision. Let us begin by reviewing a topic that we discussed in an earlier chapter.

Groups versus Individuals

As you will recall, in Chapter 8, "Group Dynamics," we listed a number of ways in which individuals working in groups are different from individuals working alone. People are aroused in groups, individual contributions to the group tend to be uneven, and groups frequently have more extreme attitudes and opinions than individuals. All these factors can influence whose beliefs and values dominate, whether there will be a tendency toward risk-taking or conservatism in the group, and the process by which an actual choice is made.

Reviews of the empirical research suggest that groups can have both beneficial and harmful characteristics with respect to the decision process. In what is perhaps the best known summary of this research, Maier (1967) describes the advantages and drawbacks of group decision making. Figure 12-1 presents this summary. As you can see, groups can both help and hurt. The question is, how can a manager evaluate the overall benefits of group participation? Furthermore, given that a group is used, how can the assets be maximized and the liabilities minimized?

Let us return to our example. You are sure that having the department participate in the position allocation decision will be an asset, since it will provide a rich source of information. Because your background is in personnel, it is hard to know what is happening in other fields. A group meeting would help generate new information and a broader perspective. Having the department meet and participate will also increase support and acceptance of whatever decision is made.

On the other hand, departmental groups typically take a long time to make decisions. There may be disagreement and conflict. A few vocal full professors often dominate departmental meetings. You also remember an occasion 10 years ago when there was a position to be allocated, and two powerful

Assets	Liabilities
1. Groups can accumulate more knowledge and facts.	1. Groups tend to work more slowly. They take more time to reach a decision, and time costs money.
2. Groups may have a broader perspective and consider more approaches and alternative solutions.	2. Group effort frequently results in compromises that are not optimal from an effectiveness perspective.
3. Individuals who participate in the decision process are more likely to be satisfied with the decision and support the decision.	3. Groups are frequently dominated by one individual or a small clique.
4. The group decision process serves as an important communication and political device.	4. Too much dependence on group decisions can limit management's ability to act quickly and decisively when necessary.

Figure 12-1
Positive and negative aspects of group decision making. (*Adapted from Maier, 1967.*)

subgroups fought actively for the slot. A compromise was reached in which one subgroup was promised the "next" position. When the next slot became available 3 years later, the needs of that subgroup were not as great as those of other subgroups, but the department was locked into the compromise. Finally, you know that the decision must be made quickly. In fact, the last time the department had a position to fill, it took so long to decide which subarea should get the slot that an economic downturn caused the governor to institute a hiring freeze before anyone could be interviewed. You lost that position forever, while another department that had decided quickly, searched quickly, and made an offer in writing was able to keep its faculty position.

The decision about whether to use participation (group decision making) is not an easy one. It involves many factors. Whether or not a decision-making group will be effective depends on the abilities of the members, the information they share (some members may have more or less information, some may be more or less willing to share it), the size of the group, and the nature of the decision problem. As we shall see, all of these factors are important in determining when and how groups perform well (Yetton & Bottger, 1983; Miner, 1984).

PARTICIPATION IN DECISION MAKING

Perhaps the first question to ask is simply whether there is any evidence that group participation is effective as a *general management strategy*. That is, does an overall participative management policy lead to positive outcomes such as higher productivity and more satisfied, committed employees?

Research on Participation

There is a rather large body of research dealing with this general question. A comprehensive review of this literature was done by Locke and Schweiger

Figure 12-2
Summary of the empirical research on participation. (*Adapted from Locke & Scheiger, 1979.*)

	Positive Effect	No Effect	Negative Effect
Laboratory studies:			
Productivity criteria	4	6	4
Satisfaction criteria	5	0	2
Correlational field studies:			
Productivity criteria	3	10	3
Satisfaction criteria	13	8	1
Controlled field experiments:			
Productivity criteria	3	10	3
Satisfaction criteria	8	5	1
Combined results:			
Productivity criteria	22%	56%	22%
Satisfaction criteria	60%	30%	9%

(1979). These authors classified the research into four categories: laboratory studies, correlational field studies, controlled experimental field studies, and multivariate field studies in which participation was changed as just one part of a more comprehensive organizational change effort. Since the multivariate field studies do not allow one to draw any firm conclusions about the separate effects of participation, Locke and Schweiger (1979) left these results out of their overall summary. Figure 12-2 shows a compilation of their findings.

The implications of these findings are rather clear. First, in terms of actual *productivity* changes, participation had no effect in more than 50 percent of the studies. Moreover, there seem to have been just as many decreases in productivity caused by participation as there were increases. On the other hand, participation had a positive impact on *satisfaction* more than 60 percent of the time. Overall, this research indicates that participative management may not increase productivity, but it is likely to increase satisfaction.

The Complexity of Participation

It is important to recognize that participation is not a unidimensional construct. Rather, it has a number of distinct facets. For example, participation can be either forced or voluntary. In some cases participation is legally mandated. For example, when certain decisions are made by our local, state, and national governments (e.g., regarding nuclear power plants, school closures, and the like) input must be solicited from different groups, and in some cases those groups must be represented in the decision-making body itself. Union contracts may also build in participation on some issues. In short, there are times when people have to participate in the decision-making process whether they want to or not.

Participation can also be either direct or indirect. The more that representatives are used, the less direct the participation. Many decision-making bodies are composed of representatives from unions, company departments, technical specialties, and so on. In general, the more the decision-making process is legally specified, the more formal and indirect the participation is likely to be.

Finally, participation varies in its degree, content, and scope. Participation might involve information gathering or actual decision making. One might participate in certain stages of the process but not in others. Also, participation can be about various types of decisions such as personnel matters (e.g., hiring, firing, job description), job matters (e.g., assignments, work methods, deadlines), working conditions (e.g., hours, safety, breaks), and organizational policy (e.g., expansion, profit sharing, layoffs).

What we are saying, then, is that participation is a rather complex variable. This is important, because it suggests why participation sometimes has a positive effect on productivity and satisfaction, why it sometimes has a negative effect, and why it sometimes has no effect at all. Specifically, it seems likely that certain types of participation work better in some situations than in others. Consequently, if the wrong type of participation is used in a given situation, neutral or even negative effects are likely to be the result. But what are some of the situational factors that limit the effectiveness of participation?

Limitations on Participation

In-depth reviews of the literature provide us with a number of clues about the conditions under which employee participation seems to run into trouble. For example, management must believe in the value of participation and be committed to it. One survey of senior business executives showed that 79 percent felt that top managers know best what needs to be done, and have the right to make organizational decisions as they see fit. In situations in which management is dead set against participation, it is not likely to succeed (Krishnan, 1974).

There are also some limiting factors from the employee's perspective. Employees must have some interest in and knowledge about the subject under consideration. Asking for participation in decisions about which an employee either knows or cares little is likely to lead to resentment. There is also evidence that too much participation can lead to stress, dissatisfaction, and lower performance (Hespe & Wall, 1976).

CONTINGENCY MODELS OF PARTICIPATION

In the last 10 to 15 years a number of researchers have analyzed the different types of participation and the various situational limitations in an attempt to develop contingency models of participation. The purpose of these models is to help the manager predict when participation is most likely to be effective.

The Vroom and Yetton Model

Perhaps the most well known and best articulated of these models is the one developed by Vroom and Yetton (1973). On the basis of the same research results we reviewed previously, they developed a procedure that managers can use to help them decide when and how much participation should be employed.

The first point these authors make is that there are five degrees or forms of participation that are possible. Figure 12-3 presents these five alternatives. As

Figure 12-3
Different degrees of participation possible. (*Adapted from Vroom & Yetton, 1973.*)

AI	Manager makes the decision alone.
AII	Manager asks for information from subordinates but makes the decision alone. Subordinates may or may not be told about what the problem is.
CI	Manager shares the problem with subordinates and asks for information and evaluations from them. Meetings take place with each subordinate separately, not as a group, and the manager makes the decision.
CII	Manager and subordinates meet as a group to discuss the problem, but the manager makes the decision.
GII	Manager and subordinates meet as a group to discuss the problem, and the group as a whole makes the decision.

Note: A = alone; C = consultation; G = group.

you can see, they range from no participation at all, to consultation, to full participation in which the group as a whole makes the decision.

Vroom and Yetton (1973) argue that the most appropriate choice from among these five alternatives depends on the decision problem itself. More specifically, they provide seven diagnostic questions that the manager should ask about the problem before the form of participation is chosen. Figure 12-4 lists these questions and provides a decision tree that shows which forms of participation are most feasible for various combinations of answers. The seven diagnostic questions deal with two main issues: (1) the quality of the decision (questions A, B, C, and F), and (2) the subordinates' likely acceptance of whatever decision is made (questions D, E, and G). The decision tree is structured in such a way that if a particular form of participation would be likely to reduce either the overall quality of the decision that is made or the

Figure 12-4
Summary of the Vroom and Yetton model. (*Adapted from Vroom & Yetton, 1973.*)

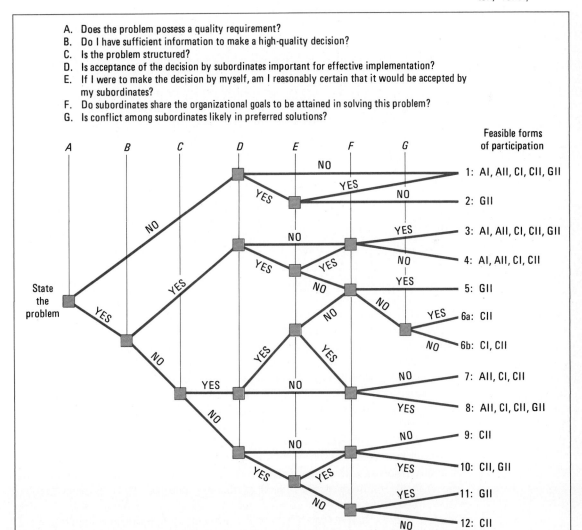

A. Does the problem possess a quality requirement?
B. Do I have sufficient information to make a high-quality decision?
C. Is the problem structured?
D. Is acceptance of the decision by subordinates important for effective implementation?
E. If I were to make the decision by myself, am I reasonably certain that it would be accepted by my subordinates?
F. Do subordinates share the organizational goals to be attained in solving this problem?
G. Is conflict among subordinates likely in preferred solutions?

Feasible forms of participation

1: AI, AII, CI, CII, GII
2: GII
3: AI, AII, CI, CII, GII
4: AI, AII, CI, CII
5: GII
6a: CII
6b: CI, CII
7: AII, CI, CII
8: AII, CI, CII, GII
9: CII
10: CII, GII
11: GII
12: CII

subordinates' acceptance of that decision, that form of participation is eliminated as a feasible alternative.

To understand better how this model works, let us return to the faculty position allocation decision and answer the questions from the department chairperson's point of view. To diagnostic question A, the chairperson is likely to answer *yes*. It is quite conceivable that certain allocation decisions might be better than others (e.g., deciding to allocate the position to a subarea that is currently understaffed would probably be better than deciding to allocate it to a subarea that is overstaffed). To diagnostic question B, the chairperson is likely to answer *no*. As we indicated previously, the chairperson's background is in personnel, and he or she may not be fully aware of what is going on in other fields. The chairperson is also likely to answer *no* to diagnostic question C. The problem is not structural, at least not in the sense that there is a "cookbook recipe" for making the decision. To diagnostic question D, the chairperson is likely to answer *yes*. In most departments, faculty acceptance of this type of decision is fairly important. If a decision were made that the faculty did not accept, a certain amount of conflict and animosity would probably arise, and in the extreme case, faculty members could go directly to the dean in an effort to block the decision. The chairperson's response to diagnostic question E depends a great deal on his or her interpersonal relations with the rest of the faculty in the department, and on their trust in his or her judgment. Let us suppose that in this case the chairperson answers the question *no*. To diagnostic question F, the chairperson is likely to answer *yes*. Most faculty members share the educational and research goals that would be achieved by making a new faculty appointment. Finally, the chairperson would skip diagnostic question G, since it is not relevant given the pattern of answers to previous questions. (Had we reversed the responses given to questions C and F, diagnostic question G would have been relevant.)

This pattern of answers takes us through the decision tree to decision type 11. According to the model, the only feasible form of participation in this situation is to allow the department as a whole to vote on the decision (GII). Notice that had the chairperson answered *yes* to diagnostic question E, we would have ended at decision type 10, in which case either a consultative approach (CII) or full department vote (GII) would be feasible.

Thus, it should be clear that the use of participation as a decision-making strategy is a decision in itself. Consequently, it should be thoroughly studied and rationally analyzed. According to the Vroom and Yetton (1973) model, there are times when it will be appropriate to use only full participation by the group (e.g., decision types 2, 5, and 11), and times when full group participation should definitely not be used (e.g., decision types 4, 6a, 6b, 7, 9, and 12).

The research using this model has been quite supportive. Vroom and Yetton (1973) gathered hundreds of actual decision problems from a wide variety of managers. These problems were categorized into one of the thirteen problem types described in Figure 12-4. The most interesting, relevant, and important problems were then used as training materials to help other managers increase their effectiveness in diagnosing decision problems and deciding when to use participation. The results showed that managers who had been trained to use the diagnostic questions were better able to classify decision problems and choose appropriate participation levels than managers without such training. Also, there is some evidence that this type of training increases diagnostic skills, and that the correct participation level increases effectiveness (e.g., Vroom & Jago, 1978; Field, 1982).

One interesting recent study by Heilman, Hornstein, Cage, and Herschlag (1984) showed support both for the Vroom and Yetton model as well as for the previously discussed satisfaction results presented by Locke and Schweiger (1979). In this study subjects were presented with a number of decision scenarios. When the subjects were assigned the role of manager, the level of participation evaluated as most effective fit fairly well with the prescriptions of the Vroom and Yetton model. However, when they took the role of subordinates, the subjects "never rated an autocratic leader's behavior as more effective than a participative leader's behavior, even when the situation was one in which autocratic behavior would be prescribed by the Vroom-Yetton model" (p. 50). Thus, as Locke and Schweiger's (1979) review indicated, people seem to be more satisfied with higher levels of participation, even when using a high level of participation is not the most effective strategy.

Other Contingency Models

While the Vroom and Yetton model focuses on the characteristics of the specific decision problem at hand, other models take a broader and somewhat more externally oriented approach. Although these other models are *far* less specific about telling an individual manager when and to what extent participation should be used, they do include variables not considered by Vroom and Yetton.

The two best examples of these alternative models are those presented by Nutt (1976) and Sashkin (1976). These authors argue that participation is appropriate as a *general management strategy* (as contrasted with a specific strategy for a specific problem) under certain task and environmental conditions. More specifically, they argue that when the task itself is difficult to analyze and is heterogeneous in its demands, more participation should be used. Participation is also predicted to be helpful when the external organizational environment is subject to substantial amounts of change, which creates more uncertainty and ambiguity in the decision task. Finally, the more interdependent the tasks, the more participation should be used.

Some of the factors suggested by these authors are included in the diagnostic questions used by Vroom and Yetton. For example, the need for information and the degree of structure in the problem (questions B and C) relate to the factors of uncertainty and ambiguity. But additional factors are also important. What the Nutt (1976) and Sashkin (1976) models recognize is that task demands, interdependencies, and turbulence in the external environment can also affect the need for participation.

In summary, there are several models that specify the conditions under which participation is most likely to be successful. However, as we mentioned at the beginning of the chapter, the decision to use participation is only one part of the overall problem. Of equal, and in some cases greater, importance is the way in which the group itself is run. The effectiveness of group decision making is dependent not only on the mere fact that a group is used, but also on the process by which the group arrives at its decision. We turn now to a discussion of decision processes.

GROUP DECISION PROCESSES

As we stated in the beginning of the chapter, more and more decisions are being made by groups. To some extent this is occurring because of legal and political pressures. More importantly, however, it is occurring because there is a growing awareness that group decision making can sometimes be advantageous. As the Vroom and Yetton (1973) model suggests, under some circumstances group decision making can lead to (1) higher quality decisions, and (2) greater acceptance of and commitment to whatever decision is made.

In order to realize these benefits, especially the benefit of higher quality decisions, it is important not only that group decision making be used in the "proper" situations (e.g, those specified by Vroom and Yetton), but also that the interpersonal dynamics within the group foster effective decision making. We discussed a number of group dynamics issues in Chapters 8, 9, and 10. In this section we first briefly review several topics in group dynamics that are particularly relevant for decision making in a group context, and then take a more detailed look at two extensions of these ideas.

Group Dynamics

In Chapter 8 we discussed why people join groups and how groups develop over time. Some of this information is helpful for understanding decision-making groups. For example, as a group develops, stable patterns of communication form. These patterns influence how and to whom information gets distributed, as well as who makes the greatest and the smallest contribution to the group. Obviously, when decision making is involved, we want the people with the "best" information to feel free to communicate this information to others.

A second issue of importance is the type of decision task at hand. Certain types of decision tasks require that everyone contribute fully and equally, while for others the excellence of the decision depends more on the skills of either the best or worst group member (Steiner, 1972). Also, certain types of decision tasks require creative solutions—new ideas and innovations—while others require the assimilation, integration, and analysis of information already available, with an emphasis on the evaluation of alternatives.

Another important issue is that of evaluation apprehension. People are often reluctant to speak out in a group context. They are afraid of how their ideas will be evaluated, or that they will be made to look foolish in front of others. If decision groups are to be successful, especially those that require innovative and creative thinking, people must feel comfortable about making contributions.

Finally, group members that have been together a long time often come to like one another, have a strong sense of commitment to the group, and have similar attitudes and feelings about things. We spoke of cohesive groups as groups with these characteristics. For some decision tasks a cohesive group may be just what is needed. If a routine decision is needed quickly and a unified front is important, such a group does well. However, in other cases in which new ideas are required or the wisdom of past decisions should be challenged, a cohesive group may actually be a problem. This type of problem has occurred at the highest levels of policymaking in both business and government organizations. Because of its importance, it has received a great deal of attention in the research literature, and is referred to as "groupthink."

Groupthink

As we discussed in Chapter 8, there are a number of factors that can affect the development of group cohesiveness. An organization can put people together who have similar attitudes, provide them with a common goal, structure their tasks so that they have a high degree of interaction, reward them for group success, and so on. These factors should produce a tightly knit, highly cohesive group. Is this desirable? Do we want groups like this? At first blush we might respond positively.

Irving Janis (1972) has written a highly provocative book about just such groups. He analyzed the foreign-policy decisions made by the Kennedy and Johnson administrations and came to the conclusion that many of the groups responsible for these decisions were indeed highly cohesive and close-knit. Unfortunately, their decision-making process was sometimes marred by *groupthink,* a phenomenon characterized in the following manner.

First, there was an illusion of invulnerability. The group members often came to feel that they were invincible. For example, Robert Kennedy, on the eve of the Bay of Pigs fiasco (an attempt to invade Cuba in April of 1961 that resulted in total disaster), reported that he felt that with such talent, "bold new ideas," and "common sense and hard work" they would overcome whatever challenged them. Similarly, John Dean, in discussing his role in the Watergate cover-up, mentioned that President Nixon's personal staff (also characterized by groupthink) felt that nothing could go wrong in the White House while they were there.

Second, there was a general tendency to moralize—to see the United States as the leader of the free world, and to portray the opposition as evil, weak, and stupid. Our continuing commitment to the war in Vietnam often reflected this type of atmosphere.

A third characteristic was the feeling of unanimity. The reports from inside the Executive Committee were frequently that everyone was unanimous in their support of the President's decision. It was only later that doubts were expressed. For example, both Arthur Schlesinger and Theodore Sorensen (close confidants of the President) reported that they had doubts about the decisions being made and the policies being developed with regard to Southeast Asia during the Kennedy years. Each felt, however, that everyone else was in agreement, and that he was the only one with divergent views. Rather than appear "soft" or "compromising," they kept their feelings to themselves. Both men later regretted their hesitancy.

A fourth and crucial factor was the pressure toward conformity. When discussions were held on a topic, President Kennedy would occasionally call in an "expert" and have him or her respond to the critical questions that might appear. Instead of actively inquiring about the extent of dissent or seeking divergent views, Kennedy would simply let the expert silence the critic. Also, in many cases informal pressure was placed on the President's staff. Schlesinger reports, for example, that Robert Kennedy took him aside and mentioned that while he could see that there might be some minor problems with the President's decision, the President needed unanimous support. There was an appeal for group solidarity.

Finally, because of the similarity in the attitudes of the group members, their liking for one another, and the pressure for conformity, outside criticism and relevant arguments were often dismissed prematurely. It is reported that there was a lot of evidence available that suggested that the Bay of Pigs invasion would fail. However, due to the factors mentioned above, this evidence was never given proper consideration.

In summary, the decision-making process that occurred within these high-level policy groups was sometimes severely hindered in effectiveness by the group's internal cohesiveness and conformity. They closed themselves off from others. They rejected both internal and external dissent. They failed to recognize valuable criticism when it appeared. They overlooked important details. They felt they could do no wrong.

And they made all this clear in public. A study by Tetlock (1979) analyzed the content of the public statements of the members of these decision-making groups. Their statements were contrasted with those of people who were also government supporters but who were not members of the particular group in question. It was found that the decision makers subjected to groupthink were more simplistic in their analyses and made more positive references to the United States and our allies than was the case for those who had not suffered from groupthink.

Thus, groupthink can be an ineffective and sometimes dangerous state for a group to be in. This is especially true when it is vitally important that different viewpoints be expressed and multiple alternatives considered. Janis has discussed in more detail those factors that cause groupthink, the consequences of groupthink, and ways to avoid it (Janis & Mann, 1977). Figure 12-5 presents an overview of the groupthink process.

As you can see from the figure, the causes of groupthink include cohesiveness, a dominating leader, stress or pressure to decide, and lack of a

Figure 12-5
Causes, symptoms, and consequences of groupthink. (*Adapted from Janis & Mann, 1977.*)

CAUSES OF GROUPTHINK	GROUPTHINK SYMPTOMS	DEFECTIVE DECISION PROCESSES
1. Cohesive group	1. Belief in own group's moral and rational correctness	1. Limited and/or biased search for information
2. Strong leadership	2. Perceived invulnerability	2. Incomplete list of alternatives
3. Unstructured group process	3. Us-versus-them thinking	3. Inadequate evaluation of alternatives
4. Pressure for solution	4. Pressure brought to bear on those who disagree	4. Maintenance of the status quo
5. Perceived narrow range of solutions	5. Self-censorship	5. Poor planning for contingencies
	6. Perception of unanimity	

systematic process for making the decision that will avoid the pitfalls of groupthink. The symptoms are those we discussed above, and the consequences are often decisions that are poorly researched and evaluated and for which no contingency plans have been made.

Other empirical research on groupthink generally supports Janis' (1972) conclusions. For example, Flowers (1977) demonstrated that groups with a directive leader suggest fewer solutions, consult fewer outside sources of information, and use more rationalization than groups with a nondirective leader. And Courtright (1978) demonstrated that highly cohesive groups have less disagreement than groups that are low in cohesiveness.

These findings raise two questions. First, how do we avoid groupthink? Janis (1972) mentions a number of factors that may decrease groupthink. He suggests that a leader should try to stay neutral and should encourage criticism and new ideas. Small subgroups or outside consultants may come up with a different viewpoint. People sympathetic to alternative views should be encouraged to present their perspectives. And contingency plans should be built into the process. Several additional strategies that may be useful in combatting groupthink will be discussed in a later section of the chapter.

A second important question is, when do cohesiveness and directive leadership lead to effective decisions, and when do they lead to groupthink? The answer seems to be that it depends on the task. When we have a complex problem for which we need to examine multiple alternatives, have creative and diverse inputs, avoid premature closure, and make sure we have contingent plans in case of failure, then excessive cohesiveness and directive leadership can lead to groupthink. On the other hand, if a group has a routine problem about which consensus is obvious and there is a need to act quickly, we may find that a cohesive group and directive leadership are necessary ingredients for a good decision. In short, some sort of match between the *group process* and the *group problem* is needed.

Image Theory

While not as richly described for group decision processes as Janis' work, the notions of image theory presented in the last chapter in connection with individual decision making are also applicable for groups (Mitchell, Rediker, & Beach, 1986). It is fairly easy to draw parallels between the individual decision process and the group process, especially when we are describing policy or strategic decision making.

First, an organization usually has a self-image that can be readily articulated by its members (Selznick, 1957). Second, the trajectory image refers to the key goals the organization is trying to achieve. Third, the projected image is the extent to which the organization feels it is on track (various marketing, production, and accounting procedures constantly provide data on this issue). And finally, the action image consists of the plans and tactics being used for goal attainment.

Although image theory is very different from the theory presented by Janis (1972), it leads to some of the same conclusions. For example, Mitchell, Rediker, and Beach (1986) argue that when there is a strong culture in the organization, groups will use fittingness or congruence as the decision criterion and that in most cases they stay with the status quo. The term *strong culture* simply means that there exists in the organization a set of clearly defined and well-developed norms of behavior that is shared by a majority of the organization's members (see Chapter 9, pp. 279–280). High cohesiveness is often a concomitant of strong culture. Staying with the status quo implies that competing alternatives are usually rejected (quickly and without much analysis) and that if a new course of action is to be adopted, it must be substantially (as opposed to marginally) better than continuing with the status quo.

Thus, image theory also suggests that groups with strong cultures (high cohesiveness) may have difficulty dealing with decisions that require (1) substantial input, (2) creative and new ideas, (3) consideration of alternatives that deviate from the group's current course or direction, and (4) actual change from the status quo. Again, the question that confronts us is how to introduce formal procedures to help groups make good decisions in the face of these forces that limit their effectiveness.

FORMAL PROCEDURES FOR CHANGING GROUP PROCESS

Over the last 20 years, a number of techniques have been developed to help groups make decisions without being hindered by such factors as strong leadership and/or group cohesiveness (although these can be beneficial in some circumstances). Some of these techniques are designed to deal with the problem of evaluation apprehension (people's fear of speaking up or being criticized). Others are designed to generate more creative ideas, more information, and more alternative solutions (Van Gundy, 1984). Still others are designed to facilitate quality and productivity improvements in the workplace. The most well known of these techniques are described below.

Generating New and Creative Ideas

Let us begin with those situations in which new, fresh ideas are needed. As we have mentioned, in many groups not everyone is heard, in part because certain people may dominate the discussion. Also, there is a tendency for group members to prejudge suggestions as they are made, which can inhibit the free flow of ideas. Osborn (1963) was the first to propose a technique for facilitating the generation of ideas in a group. He called this technique *brainstorming*. The general procedure for brainstorming is as follows: (1) ideas are generated without reference to quality, (2) evaluation of ideas takes place only after all the ideas have been produced, and (3) people are encouraged to elaborate on the ideas of others. Under these conditions, it was hoped that more new and creative ideas would be elicited. Not only would the group have access to all the individual ideas that might be thought of alone, it would also have ideas that were triggered by other group members—ideas that an individual might not have thought of alone or while under group pressure for conformity.

The research on the use of brainstorming suggests that this technique can work. Delaying the evaluation of ideas until all the ideas have been produced can lead to more and higher quality ideas being generated. When brainstorming, people express less evaluation apprehension and are able to use creatively the ideas of others (Parnes, Noller, & Biondi, 1977).

Generating and Evaluating Alternatives

A number of techniques have been developed that attempt to regulate not only the process of idea generating and evaluation, but also the making of the decision itself—the choice of a preferred alternative. By far the most well known are the *nominal group technique* (NGT) and the *delphi technique.* Both are used when creative and independent ideas or judgments are needed. NGT is designed for a group meeting and includes the following format: (1) individuals silently and independently generate their ideas about a task or problem; (2) each member in turn presents his or her ideas to the group, and the ideas are recorded on a blackboard or flip chart; (3) after all the ideas are presented, they are discussed for clarification and evaluation; and (4) the meeting ends with a silent, independent vote on the ideas presented. The group decision is determined by various mathematical procedures using the results from the final vote (Delbecq, Van de Ven, & Gustafson, 1975).

The delphi technique is similar in many ways, but it does not require the

---

SPECIAL REPORT

Sex and Problem Solving

Your company has a problem and you need to appoint a committee to look into it. But should you choose men or women to sit on the committee? The answer, according to psychologist Wendy Wood, depends on whether you want brainstorming or a few creative solutions.

Wood and two colleagues arranged 90 male and 90 female college students into single-sex groups of three and asked them to come up with answers to three problems: the personality traits of successful people, the factors to consider when deciding on an academic major and the features (other than price) to think about when buying a house. Half of the groups were instructed to come up with as many answers as possible, and the other half were told to write down only the best answer the team could devise.

The researchers report that the average all-male group came up with 58 answers in the half-hour allotted, compared with 47 answers for women. "Men are generally more 'task-oriented' than women are," Wood says, and because men achieve status through actions calling attention to themselves, it gives them the advantage at this task, she explains.

But when the researchers analyzed the results of the discussion groups that needed to come to a consensus, the answers arrived at by the all-women groups were slightly longer, better-presented and "more creative" than those given by the men's groups. "Women in groups spend a great deal of time seeking harmony and getting everyone involved," Wood says. She says that "more positive social behavior by the women may have contributed to the success of their discussions."

The researchers note that some women tend to be extremely task-oriented, and some men are highly affiliative in groups. But on average, they say, "When the people don't know each other, men are better choices for brainstorming groups and women are better candidates when the quality of the solution is important."

Wood is at Texas A & M University. The study was published in the *Journal of Personality and Social Psychology* (Vol. 48, No. 1).

Source: J. Meer. (1985, July). *Psychology Today,* p. 13. Reprinted with permission from *Psychology Today,* Copyright © 1985 (American Psychological Association).

physical presence of the group members. Usually the procedure is as follows: (1) a questionnaire designed to solicit opinions and ideas on an issue is sent to a group of people who are unknown to one another, (2) the responses are tabulated and summarized, and a report of this information is returned to the respondents along with a second questionnaire designed to probe any issues that need further clarification or consideration, (3) the feedback report is evaluated, and respondents rate the various ideas presented, (4) the data are again tabulated, a decision is made, and a summary of the data and the decision are returned to the respondents.

There are many similarities between the two techniques. They both utilize independent work for idea generation and evaluation. All the individuals' judgments are treated equally. Both techniques separate the idea generation and evaluation stages. And both use mathematical procedures to arrive at a group decision. In short, they are designed to get maximum idea generation, equal treatment, separate evaluation, and a decision based upon mechanically pooled responses.

The differences are relatively minor. NGT members know one another, they meet face-to-face in a group, and much of their communication is direct and verbal. Delphi members are anonymous. They are physically dispersed, and they communicate only in writing. The choice of which technique to use is partly dependent upon how easy it is to assemble the group in one place, and whether the issue is so sensitive that anonymity is necessary.

The research on these techniques has been very encouraging. Comparisons with regular interacting groups or committees show that NGT and delphi groups are often superior. More ideas are generated, and people are often more satisfied with the decision process in NGT and delphi groups. Interacting

Figure 12-6
Brainstorming en-
courages people to
elaborate on the
ideas of others.

"It's our new assembly line. When the person at the end of the line has an idea, he puts it on the conveyor belt, and as it passes each of us, we mull it over and try to add to it."

groups seem to waste too much time on interpersonal relationships, ideas are evaluated prematurely, a few individuals tend to dominate the group, too much time is spent on tangential discussions, conformity often inhibits idea generation, and accomplishment is often felt to be too low (Huber, 1980; Scott & Deadrick, 1982). NGT and delphi, on the other hand, seem to ensure that everyone is heard, that the focus of the group remains on the task, that each idea gets evaluated, and that everyone has an equal vote in the final decision. The implications are clear: When confronted with decision problems in which ideas need to be creative, and criticism held to a minimum, some sort of NGT or delphi technique should increase effectiveness.

Finally, one recent study by Basadur, Graen, and Green (1982) attempted to train people to be creative not only in problem solving, but also in problem finding. The training program involved 2 days of intensive work, mostly with experiential materials (case studies, discussions, exercises to prompt divergent thinking, and so on). The trainees were engineers, their managers, and technicians in an engineering department of a large consumer goods industrial company. The design of the study involved three groups of sixteen managers each, only one of which received creativity training (the other two were control groups). The dependent variables consisted of a wide variety of measures gathered through questionnaires, interviews, and tape recordings. Some of these variables included supervisors' ratings of the subjects' creativity in the two phases of the decision-making process (problem finding and problem solving). Data were gathered both immediately following the training and 2 weeks later.

The results were very positive. They clearly showed that the trained group was more creative in both phases of the decision process. Moreover, the effect seemed to be fairly general. "There is evidence of changes in cognitive (e.g., time spent in different modes of thinking), attitudinal (e.g., openess to ideas), and behavioral (e.g., number of negative judgments made on ideas, not jumping to conclusions) processes" (p. 65). Thus, while the training program was relatively short, and the sample small, the results are quite encouraging. They suggest that individuals as well as groups can be trained to be more creative decision makers.

New Strategies for Improving Quality and Performance

A technique that has received considerable attention in recent years is the quality circle. *Quality circles* (QCs) are groups of employees that meet regularly for a total of about 4 hours a month on company time to generate and discuss potential solutions for problems affecting their work. The group usually consists of five to ten volunteers who have received some training in problem solving and group process. The reason the groups are called quality circles is that they were originally designed to deal with problems of product quality. However, more recently problems of productivity improvement and employee involvement have also been included (Yager, 1981).

A 1982 study commissioned by the New York Stock Exchange reported that 44 percent of all companies with 500 or more employees have QC programs (Lawler & Mohram, 1985). It is estimated that over 90 percent of the Fortune

500 companies have such programs, including IBM, TRW, Honeywell, Westinghouse, and Xerox. Thus, QCs are clearly popular.

On the other hand, the results regarding the effectiveness of QCs are quite mixed. For example, Ingle (1982) reports a number of successes at Mercury Marine (e.g., in eliminating damage to pistons). Another group working on the General Dynamics F-16 aircraft came up with ways to reduce defects. However, as Lawler and Mohrman (1985) report, "in our experience, few QC programs turn into other kinds of programs. More commonly, decline sets in" (p. 69). The group meets less, they become less productive, and supportive resources begin to dwindle.

A number of authors have suggested ways to improve the effectiveness of QCs. First, the groups need management support. Second, management should be patient and accepting of failures. Also, participation should be voluntary, circle leaders should be carefully chosen, and QCs should be used only in those contexts in which they are most likely to be helpful (e.g., when there are clear problems, the employees are enthusiastic about the idea, and management is committed to quality improvement). In short, QCs have sometimes been of considerable help, and they can continue to be so. But they are not a panacea for all problems. Like everything else, they need to be well managed, supported, and designed to work on appropriate issues.

Finally, a fairly recent procedure for facilitating group functioning on particular decision-making tasks is called *automated decision conferencing* (ADC). This procedure can be used for urgent, important, and complex decisions for which there are clearly different points of view. The conferences usually involve two or three day-long sessions with an executive team or work group aided by staff members trained in management science techniques, computer technology, and organizational change interventions. The objectives are to reach consensus on a solution and to document the process by which the solution was reached (Rowe, Boulgarides, & McGrath, 1984).

These groups usually involve five to fifteen people along with two or three staff support members. The staff people aid in the decision process (e.g., suggest various techniques such as brainstorming), operate the computer (e.g., call up data, make forecasts, use models), and record the decision process. The process moves through a series of distinct phases, including (1) identifying and defining the problem, (2) identifying and using computer data bases and analyses, and (3) discussing and refining the solution until consensus is reached.

It should be clear that ADC is a technique that is useful primarily for technical problems in which computer technology, decision aids, models, and formulas can be of help. Large amounts of information can be processed, and divergent views can be tested with data. Although the applications of this technique are somewhat limited, in the right situations it can be very helpful.

Thus, there are a number of formal procedures that can help to improve the quality of decision making in certain special circumstances. But what about decision making in more routine situations? For example, how can we help to improve the everyday meetings that take place to deal with run-of-the-mill operating problems in marketing, personnel, production, and so on. The next section suggests some general strategies for making ordinary group meetings more effective.

MANAGING GROUP MEETINGS

387

Chapter 12:
Group
Decision
Making

Running a group meeting requires that a lot of work be done well. Unfortunately, it is one of the things that managers do least well. If managers would simply take the time to do the necessary preliminary work, the decision processes that take place in the meeting would be much more effective.

Three factors are important for an effective group meeting: planning, staffing, and handling the meeting itself. Time spent on planning what is to be done, who should be there, and what sort of interaction should evolve can be crucial for success. We discuss each of these topics in turn (see Huber, 1980, for a review).

Planning

The first issues to be dealt with are the questions of why the group is meeting and what is expected. Although some sort of participation has already been decided upon, the question remains, How much participation? The manager must make clear exactly what the group's function is. The group members should all know whether they are expected to (1) generate ideas, (2) advise the manager, or (3) come to some sort of decision. This information should be shared explicitly and early in the group interaction.

Other planning activities involve preparing the necessary background information. Short, but precise, summaries in hand-out or slide form can be used to communicate this information. Also, time limits, deadlines for reports, and other such requirements should be thought about beforehand.

Staffing

The second premeeting issue of importance concerns who should be part of the group. There are at least four specific questions that ought to be asked. The first is, Which individuals have the necessary information? This questions focuses on the technical aspects of the decision. Clearly, those people with relevant information should be included. The second question is, who should be there for political reasons? It may be important that people who are affected by the decision, who will have to support it, or who will have to implement it be included in the process of deciding.

A third question is, How large should the group be? A group of five to seven is probably best. It is likely to yield the most effective exchange of information. A final question is, How heterogeneous should the group be? The answer to this question entails a trade-off. The more heterogeneous the group (i.e., the more different types of people included), the more the group is likely to come up with different ideas and new points of view. However, it is also true that heterogeneous groups have more conflict and have greater difficulty in reaching agreement. The implication is that the manager must match the heterogeneity of the group with the purpose he or she wants to achieve. If the purpose is simply idea generation, a heterogeneous group may do well. If, on the other hand, a decision is required about which there must be agreement, harmony, and commitment, a homogeneous group (similar people) may be more appropriate.

Group Process

The final area of preliminary work is designed to handle and structure the actual group interaction. You may recall that in our discussion of group dynamics we mentioned a number of problems that occur in groups. Some of these are that (1) certain individuals talk more than others, (2) high-status individuals have more impact on decisions than low-status individuals, (3) groups often spend a great deal of time on interpersonal smoothing, (4) groups may lose sight of their goal and get off on irrelevant issues, and (5) group members often experience extreme pressure to conform. Anyone who has tried to run a meeting is probably familiar with these problems.

A manager cannot always make these problems go away. However, with proper preparation, he or she can minimize their disruptiveness. First, make sure everyone is acquainted. This may entail having people give a short description of who they are, what they do, and why they are there. Second, make sure people know the purpose of the meeting, the goals, the agenda, and the time limitations. This information will help structure the process. Start the meeting with a short synopsis, stick to the agenda, and summarize at the

Figure 12-7
Decision making is
often performed in
groups.

end. Make sure that people have an opportunity to speak by using a round robin technique or other similar procedure designed to solicit input.

Also remember that the physical setting can make a difference. A rectangular conference table with one chair at the head sets a very different tone from a round table. Comfortable chairs with coffee and doughnuts implies something different from straight-back chairs without refreshments. Tape-recording the meeting or having a secretary take detailed notes has an impact on the freedom of the discussion. In short, both the personal characteristics of the group members and the physical properties of the setting can be manipulated to influence the type of process that evolves.

Running a meeting requires a lot of work. What is often not recognized is that those people who are good at running meetings are usually successful because they have prepared in advance. They have thought ahead of time about how to control those who are difficult or disruptive, draw out information from the timid or powerless, and encourage a clash of ideas and creativity. With careful planning about who should be there and how the group meeting should be run, many problems can be avoided or at least minimized.

CONTINGENCY MODELS FOR GROUP DECISION MAKING

Earlier in the chapter we described several contingency models that have been developed around the participation question. We pointed out, however, that the effectiveness of group decision making depends on far more than just the degree of participation. Group process is equally important. To date, there has been only one major contingency model that has focused on the question of group process. This model was proposed by Stumpf, Zand, and Freedman (1979).

These authors present their model as a summary of many of the factors we have already mentioned. Thus, they suggest that in preparing for a group meeting, a manager should (1) identify and formulate the problem, (2) define the decision criterion, (3) decide on how the situation should be structured (where, when, size of group, physical characteristics of the rom), and (4) select both the group members and the group decision-making process to be used. They lay out some of the possible alternatives that exist when different types of group composition are crossed with different types of decision-making processes. Figure 12-8 shows how these various combinations result in nine types of groups.

Criterion for Selection of Group Members	Decision-Making Procedure		
	Interacting (Discussion in All Phases)	Nominal (Discussion in Evaluation Only)	Delphi (No Face-to-Face Exchange)
Expertise	1	2	3
Political representation	4	5	6
Coworkers	7	8	9

Figure 12-8
Types of decision-making groups. (*Adapted from Stumpf, Zand & Freedman, 1979.*)

The question before the manager is how to decide which type of group to use. The authors, in reviewing previous research, develop eight basic design propositions for helping in this selection process. Each proposition examines the feasibility of using one or more types of group based on information about (1) the need for a high-quality decision, (2) the scope (span) of the decision problem, (3) the availability of expertise, (4) the possibility of group conflict, (5) the need for originality, and/or (6) the need for acceptance. Figure 12-9 gives a summary of these propositions and how they narrow down the choice of the appropriate type of group.

As can be seen, this model is similar to the Vroom and Yetton (1973) model in a number of ways. It is basically a diagnostic approach. That is, it gives the manager a set of questions to ask before the group convenes. With a proper diagnosis, the manager may be able to narrow down considerably the list of preferred alternatives regarding both group membership and group process. While this model falls short of specifying exactly what type of group should be used for each type of problem, it does an excellent job of laying out some of the parameters for diagnosing the situation.

One large empirical study tested this model (Stumpf, Freedman, & Zand, 1979). In this study 540 business students worked in five-person groups. Six different types of groups were established. Half of the groups used a regular interacting group process and half used a nominal group technique. Within each of these categories, group members were either subject-matter experts, representatives of special interest groups, or coworkers for whose work the decision was relevant. Each group was confronted with one of six problems (cases), which varied on the dimensions of (1) required acceptance, (2) required originality, (3) effect of decision on external consultants, and (4) availability of expertise. The effectiveness of the group decisions (as rated by independent judges) served as the criteria.

The findings provided preliminary support for the model. The decisions of groups predicted by the model to be least effective were actually rated less favorably than were the decisions of groups predicted by the model to be most effective. For example, when acceptance was not needed, representative groups did not do as well as expert or coworker groups. When creativity and originality were needed, a nominal group method did better than an interacting group method. When acceptance was needed but originality was not, an interacting group method did better than a nominal group method. These results are consistent with a more recent analysis done by Murnighan (1981).

While more work needs to be done with this model, the approach is laudable. Very little research has so far tried to match group process and membership with the decision at hand. The work of Stumpf and his colleagues, along with research by Hackman and Morris (1975), represents a significant beginning in this important area.

We close by noting that diagnostic skills can be learned through experience as well as through the use of formal models. Earlier in the chapter we mentioned that groupthink can be blamed for some of the faulty decisions made at the highest levels of our government. However, President Kennedy seemed to have learned something from the decision-making problems he encountered in the Bay of Pigs fiasco. You will recall that during that episode little disagreement was expressed by the president's advisors (although much

Proposition	Characteristics
P1 Quality and acceptance needed: A∩B→eliminate delphi method	When the quality of the decision and its acceptance by those affected by it are important, a group method permitting discussion in the evaluation phase is desirable. The delphi method is eliminated from the preferred set.
P2 Quality but not acceptance needed: A∩B̄→eliminate representative groups	When the quality of the decision is important but acceptance is not, representative membership is unnecessary. Representative groups are eliminated from the preferred set.
P3 Acceptance but not quality relevant: B∩Ā→eliminate expert groups	When quality is not relevant but acceptance is, expertise is redundant and a representative group is most likely to formulate an acceptable decision. External expert group members are eliminated from the preferred set.
P4 Quality and originality needed: A∩D→eliminate interacting method	When a creative or original decision is required, groups that do not inhibit originality are desirable. The interacting method is known to produce fewer original ideas than other methods. The interacting method is eliminated from the preferred set.
P5 Quality, acceptance, and broad span: A∩B∩C→eliminate coworker groups	When the decision has a broad span and acceptance is critical, the membership of the group should include individuals from all relevant constituencies. Coworker groups are eliminated from the preferred set.
P6 Quality, acceptance, and narrow span: A∩B∩C̄→eliminate expert groups	When the decision has a narrow span and acceptance is critical, experts outside the affected group are not required. Expert groups are eliminated from the preferred set.
P7 Quality but no internal expertise: A∩Ē→eliminate coworker groups	When knowledge and information are required for a high-quality decision but are not available within the convener's immediate resources, outside experts are required. Coworker groups are eliminated from the preferred set.
P8 Quality, acceptance, no originality, but conflict: A∩B∩D̄∩F→eliminate nominal and delphi methods	When disagreement among members concerning the synthesis of a solution is likely, and when acceptance is critical and innovativeness is not necessary, an interactive method (which helps resolve differences) should be used. Nominal and delphi methods of group functioning are eliminated from the preferred set.

Note: A = quality; B = acceptance; C = decision span; D = originality; E = expertise; F = conflict. The sign ∩ is set theory notation for "intersection," meaning both conditions apply simultaneously. A bar over a letter signifies "no" or elimination; for example, A∩B̄ means "quality but not acceptance."

Figure 12-9
Propositions underlying the Stumpf, Zand, and Freedman (1979) decision-making model.

was reportedly felt), that all those involved believed they were morally correct in their actions, and that there was a great deal of pressure to support the President.

When the Cuban missile crisis subsequently arose, Kennedy apparently used a very different strategy. First, he thought systematically about the group membership. He went out of his way to have people with different opinions present. Second, he tried to influence the group process in a number of ways. For example, he was adamant about not expressing his own opinion. He also actively encouraged disagreement and dissent. In some cases he absented himself from the sessions altogether so that people would be encouraged to say what they felt. Kennedy was also aware of the trappings of his office and the status that was attached to it.

In short, his experience with the Bay of Pigs decision made him very sensitive to the issues described in this chapter, and probably made him a more effective decision maker. His handling of the Cuban missile crisis is recognized as an example of superb decision making under extreme stress. Part of that excellence can be attributed to Kennedy's having learned from experience how to get the best information out of those people intimately involved in the decision.

Summary

Chapter 11 and 12 are really a package, in the sense that they both deal with decision making. The highlights of Chapter 12 are as follows:

1. Group decision making is similar to individual decision making in that the stages of problem recognition, information gathering, generation and evaluation of solution alternatives, and choice all occur. However, group decision making is more complex, since multiple judgments must be combined in some or all of these phases.
2. The effectiveness of group decision making depends both on the right degree of participation being used and on the group process itself. The former has been more thoroughly studied than the latter.
3. The research on participation shows that, in general (i.e., for different types of problems and people), participation creates greater satisfaction but may or may not affect performance.
4. When participation works, it does so because there is more information, a broader perspective, better understanding, and higher commitment. When it fails, it is often because participative decision making is slow, conflicts develop, or individuals have little interest or knowledge about the issues involved.
5. Contingency models developed by people such as Vroom and Yetton (1973), Nutt (1976), and Sashkin (1976) can help managers choose the appropriate amount of participation.
6. Once participation is decided upon, the second crucial step for effective group decision making is to manage the group process and procedures. Proper planning, staffing, and the structuring of the group interaction can help in this regard.
7. Specific techniques for creative decision making are available. Brainstorming, the delphi method, and the nominal group technique (NGT) all are designed to maximize idea generation and minimize early criticism and evaluation.
8. Quality circles are sometimes helpful for dealing with issues of performance quality, while automated decision conferencing can be helpful for dealing with divergent views when computer technology can be brought to bear.

9. Diagnostic contingency models for the management of group process in decision making are not as well developed as are those for choosing the level of participation. However, the work of Stumpf, Zand, and Freedman (1979) is a positive move in that direction.

IMPLICATIONS FOR RESEARCH

A number of issues need to be addressed by researchers interested in group decision making. First, we need substantially more knowledge about group process, that is, about how information is generated, processed, analyzed, communicated, and used in groups. Because decision making in groups requires the exchange and integration of ideas, beliefs, and values, we need to know more about how and under what circumstances people change their opinions. We suspect that much of the literature on bargaining and attitude change may be helpful here, but its application to group decision processes needs to be pursued.

A second area of research that would be extremely helpful is the development of more refined diagnostic contingency models. Basically, this approach requires a good understanding of the decision task and its requirements. This is an area of research that has received little attention in recent years, partly due to its incredible complexity and difficulty. McCormick and Ilgen (1985) and McGrath (1984) discuss ways to classify tasks in general, and the work on structural role theory (Oeser & Harary, 1962) and on job enrichment (Hackman & Oldham, 1980) also includes some general dimensions for describing tasks. But more work specifically focused on group decision-making tasks is needed if we are going to develop contingency models of effective decision-making processes.

Finally, while the development of techniques such as NGT and delphi have certainly been useful, they are designed to deal with a fairly specific type of task—one that requires creative input and in which premature criticism of alternatives needs to be avoided. There are obviously other types of decision tasks, and we need to develop techniques that will help us solve these kinds of problems too. The automated decision conferencing technique is an example of a procedure to use when disagreement is already present (as opposed to techniques designed to reduce groupthink when too much agreement is present). More research is needed in these areas if we are to evolve a truly complete understanding of group decision processes.

IMPLICATIONS FOR PRACTICE

This chapter is important for a variety of reasons. The first and perhaps most important reason is the fact that participation in decision making is dramatically increasing in organizations. The explanations for this increase are numerous. One is the inherent political nature of participation. Because participation implies power sharing, it is at the heart of a democratic system.

As employees demand more and more say in the decisions that affect their lives, we will see greater pressure for widespread participation.

The second reason this chapter is important is that it suggests that managers can do far more than they presently do to increase the effectiveness of the group decision-making process. The diagnostic models presented in this chapter should make it clear that choices about the level and amount of participation can be made rationally and with some degree of confidence. When managers resent participation, when a quick decision is needed, when subordinates have little information or interest, or when conflict is likely, participation should not be used. On the other hand, when information and commitment are needed, conflict is unlikely, and time is available, participation can be quite beneficial.

One final point cannot be understated: *The group process can and should be managed.* The time spent prior to the actual meeting can be crucial. Planning objectives; developing summaries, handouts, and displays; choosing the members of a group with regard to the objectives—these are all important, yet they are frequently overlooked. The one factor that receives perhaps the least attention is the group process itself. In very few meetings is the interaction process actively discussed or controlled.

It is not difficult to diagnose the decision situation. When faced with a decision about participation, one can refer to six or seven simple questions and in a short amount of time make a reasonable choice. When a group meeting is being planned, there are also simple diagnostic questions available to help deal with planning, staffing, and most important of all, managing the group process. Adequately preparing for a meeting can dramatically increase the effectiveness of the group decision process.

Discussion Questions

1. In what ways is group decision making more complex than individual decision making? Describe some group decisions with which you have been involved in which the process was particularly difficult.
2. Should students be part of the decision process when faculty make decisions on (1) course offerings, (2) teaching schedules, (3) hiring and promotion, or (4) compensation? Why or why not?
3. Have you ever been in a group in which someone deliberately tried to influence or structure the group process? What happened? Did it work?

CASE: GUIDELINES AND STANDARDS—WHO DECIDES?

Jack O'Brian was the regional manager of a larger chain of retail grocery stores. Two constant problems faced by the company over the years were the haphazard way that products were stacked and stored when delivered, and incorrect placement of the merchandise in the store itself. O'Brian's boss felt strongly that these procedures could be handled more systematically and efficiently, and she assigned the responsibility to Jack to find out how this could be done.

The first thing that O'Brian did was to hire an outside consultant to analyze the system as it currently operated. Roving observers with stopwatches and cameras were sent to gather data. Each activity was filmed and timed. The number of boxes stored and where they were stored were recorded. Time spent on breaks, rest pauses, and social interactions was computed. In short, a thorough time and motion study was conducted.

The consultants took all of this information and fed it into the computer. After many weeks of analyzing the data, they wrote a 200-page report for O'Brian and sent it to him along with their recommendations.

O'Brian got the report on a Thursday morning and read quickly through the summary and "action steps" section. It was clear from this report that (1) new guidelines needed to be established for performance on the job, and (2) performance was significantly below what was optimal. He was so agitated by the report that he called up Ian Cooper, the supervisor of the loading crew at one of the stores. He was informed that Cooper was at a district meeting of all loading crew supervisors and would be unavailable until later in the day.

Jack decided that something needed to be done quickly. He picked up the report and drove over to the store where the supervisors were meeting. He broke into their meeting and asked them if they could meet again the following day at 8 A.M. to discuss the report. He briefly summarized what the report said and indicated his distress.

The next morning O'Brian met with the supervisors. He had made copies of the consultants' report for everyone, and he distributed these immediately. He told them he felt strongly that new guidelines were needed and that the supervisors should help him set them up.

To make a long story short, this meeting and the two that followed were disasters. The supervisors disagreed with just about every recommendation made by the consultants. They voted down every proposal that was seriously considered. From their perspective, they thought that the standards might even be lowered rather than raised. When O'Brian finished with this series of meetings he felt that somehow he was in worse shape than when he started. He did not know where he had gone wrong or what to do next.

Questions about the Case

1. Was Jack O'Brian's preparation for this meeting adequate? Did he have all the information he needed?
2. Was the composition of the group the best possible?
3. How about the group process—could it or should it have been structured? Should decisions have been made by a majority-rule voting procedure?
4. All in all, had O'Brian chosen the right level of participation?

References

Basadur, M., Graen, G. B., & Green, S. G. (1982). Training in creative problem solving: Effects on ideation and problem finding and solving in an industrial research organization. *Organizational Behavior and Human Performance, 30,* 41–70.

Courtright, J. A. (1978). A laboratory investigation of groupthink. *Communication Monographs, 45,* 229–246.

Dachler, H. P., & Wilpert, B. (1978). Conceptual dimensions and boundaries of participation in organizations: A critical evaluation. *Administrative Science Quarterly, 23,* 1–39.

Delbecq, A. L., Van de Ven, A. H., & Gustafson, D. H. (1975). *Group techniques for program planning.* Glenview, IL: Scott, Foresman.

Field, R. H. G. (1982). A test of the Vroom-Yetton normative model of leadership. *Journal of Applied Psychology, 67,* 523–532.

Flowers, M. L. (1977). A laboratory test of some implications of Janis's groupthink hypothesis. *Journal of Personality and Social Psychology, 35,* 888–896.

Hackman, J. R., & Morris, C. G. (1975). Group tasks, group interaction process and group performance effectiveness. In L. Berkowitz (Ed.), *Advances in experimental social psychology* (Vol. 8, pp. 45–99). New York: Academic Press.

Hackman, J. R., & Oldham, G. R. (1980). *Work redesign.* Reading, MA: Addison-Wesley.

Heilman, M. E., Hornstein, H. A., Cage, J. H., & Herschlag, J. K. (1984). Reactions to prescribed leader behavior as a function of role perspective: The case of the Vroom-Yetton model. *Journal of Applied Psychology, 69,* 50–60.

Hespe, G., & Wall, T. (1976). The demand for participation among employees. *Human Relations, 29,* 411–429.

Huber, G. R. (1980). *Managerial decision making.* Glenview, IL: Scott, Foresman.

Ingle, S. (1982, June). How to avoid quality circle failure in your company. *Training and Development Journal,* pp. 54–59.

Janis, I. L. (1972). *Victims of groupthink: A psychological study of foreign policy decisions and fiascos.* Boston: Houghton Mifflin.

Janis, I. L., & Mann, L. (1977). *Decision making.* New York: Free Press.

Krishnan, R. (1974). Democratic participation in decision making by employees in American corporations. *Academy of Management Journal, 17,* 339–347.

Lawler, E. E. III, & Mohrman, S. A. (1985, January–February). Quality circles after the fad. *Harvard Business Review,* pp. 65–71.

Locke, E. A., & Schweiger, P. M. (1979). Participation in decision making: One more look. In B. M. Staw (Ed.), *Research in organizational behavior* (Vol. 1, pp. 265–339). Greenwich, CT: JAI Press.

Maier, N. R. F. (1967). Assets and liabilities in group problem solving: The need for an integrative function. *Psychological Review, 74,* 238–249.

McCormick, E. J., & Ilgen, D. R. (1985). *Industrial and Organizational Psychology* (8th ed.). Englewood Cliffs, NJ: Prentice-Hall.

McGrath, J. E. (1984). *Groups: Interaction and performance.* Englewood Cliffs, NJ: Prentice-Hall.

Miner, F. C., Jr. (1984). Group versus individual decision making: An investigation of performance measures, decision strategies and process losses/gains. *Organizational Behavior and Human Performance, 33,* 112–124.

Mitchell, T. R., Rediker, K. J., & Beach, L. R. (1986). Image theory and organizational decision making. In H. P. Sims, Jr., & D. A. Gioia (Eds.), *The thinking organization: Dynamics of organizational social cognition* (pp. 293–316). San Francisco: Jossey-Bass.

Murnighan, J. K. (1981, February). Group decision making: What strategy should you use? *Management Review,* pp. 55–62.

Nutt, P. C. (1976, April). Models for decision making in organizations and some contextual variables which stipulate optimal use. *Academy of Management Review,* pp. 94–98.

Oeser, O. A., & Harary, F. (1962). A mathematical model for structural role theory, *Human Relations, 15,* 89–109.

Osborn, A. F. (1963). *Applied imagination: Principles and procedures of creative thinking.* New York: Scribner's.

Parnes, S. J., Noller, R. B., & Biondi, A. M. (1977). *A guide to creative action.* New York: Scribner's.

Rowe, A. J., Boulgarides, J. D., & McGrath, M. R. (1984). *Managerial decision making.* Chicago: Science Research Associates.

Sashkin, M. (1976, July). Changing towards participative management approaches: A model and methods. *Academy of Management Review,* pp. 75–86.

Scott, O., & Deadrick, D. (1982, June). The nominal group technique: Applications for training needs assessment. *Training and Development Journal*, pp. 26–33.

Selznick, P. (1957). *Leadership in administration: A sociological interpretation.* New York: Harper & Row.

Steiner, I. D. (1972). *Group process and productivity.* NY: Academic Press.

Stumpf, S. A., Freedman, R. D., & Zand, D. E. (1979). Judgment decisions: A study of interactions among group membership, group functioning and the decision situation. *Academy of Management Journal, 22,* 765–782.

Stumpf, S. A., Zand, D. E., & Freedman, R. D. (1979). Designing groups for judgmental decisions. *Academy of Management Review, 4,* 589–600.

Tetlock, P. E. (1979). Identifying victims of groupthink from public statements of decision makers. *Journal of Personality and Social Psychology, 37,* 1314–1324.

Van Gundy, A. G. (1984, August). How to establish a creative climate in the work group. *Management Review,* pp. 24–28.

Vroom, V. H., & Jago, A. G. (1978). On the validity of the Vroom-Yetton model. *Journal of Applied Psychology, 63,* 151–162.

Vroom, V. H., & Yetton, P. W. (1973). *Leadership and decision making.* Pittsburgh: University of Pittsburgh Press.

Yager, E. G. (1981, April). The quality control circle explosion. *Training and Development Journal,* pp. 98–105.

Yetton, P., & Bottger, P. (1983). The relationship among group size, member ability, social decision schemes and performance. *Organizational Behavior and Human Performance, 32,* 145–159.

Chapter 13

Power and Politics

Nobody yields to force unless he is forced to.
—BRECHT

In Chapter 3, "Understanding Organizations," we noted that when joining an organization, people must voluntarily give up some of their individual flexibility and freedom. In order for an organization to meet its goals, compromises must be made. Not everyone can do exactly what he or she wants to do. However, reaching a compromise, channeling effort in a given direction, and getting people to do things that they might not normally elect to do are all difficult tasks. If you are to succeed in convincing a subordinate, a peer, or even your boss to do something that you personally would like to see done, you will first need to develop a base of *social power*. And if your department or organizational unit is to secure the resources it needs in order to grow and prosper (e.g., more budget, staff positions, and/or physical space), it may have to exercise some *political clout*. Power and politics are thus key ingredients for getting things done in organizations. In this chapter we discuss these concepts in detail.

There are two major areas of ambiguity surrounding the topics of power and politics that we hope to clarify in this chapter. First, there is some degree of conceptual ambiguity about the meaning of these terms—different authors use rather different definitions. One of our goals will be to clear up this confusion by showing what these definitions have in common and where the major areas of disagreement lie. It is hoped that this exercise will provide answers to such questions as, how is power different from social influence or leadership? and is organizational politics a good thing or a bad thing?

Second, there is ambiguity in practice. People in organizations are often unsure about how much freedom they have and how much they should relinquish. The agreement they have with the organization regarding their latitude of action is for the most part informal, implicit, and unclear. Because of this ambiguity, a great deal of controversy often revolves around the use of power and politics. Yet every manager knows that these are a necessary part of organizational life. Therefore, we will not only describe these processes and their effects, but also evaluate them. We will indicate how power and politics can be used both constructively and destructively. Thus, we hope to provide a more balanced picture of how they influence organizational effectiveness.

SOCIAL POWER

The topic of social power has intrigued scientists and philosophers throughout history. "That some people have more power than others is one of the most palpable facts of human existence," wrote Robert Dahl in his discussion of social power (1957, p. 201). "Because of this," he continued, "the concept of power is as ancient and ubiquitous as any that social theory can boast."

But what is this thing called "social power," and how does it differ from such related concepts as social influence, leadership, and politics? The answer is that all are concerned with behavior change in organizational settings, but differ with respect to the initiator and target of the change. Look at Figure 13-1. Across the top of this figure we have distinguished between individuals and groups as initiators of behavior change, while down the side we have distinguished between individuals and groups as targets of the change attempt. When a group tries to change the behavior of an individual, that process is called *social influence*. Many of the mechanisms of social influence were

Target of Change Attempt	Initiator of Change Attempt	
	Individual	**Group**
Individual	Social power	Social influence
Group	Leadership	Political behavior

FIGURE 13-1
A Classification of Social Power and Related Concepts

discussed previously in Chapters 8 and 9 (e.g., roles, norms, group cohesiveness). When one individual tries to affect the behavior of a group, the process is called *leadership*—a topic to be discussed in Chapter 14. When one group tries to influence another group, the process is often placed under the heading of *political behavior*. Organizational politics are discussed more fully later in this chapter. Finally, we come to *social power*—the situation in which one individual tries to change the behavior of another individual. Thus, social power focuses on those relationships among people in which one person tries to get another to do something.

A Decision Theory Analysis of Social Power

There are a number of different theoretical perspectives on the nature of social power (e.g., Emerson, 1962; Kelley & Thibaut, 1978; Lewin, 1951; March, 1955). One that we find particularly useful involves a decision theory analysis and makes use of the expected-value formulation previously discussed in Chapters 6 and 11 (cf. Pollard & Mitchell, 1972). According to this perspective, a person (B) who is the target of an influence attempt can be seen as making a choice between two alternatives: compliance and noncompliance. B should choose the alternative that has the highest expected value—the one that has the *highest probability* of leading to outcomes that B *values*. Individual A has power over B to the extent that A can increase the expected value of compliance and decrease the expected value of noncompliance.

This decision theory analysis has several important implications. First, the power of A is defined in terms of what B values and feels is likely to happen as a result of his or her behavior. Strictly speaking, A's feelings and actual behavior are not relevant. Second, B can respond both to an anticipated request and to an actual one. What is important is B's *feeling* that A wants something. Third, B does not actually have to comply in order for A to be considered to have power. The power of A is defined in terms of the pressure B feels. This pressure is a result both of how much B values the outcomes he or she believes A may control, and of B's beliefs about the likelihood of their occurrence. Also, whether B would have performed the act without A requesting it is not critical. Power is defined in terms of the *pressure* A brings to bear on B to comply. Even if the expected value of compliance exceeded that of noncompliance *before* A requested it, if the expected value of compliance *increases* and the expected value of noncompliance *decreases* after the request, then A has power. Finally, power can be reciprocal. That is, B can also have power over A by controlling outcomes that A values.

Some Examples of Social Power

To help clarify this decision theory analysis of social power, consider the following situation. Imagine that you are at home on a Saturday morning thinking about whether you should finish up some work or go out to play handball. You decide that the work can wait, and you get ready to go over to a nearby gym. Just as you are about to leave, the phone rings. It is your boss, inquiring about the status of a report that you know needs to be finished. Your boss reminds you that the report is due on Monday. What do you do?

If you decide to forgo playing handball and go to the office instead, this is a clear-cut case of social power. Your boss (individual A) has brought pressure to bear on you (individual B), and you have changed your behavior.

But what if the handball match is a crucial one? You belong to a team and you have a shot at the city championship. If you are not there, the team will forfeit, and there will be no hope of competing in the playoffs. The alternative of going to work is made more attractive by your boss's call (due to the potential rewards for complying and punishments for not complying), but the handball match is very important. Instead of an easy decision (one with a large difference in expected value between compliance and noncompliance), you now have a very difficult decision (the expected values of both alternatives are nearly equal).

Suppose you decide to play handball. Now the question is, Did A have power over B in this situation even though B did not comply? According to a decision theory analysis, the answer is *yes*. And according to common sense, the answer is *yes*. Research has shown that if you ask B whether A has power in such situations, B will respond affirmatively. The pressure was felt—it just was not enough to ensure compliance.

The same would be true if you had decided to go to work *before* your boss called. Perhaps before the call the decision was a tough one, but work still had a slightly higher expected value than handball. However, after the call there is little dilemma. You are still going to go to work, but now it is an easy choice—the pressure brought to bear by A on B increased the expected value of compliance. Again, theory, common sense, and research suggest that A has power in such situations.

One final point: Let us say that part of the reason you decide to go to work is that you think your boss will put in a good word for you to the vice president of your division, and perhaps you will get that raise you want (a positive outcome). For various reasons you may have come to believe that your boss and the vice president are on good terms and that they see each other frequently. In reality it may be that your boss seldom sees the vice president, and when they do meet, your boss rarely discusses the work of subordinates. However, the reality of the situation is not what influences you. It is what *you think* your boss can do, not what your boss *actually* can do that influences your decision.

To summarize, a decision theory definition of social power focuses on the force that A can bring to bear on B to act in accordance with A's wishes. This force is determined by asking B about his or her perceptions of what A wants and is likely to do if B complies or does not comply, and how important those consequences are to B. If A's perceived or actual request in some way increases B's desire to comply, or decreases B's desire not to comply, then A has exerted power over B. Thus, someone has power over you to the extent that (1) you think that person controls, and will make use of, outcomes (resources) to back up his or her request, (2) you value the outcomes that may result, and (3) you have few alternatives, that is, complying with the request is the only way you can obtain those outcomes.

POWER IN USE

Having examined some of the complexities of defining what social power is, we are now better prepared to discuss how it is used in organizations. As we have seen, some of the important components of the power relationship are the resources at A's disposal, B's dependency on those resources, and B's alternatives. The next three sections discuss these factors.

Power Resources

What are some of the resources that B might perceive A to have that would be important for B's decision? French and Raven's (1960) classic analysis of this issue suggests the following six categories of resources:

1. *Rewards.* Reward power refers to the number of positive incentives B thinks A has to offer. Can A promote B? To what degree can A determine how much B earns or when B takes a vacation? To some extent, A's reward power is a function of the formal responsibilities inherent in his or her position.

2. *Punishment.* Punishment power has to do with the negative things that B believes A can do. Can A fire me, dock my pay, give me miserable assignments, or reprimand me? These factors are again often organizationally and formally determined as part of A's position.

3. *Information.* As we suggested in Chapter 10, "Communication," information can be a source of power. This is especially true for information gatekeepers. They can decide who should know what. To the extent that B thinks A controls information B wants and perhaps needs, then A has power. This information can be both formally *and* informally gathered and distributed.

4. *Legitimacy.* Legitimate power as a resource stems from B's feeling that A has a right to make a given request. Legitimate power is sometimes described as authority. The norms and expectations prevalent in the social situation help to determine A's legitimate power: Has A done this before? Have others complied? Is the request job related? Is the request appropriate given A's status in the organizational hierarchy?

5. *Expertise.* A may be an expert on some topic or issue. If so, B will often comply with A's wishes simply because B believes that A "knows best" what should be done in this situation. Expertise and ability are almost entirely a function of A's personal characteristics (e.g., training, experience) rather that A's formal position in the organization.

6. *Referent power.* In some cases B will look up to and admire A as a person. B may want to be similar to A and be liked by A. In this situation, B may comply with A's demands because B identifies with A and wants to achieve whatever goals and objectives A wants to achieve. Note again that this resource is mostly a function of A's personal qualities (e.g., charisma).

Several examples might help to clarify how these resources work. A large industrial organization once hired as one of its vice presidents an individual who had been a prominent cabinet member during Gerald Ford's tenure as

President of the United States. After talking with this individual's subordinates, it became clear that he had much more power than other vice presidents in similar positions in the company. The reason was that he had both expertise and referent power. This individual was a recognized expert who had a charismatic personality. People were more than willing to respond to both anticipated and actual requests.

Another example comes from our observations at a military base. In this instance a number of junior officers had indicated that their commanding officer was a "cold fish" (low referent power) and had limited knowledge about the type of aircraft the men were flying (low expert power). However, one had only to watch the interactions between this commanding officer and his junior officers to see that there was politeness, obedience, and high motivation to meet the commander's demands. The explanation given by these men when interviewed was that their commander had control over important rewards and punishments, knew the "organizational ropes" and how to use them, and would act upon his judgments. In short, he could make or break them and would not hesitate to do so.

Finally, an example cited by Salancik and Pfeffer (1977) shows the importance of information. These researchers were investigating patterns of power and influence in an insurance company. They found that one of the most powerful individuals in the company was the woman in charge of the coding function. Her department rated, recorded, and kept track of the codes of all policy applications and contracts. The information she had and the speed with which she retrieved and distributed it affected virtually every other department in the company. Because of other people's dependence on this information, this woman was seen as the third most powerful department head (out of twenty-one), even though her place in the organizational chart was substantially lower.

Research on the Bases of Power

In comparing the six bases of social power discussed, it should be clear that one's level of reward and punishment power depends to a large extent upon one's access to organizational resources. One's informational and legitimate power, on the other hand, depend more simply upon one's position in the organization. In the case of informational power, it is one's position in the communication network that is crucial, while legitimate power depends on one's position in the formal organizational authority structure. Finally, one's expert and referent power are not dependent on the organization at all. Rather, these are totally dependent upon one's personal characteristics.

The empirical research on these six bases of social power shows that, while all of the power bases are used, the particular mix employed in any given situation depends upon the circumstance and the people involved. In general, people prefer to use expert and legitimate power rather than negative sanctions or appeals to friendship. For example, one study showed that M.B.A.s prefer the use of data and evidence first, reason second, and the "big picture" (legitimacy) third. Rewards and friendship follow, with threats, anger, and punishment at the bottom (Dyer, 1979). A study of the influence tactics used by 360 first- and second-line managers from the United States, Australia, and

Great Britain revealed similar results (Kipnis, Schmidt, Swaffin-Smith, & Wilkinson, 1984). When these managers were asked how often they use various strategies for influencing their subordinates, they reported using reason most often and the threat of punishment least often. Appeals based on friendship were used an intermediate amount.

Not only do managers use different bases of power in different amounts, their ability to use these power bases varies dramatically depending on who they are trying to influence. This point was nicely demonstrated in a study by Kahn, Wolfe, Quinn, Snoek, and Rosenthal (1964). These authors asked managers the extent to which they were able to use four different bases of power to influence (1) a subordinate, (2) a peer in their work unit, and (3) their supervisor. The results are presented in Figure 13-2. Two aspects of these results deserve comment. First, the managers reported being able to use more bases of power for influencing their subordinates than for influencing either their peers or their supervisors. Second, the managers felt they were able to use expert power equally well with subordinates, peers, and supervisors. Thus, the bases of power that managers use in a given situation are likely to be strongly affected by who it is they are trying to influence.

There are also some individual differences in the use of various bases of power. For example, managers who are less authoritarian and more participative in their style tend to rely on expertise and referent power to get things done, while more authoritarian, less participative managers tend to use more formal resources such as rewards and punishments. Additionally, people with an internal locus of control are often more likely to use personal persuasive powers (e.g., expert and legitimate power) when dealing with problem

FIGURE 13-2

Managers reported being able to use more bases of power for influencing their subordinates than for influencing either their peers or their supervisor. Note: Higher numbers indicate a greater ability to use the power base rated. (*Based on data presented by Kahn, Wolfe, Quinn, Snoek, & Rosenthal, 1964.*)

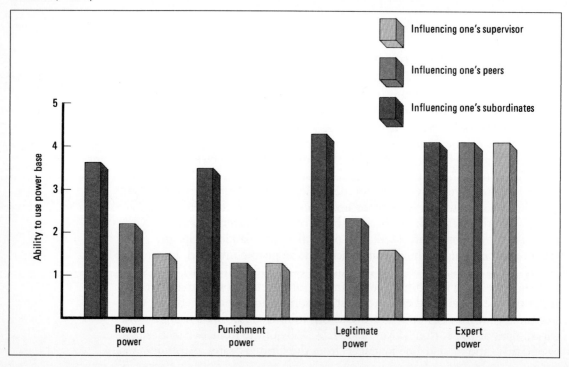

subordinates, while those with an external locus of control are more likely to use punishment power (Goodstadt & Hjelle, 1973). (For a review of authoritarianism and locus of control see Chapter 4, pp. 102–106).

Finally, the nature of the organization itself is likely to affect the bases of power that organizational members use. In highly formalized organizations, for example, in which rules, regulations, standard operating procedures, and job responsibilities are all very clearly specified, it is likely that there will be a higher reliance on reward and punishment power than is the case in informal organizations, in which there are fewer rules, regulations, and standard operating procedures, and in which job responsibilities are less clearly defined. Formalization serves to clarify exactly what job behaviors are expected and when it is and is not appropriate to use rewards and sanctions. It is the increased clarity about when to use these two bases of power that leads to their actually being used more often.

In summary, which bases of social power managers draw on to exert influence in organizations depends on many things. It depends on (1) their access to organizational resources, (2) their location in both the communication network and the formal organizational structure, (3) who they are trying to influence, (4) their own personal characteristics, and (5) the characteristics of the organization itself.

Power and Dependence

So far we have focused on what B thinks are the reasons for A's request and the possible outcomes that may occur as a function of compliance or noncompliance. An equally important question has to do with B's dependence upon A. That is, to what extent does it matter to B what A does? There are a number of factors that contribute to this dependency, including B's values, the nature of the relationship, and B's ability to counter the pressure being exerted.

B's Values. If the outcomes that A can influence are important to B, the pressure to comply will be greater than if the outcomes are irrelevant to B. If A is B's boss, then A should be able to control some important outcomes for B. B may want a raise, a promotion, to be "in the know," or to be socially accepted. One mark of an excellent manager is that he or she understands and uses the resources that people value. And because different individuals are likely to value different things, this means that a good manager will treat people *differently*. He or she will use different—but appropriate—resources for influencing different people.

The Relationship. Another factor is the type of relationship that A and B are in. Are they peers, or a boss and a subordinate? Is this a paying job or a volunteer group? Is this summer work or one's first professional position? The question here is, how important to B is the relationship itself? Short-term jobs are generally less important than long-term ones. A volunteer group may be less important than a position that provides one with steady income. It may be less damaging to refuse a peer than a superior. Thus, part of B's considerations are often about the relationship itself. If B decides that the relationship is not very important or that it is short-term, B will be less likely to comply.

Counterpower. A final issue is B's ability to change the pressure being brought to bear by A. This is referred to as B's *counterpower*. Counterpower exists when B controls resources that are important to A. The classic example is the secretary who has some measure of power over his or her boss. The power resides in the secretary's informational resources. The secretary is often the only one who knows where things are filed, how to get through the administrative maze, and/or whom to call to get things done. Thus, B may be able to change A's request by asking for favors in return or by putting subtle pressure on A to ease up.

Thus, apart from the bases of power A may have, A's power over B depends on B's values, the importance of the relationship to B, and B's counterpower. The more B values A's resources, the greater A's power. The more important the relationship is to B, the greater A's power. And, the fewer resources B can muster against A, the greater A's power.

Empirical research generally supports these propositions. In one study, for example, a number of stories were written in which one individual was trying to get another individual to do something (Michener, Lawler, & Bacharach, 1973). The stories focused on the relationship between a salesperson and a regional sales manager, a newspaper editor and a local judge, and two members of Congress. The researchers were interested in the effects of four factors: (1) A's resources, (2) A's probability of using the resources to influence B, (3) B's ability to block the use of A's resources, and (4) B's ability to bring counter-measures to bear. Each of these four factors was manipulated in the stories. Thus, for example, in some of the cases B could block A's use of power or bring countermeasures to bear, while in other cases B did not have this power. Students read these various stories and then rated A's power. It was found that A's power was rated highest when A had many resources and was likely to use them, when B could do little to block A's efforts, and when B had little ability to bring countermeasures to bear. Thus, power is a joint function of A's resources, the nature of the relationship, and B's ability to change or counter A's request.

Tactics for Lateral and Upward Influence

In thinking about power relationships in organizations, we all too often focus exclusively on downward influence. As the results of the study by Kahn et al. (1964) reported earlier show, managers have multiple bases of power and multiple influence tactics they can use to gain compliance from individuals at lower organizational levels. In comparison, they have many fewer bases of power for influencing their peers and superiors. However, the prospects for lateral and upward influence are by no means hopeless. We have already mentioned that one way organizational members can exert both lateral and upward influence is by gaining access to critical sources of information. Information is power, and this power can be put to use (Pondy, 1977). Similarly, individuals who have special expertise in areas that are important for the functioning of their organizational unit can draw on this expertise in order to influence others who are at or above their hierarchical level. In addition to relying on these two power bases, there are several specific tactics that organizational members can use to gain compliance with the requests they direct toward either their peers or their superiors.

Alternative Sources of Legitimate Power. As we stated previously, legitimate power arises from B's feeling that A has a right to make a given request. To a large extent, this "right" or legitimacy is tied to the particular position an individual occupies. Thus, it may be quite legitimate for the vice president in charge of manufacturing to request that a plant manager increase production rates in order to increase the company's inventory of finished goods. This same request would probably not be legitimate if made by the director of marketing. In addition, however, requests can also be legitimated by clearly linking them to (1) important organizational goals, (2) formal organizational rules or procedures, and/or (3) valued societal norms.

One way to give a request legitimacy is to point out how the request is consistent with broader organizational goals. An employee might ask his or her boss to add into next year's budget sufficient funds to purchase a new desktop computer for the employee. The employee can make this request more legitimate by noting that the computer will make him or her more productive and thereby help to achieve the organization's goal of improved performance.

Requests can also be legitimated by invoking formal organizational rules or procedures. For example, suppose an employee requests his or her boss's permission for a day off from work during a particularly busy period. Suppose also that there is a formal organizational rule that states every employee is entitled to two "personal holidays" during any given calendar year, that is, two days off in addition to regular holidays and vacation days that are selected by the employee (e.g., some employees may take a "personal holiday" on their birthday). The employee will be more likely to get the desired day off if he or she prefaces the request with a statement such as, "According to company policy, I am entitled to. . . ."

Finally, requests can also be legitimated by invoking valued societal norms. This happens, for example, when one begins a request by saying, "I think it is only fair" or "in all fairness." Besides the norm of fairness, there are the norms of altruism and reciprocity. One can invoke the altruism norm by seeming to be in great need, or the reciprocity norm by reminding the person you would like to influence of a recent favor you performed. The norm of reciprocity is a particularly powerful one for gaining compliance with a request (Cialdini, 1985), but of course it requires that you have actually done the other person a favor in the recent past. In all of these situations, A is depending on social norms and expectations to legitimate his or her request and thereby gain B's compliance.

Getting Your Foot in the Door. A second general strategy for influencing others has to do with the way in which you position your request vis-à-vis other requests. Consider the following scenario. You have a job waiting on tables in a local restaurant. It is a moderately priced establishment that tries hard to project a more "expensive" image (e.g., low lights, linen tablecloths,

How to Manage Your Boss

In recent years, a surprising amount has been written about managing the boss, mostly by psychologists, business school professors, and consultants. Their advice typically begins with the arresting thought that you the underling can manage, if not your boss, exactly, then at least your relationship with him or her. . . . Managing upward has all sorts of attractions. It can give you greater freedom to do your own work, while ensuring that you both are toiling toward the same goals.

Start working on the relationship, the experts say, by studying your boss's style, a managerial euphemism for how he thinks and acts. What tends to rattle him? How does he treat people? Then, the advice goes on, consider your own style. In reviewing your psychology, dwell especially on how you have got along with so-called authority figures—no use repeating the mistakes you made with Dad and Mom. This done, about all that's left is for you to adjust your behavior so that the boss finds it easy to go along with what you want to do. Let us call this approach to managing upward Theory Y, in that it slightly resembles Douglas M. McGregor's famous hypothesis about the proper way to motivate subordinates—by helping them satisfy needs for self-esteem and self-fulfillment.

There is, however, another approach to managing the boss. Call it Theory X, in that it more closely resembles McGregor's notion of how management has traditionally wrung work from employees—by cajoling, rewarding, punishing, and controlling. Theory X of boss management takes as its initial premise that you can in fact do something to shape not just your relationship with this exalted personage but the personage's behavior as well. You can't simply order him around, of course; he is the boss. But you can subtly direct his efforts, or at least so say some businessmen and -women who have wrestled with the challenge. The conclusion reached by a former Atari executive who worked for a martinet might be taken as the watch word of Theory X's proponents: "Bosses have problems with wimps." So don't be one.

In pursuing Theory X, the opposite of wimpery is not idiot machismo—full of bluster, overbearing—but rather an aggressive yet artful straightforwardness. After getting the requisite facts, and giving their presentation a bit of crafty thought, "be straight up in the boss's face," as one Silicon Valley manager puts it.

Robert C. Bleke, a management psychologist who seems more comfortable with Theory X than most of his professional brethren, elaborates: "It is very important that a subordinate not try to play psychologist with his boss. Don't try to interpret, outguess, or read something into what he may say or do."

Academic experts and businessmen alike attest to the overriding importance of achieving agreement with the boss on what you should be trying to accomplish in your job. Take the advice of one who has helped pick up the pieces of many a failed boss-subordinate relationship—Stephen Morris of Drake Beam Morin, an out-placement firm. Morris suggests easing by the boss's office door early in the week and saying something like, "You know, over the weekend I gave a lot of thought to what I ought to be doing with the job. I made a brief list and I'd like to bounce it off you, now or whenever." You and the boss then proceed to play a friendly but meaningful game of intellectual medicine ball, and with your ball. "What you're doing is writing a contract," observes Morris.

A similar subtlety should inform any attempt to procure that most-precious-because-most-scarce object of desire among subordinates, an honest performance appraisal. An adept proponent of Theory X gets his appraisals by being observant when working on assignments with the boss. "In my 35 years of business, I've only had one decent formal performance review," says one savvy executive. "You get feedback in a task-oriented situation," the man concluded. "From the way your boss responds to things that you do, even from his body language." And don't forget that bosses need bolstering too. If you think he did a job particularly well, tell him so.

Most bosses are interested in the progress made on assignments, not in what subordinates have done to achieve that progress—results, in short, not the hours you've put in. They are also interested, believe it or not, in problems, threats, and obstacles, but here be careful. As devotees of Theory X know better than cut flowers on each table. The owner is very concerned about the "look" of both the restaurant and its employees. She has chosen a conservative decor and insists that her staff be very well groomed.

Now, suppose that your next-door neighbor, who works at the city's art museum, has asked you to help get a poster advertising an upcoming museum fund raiser displayed in the restaurant's front window. You agree to ask the owner about it but recognize that there are two problems. One is that the poster is very large and not all that attractive (it consists of a photograph of a rather bizarre orange and black painting from the museum's modern art collection). The second problem is that in all the time you have worked in the restaurant you have never seen anything but the restaurant's name posted in the front window. Thus, because you know that the owner is very particular about the appearance of the restaurant, and the poster you want her to display is very large and not terribly attractive, you worry that she will not agree to your request.

One thing you can do to increase the owner's willingness to display the poster is to get her first to agree to a preliminary, "smaller" request that is in some way related to the poster request. For example, after the restaurant closes one night you might ask her for a small donation (say, $5) to help the museum mount its fund raiser. Because your request is for a small amount of money, and because it does not affect the "image" of the restaurant, it should be much easier for her to agree to. Once she agrees to this preliminary request, you can come back later (say, after a week) and make the poster request that you are primarily interested in. Using this smaller-request-first/larger-request-second tactic does not guarantee that the owner will agree to display the poster, but it will significantly increase the probability that she will do so.

Salespeople are well aware of the effectiveness of this influence strategy (Green, 1965). They call it the "foot-in-the-door" technique. The name comes from the traveling salesperson who gets his or her "foot in the customer's door" by making a small request that is easy to agree to (Can I come in just to demonstrate how well this product works?). Once inside, it is much simpler to get the customer to agree to larger, more difficult requests (Would you be interested in buying one of these?).

Although there are several competing explanations for the success of the foot-in-the-door strategy, one that seems particularly cogent is that the act of agreeing to the initial small request affects people's self-perceptions (Freedman & Fraser, 1966; Snyder & Cunningham, 1975). In our example, after giving you $5 for the museum, the owner is somewhat more likely to perceive herself

409

as the type of person who supports this kind of cause. With this self-image in place, you later approach her about the poster. Turning you down would now be inconsistent with her recently enhanced self-image as a patron of the arts. Consequently, she is more likely to agree to display the poster. Had the initial small request not been made and agreed to, this particular self-image would not have been salient, and there would have been no issue of consistency— hence less likelihood of agreement. Thus, once again we see that psychological consistency can play a significant role in determining behavior. (Recall that psychological consistency was discussed in some detail in Chapter 5, "Attitudes.")

Getting the Door in Your Face. The foot-in-the-door tactic can be very effective, but in many situations it is difficult to implement. It requires that you be able to come up with a small preliminary request that is somehow related to the larger request you are really interested in. Also, a certain amount of time should elapse between the two requests. If you make the two requests one right after the other, this strategy will not work. Finally, it is essential that the preliminary request be agreed to. If it is not, the foot-in-the-door tactic will backfire, and your chances of getting what you want from the second request will be worsened by having attempted to use this influence strategy.

There is, however, a related influence tactic that does not have these limitations. This alternative strategy also involves the relative positioning of larger and smaller requests. It is called the "door-in-the-face" technique. Let us go back to the restaurant to see how this influence strategy works.

Suppose that one of your friends is getting married in another city, and you want to go to the wedding. Because of the distance, you will have to take 3 days off from work to attend. The owner has agreed to give you the days off, but only if you can arrange to have someone else cover for you. As it turns out, there are three people who can take your place. The current work schedule is such that each of these three individuals can potentially take all three of your shifts. However, this would be too big a favor, and you are certain that none of them will be willing to do it. Indeed, because all of the restaurant's employees so jealously guard their time off, you are not even sure that you can get each person to take just one shift. If you cannot influence all three individuals to take a shift, you will not be able to go to the wedding.

One way to approach this situation is simply to ask each of these people to take one shift. Your chances of getting each person to comply with this request will increase significantly, however, if you first make a larger request that you are sure they will *turn down*. Thus, you might first ask each person if he or she would be willing to work all three shifts for you. Although you know that no one will do this, you should make an earnest attempt to convince each person to comply. After you are turned down, you make the more modest request of taking only one of your shifts. Research clearly shows that if you precede a request with a preliminary one that is substantially larger, and that larger request gets rejected, you are more likely to gain compliance with the subsequent, more moderate request (Cialdini, 1985; Cialdini et al., 1975).

There are two reasons why the door-in-the-face tactic works, and they are both different from the self-perception explanation underlying the foot-in-the-door strategy. One is that when you make a large request and follow it with a second one of more moderate size, you provide a frame of reference for judging the magnitude of the second request. In our example, for instance, your coworkers in the restaurant can now think to themselves, "Well, I guess taking one shift isn't so bad, especially when you compare it with taking three." You have in essence created a *perceptual contrast effect*—in contrast to the first request, the second one does not seem so big. This fact alone should increase the probability of compliance.

The second reason the door-in-the-face strategy works is that it evokes the norm of reciprocity mentioned earlier. If you do someone a favor, that person should be willing to do you a favor. Likewise, if you make a concession when negotiating over some point, the other individual should also be willing to make concessions. Now, if you make a request that someone is unable to comply with and then come back with a more modest request, you have in a sense made a concession—you have demonstrated a willingness to reduce the magnitude of your request. In order to reciprocate, the other individual should be willing to give in a little too, which he or she can do by becoming more agreeable. Hence, the other individual should be more willing to comply with the second request. Figure 13-3 compares the essential features of the foot-in-the-door and door-in-the-face influence tactics.

An understanding of how these tactics operate is useful in two respects. First, it can increase your chances of being able to influence other organization members successfully, even when you have relatively few bases of social power on which to draw. Equally important, however, is that a thorough understanding of these strategies should also help you *avoid the influence of others*. Both tactics are frequently used, both in organizational settings and elsewhere. What is important is that you can learn to recognize when these two tactics are being used on you. If you are aware of the relationship between the requests that are being made by other people, you should be able to avoid the effect of these two influence tactics. Forewarned *is* forearmed! And by being forearmed you increase your ability to make decisions without being unduly influenced by the way in which those decisions are presented. In effect, you gain more control over your own behavior. Thus, an understanding of these

	Influence Tactic	
	Foot-in-the-Door	**Door-in-the-Face**
Size of preliminary request	Small	Large
Response required to preliminary request	Compliance	Noncompliance
Size of second (main) request	Moderate	Moderate
Expected response to second (main) request	Compliance	Compliance
Reasons why tactic works	Self-perception and psychological consistency	Perceptual contrast and reciprocity norm

FIGURE 13-3.

Comparing the foot-in-the-door and the door-in-the-face influence tactics.

two influence tactics is useful from both an offensive and a defensive perspective.

The Effects of Power

Two final questions we address here concern the effects of power on the power holder and people's reactions to the use of power. How do people act when they attain power? And how do they feel when power is used on them?

Behavioral Changes in the Power Holder. Over the years there has been some debate about whether power is corrupting or ennobling. Some people have argued that power brings with it responsibility, and that as a consequence the powerful may be more compassionate and understanding than other people (e.g., Berle, 1967). Also, a number of books have suggested that it is okay both to seek and to obtain power. Books with titles such as *Power: How to Get It, How to Use It; Winning through Intimidation;* and *Looking Out for Number One* have become increasingly popular. On the other side of the argument are those who say that power is corrupting and that power induces people to act in an inequitable and exploitative manner (e.g., Hobbes, 1968).

Empirical research on this topic indicates that access to bases of social power, especially organizational resources, does indeed affect the behavior and perceptions of the power holder. A number of studies have reported on the behavior of people who have either attained power or who have more power than others around them. The data suggest that power holders actually try to exert their influence more, devalue the less powerful, and decrease their interpersonal associations with them.

Some of the best work in this area has been done by David Kipnis (1976). For example, in one study he had twenty-eight undergraduate business school students act as managers in an industrial simulation (Kipnis, 1972). Each manager was in charge of four workers who were performing a coding task in another room. Each worker's output was known to the manager, and while the manager could not see the workers, he or she could communicate with them through an intercom. The manager's job was to operate the company at a profitable level by maintaining the efficiency of the workers.

All twenty-eight managers had the same job. However, fourteen of them were delegated a range of institutional powers. They could award small pay increases, transfer workers, give additional instructions, deduct pay, and terminate employment. The other fourteen managers could only use their powers of persuasion and expertise. They had no formal power.

In fact, as in several studies we have seen, the workers in the other room were fictitious. In this way, the experimenter could bring in exactly the same performance data to every manager. The only difference between the two groups of managers was their power.

The results of the study were quite clear. The managers with power (1) made more attempts to influence their workers, (2) rated their workers less highly on an overall performance appraisal, (3) indicated less willingness to meet socially with the workers, and (4) were more likely to attribute the workers' performance to their own managerial expertise than were their less powerful counterparts. The first two of these results are shown in Figure 13-4.

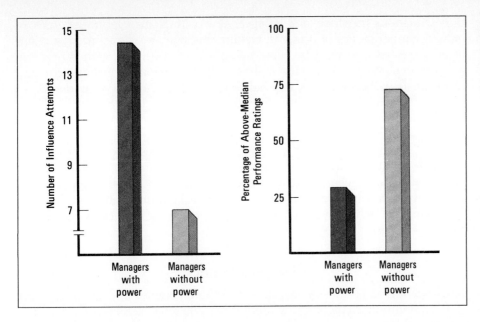

FIGURE 13-4
Managers who were delegated institutional power made more attempts to actually influence the workers, and evaluated their performance less positively, than did managers who were not delegated institutional power. (*Based on data presented by Kipnis, 1972.*)

What these results suggest is that power may inhibit social relationships, and that powerful people actually use their power, devalue the efforts of less powerful people, and reevaluate their own efforts in a more positive light.

Reactions to the Use of Power. In general, people do not like power to be used on them. Any attempt to alter another's behavior produces, initially at least, a small amount of resistance (Brehm, 1966). When strategies are used based on legitimate, expert, or information resources, this resistance is relatively low. However, the more that coercion and punishment are used, the greater the resistance. There is even evidence that the direct and manipulative use of rewards may make the task of compliance less pleasant. It is nicer to do something for someone else because we want to—not because we think we have to.

To summarize, social power is used in organizations all the time. It is necessary to get things done. However, people react to the use of different types of power in different ways. Power strategies based on coercion may bring compliance, but they are less satisfactory to both parties, especially the less powerful. Strategies based on expertise, legitimacy, and information are more readily accepted.

POLITICS

So far our focus has been on situations in which one individual tries to influence another. We have examined the various bases of social power that individual organizational members draw on when trying to exert their influence, and we have discussed several potential consequences of having access to power.

We now wish to shift our focus to the group level of analysis, and consider those situations in which one group or unit within an organization tries to influence other groups or units. In making this shift, we move into the realm of *organizational politics*. The term *politics* carries with it a rather negative connotation. We tend to view politics with suspicion in government and condemn it in business. As we shall see, however, such a view denies an important organizational reality: *All organizations are inherently political.* To be sure, some organizations are more political than others, but a certain amount of political behavior can be found in all organizations.

In this second half of the chapter we discuss the causes of political behavior, why politics are an inevitable consequence of organizing, several political tactics that groups can use to influence the behavior of other groups, and factors that can help to reduce (but not eliminate) political behavior. But first, we attempt to define more clearly what we mean by the terms *politics* and *political behavior*.

Defining Politics

The literature on politics in organizations is both complex and confusing. Part of the confusion stems from a fundamental lack of agreement about the meaning of the term *politics*. Different authors use this term in very different ways, and as a consequence there has been a good deal of open debate on such issues as whether political activity is good or bad and whether it should (or can) be eliminated from organizational life. It is useful to introduce this debate by briefly examining two alternative definitions of politics.

Consistent with the connotation that politics is somehow bad and to be avoided, at least in rational organizations, some authors have defined this concept in terms of behavior that departs from what is normative, expected, or sanctioned. For example, Mayes and Allen (1977) define politics as "the management of influence to obtain ends *not sanctioned* by the organization or to obtain sanctioned ends through *nonsanctioned* influence means" (emphasis added). However, as Pfeffer (1981) has noted, there is a major problem with this type of definition. What is and what is not sanctioned in an organization is itself often the result of political activity. For example, in a university several key academic departments might form a coalition and set out to lobby the university administration to divert funding away from a proposed new library and build instead a new computer facility. On a purely intuitive basis, most people would agree that the formation and activity of the coalition are political, since their sole purpose is to pursue a goal not currently sanctioned by the university—building a new computer facility.

But what if the coalition is successful? Suppose the university administration gives in to the coalition and agrees to commit funds to the construction of a new computer center instead of a library. Certainly, many more decisions need to be made before the facility can actually be built (e.g., decisions regarding location, access, the division of resources among different types of computing needs, budgets, staffing). Is the further work of the coalition on these issues suddenly nonpolitical? Mayes and Allen (1977) would say *yes*. Yet, it seems likely that much of the important behavior of the coalition that was previously labeled "political" (e.g., bargaining, lobbying, compromise, co-optation) will continue as the members wrestle with these additional questions. Mayes and Allen's definition of politics would suddenly have us ignore these behaviors.

It should also be noted that the most powerful groups in an organization are the very ones that are most likely to have their own preferred goals, and the means to attain those goals, sanctioned by the rest of the organization. Thus, Mayes and Allen's (1977) definition of organizational politics inevitably draws our attention to the activities of groups that are less powerful and less successful in getting their own preferred goals and means sanctioned. This seems unnecessarily restrictive, and would cause us to overlook many important acts of influence exhibited by very powerful organizational groups.

Pfeffer (1981) offers an alternative definition of organizational politics that we believe is somewhat more useful. He suggests that political behavior is best defined as "those activities taken within organizations to acquire, develop, and use power and other resources to obtain one's preferred outcomes in a situation in which there is uncertainty or dissensus about choices." Three important aspects of this definition are worth noting. First, political activity involves the use of power in order to obtain outcomes. In this respect, organizational politics and social power are very much alike. They are distinguished primarily by the unit of analysis involved. When our focus is on individuals influencing other individuals, we are talking about social power. When our focus is on groups influencing other groups, we are talking about organizational politics. Second, political behavior occurs in situations characterized by uncertainty. When there is no uncertainty or disagreement about what course of action should be taken, there is little room for political behavior. Uncertainty is thus a necessary (although not sufficient) condition for the appearance of political behavior. Finally, Pfeffer's definition does not pass judgment on the merits of organizational politics. It does not suggest that political behavior is inherently either good or bad. Instead, we must examine the *outcomes* associated with a given political act in order to decide whether that act was a good or bad one (cf. Cavanagh, Moberg, & Velasquez, 1981).

The Causes of Political Behavior

Imagine the following situation. A wealthy business executive makes a $500,000 gift to a local university. The executive stipulates only that the money is to be used "in whatever way the university judges will best serve the needs of undergraduate education." There are many possible ways this money might be spent. It could be used to endow a new faculty chair, purchase new computer equipment, expand the holdings of the library, obtain new classroom equipment, or refurbish the university's deteriorating athletic facility. The university has needs in all of these areas, and it is virtually impossible to say which is objectively most critical. Moreover, various groups within the university have conflicting opinions about how the money should be spent. The library staff, for example, believes that the university's most serious need is for books and journals. Various academic departments, by contrast, see new faculty positions as the most pressing need. And the computer center staff views the need for new computing equipment as the most acute.

This situation has a number of features that make it ripe for the appearance of political behavior. First, it is characterized by uncertainty. There is no obvious "correct" or "best" way to spend the money. It is difficult to decide *objectively* what should be done. Second, different groups have different and conflicting preferences regarding the specific use to which the money should be put. These preferences are in conflict in the sense that fully satisfying one group (e.g., putting the entire sum of money toward the purchase of new computer equipment) is mutually exclusive with fully satisfying the other groups. Third, it is an important decision. Such a large sum of money is likely to reap substantial benefits in whichever area it is committed. Finally, the various groups vying for this money all have some measure of power within the organization. No one group has absolute power over any of the others.

These four conditions (uncertainty, conflicting preferences, decision importance, and distributed power) all are necessary for the appearance of political behavior. As Pfeffer's (1981) definition suggests, whenever political activity occurs, it always revolves around a decision in which the affected parties have conflicting preferences as to which choice alternative should be selected. In this sense, conflicting opinions and preferences are perhaps the single most important cause of political behavior. But such conflicts can exist only if there is some degree of uncertainty about what is objectively the best or most appropriate course of action. (Note that there would have been no uncertainty, and hence no conflict, had the university's benefactor stipulated a specific use for the money, e.g., to purchase new books for the library.) In addition, the decision must be an important one. If it were not important (e.g., had the executive given the university only $100), there would be little interest in the decision outcome, and hence little likelihood of political behavior. Finally, it is also necessary that power be distributed roughly equally among the groups affected by the decision. If all or most of the power were concentrated in the hands of only one group, that group would be able to take unilateral action to attain its preferred outcomes without recourse to bargaining, negotiation, compromise, or the like.

It is important to recognize that although conflicting preferences can exist only when there is some uncertainty about what is objectively the most correct or appropriate course of action, uncertainty is not itself the source of the conflicting preferences. Rather, uncertainty simply provides an environment in which conflicting preferences can develop. The real causes of the conflicting opinions and preferences are *differentiation* and *resource scarcity* (cf. Pfeffer, 1981).

Differentiation. As we discussed in Chapter 3, "Understanding Organizations," almost every organization is divided into multiple units, with different units performing different tasks. This differentiation is a natural result of organizational growth. As organizations grow larger, they evolve more and more subunits, and these subunits focus on more and more narrowly defined sets of activities. This differentiation has two interrelated consequences, both of which increase the likelihood that the different subunits will have conflicting opinions and preferences about various choice alternatives.

First, while the process of differentiation separates people into different groups or organizational units, the tasks they perform often remain relatively *interdependent*. Thus, for example, the specific production activities performed in a company's manufacturing division depend to a certain extent on both the particular product designs developed in its research and development unit and the performance of its sales force. Similarly, some of the research activities performed by a university's faculty depend upon the work that is done by the staff of both the library and the computer center. One implication of this type of interdependence is that decisions made in one part of the organization often affect many different groups. Thus, a decision to expand the size of the company's sales force will be likely to affect not only those in sales, but also those in manufacturing. And the budgetary, staffing, and purchasing decisions made by those who run the university's library and computer center will ultimately impact upon the faculty.

The second consequence of differentiation is that it encourages various subgroups to develop rather *parochial perspectives* on organizational problems and opportunities. In part, these parochial perspectives reflect the fact that different tasks carry with them rather different goals and objectives, and that the people working on these tasks come to have somewhat different orientations (i.e., toward uncertainty and time span of feedback; Lawrence & Lorsch, 1967). The parochial perspectives also reflect the fact that different types of tasks afford somewhat different means of coping with problems. Thus, to repeat an example we have used before, those in manufacturing may become accustomed to dealing with organization-level performance problems by trying to reduce production costs (the one variable they are likely to have the greatest degree of control over), while those in marketing and sales may become accustomed to dealing with the same problem by trying to increase flexibility and responsiveness to customer needs.

In addition, differentiation encourages the development of parochial perspectives by fostering a biased distribution of information and communication. Within a university, for example, members of the faculty are more likely to receive detailed information about course enrollments and student-teacher ratios than about library acquisitions or computer hardware problems. Moreover, the day-to-day activity of the faculty gives them many first-hand experiences that make the meaning of enrollment figures more vivid (e.g., changes in course enrollment often force instructors to make last-minute changes in their preferred method of instruction, the nature of homework assignments, and/or the number and style of exams). The faculty are not likely to appreciate

FIGURE 13-5
One consequence of differentiation is the development of parochial perspectives.

ANIMAL CRACKERS

in quite the same way information concerning either the library or the computer center. Of course, the reverse will also be true. The staffs of both the library and computer center are likely to receive and fully appreciate only information relevant to their own particular spheres of operation.

Thus, differentiation leads to both task interdependence and parochial perspectives. Task interdependence means that organizational decisions will often affect multiple groups, and the presence of parochial perspectives means that the affected groups are likely to have a variety of different opinions and preferences regarding the various decision alternatives.

Resource Scarcity. In some cases, task interdependence and parochial perspectives are not enough to create conflicting preferences. Groups can frequently have different preferences without those preferences being in conflict, as long as there are adequate resources available. When resources become scarce, on the other hand, and the various preferences of the different groups cannot all be satisfied simultaneously, a situation of conflict exists. Thus, had the university's benefactor given enough money to satisfy simultaneously the academic departments' desire for additional faculty positions, the library's desire for more books and journals, and the computer center's desire for new equipment, there would be no conflict among these three groups. They all could have gotten what they wanted. It is only when they cannot all simultaneously obtain the outcomes they want that their preferences come into conflict.

The preceding discussion is summarized in the model presented in Figure 13-6. This model outlines the various factors contributing to the emergence of political behavior in organizations. Tracing through this model, it can be seen that one of the root causes of political behavior is differentiation. Differentiation has two consequences: task interdependence and the development of

FIGURE 13-6
A model of the
factors that con-
tribute to the
emergence of po-
litical behavior in
organizations.
(*Adapted from
Pfeffer, 1981.*)

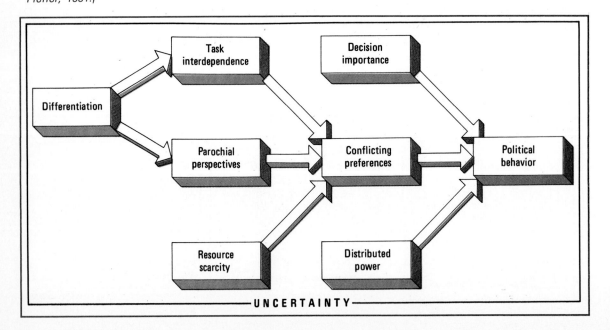

parochial perspectives. These, together with resource scarcity, make it highly probable that there will be conflicting preferences among the various groups affected by a given decision. This conflict will lead to political behavior if the decision is an important one and if power is distributed more-or-less equally among the affected groups. Finally, this entire process occurs only when there is uncertainty about which choice alternative is objectively most correct or appropriate.

It is important to note here that since differentiation is a natural consequence of organizational growth, and since both uncertainty and resource scarcity are the rule rather than the exception in organizations, it must be concluded that *both conflict and political activity are inevitable group-level outputs that can be found in virtually any organization.* The *amount* of conflict and political behavior that occurs in a given organization will depend upon the *severity* of the prerequisite conditions (i.e., the degree to which there exist task interdependence, parochial perspectives, resource scarcity, and so on). However, since at least moderate levels of these prerequisite conditions are likely to exist in *all* organizations, all organizations are likely to exhibit at least some degree of both conflict and political activity.

The Consequences of Conflict

As Figure 13-6 suggests, the emergence of political behavior is one important consequence of the group-level conflicts that often develop in organizational settings. Shortly, we will discuss several political tactics that groups use to resolve such conflicts. Before doing so, however, it is useful to examine briefly some of the other consequences that conflict can have. These can be categorized into two types: functional consequences and dysfunctional consequences.

Functional Consequences of Conflict. As is true with politics, we often think of conflict as a dysfunctional event that should be avoided in organizations. And indeed, this was the dominant view among behavioral scientists until relatively recently (Thomas, 1976). Gradually, however, this perception is changing. More and more behavioral scientists are recognizing that conflict can sometimes have functional as well as dysfunctional consequences.

At a very basic level, one potentially functional consequence of conflict is that it can generate a great deal of arousal among organizational participants. It can energize them and mobilize them to take action. Recall from Chapter 6 that arousal is the starting point in the overall motivation process. Unless people are aroused, they will have little interest in performing well or achieving goals. Arousal by itself, however, does not dictate *how* organization members will behave. It only increases the likelihood that they *will* behave. Thus, in order for conflict-generated arousal to have functional value, that arousal must be channeled toward the achievement of desired organizational goals.

One such goal is the development of innovative solutions to the very problems giving rise to the conflict. Hall (1971) has suggested that when properly managed, conflict may not only increase the motivation to seek problem solutions, it can often result in more creative solutions. For example, in one study it was found that problem-solving groups composed of members with conflicting points of view generated significantly higher quality solutions than did problem-solving groups composed of members who all had essentially the same point of view (Hoffman & Maier, 1961).

Apart from the arousal generated by conflict and the possibility that such arousal can be directed toward creative problem solving, conflict can also be functional for group development. In a now classic study, Sherif and Sherif (1953) found that when groups come into conflict, members become more loyal to their respective groups and identify with their groups more strongly; as a result, each group becomes more cohesive. In addition, there is also evidence that group members become more task oriented, perhaps as a result of the increased arousal.

Dysfunctional Consequence of Conflict. Of course, not all of the consequences of conflict are beneficial for the organization. Often it is difficult to channel the energy generated by conflict toward creative problem solving. The reason is that the presence of conflict also has a tendency to affect how the conflicting groups perceive and behave toward one another.

When the conflict between two or more groups persists over even a moderate length of time, there is a tendency for the conflicting groups to adopt a *win-lose orientation* (Filley, 1977; McCallum et al., 1985). The group members begin to think in terms of "us versus them" and "victory versus defeat." Emphasis often gets placed on "coming out a winner" rather than on finding a solution that will best meet the needs of all parties to the conflict.

This win-lose orientation is frequently accompanied by distorted perceptions, both of the other groups involved in the conflict and of one's own group. In evaluating the behavior and motives of the other parties to the conflict, groups often invoke negative stereotypes ("Those guys in marketing are only interested in their own personal careers. They don't give a damn about what is really best for the company"). The group members then selectively attend to information consistent with these stereotypes. At the same time, they often fail to perceive the faults in their own behavior or positions. Thus, the other groups involved in the conflict come to be viewed more negatively than they really are, while one's own group comes to be seen more positively than it really is.

Finally, there is also a tendency for the conflicting groups to decrease their level of interaction and to communicate less with one another. Occasionally this is taken to such extremes that only the official representatives of the various groups communicate, and then only in formal, carefully planned meetings (e.g., in labor contract negotiations). When this happens, the reduced interaction serves to maintain the distorted perceptions noted above. In the absence of free-flowing communication and regular interaction, little information is likely to come to light that will contradict the stereotypic perceptions held by the conflicting groups (cf. Stephen, 1985).

Thus, while the arousal that is generated by conflict can benefit an organization, the benefits are likely to be realized only when the dysfunctional perceptual consequences of conflict can be overcome. If these cannot be overcome, the conflict will be more difficult to resolve, and under some circumstances it may evolve into open hostility—groups taking overt action to disrupt the operations of other groups.

Political Strategies for Resolving Conflict

Barring the occurrence of open hostility, there are several political strategies that groups can use to resolve conflict. These include compromise, the formation of coalitions, and co-optation.

Compromise. Compromise is actually one of a family of related conflict-resolution strategies. The other members of this family include domination, collaboration, avoidance, and accommodation (Thomas, 1976). The relationship among these various strategies can be expressed in terms of two underlying dimensions, as shown in Figure 13-7. The first dimension is the extent to which the group desires to attain its own preferred outcomes. This dimension predicts how assertive the group will be in pursuing these outcomes. When a decision is important to a group, and consequently the group has a strong desire to attain its preferred outcomes, the members are likely to be very assertive in their efforts to secure those outcomes. When, on the other hand, the decision is relatively unimportant, and thus the group does not have a strong desire to attain its preferred outcomes, the members are not likely to be very assertive in pursuing those outcomes. The second dimension is the extent to which the group desires to satisfy the concerns of the other groups involved in the conflict. This dimension predicts how cooperatively the group will behave. A group that has a strong desire to satisfy the concerns of the other groups involved in the conflict will be very cooperative, whereas one that has little or no interest in satisfying the concerns of other groups will be rather uncooperative.

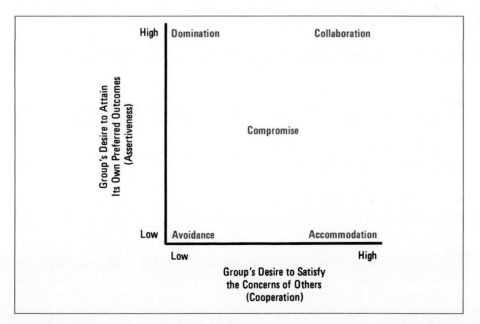

FIGURE 13-7
Five conflict-handling orientations. (*Adapted from Thomas, 1976.*)

As Figure 13-7 suggests, various combinations of these two dimensions (i.e., the group's desire to attain its own preferences, and its desire to satisfy the concerns of others) result in the five different conflict-resolution strategies. The most extreme combinations are listed in the four corners of the figure. When a group has a very strong desire to attain its own preferred outcomes, and it has little or no desire to satisfy the concerns of the other groups involved in the conflict, the group will be oriented toward *domination*. It will seek to satisfy its own concerns at the expense of others. Conversely, when a group has little desire to attain its own preferred outcomes but has a very strong desire to satisfy the concerns of the other groups involved, it will be oriented toward *accommodation*—working toward the satisfaction of the concerns of the other groups, even if this means sacrificing all of its own preferred outcomes. This strategy seems most likely to be used when a group strongly abhors conflict and desires agreement and harmony for its own sake. When a group has a very strong desire both to attain its own preferred outcomes and to satisfy the concerns of the other groups involved in the conflict, it will be oriented toward *collaboration*. The collaborative strategy implies an attempt at joint problem solving in which the conflicting groups work together to develop a solution that meets *all* of the preferences of *all* parties to the conflict. Before this strategy can be used, however, the various parties involved in the conflict must all believe that it is possible to find such a solution. Finally, when a group has little or no interest either in attaining its own preferred outcomes or in satisfying the concerns of the other groups involved, it will be oriented toward *avoidance*. It will simply ignore the conflict.

These four strategies—domination, accommodation, collaboration, and avoidance—represent extreme orientations to conflict resolution, and as such, they do not frequently appear in their pure form. Instead, the most common strategy is *compromise*. This strategy reflects a moderate desire by a group both to attain its own preferred outcomes and to satisfy the concerns of the other groups involved in the conflict. Compromise implies that the group is willing to give up some, but not all, of what it desires in order that the other groups involved can satisfy some of their concerns. It is a willingness to share outcomes in order to resolve the conflict. Note that in any given situation, a group's orientation toward compromise is likely to lean in the direction of either domination, accommodation, collaboration, or avoidance. However, unless these "leanings" are extreme, the strategy essentially remains one of compromise.

It is important to recognize that compromise (along with domination and collaboration) implies the use of power by the conflicting groups. Their power may reside in their control of resources that others depend upon, their ability to cope with uncertainty, the unique skills they possess, or the services they offer (Pfeffer, 1981). Regardless of the source, however, the possession and use of power is central to the effectiveness of compromise as a strategy for conflict resolution. If one of the groups involved in a conflict were to have no power, that group would have no way to compel others to give it what it desires. In terms of the diagram shown in Figure 13-7, it would have no way to assert itself in order to attain its preferred outcomes. In this situation, the group or groups holding all the power would dominate. On the other hand, if the conflicting groups have roughly equal amounts of power, compromise will become a highly (and perhaps the only) viable conflict-resolution strategy. Thus, because it involves the use of power to obtain preferred outcomes, compromise fits the definition of political behavior given earlier.

Coalition Formation. When there are multiple groups affected by a decision, and when these groups all have roughly the same amount of power, a simple compromise may sometimes be difficult to achieve. There may be too many diverse interests to take into account, and no one group is likely to have sufficient power to be able to force its preferences on the others. In such a situation, compromise can be facilitated through the use of *coalitions*. Coalitions are loose alliances among groups. The formation of a coalition is a way to gather or concentrate power (Bacharach & Lawler, 1980). The coalition, once formed, acts as a single body, but with the combined power of all its component groups.

Earlier, we used as an example a situation in which several academic departments formed a coalition in order to influence the university administration to divert funds away from a proposed new library and to build instead a new computer center. It seems quite unlikely that any single department, no matter how large, would be able to exert enough power and influence to get what it wanted in this situation. However, by bringing together into one coalition a sufficient number of key departments, it is quite possible that enough political power could be amassed to influence the administration successfully. Note that this strategy does not hinge on bringing a numerical majority of the faculty into the coalition. It is only necessary that enough groups be brought together that their combined power equals or exceeds that of the opposing group, which in this example is the university administration. Fewer groups, and a smaller percentage of the total faculty, will be needed for this purpose if the individual departments brought into the coalition are themselves all relatively powerful.

The function of forming a coalition—the concentration of power—is the same at both the individual and group levels of analysis. A good example of coalition formation at the individual level of analysis is a labor union. As individuals, people have very little power, at least compared to the power of an entire organization. Thus, they have very little means of influencing the terms of a labor contract when acting on their own. But when these same people come together to form a union, the threads of power held by thousands of individuals can be woven together into a political fabric that is not easily ignored.

It should be noted that the process of forming a coalition itself often involves compromise. In forming the coalition, member groups generally agree (usually informally) to sacrifice objectives that are of interest only to themselves in order to concentrate on the pursuit of objectives common to all. Furthermore, some groups may agree to pool their political resources with others only if they are granted certain concessions in exchange. For example, an academic department may agree to join a coalition seeking the construction of a new computer center only if it receives assurances from the other departments that it will have their support for a new program expansion it is planning (e.g., offering a new postgraduate degree). Also, the coalition may involve groups that are not directly affected by the decision and who thus were not previously involved in the conflict. Indeed, coalitions may even involve groups who are not formally a part of the organization, such as professional or community groups, customer groups, governmental groups, or in the case of a university, the alumni. From the point of view of the coalition, it generally does not matter that all of its member groups are not directly affected by the decision. What does matter is that the member groups all have some degree of power vis-à-vis the opposition, and that they are willing to exert their political influence in the direction desired by the rest of the coalition.

Co-optation. Unlike coalition formation and compromise, which are political strategies for building and using power, respectively, *co-optation* is a strategy that groups can use to *dissolve opposition* to their preferred decision alternatives. Co-optation involves an attempt to secure the cooperation of an opposing group by giving that group a small measure of power *within* the co-opting group. The goal of the co-opting group is to relinquish a small amount of control over its own actions in order to gain a large degree of cooperation.

An excellent example of co-optation is discussed by Feldman and Arnold (1983). They cite the case of university administrations that used co-optation as a strategy for controlling vocal student groups during the campus unrest of the late 1960s and early 1970s. During that period, both the war in Vietnam and the civil rights movement were important political issues. Student groups all across the United States were demanding that their university administrations divest themselves of defense industry stocks, respond more quickly and affirmatively to the needs of minorities and women, and loosen up on rigid curricular requirements. To manage this conflict, many universities put students on all types of committees dealing with these issues. In doing so, the universities in effect made the students a part of the administrative machinery. Because they now had committee representation, the student groups could no longer protest that they were not being heard by the administration. On the other hand, the students elected to these committees were in such a minority position that they had little real power with which to influence decisions. Thus, by relinquishing a rather small amount of decision-making power to the students, the universities were effectively able to dissolve most of their opposition.

Another example of co-optation occurred in 1980 when Chrysler Corporation appointed Douglas Fraser, then president of the United Auto Workers union, to its board of directors (Iacocca & Novack, 1984). At the time, Chrysler was in serious financial trouble, and it intended to seek major wage and benefit concessions from the UAW in order to maintain solvency. The union's membership would certainly oppose such concessions, and it was by no means certain that persuasive arguments from top company officials would gain their cooperation. By putting Fraser on its board, Chrysler gave him a personal stake in the company's future that went well beyond his role as union president. Furthermore, as a board member, Fraser had access to detailed financial information that revealed the true severity of the company's position. Because he was a highly credible source in the eyes of the union's membership, he could be much more persuasive than other company officials in communicating this information to them. Thus, in exchange for a relatively small degree of power, Chrysler gained an ally who could play a key role in dissolving the union's opposition to subsequent company demands for concessions.

There are several features of the co-optation process that lead to its effectiveness as a conflict-resolution strategy (cf. Pfeffer, 1981). First, it serves to bring the conflicting groups together, thus helping to eliminate whatever distorted perceptions and stereotypes may be present, especially within the co-opted group. In a similar fashion, co-optation helps to break down the "us versus them" orientation. The co-opted group suddenly finds that "us *is* them!" Second, by accepting a formal role in the governance of the co-opting group, representatives of the co-opted group implicitly volunteer their cooperation. This, in conjunction with a desire not to lose their new-found status, should motivate these representatives to avoid behaving in ways that might appear antagonistic toward the co-opting group. Finally, because the representatives of the co-opted group are generally a small minority in comparison to others who share control over the actions of the co-opting group, they are not likely to be very influential. Furthermore, they will undoubtedly experience a great deal of conformity pressure from the majority. The result will often be that the representatives of the co-opted group are not only unable to change the preferences of the majority, they will in the end voluntarily (although perhaps reluctantly) consent to go along with those preferences. (Note that this is exactly what was found in the conformity research of Solomon Asch, 1955, discussed in Chapter 9.)

Approaches to Minimizing the Opportunity for Conflict and Organizational Politics

Earlier we stated that conflict, and hence political behavior, are inevitable consequences of organizing. Some degree of both conflict and political activity can be found in all organizations. Yet, experience tells us that organizations are not all equally political. Some appear to be more political than others. The model shown in Figure 13-6 suggests that if an organization can take action to reduce the severity of the conditions that give rise to conflict, less political behavior should occur.

There are several approaches that can be taken for doing this. One is to structure the organization so as to minimize the degree to which tasks are interdependent. It is seldom the case that task interdependence can be totally eliminated. At the same time, the degree of task interdependence between groups is often greater than it needs to be. The opportunity for conflict and political behavior will be reduced if organizations strive to combine interdependent tasks so that they are performed within the same group, and separate those that are independent. The pattern of task independence/interdependence provides natural lines of fracture upon which the organization can be differentiated. If these lines are followed, the opportunity for conflict and organizational politics will be reduced. If they are not followed, the opportunity for conflict and political behavior will increase. In this regard, it seems likely that when groups are differentiated on the basis of function, there will often be more conflict and political activity than when they are differentiated on the basis of product, customer, or geography. (Recall that the various bases of horizontal differentiation were discussed in Chapter 3, "Understanding Organizations.")

A second tactic that organizations can employ to help reduce the likelihood of conflict and politics is to create *slack resources.* As indicated in Figure 13-6, one cause of conflict is resource scarcity. Resource scarcity intensifies the degree to which groups are interdependent (Galbraith, 1977), and interdependence leads to conflict. Thus, one way to reduce interdependence is to provide more resources. The particular resources involved will depend on the situation, but they may include such things as money (budget), raw materials, inventory, or time. For example, a company's sales force can remain responsive to fluctuations in customer demand without disrupting the operations of the manufacturing division if the company maintains a large inventory of finished products. Carrying a large inventory is costly, but it may be an expense the company is willing to incur in order to minimize the potential for internal conflict.

Finally, organizations can also help reduce the likelihood of conflict and politics by establishing *integrator roles* and by using systematic *job-rotation programs.* Both of these tactics help to address the "parochial perspectives" problem. Integrator roles are formal positions created to facilitate the coordination of interdependent groups. In business firms with diverse product lines, a commonly found integrator role is that of "product manager." Governmental agencies often have "program managers." And hospitals usually have a number of different "unit coordinators." All of these are integrator roles. The integrator's job is to see to it that information passes smoothly and in a timely manner between the interdependent groups. The integrator works closely with each group but is usually not him- or herself a formal group member. As a result, he or she can remain objective, and can help to ensure that information and perceptions are accurate and that each group's behavior and motives are correctly understood by others.

This same goal can also be achieved by systematically rotating managers through a series of jobs in different groups (cf. Edstrom & Galbraith, 1977). By being a member of each group for a period of time, a manager will come to understand better each group's needs, as well as the various constraints under which each group operates. This experience will give the manager a broader perspective on organizational problems, and as a consequence, his or her preferences regarding various decision alternatives are likely to be less parochial. It is interesting to note that the systematic rotation of managers through jobs in different organizational units is much more common among Japanese firms than among American firms (Ouchi & Jaeger, 1978).

In summary, we have argued that conflict is inevitable in organizational settings. Some organizations experience more conflict than others, but all organizations experience some conflict. There are a variety of political strategies groups use to help resolve conflicts. These include compromise, the formation of coalitions, and co-optation. Finally, the opportunity for conflict can be reduced, although not completely eliminated, by choosing patterns of differentiation that reduce task interdependence, by supplying slack resources, and by establishing integrator roles and job-rotation programs. These latter tactics can be thought of as formal organizational mechanisms for controlling conflict and political behavior.

427

Chapter 13:
Power and
Politics

Summary

Listed below are some of the major points discussed in the chapter:

1. Power is defined as the force that A can bring to bear on B to modify B's behavior. It is based on B's perceptions. If B thinks that A will provide valued outcomes as a result of compliance, then A has power over B.
2. The outcomes that A controls are based on A's resources. These resources include rewards, punishments, information, expertise, legitimacy, and attractiveness (referent power). If B values these outcomes, values the relationship, and has few other options or little counterpower, B is likely to comply with A's demands.
3. Specific behavioral strategies are often used by A to indicate to B what power resources are operating. Norms may be invoked (e.g., fairness, reciprocity), information manipulated, expertise illustrated, threats or promises uttered, or legitimacy demonstrated. The particular strategy used depends on the person and the setting.
4. Social power in organizations operates not only downward (from superiors to subordinates) but laterally and upward as well. Information and expertise are important sources of social power for influencing laterally and upward. Individuals can also exert influence laterally and upward by seeking to legitimate their requests, and by making use of the foot-in-the-door and door-in-the-face tactics.
5. Organizational politics is defined as the use of power by groups to obtain their preferred outcomes in situations where there is uncertainty or disagreement about choices. Political behavior is not inherently either good or bad. The goodness or badness of a given political act must be judged by its outcomes.
6. Some degree of political activity is inevitable in all organizations. Politics is rooted in conflict, which in turn is the result of differentiation, task interdependence, parochial perspectives, and resource scarcity.
7. Political strategies for resolving conflict include compromise, the formation of coalitions, and co-optation. Organizations can often reduce (although not eliminate) the opportunity for political activity by minimizing the prerequisite conditions that lead to conflict.

IMPLICATIONS FOR RESEARCH

A large volume of research has been done on the topics of social power and organizational politics. Yet there still remain many things that we do not understand. There are many questions that need to be answered, and much research that needs to be done.

One set of questions concerns the behavioral, perceptual, and attitudinal changes that occur in power holders. The research discussed in this chapter suggests that access to various sources of power can change (1) the extent to which a power holder attempts to influence a target, (2) the power holder's perceptions of the quality and underlying causes of the target's performance, and (3) the power holder's overall attitude toward the target (Kipnis, 1972). It seems unlikely, however, that such changes will occur in every single instance. The question is, what determines whether or not the access to power will affect the power holder? Perhaps there are situational factors that should be considered. The presence of a role model (i.e., a person who already has access to power), for example, may strongly affect how a new power holder behaves. It also seems likely that various personality traits may be important. The need for power (McClelland, 1985) and Machiavellianism (Christie & Geis, 1970) are two traits that seem particularly relevant in this regard. The point we are trying to make here is that results such as those found by Kipnis (1972), while intriguing, are unlikely to hold for everyone in every situation. A truly complete understanding of social power phenomena requires that we learn exactly when these findings do and do not hold.

Another topic that requires more research is that of "empowerment." How do managers go about conferring social power on others, especially their subordinates? How willing are managers and other power holders to share the social power they have? Are some types of managers or situations more given than others to power sharing? And does the sharing of power with subordinates increase or decrease the power of a manager? At first blush, the answer to the last question would seem to be that when power is shared among more people, each individual holds less of it. But this is not necessarily the case. There are some social scientists who believe that social power is not a fixed commodity, and that sharing it can actually increase a manager's power. This is an interesting idea that deserves more research.

A related issue has to do with giving up power and authority. There are some situations in which individuals must take action to reduce their power, at least in some spheres of organizational activity. For example, entrepreneurs who start successful businesses usually find that after a time it is necessary to add intermediate layers of management. They can no longer afford the time required to be personally involved in the ever-increasing complexity of day-to-day operating problems. These managers need to spend their time instead on the "big picture," developing long-term goals and strategic plans. Yet, there is anecdotal evidence that they find this difficult to do, in part because they hate to give up power in the realm of day-to-day operations (e.g., Hymowitz, 1985). Research is needed to investigate this problem systematically. In general, we need to know more about the problems and prospects for gaining power, transferring power, and decreasing power.

A final topic on which there is relatively little empirical research is the stability of power over time. Does social power change over time, even in the absence of efforts by the power holder to increase or decrease it? Again, the evidence on this question is largely anecdotal. What limited research does exist, however, suggests that in order to maintain their power, power holders must exercise it on a regular basis (e.g., Biggart & Hamilton, 1984). Like physical health, without regular exercise, power may fade over time. This possibility also deserves more careful attention.

IMPLICATIONS FOR PRACTICE

A point we have made repeatedly throughout the chapter is that social power and organizational politics are both used to get things done. In that respect they are organizational necessities. An effective organization invariably uses power and politics to its advantage. Thus, one general implication is that in order to be successful, the individual manager will need to understand and be able to make good use of social power and political processes.

There are also several implications of a more specific nature that should be discussed. First, with regard to social power, it is very useful to be able to identify who in the organization has power and who does not. Yet, this task is not always an easy one. There are three reasons for this. One is that a manager's power cannot be determined by direct observation. Rather, it must be inferred from the behavior of those individuals the manager tries to influence. A second reason is that power is defined in terms of felt pressure to comply with a request. This felt pressure is not always accurately reflected in behavior. For example, sometimes a subordinate may feel a great deal of pressure to comply with a manager's requests (thus, the manager has great power over that subordinate), yet he or she may not be able to comply due to external constraints (e.g., the subordinate may not have the skills to do what the manager wants). Or a subordinate may have intended to behave in a particular way even if the manager had not made the request. The point is that behavior is not always the best indicator of the compliance pressure someone feels. Finally, power is always defined with reference to specific others. Thus, a manager may have a great deal of power over one set of individuals, but this does not guarantee that he or she will have power over some other set of individuals in some other context. Power is a relational phenomenon, not an absolute one. Thus, when trying to determine who has power, one must further specify (1) over whom, and (2) with regard to what sorts of behavior.

Besides knowing who has power, there is also the question of its use. The research is clear on this topic. People prefer to use and to have used on them the resources of expert, referent, and legitimate power. Both the powerful and the powerless generally find the use of reward and punishment resources to be distasteful. The extensive use of rewards and punishment is often perceived to be manipulative or coercive, and people usually resent the feeling of being coerced.

We are not saying that rewards and punishments are not needed. They serve a very important function as the resource of last resort and as a feedback mechanism. However, it should be recognized that when promises and threats are used extensively as inducements, negative consequences are likely to occur. Rarely will B come to like what he or she is doing, and the relationship between A and B will probably become strained and uncomfortable. The prognosis for long-term effectiveness is poor when rewards and punishments are the sole bases of power that a manager uses. The use of power is a question of style. To be effective, a manager must learn to utilize the right power bases in the right settings. As we shall see in Chapter 14, "Leadership," this question of matching actions to problems is broader than the single issue of power.

Finally, with regard to organizational politics, managers must learn how to wield power and influence at the group level of analysis. One important role that most managers play is that of spokesperson. As a spokesperson, a manager represents his or her unit to the rest of the organization (cf. Mintzberg, 1973). The manager is responsible for seeing to it that his or her unit gets the resources it needs to function, and that it is able to secure its preferred outcomes when important decisions arise. In order to do this, the manager may have to engage in frequent negotiations (both formal and informal) with the representatives of other groups. A manager will succeed in these negotiations only to the extent he or she is facile with such basic political tactics as compromise, coalition formation, and co-optation. The use of these tactics is an art, and it is one in which managers would do well to hone their skills.

Discussion Questions

1. Think of the people who have power over you. What power bases do they use? Which ones are most effective?
2. Do you think power corrupts? Does it ruin effective interpersonal communication? Can we get things done without it?
3. Describe the various political strategies used in organizations. What factors make political activities more acceptable?

CASE: OBEDIENT BETTY

Mr. Musgrave was having one of his tantrums. He had been harassed all morning with petty details and he had not gotten anything done. He was ready to snap at anyone.

Just then his secretary buzzed him on the intercom. "Yeah, what do you want?" growled Musgrave. "It's Casey Templeton on the phone sir," replied his secretary, Betty Odland. "He says he's not happy with the last shipment we sent him and he's ready to cancel his contract. He sounds angry."

"Tell that SOB to jump in the lake. I can't be bothered with his moaning and groaning. And don't interrupt me again until after lunch," yelled Musgrave.

Ms. Odland was fed up. She did not like being treated that way. So, with the intercom still on, she calmly picked up the phone and said, "Mr. Templeton? Mr. Musgrave said you should go jump in the lake. He can't be bothered with your moaning and groaning."

Questions about the Case

1. Should Betty have done what she did?
2. Who is responsible in this situation? How literally should we follow instructions or orders?
3. Is there a point at which we can and should refuse to obey? What is that point?

References

Asch, S. E. (1955). Studies of independence and conformity: A minority of one against a unanimous majority. *Psychological Monographs, 20*(Whole No. 416).

Bacharach, S. B., & Lawler, E. J. (1980). *Power and politics in organizations*. San Francisco: Jossey-Bass.

Berle, A. A. (1967). *Power.* New York: Harcourt, Brace, & World.

Biggart, N. W., & Hamilton, G. G. (1984). The power of obedience. *Administrative Science Quarterly, 29,* 540–549.

Brehm, J. W. (1966). *A theory of psychological reactance.* New York: Academic Press.

Cavanagh, G. F., Moberg, D. J., & Velasquez, M. (1981). The ethics of organizational politics. *Academy of Management Review, 6,* 363–374.

Christie, R., & Geis, F. L. (1970). *Studies in Machiavellianism.* New York: Academic Press.

Cialdini, R. B. (1985). *Influence: Science and practice.* Glenview, IL: Scott, Foresman.

Cialdini, R. B., Vincent, J. E., Lewis, S. K., Catalan, J., Wheeler, D., & Darby, B. L. (1975). Reciprocal concessions procedure for inducing compliance: The door-in-the-face technique. *Journal of Personality and Social Psychology, 31,* 206–215.

Dahl, R. A. (1957). The concept of power. *Behavioral Science, 2,* 201–215.

Dyer, W. (1979, Summer). Caring and power. *California Management Review,* pp. 84–89.

Edstrom, A., & Galbraith, J. (1977). Transfer of managers as a coordination and control strategy in multinational organizations. *Administrative Science Quarterly, 22,* 248–263.

Emerson, R. M. (1962). Power-dependence relations. *American Sociological Review, 2,* 31–41.

Feldman, D. C., & Arnold, H. J. (1983). *Managing individual and group behavior in organizations.* New York: McGraw-Hill.

Filley, A. C. (1977). Conflict resolution: The ethic of the good loser. In R. C. Huseman, C. M. Logue, & D. L. Freshly (Eds.), *Readings in interpersonal and organizational behavior* (pp. 234–252). Boston: Holbrook.

Freedman, J. L., & Fraser, S. C. (1966). Compliance without pressure: The foot-in-the-door technique. *Journal of Personality and Social Psychology, 4,* 195–202.

French, J. R. P., Jr., & Raven, B. (1960). The bases of social power. In D. Cartwright and A. F. Zander (Eds.), *Group dynamics* (2d ed., pp. 607–623). Evanston, IL: Row, Peterson.

Galbraith, J. R. (1977). *Organization design.* Reading, MA: Addison-Wesley.

Goodstadt, B. E., & Hjelle, L. A. (1973). Power to the powerless: Locus of control and the use of power. *Journal of Personality and Social Psychology, 27,* 190–196.

Green, F. (1965). The foot-in-the-door technique. *American Salesman, 10,* 14–16.ep

Hall, J. (1971, November). Decisions, decisions, decisions. *Psychology Today,* pp. 51–54.

Hobbes, T. (1968). *Leviathan.* Middlesex, England: Penguin.

Hoffman, L. R., & Maier, N. R. F. (1961). Quality and acceptance of problem solutions by members of homogeneous and heterogeneous groups. *Journal of Abnormal and Social Psychology, 62,* 401–407.

Hymowitz, C. (1985, May 5). Small-business owners discover giving up authority isn't easy. *The Wall Street Journal,* p. 33.

Iacocca, L., & Novack, W. (1984). *Iacocca: An autobiography.* New York: Bantam.

Kahn, R. L., Wolfe, D. M., Quinn, R. P., Snoek, J. D., & Rosenthal, R. A. (1964). *Organizational stress: Studies in role conflict and ambiguity.* New York: Wiley.

Kelley, H. H., & Thibaut, J. W. (1978). *Interpersonal relations: A theory of interdependence.* New York: Wiley.

Kipnis, D. (1972). Does power corrupt? *Journal of Personality and Social Psychology, 24,* 33–41.

Kipnis, D. (1976). *The Powerholders.* Chicago: University of Chicago Press.

Kipnis, D., Schmidt, S. M., Swaffin-Smith, C., & Wilkinson, I. (1984, Winter). Patterns of managerial influence: Shotgun managers, tacticians, and bystanders. *Organization Dynamics,* pp. 58–67.

431

Chapter 13:
Power and
Politics

Lawrence, P., & Lorsch, J. (1967). *Organization and environment.* Boston: Harvard Business School, Division of Research.

Lewin, K. (1951). *Field theory in social science.* New York: Harper & Row.

March, J. G. (1955). An introduction to the theory and measurement of influence. *American Political Science Review, 49,* 431–451.

Mayes, B. T., & Allen, R. W. (1977). Toward a definition of organizational politics. *Academy of Management Review, 2,* 672–678.

McCallum, D. M., Harring, K., Gilmore, R., Drenan, S., Chase, J. P., Insko, C. A., & Thibaut, J. (1985). Competition and cooperation between groups and between individuals. *Journal of Experimental Social Psyhology, 21,* 301–320.

McClelland, D. C. (1985). *Human motivation.* Glenview IL: Scott, Foresman.

Michener, H. A., Lawler, E. J., & Bacharach, S. B. (1973). Perceptions of power in conflict situations. *Journal of Personality and Social Psychology, 28,* 155–162.

Mintzberg, H. (1973). *The nature of managerial work.* New York: Harper & Row.

Ouchi, W. G., & Jaeger, A. M. (1978). Type Z organization: Stability in the midst of mobility. *Academy of Management Review, 3,* 305–314.

Pfeffer, J. (1981). *Power in organizations.* Marshfield, MA: Pitman Publishing.

Pollard, W. E., & Mitchell, T. R. (1972). Decision theory analysis of social power. *Psychological Bulletin, 78,* 433–446.

Pondy, L. R. (1977). The other hand clapping: An information processing approach to organizational power. In T. H. Hammer & S. B. Bacharach (Eds.), *Reward systems and power distributions.* Ithaca, NY: Cornell University Press.

Salancik, G. R., & Pfeffer, J. (1977, Winter). Who gets power—and how they hold on to it: A strategic contingency model of power. *Organizational Dynamics,* pp. 3–21.

Sherif, M., & Sherif, C. W. (1953). *Groups in harmony and tension.* New York: Harper.

Snyder, M., & Cunningham, M. R. (1975). To comply or not comply: Testing the self-perception explanation of the foot-in-the-door phenomenon. *Journal of Personality and Social Psychology, 31,* 206–215.

Stephan, W. G. (1985). Intergroup relations. In G. Lindzey & E. Aronson (Eds.), *The handbook of social psychology* (3d ed., Vol. 2, pp. 599–658). New York: Random House.

Thomas, K. (1976). Conflict and conflict management. In M. D. Dunnette (Ed.), *Handbook of industrial and organizational psychology* (pp. 889–935). Chicago: Rand McNally.

Chapter 14

Leadership

Better to reign in hell than serve in heav'n.
—JOHN MILTON

In the last chapter we examined two important influence processes that occur in organizations: (1) the process by which individuals influence the behavior of other individuals (social power), and (2) the process by which groups influence the behavior of other groups (organizational politics). In addition, in an earlier chapter (Chapter 9) we examined how groups influence the behavior of individuals through the systematic enforcement of group norms. In the present chapter we examine one final influence process—the way in which individuals influence the behavior of groups. This process is called *leadership*.

Leadership is a key element in the functioning of any organization. The success or failure of an organization is often attributed to the quality of its leadership. When a business venture, a university, or an athletic team is successful, it is the CEO, president, or coach who often receives the credit. When failure occurs, it is usually the same individual at the top that is replaced. Thus, one major concern of any organization is how to attract, train, and keep people who will be effective leaders.

This concern is justified by research data. Numerous studies show that variations in leadership are related to variations in group morale and group productivity. What we need to know, then, is how to select those people who will be effective leaders, how to train them, and where to place them in the organization. To do this well demands that we define clearly and precisely what we mean by leadership.

DEFINING LEADERSHIP

The term *leadership* has been defined in many different ways by many different people. Common to most definitions, however, is the notion that *leadership is a process whereby an individual influences the group toward the attainment of desired group or organizational goals* (cf. Hollander, 1985). Several aspects of this definition are worth noting. First, leadership refers to a *process*, not to a person. Thus, the formal leader of a group (i.e., the individual who occupies the position of formal power and authority—captain, manager, chairperson, coach) may or may not exhibit leadership. Conversely, in order to exhibit leadership one does not have to be a formal leader. This latter point raises the possibility that a group may have one or more *informal leaders.* Second, leadership implies a degree of legitimacy. That is, the rest of the group must either explicitly or implicitly consent to the leader's influence. They must allow themselves to be influenced. If the leader does not have legitimacy in the eyes of the rest of the group, the group is likely to ignore the leader's influence attempts, or worse, may actively behave in ways that run counter to the leader's wishes. The implication is that a leader's power is ultimately rooted in the group itself. Finally, leadership is defined in terms of goal attainment. If a leader is unable to move the group toward its desired goals, he or she is not exerting leadership.

Given this definition, there are a number of important questions that can be asked about the leadership process. One has to do with leader legitimacy. How do leaders gain legitimacy? Is it enough to be appointed to a formal position of power and authority by those who are higher up in the organization (e.g., as a promotion), or is something else required? And what about informal leaders? How do they gain legitimacy? A second question concerns how the leadership process fits into the overall job of a manager or supervisor. Are all managers leaders? If so, is there something called a "leadership role" that is distinct from all the other roles that a manager plays? A third question concerns the emergence of informal leaders in a group. What are the personal and situational factors that contribute to leader emergence? Finally, and perhaps most important, is the question of leader effectiveness. What are the factors that determine who will and who will not be an effective leader? In this first section of the chapter we examine the questions of leader legitimacy, leadership as a managerial role, and leader emergence. After that, we devote most of the rest of the chapter to the question of leader effectiveness.

Leader Legitimacy

The question of leader legitimacy is a question of right: What gives a particular individual the right to exert influence over the rest of the group? In the case of a formal group leader, the right to influence is conferred partly by the organization. When an individual is appointed to the position of bank manager, head nurse, supervisor, superintendent, commander, captain, or any other such position, he or she is implicitly given the authority to exert influence over his or her subordinates within a limited area. This implicit authority is called *institutional legitimacy*. Thus, a manager has a right to make certain requests, and his or her subordinates have a corresponding obligation to comply. Institutional legitimacy is tied to the *position* that the individual occupies. Consequently, anyone in that position would have exactly the same degree of formal authority to influence others.

Institutional legitimacy tells only part of the story, however. Experience provides many examples in which different individuals occupy virtually identical positions (e.g., the heads of various academic departments within a university), and yet those individuals are not equally accepted by the members of their respective groups. The less-accepted leaders are able to command little more than perfunctory compliance with requests, while the more-accepted leaders are able to command not only compliance, but also a genuine enthusiasm and eagerness to strive for desired goals. Such differences obviously cannot be explained in terms of the institutional legitimacy inherent in the formal positions occupied by the leaders. Nor can institutional legitimacy explain the acceptance of informal group leaders, who may have no formal authority at all. Thus, in addition to institutional legitimacy, there must also be a process by which leaders build a *personal* base of legitimacy and acceptance among their group members (cf. Rasinski, Tyler, and Fridkin, 1985).

An Exchange Theory Perspective. The process by which leaders build personal legitimacy and acceptance can be understood in terms of an *exchange theory* analysis. The central tenet of exchange theory is that all social relationships involve some sort of economic-like exchange, in which the various parties both give and receive benefits. In the case of leadership, the exchange is between the leader (formal or informal) and the rest of the group. In this relationship, the leader gives the group direction, coordination, expertise, access to special resources, or other similar benefits that will help the group achieve desired goals. In exchange, the leader gets from the group status, recognition, esteem, compliance, and the potential for even greater influence in the future (Hollander, 1978).

An important element of this exchange theory analysis is the concept of *idiosyncrasy credits*. Idiosyncrasy credits can be roughly defined as hypothetical units of legitimacy, status, or acceptance within the group (cf. Hollander, 1964). Whenever a leader (or any other group member) does something that contributes to the group's primary task or demonstrates loyalty to the group's norms, he or she earns idiosyncrasy credits (i.e., gains legitimacy, status, and acceptance). Conversely, whenever a leader does something that detracts from the group's primary task or deviates from the group's norms, he or she loses idiosyncrasy credits (i.e., loses legitimacy, status, and acceptance).

The usefulness of this concept becomes clear when it is recognized that in order to better achieve a desired goal, it is often necessary for the leader to introduce some type of innovation or change in the group's current mode of operation. This might involve asking the group members to exert more effort on the job (e.g., work longer hours) or perhaps to alter the way they go about doing their work. But change, by definition, means a deviation from existing group norms—a departure from the status quo. Furthermore, before a change is implemented and allowed to exist for a period of time, it is often not apparent that the change will actually work (i.e., that it will help the group more effectively attain its goal). For both of these reasons, the introduction of a change is usually costly for a leader in terms of idiosyncrasy credit. That is, a leader will generally "spend" idiosyncrasy credits simply by introducing a change, and he or she risks losing additional credits if the change does not prove effective. On the other hand, if the change yields positive results, those credits will be earned back. Indeed, more idiosyncrasy credits will usually be earned back than were spent to initiate the change in the first place.

Two important points about this process should be noted. First, in order to introduce a change, a leader must have some degree of idiosyncrasy credit to begin with. A leader can initially begin to earn a few credits just by putting time and energy into running the group and maintaining the status quo. Idiosyncrasy credits accrued in this way (in combination with the leader's institutional legitimacy) can then be used to initiate one or two small changes—changes that do not depart radically from the current mode of operation and that consequently do not "cost" many idiosyncrasy credits. The second point is that a successful innovation usually earns for the leader more idiosyncrasy credits than it originally costs to implement. Consequently, as small changes are introduced and proved effective, the leader will accumulate more and more credits. The leader's growing idiosyncrasy credit can then be used to introduce more substantial changes in the future. These more substantial changes would not have been possible earlier, since the leader did not have sufficient credit for them to be accepted by the group. However, now that the leader has demonstrated his or her competence and has gained more credit, the group will be more willing to go along with his or her suggestions. Thus, a string of successes will build the leader's personal legitimacy and acceptance, and he or she will be able to exert more and more influence over the group as time goes on. Of course, the opposite is also true. A string of failures will destroy a leader's personal legitimacy, and he or she will exert less and less influence over the group as time goes on.

Although leaders do not use the term *idiosyncrasy credit* when talking about their personal legitimacy or acceptance in the group, it is clear that they are aware of the basic concept and that they behave in accordance with the predictions of the idiosyncrasy credit model. For example, one prediction made by this model is that in comparison to those who are *appointed* by the organization to the position of group leader, those who are *elected* to that position by the members of the group should feel more freedom to introduce the changes they think will be beneficial. The reason is that election is an explicit statement of the group's acceptance of the leader. It is, if you will, a sign that the leader has idiosyncrasy credits to spend. Appointed leaders do not have this clear statement of group acceptance, and thus they are likely to be unsure of just how much idiosyncrasy credit they have.

This prediction was borne out in a laboratory experiment conducted by Hollander and Julian (1970). In this experiment forty male university students served as the leaders of four-person problem-solving groups in what appeared to be a study concerned with decision making and urban planning. Each group's task was to evaluate several different solutions proposed for each of ten specific "urban problems" (e.g., education, welfare, housing) and to decide which solution for each problem was the best. It was the leader's responsibility to make the final decision for the group, but he was to take the opinions of the rest of the group into consideration. Among the alternatives presented for each problem was one solution that most people agree is clearly the best and one that most people agree is clearly the worst.

The independent variable manipulated in this study was the way in which the leader got his job. Half of the leaders were appointed to their positions by the experimenter, while the other half were elected (or so they believed) by the other members of their group. As the experiment progressed, the leaders in both conditions found themselves in a curious position. On seven of the ten problems, the solution that the other members of the group favored most was the very one that most people would say was the worst, while the solution that the group favored least was the one that most people would say was the best. Thus, all of the leaders knew that if they went along with the preferences of the other members of their group, there was a strong possibility that they would be choosing the wrong alternative. The research question was, therefore, what percentage of the time would the leaders countermand the preferences of the rest of their group, and pick instead the alternative they (like most people) believe to be the best? And more importantly, would this percentage vary as a function of having been elected versus appointed to their leadership position?

The results are presented in Figure 14-1. As you can see, approximately one-third of the time the leaders made decisions opposite to the preferences expressed by the rest of the group. But this happened much more often when the leaders were elected than when they were appointed. These results are in agreement with the predictions of the idiosyncrasy credit model. Election is an explicit statement of acceptance that gives a leader more latitude to make the changes that he or she believes are in the group's best interest—even when

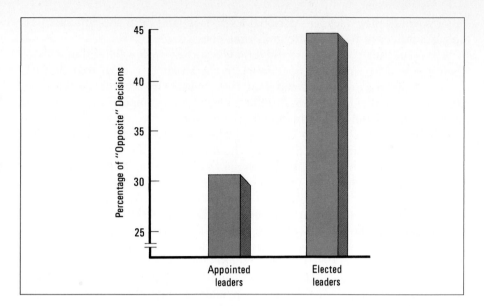

these changes involve choices that the rest of the group may not initially agree with. If these changes turn out to be beneficial for the group, the leader will accrue additional credit, and thus build more personal legitimacy for making further changes.

One final point about idiosyncrasy credits should be noted. A leader cannot "sit on" his or her credits indefinitely. Leaders are generally *expected* to introduce change and do things that will help the group better achieve its goals. In terms of idiosyncrasy credits, this means that leaders are expected to spend the credits they earn. If credits are earned but never spent, those credits will gradually evaporate. Thus, inaction ultimately destroys a leader's personal legitimacy, and consequently, his or her ability to introduce innovative changes in the future.

Vertical Dyad Exchanges. While an exchange theory analysis is a useful way of conceptualizing the leadership process, it is somewhat misleading to view this process as an undifferentiated exchange between the leader and the group *as a whole.* Rather, we would do better to focus on the exchange that takes place between the leader and *each individual member of the group* (e.g., Dansereau, Graen, & Haga, 1975; Graen & Cashman, 1975). By focusing on the exchange relationship within each leader-subordinate pair—called a *vertical dyad*—it is possible to determine whether leaders have different types of exchange relationships with different types of subordinates. It seems highly likely, for example, that leaders exchange more benefits with some subordinates than with others. Thus, a leader may systematically give certain subordinates more desirable job assignments, more autonomy, greater responsibility and authority, better resources, greater access to "privileged information," and so on. The subordinates that get these special benefits are likely to give the leader in return greater loyalty, more effort and commitment to achieving group goals, and greater involvement in the overall functioning of the group.

Those that do not get these special benefits are likely to be less loyal, less committed, and less involved in the group.

Research generally supports the usefulness of this more differentiated view of the leader-subordinate exchange process. Subordinates that receive special benefits from the leader are called *in-group* subordinates, and they are the ones who become the leader's chief lieutenants. Those that do not get special benefits from the leader are called *out-group* subordinates. In comparison to in-group subordinates, out-group subordinates have been found to be less productive, less satisfied with their jobs, and more likely to quit (e.g., Graen, Novak, & Sommerkamp, 1982; Graen, Liden, & Hoel, 1982; Vecchio & Gobdel, 1984).

Leadership as a Managerial Role

An exchange theory analysis tells us something about the basic process of leadership and about how leaders build personal legitimacy and acceptance within their groups. In order to be successful, managers must learn to master this process.[1] Being a leader, in other words, is an important managerial role. But it is not the only role that a manager plays. There are others. Mintzberg (1973), for example, has identified ten distinct roles that are played by almost every manager. Managers differ in the relative amount of time they devote to these various roles, but most devote at least some time to each one. These ten roles fall into three categories: informational roles, decisional roles, and interpersonal roles.

Informational Roles. Three of the roles that managers play have to do with acquiring and transmitting information. One of these is called the *monitor* role. This role is concerned with the acquisition of information. Managers must continually monitor their environment for information that will help them understand what is happening both inside and outside their work group. They need information that tells them about problems and opportunities facing their group, and about pressures and constraints that limit their group's scope of action. Much of this information is "soft" (nonquantified), undocumented, and transmitted by word of mouth. To be effective in this role, it is essential that a manager be "well connected" in the organization's informal communication network.

The other two roles in this category are the *disseminator* and *spokesperson* roles. Both involve the transmission of information. The disseminator role involves transmitting information to those individuals within the group who need it and/or can act on it. This information might be of a factual nature, or it might consist of the values, preferences, and goals of either the manager or important individuals outside the group (e.g., the manager's boss). In the spokesperson role, the manager communicates in the opposite direction. He or

---

[1]We use the term *manager* in a generic sense here to refer to anyone who is the formal head of a group, and who is responsible for the work done by the group's members. This usage thus includes many individuals who do not normally carry the formal title of manager (e.g., airline captains, construction supervisors, company vice presidents, school principals, army lieutenants). Conversely, it excludes those individuals who are formally called managers, but who do not have any subordinates (e.g., certain account managers in financial services organizations).

she transmits important information about the group to other units in the organization or to relevant individuals and groups outside the organization (e.g., customers and suppliers).

Decisional Roles. Decision making is a crucial aspect of most managerial jobs. Four separate decisional roles can be identified. The first is the *entrepreneurial* role. In this role the manager initiates and designs innovative changes that take advantage of significant opportunities facing the group. The focus of this role is the decision making that surrounds the initial phases of designing the innovation. Implementation, which may include gaining the acceptance and commitment of subordinates (part of the leadership role), is not of prime concern. On the other hand, an innovation is worthless unless it can be successfully implemented. Thus, the entrepreneurial and leadership roles are often closely related.

A second decisional role is that of *disturbance handler*. Managers must often deal with unforeseen disturbances (problems) that appear quite suddenly. These may involve conflicts among subordinates, conflicts between the manager's own group and another, or the threatened or actual loss of important resources. As a disturbance handler, the manager must rapidly (and accurately) diagnose the problem and decide on a remedy.

Finally, there are two decisional roles that are primarily concerned with resource usage. One is the role of *resource allocator*. In this role, the manager makes frequent decisions about which subordinates get what resources, and about what projects or programs are to receive priority. The second role is that of *negotiator*. Here, the manager participates in and directs the group's negotiations and exchanges (both formal and informal) with other groups in the organization. As a negotiator, the manager has the responsibility for making decisions that commit group resources and that obligate the group to perform certain actions. It is in this role that the manager gets involved in the political activities discussed in Chapter 13.

Interpersonal Roles. Finally, there are three roles that focus primarily on the manager's position in the group and his or her interpersonal relationships with others. The first of these is the *figurehead* role. In this role the manager performs tasks that are often of a legalistic or symbolic nature (e.g., introducing guest speakers, writing letters of appreciation to retiring employees). Such activities frequently have little to do with the real work of managing, but fall to the manager simply because he or she is the formal head of the group.

A second interpersonal role is that of *liaison*. In this role, the manager serves as a link between his or her own group and other important groups throughout the rest of the organization. It is essential that managers build and maintain an informal network of contacts with individuals in other groups, because these relationships serve as the foundation upon which some of the manager's other roles rest (e.g., monitor, disseminator, spokesperson, and negotiator).

Finally, we come to the *leadership* role. Leadership is properly classified as an interpersonal role, since, as we have seen, it involves an interpersonal exchange relationship between the manager and each of his or her subordinates. The purpose of this exchange, from the manager's perspective, is to motivate the group members and to get them to work together effectively in the pursuit of desired group or organizational goals. In many respects, however, this is the least distinct of the ten roles identified by Mintzberg (1973). The leadership role pervades virtually all managerial activity. It is frequently the case that an action performed primarily in the service of some other role also serves the manager's leadership role. For example, providing the group with critical information on a timely basis (part of the disseminator role) is likely to earn idiosyncrasy credits for the manager. Idiosyncrasy credits will also be earned when the manager develops creative innovations in work procedures and objectives (part of the entrepreneurial role) that turn out to be successful. The credits earned as a function of performing these other roles well will increase the manager's personal legitimacy and will make it easier for him or her to perform the leadership role.

The Emergence of Informal Leaders

It should be clear that the exchange process we have outlined here applies just as well to informal leaders as it does to formal leaders. Thus, an individual who has no formal power or authority in the group can nevertheless emerge as an informal group leader by making a series of unique contributions to the attainment of group goals, and by adhering to important group norms.

There are two basic types of "contributions" that increase an individual's chances of emerging as an informal group leader. One is contributing special expertise or ability to the group (Shaw, 1981). If an individual has some specialized knowledge or skill that is relevant to the group's task, and this knowledge or skill is not possessed by other group members, he or she may be able to make an important contribution to the performance of the group that is over and above what others are able to contribute. This may be a direct contribution (e.g., being the only person on a research team with enough programming background to solve certain computer software problems), or it may be an indirect contribution that involves influencing the actions of others (e.g., instructing other group members on how to handle a new piece of equipment correctly). In either case, if as a result of this individual's expertise the group makes noticeable progress toward its goal, he or she will earn idiosyncrasy credits from the other group members. After making several such contributions, this individual is likely to have accumulated a sufficient number of credits to begin expanding his or her scope of influence to areas beyond those in which he or she is the sole expert. As long as these subsequent influence attempts continue to benefit the group, this individual's idiosyncrasy credit will continue to grow, and his or her role as an informal group leader will be established.

The second type of contribution that will increase an individual's chances of becoming an informal group leader is exerting effort on behalf of the group. Even though an individual may have only average skills and abilities, he or she can still earn idiosyncrasy credits by putting an unusually high level of effort into the group's task. There are several ways in which this can be done. One is to spend more time on the task than is spent by other group members. This, of course, does not mean working slower than others. It means working at the same (or faster) rate but doing so for a longer period. Someone who contributes more of his or her time to the group's task will be seen as exerting more effort than someone who spends less time. And more to the point, those who volunteer more time are more likely to be perceived as informal group leaders (cf. Bass, 1981).

Another way in which an individual can contribute more effort to the group is by being more participative in group problem-solving discussions. In general, the more someone talks during a group discussion, the more likely it is that he or she will be perceived by the rest of the group as having influence and as being an informal leader (Stein & Heller, 1979). It is interesting to note that this occurs independently of the *quality* of the ideas that are contributed. This point was demonstrated in a study by Sorrentino and Boutillier (1975). They had 16 four-person groups work on a problem-solving task for about an hour. Unknown to the others, one member of each group was a confederate of the researchers who was coached to exhibit one of four patterns of verbal behavior during the group discussion: (1) being relatively talkative and contributing a number of high-quality ideas, (2) being relatively talkative but contributing few high-quality ideas, (3) being relatively quiet but still contributing a number of high-quality ideas, and (4) being relatively quiet and contributing few high-quality ideas. Of interest are the ratings that were made by the other group members of this individual's influence in the group. Remember that the ability to influence the group is central to the definition of leadership. The results are shown in Figure 14-2. As can be seen, when the confederate was talkative the influence ratings were higher than when he or she was quiet. Furthermore, this effect occurred regardless of how many high-

Figure 14-2
Those who were
more talkative
were rated as hav-
ing more influence
in the group.
(*Based on data
presented by Sor-
rentino &
Boutillier, 1975.*)

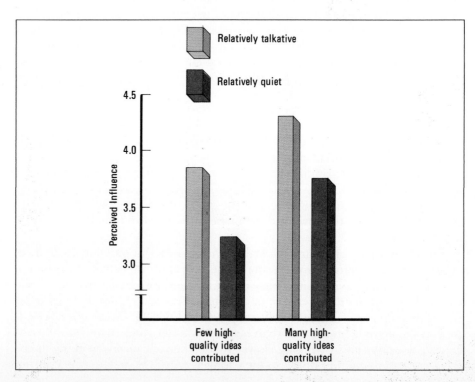

quality ideas were contributed. This does not mean that the quality of the ideas was unimportant. On the contrary, contributing many high-quality ideas resulted in higher influence ratings than contributing few high-quality ideas (cf. Bottger, 1984). Over and above the issue of quality, however, it is clear that the *amount* of verbal participation significantly affected the influence ratings, and by implication, the emergence of the confederate as an informal group leader.

Finally, we should note that there are several situational variables that also affect the likelihood that a group member will emerge as an informal leader. For example, there is evidence that occupying a physical space usually identified with leadership (e.g., the head of a table) increases one's chances of emerging as an informal group leader (Strodtbeck & Hook, 1961). Also, those who are at the center of a communication network are much more likely to emerge as informal group leaders than those at the periphery (Bales, 1953; Shaw, Rothschild, & Strickland, 1957). This latter effect is very robust, and is quite consistent with the verbal participation results cited previously. When at the center of a communication network, one spends more time interacting with others. Furthermore, being at the center of a communication network makes it easier to perform some of the managerial roles previously discussed (e.g., monitor, disseminator, spokesperson, disturbance handler, negotiator). It is thus not surprising that group members at the center of a communication network are more likely to become informal group leaders. Apparently, when group members behave in ways that are similar to how formal group leaders behave (e.g., sitting in the "leader's" chair, performing important managerial roles), their own role as informal leaders is enhanced in the eyes of the rest of their group.

Figure 14-3
By behaving in ways that formal leaders do, group members who do not have formal power and authority can often enhance their status as informal group leaders.

LEADER EFFECTIVENESS:
A CONCEPTUAL FRAMEWORK

So far we have examined (1) the process by which leaders gain personal legitimacy and acceptance in their group, (2) how the leadership role fits in with the other roles a manager must play, and (3) how group members who may have no formal power or authority in the group nevertheless emerge as informal group leaders. Central to our discussion has been an exchange theory analysis of the leader-member relationship. As we have seen, this type of analysis is extremely useful for understanding the basic process of leadership. However, except in a very general way, an exchange theory analysis does not explain why some individuals perform the leadership role better than others. It does not provide any details about the personal and/or situational factors that contribute to leader effectiveness. It is this question of effectiveness to which we now turn.

Social scientists have taken several different approaches to the study of leader effectiveness, four of which will be discussed here. Underlying these four approaches are very different assumptions about the nature of leadership. Furthermore, each of these assumptions has its own unique implications for how leader effectiveness ought to be managed. A framework for understanding the interrelationship among these four approaches, as well as the implications of their underlying assumptions, is shown in Figure 14-4. This framework defines each approach in terms of two basic dimensions. The first dimension, represented along the side of the figure, is whether the approach focuses on the leader's personality traits or on the leader's observable behavior. The second dimension, represented across the top of the figure, is whether the focal

Figure 14-4
A framework for
understanding the
interrelationship
among various ap-
proaches to the
sudy of leader ef-
fectiveness and
their implications.
(*Adapted from
Jago, 1982.*)

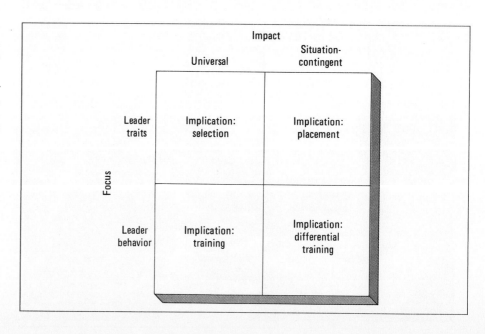

construct (i.e., trait or behavior) is assumed to have an impact in all situations (universal) or only in some situations (situations contingent).

The intersection of these two dimensions describes the essential character of each of the four approaches to studying leader effectiveness. The first approach, studying *universal traits*, seeks to find personality traits that improve leader effectiveness across many diverse situations. If such traits can be found, the implication for managing leader effectiveness would be to select those individuals for leadership positions who have the appropriate set of traits— those with the "right stuff." In other words, the organization should concentrate its energies on developing and refining its leader *selection* procedures.

The second approach, studying *universal behaviors*, seeks to find specific behaviors or behavior styles that increase leader effectiveness across many diverse situations. If such behaviors can be identified, the implication for managing leader effectiveness would be to focus on leadership *training*. That is, because behavior is much more modifiable than personality, organizations ought to be able to teach managers how to perform those behavior patterns that research identifies as being most effective. Since these behaviors are potentially learnable by anyone, the organization would not have to worry about selecting the right type of person. Anyone would do, so long as he or she could be trained.

The third approach, studying *situation-contingent traits*, seeks to find the personality traits that improve leader effectiveness in specific situations. Unlike the universal trait approach, the situation-contingent trait approach does not assume that any one set of traits will be appropriate in all situations. Rather, different situations are assumed to require different trait combinations. If sets of situation-specific traits can be identified, the implication would be that organizations can manage leader effectiveness through the use of carefully designed *placement* programs. There would be no need to hire only a few individuals of the "right" type. Many different types of individuals could be hired, as long as they were placed in different leadership positions according to what is best for them, that is, in situations in which their traits would result in the most effective performance.

The last approach, studying *situation-contingent behaviors*, seeks to identify the particular behaviors that increase leader effectiveness in specific situations. This approach is similar to the situation-contingent trait approach; however, its implication for managing leader effectiveness is somewhat different. Instead of concentrating on placing leaders in the right situation, organizations could manage leader effectiveness most easily through *differential training*. That is, managers could be trained to use the behaviors that are most appropriate for their own particular leadership situation. Furthermore, if managers are moved from one situation to another, as often happens in large organizations, they could simply be retrained to perform the behaviors that are most appropriate for their new situation.

Thus, we have four different approaches to studying leader effectiveness. It is important to note that these four approaches, and the assumptions that underlie them, reflect not only the differing views of social scientists, but also basic differences in the way organizations view leadership. That is, all organizations implicitly operate under one or the other of these four sets of assumptions, and these assumptions guide their decisions with respect to committing resources to leader selection, training, and placement programs. The critical question, then, is which of these four approaches is actually the correct one? We review the research on each approach in the next four sections.

UNIVERSAL TRAITS

> *Young men are fitter to invent than to judge, fitter for execution than for counsel,*
> *and fitter for new projects than for settled business.*
> —FRANCIS BACON

The universal trait approach to the study of leader effectiveness is by far the oldest of the four approaches covered here. This approach is sometimes called the "great man" theory of leadership. It assumes that effective leadership is ultimately rooted in some combination of enduring personal characteristics or traits of the leader. Situational factors have little to do with it. According to this view, great leaders are born, not made. Thus, proponents of this approach would argue that individuals such as Winston Churchill, Indira Gandhi, and Mao Tse-tung would have become great leaders no matter what particular political circumstances surrounded them.

A Summary of Research Findings

The basic research strategy associated with this approach is to observe effective leaders, measure their personality traits and other related characteristics, and determine which traits differentiate them from leaders who are not very effective. Literally thousands of studies have been done in this way. Physical traits such as age, height, weight, and energy have been investigated, along with social background (e.g., education, social status), intelligence, and a long list of personality variables (e.g., assertiveness, dominance, independence, self-confidence, objectivity) and social characteristics (e.g., attractiveness, popularity, tact).

The initial reviews of this literature that appeared in the late 1940s and early 1950s were rather devastating (e.g., Stogdill, 1948). They indicated that there was very little consistency in the results. In many cases a particular trait would be positively related to performance in one study, but negatively related to performance in another. However, a more recent review by Stogdill (1974) based on a newer set of studies is somewhat more encouraging. While different situations may indeed require somewhat different types of leaders, there are nevertheless a number of general characteristics that seem to be present in most effective leaders in most situations. According to Stogdill (1974), effective leaders have

> a strong drive for responsibility and task completion, vigor and persistence in pursuit of goals, venturesomeness and originality in problem solving, drive to exercise initiative in social situations, self-confidence and sense of personal identity, willingness to accept consequences of decision and action, readiness to absorb interpersonal stress, willingness to tolerate frustration and delay, ability to influence other persons' behavior, and capacity to structure social interaction systems to the purpose at hand (p. 81).

Figure 14-5
Having the "right" traits does not always guarantee that one will be a leader.

A Contemporary Application

A contemporary application of the universal trait approach can be found in many assessment centers. An *assessment center* is an employee evaluation technique that uses multiple methods to assess the skills and traits known to be related to managerial effectiveness. As part of an assessment center evaluation, individuals who are candidates for selection or promotion to managerial positions are asked to complete a number of personality questionnaires, as well as to participate in a variety of group exercises, simulations, and management games over a period of several days. (A more detailed description of assessment centers is given in Chapter 15, pp. 486–487.)

The degree to which personality traits and other characteristics measured in assessment centers actually predict managerial effectiveness is illustrated in a study by Ritchie and Moses (1983). These authors examined a variety of measures obtained in a 2-day assessment center conducted at AT&T. In all, more than 1200 Bell System employees were involved. These scores were correlated with a measure of managerial success collected 7 years later. Managerial success was defined as how high the employee had risen in the Bell System management hierarchy. (Note that in using this measure of success the authors make the tacit assumption that individuals who are promoted to higher levels of management are in fact more effective managers than those who are not promoted.) The results of the study are shown in Figure 14-6. As you can see, most of the traits that were assessed show a significant positive correlation with managerial success after 7 years. On almost every trait dimension, those who had originally attained a high score were likely to achieve a higher managerial rank after 7 years than those who attained a low score. This was just as true for women as it was for men. On the other hand, none of the correlations reported in Figure 14-6 are really very high. (A correlation coefficient can range as high as $r = 1.00$.) Furthermore, these trait dimensions account for an average of only about 8 percent of the variance in managerial success.

The conclusion to be drawn from all of this is that the universal trait approach, while helpful in some ways, falls well short of explaining all there is to know about leadership and managerial effectiveness. The ability to predict, and therefore select, managers who will be effective across many different

Figure 14-6
Traits measured in
an assessment
center showed a
significant positive
correlation with
managerial suc-
cess 7 years later.
(*Adapted from
Ritchie & Moses,
1983.*)

Trait Dimension	Males	Females
Oral communication	.33	.27
Leadership	.32	.36
Energy	.28	.34
Self-objectivity	.04	.28
Awareness of social environment	.17	.28
Behavior flexibility	.21	.36
Inner work standards	.21	.30
Resistance to stress	.31	.32
Tolerance of uncertainty	.30	.32
Need for advancement	.31	.29
Range of interests	.23	.17
Organizing and planning	.28	.30
Decision making	.18	.26
Scholastic aptitude	.19	.25

situations is at best quite modest. Perhaps what is needed, then, is an approach that takes the situation into account.

SITUATION-CONTINGENT TRAITS

A large number of studies have demonstrated that personality traits do a better job of predicting leader and managerial effectiveness when the characteristics of the situation are taken into account. For example, research indicates that different types of psychological needs predict managerial effectiveness in different types of organizations. A moderate-to-high need for power is an important ingredient for managerial effectiveness in large bureaucratic organizations but not in small entrepreneurial firms, while a high need for achievement is predictive of managerial effectiveness in small entrepreneurial firms but not in large bureaucracies (McClelland, 1985; Miner, 1980).

But one need not be limited to broad organizational differences to find important situational characteristics related to leader effectiveness. In almost any organization managers are faced with many different types of leadership situations, and different traits seem to be associated with success in these various situations. The most extensive program of research taking a situation-contingent trait approach is that conducted by Fiedler and his colleagues (Fiedler, 1967, 1978; Fiedler & Chemers, 1974). Fiedler's theory is called (not surprisingly) the *contingency model* of leader effectiveness.

Fiedler's Contingency Model

Consistent with the definition of leadership given at the beginning of the chapter, the contingency model defines leader effectiveness in terms of group performance. Other things being equal, leaders whose groups perform well are considered to be more effective than those whose groups perform poorly. The basic proposition of the model is that in order to be effective, a leader's "style" must match the demands of the situation. To understand fully what this means, we need to know how the model defines "leadership style" and what the relevant characteristics of the situation are.

Leadership Style. The contingency model is concerned with two basic leadership styles or orientations. The first is the *task-oriented* style. A person who is task-oriented sees work primarily in terms of goal attainment. Task performance is of paramount importance to the task-oriented leader. In contrast, there is the *relationship-oriented* style. A person who is relationship-oriented sees work not only in terms of performance, but also in terms of people. The quality of interpersonal relations within the work group is much more important to the relationship-oriented leader than to the task-oriented leader.

These two leadership styles are measured by a questionnaire known as the *least preferred coworker* (LPC) scale. This questionnaire consists of from sixteen to twenty-four bipolar adjective scales such as the following:

Unpleasant :____:____:____:____:____:____:____:____: Pleasant
              1   2   3   4   5   6   7   8

Tense :____:____:____:____:____:____:____:____: Relaxed
        1   2   3   4   5   6   7   8

When filling out this questionnaire, the leader is asked to think of all the people with whom he or she has ever worked and to describe the one person that he or she would least like to work with again—his or her least preferred coworker. For the task-oriented leader, the overriding importance of task accomplishment colors his or her perceptions of the least preferred coworker, and consequently that person is described in universally negative terms (e.g., very tense and unpleasant). This results in a low score on the LPC scale. Thus, "low LPC leaders" are task-oriented leaders. The relationship-oriented leader, on the other hand, looks at his or her least preferred coworker in a more complex manner—in terms of more than just whether or not that person can get a job done. Consequently, he or she is likely to describe that person in more differentiated terms—some positive and some negative (e.g., very tense, yet moderately pleasant). This results in a relatively higher score on the LPC scale. Thus, "high LPC leaders" are relationship-oriented leaders (Fiedler, 1978).

Characterizing the Situation. Since leadership is essentially an influence process, the contingency model attempts to characterize various leadership and managerial situations in terms of one underlying dimension: the degree to which it is easy or difficult for the leader to influence his or her group members. This influence dimension is composed of three major factors. The first and most important factor is the quality of *leader-member relations*. In situations in which relations are good, the leader has greater influence than in those in which they are poor. The second factor is the degree to which the task is *structured or unstructured*. The greater the structure, the easier it is for the leader to tell group members what to do. The last factor is the leader's *formal position power*. The more formal power and authority the leader can use, the more influence the leader will have.

These three factors are the basis for the classification system shown in Figure 14-7. Note that this system says nothing about how intrinsically difficult the group's task may be. A structured task, for example, assembling an electronic computer, may be much more difficult than a more unstructured task, such as preparing an entertainment program. But a leader is likely to have more problems directing the task-related behavior of an entertainment committee than that of an electronics assembly team. Similarly, it is somewhat easier to lead if you are the liked and trusted captain of any army surveying crew (cell 1) than if you are the informal leader of a recreational basketball team (cell 4). And it will be very difficult indeed to be the disliked and distrusted leader of a volunteer group that is asked to plan a new nursing school curriculum (cell 8). In other words, the cells are ordered on the basis of how favorable or unfavorable the situation will be for the leader in terms of ease of influence.

Empirical Results. Now that we have a measure of leadership style (LPC) and a situational classification system, the next step is to combine the two. The combination will allow us to predict what sort of style is best for a particular situation. Research with well over 800 groups has provided fairly consistent results in this regard (e.g., Peters, Hartke, & Pohlmann, 1985; Strube & Garcia, 1981). Using basketball teams, tank crews, surveying parties, boards of directors, and many other types of groups, it has been found that the relationship between leaders' LPC scores and their groups' performance changes systematically with the situation. These results are summarized in Figure 14-8.

The correlation between LPC and performance is positive in situations of moderate favorability (i.e., cells 4, 5, and 6). The more relationship-oriented the leader (i.e., the higher the LPC score), the better the group's performance. On the other hand, the correlation between LPC and performance in both more favorable situations (i.e., cells 1, 2, and 3) and in highly unfavorable situations (i.e., cell 8) is negative. In these situations the more task oriented the leader (i.e., the lower the LPC score), the better the performance.

Taken as a whole, Figure 14-8 shows that task-oriented leaders are most

Figure 14-7
Classification of situations according to Fiedler's contingency model. (*Adapted from Fiedler, 1967.*)

Elements of the Situation	Leader-Member Relations	Good				Poor			
	Task Structure	High		Low		High		Low	
	Position Power	Strong	Weak	Strong	Weak	Strong	Weak	Strong	Weak
	Cell Number	1	2	3	4	5	6	7	8

Very Favorable ⟵ **Situational Favorableness** ⟶ Very Unfavorable

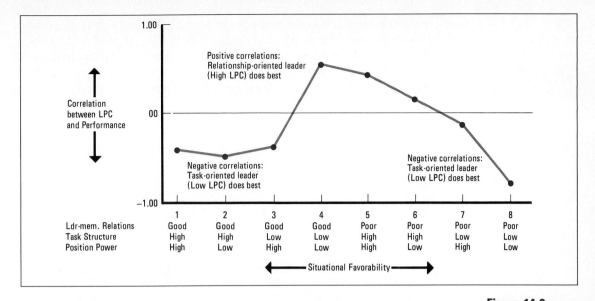

Ldr-mem. Relations	1 Good	2 Good	3 Good	4 Good	5 Poor	6 Poor	7 Poor	8 Poor
Task Structure	High	High	Low	Low	High	High	Low	Low
Position Power	High	Low	High	Low	High	Low	High	Low

◄——— Situational Favorability ———►

Figure 14-8
Results from the contingency model research. (*Adapted from Fiedler, 1967.*)

effective in situations in which they have either quite a lot or very little influence. In contrast, relationship-oriented leaders are most effective in situations in which they have a moderate amount of influence. It would appear, then, that in both very favorable and very unfavorable situations, task-oriented leadership is needed to be effective. In situations of moderate favorability, the leader who is concerned about interpersonal relationships in the group will be most effective. Thus, the model gives us some idea about what type of person should be best for a particular setting.

Fiedler (1978) has attempted to extend the findings of the contingency model so they may be used in organizational programs for training or rotating leaders in order to improve their performance. The contingency model predicts that any general training or rotation experience that is similar for all leaders will increase the effectiveness of some and decrease the effectiveness of others. For example, if all the upper-level managers of a particular organization gain interpersonal skills through sensitivity training, this will in some cases make a better match between leaders and their situation and in some cases make a poorer match. A high-LPC, relationship-oriented leader in a very unfavorable situation may be able to make leader-member relations better with such training. The leader would then be in a situation of moderate favorability in which a good match occurs (a move from cell 8 to 4). However, the same training with the same change in situational favorability will result in relatively worse performance for a low-LPC, task-oriented leader (who does not perform well in cell 4).

Fiedler has developed a training manual called *Leader Match* (Fiedler, Chemers, & Mahar, 1976). This manual helps a manager diagnose (1) his or her own style, and (2) the setting in which he or she works. If there is a mismatch between the style and the setting, the individual learns various techniques for changing the setting so that it matches his or her style. The training program provides numerous cases and examples to help the trainee learn the diagnostic skills, as well as how to change the interpersonal relations, task structure, and position power in a group so that a good fit occurs. Empirical studies using this approach suggest that managers who have been trained with the *Leader Match* manual perform significantly better than those without such training (Fiedler & Mahar, 1979).

Finally, it is important to note that the contingency model has its critics as well as its proponents (e.g., Schriesheim & Kerr, 1977). The use of the LPC scale has been questioned by many researchers. They argue that better, more reliable measures of actual leader behavior are available. A second criticism is that the situation classification system is too simplistic. Other factors besides the three suggested by Fiedler seem important. But these criticisms notwithstanding, the contingency model has made an important contribution to our understanding of leadership. It represents one of the first major attempts to combine estimates of the leader's style with estimates of the situation. This is a major step forward.

UNIVERSAL BEHAVIORS

Although the situation-contingent trait approach is helpful for predicting who will and who will not be an effective leader in a given situation, it still leaves unanswered the question of what leaders actually do in various situations that makes them effective. For example, although high LPC leaders are said to be relationship oriented and low LPC leaders task oriented, the LPC score itself generally does not predict how these two different types of leaders behave (Fiedler, 1978). Thus, while measuring LPC may tell us something about leaders' orientation toward work, it does little to clarify what they actually do at work.

An understanding of how effective leaders actually behave is important for several reasons. First, it would allow us to clarify once and for all the details of the exchange relationship between the leader and the group. If we know how a leader behaves, we can say precisely what it is that he or she is giving to the group. Second, describing leadership in terms of behavior rather than in terms of the leader's orientation, traits, or skills allows for the possibility that someone else in the group besides the formal leader may share in the leadership process (Yukl, 1981). In other words, a behavioral orientation is likely to have the added benefit of telling us something about informal group leaders. Finally, a behavioral orientation has the potential for expanding our capacity to train effective leaders. Note that the *Leader Match* training manual developed by Fiedler, Chemers, and Mahar (1976) trains leaders to change the situation to fit their own personal styles. This strategy may not always be feasible. There are likely to be some situations that are impossible to change. Therefore, it would seem useful to be able to train leaders to change their style to fit whatever situation is at hand. But this can be done only if "style" is defined in very explicit behavioral terms.

The Ohio State Studies

A program of research begun in the late 1940s at The Ohio State University was one of the earliest and most significant attempts to study the actual

Two Executives: A Study in Contrasts

The two case histories that follow are told in the words of corporate executives who knew them well.

One who arrived

THE MAN
"He was an intelligent guy with a delightful twinkle in his eye. He could laugh at himself during the toughest of situations."

NOTABLE STRENGTHS
"He was a superb negotiator. He could somehow come out of a labor dispute or a dispute among managers with an agreement everyone could live with. I think he did this by getting all around a problem so it didn't get blown. People knew far in advance if something might go wrong."

FLAWS
"He was too easy on subordinates and peers at times. Line people wondered whether he was tough enough, and sometimes, why he spent so much time worrying about people."

CAREER
"He was thrown into special assignments—negotiations, dealing with the press, fix-it projects. He always found a way to move things off dead center."

AND ENDED UP . . .
Senior Vice President

One who derailed

THE MAN
"He got results, but was awfully insensitive about it. Although he could be charming when he wanted to be, he was mostly knees and elbows."

NOTABLE STRENGTHS
"He was a superb engineer who came straight up the operations ladder. He had the rare capability of analyzing problems to death, then reconfiguring the pieces into something new."

FLAWS
"When developing something, he gave subordinates more help than they needed, but once a system was set up, he forgot to mind the store. When things went awry, he usually acted like a bully or stonewalled it, once hiring a difficult employee and turning him over to a subordinate. 'It's your problem now,' he told him."

CAREER
"He rocketed upward through engineering/operations jobs. Once he got high enough, his deficiencies caught up with him. He couldn't handle either the scope of his job or the complexity of new ventures."

AND ENDED UP . . .
"Passed over, and it's too bad. He was a talented guy and not a bad manager, either. I suppose that his overmanaging, abrasive style never allowed his colleagues to develop and never allowed him to learn from them."

Source: M. W. McCall, Jr. & M. M. Lombardo. What makes a top executive? *Psychology Today*, (1983, January), p. 31. Reprinted with permission from *Psychology Today*. Copyright © 1983 (American Psychological Association).

behavior of leaders (Shartle, 1950; Hemphill & Coons, 1957). The initial goal of this research was to identify the basic types or categories of behavior that all effective leaders use. Since little attention was paid to situational differences, this research was essentially a universal behavior approach to the study of leader effectiveness.

During the early phases of this research program some 1800 descriptions of leader behavior were collected. Through a process of both expert judgment and statistical analysis, this list was shortened to approximately 150 behaviors that seemed to be good examples of leader functioning. These 150 descriptions were rewritten as questions (e.g., How often does your boss request group members to follow uniform procedures? How often does your boss put suggestions made by the group into operation?) and assembled in the form of a questionnaire. This questionnaire, known as the *leader behavior description questionnaire* (LBDQ), was then used in subsequent field research to help identify the salient behavior patterns used by both effective and less effective leaders.

The behaviors listed in the LBDQ fall into several different categories. By far the most important of these are the categories of *consideration* and *initiation of structure*. Consideration includes such behaviors as helping subordinates, doing favors for them, looking out for their welfare, explaining things, and being friendly and available. These are thus primarily people-oriented behaviors. Initiation of structure, on the other hand, includes such behaviors as getting subordinates to follow rules and procedures, maintaining performance standards, and making the roles of various group members explicit. These behaviors are thus more task-oriented in nature. It is important to note that these two groups of behaviors are not opposites of one another. It is quite possible for a given leader to engage in both types of behavior at more-or-less the same time, that is, to be both considerate and structuring. The important research question is, therefore, how do leaders who are more effective compare to leaders who are less effective on these two types of behavior?

The results from this program of research have been rather disappointing. A few early studies seemed to indicate that in comparison to less effective leaders, more effective leaders engage in both more considerate behavior and more structuring behavior. However, a substantial amount of subsequent research has cast doubt upon this initial conclusion. Several reviews of the empirical literature show that different studies often yield widely different results (e.g., Bass, 1981; Kerr & Schriesheim, 1974; Korman, 1966). Thus, when group performance is used as the criterion, there is little consistent evidence that either consideration or initiation of structure, whether taken individually or in combination, is *universally* related to leader effectiveness.

On the other hand, there *is* some evidence that consideration (but not initiation of structure) is related to subordinate satisfaction. Subordinates usually report being more satisfied with leaders who behave considerately than with leaders who do not behave considerately. Since high satisfaction is usually related to low rates of employee absenteeism and turnover (see Chapter 5), it seems likely that considerate leader behavior can be helpful in an indirect way.

The Michigan Research

Ohio State did not have the only program of research aimed at discovering patterns of effective leader behavior. Similar work was going on at about the same time at other universities. For example, research at the University of Michigan eventually led to the development of a four-factor theory of leadership (Bowers & Seashore, 1966). Central to this theory are four categories of leader behavior hypothesized to be directly related to leader effectiveness. These four categories are as follows:

Support. Behaviors that enhance group members' feelings of personal worth and importance

Interaction facilitation. Behaviors that encourage group members to develop close, mutually satisfying relationships

Goal emphasis. Behaviors that stimulate an enthusiasm for meeting group goals and achieving high performance

Work facilitation. Behaviors that directly aid goal attainment by providing resources such as tools, materials, and technical knowledge

Notice that the first two categories, support and interaction facilitation, are primarily person-oriented behaviors, while the last two, goal emphasis and work facilitation, are primarily task oriented. Thus, there is some degree of conceptual overlap between these four categories and the two that were identified in the Ohio State studies (consideration and initiation of structure). As with the Ohio State studies, the initial research using this four-factor breakdown seemed to support its usefulness. However, later studies produced many conflicting results (Yukl, 1981). Few studies found all four behavior categories to be important, and no single category was shown to be universally important in all situations.

The programs of research conducted at Ohio State, Michigan, and elsewhere thus leave us with a legacy of confusing, and in many cases, conflicting findings. This legacy is at once disappointing and encouraging. It is disappointing because it indicates that there is probably no one set of behaviors that will universally predict leader effectiveness. On the other hand, it is encouraging because so many of these studies did find *something.* That is, although the relationships observed between various patterns of leader behavior and measures of leader effectiveness have not always been consistent from one study to the next, the fact that so many studies have found at least some sort of relationship suggests that a behavioral approach to leadership may yet prove successful. As with leadership traits, however, the characteristics of the situation need to be taken into account.

SITUATION-CONTINGENT BEHAVIORS

The behavioral approach to the study of leader effectiveness, like the trait approach, benefits greatly when the leader's situation is taken into account. Many of the studied conducted as part of the Ohio State and Michigan research programs point to the conclusion that various patterns of leader behavior are effective in some types of situations but not in others. Thus, what is needed is a theoretical framework that tells us which situational variables are most important, and then systematically links different categories of leader behavior to leader effectiveness in these different situations.

The Vroom and Yetton Model (A Review)

One such framework is the Vroom and Yetton (1973) model of participative decision making. Recall that this model was discussed in some detail in Chapter 12. The goal of the Vroom and Yetton model is to predict when leaders should and when they should not invite group members to participate in the decision-making process. Although we originally discussed this model in conjunction with group decision making, it can be legitimately considered a situation-contingent behavior approach to understanding leader effectiveness. It simply has a narrower focus than do some of the other theories and research programs we have seen.

The model focuses on a single class of situations—those in which some sort of decision must be made. Situations that do not involve a decision are not covered. Several aspects of these situations are of concern, including:

1. The importance of decision quality
2. The amount of decision-relevant information possessed both by the leader and by the group members
3. The degree to which the decision problem is structured
4. Whether group acceptance and/or commitment is necessary in order to implement the decision effectively
5. The degree to which the group is motivated to attain the objectives valued by the leader or the organization
6. The level of disagreement within the group about preferred alternatives
7. The amount of time available to make the decision

The behavior of interest in this model is the degree to which the leader permits the members of the group to get involved in the decision-making process. At one extreme, the leader may choose to make the decision him- or herself, using the group only as an information resource. Here, group involvement is minimal. Alternatively, he or she might give the group an advisory role but still make the final choice alone. Or he or she might invite the group to participate fully in the decision (e.g., by allowing the group members to vote on the various decision alternatives). Vroom and Yetton (1973) predict that these different levels of group participation will be appropriate (i.e., effective) under different conditions (the exact predictions are shown in Figure 12-4 on p. 375).

Although less research has been done on this model than on other theories of leader behavior, that which has been done is generally supportive (e.g., Chemers, 1983; Jago, 1982). In most cases, leaders are more effective when they behave in accordance with the dictates of the model than when they behave otherwise. Thus, when faced with different types of decision situations, effective leaders will use different levels of participation. Sometimes they may encourage a great deal of participation (e.g., GII), while at other times they may allow very little (e.g., AI). It all depends on the characteristics of the particular situation they face.

House's Path-Goal Theory

Another theory that takes a situation-contingent behavior approach to understanding leader effectiveness is House's *path-goal theory of leadership* (House,

1971; House & Dessler, 1974; House & Mitchell, 1974). This theory argues that leader effectiveness is the result of leaders' ability to influence positively their subordinates' satisfaction and motivation. Subordinate satisfaction and motivation are hypothesized to be affected by the degree to which leaders either (1) directly meet their subordinates' *goals,* or (2) clarify the *paths* to attaining those goals (hence the title "path-goal" theory). As it is used here, *goal attainment* refers to the satisfaction of important subordinate needs. Thus, leaders will be *acceptable and satisfying* to subordinates to the extent that they are either an immediate source of need satisfaction or instrumental to future need satisfaction. Similarly, leaders will be *motivating* for subordinates to the extent that they make the satisfaction of subordinates' needs contingent on effective performance, and complement the subordinates' environment by providing the coaching, guidance, support, and rewards necessary for effective performance (House & Mitchell, 1974).

Note the importance of the phrase "complement the subordinates' environment" in the preceding sentence. It means that leader behavior will be effective in promoting subordinate satisfaction and motivation only if it provides something that is not already provided by the situation. If a leader's behavior is completely redundant with the situation, it will have no marginal utility, and may even have disutility, that is, a negative impact on satisfaction and motivation. Thus, according to path-goal theory, it is essential to take the characteristics of the situation into account.

A diagram of the theory is presented in Figure 14-9. As can be seen, the

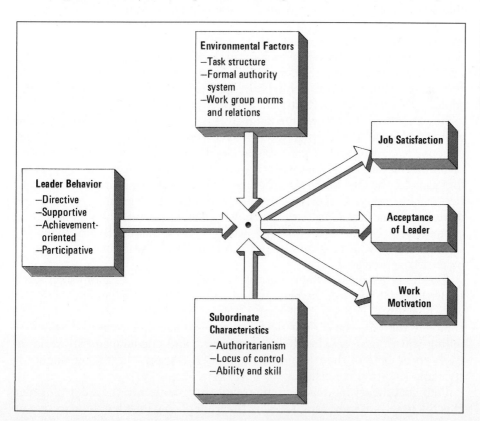

Figure 14-9
Path-goal theory of leader effectiveness. (*Adapted from House & Mitchell, 1974.*)

theory predicts that four categories of leader behavior will interact with two types of situational variables to influence subordinate job satisfaction, acceptance of the leader, and work motivation. The first two leader behavior categories, *directive* and *supportive behaviors*, are equivalent to the Ohio State categories of initiating structure and consideration, respectively. *Achievement-oriented behaviors* include seeking performance improvements, setting challenging goals, emphasizing excellence, and showing confidence that subordinates will achieve these high standards. *Participative behaviors* include consulting with subordinates, soliciting their suggestions and opinions, and taking these seriously into consideration before making a decision.

The situational variables important in the theory are of two types: (1) *environmental factors,* such as the structure of the task, the nature of the formal authority system in the organization, and the norms and interpersonal relationships that exist in the network group, and (2) *subordinate characteristics,* such as personality traits (e.g., authoritarianism and locus of control), skills, and abilities. The importance of these various situational factors is that they determine which leader behaviors will be effective and which will not. To help clarify this, let us consider two examples, one involving a subordinate personality trait, and one involving an environmental factor.

One set of research studies has shown that employees with an internal locus of control (i.e., those who believe that what happens to them occurs as a function of their own behavior) are more satisfied with a participative leader than are employees with an external locus of control (i.e., those who believe that what happens to them occurs because of chance or luck). Externals, on the other hand, are more satisfied with a directive leader than are internals. Intuitively, these findings make sense. A more independent, internal type of person prefers more autonomy and say in decisions, while a more dependent, external type of person prefers a leader who structures the environment. The best match thus depends upon both the leader's behavioral style and the subordinate's personality (Mitchell, Smyser, & Weed, 1975).

Research with the environmental factors has produced similar findings. For example, House and Dessler (1974) have shown that a more structuring, directive leadership style is generally more effective when the group is working on an unstructured task than when it is working on a structured task. Suppose, for example, that you are given a number of blueprints depicting the construction of new mobile homes, and you are asked for an estimate of needed raw materials. What if you do not know how to read blueprints, how to make the computations, or how to find out what types of materials are available. Guidance from your boss that helps to structure and direct your efforts would be greatly appreciated.

On the other hand, when the task is more structured, a more supportive leadership style seems to be best. If you have had a lot of experience working with blueprints, and you understand how to do all of the steps required to complete the job, you do not need a supervisor standing over your shoulder telling you things you already know. Support and encouragement are more likely to be helpful than redundant reminders. Again, the proper match of style and situation is needed.

Path-goal theory has made an important contribution to the study of leader effectiveness. Not only does it specify the leader behaviors that are effective in a given situation, it also provides us with an insight into *why* those behaviors are effective. In doing so, it tells us something about the underlying nature of leadership and what leaders contribute to the leader-member exchange. The leader's contribution is, in a nutshell, the satisfaction of important subordinate needs (cf. Fulk & Wendler, 1982). Of course, which needs are important will depend on the characteristics of both the subordinate and the environment. A crucial task for any leader, therefore, is to discover what those needs are. If this can be done, and if the leader is able to satisfy those needs, then in return he or she can expect subordinate acceptance and esteem. In addition, if the leader makes the satisfaction of important needs contingent upon successful task performance, *and* he or she makes the path to successful performance easy to follow (e.g., by providing structure when the task is ambiguous), then he or she can also expect to see high levels of motivation and commitment in subordinates. In the long run this will lead to a higher probability of being able to achieve important group and organizational goals.

Further Refinements

One mark of a good theory is that over time it continues to stimulate both new research and fresh insights into significant organizational problems. In this regard, path-goal theory has been moderately successful. It has given rise to new ideas about how situational factors can act as substitutes for leader behavior, and it has stimulated new research, some of which has refined and extended the basic concepts underlying path-goal theory.

Substitutes for Leadership. One of the central ideas in path-goal theory is that in order to be effective, a leader's behavior must complement the situation—it must provide something that is not already provided by other situational factors. Thus, for example, structuring behavior on the part of a leader will be effective only when the group's task is unstructured. Said differently, it is unnecessary for the leader to engage in any structuring behavior—at least with regard to the task at hand—if the task itself is highly structured. In a sense, high task structure acts as a sort of *substitute for leadership.*

The notion that various aspects of the situation might act as substitutes for leadership was developed by Kerr and Jermier (1978; see also Howell, Dorfman, & Kerr, 1986). They define a substitute for leadership as any situational variable that makes leader behavior *unnecessary and redundant.* Substitutes might include subordinate characteristics (e.g., their experience with the task), task characteristics (e.g., its inherent structure), work group characteristics (e.g., its cohesiveness), or characteristics of the organization (e.g., its degree of formalization). Substitutes for leadership are contrasted with *neutralizers of leadership.* A neutralizer is defined as any situational variable that *prevents* a leader from behaving in a particular way (as opposed to making that behavior unnecessary). Thus, for example, union contracts often act as neutralizers, in that they frequently make it impossible for managers to use either pay or (to a lesser extent) promotion as a reward for good performance.

Figure 14-10 lists a number of variables that are likely to act either as substitutes or neutralizers for two broad categories of leader behavior. The first of these two categories, *supportive behavior,* is equivalent to the "considera-

Figure 14-10
Substitutes and
neutralizers for
supportive and in-
strumental leader
behaviors.
(*Adapted from
Yukl, 1981.*)

Substitute or Neutralizer	Supportive Leadership Behavior	Instrumental Leadership Behavior
1. *Subordinate characteristics*:		
a. Experience, ability, training		Substitute
b. "Professional" orientation	Substitute	Substitute
c. Indifference toward rewards offered by organization	Neutralizer	Neutralizer
2. *Task characteristics*:		
a. Structured, routine, unambiguous task		Substitute
b. Feedback provided by task		Substitute
c. Intrinsically satisfying task	Substitute	
3. *Work group characteristics*:		
a. Cohesiveness	Substitute	Substitute
b. Skill heterogeneity		Substitute
4. *Organization characteristics*:		
a. Low position power (leader lacks control over organizational rewards)	Neutralizer	Neutralizer
b. Formalization (explicit plans, goals, areas of responsibility)		Substitute
c. Inflexibility (rigid, unyielding rules and procedures)		Neutralizer
d. Leader located apart from subordinates with only limited communication possible	Neutralizer	Neutralizer

tion" category defined in the Ohio State research. The second category, *instrumental behavior,* includes such previously defined behaviors as "initiation of structure" (Ohio State), "goal emphasis" and "work facilitation" (Michigan), and "directive" and "achievement-oriented" behavior (path-goal). For each behavior category, the figure indicates which variables are likely to be substitutes and which are likely to be neutralizers.

For example, subordinate experience, ability, and training will all serve as substitutes for instrumental leader behavior—they make such behavior largely unnecessary (e.g., a mechanic who has had a great deal of experience maintaining jet engines does not need close technical supervision from his or her supervisor). Group cohesiveness, on the other hand, is predicted to act as a substitute for supportive leader behavior. To the extent that a group is cohesive, its members will provide each other with a great deal of mutual support, rendering additional supportiveness from the leader unneeded, or at least unessential. An example of a neutralizer is physical separation between the leader and his or her subordinates (e.g., the subordinates are all sales representatives who spend the majority of their time on the road). Physical separation makes interpersonal communication difficult (see Chapter 10) and severely limits the amount of supportive and instrumental behavior the leader can engage in.

That situational variables may sometimes act as either substitutes or neutralizers of leadership is a relatively new concept. Nevertheless, the preliminary research testing this idea is generally supportive. For example, in one recent study of 670 staff nurses it was found that the nurses' education, the cohesiveness of their floor units, and technological aspects of their tasks all served as substitutes for head nurse leadership behavior. The administrative climate of the hospital, on the other hand, acted to neutralize the effectiveness of head nurse leadership attempts (Sheridan, Verdenburgh, & Abelson, 1984; see also Howell & Dorfman, 1981).

The substitutes/neutralizers model draws attention to two important points. One of these echoes the main conclusion from our discussion of the universal behavior approach to understanding leader effectiveness. That is, there is no one category of leader behavior that is needed in all situations. In many cases there are aspects of the situation that serve as substitutes for leadership, making certain leadership behaviors unnecessary (and sometimes dysfunctional). The second point is that leaders do not always have the latitude to engage in the behaviors that might otherwise be most beneficial from a performance standpoint. There are often situational constraints that neutralize their best efforts, thus limiting their effectiveness as leaders.

Refinements and Extensions. In addition to examining leadership substitutes and neutralizers, recent research has sought to refine and extend the basic contingency concepts underlying path-goal theory. These refinements and extensions have been of two types. The first includes refinements that expand the number and type of situational factors hypothesized to moderate the relationship between leader behavior on the one hand, and subordinate satisfaction and motivation on the other. Thus, for example, Schriesheim and DeNisi (1981) have shown that in addition to the environmental factors listed in Figure 14-9, the relationship between directive leader behavior and subordinates' satisfaction may also depend upon the degree of variety and feedback in the subordinates' tasks, and on the extent to which the subordinates' jobs give them an opportunity to interact with other people.

The second type of refinement includes extensions of the basic contingency notion that encompass a greater variety of leader behaviors and/or subordinate performance variables. For example, research by Wofford and Srinivasan (1983) has examined the effects of leader behavior on several subordinate performance variables not explicitly addressed by path-goal theory. Thus, whereas subordinate motivation is the primary performance variable considered by path-goal theory, Wofford and Srinivasan (1983) also investigated the way in which actions of the leader influence subordinate ability, role perceptions (what the subordinate believes he or she is supposed to do), and environmental constraints. They argue that subordinate performance is influenced by all of these variables, not just by motivation, and that leader effectiveness therefore depends on the leader's ability to influence each and every one of them positively.

Overall, the situation-contingent behavior approach represents an extremely useful way of looking at the leader-effectiveness question. This approach has given rise to several theories that make specific predictions about which leader behaviors will be effective in which situations. It has also been helpful in clarifying the specific nature of the exchange process that underlies leader effectiveness. Finally, it continues to spawn new research and new ideas that further improve our understanding of leadership in organizations.

Summary

Some of the most important points made in the chapter are listed below:

1. Leadership refers to the process whereby an individual influences a group toward the attainment of desired group or organizational goals.

2. At the heart of this process is an exchange relationship in which the leader gives something to the group and the group gives something in return. In simplest terms, the leader gives need satisfaction to the group, and the group gives motivation, commitment, and high levels of performance.

3. Leadership is just one of a number of roles that any manager must play. Managers differ in the total amount of time they devote to this role, but all successful managers devote at least some time to it.

4. The same basic exchange process that takes place between a formal leader and the group also takes place between informal leaders and the group. The difference is that informal leaders have no institutional legitimacy. Thus, the influence of informal leaders is based solely on their personal legitimacy.

5. There are a number of different ways to approach the question of leader effectiveness. Each approach has its own unique set of implications for how organizations might best go about the task of managing leader effectiveness.

6. Neither the universal trait nor the universal behavior approach has been very successful. In both cases, the ability to predict leader effectiveness is greatly enhanced when the characteristics of the situation are taken into account.

7. One advantage that the situation-contingent behavior approach has over other approaches is that it does a better job of clarifying the basic nature of the leader-member exchange relationship. As such, it provides us with greater insight into the fundamental nature of leadership.

8. The two categories of leader behavior that have been found to be most important across many different types of studies are the supportive and instrumental behavior categories.

IMPLICATIONS FOR RESEARCH

Research conducted during the last 25 years has told us a great deal about the overall process of leadership. In certain areas, however, we still have much to learn. There are many questions that remain to be answered and many issues that need to be resolved. Consequently, there is still a need for a great deal more research. Two areas in which this need is especially strong are discussed briefly here.

When thinking about managers as leaders, our inclination is to focus on their role as causal agents. For example, when a manager's group performs well, we want to know what he or she did that contributed to the success. And when the group performs poorly, we want to know what the manager did wrong. We focus on the manager as the cause (or potential cause) and the group's performance as the effect. What is often overlooked in such an analysis is that the causal arrow can also point in the other direction. More generally, we frequently lose sight of the fact that leader behavior, like any other behavior that occurs in organizations, is subject to the influence of a wide variety of situational factors, one of which is group performance. Thus, leader behavior not only shapes events, it is shaped by events.

This point is implicit in the exchange theory analysis of leadership discussed in the first section of the chapter. If leadership is really based on a true exchange relationship, it seems reasonable that the responses of *either* party to the exchange should be affected by the contributions of the other. Thus, if the group contributes to the exchange in one way (e.g., by exerting high effort), it is reasonable to expect a different type of response (behavior) from the leader than would be the case had the group contributed in some other way (e.g., by exerting little effort). A similar conclusion can be derived from the substitutes/ neutralizers model. If the situation facing the leader contains significant substitutes and/or neutralizers of leadership, and if the leader is aware of these, then it seems reasonable that he or she might behave differently than would be the case if these substitutes and/or neutralizers were not present.

Although this point may seem obvious, it is interesting to note that much less research has focused on the variables *influencing* leader behavior than on the variables *influenced by* leader behavior. Furthermore, there are few formal theories of leadership that deal with the causes of leader behavior (for an exception see Hunt & Osborn, 1978). Consequently our understanding of the various factors influencing leader behavior is not very well developed. What is needed is more research on the causes of leader behavior. Additionally, it would be extremely useful if this research could be integrated with research on the effects of leader behavior. By simultaneously considering both the causes and the effects of leader behavior, a more dynamic (and hence realistic) picture of the overall leadership process is likely to emerge (cf. Larson, 1984). The addition of a dynamic component to existing leadership theories would be of great benefit.

A second area in which there is a need for more research is the measurement of leader behavior. If we are to make significant advances at either a theoretical or practical (e.g., leadership training) level, we desperately need better measures of the leader behaviors we are interested in. Current research relies very heavily on questionnaire measures such as the LBDQ described in the chapter. Yet such measures are notoriously unreliable. Responses to these questionnaires have been shown to be affected by many things that have nothing to do with leader behavior. For example, simply knowing how well a group has performed can significantly influence the way its leader's behavior is described. When a leader's group is known to have performed well, the leader is apt to be described as having behaved more considerately toward group members and as having provided more structure than when the group has performed poorly. This can occur even though there may be *no objective difference* in the way the leader behaves in these two situations (e.g., Lord, 1985). It should be apparent that such effects can contaminate, if not completely invalidate, the research findings using these questionnaires.

We therefore need to develop alternatives to such questionnaires. One possibility is to use more rigorous observational systems. Such systems provide measures of leader behavior based on direct observation and time-sampling procedures (e.g., observing and recording what a manager actually does during random 10-minute observation periods over a 2-week interval). Because such systems do not rely on (extremely fallible) group-member memories, as questionnaires do, they hold the promise of being much more accurate and thus much more useful for both theory development and application. To date, relatively little research has been done on such measurement techniques, but that which has been done is encouraging (e.g., Luthans & Lockwood, 1984). More effort is needed in this direction. This, is concert with a broader focus on both the causes and consequences of leader behavior, is likely to contribute significantly to our overall understanding of the leadership process.

IMPLICATIONS FOR PRACTICE

The conclusions drawn from this chapter have major relevance for the on-going organizational processes of selection, promotion, and training. The traditional approach of selecting leaders based on some universally agreed upon set of ideal characteristics does not work very well. The best person to select is not necessarily the person with the highest intelligence, gregariousness, and assertiveness scores. It is far more important to know the specifics about the particular job for which the individual is being selected. With this information, an individual can be selected who has the behavior style or set of skills and traits that best matches the actual requirements of the job.

This conclusion is also true with regard to promotions and transfers. Simply to promote someone who has done well in the past does not ensure that his or her high level of performance will be sustained. Past performance is not necessarily a good predictor of how an individual will do on a new job, especially if the new job differs widely from the previous one. Again, it is important to match the job demands with the behavior style of the prospective job holder. A good job analysis is needed both for selection and for promotion and transfer.

To some extent companies are beginning to recognize these points. For example, Texas Instruments (TI) has developed a manpower planning policy that fits well with what we have said. Charles Phipps, manager of strategic planning, explained that "as a product moves through different phases of its life cycle, different kinds of management skills become dominant." While entrepreneurs may be best suited to manage the initial development and marketing of a product, a person with long-standing administrative skills may be needed for an established product. TI currently employs a review procedure in which the president of the company reviews the records of top managers and actively tries to match management orientations with job needs ("Wanted," 1980).

There is also more recognition that in some cases an aggressive, hard-nosed style is appropriate. Companies that are struggling, faced with the need for quick decisions, or confronted with cutbacks or reorganizations may require a tough, task-oriented style. A *Fortune* article, for example, describes the "ten toughest bosses" in American business, based on interviews with large numbers of subordinates (Menzies, 1980). These people are seen as inspiring awe, respect, and fear. They are devoted to their work and they expect the same devotion of others. They have an unrelenting demand for continued and increased excellence. Several have done magnificently (e.g., Andrall Pearson, president of Pepsi Co.), while others have been less effective. The point to be recognized is that in some cases this style may be the best for the situation.

Finally, similar generalizations are applicable for training programs. To send all top-level managers to the same training program disregards the fact that different managers work in different settings with different subordinates. Giving everyone the same training may help some and hinder others. As we have seen, Fiedler (1978) argues that one way to solve this problem is to use a new type of training: Teach managers how to diagnose their own styles and situations, and then teach them how to change the situation so they can create a better style-situation match.

At the heart of all three issues—selection, promotions and transfers, and training—is the central idea of job analysis. First and foremost, one must analyze the job. What skills are needed? What behaviors work best? While job analysis is covered more fully in personnel courses, we will give some attention to this topic in the next chapter.

Discussion Questions

1. What do we mean by effective leadership? How would you select the most effective leaders from among a group of managers?
2. Are leaders made by their times or do they make their times? Which is most important, the person or the situation?
3. Should we use training programs to change people or to teach people how to change the situation? What are the implications of your answer for other processes such as selection, placement, and promotion?

CASE: A SCIENTIST'S SCIENTIST

Lee Ross was an engineer-scientist in the research and development department of a large wood-harvesting company. He had worked for the company ever since he received his degree 15 years earlier, and he was clearly recognized as one of the best researchers in the area. He spent many hours keeping current on the literature, and he knew how to set up tight research designs. Knowledgeable in statistics and computer processing, he had a reputation for sticking to his guns about how specific research studies should be conducted. He believed that if something wasn't done well, it shouldn't be done at all.

Because of his expertise, Lee had written articles for numerous publications and many technical reports. A number of his discoveries had saved the company millions of dollars. His colleagues frequently came to him for advice about how to proceed on various projects. He was convinced about the correctness of his advice, which he gave readily. In short, Lee was the star of the department.

Early in the spring of 1980, it became clear that Lee's boss, Melissa Lansford, would retire as head of R&D. The decision about Melissa's successor was in the hands of her boss, Bob Daley. Melissa recommended Lee because his record of outstanding service made him well qualified for her position. The new position required large amounts of administrative work and less research, but they both felt he deserved the promotion and the recognition.

Melissa and Bob discussed some of these issues with Lee. He would no longer be in charge of specific research projects, but because everyone came to him anyway for advice, he could still be actively involved. Lee thought long and hard about the offer. The promotion meant more money and recognition. He just couldn't say no. Starting on July 1, Lee became the head of the R&D department.

It was not long before things started to go wrong. First of all, Lee had more difficulty keeping up with the literature. Other priorities always seemed to interfere with his reading time. He also noticed a distinct cooling in the way his colleagues treated him. At first they had continued to come to him with questions and problems. Lee responded as he always had—"Here's how it ought to be done." In a few cases his advice was not followed, and Lee was critical of the work that was done. He even shut one project down that had been running for over a year because of improper sampling.

He also got into a number of arguments with Bob, his boss. In many cases he demanded more financial support from Bob to conduct various research projects in the way he felt they needed to be done. Bob, who was restricted by financial limitations and organizational priorities, was frequently unable to generate the additional support. It got to the point that almost every interaction between the two resulted in an argument.

Finally Bob knew that something had to be changed. He went to Lee and told him that he had to (1) compromise more and accept the realities of his job, (2) step down from his position, or (3) leave the company. Three months later, Lee handed in his resignation.

Questions about the Case

1. Why do you think Lee was not successful at this job?
2. Why did problems start to occur between Lee and his colleagues?
3. Do you think the selection of Lee for the position of R&D head was the right move? How should this process of selection have been conducted?

References

Bales, R. R. (1953). The equilibrium problem in small groups. In T. Parsons, R. F. Bales, & E. A. Shils (Eds.), *Working papers in the theory of action.* New York: Free Press.

Bass, B. M. (1981). *Stogdill's handbook of leadership: A survey of theory and research* (rev. and expanded ed.). New York: Free Press.

Bottger, P. C. (1984). Expertise and air time as bases of actual and perceived influence in problem-solving groups. *Journal of Applied Psychology, 69,* 214–221.

Bowers, D. G., & Seashore, S. E. (1966). Predicting organizational effectiveness with a four-factor theory of leadership. *Administrative Science Quarterly, 11,* 238–263.

Chemers, M. M. (1983). Leadership theory and research: A systems process integration. In P. B. Paulus (Ed.), *Basic group processes* (pp. 9–39). New York: Springer-Verlag.

Dansereau, F., Graen, G., & Haga, W. J. (1975). A vertical dyad linkage approach to leadership within formal organizations: A longitudinal investigation of the role making process. *Organizational Behavior and Human Performance, 13,* 46–78.

Fiedler, F. E. (1967). *A theory of leadership effectiveness.* New York: McGraw-Hill.

Fiedler, F. E. (1978). The contingency model and the dynamics of the leadership process. In L. Berkowitz (Ed.), *Advances in experimental social psychology* (Vol. 11, pp. 59–112). New York: Academic Press.

Fiedler, F. E., & Chemers, M. M. (1974). *Leadership and effective management.* Glenview, IL: Scott, Foresman.

Fiedler, F. E., Chemers, M. M., & Mahar, L. (1976). *Improving leader effectiveness: The leader match concept.* New York: Wiley.

Fiedler, F. E., & Mahar, L. (1979). The effectiveness of contingency model training: A review of the validation of Leader Match. *Personnel Psychology, 32,* 45–62.

Fulk, J., & Wendler, E. R. (1982). Dimensionality of leader-subordinate interactions: A path-goal investigation. *Organizational Behavior and Human Performance, 30,* 241–264.

Graen, G., & Cashman, J. (1975). A role-making model of leadership in formal organizations: A developmental approach. In J. G. Hunt & L. L. Larson (Eds.), *Leadership frontiers* (pp. 143–165). Kent, OH: Kent State University Press.

Graen, G., Liden, R., & Hoel, W. (1982). Role of leadership in the employee withdrawal process. *Journal of Applied Psychology, 67,* 868–872.

Graen, G., Novak, M., & Sommerkamp, P. (1982). The effects of leader-member exchange and job design on productivity and satisfaction: Testing a dual attachment model. *Organizational Behavior and Human Performance, 30,* 109–131.

Hemphill, J. K., & Coons, A. E. (1957). Development of the leader behavior description questionnaire. In R. M. Stogdill & A. E. Coons (Eds.), *Leader behavior: Its description and measurement.* Columbus, OH: The Ohio State University, Bureau of Business Research.

Hollander, E. P. (1964). *Leaders, groups, and influence.* New York: Oxford University Press.

Hollander, E. P. (1978) *Leadership dynamics: A practical guide to effective relationships.* New York: Free Press.

Hollander, E. P. (1985). Leadership and power. In G. Lindzey & E. Aronson (Eds.), *The handbook of social psychology* (3d ed., Vol. 2., pp. 485–537). New York: Random House.

Hollander, E. P., & Julian, J. W. (1970). Studies in leader legitimacy, influence, and innovation. In L. Berkowitz (Ed.), *Advances in experimental social psychology* (Vol. 5, pp. 33–69). New York: Academic Press.

House, R. J. (1971). A path-goal theory of leader effectiveness. *Administrative Science Quarterly, 16,* 321–339.

House, R. J., & Dessler, G. (1974). The path goal theory of leadership: Some post hoc and a priori tests. In J. G. Hunt & L. L. Larson (Eds.), *Contingency approaches to leadership.* Carbondale, IL: Southern Illinois University Press.

House, R. J., & Mitchell, T. R. (1974). Path-goal theory of leadership. *Journal of Contemporary Business, 3,* 81–99.

Howell, J. P., & Dorfman, P. W. (1981). Substitutes for leadership: Test of a construct. *Academy of Management Journal, 24,* 714–728.

Howell, J. P., Dorfman, P. W., & Kerr, S. (1986). Moderator variables in leadership research. *Academy of Management Review, 11,* 88–102.

Hunt, J. G., & Osborn, R. N. (1978). A multiple influence approach to leadership for managers. In J. Stinson & P. Hersey (Eds.), *Leadership for practitioners.* Athens, OH: Center for Leadership Studies.

Jago, A. G. (1982). Leadership: Perspectives in theory and research. *Management Science, 28,* 315–336.

Kerr, S., & Jermier, J. M. (1978). Substitutes for leadership: Their meaning and measurement. *Organizational Behavior and Human Performance, 22,* 375–403.

Kerr, S., & Schriesheim, C. A. (1974). Consideration, initiating structure, and organizational criteria: An update of Korman's 1966 review. *Personnel Psychology, 27,* 555–568.

Korman, A. K. (1966). Consideration, initiating structure, and organizational criteria: A review. *Personnel Psychology, 19,* 349–362.

Larson, J. R., Jr. (1984). The performance feedback process: A preliminary model. *Organizational Behavior and Human Performance, 33,* 42–76.

Lord, R. G. (1985). An information processing approach to social perceptions, leadership, and behavioral measurement in organizations. In L. L. Cummings & B. M. Staw (Eds.), *Research in organizational behavior* (Vol. 7, pp. 87–128). Greenwich, CT: JAI Press.

Luthans, F., & Lockwood, D. L. (1984). Toward an observation system for measuring leader behavior in natural settings. In J. G. Hunt, D. Hosking, C. A. Schriesheim, & R. Steward (Eds.), *Leaders and managers: International perspectives on managerial behavior and leadership* (pp. 117–141). New York: Pergamon.

McClelland, D. C. (1985). *Human motivation.* Glenview, IL: Scott, Foresman.

Menzies, H. D. (1980, April 2). The ten toughest bosses. *Fortune,* p. 62ff.

Miner, J. B. (1980). *Theories of organizational behavior.* Hinsdale, IL: Dryden Press.

Mintzberg, H. (1973). *The nature of managerial work.* New York: Harper & Row.

Mitchell, T. R., Smyser, C. M., & Weed, S. E. (1975). Locus of control: Supervision and work satisfaction. *Academy of Management Journal, 18,* 623–630.

Peters, L. H., Hartke, D. D., & Pohlmann, J. T. (1985). Fiedler's contingency theory of leadership: An application of the meta-analysis procedures of Schmidt and Hunter. *Psychological Bulletin, 97,* 274–285.

Rasinski, K., Tyler, T. R., & Fridkin, K. (1985). Exploring the function of legitimacy: Mediating effects of personal and institutional legitimacy on leadership endorsement and system support. *Journal of Personality and Social Psychology, 49,* 386–394.

Ritchie, R. J., Moses, J. L. (1983). Assessment center correlates of women's advancement into middle management: A 7-year longitudinal analysis. *Journal of Applied Psychology, 68,* 227–231.

Schriesheim, C. A., & DeNisi, A. S. (1981). Task dimensions as moderators of the effects of instrumental leadership: A two-sample replicated test of path-goal leadership theory. *Journal of Applied Psychology, 66,* 589–597.

Schriesheim, C. A., & Kerr, S. (1977). Theories and measures of leadership: A critical appraisal of current and future directions. In J. G. Hunt & L. L. Larson (Eds.), *Leadership: The cutting edge* (pp. 9–45). Carbondale, IL: Southern Illinois University Press.

Shartle, C. L. (1950). Studies of leadership by interdisciplinary methods. In A. G. Grace (Ed.), *Leadership in American education.* Chicago: University of Chicago Press.

Shaw, M. E. (1981). *Group dynamics: The psychology of small group behavior* (3d ed.). New York: McGraw-Hill.

Shaw, M. E., Rothschild, G. H., & Strickland, J. F. (1957). Decision processes in communication nets. *Journal of Abnormal and Social Psychology, 54,* 323–330.

Sheridan, J. E., Verdenburgh, D. J., & Abelson, M. D. (1984). Contextual model of leadership influence in hospital units. *Academy of Management Journal, 27,* 57–78.

Sorrentino, R. M., & Boutillier, R. G. (1975). The effect of quantity and quality of verbal interaction on ratings of leadership ability. *Journal of Experimental Social Psychology, 11,* 403–411.

Stein, R. T., & Heller, T. (1979). An empirical analysis of the correlations between leadership status and participation rates reported in the literature. *Journal of Personality and Social Psychology, 37,* 1993–2002.

Stogdill, R. M. (1948). Personality factors associated with leadership: A survey of the literature. *Journal of Psychology, 25,* 35–71.

Stogdill, R. M. (1974). *Handbook of leadership.* New York: Free Press.

Strodtbeck, F. L., & Hook, L. H. (1961). The social dimensions of a twelve-man jury table. *Sociometry, 24,* 397–415.

Strube, M. J., & Garcia, J. E. (1981). A meta-analytic investigation of Fiedler's contingency model of leader effectiveness. *Psychological Bulletin, 90,* 307–321.

Vecchio, R. P., & Gobdel, B. C. (1984). The vertical dyad linkage model of leadership: Problems and prospects. *Organizational Behavior and Human Performance, 34,* 5–20.

Vroom, V. H., & Yetton, P. W. (1973). *Leadership and decision making.* Pittsburgh: University of Pittsburgh Press.

Wanted: A manager to fit each strategy. (1980, February 25). *Business Week,* p. 166ff.

Wofford, J. C., & Srinivasan, T. N. (1983). Experimental tests of the leader-environment-follower-interaction theory of leadership. *Organizational Behavior and Human Performance, 32,* 35–54.

Yukl, G. A. (1981). *Leadership in organizations.* Englewood Cliffs, NJ: Prentice-Hall.

Part Five

Individual and Organizational Effectiveness

In this final part of the book we focus on applying much of the preceding material. By now you should have a fairly firm understanding of individual and group behavior. Part 5 examines ways to apply these principles so that both individual and organizational effectiveness are enhanced.

Chapter 15, "Formal Systems for Managing Employee Performance," focuses on three important problems that organizations must deal with in order to maintain their overall effectiveness. The first problem discussed is that of selection—how we get the right person into the organization in the first place. The most promising techniques are those that assess the degree to which a job applicant actually possesses the skills necessary to perform effectively in a particular position. The closer the match between the job's requirements and the applicant's skills, the higher the performance and satisfaction.

Two other topics discussed in Chapter 15 are performance appraisal and reward systems. Performance appraisals can be used both as an evaluation mechanism and for counseling and development purposes. We emphasize the importance of having a fair evaluation and a continuing process of feedback. Reward systems provide the organiza-

tion with a formal means of influencing motivation. Different sorts of compensation systems are discussed and evaluated. One important point we make is that the particular reward system should match the requirements of the situation.

Whereas Chapter 15 examines formal organizational systems for managing employee performance, Chapter 16 discusses the role that individual line managers play in this process. Again, three important problem areas are covered. The first is that of socializing new employees—teaching them the values, norms, and patterns of behavior judged to be important in the organization. Line managers usually have a great deal of discretion in deciding how to structure the socialization process, and there are specific things they can do to help ensure its success. We spend some time discussing these.

In Chapter 16 we also discuss the problem of managing poor performers. The empirical literature indicates that managers make many errors in evaluating and responding to poorly performing employees. Suggestions are offered regarding how some of these errors can be avoided, and a number of specific strategies for dealing with poor performers are covered.

Finally, in Chapter 16 we emphasize the important role that managers play in maintaining the performance of effective employees. We note that managers should be just as active in trying to maintain the good performance of their effective employees as they are in trying to socialize new employees and/or improve the performance of poorly performing employees.

The last chapter, Chapter 17, deals with organizational change. In order to implement many of the ideas and recommendations made throughout the text, it is necessary to introduce some type of change. This chapter takes a close look at the process of change and discusses a number of specific strategies and techniques for accomplishing change. The chapter covers strategies for changing people, jobs, informal group relations, and, to a lesser extent, the formal organizational structure.

In combination, the chapters in Part 5 show that with a proper diagnosis of the situation, the basic principles governing the behavior of people in organizations can be applied in a manner that will enhance both individual and organizational effectiveness.

Chapter 15

Formal Systems for Managing Employee Performance

*We are being whipsawed by both inflation and recession, and pressured
by powerful foreign economic forces. . . . At the heart of our problem
is the need to improve productivity.*
—GERALD FORD, 1975

A number of years ago a Gallup poll reported that over 50 percent of the
adult population of the United States thought that American workers
were not producing as much as they should. People seemed to feel that we
were not working up to our capacity and that there was room for significant
improvement in productivity.

This issue is of central importance because it bears directly on our standard
of living. If we are more productive we can increase the profits that a company
makes, and as a consequence increase the salaries that its employees earn.
However, increases in salaries without increases in productivity usually lead to
increased prices, inflation, and, therefore, a decreased standard of living. It is
thus in everyone's best interest to increase our overall level of productivity.

It is painfully obvious that productivity is down. According to data provided by the United States Bureau of Labor Statistics, the average compound
annual rate of growth of output per hour of all persons in the business sector for
the years 1973–1985 was only .8 percent. In comparison, for the years
1947–1973 the average rate was 3.0 percent—nearly four times as high!
Unquestionably, much of the earlier rise in productivity was due to technology, and to some extent the more recent lower levels reflect the fact that
the rate of dramatic technological innovation may have leveled off. However,
a major part of productivity is also people—how hard they work and how
much they produce. It is this aspect of productivity, along with the formal
systems that organizations use to manage it, that is the focus of this chapter.

DETERMINANTS OF PERFORMANCE

In the chapter on motivation (Chapter 6) we pointed out that one can often
observe wide variations in performance among employees working on exactly
the same job. Some people produce twice as much as their coworkers. In that
chapter we suggested that both personal abilities *and* motivation contribute to
effectiveness, and that both must be present for good performance to occur.
Ability without motivation or motivation without ability is not likely to lead
to a high level of output. In the first case, the employee knows what to do but
does not care, and in the second case he or she works hard but does not have
the necessary skills.

A simple example might help to illustrate this idea. Imagine a young boy or
girl coming up to bat in a baseball game. The performance criterion is usually
clear: hit the ball where there are no fielders. However, in order to accomplish
this goal both ability (e.g., eye-hand coordination, a level swing) and effort
(the bat has to be swung vigorously) are required. If the child has the skill but
no enthusiasm, or plenty of enthusiasm but little skill, the result should be the
same: an out. In contrast, skill combined with effort increases the chances of a
hit. The present chapter focuses on the formal policies, systems, and procedures that an oganization can establish to ensure that it has highly qualified
and motivated employees.

Chapter 15:
Formal
Systems for
Managing
Employee
Performance

Before we proceed further, we should note that our assumption about ability and motivation as joint contributors to performance is a fairly recent idea. Through the years there have been numerous other theories with very different views of employee performance. Some of these positions are reviewed below.

The Great-Man Theory. For many years it was assumed that motivation is primarily based on economic concerns, and that most employees want the same thing from their jobs (money). Differences in performance were attributed to individual differences in personality traits, abilities, and skills. According to this approach, we have only to identify the personal characteristics of our most effective employees. Once this set of characteristics is known, we can select similar people to fill other jobs, and we will soon have an organization staffed with superperformers, or "great men." (Notice the similarity here to the universal-trait approach to the study of leader effectiveness discussed in Chapter 14.)

Unfortunately, this theory does not hold up. Research results show that different characteristics are important for different jobs. Some characteristics that clearly lead to good performance in one type of job actually produce poor performance in others. Even a trait such as intelligence is occasionally a drawback. In addition, even when a list of desirable characteristics is generated *for a particular job,* selecting people who possess these characteristics does not invariably mean they will all be successful. Thus, over time it gradually came to be recognized that motivational differences are equally important factors in the overall performance equation.

Satisfaction Produces Effectiveness. Another outdated perspective is one that was strongly advocated by those in the *human-relations* movement, a philosophy of management that evolved partly in response to the Hawthorne studies done during the Depression era (see Chapter 3). This view assumed that employees are motivated not only by money, but also by the social and interpersonal aspects of the job. Thus, it was proposed that a pleasant physical and social environment would produce highly motivated employees. As Parker and Kleemeier (1951) stated it, "Management has at long last discovered that there is greater production, and hence greater profit, when workers are satisfied with their jobs. Improve the morale of a company and you improve production" (p. 10).

In essence, this view proposes that satisfaction *causes* productivity: A happy employee is a motivated and productive employee. The role of management, then, is to design an environment that is physically and socially satisfying. Unfortunately, research results have not supported the human-relations position either. It is just too simple an explanation. Numerous studies have shown that performance and satisfaction are only weakly related, and there is very little evidence that satisfaction causes increased productivity (e.g., Iaffaldano & Muchinsky, 1985).

These findings are not really surprising. The satisfaction-causes-productivity thesis omits almost all concern for an employee's ability and personal traits.

Many people can be happy with a high-paying, interpersonally pleasant job but not have the skill to perform well. Also, the human-relations explanation gives no attention to goals, equity, reinforcement, or other major factors that motivate individuals. The focus on satisfaction alone is too narrow.

Past Performance Predicts Future Performance. The final dated proposition that we will discuss focuses on the *selection* and *placement* of employees. It is sometimes argued that if people have performed well on other jobs, they should do well on any new job. This approach is still used today as the major factor in personnel decisions in many organizations. We look at an employee's résumé and letters of recommendation, and we base our prediction of future performance on past performance. To ensure good performance in the future, all we have to do is select people who were good performers in the past.

This idea has some merit. As it turns out, this *is* a very good strategy under a restricted set of conditions. When the prospective employee is being asked to do a job that is *highly similar* to one in which he or she has previously been effective, past performance may be a good predictor of future performance. In many cases, however, the jobs will differ dramatically. And there is no reason to believe that the traits and skills that are effective in one job will necessarily be effective in another. Also, what motivated the individual previously may have been specific to the first job. A new and different job may present very different conditions that will influence the employee's effort differently.

The *Peter principle,* an amusing theory developed by Peter and Hull (1969), describes a logical extension of this proposition. Peter and Hull argue that since we continually use past performance to predict future performance, eventually we will select or promote people to jobs in which they are not effective. At this point, they no longer receive further promotions, because they are no longer performing well. In the long run, they suggest, everyone is promoted to his or her level of incompetence, and the effectiveness of organizations suffers accordingly.

The Peter principle is overly pessimistic. Past performance is not the only factor in selection and promotion decisions. However, Peter and Hull's (1969) work does call attention to the problem that arises when past performance is used to predict future performance on a job that is substantially different from the one the person is leaving.

A New Perspective

Rejection of the great-man and human-relations perspectives leads us inevitably to a *contingency approach* to performance effectiveness. At the heart of this new approach is the proposition that *effective performance depends upon the proper match between the individual and the job.* Thus, in order to achieve maximum productivity, an organization must ensure that the right people are working in the right jobs under the right conditions. In part, this means that the organization must strive to match the skills of the employee with the demands of the job. To accomplish this, the job itself must be carefully analyzed so that its requirements are thoroughly understood. Once this is done, employees with the proper skills and abilities can be selected. In addition, the organization must also attend to the motivational aspect of performance. One way to do this is to establish good performance appraisal and reward systems. These contribute to motivation by providing employees with the performance feedback they need for evaluation, reward, and development purposes.

Note that this contingency idea is wholly compatible with the open systems theory view of organizations and the concept of congruence outlined in Chapter 3. In terms of the open systems theory framework, procedures for job analysis, employee selection, performance appraisal, and reward administration can all be classified as part of the formal organizational structure. They are, in effect, all formal systems designed to help the organization manage employee performance. In the remainder of the chapter we examine these formal systems in more detail.

EMPLOYEE SELECTION SYSTEMS

Suppose you are an entrepreneur with a new product—a collapsible bicycle. You and some friends have developed a couple of prototypes, and it turns out that a large sporting goods company has decided to finance the production of your product. You know it will take thirty or forty people to produce the bicycles, and that these people will have to work on a variety of jobs. You will need one or two engineers, several managers and supervisors, a financial expert, some skilled employees for the actual construction process, and so on. You need to attract, select, and keep people who will do a good job.

How do you do it? How do you get the right people matched up with the right job? Probably the first thing you would do is to imagine what sorts of tasks are actually to be performed in the various jobs. That is, you would try to analyze the jobs in terms of their specific requirements. This process is called *job analysis*, and it should provide a rough idea of the characteristics your employees will need.

The next step is the actual *selection* of people. This process requires that you find out something about the job applicants. Somehow you must discover whether the potential employees possess the characteristics that are important for successful performance. You might use an interview, psychological tests, or an on-the-job simulation to gather this information. There are strengths and weaknesses in all these techniques.

Finally, after you have analyzed the job and selected the people, you want to be able to check on how good a selection job you did. Some of the people you hire may not work out. The crucial question is whether you could have predicted this from your job analysis and the information you had about the applicants. It is important that you *validate* your selection procedure. You must find out whether your selection procedure actually predicts performance on the job. If it does not, you should change it so that it does.

In the ideal situation, we want to be able to place people in positions in which they use their skills and are highly effective. If we do this, people will feel that their potential is being realized, and the organization will achieve a high level of productivity. The personal and economic benefits to both the individual and the organization will be maximized.

This is the ideal. Unfortunately, we too often fall short of this goal. The processes of job analysis, selection, and validation are far from exact sciences. People and jobs change over time. What is a good match today may be a poor match tomorrow. However, the failure to reach this ideal is not totally the fault of inadequate scientific information. It also occurs because personnel managers are often poorly informed about these processes and how to use them. A thorough understanding of job analysis, selection, and validation is a necessity for successful personnel planning and administration.

Individual Differences

It is the common wonder of all men, how among so many millions of faces, there should be none alike.
—Sir Thomas Browne

At the heart of the selection process is the idea of *individual differences.* Human beings vary on every dimension we can measure. This includes their physical, psychological, biological, emotional, and behavioral characteristics. Any individual that applies for a job possesses a *unique* combination of characteristics—there is no one else who is exactly the same. Thus, the job of the personnel manager is to (1) assess accurately what characteristics the applicant possesses, and (2) determine whether those characteristics are important for a particular position.

The presence of individual differences has important implications for both the individual manager and the organization as a whole. First, managers must

FIGURE 15-1
People look for jobs they think will be a good match with their skills, interests, and aspirations.

realize that there will always be some people who perform better than others. Not everyone can perform at the level of the best employee. By firing the worst performer you simply make another individual the worst.

On the other hand, if everyone *is* producing exactly the same amount, one should be on the lookout for informal work-group norms that are artificially suppressing the performance of some employees (recall that this topic was discussed in detail in Chapter 9). The lack of variability in performance is often due to enforced norms concerning how much work should be done. Left to their own initiative, individuals almost always show some variability.

Individual differences also have an impact at the organizational level of analysis. Different productivity rates result in different labor and overhead costs. Also, the cost of selecting and training people for different jobs varies widely. It may be relatively easy and inexpensive to find and train a shipping-room packer, while an electronics engineer may cost 100 times as much.

Finally, individual differences are also important from the employee's point of view. It must be remembered that people are happiest and most satisfied with their jobs when they are using their skills and talents optimally. They become dissatisfied both when they are put into jobs that do not make use of their skills, and when they are put into jobs that require skills they do not possess. Although job dissatisfaction is not a direct cause of poor performance, it can lead to increased rates of tardiness, absenteeism, and turnover (see Chapter 5). Thus, finding the optimal match between the employee and he job is of mutual benefit to both the individual and the organization at large.

Job Analysis

The first step in any successful selection procedure is to obtain an accurate description of the jobs we wish to fill. Before we can select people, we must have a good idea about what we want these people to be able to do. The process of developing a detailed description of a job is called a *job analysis*.

Sources and Methods. The process of job analysis demands that we gather data about particular jobs and about the kinds of things that people do in order to be successful in those jobs. Any number of methods can be used to gather such information. One commonly used strategy is simply to *observe* one or more employees while they are actually performing their jobs. Another method is to conduct *interviews*. Job holders can be asked to describe in their own words what it is they do on the job. Training manuals, reports, records, and other printed sources might also be consulted. From all of this information one can write a *job description*. A job description is a written narrative that enumerates the various types of activities actually performed on the job. Job descriptions are useful because they outline the various roles the job holder must play, suggest how these roles relate to overall organizational objectives, and in a general way indicate what the employee must do to fulfill these roles (McCormick & Ilgen, 1985). On the other hand, job descriptions often suffer from a lack of detail. While they describe what is generally done on the job, they usually provide little information about those areas of behavior that separate good performers from poor performers.

In response to this criticism, several more thorough job analysis procedures have been developed. These involve the use of highly structured questionnaires that are completed by professionals familiar with the job being analyzed (e.g., McCormick, Jeanneret, & Mecham, 1972). These questionnaires yield a much more detailed and quantifiable description of the behaviors required for the job. For example, an ordinary job description for a college-level chemistry instructor might include the phrase "teach introductory course in organic chemistry." In contrast, a more detailed job analysis using one of the structured questionnaires might also include such statements as "speak audibly without a microphone to a class of up to 220 students," "construct both true-false and multiple-choice type exams," and "operate an overhead projector." The amount of time spent in these various activities might also be recorded, along with an estimate of each activity's overall importance to the job.

One other job analysis method that is often quite helpful makes use of what is called the *critical incident technique* (Flanagan, 1954). In using the critical incident technique, employees are asked to describe actual behaviors that led to either success or failure on the job. After a large number of these incidents are collected, they can be sorted and categorized to produce a behavioral description of the good performer and the poor performer. A good job analysis should reveal not only the general behavioral requirements of the job, but also what types of behaviors distinguish high performers from low performers. A well-done critical incident study can meet these criteria.

Suppose you wanted to do your own job analysis for college instructors. You might start by taking the best criteria of excellence you can find (e.g., a combination of student ratings, faculty opinions, and demand for classes) and divide your faculty into three groups: outstanding, average, and poor teachers. Through interviews, observations, and gathering critical incidents, you might find that good instructors all (1) come to class on time; (2) put an outline on the board; (3) are well organized; (4) use a variety of different teaching media, such as films, exercises, and visual aids; (5) use language that is easily understood by students; (6) respond helpfully to questions; and (7) finish each class period on time. Poor instructors, by contrast, might be found to (1) be disorganized, (2) come late to class frequently, (3) read from their notes, (4) talk down to students, (5) use technical language, and (6) keep their classes late. Once you have determined the characteristics that are related to effective performance, you will have a better idea about what sorts of behaviors and abilities to look for the next time an instructor is to be hired. The combination of needed behaviors, knowledge, skills, and abilities forms the *job specification*—what a prospective employee must have or be able to do in order to get the job and be successful at it.

It should be noted that while the preceding discussion is meant to be straightforward and easy to understand, developing a good job specification is extremely difficult. Constructing a questionnaire to describe jobs may take months of work by people who are technically trained in this process. Conducting interviews designed to gather job-related data also takes training, time, and expertise. In short, a job analysis is hard to do well. It frequently demands the use of outside experts as well as substantial amounts of time. However, since the other formal systems of selection, appraisal, and reward rest on a good job analysis, it is well worth the cost.

Points for Consideration. Several summary comments about job analysis should be made. First, the most useful analyses are those that are specific and focus on behavior. They provide a detailed description of what people actually do, and they generate behavioral dimensions that will distinguish good performance from poor performance. Second, a good job analysis can be used for many things. It can be helpful for selecting employees, generating a performance-appraisal instrument, and pinpointing individual needs for counseling and training. Third, from the prospective employee's point of view, a job specification can be very helpful. It gives a realistic description of what will be required on the job, and it can reduce uncertainty. It is a powerful and important tool.

481

Chapter 15:
Formal
Systems for
Managing
Employee
Performance

Finally, a word of caution. People and jobs change over time. Some of this change is systematic and planned, and some of it is not. The point is that a job analysis, especially one that describes very specific behaviors, may become obsolete with the introduction of new technology or other factors. The process of analyzing jobs should be an ongoing activity rather than something that is performed once and then used without modification for 20 years. Periodic checks are needed to ensure that job descriptions and job specifications continue to be accurate statements of what is required for good performance.

Candidate Assessment

Once a job specification has been developed, the next step is to establish a procedure that will generate the information about job candidates needed to make a personnel decision. Job candidates provide some of this information in the form of biographical data, work histories, and letters of recommendation. But most companies actively pursue additional information through the use of interviews, psychological tests, work simulations, and other procedures. These techniques are designed to reveal whether or not a particular candidate fits the job specifications, and thus whether or not he or she is a good bet to succeed. Four of the most important strategies for gathering such information are reviewed below.

Interviews. Perhaps the most widely used selection technique is the interview. Job candidates sit down and talk with a company representative about a variety of topics that are usually chosen by the interviewer. It is meant to provide both the prospective employee and the employer with a more personal feel for one another. It may also be used by the interviewer to gather information that is not available from other sources. After the interview is over, the interviewer typically makes a series of judgments based on his or her notes, and this information is entered into the candidate's file and becomes part of the decision-making process.

Besides providing the organization with information about the applicant, an interview may also be used to "sell" the organization to the applicant. In this sense, the interview should also be considered a part of the recruiting process. The candidate is not the only one who is being evaluated. Prospective employees will be interested in the terms of employment, work conditions, and other factors that may influence their decision. Thus, the interview should be seen as a two-way exchange.

The type of interview most frequently used is called an *unstructured interview* (Dunham, 1983). As the name suggests, an unstructured interview is a rather casual, loosely organized conversation between the applicant and the interviewer. The questions asked are likely to vary from one applicant to the next and from one interviewer to the next. In contrast to the unstructured interview, there is the less frequently used *patterned,* or *structured, interview.* Here, the interviewer has a fairly well-established format or outline of questions to pursue. The questions are usually direct and unambiguous, and may require a fairly short answer (e.g., What courses in your college education did you enjoy most?). As we shall see, the more direct, structured, and unambiguous the exchange, the more reliable and useful the information turns out to be (cf. Orpen, 1985).

In some cases a different type of interviewing process is used. Occasionally a *stress interview* is employed in order to see how the candidate responds to a difficult or stressful situation. Or a *group interview* (when there are multiple candidates) or a *panel interview* (when there are multiple interviewers) might be used. These procedures are used relatively infrequently and typically in response to particular demands of the job. For example, stress interviews were used to look at possible candidates for espionage operations during World War II.

Our knowledge about the problems with interviews is extensive. In general the reliability of the unstructured interview is fairly poor. That is, different interviewers tend to make very different judgments about the same applicant. The reason for this is that the unstructured interview allows too much

FIGURE 15-2
The job interview is often an important source of data for both the organization and the job candidate.

subjectivity in interpreting the meaning of what the candidate says. To the extent that an interview requires a great deal of judgment, interpretation, and subjective assessment, it will generally produce less reliable data.

This source of error shows up in a variety of ways. The more subjective and unstructured the interview, (1) the less agreement among raters, (2) the greater the distortion of facts, and (3) the more the interviewer's personal biases enter into the decision. We know from a number of research studies that interviewers make mistakes, have biases, and are influenced by some factors more than others. For example, negative information is often weighted more heavily than positive information (e.g., Miller & Rowe, 1967). The candidate's nonverbal behavior can sometimes influence the interviewer (e.g., Imada & Hakel, 1977; note that this study was described in detail in Chapter 10, pp. 312–314). The degree of similarity between the candidate and the interviewer can also bias the decision (e.g., Rand & Wexley, 1975). And most interviewers tend to make an evaluative judgment about the candidate during the first few minutes of the exchange. This premature judgment can color their perceptions of the rest of the interview (e.g., Webster, 1964).

Finally, it should be noted that the *context* in which the interview takes place can also strongly influence the interviewer's judgment about the candidate. One context factor that can be particularly problematic is the suitability of *other candidates who have previously been interviewed*. Suppose, for example, that you are about to be interviewed for a job in the sales department of a large computer manufacturing firm. You feel moderately qualified for the position, but you are a little nervous about the interview itself. Will the interviewer's evaluation of you be influenced in any way by the qualifications of the other people he or she has already seen? Research indicates that this is in fact quite likely to happen.

For example, Wexley, Yukl, Kovacs, and Sanders (1972) had 80 subjects watch videotapes of three different job candidates being interviewed for the position of "office systems salesman." Prior to seeing any of the interviews, the subjects were given a detailed description of the sales job. After seeing each interview, the subjects rated the candidate's suitability for the job on a 9-point scale. Some of the subjects first saw two other candidates who were very highly qualified for the job and then a third candidate who had either very high, average, or very poor qualifications. Others first saw two candidates who were very poorly qualified for the job and then a third who had either very high, average, or very poor qualifications. Of interest are the ratings given to the last of the three candidates. (All of the candidates were males.) These ratings are shown in Figure 15-3.

As can be seen, regardless of the third candidate's actual qualifications for the job, he was rated less favorably when the first two candidates were highly qualified in comparison to when the first two candidates were poorly qualified. This effect was quite extreme when the third candidate had only average qualifications. When the third candidate had average qualifications and followed two other candidates who were very highly qualified, he was rated very unfavorably. When, on the other hand, the third candidate followed two others who were very poorly qualified, he was rated very favorably. (The moral of the story, of course, is that whenever you go into an interview, arrange to have two poorly qualified applicants precede you!)

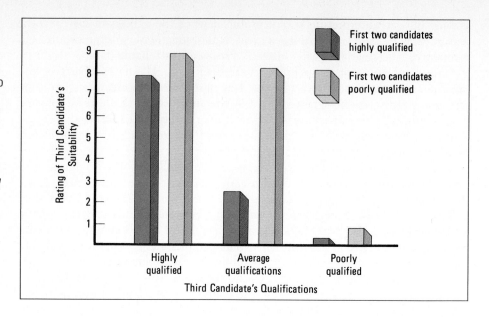

Given these problems, what can be done to increase the reliability of the interview? We can offer several suggestions. First, the construction of a structured, preplanned, and agreed-upon interview format is the most important consideration. At least under this strategy, the same questions will be asked of all the candidates. The person being interviewed will feel that the situation is fairer if everyone is asked the same questions and evaluated on the basis of the same criteria. The candidates' responses should, of course, be accurately recorded. There is also evidence that interviewers can be trained to avoid some of the errors just described (e.g., Wexley, Sanders, & Yukl, 1973). Finally, the interview should be seen as only one part of the overall selection process, and therefore should be designed to obtain specific information. This information can fill in gaps that were not covered by other sources. When used in this way, the interview can make a unique contribution and can help with the exchange of information.

Psychological Tests. Information about job candidates can also be provided by psychological tests. Psychological tests can be used to assess applicants' characteristics in four main areas: (1) mental abilities, (2) muscular or motor coordination, (3) personality traits, and (4) physical and sensory capacities. The choice of which tests to use depends on the job specification. The scores on these tests are used to supplement the interview, biographical, and job-history data already gathered.

The number of psychological tests is vast. There are far too many to include any sort of comprehensive review here. But we can mention some typical examples of tests frequently used. The most comprehensive measures of mental abilities are the intelligence tests. Intelligence test results are closely associated with success in school and academic-related activities. Tests of motor coordination might assess such functions as muscular control, manual dexterity, and other manipulative activities. These tests are highly specific

485

Chapter 15:
Formal
Systems for
Managing
Employee
Performance

(while intelligence tests are more general), and often involve rather complex equipment. Personality tests are designed to measure the types of personal characteristics that we discussed in Chapter 4, such as sociability, dominance, extroversion, and dogmatism. Finally, tests designed to measure sensory capacities might test for judgments of distance, night vision, color differentiation, hearing acuity, or sense of smell (e.g., for wine tasters).

The critical questions to ask about psychological tests concern their reliability and validity. *Reliability* refers to the amount of error in a test score. If you take an intelligence test today and get a high score will you get the same high score if you take the test tomorrow? A reliable test is one that we can count on. It is one that is subject to little error in measurement and therefore will produce very similar results upon retesting.

However, the fact that the scores from a psychological test contain very little error (i.e., are reliable) does not mean that those scores will necessarily be useful for the purpose of selecting employees. In addition to being reliable, a test must also be *valid*. There are several different types of validity, each with a slightly different meaning. One type is called content validity. *Content validity* refers to whether or not the test actually measures what we think it measures. For example, does the test depicted in Figure 15-4 really measure intelligence? If we are able to answer this questions affirmatively, we are saying that the test has content validity.

An even more important type of validity, at least from the standpoint of employee selection, is called *predictive validity*. Predictive validity refers to whether or not the test is really able to predict performance on the job. A thermometer placed under the tongue may be a reliable and content-valid measure of body temperature, but it is not likely to predict one's performance as a manager—it has little predictive validity for this purpose. (Note that it does have predictive validity for other purposes, such as assessing short-term physical well-being.) In order to be effective as a selection tool, a psychological test must be shown to have predictive validity. Indeed, predictive validity is an essential requirement for *any* selection procedure, whether or not it includes psychological testing.

A more detailed description of psychological tests is available in most industrial psychology textbooks (e.g., McCormick & Ilgen, 1985; Wexley & Yukl, 1984). The important points to emphasize here are that there are

FIGURE 15-4

Intelligence *can* sometimes be a valid predictor of an applicant's suitability for a job.

numerous tests and that they vary in quality (i.e., reliability and validity). A personnel manager must treat psychological tests like any other tool. They are not a panacea or cure-all. For some specific jobs, some specific tests will be fairly good predictors of job performance. For other jobs, there may be no tests that are good predictors. Again, psychological tests are only one means of predicting future job behavior.

Work Samples. A rather innovative strategy for employee selection is the use of *work samples*. The basic idea is to simulate as closely as possible the actual conditions of the job. Job candidates participate in the simulation exercise, and measures of their behavior are gathered. The underlying premise is that samples of actual behavior for a specific job will be the best predictor of later behavior on that same job.

For some types of positions, such as that of a typist, work samples have been a routine element of the selection process for many years. However, more recently we have seen this technique employed to assess the behavior of people applying for other types of jobs. One of the most popular work-sample techniques for managerial jobs is known as the "in-basket" test. From a thorough job analysis, a set of "action items" (e.g., letters, memos, routine forms) can be put together that reflect the types of problems and issues that a manager in a particular company at a particular level might have to deal with. These items are placed in an in-basket, and the job candidate is asked to play the role of the manager and make decisions about each item. The way in which these items are handled provides a quantitative score that can be used to predict later performance on the job.

In some research, work samples have been shown to be a more effective predictor of performance than other procedures such as psychological tests (e.g., Hunter & Hunter, 1984). Campion (1972), for example, used a work sample to predict the performance of maintenance mechanics employed by a food-processing company. After a thorough job analysis, several tasks were selected that were deemed to be representative of actual on-the-job behavior (e.g., repairing a gearbox; installing and aligning a motor). Measures of proficiency on this work sample turned out to be better predictors of performance on the job than more traditional testing techniques designed to assess mental abilities and mechanical comprehension. Also, applicants thought the work sample was fairer than traditional techniques.

Work samples are most useful when there are specific, observable behaviors that are known to be necessary for good performance. Some positions are difficult to define behaviorally in this way. In these jobs one must rely on some of the other techniques discussed previously.

Assessment Centers. One further development in the use of selection techniques is the assessment center. An *assessment center* combines interviews, psychological tests, and work samples into an integrated evaluation package. The data generated from an assessment center can be used for selection, promotion, training, and development. Assessment centers have become increasingly popular and are in use by companies such as AT&T, IBM, AMOCO, Sears, and Caterpillar Tractor.

487

Chapter 15:
Formal
Systems for
Managing
Employee
Performance

The typical assessment center takes from 1 to 3 days to complete. There are usually four to six professionals in charge of the assessment process who have been trained to administer and score the various assessment tools. In most cases the participants are candidates for management jobs, either from within the company or from outside, and the ratio of candidates to assessors is usually small (e.g., 3 to 1). The candidates participate in a number of group exercises, simulations, and management games. They take a battery of tests, and they are interviewed by a number of assessors. Their performance is rated by themselves, their peers, and the assessors. All this information is then combined to allow predictions to be made about future managerial performance.

Research results on the assessment center technique are encouraging. Reviews of this literature suggest that assessment centers can predict later managerial success (e.g., Bray, 1982; Ritchie & Moses, 1983). For example, Hinrichs (1975) reported on a follow-up study conducted with forty-seven individuals in a marketing department of a large manufacturing company. In 1967 these individuals went through an extensive assessment center involving tests, simulations, and group exercises. At that time, an overall assessment-center rating and a management potential evaluation (made without knowledge of the assessment-center results) were gathered. Eight years later these two predictors correlated positively ($r = 0.58$) with the position level attained for the thirty individuals still with the company. Those that had risen the highest were characterized as self-assured, persuasive, facile in interpersonal communication, and aggressive. While these results are impressive, we should hasten to point out that promotability is only one index of managerial success. Furthermore, it is an index that may measure more than just managerial performance. That is, one's rate of promotion may be determined by other things besides being a good manager (e.g., knowing how to project a good image to one's boss). Thus, additional research is needed that also looks at other measures of managerial performance (e.g., work-unit output, ratings by the manager's peers and subordinates). If assessment centers are as effective as the preliminary research indicates, they should be able to predict these other performance indices.

Assessment centers are not without their problems, however. One obvious drawback is their cost—they are quite expensive to run. This cost must be balanced against their potential gain. Thus, an assessment center must be shown to have high validity for the particular organization involved, and it should be used only for positions that are expensive, in terms of recruitment and training costs, and important for the smooth running of the organization.

Assessment centers can also create a great deal of anxiety for the participants. The candidates are not only being thoroughly tested, they are also competing with one another. Moreover, when candidates are selected from within the company to participate in an assessment center, the nomination and assessment process itself may cause problems. The person who is not nominated to participate in the assessment center at all may become labeled as someone who does not have management potential. The candidate who participates and does well in the center may carry a positive stereotype throughout his or her career. And the candidate who does poorly may never be considered again.

Thus, there are many different procedures for generating information about job candidates. Interviews, psychological tests, work samples, and assessment centers can all provide valuable data. Given a thorough job analysis and a thorough assessment strategy, the personnel manager should be in a fairly good position to place the right people in the right jobs. But, as we noted previously, there are other factors that contribute to performance. Specifically, motivation and the situational factors that affect motivation also need to be taken into consideration. There will be a ceiling on the effectiveness of any selection procedure in terms of its ability to predict performance. No selection procedure is ever likely to be 100 percent effective.

Job Previews

Besides job analysis and candidate assessment, there is one other preselection strategy that can be helpful for getting the right person into the right job. This is called a *job preview*. Job previews involve the presentation of information about the job to the candidate. Simulations, printed material, videotapes, and interviews with current job holders have all been used. The most effective type of job preview is one that is *realistic*, in the sense that it presents *both the desirable and undesirable* aspects of the job and the organization. This strategy may cause some people who were undecided in the first place to drop out, but it increases the commitment of those who do finally choose to enter. That is, although initial expectations may be lowered, those people who do decide to join are more likely to stay.

The criterion of success for job previews is job tenure. While selection procedures are validated against performance measures, previews are validated against turnover data. A successful job preview increases the chances that people will stay on the job.

John Wanous (1977), who is well known for his work in this area, summarized five studies that compared employees who had realistic job previews to those who did not. In general, people who had job previews seemed to be more satisfied and more likely to stay on the job. Wanous summarized these results as follows:

1. *Life and Casualty Insurance Company of Tennessee—life insurance agents:* 68 percent with previews stayed over 5 months; 53 percent without previews stayed.
2. *Prudential Insurance Company—life insurance agents:* 71 percent with previews stayed over 6 months; 57 percent without previews stayed.
3. *West Point—first-year cadets:* 91 percent with previews stayed over 1 year; 86 percent without previews stayed.
4. *Southern New England Telephone Company—telephone operators:* 62 percent with previews stayed over 3 months; 50 percent without previews stayed.
5. *Manhatten Industries—sewing machine operators:* 89 percent with previews stayed over 6 weeks; 69 percent without previews stayed.

These findings clearly suggest that realistic previews can help (see also Premack & Wanous, 1985). So, analyze the job to determine what is needed, assess the candidate, and then give a realistic job preview. These three strategies should increase the chances for matching the person and the job.

PERFORMANCE APPRAISAL SYSTEMS

489

Chapter 15:
Formal
Systems for
Managing
Employee
Performance

*An ounce of image is worth a pound
of performance.*
—LAWRENCE J. PETER AND RAYMOND HULL

As we stated at the beginning of the chapter, performance depends jointly upon employees' ability and motivation. Once we have selected and hired those individuals with the required skills and abilities, we can switch our attention to the motivational aspects of the job. Two factors that are important for successfully motivating employees are (1) the ease with which the correct job behaviors can be learned, and (2) the rewards that are made contingent upon those behaviors. Employees want to know how well they are doing. They want feedback so that they can learn what they are doing right, what they are doing wrong, and how they can do things better. In addition, they want to be recognized and rewarded for a job well done. The process of evaluating employee performance can serve both of these functions. It can provide feedback for counseling and learning, and it can provide evaluative information upon which rewards can be based. This section of the chapter describes the performance-appraisal system in some detail.

Purposes

Performance appraisals serve two main purposes. First, they serve as the basis for important *administrative decisions.* For example, evaluations of employee performance are used for making decisions about promotions, transfers, dismissals, wage and salary administration, and bonus pay. They are also used as the primary criterion against which employee-selection procedures are validated. Second, performance appraisals also serve as a basis for *employee development.* The information obtained from a performance appraisal can serve as feedback to the employee and as a guide for defining training needed. It can also be used as a basis for establishing performace goals. It is important to recognize that because a performance appraisal can serve as the foundation for both goal setting and reward administration, it is an important mechanism that organizations can use to influence employee motivation.

Appraisal Techniques

There are many different ways to evaluate employee performance. Both *objective* and *subjective* measures exist. The objective measures include (1) measures of volume or quantity of output, such as items produced or words typed; (2) measures of quality, such as spoilage or items rejected; (3) measures of lost time, such as absenteeism or tardiness; and (4) measures involving training or promotion time, such as time in a particular position. In jobs in which there are unambiguous, objective measures of the quantity or quality of output, these measures are frequently used. In many cases, however, such measures either are not available at all or are not clearly indicative of individual performance. For example, some employees work in teams, where each individual's output is highly dependent on the output of all the other team members. Under these circumstances, the subjective judgments of a supervisor about the performance of individual group members are usually required.

The criteria used for subjective performance judgments fall into two main categories: *Other people* and *absolute standards*. When other people are used as the criterion, the assessor is often asked to compare the employee with other employees on a number of personal traits. Figure 15-5 presents an example of a form used for this purpose. Another type of comparison procedure is to have the rater rank-order all the employees in terms of their overall performance. Or a paired comparison procedure might be used, in which each employee is specifically compared to each of the other employees in the group who do the same job. Finally, some sort of forced distribution system could be used. With this technique, the rater is asked to sort employees into several groups, such as the top 10 percent, the next 20 percent, the middle 40 percent, the next 20 percent, and the bottom 10 percent. All these techniques yield performance measures that indicate who is doing *relatively* well and who is doing *relatively* poorly (i.e., relative to others).

One criticism that is often leveled at these comparison techniques is that the basis for the judgments is ambiguous and may be quite idiosyncratic. Consequently, different raters may produce somewhat different rank orders or forced distributions. To remedy this problem, many personnel experts suggest that performance ratings be based upon absolute standards.

Most appraisal instruments using absolute standards are founded upon a preliminary job analysis. As we discussed earlier, a job analysis can provide a detailed description of the behaviors necessary for effective performance. The criterion then becomes the actual presence of the required behavior, rather than a comparison with other employees.

FIGURE 15-5

A personal-trait
rating form.

NAME OF EMPLOYEE					
	Rating				
	1	2	3	4	5
Personal Trait	Exceptional	Above Average	Average	Below Average	Poor
1 Aggressiveness					
2 Tolerance of stress					
3 Physical energy					
4 Creativity					
5 Self-confidence					
6 Adaptability					
7 Leadership					
8 Personal integrity					
9 Emotional balance					
10 Enthusiasm					

A common format for this type of evaluation is some sort of *behavioral checklist*. The behaviors necessary for effective performance in a number of areas are described, and the rating is made. Figure 15-6 presents a humorous example of how a Superhero might be evaluated on such a scale. More elaborate procedures, such as weighted checklists and behaviorally anchored rating scales, are also available. These strategies demand a thorough job analysis that generates a large number of behaviors actually required for the job, some sort of weighting as to the relative importance of these behaviors for good performance, and a categorization process that places similar behaviors into dimensional groupings.

Let us consider an example. Latham and Mitchell (1976) developed a performance appraisal instrument for the members of a research and development department of a large forest products company. Each employee in the department was asked in an interview to provide five specific examples of behavior that led to good performance on their job and five that led to poor performance. All of these behavioral incidents (about 750) were then classified by judges (R&D employees) into a relatively small set of homogeneous categories. Redundant and irrelevant items were discarded, and the sorting procedure was performed again by different judges to make sure that there was a high level of agreement. After a number of other validation checks, an appraisal instrument was developed that consisted of eight dimensions represented by about five behaviors each. For example, one dimension was planning and scheduling, which was represented by the following behaviors: (1) develops a project plan prior to conducting the project, (2) prepares in advance for meetings, and (3) can work on two or more projects effectively at the same time.

The advantages of such a technique are numerous. First, it refers to actual behavior rather than to a subjective estimate of excellence. Second, it can be reliably constructed, and the construction method ensures that a satisfactory instrument is produced. Third, it usually involves the input of the employees who are actually going to be evaluated. As a result, the employees are more

491

Chapter 15:
Formal
Systems for
Managing
Employee
Performance

FIGURE 15-6
A guide to Super-hero performance appraisal.

Area of Performance	Far in Excess of Job Requirements	Exceeds Job Requirements	Meets Job Requirements	Needs Improvement	Does Not Meet Minimum Requirements
Quality of work	Leaps tall buildings in a single bound	Leaps tall buildings with a running start	Can leap short buildings if prodded	Bumps into buildings	Cannot recognize buildings
Promptness	Is faster than a speeding bullet	Is as fast as a speeding bullet	Would you believe a slow bullet?	Misfires frequently	Wounds self when handling guns
Initiative	Is stronger than a locomotive	Is as strong as a bull elephant	Almost as strong as a bull	Shoots the bull	Smells like a bull
Capability	Walks on water	Keeps head above water	Washes with water	Drinks water	Passes water in emergencies
Communication	Talks with God	Talks with the angels	Talks with self	Argues with self	Loses arguments with self

likely to be committed to the evaluation process (cf. Silverman & Wexley, 1984). Fourth, the behaviors that are evaluated are directly tied to performance. Irrelevant behaviors are not included. Finally, this type of procedure can provide the employee with much more specific feedback about what improvements are needed. It may be difficult for an employee to know how to become more aggressive (as rated on a personal-trait form), but it is fairly obvious what needs to be done about a low rating on preparation for meetings and developing project plans.

Problems and Remedies

Thus, there are both objective and subjective measures of performance, and among the subjective measures there are both employee comparison and absolute standard methods. Although some of these measures are better than others for the purpose of performance appraisal, none of them are perfect. It is important to be aware of the types of problems that affect the validity of each one.

Rater Errors. People who evaluate others, either in selection interviews or performance appraisals, tend to make a number of *systematic errors*. For example, individuals who are seen as being similar to the rater tend to receive higher scores (called the "similar to me" error). This is not surprising. We generally like people who are similar to ourselves. Another type of error is called the *halo error*. Raters often allow some outstanding single characteristic (either good or bad) to influence their evaluation of other dimensions. This is most problematic when non-job-related qualities (e.g., athletic accomplishments) are permitted to influence judgments about job-related dimensions. Finally, there are also errors of *leniency*, *strictness*, and *central tendency*. Some raters tend to place most or all of their ratings at the positive end of the rating scale (leniency). Others stick to the negative end of the scale (strictness). Still others stay very close to the middle (central tendency). While there are a few employees who genuinely deserve one or the other of these three patterns of ratings, these will be the exception rather than the rule. Most often, employees show some degree of variability across rating dimensions, being higher on some than others. Thus, a manager who gives one of these three patterns of ratings to more than just a few employees is probably committing a rater error, thereby decreasing the validity of those ratings.

These rating errors can be avoided. When hard productivity data are available (e.g., absences or quantity of output), there is little room for subjective judgment. Also, on those jobs for which behavioral ratings are gathered, the errors can be minimized by properly training the people making the judgments (Smith, 1986). Understanding the nature of these errors is an important step toward eliminating their influence in the performance appraisal process.

Single Criterion Problems. Performance on most jobs cannot be adequately described by the use of just one criterion measure. The reason is that most measures suffer from two related problems: deficiency and contamination. A performance measure is *deficient* to the extent that it does not assess all relevant aspects of the person's performance, and it is *contaminated* to the extent that it assesses things that are irrelevant to the person's performance.

493

Chapter 15:
Formal
Systems for
Managing
Employee
Performance

The nature of these two problems will perhaps become clearer if we consider an example. Suppose you want to evaluate the performance of a baseball player. If you were to use the player's batting average as the sole measure of performance, your performance appraisal would be seriously deficient. Although a batting average is an objective measure that cannot be easily influenced by any of the rater errors listed above, it nevertheless gives only a partial view of a player's overall performance. For instance, it says nothing about how well a player performs as a fielder. Furthermore, a batting average may also be contaminated. If a player bats in a league in which the pitchers are all rather poor (i.e., easy to get a hit off of), he or she is likely to have a higher average than someone who bats in a league in which the pitchers are all rather good (i.e., difficult to get a hit off of). The difference between the batting averages of these two players is partly a reflection of the quality of the pitching in the two leagues, which, of course, is not a part of either player's performance.

The concepts of deficiency and contamination can also be presented graphically by using a Venn diagram. Look at panel A of Figure 15-7. The circle on the left represents the individual's true performance, that is, the sum of all the various aspects of his or her overall performance (e.g., hitting, fielding, attending practice). The circle on the right represents the individual's measured performance, that is, all those factors that influence scores on whatever index of performance is being used (e.g., hitting quality and pitching quality). As can be seen, the measured performance does not completely overlap with the true performance. That part of the *true* performance that is not captured in the measured performance is labeled the "area of deficiency." The larger the area of deficiency, the less valid the appraisal. That part of the *measured* performance that is irrelevant to true performance is labeled the "area of contamination." The larger the area of contamination, the less valid the appraisal.

The situation described in this example is not unusual. Virtually every objective and behavioral performance measure is both deficient and contaminated to a certain extent. The implication, then, is that any *single* measure is only partially valid as an index of performance. This does not mean, however, that the validity of an overall performance appraisal must necessarily be low. The validity of a performance appraisal can be significantly increased if *multiple performance measures* are used, and these measures each capture a *different* aspect of the individual's true performance. This is illustrated in panel B of Figure 15-7. When using multiple measures of performance, the area of deficiency decreases in size, while the area of validity increases in size. (The two areas of contamination are assumed to be independent and random, so that their effects cancel each other out.) Thus, a good rule of thumb is always to use multiple measures of performance. This is true whether one is using objective measures or behaviorally anchored judgments.

Besides the problems of deficiency and contamination, there is one other reason for avoiding the use of a single criterion. When employees see that only one aspect of their performance is being assessed, they tend to focus on that one aspect to the exclusion of others, even though those other, unmeasured

FIGURE 15-7
Performance ap-
praisal deficiency,
contamination, and
validity when one
(panel A) and two
(panel B) perform-
ance measures are
used.

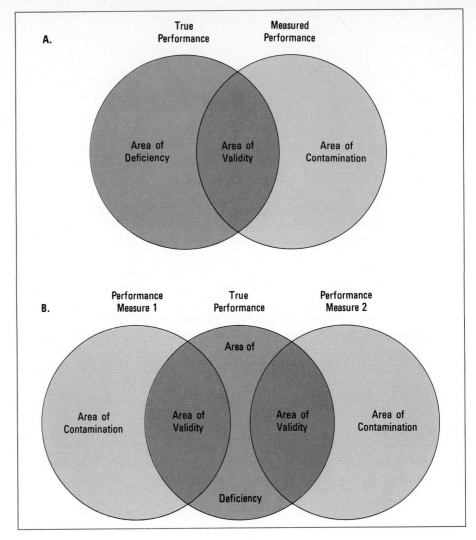

aspects may be important to the long-run success of the organization. Thus, if batting average is used as the sole measure of a baseball player's performance, players can be expected to spend most of their time in batting practice and relatively less time practicing their fielding skills. Similarly, if the number of new accounts obtained is the sole measure of an insurance agent's perform-ance, agents can be expected to spend most of their time talking to prospective customers and relatively less time servicing existing accounts. These results point out an important consequence of performance appraisal—what you measure is what you get!

Differences among Jobs and Raters. What can you do when one supervisor seems consistently to rate people higher than another supervisor and these differences cannot be corrected by rater training? Or how about the situation in which exactly the same evaluation form is used for very different positions. The question here is one of standardization. The employee should not be subject to the whims of a "tough judge" or to the bias of doing something that is different from the rest of the group.

495

Chapter 15:
Formal
Systems for
Managing
Employee
Performance

One way to handle these problems is through statistical techniques. If over a number of evaluation sessions it becomes clear that there are several particularly tough raters or jobs, you can sometimes make a mathematical adjustment. For example, when it is clear that there is no difference between jobs, but there are differences in ratings attributable to rater error (and not to supervision or other factors), a constant can be added to (or subtracted from) the affected performance appraisal scores. In this way employees are less likely to feel they are the victims of circumstances beyond their control.

Employee Feedback. The final problem we will address is caused by the necessity of giving employees feedback about the results of a performance appraisal. Whether or not employees should be given feedback about appraisal results depends largely upon the reason the appraisal was done in the first place. If employee counseling, development, and training are of concern (and they usually are), feedback can be quite helpful and should be given. However, knowing that employees will see the appraisal can have a negative influence on the quality of the ratings given. More specifically, there is evidence that supervisors give significantly higher ratings when they know that those ratings will later be seen by the employee. This is especially true when the employee's performance is poor to begin with (Fisher, 1979) and when the ratings are also used as the basis for making decisions about promotions and financial rewards (Ilgen & Feldman, 1983).

There is no easy solution to this problem. The best strategy is to minimize the degree of subjectivity in the appraisal procedure itself. The more objective and observable the performance criteria, the easier it is to justify a performance evaluation. And when subjective judgments are necessary, they should be based on clearly specified behavioral standards defined through a careful job analysis. Finally, allowing employees to participate in the development of the appraisal instrument will increase the likelihood that they will preceive it as being fair and equitable. All of this should serve to reduce the rater's tendency to inflate the performance ratings when those ratings are to be fed back to the employee.

Other Considerations

There are several additional issues related to the appraisal process that should be briefly discussed. The first topic concerns *who is doing the evaluation*. In the overwhelming majority of cases, the immediate supervisor is the person who does the ratings. From a legitimacy point of view, this makes sense. We expect and more readily accept evaluative feedback from our boss.

However, research on the evaluation process suggests that in some cases peer reviews, self-ratings, and/or outsider assessments may also be appropriate (e.g., Kane & Lawler, 1978). When individuals rate themselves, and this rating is actually used as part of the evaluation, there is frequently an increased sense of commitment and increased feelings of fairness on the part of the employees. Outside raters are often seen as unbiased. Peer ratings can be helpful when the supervisor is frequently separated from the group, and when group members trust one another. The important point is that those who are in the best position to see what an employee actually does ought to be included in the evaluation process. Perhaps the best strategy is to gather different types of ratings (e.g., superior, peer, and self) and use each rating as a source of valuable information.

Another consideration is the *frequency* of evaluation. Since both people and jobs change over time, some sort of annual review is probably the minimum requirement. In support of this, Landy, Barnes, and Murphy (1978) found that employees perceive the performance appraisal process to be more fair and accurate when the appraisals are done at least once a year. In some cases a quarterly or semiannual assessment will make the most sense. A balance has to be struck between evaluating too frequently (the employee feels constantly threatened) and evaluating too infrequently (the employee feels that the evaluation does not provide timely feedback and recognition of improvement).

Finally, there are *legal issues* that must be considered. More and more companies are having to defend their personnel decisions in court. As a consequence, all organizations are feeling pressure to make personnel decisions that they can document and justify empirically. For example, many companies report that before 1970 they had neither a personnel manual nor an affirmative-action manual. Now they have both. Companies are becoming more thorough, more systematic, more cautious, and more procedure conscious. In the long run, these are probably good signs.

SYSTEMS OF REWARD

So far we have discussed two formal organizational systems for managing employee performance: the employee selection system and the performance appraisal system. While employee selection systems are directed toward the skill and ability side of the overall performance equation, performance appraisal systems are directed toward the motivational side. However, appraisal systems cannot affect motivation by themselves. Something must be done with the information generated by those systems. At minimum, the performance information should be fed back to the employee and/or used as a basis for goal setting. In addition, it should also be used as a basis for rewarding employees. When used in combination, the appraisal and reward systems represent a very powerful mechanism that organizations can use to influence the motivation of their employees. In this final section of the chapter, we will discuss systems of reward in some detail.

Compensation is a key element of the implicit contract that every employee has with the organization. In exchange for the employee's services, the organization agrees to compensate him or her in certain specific ways (e.g., wages, fringe benefits). Thus, if the organization's system of rewards is poorly designed, other factors such as selecting the right people, placing them in the right jobs, and fairly evaluating their performance may be irrelevant. Unless rewards are perceived as attractive and clearly linked to performance, employee motivation is likely to be comparatively low.

From the organization's point of view, the reward system can serve a number of functions. First, it can be used to attract and keep high-quality employees. Everything else being equal, people want to go where the rewards are greatest. Second, it can be used to acknowledge past performance and accomplishments. Finally, it can serve as a motivator for future performance. Rewards can be explicitly tied to future goal attainment, thereby stimulating higher levels of work motivation.

497

Chapter 15:
Formal
Systems for
Managing
Employee
Performance

From the individual's perspective, the reward system also serves a number of functions. First, it provides a sense of security. Pay, pensions, sick leave, and other parts of the compensation package ease the psychological burden of trying to make a living for oneself and one's dependents. Second, rewards are a source of recognition. They let individuals know how well they are doing. In this sense, the reward system serves as an important feedback mechanism. Finally, rewards can serve as important personal goals to attain. A certain level of pay or promotion may be a significant lifelong ambition.

Types of Rewards

There are two main types of rewards that an individual receives on the job. Those that come as an inherent part of doing the job itself are called *intrinsic rewards.* We discussed these in our chapter on learning (Chapter 2). They include such things as feelings of competence, accomplishment, and self-fulfillment. While the organization can have some control over the intrinsic aspects of one's job, these are not usually discussed as part of the formal organizational reward system.

The second class of rewards that are received on the job are called *extrinsic rewards.* These are tangible external reinforcers that are controlled by the organization. In terms of compensation systems, extrinsic rewards fall into two subcategories: *pay and promotions* and *"other benefits."* The latter includes (1) legally required benefits, such as unemployment compensation, disability insurance, and medicare hospital benefits; (2) private health and security benefits, such as a retirement plan and life insurance; (3) employee services, such as discounts, meals, and transportation; and (4) compensation for time not worked, such as during vacations, sick leave, jury duty, and lunchtime.

The interesting point about most "other benefits" is that they are usually the same for all of the employees in a specific classification. There is little attempt to differentially distribute these rewards as a function of past performance, or to use them as motivators for better performance in the future. Instead, they serve to meet legal requirements, attract people to the organization, and provide a certain level of security for them once they are on the job.

The pay and promotions subcategory, on the other hand, is often used to recognize excellence and encourage greater effort. The rewards in this subcategory are distributed in a number of different ways, with differing requirements and impact. Promotions often involve both a change in job and a change in pay, and it is therefore difficult to tease out which factor serves as a motivator. The effects of financial payments, by contrast, are more easily identified. The next section briefly describes the major types of pay systems used in organizations today.

Systems of Pay

Most managers, professionals, and upper-level employees receive a salary or some sort of time-based pay. The amount they earn is dependent on the amount of time they work, by the hour, day, week, or month. Note that money is not tied to performance in these cases. It is not how much you produce that matters but how long you work.

Organizations with time-based pay systems are usually forced to find other rewards to motivate their employees. Promotions, recognition, and intrinsic rewards (such as assigning interesting or challenging tasks) may be used. But more frequently, some sort of bonus system is installed to provide additional pay based on merit. These bonus systems tie money as directly as possible to productivity. The idea is to reward past performance in order to encourage excellence in the future. This type of system is easiest to set up and administer in those situations in which good performance is easily defined and measured.

Individual Plans. The simplest and most direct individual incentive plan is the piece-rate system. Here the employee is paid for the number of items or pieces completed, regardless of the amount of time or effort expended. Those who produce a lot get a lot, while those who produce less get less.

Piece-rate incentive plans have intuitive appeal, but they also have drawbacks. In many cases employees are not entirely independent of other individuals or machines. Thus, their output may not always be a direct reflection of their effort. Also, unless there is substantial agreement and trust about how the rate-per-piece is determined, there may be dissatisfaction. Employees may establish informal norms to hold down production if they feel that higher levels of performance will ultimately lead management to lower the rate paid for each piece produced.

Other individual incentive plans (used when piece rates are not feasible) base the incentive on some subjective measure of performance. It is in these settings that a reliable and valid performance appraisal system is most important. The employees must feel that the incentive is in fact based on what they actually do, rather than on chance or the whims of the rater. The system usually includes both a time-based wage and an incentive, and the incentive may be distributed daily, weekly, or monthly. In some cases it even takes the form of an end-of-the-year bonus.

Group Plans. In many organizations people work together in teams or groups, and everyone is highly dependent upon everyone else. In order to perform well everybody must contribute. Recall that in our discussion about task demands for interaction and cooperation in Chapter 8, "Group Dynamics," we mentioned that in highly interdependent groups, rewards should not be highly differentiated. For motivation to be high in this sort of situation, rewards should be distributed to the group members fairly equally (see pp. 239–241).

There are a number of compensation systems that are specifically designed to reward individuals according to their group's productivity. At the extreme end of this continuum are companywide profit-sharing plans, in which a percentage of the company's profits is distributed to all employees as a function of their position (level) within the organization. Some well-known profit-sharing systems such as the Scanlon Plan and Improshare use variants of this idea ("Productivity Sharing," 1981). A basic goal of this type of system is to instill in employees a sense of organizational commitment. The assumption is that if employees see that their own pay is tied to the overall success of the company, they are more likely to help in increasing the company's effectiveness.

499

Chapter 15:
Formal
Systems for
Managing
Employee
Performance

New Ideas in Compensation. Two relatively new ideas in pay administration are *cafeteria-style compensation plans* and *skill-evaluation plans.* The cafeteria plans tell the employee how much is in the total pay package, but allow the employee to spend this money however he or she wants. An employee may take it all in cash or may place more of the money in fringe benefits. In some plans, the choice only occurs within the fringe-benefit category. This type of system is designed to ensure that employees are working for rewards they really want. In expectancy theory terms, the system should increase the valence of the outcomes (see pp. 163–164).

The skill-evaluation plans pay people for the skills they have learned rather than for the job they are currently doing. Used mostly in manufacturing plants that employ autonomous work groups in which there is a high possibility of job rotation, this type of system encourages individuals to learn more skills.

For example, in one experiment with this type of system at the General Foods plant in Topeka, Kansas, employees were started at a specified base pay rate. After learning five different jobs they were moved up to the next higher pay rate. After they could do all the production tasks in the plants (these usually took about 2 years to learn) they would get the top pay rate in the plant. In effect, these people were being rewarded for learning new skills. These skills in turn allowed them to have more variety on the job and to fill in when absences occurred (Lawler, 1976; see also Walton, 1985). Note that this type of system assumes that there are other motivators for good performance, such as intrinsic rewards from the work itself, and/or favorable group norms.

Performance-Based Pay: Strategic Issues

From a motivational point of view, tying a certain portion of an employee's total compensation to performance makes a great deal of sense. If employees see that high levels of performance lead to high levels of pay, it is likely that they will actually strive to achieve higher levels of productivity than they would if there were no connection between the two. There are, however, several strategic issues to consider when establishing a performance-based pay system. These include the equity of the system, the level of aggregation at which performance is measured, the use of salary increments versus bonuses, and whether or not information about pay awards should be kept secret. Each of these issues is discussed below.

Equity. If a performance-based pay system is to succeed, it must be perceived as being equitable. At the core of every incentive system is the fact that different people get different rewards. It is essential that these differences match up with actual differences in performance. If there are clear differences in how well people perform and in how much they are paid, but the pay differences bear no relationship to the performance differences, then the pay

A Varied Menu of Benefits

As the summer vacation season arrives, employees at Fluor Corp. (1982 revenues: $7.3 billion) face a tough decision. Do they want more money or more time off? Those working for the Caifornia-based construction firm can add unused holidays and sick leave to their vacations and take extra, paid time off. On the other hand, they can sell their vacations back to the company for cash and spend their summers on the shop floor or behind their desks.

Such choices are part of a growing corporate trend toward flexible, or "cafeteria-style," benefits. Instead of dispensing rigidly fixed programs to everyone on the payroll, some 100 major U.S. firms now offer or plan to offer expanded menus of alternatives. Employees whose working husbands or wives already have family medical insurance, for example, might prefer legal insurance or added vacation instead of more health coverage.

The options can be as varied and innovative as personnel departments can make them. At Detroit's Comerica Inc. (1982 assets: $7.4 billion), Michigan's second largest bank holding company, employees can tailor their benefit packages to help pay for child care. At Baker Packers, a unit of California-based Baker International (1982 revenues: $2.5 billion), workers can cash in up to a week of vacation and deposit the proceeds in company-sponsored savings plans that invest in stocks and other securities.

A main appeal of the flexible programs is tax savings. Employees who opt for child care or other services may receive them in place of higher salaries. But since the benefits are not considered taxable income, the workers are not pushed into a higher tax bracket.

Another driving force behind the new policy has been the mushrooming cost of traditional benefit plans, especially for health programs. U.S. companies paid an average of $6,627 per employee for benefits in 1981, according to a study released last year by the U.S. Chamber of Commerce. Those payments equaled 37% of the typical worker's salary, up from about 30% a decade ago. Wyatt Co., a consulting firm based in Washington, notes that health-care expenses have climbed at an annual rate of 18% over the past five years. Says Lance Tane, a Wyatt analyst: "Benefits used to be considered the condiments of any pay package, but suddenly they were becoming part of the meat and potatoes."

The flexible fringes save firms money mainly by shifting corporate outlays away from medical plans with rapidly rising costs. Executives at SCM Corp. (1982 sales: $1.9 billion), a New York City-based conglomerate, expect that the cafeteria-style program launched this year will save the firm $600,000 in 1983 and $1.2 million each year after that. The new package requires employees to pick up part of their health insurance premiums, which the company had previously absorbed, but increases the benefits available under SCM's employee savings plans.

The new programs, in part, reflect the changing U.S. work force. Traditional benefit plans have been mainly geared to single-income homes in which husbands work and wives tend to the children. But a survey of Comerica's 5,200 employees, for example, showed that only about 13% were living in such once typical households. The 1980 census reported that 51.3% of U.S. women over the age of 16 had joined the labor force, compared with 37.7% in 1960. The number of families supported by one breadwinner, meanwhile, dropped to 33% from 48.3% over the same period. Says Philip M. Alden Jr., a benefits specialist with the New York City consulting firm of Towers, Perrin, Forster & Crosby: "Benefits had to change with the times."

Workers, so far, seem pleased with the cafeteria-style plans. Says Gene Cincotta, director of compensation and benefits for electronics and defense operations of TRW (1982 sales: $5.1 billion): "The programs show that the company trusts its employees to make their own decisions, and that becomes part of the working climate." Last year a poll of the unit's employees found that some 96% of them said they were "moderately or very satisfied" with the firm's flexible benefits. The TRW program included extra life insurance at favorable rates and a wide range of medical and dental choices. Says Carol Schamp, a department manager: "It's a very good plan. I've found no problems selecting just the kind of benefits that I need."

Companies report, though, that cafeteria programs can be expensive and time consuming to introduce, and some firms are hanging back because the start-up costs are too high. SCM spent $100,000 simply for an information campaign to explain its new plan to employees. Companies must also make substantial investments in computer software in order to administer the complex benefits programs. Even then, keeping track of who gets what can create headaches.

Another company concern is that the IRS will decide to tax the employee benefits in the flexible plans. The IRS has not yet issued a permanent ruling on the practice of exempting most of the funds from taxes, and some firms fear that it may eventually decide to crack down on the procedure. The federal agency, which has been preparing regulations covering the plans, hopes to issue them later this year.

Many firms, however, seem willing to push forward with flexible programs no matter what the IRS decides. Says Martha McDonald, personnel services manager of the Public Service Co. of New Mexico in Albuquerque, which has been considering switching to a cafeteria plan: "We feel we could implement one based on current proposed regulations and then change the program if we needed to." McDonald adds that she personally would like such a package. "I never get around to taking my vacation," she says, "so I would certainly rather be paid for the vacation I don't take."

Source: J. Greenwald. (1983, June 27). *Time,* p. 54. Copyright © 1983 by Time Inc. All rights reserved. Reprinted by permission.

system will be seen as being grossly unfair, and the result will be low motivation, dissatisfaction, and turnover.

To a large extent, the equity of a pay system rests on the quality of the performance appraisal system. An organization must have a valid appraisal system if it wants to use performance-based pay. In terms of the model presented in Figure 15-7, the appraisal system should be neither deficient nor contaminated. If this requirement cannot be met, the organization should either (1) improve the performance appraisal system, or (2) abandon the idea of using a performance-based pay system. If differences in performance cannot be accurately measured, the best strategy is to pay people equally.

Level of Aggregation. As our review of pay systems in use suggests, pay can be tied to performance at many different levels of aggregation. At the lowest level, pay can be tied to individual performance. Here, performance is aggregated only across the individual's own behavior (e.g., over time or over different types of behavior). One level up, pay is tied to the performance of the work group. Successively higher levels of aggregation might include the performance of the manufacturing plant, the division, and the company as a whole. The level of aggregation one should choose as the basis for incentive pay depends on a number of considerations.

There are several reasons why it may be desirable to measure performance at a higher rather than lower level of aggregation. One is that higher levels of aggregation may offer more objective and reliable performance measures than are available at lower levels. Indeed, there may simply be no good measure of performance at the lower levels. This is likely to be the case, for example, when employees work in groups that are extremely interdependent. In such situations, one must search for an acceptable performance measure at some level of aggregation higher than the individual.

Even when there are valid performance measures at lower levels of aggregation, however, it may still be desirable to base pay on performance aggregated at some higher level. For instance, one benefit of basing pay on performance at the group or plant level is that it will, up to a point, increase cooperation among employees and/or reduce conflict. Tying pay to performance at a higher level of aggregation may also be necessary in order to be acceptable to some types of employees. This is likely to be especially true for unionized employees (cf. Lawler, 1981). Labor unions have traditionally opposed management systems that attempt to differentiate employees on the basis of performance. Tying pay to plant or company performance reduces the amount of individual employee differentiation that occurs.

While these are all legitimate reasons for basing pay on a higher as opposed to lower level of aggregation, it is important to recognize that higher levels of aggregation have one very significant drawback. The higher the level at which performance is aggregated, the more difficult it is for individual employees to see the connection between the effort they expend and the rewards they receive. The benefits of measuring performance at a higher level of aggregation (e.g., greater objectivity, cooperation, and acceptance) may therefore be offset by a decrease in the effectiveness of performance-based pay as a motivator. Thus, measurement objectivity and acceptance, task demands for cooperation, and motivational impact all need to be taken into consideration when deciding on a level of aggregation for a performance-based pay system.

Salary Increments versus Bonuses. Another issue is whether performance-contingent pay should be given as a salary increment or a bonus. Salary increments are by far the most commonly used form, with high performers getting a higher annual salary increase than low performers. From a motivational point of view, however, a bonus system may actually be more effective (Lawler, 1981; Overstreet, 1985). One reason for this is that a bonus system links pay to performance much more closely than does a salary increment system. Suppose, for example, that an employee performs moderately well in one year and receives a 6 percent salary increase. That 6 percent will stay in the employee's paycheck permanently. Organizations generally do not reduce employees' salaries, even for reasons of poor performance. If in the following year the employee performs very poorly, the worst that can happen (short of being fired) is that he or she will be given no salary increase at all. But the 6 percent from the first year is still there. In other words, in a salary increment pay system, poor performance does not decrease one's total pay.

If we shift to a bonus pay system, this scenario is likely to change in two respects. First, the bonus given in the first year can be much larger than 6 percent of the employee's base salary, since the organization now does not have to commit itself to continuing the bonus in subsequent years. (Note that a 6 percent salary increase given in 1987 is at the end of 10 years equivalent to a 22 percent one-time bonus—adjusted to 1987 dollars using a 10 percent discount rate; cf. Overstreet, 1985.) Second, if because of poor performance the employee gets no bonus in the second year, the total pay in the second year is very likely to be lower than it was in the first year (this can be true even if a cost-of-living adjustment is automatically given to all employees). Remember, unlike salary increments, bonuses do not carry over from one year to the next.

Thus, year-to-year changes in total pay are much more closely tied to year-to-year changes in performance in a bonus system than in a salary increment system. In a salary increment system, changes in performance can lead to moderate positive but not negative changes in total compensation, while in a bonus pay system changes in performance can lead to both large positive and large negative changes in total compensation. Bonus pay systems should therefore have a much more powerful effect on the motivation to perform well, since changes in performance have a much more dramatic, visible, and immediate effect upon rewards.

503

Chapter 15:
Formal
Systems for
Managing
Employee
Performance

Secrecy. A final issue is whether information about performance-based pay should be kept secret or made public. The norm in most organizations is to keep pay information confidential, at least within the managerial ranks. Managers are usually told only about their own individual bonuses or salary increments. Again, however, what is normative may not be optimal from a motivational standpoint. For example, in one survey of 1205 managers it was found that the overwhelming majority (86 percent) felt that employees should be told the ranking of their salary within their pay grade (Lawler, 1981). This is quite understandable. If a manager receives a $1500 end-of-the-year bonus, he or she will undoubtedly want to know what that bonus means. Is it a good bonus (higher than many others), or is it rather poor (lower than many others)? This is important information, because it will reveal something about the link between performance and rewards. Most managers have a general sense of how well they are performing relative to others. Therefore, if the *relative* magnitude of the bonus is commensurate with the manager's self-assessment of his or her *relative* performance, he or she is likely to infer that pay is closely tied to performance. This will motivate the manager to perform well in the future. If, on the other hand, the relative magnitude of the bonus is not commensurate with the manager's self-assessed performance (and the manager is sure about how his or her performance compares to that of others), he or she will be less motivated to perform well in the future.

Thus, secrecy can defeat the purpose of a well-designed performance-based pay system. Such a system will have a positive influence on motivation only if employees believe that pay is indeed tied to performance. There is no better way to convince them of this than to let them see for themselves that high performers actually do get higher bonuses or salary increments than low performers. Of course, the opposite is also true. Secrecy can be used to cover up the fact that pay is unrelated to performance. In this case, however, secrecy does not build motivation, it simply prevents motivation from evaporating as fast as it otherwise might.

Summary

Some of the most important points made in the chapter are listed below:

1. An individual's performance on the job is a joint function of his or her personal characteristics (e.g., skills and abilities) and his or her motivation to do a good job. Both factors are needed for good performance.
2. The underlying principle for managing effective performance is getting the right person working on the right job under the right conditions.
3. Selection systems are designed to find the people with the right characteristics for the job. A good selection system involves a thorough job analysis, comprehensive candidate assessment, and a realistic job preview.

4. Performance appraisal serves a dual function: It is both an evaluation mechanism on which rewards may be based, and a counseling tool for feedback and personnel development.

5. Appraisals often involve comparisons with other employees or with some absolute standard. If a behavioral criterion is thoughtfully and scientifically developed, it can be reliable, valid, and accepted.

6. Pay is an important source of motivation and satisfaction. Properly administered rewards will increase productivity.

IMPLICATIONS FOR RESEARCH

Designing and administering formal systems for employee selection, performance appraisal, and reward is a major focus of the work done in the human resources departments of most large organizations. These are essential components of the formal organizational structure that must function well if the organization is to be effective in managing its employees. Given the importance of these systems, it is not surprising that a great deal of research attention has been devoted to them. Despite the vast amount of research that has already been done, however, there still remain many significant issues that have not been resolved. Here we will briefly mention three, one from each area covered in the chapter.

The process of employee selection is really a two-way street. The organization has to decide which applicant to hire, while the applicant has to decide which job to accept. Unfortunately, our knowledge about how to assess and select applicants far outdistances our knowledge about how to provide applicants with the information they need to assess and select a job. Yet, as we indicated in the chapter, preliminary research shows that helping the applicant with the job-selection decision by providing a realistic job preview can be a very useful way to ensure that the right person is working at the right job. What we need to know is how to do this more efficiently. For example, there is evidence to suggest that receiving job information from a current employee is often more effective than getting it from other sources (e.g., Breaugh & Mann, 1984; Colarelli, 1984). What is it that makes job holders more effective sources? Are they simply more credible, or do they provide important information that is difficult to obtain elsewhere (e.g., information about the informal work-group environment)? Discovering the answers to such questions may allow us to develop better and more effective non-employee-based job-preview methods. In the long run, this is likely to have substantial payoffs, both for individuals and for organizations.

With regard to performance appraisal, one area that deserves more research attention is the use of employee self-appraisals. We argued in the chapter that those who are in a position to see what an employee does on the job should be involved in the appraisal process. Who is in a better position to know what the employee does than the employee him- or herself? Unfortunately, past attempts to use self-appraisals have shown them to be both inflated and in poor agreement with supervisory ratings. In short, their validity has been rather low. However, there may be techniques that can be used to help combat these problems. For example, Steel and Ovalle (1984) conducted a study using a self-appraisal system that asked employees to rate themselves from the perspective of their supervisor. In comparison to conventional self-appraisals, this new method yielded ratings that were less subject to leniency errors, showed greater agreement with the ratings of superiors, and were more strongly correlated with objective performance criteria. These results are encouraging. Although preliminary, they suggest that it may indeed be possible to improve the validity of self-appraisal ratings. If so, self-appraisals should be put to greater use in the performance evaluation process. They might also serve an important function in self-development and self-management. Self-management is a concept that is likely to become an increasingly important topic in the years ahead.

Finally, we recommended in the chapter that pay be tied to performance aggregated at the lowest level possible. In many cases it is possible to tie pay to the performance of the individual. Sometimes, however, the best that can be done is to tie pay to the performance of the plant, the division, or the company as a whole. Although there exist a number of specific plans for linking pay to the performance of large organizational units (e.g., Scanlon, Improshare, Rucker), research on the relative effectiveness of these plans has been lacking. What little research has been done suggests that such plans do increase motivation and productivity. At the same time, some plans seem to be more effective than others, and no one plan is effective 100 percent of the time ("Productivity Sharing," 1981).

What are the factors that determine whether a group incentive plan will be effective (i.e., increase productivity)? A great deal more needs to be learned before a satisfactory answer to this question can be offered. Group incentive plans have been around since at least the 1930s, yet they have been slow to catch on. In recent years more and more companies have installed such plans, but they still are not in widespread use. Perhaps this state of affairs would change if we knew more precisely what the strengths and weaknesses of the various plans are and could demonstrate more clearly the benefits that they produce. This, then, is a third area in which a great deal more empirical research is needed.

IMPLICATIONS FOR PRACTICE

The workforce is becoming more and more heterogeneous. There are more women and minority-group members at all organizational levels. And work habits are changing as well. There are more families in which both husband and wife work. There are more people seeking part-time employment. Work hours are becoming more flexible. Retirement is no longer mandatory at age 65. In short, there are more different types of people seeking more different types of employment.

The consequences of this heterogeneity are twofold. First, organizations must do a better job of assessing individual needs and interests. A valid selection system can reduce the effects of heterogeneity through clearer specifications of job requirements. Second, when heterogeneity exists, the organization must provide a more flexible and responsive motivational system. This is an issue that concerns both appraisal and compensation.

505

Chapter 15:
Formal
Systems for
Managing
Employee
Performance

In the area of selection there are three important factors with which organizations should be concerned. The first is a good job analysis. Almost everything else follows from knowing what is expected on a job: selection (whom to look for), appraisal (what to evaluate), and compensation (what to reward).

Given a good job analysis, one must next assess the characteristics of the job candidate. It is becoming increasingly popular to do this through assessment centers, which attempt to provide a comprehensive view of the abilities, traits, and behavioral skills of the participants. Since 1970 the use of these centers has expanded dramatically. By one estimate there are currently more than 2000 corporate-run assessment centers. Unfortunately, some of these centers can cost up to $1500 per job candidate, which may make them prohibitive for smaller companies to use.

The third important step in a good selection process is the use of realistic job previews. Previews can give people accurate information about what to expect on the job—both the good and the bad. We should note that a good job analysis provides much of the material around which a preview can be structured.

Once the candidate is hired, the focus shifts to the topic of motivation. How can a desire to work hard be instilled and maintained? The two organizational systems that are critical for high motivation are accurate appraisals and equitable compensation. There are many types of appraisal instruments available. But besides a good instrument, one needs accurate judges. Managers should be trained so that their performance judgments will be reliable and valid. Such training programs are available commercially. For example, General Telephone and Electronics Corporation (GTE) had 400 of its managers take a 2-day course on performance appraisal. The course provided lectures, films, and exercises designed to correct typical rating errors (e.g., halo, central tendency, similar-to-me), as well as to show managers how appraisal information can be communicated. Donald A. Mitchell, vice president for planning and marketing at GTE, commented that the course taught him "what to say and how to say it" and "how to criticize without emasculating someone" ("Training," 1980).

Finally, one must tie rewards to good performance. Compensation systems are needed that reward people for doing well, and that are flexible enough to encourage development and provide the rewards that are wanted. The important point is that the task and the type of people should be matched to the compensation program. When people are highly interdependent, use group rewards. When people are independent, use individual rewards. If the workforce is highly heterogeneous, provide some flexibility in the choice of rewards (e.g., cafeteria-style plans). If absenteeism is a problem and skill interchangeability is needed, reward the learning of new skills. Again, it is the match between these factors that must be sought. There is no one best system.

Discussion Questions

1. What are the two major factors that contribute to performance? Which do you think is most important in an academic setting and why?

2. What are the problems with job interviews, and how can interviews be made more effective? Why do you suppose interviews are used so extensively?
3. How should students in a classroom setting be evaluated? Should progress or absolute amount learned be the criterion? Could group rewards or bonuses be helpful?

507

Chapter 15:
Formal
Systems for
Managing
Employee
Performance

CASE: AFFIRMATIVE ACTION IN ACTION

The undergraduate curriculum committee at a large Midwestern university is in charge of setting policy and guidelines for all aspects of the undergraduate program in the school of business. Over the last few years the demand to get into the business school has increased dramatically. In fact, it has gotten so intense that 50 percent of the applicants are being turned away. There are 1400 possible slots, and more than 3000 people tried to get in for the current year.

The result of this pressure has been twofold. First, since entrance is competitively determined, the grade point average (GPA) required for entrance is now over 3.0 in the first 2 years of college. People with 2.8s and 2.9s who would have been received with open arms a few years ago are now being turned away. The second result is that it is hard to decide on a clear policy for selecting students, especially with respect to affirmative action.

Here is the rub: Many applications from women and minority group members are being received, but a large percentage of these students do not meet the 3.0 cutoff. In some cases there are obvious hardship reasons for the lower grades. But how does one justify turning away a student with a higher average in order to accept one with a lower GPA? The task of the committee is to develop legally and morally sound policies with which they can live.

Everyone on the committee is aware of the DeFunis case of a few years ago. In that situation, a law school rejected a white student who had a better academic record than a number of minority students who were accepted. Several lower state courts supported DeFunis and ordered the university to accept him, which it did. By the time the case reached the Supreme Court, however, DeFunis was about to graduate. The Court refused to hear the case.

The question raised by the case is still unanswered. How can the number of women and minority group members be increased? How can affirmative action take place without "reverse discrimination?" Arbitrary quotas are unsatisfactory to almost everyone.

One of the women on the committee is a student, and she feels very strongly about the situation. There is a rumor circulating that women are being accepted with lower GPAs than men, and she is angry about it. "The men look down their noses at you," she says. "They think you got in the easy way. I don't think anyone should be accepted below the cutoff—hardship or not. We either make it or we don't, just like anybody else."

Another committee member disagrees. She feels that the grade point average is a poor criterion for selection. She thinks that many people, especially minority group members and women, frequently face economic hardships. They are forced to go to school and work at the same time. They may also have a family for whom they are responsible. Therefore, the GPA may not be a good reflection of either potential performance in school or success on the job.

Questions about the Case

1. What sort of selection program would you suggest? How can you justify your policy?
2. What is "reverse discrimination"? How do you feel about it?
3. Is the student member of the committee right? Should there be any special treatment of women and minorities? If so, how do you deal with rumor and innuendo? What is a fair selection procedure?
4. Can people be accepted on an "overload" basis, that is, fill the first 1400 spots competitively and then accept a few petitions based on some set of agreed-upon criteria?

References

Bray, D. W. (1982). The assessment center and the study of lives. *American Psychologist, 37,* 180–189.

Breaugh, J. A., & Mann, R. B. (1984). Recruiting source effects: A test of two alternative explanations. *Journal of Occupational Psychology, 57,* 261–267.

Campion, J. E. (1972). Work sampling for personnel selection. *Journal of Applied Psychology, 56,* 40–44.

Colarelli, S. M. (1984). Methods of communication and mediating processes in realistic job previews. *Journal of Applied Psychology, 69,* 633–642.

Dunham, R. B. (1983, November). Organizational practices. *The Industrial-Organizational Psychologist, 21,* 42–47.

Fisher, C. D. (1979). Transmission of positive and negative feedback to subordinates: A laboratory investigation. *Journal of Applied Psychology, 64,* 533–540.

Flanagan, J. C. (1954). The critical incident technique. *Psychological Bulletin, 51,* 327–358.

Hinrichs, J. R. (1975). An eight year follow-up of a management assessment center. *Journal of Applied Psychology, 63,* 596–601.

Hunter, J. E., & Hunter, R. F. (1984). Validity and utility of alternative predictors of job performance. *Psychological Bulletin, 96,* 72–98.

Iaffaldano, M. T., & Muchinsky, P. M. (1985). Job satisfaction and job performance: A meta-analysis. *Psychological Bulletin, 97,* 251–273.

Ilgen, D. R., & Feldman, J. M. (1983). Performance appraisal: A process focus. In L. L. Cummings & B. M. Staw (Eds.), *Research in organizational behavior* (Vol. 5, pp. 141–197). Greenwich, CT: JAI Press.

Imada, A. S., & Hakel, M. D. (1977). Influence of nonverbal communication and rater proximity on impressions and decisions in simulated employment interviews. *Journal of Applied Psychology, 62,* 295–300.

Kane, J. S., & Lawler, E. E. III. (1978). Methods of peer assessment. *Psychological Bulletin, 85,* 555–586.

Landy, F. J., Barnes, J. L., & Murphy, K. R. (1978). Correlates of perceived fairness and accuracy of performance evaluation. *Journal of Applied Psychology, 63,* 751–754.

Latham, G. P., & Mitchell, T. R. (1976). Behavioral criteria and potential reinforcers for the engineer/scientist in an industrial setting. *JSAS Catalog of Selected Documents in Psychology, 6,* 316.

Lawler, E. E. III. (1976, September–October). New approaches to pay administration. *Personnel, 53,* 11–23.

Lawler, E. E. III. (1981). *Pay and organization development.* Reading, MA: Addison-Wesley.

McCormick, E. J., & Ilgen, D. R. (1985). *Industrial and organizational psychology* (8th ed.). Englewood Cliffs, NJ: Prentice-Hall.

509

Chapter 15:
Formal
Systems for
Managing
Employee
Performance

McCormick, E. J., Jeanneret, P. R., & Mecham, R. C. (1972). A study of job characteristics and job dimensions as based on the Position Analysis Questionnaire. *Journal of Applied Psychology, 56,* 347–368.

Miller, J., & Rowe, P. M. (1967). Influence of favorable and unfavorable information upon assessment decisions. *Journal of Applied Psychology, 51,* 432–435.

Orpen, C. (1985). Patterned behavior description interviews versus unstructured interviews: A comparative validity study. *Journal of Applied Psychology, 70,* 774–776.

Overstreet, J. S. (1985, May–June). The case for merit bonuses. *Business Horizons,* pp. 53–58.

Parker, W. E., & Kleemeier, R. W. (1951) *Human relations in supervision: Leadership in management.* New York: McGraw-Hill.

Peter, L. J., & Hull, R. (1969). *The Peter principle: Why things go wrong.* New York: Morrow.

Premack, S. L., & Wanous, J. P. (1985). A meta-analysis of realistic job preview experiments. *Journal of Applied Psychology, 70,* 706–719.

Productivity sharing programs: Can they contribute to productivity improvement? (1981). Washington, D.C.: U.S. General Accounting Office.

Rand, T. M., & Wexley, K. N. (1975). A demonstration of the Byrne similarity hypothesis in simulated employment interviews. *Psychological Reports, 36,* 535–544.

Ritchie, R. J., & Moses, J. L. (1983). Assessment center correlates of women's advancement into middle management: A 7-year longitudinal analysis. *Journal of Applied Psychology, 68,* 227–231.

Silverman, S. B., & Wexley, K. N. (1984). Reaction of employees to performance appraisal interviews as a function of their participation in rating scale development. *Personnel Psychology, 37,* 703–710.

Smith, D. E. (1986). Training programs for performance appraisal: A review. *Academy of Management Review, 11,* 22–40.

Steel, R. P., & Ovalle, N. K. (1984). Self-appraisal based on supervisory feedback. *Personnel Psychology, 37,* 667–685.

Training managers to rate their employees. (1980, March 17). *Business Week,* p. 178.

Walton, R. E. (1985, March–April). From control to commitment in the workplace. *Harvard Business Review,* pp. 77–84.

Wanous, J. P. (1977). Organizational entry: The individual's viewpoint. In J. R. Hackman, E. E. Lawler III, & L. W. Porter (Eds.), *Perspectives on behavior in organizations.* New York: McGraw-Hill.

Webster, E. C. (1964). *Decision making in the employment interview.* Montreal: McGill University Press.

Wexley, K. N., Sanders, R. E., & Yukl, G. A. (1973). Training interviewers to eliminate contrast effects in employment interviews. *Journal of Applied Psychology, 57,* 233–236.

Wexley, K. N., & Yukl, G. A. (1984). *Organizational behavior and personnel psychology* (rev. ed.). Homewood, IL: Irwin.

Wexley, K. N., Yukl, G. A., Kovacs, S., & Sanders, R. E. (1972). The importance of contrast effects in employment interviews. *Journal of Applied Psychology, 56,* 45–48.

Chapter 16

The Line Manager's Impact on Employee Performance

Key Terms to Watch For:

Organizational Socialization

Collective versus Individual Socialization

Formal versus Informal Socialization

Sequential versus Random Socialization

Fixed versus Variable Socialization

Serial versus Disjunctive Socialization

Investiture versus Divestiture Socialization

Internal Attributions

External Attributions

Distinctiveness

Consistency

Consensus

Actor-Observer Bias

Self-Serving Bias

Employee Development

Mentoring

Chapter Outline

I n the last chapter we examined three important problems that organizations must deal with in order to maintain their overall effectiveness: (1) selecting new employees, (2) assessing people's performance on the job, and (3) rewarding them. As we saw, formal systems can be created to help manage each of these problems. In most large organizations, these systems are centrally developed and administered by personnel specialists in the company's human resources department. This means that it is the personnel specialist who is primarily responsible for most of the important decisions that affect the ultimate success of these systems (e.g., decisions about the types of work samples or tests to be used in selecting employees and the types of rating scales or objective measures to be used in assessing on-the-job performance). By contrast, the line manager's responsibility with regard to these systems is usually quite limited. When doing a performance appraisal, for example, he or she is expected simply to follow a set of preestablished procedures. The line manager has little choice about which behavioral dimensions to rate or what sort of evaluation form to use.

511

Chapter 16:
The Line
Manager's Impact
on Employee
Performance

In the present chapter we examine three rather different problems that must also be successfully dealt with if the overall effectiveness of the organization is to be maintained. Unlike those discussed in Chapter 15, however, the problems examined here are not easily handled by formal organizational systems. As a consequence, a great deal more is demanded of the individual line manager as far as diagnosing each problem and choosing a solution. The line manager usually has wide discretion concerning how these problems are handled, and he or she is primarily responsible for their eventual outcomes.

The first problem is that of socializing the new employee—teaching him or her the values, norms, and behavior patterns judged to be important in the organization. In order to maintain its long-term stability and effectiveness, an organization must do more than select the right (i.e., technically qualified) people. It must also ensure that those people adopt the values and standards upheld by the rest of the organization. It is only in this way that an organization can expect to maintain a sense of identity and continuity in the face of an ever-changing membership. This is accomplished through the process of socialization.

Since the socialization process is essentially one of learning new norms and role behaviors, the material covered in this chapter is closely related to, and builds upon, the concepts previously discussed in Chapter 9. The present chapter goes beyond our previous discussion, however, by calling special attention to the line manager's impact on this process. As we will see, the line manager is in a unique position to influence the outcome of the socialization process. We will examine some of the decisions that line managers face with regard to structuring this process, as well as several specific tactics they can use to help ensure its success.

A second problem examined in the present chapter is that of managing the poorly performing employee. A primary function of virtually every managerial job is the maintenance of an acceptable level of subordinate performance. When subordinate performance falls below some critical level, it is incumbent upon the manager to take corrective action in order to bring that performance back up. Yet it is here that managers often encounter a great deal of difficulty and frustration. In this chapter we will review some of the issues involved in dealing with poor performance. These include how performance is defined and recognized, the types of information that managers use to make judgments about the causes of poor performance, and what managers do to correct the situation. We will emphasize the kinds of decisions a manager must make, the factors that influence those decisions, the places in which errors are often made, and how those errors can be corrected.

The third and final problem examined in the present chapter is that of managing the effective employee. We define this as a "problem" not because effective performance is in any way detrimental to the organization, but because we wish to emphasize that managers should be just as active in trying to maintain the good performance of effective employees as they are in trying to socialize new employees and improve the performance of ineffective employees. Thus, continued diagnosis and managerial action are needed. In connection with managing the effective employee, we briefly discuss employee development and mentoring.

SOCIALIZING THE NEW EMPLOYEE

As we stated repeatedly in the last chapter, in order to be effective, an organization must ensure that it has the right people working in the right jobs. Or, in the language of open systems theory, it must ensure that there is a good "fit" between each person and the job he or she is performing. An organization can begin to achieve this goal by establishing a carefully validated employee-selection system. Through such a system, it can significantly increase its chances of selecting employees who have the technical skills, abilities, and knowledge necessary to perform well on the job.

By itself, however, a selection system will provide only a rough approximation of the person-job fit that is ultimately needed for organizational effectiveness. The reason for this is that in addition to *task-related* skills and abilities (which are the primary focus of selection systems), there is also a great deal of nontechnical, *social* knowledge that the new employee must have in order to function well on the job. This social knowledge includes an understanding of (1) the basic goals of the work group and/or organization, (2) the preferred means by which these goals should be attained, (3) the role responsibilities associated with the new job, (4) the behavior patterns that are required for effective performance in the role, and (5) the rules or principles that pertain to the maintenance of the identity and integrity of the organization (Schein, 1968). This type of knowledge is often highly specific to the particular organization, work group, and/or position in question, and as such, it can usually be obtained only through direct experience on the job. The process by which a new employee comes to acquire this knowledge and adopt the desired behavior patterns is called *organizational socialization*. Through this process the employee's attitudes and behavior are gradually shaped until they conform to prevailing norms and role expectations. Thus, organizational socialization can be thought of as a process that completes the work started by the selection system. It serves to "fine tune" the fit between the employee and the job by clarifying which behaviors are acceptable in the work setting and which are not.

It is important to recognize that some of the attitudes and behaviors that are shaped through the socialization process are extremely subtle. For example, we recently heard of a newly hired 25-year-old male engineer who, when first introduced to female coworkers, had a habit of asking, "So, what does Mr. X do?" On two occasions this happened with women who were senior managers

513

Chapter 16:
The Line
Manager's Impact
on Employee
Performance

in this Fortune 100 company. When one of these managers commented that she had kept her own name when getting married, and thus technically there was no Mr. X, he retorted, "Ah! So you're one of *those!*" Not surprisingly, these interactions raised the ire of both managers. A short time later this young engineer was taken aside and spoken to by one of the female members of his work group. It seems clear that unless this individual learns more acceptable ways of interacting with the female members of his organization, especially those who are his superiors, he is likely to experience a certain degree of difficulty on the job.

A second example is that of a new female employee who, although performing the technical aspects of her job well, had not yet learned the "proper" way to dress for her corporate position. It seems that she frequently came to work in clothes that were judged as too informal and/or sloppy. In a conversation with her boss we were told that this employee's failure to learn the corporate dress code could affect her overall performance evaluation. Her boss subsequently discussed this problem with her in private. Of course, the problem with this woman's style of dress was not its informality or sloppiness per se. The problem was that it simply did not fit the prevailing norms. John Z. DeLorean had a similar problem when he was a senior executive at General Motors, only in his case his clothes were judged to be too stylish. According to DeLorean, "The corporate rule was dark suits, light shirts, and muted ties. I followed the rule to the letter, only I wore stylish Italian-cut suits, wide-collared off-white shirts, and wide ties" (Wright, 1979, p. 9). While he may have followed the "rule," DeLorean certainly did not adhere to the norm, and on more than one occasion his superiors suggested that he change his style of dress.

In a similar manner, newly hired sales clerks learn what they should do with their time when not waiting on customers, new marketing managers learn how best to present their ideas to senior executives, and newly hired nurses learn the preferred way to keep patient records. Even one's vocabulary and pronunciation are subject to socialization. For example, the new sailor quickly learns to say "line" instead of "rope," to say "block" instead of "pulley," and to use the pronunciation "loo'ard" instead of "leeward." Thousands of other examples could be cited.

Of course, the socialization process is not something that occurs only when an employee first enters the organization. Rather, as the DeLorean example suggests, it takes place continuously throughout one's career (cf. Feldman, 1976; 1981; Schein 1971). However, this process generally becomes more intense when an employee crosses an organizational boundary (Van Mannen & Schein, 1979). Crossing an organizational boundary implies taking on a new role and/or working with new individuals or groups. Examples include moving from outside the organization to inside (i.e., being hired), moving from one functional area to another (e.g., from production to marketing), and moving from one level in the organizational hierarchy to the next (e.g., from area supervisor to department head). Of these, passing from outside to inside the organization is perhaps the most critical from a socialization standpoint, since it is here that the greatest amount of learning is likely to be required (Hall, 1976). Since some degree of new learning will be needed for every boundary crossing, however, the socialization process should be viewed as an important mechanism for maintaining the person-job fit throughout an employee's career.

Structuring the Socialization Process

The socialization process can take many different forms, and each form has its own set of strengths and weaknesses. Since line managers often have a great deal of latitude in deciding how to structure the socialization process for their newly hired subordinates, it is of interest to examine more closely some of the specific forms the process can take.

Van Mannen and Schein (1979) discuss six structural dimensions along which the socialization process can vary. These dimensions define a set of choices that a manager can make regarding how to organize the experiences of new employees so that they learn the important values, norms, and behavior patterns expected of them on the job. Each of these six dimensions is described below.

Collective versus Individual Socialization. This first dimension refers to whether or not new employees are socialized in groups. *Collective* socialization involves taking a group of new employees and putting them through a common set of experiences together. Perhaps the best example of this strategy is the boot camp or basic training experience common to most military organizations. Certain types of management and professional training also fall into this category. The alternative is *individual* socialization, which means taking new employees one at a time, in isolation from one another, through a more-or-less unique set of experiences. An apprenticeship arrangement is a good example of the individual strategy. Here, each new employee works under the watchful guidance of a more experienced person in order to learn the behaviors that are required on the job.

The decision about whether to use a collective or individual socialization strategy is often driven by considerations of cost, efficiency, and logistics. Individual socialization tends to be the more expensive alternative, in terms of both time and money. As a consequence, managers often prefer to use some type of collective strategy. However, collective socialization strategies are feasible only when a number of new employees are hired to perform essentially the same type of job. And even when many new employees are hired, individual socialization may still be desirable if the job is highly complex and/or involves many nuances. Extremely complex tasks are often easier to teach on an individual basis.

Apart from the trade-offs of cost and effectiveness, there is one important psychological factor that should be taken into consideration. In comparison to individual socialization strategies, collective strategies provide each new employee with a ready-made peer group to which he or she can turn for social support. This is often a distinct advantage. An employee's initial entry into an organization can be an anxiety-provoking experience. Everything is new, he or she doesn't know what to expect, demands that are made may seem unrealistic, and there may be a great deal of uncertainty about whether or not he or she can "make it." This is especially true when the work required is very

515

Chapter 16:
The Line
Manager's Impact
on Employee
Performance

demanding, either mentally or physically. The comradeship and group solidarity that often develop among new employees who are socialized collectively
can be a significant aid in helping them cope with their anxieties and deal
with the frustrations and uncertainties of the new job (cf. Sarason, Levine,
Basham, & Sarason, 1983). Thus, if it seems desirable to build a sense of group
identity and support among new employees, a group socialization strategy
should be used.

Formal versus Informal Socialization. This second dimension refers to the
extent to which the new employee is segregated from regular organizational
members while being put through a set of experiences specifically tailored for
the newcomer. Highly *formal* socialization strategies completely separate the
new employee from the regular day-to-day operation of the organization during
the socialization period (e.g., boot camp), while *informal* socialization strategies do not. Formal socialization strategies make it clear to everyone that the
new employee is a "trainee," "apprentice", or "novice." In contrast, an
informal socialization strategy does not clearly distinguish the newcomer's
status, and at least on the surface, it is often difficult to differentiate the new
employee from those who have more experience.

It should be noted that while the collective socialization strategies discussed
in the previous section also tend to be formal in nature, individual socialization can be either formal or informal. For example, a new clerk in a medical
office may be individually socialized in a manner that is very informal, or
laissez-faire. This person may not be outwardly distinguishable from other,
more experienced clerks in that office. On the other hand, a student nurse
working in the same office may go through a period of very formal individual
socialization. Furthermore, he or she may be compelled to wear a special
uniform or nameplate that clearly signifies his or her "student" status.

While formal socialization experiences are usually organized around the
teaching of technical skills (e.g., in specially designed training programs
offered either in-house or elsewhere), they also have a very important function
with respect to values and attitudes. Specifically, going through a rigorous
training program before becoming a full-fledged member of the organization
often serves to increase the new employee's commitment and attraction to the
organization. The reason has to do with the arousal of psychological dissonance (for a review of dissonance theory, see Chapter 5, pp. 125–131). After
going through a lengthy and perhaps difficult formal socialization period (e.g.,
to become a police officer), it would be psychologically uncomfortable to
acknowledge that the organization is less attractive than one had initially
estimated. ("How could I have been so blind and/or foolish as to struggle to
attain something that I don't really like?") This state of affairs can be most
easily avoided by convincing oneself that the organization really is not that
bad—in fact, it may actually be a bit *better* than was first expected! Thus,
those who undergo a formal socialization experience are likely to have a
stronger and more positive attitude toward the organization than those who do
not undergo such an experience. This effect will tend to be most pronounced
when the socialization experience is fairly rigorous and requires a substantial
amount of effort and sacrifice on the part of the new employee (cf. Aronson &
Mills, 1959; Gerard & Mathewson, 1966).

FIGURE 16-1
Going through a rigorous formal training program often serves to increase the new employee's commitment and attraction to the organization.

In addition to facilitating commitment, formal socialization strategies have one other benefit: They minimize the negative consequences of mistakes made by the new employee. Because formal socialization removes the employee from the day-to-day operation of the organization, there is less likelihood that errors made during the training period will be serious. Thus, formal socialization strategies should be especially useful when the nature of the work involves a high level of risk either for the new employee, the organization, or the organization's clients (e.g., police work, health care work, certain kinds of construction work). When the level of risk is lower, and hence potential mistakes are less costly, formal socialization strategies are less critical (Van Mannen & Schein, 1979).

Sequential versus Random Socialization. This dimension has to do with the temporal ordering of the new employee's socialization experiences. *Sequential* socialization involves putting the new employee through a prescribed, step-by-step sequence of discrete experiences in preparation for his or her new role. *Random* socialization occurs either when the socialization process cannot be broken down into clearly identifiable discrete steps, or when no particular sequence is followed. An example of the latter situation would be the specialized management training programs that many large corporations have, in which recently hired employees with M.B.A.s are rotated through a variety of jobs in a number of functional areas over a period of several years. It is important that the trainee learn the operations and customary modes of behavior in each area before being assigned to a permanent job. However, the particular order in which these various socialization experiences occur does not matter. Thus, different trainees will be moved in and out of different functional areas and jobs at different times and in different sequences depending on "random" events, such as where and when openings become available.

A manager should choose a sequential socialization strategy whenever learning in one socialization step requires prior knowledge obtained in some preceding step. For example, if a full appreciation of the perspectives and traditions that exist within the market research department cannot be obtained unless one has already been socialized in the sales division, a sales-marketing socialization sequence makes sense. If there is no such dependency, however, it should not matter whether the socialization sequence is sales-marketing or marketing-sales.

Fixed versus Variable Socialization. This dimension refers to whether or not there is an established timetable for completing the socialization process. A *fixed* socialization schedule is one in which there is a specific timetable that is known to the new employee. By contrast, a *variable* schedule is one in which the new employee is given no clear sense of when the socialization process will be completed.

A major benefit of a fixed socialization process is that it reduces ambiguity for the new employee. A new employee who enters a 2-year management training program knows just how long it will be before he or she is accepted as a full-fledged member of the organization. Moreover, the timetable provides a standard by which the trainee can judge his or her performance during the socialization period. A timetable serves as an operational definition of what "normal" progress is. Thus, if the trainee is scheduled to rotate to a new job every 4 to 6 months, the organization's adherence to this pace can be interpreted as a signal that the trainee's performance has so far been acceptable.

While a fixed socialization schedule can be beneficial, it is sometimes quite difficult to establish a set timetable. The reason is that there may be wide individual differences in the amount of time that is necessary for the socialization process to "take." Thus, for example, there are some apprenticeship programs that specify the minimum amount of time one must stay in the program in order to attain journeyman status, but no maximum time is specified. If in the minimum allowable time the new employee has not shown sufficient progress, he or she may be held in the program until such time as his or her performance meets standards.

Serial versus Disjunctive Socialization. This dimension refers to whether or not the new employee is socialized under the tutelage of a more experienced member of the organization who has recently occupied the same position. When a more experienced person is available to guide the new employee and to act as a role model, the process is referred to as *serial* socialization. When no such individual is available, it is called *disjunctive* socialization.

Serial socialization has benefits for both the employee and the organization.

517

Chapter 16:
The Line
Manager's Impact
on Employee
Performance

First, from the new employee's point of view, the presence of a tutor or role model can eliminate a great deal of ambiguity about what one is supposed to do on the job. Without the benefit of such a person, learning what behaviors are appropriate and expected becomes much more difficult and can be a great source of anxiety. Thus, in comparison to disjunctive socialization, serial socialization is significantly less anxiety-provoking.

From the organization's point of view, a serial process is likely to lead to greater continuity and stability over time. There will tend to be less deviation from established traditions and norms, and a much greater likelihood that things will be done pretty much as they have always been done. It should be noted, however, that while this is generally beneficial for the organization, there are circumstances under which it can be detrimental. For example, serial socialization usually has the effect of reducing innovation and creative problem solving. Hence, to the extent that creative solutions to significant role problems are needed, serial socialization can be undesirable. Also, serial socialization will be harmful to the extent that the tutor him- or herself behaves in undesirable ways (see Figure 9-4 on page 269). Through a serial socialization process, the new employee will come to adopt both the desirable *and* the undesirable aspects of the more experienced person's behavior. Thus, the choice of who will socialize the new employee should be carefully thought out.

Investiture versus Divestiture Socialization. This final dimension has to do with the degree to which the socialization process is oriented toward changing the new employee as opposed to accepting him or her pretty much as is. *Investiture* socialization strategies are designed to confirm and document for the new employee the high value the organization places on his or her personal characteristics. In essence, they are intended to communicate to the new employee, "We like you as you are." Rather than developing compliance with established norms and ways of doing things, investiture socialization strategies encourage the new employee to introduce innovation and change.

Investiture socialization strategies are structured to make the new employee's transition from outside the organization to inside as smooth as possible. Every effort is made to accommodate whatever special needs the new employee may have (e.g., with regard to living allowances or moving expenses). This transition is also likely to be accompanied by such symbolic events as news releases that announce the new employee's arrival and list his or her past accomplishments (e.g., published internally in the company's own newspaper and/or externally in the local business press), special receptions or dinners held in honor of the new employee, and ceremonial meetings with the company's president or CEO. Such fanfare will obviously be reserved for those entering the organization at very senior levels.

Divestiture socialization strategies, by contrast, are those that are designed to produce significant change in the new employee, especially with regard to his or her values, attitudes, and self-image. Through divestiture socialization the organization attempts to strip away certain personal characteristics of the new employee and replace them with other, more desirable characteristics. Such a strategy is intended to communicate to the new employee, "We think you have potential, but you must make some changes if you want to be successful in realizing that potential." Often the divestiture is accomplished through what are known as "up-ending" experiences. Schein (1968) describes an example of one such experience.

519

Chapter 16:
The Line
Manager's Impact
on Employee
Performance

> The most vivid example came from an engineering company where a supervisor had a conscious and deliberate strategy for dealing with what he considered to be unwarranted arrogance on the part of engineers whom they hired. He asked each new man to examine and diagnose a particular complex circuit, which happened to violate a number of textbook principles but actually worked very well. The new man would usually announce with confidence, even after an invitation to double-check, that the circuit could not possibly work. At this point the manager would demonstrate the circuit, tell the new man that they had been selling it for several years without customer complaint, and demand that the new man figure out why it did work. None of the men so far tested were able to do it, but all of them were thoroughly chastened and came to the manager anxious to learn where their knowledge was inadequate and needed supplementing. According to this manager, it was much easier from this point on to establish a good give-and-take relationship with his new man (p. 5).

Summary. From the preceding it should be clear that the socialization process can take many different forms. The six structural dimensions we have discussed represent six different ways in which this process can vary. Any new employee's socialization experience can be characterized in terms of all six dimensions. For example, the typical process by which newly hired college professors are socialized could be described as being individually oriented, informal, random, variable, and more directed toward investiture than divestiture. This process might be either serial or disjunctive, depending on the particular characteristics of the hiring department. In comparison, the process for socializing new recruits in the U.S. Navy might be characterized as being collective, primarily formal and sequential, fixed, serial, and oriented much more toward divestiture than investiture.

While these six dimensions are helpful as an aid in describing various socialization experiences, their real value lies in that they define an important set of options that managers have when faced with the task of bringing new employees into the organization. They clarify the possible alternatives for structuring the socialization process. Of course, not all of these alternatives will be available all of the time. As we indicated previously, for example, when only one new employee is hired, collective socialization is ruled out. However, when ten new employees are hired, both collective and individual socialization become viable options. Managers should be aware of the strengths and weaknesses of each, and be prepared to make an informed decision that best suits their own needs and the needs of the organization. To ignore these decisions is to relinquish control over an important aspect of organizational behavior.

Tactics for Ensuring Effective Socialization

Before concluding our coverage of organization socialization, we would like to discuss several specific tactics that managers can use to help ensure the success of the socialization process. These tactics are useful regardless of the specific form the socialization process takes. Furthermore, while they focus primarily on the socialization of new employees in entry-level positions (rather than middle or top management positions), they are applicable in a general way to higher level positions as well.

Training. Regardless of what form the socialization process takes, it is essential that new employees get whatever specialized technical training they need in order to perform well on the job. As we discussed in Chapters 6 and 15, employee effectiveness depends on more than just motivation. Skill is also necessary. Either one without the other is unlikely to yield satisfactory results.

Of course, part of the responsibility for ensuring that new employees have the necessary skills and abilities to perform well on the job rests with the organization's employee-selection system. However, it is not always possible to select new employees who already have all of the skills necessary for the job. The reason is that some skills are highly specific to the particular job involved, and there is nowhere else the new employee could have learned them before being hired. This will be true, for example, when the technology used on the job is unique or nearly so, and/or when the organization has its own work methods and procedures that it wants the new employee to follow. Hence, there are many instances when special skills must be acquired after the employee is hired. It is essential that the manager be sensitive to this need and see to it that the new employee learns these skills. There is no motivational technique in the world that will be able to make up for deficits in this area.

A Challenging First Job. A second tactic that will help to ensure the success of the socialization process is to give the new employee a challenging first job. Research indicates that new employees who are given relatively demanding work assignments when they first arrive in the organization generally perform better on the subsequent assignments they receive (Hall, 1976). However, it is also essential that the first job assignment be one that the employee is able to perform well on. If an employee performs poorly on the first job assignment because it was too difficult, he or she is likely to feel frustrated and be dissatisfied with both the job and the organization. On the other hand, the first assignment should not be too easy. Although an easy task ensures success, the employee is likely to be disillusioned by the fact that the organization is not making adequate use of his or her talents. What is needed, then, is a first job experience that is difficult enough to stretch the new employee—to make full use of his or her special skills and talents—but that is not so difficult that the employee is likely to fail. This can sometimes be a hard balance to achieve.

Specific Performance Goals. Another important tactic is to set specific work goals for the new employee. Many new employees will be unfamiliar with the prevailing work norms in the organization (e.g., how fast to work, the importance of deadlines, the level of quality expected). The manager can begin to inculcate the desired norms very early by establishing performance goals for the new employee. These goals should be very specific and expressed in terms that make it easy to determine when the goal has been met. In this regard, saying to a new employe, "I would like you to get the report written as soon as you can" is not very satisfactory. How will you know when the goal has been met? It is conceivable that the employee may not even know. A much better approach would be to say, "I would like you to get the report written by the 15th." This more specific goal has several advantages. First, it makes it perfectly clear to the new employee exactly what you expect. Second, the employee's performance, at least as far as getting the report turned in on time, will be quite unambiguous. Thus, it will be much easier for you as a manager to know whether praise or a reprimand is appropriate. It should also be much more apparent to the new employee whether or not he or she deserves to feel good about having met the goal. Finally, and perhaps most important, the specific goal is likely to yield higher performance—you are likely to actually get the report more quickly. As we discussed in Chapter 6 and elsewhere, specific goals, especially those that are moderately difficult, lead to higher performance than nonspecific "do your best" goals (e.g., see Figure 6-4 on p. 168).

Performance Feedback. The fact that specific goals can lead to better performance than nonspecific goals indicates that goal setting has an important motivational benefit (Locke & Latham, 1984). This benefit is not likely to be realized, however, unless the new employee also receives some sort of feedback about his or her progress toward meeting those goals (cf. Matsui, Okada, & Kakuyama, 1982). In some cases, goal attainment can be directly observed by the new employee, such as when an assigned deadline is met or when a target number of orders is placed. These goals are motivating in part because feedback about progress toward the goal is so easy to obtain. In other cases, however, the new employee may have great difficulty independently assessing whether or not the goal has been achieved. A newly hired typist, for example, may have a goal of averaging no more than one error per finished page of text over the course of a month. Yet, it will be difficult for the typist to see any progress toward attaining this goal, and hence to be motivated by it, unless he or she is also given regular, specific feedback about the number of errors actually made.

Beyond its *motivational* effect, feedback is also essential because it *guides and directs* employee behavior. That is, feedback tells employees what they are doing right and what needs to be changed. This information is especially valuable for the new employee, since so much of what he or she is experiencing on the job is unfamiliar. Feedback may be required about widely varying aspects of the individual's behavior, ranging from matters that bear directly on the tasks being performed (e.g., the accuracy of financial records, how customer complaints are handled) to matters that, while not directly task related, nevertheless influence the new employee's overall effectiveness in the organization (e.g., the way the employee interacts with coworkers, how the employee dresses).

Thus, the manager should see to it that the new employee gets adequate feedback about his or her behavior on the job. In doing this, the manager should be particularly attentive to three important issues. First, attention should be paid to the frequency with which feedback is given to the new

521

Chapter 16:
The Line
Manager's Impact
on Employee
Performance

employee. New employees often require more frequent feedback than do veteran employees. Unlike the veteran, the new recruit may not have a long history of personal experience on which to base judgments about his or her performance in relation to others. Consequently, the new recruit is usually more heavily dependent on external feedback to guide his or her behavior. The manager should be alert to this, and should make sure that the new employee gets the frequent feedback he or she needs.

Second, it is important that positive as well as negative feedback be given. The manager should not assume that just because the new employee is performing well, no feedback is required. New employees often do exactly what is desired without being certain that what they are doing is actually correct. Thus, positive feedback is essential. Positive feedback is reinforcing and helps to ensure that desired behaviors continue to occur.

Finally, specific feedback will be more effective than nonspecific feedback. Specific positive feedback tells the new employee exactly what aspects of his or her behavior are desirable and should remain the same, while specific negative feedback clarifies exactly what behaviors need to change. Interestingly, managers may be somewhat more conscientious about being specific when they give negative feedback than when they give positive feedback (cf. Larson, 1986).

The Work Group. A final tactic that managers can use to help ensure the effectiveness of the socialization process is to assign the new employee to a work group that has high morale and exhibits a pattern of behavior that is desired by the organization. In Chapter 8 and 9 we discussed the powerful influence that work groups can have on the behavior of their members. With regard to shaping the behavior of a new employee, it is highly likely that the group will have at least as much influence as the manager, if not more. The work group is an important source of information about informal standards and norms of behavior, and it can be a valuable source of performance feedback, social support, rewards, and punishment for the new employee. The manager can capitalize on the potential power of the work group as a socializing agent by carefully choosing which group the new employee is allowed to work with. As we have stated before, new employees will usually learn and adopt whatever norms of behavior exist in the work group they are in. It thus makes sense to place them in groups in which they will learn the attitudes, values, and behaviors that are most desirable from the organization's point of view.

To summarize, in addition to shaping the general structure of the new employee's socialization experiences, there are several specific tactics that managers can use to help ensure the success of the overall socialization process. These include providing needed technical training, giving the new employee a challenging first job, setting specific performance goals, providing frequent and specific feedback about both the positive and negative aspects of the employee's behavior, and placing the new employee into a work group that itself exhibits desired patterns of behavior.

Of course, managing the socialization of new employees is not the only problem facing the line manager. Another is managing the poorly performing employee, and it is this problem to which we turn next.

MANAGING THE POOR PERFORMER

523

Chapter 16:
The Line
Manager's Impact
on Employee
Performance

Imagine the following situation. You work for a large communications equipment manufacturer and have recently been promoted to the position of director of management training. The mission of your department is to provide the company's lower- and middle-level managers with educational courses that will keep them up to date on the latest trends and techniques in business management. Among other things, your department offers courses in finance, accounting, quality control analysis, and managerial skills.

One member of your staff is a woman named Jill. She has been with the company for 6 years and is responsible for all of the accounting and finance courses you offer. Jill teaches two of the courses herself, and makes arrangements for faculty members from nearby universities to teach the others. Although Jill does not teach all of the courses, she is nevertheless held responsible for their content and quality. Thus, she is expected to be involved in all aspects of the development of each course within her jurisdiction. These courses are offered on a rotating basis at several of the company's regional offices around the country, which means that Jill must spend as much as 40 percent of her time traveling.

Ever since arriving in the department you have seen signs of trouble with the way Jill handles her job. For example, you have heard several complaints about the quality of her courses from senior managers in other departments. In order to get more objective evidence about this, you have asked Jill to provide you with course evaluations. So far, however, she has been very lax in conducting these evaluations. Moreover, she always seems to have an excuse for why they were not done (e.g., "This professor is an old friend. I know he is very good, and besides, I didn't want to offend him."). Jill also has difficulty keeping within her assigned budget, especialy in the area of supplies and equipment. In one case she even took it upon herself to lease a personal computer for her office when she had no formal authority to do so. Finally, Jill does not seem to get along well with the other six members of the department. They complain that in the past she has taken advantage of them in order to make herself look good, and that she is reluctant to help them out on projects that could benefit from her expertise. In casual discussions with Jill about some of these issues you notice that she seems to chafe at your "meddling" in her affairs.

Jill is a performance problem. Not only is there a question about the quality of her own work (i.e., her courses), her lack of cooperation and the bad reputation she seems to be creating in the organization decrease the effectiveness of your department as a whole. As Jill's boss, it is your responsibility to take action to correct the problem. What do you do? How should you proceed?

Dealing with performance problems such as this one can consume an inordinate amount of time and energy. And it can be one of the most difficult and unpleasant aspects of a manager's job. Part of the reason for this is that the causes of the poor performance and the appropriate corrective actions are often very hard to pinpoint. Furthermore, confronting the poor performer can be a stressful experience that has the potential for generating a great deal of interpersonal unpleasantness.

An Overview of the Process

On the basis of interviews, case studies, and the descriptive literature on union-management disputes, it is possible to construct a fairly clear picture of both the types of performance problems that managers face and the way they deal with these problems when they occur. One can get a feel for the range of performance problems that can develop by analyzing the performance issues that have been taken to formal, third-party arbitration. For example, Figure 16-2 shows Wheeler's (1976) categorization of arbitration cases reported over a 5-year period. Note that categories 1 and 4 deal directly and explicitly with substandard productivity, while categories 7 and 8 are indirectly related to productivity (a total of 54 percent). Other performance problems, such as fighting and dishonesty, make up the remaining 46 percent of the cases. These percentages probably do not accurately reflect the exact breakdown of performance problems that *do not* go to arbitration, since arbitration cases are usually much more extreme than average. However, they do represent fairly accurately the various *types* of performance problems that can confront a manager.

Assuming that a performance problem of the sort listed in Figure 16-2 has occurred, we can describe in step-by-step fashion the general process that managers go through in dealing with the problem (cf. Arvey & Jones, 1985). The very first step is that the performance problem must be recognized. This implies that there exists some definition of what constitutes poor performance. Perhaps the simplest way to define poor performance is as a deviation from expectations. Most managers have fairly clear expectations for how they want their subordinates to behave. These expectations might be expressed in terms of performance goals (e.g., sell $40,000 worth of merchandise per month) or as norms of behavior (e.g., always wear a business suit to work). When a manager judges that his or her expectations have not been met, a performance problem is perceived to exist. Note that the definition of the problem is both *subjective* and from the *manager's* perspective. It is quite conceivable that a pattern of behavior that is perceived to be a problem by the manager is not seen as a problem by the employee (e.g., "What does it matter that I don't always wear a suit if I am still making my $40,000 monthly quota?").

Once the performance problem is recognized, the natural question to ask is,

FIGURE 16-2
Types of arbitration cases.
(*Adapted from Wheeler, 1976.*)

Offense	Number	Percent
1. Insubordination, refusal of a job assignment, refusal to work overtime, or altercation with supervisor	98	29
2. Rule violations	48	14
3. Dishonesty, theft, falsification of records	43	13
4. Incompetence, negligence, poor work	37	11
5. Fighting, assault, horseplay, troublemaking	34	10
6. Illegal strikes, strike violence, deliberate restriction of production	31	9
7. Absenteeism, tardiness, leaving early	30	9
8. Intoxication, bringing drugs to work	18	5
Total	339	100

why did it occur? Some of the factors frequently cited by managers as reasons for poor performance are listed in Figure 16-3. An interesting aspect of this list is that some of the categories are factors that relate directly to the employee (e.g., lack of motivation or ability), while others are external to the employee (e.g., poor communications or work environment). One might suspect that managers will be more punitive when they believe that the employee him- or herself is the cause of the poor performance than when the task or setting is perceived to be the cause. In the latter situations, it would appear that job design or enrichment would be a more appropriate response (see Chapter 6).

After recognizing the poor performance and thinking about its cause, the next step for the manager is to select a response. In many cases the decision is to use some form of discipline or punishment. This is often an informal

525

Chapter 16:
The Line
Manager's Impact
on Employee
Performance

---

1. *Insufficient intellectual ability*—lack of ability to understand, learn, or express oneself well (e.g., low IQ or low verbal ability)

2. *Insufficient job knowledge*—lack of adequate information about job duties and/or job requirements or lack of experience with a particular type of job (e.g., being unaware of a company policy or production technique)

3. *Counterproductive emotional states*—emotional states that interfere with or prevent satisfactory performance on the job (e.g., severe anxiety or depression)

4. *Use of drugs or alcohol*—being under the influence of, or the aftereffect of, drugs or alcohol (e.g., drunk, under influence of amphetamines, hung over)

5. *Alcoholism or drug addiction*—dependence on a drug as well as being under its influence or the influence of its aftereffects (e.g., amphetamine addiction, alcoholism)

6. *Low work standards*—a worker defining success in terms of very low personal standards and/or experiencing satisfaction at low levels of performance (e.g., a worker being content to be the least productive employee)

7. *Low work motivation*—generally demonstrated lack of interest in the job and/or general lack of effort on the job (e.g., the "lazy" or "uninvolved" worker)

8. *Physical limitations*—insufficient personal physical capacities for a particular job (e.g., a person may be too short, too weak, blind, uncoordinated)

9. *Family crises*—unusual family situations that interfere with or prevent satisfactory job performance (e.g., divorce, sickness, death in family)

10. *Predominance of family considerations over work demands*—worker is more responsive to family demands than to job demands in noncrisis family situation (e.g., taking job time for child care, refusing to travel because of family commitments)

11. *Negative work-group influences*—informal work-group influences that are counterproductive for the organization (e.g., group norms to restrict output, a group ostracizing a worker and negatively affecting his or her work)

12. *Counterproductive work environment*—Environmental factors that interfere with or prevent satisfactory job performance (e.g., excessive heat or cold for a particular worker, excessive noise level)

13. *Inadequate communications to the worker concerning performance*—organization does not clearly communicate expectations about job performance and/or does not give feedback about deficiencies that need correcting (e.g., failing to make clear when a worker is to be at work, supervisor failing to tell a worker he or she is breaking a work rule)

14. *Conflict of personal values and job requirements*—worker's personal values, derived from family and culture, prevent or interfere with satisfactory performance (e.g., religious values proscribe a worker from working overtime on Saturday)

FIGURE 16-3
Definitions of possible causes of ineffective performance.
(*Adapted from Green, 1979.*)

process, especially when applied either within the managerial ranks or in nonunion situations. However, at lower organizational levels, or when the employee in question is part of a unionized labor force, a formal disciplinary system may exist. In such cases, the system usually consists of multiple steps that gradually increase in severity. For example, some companies use a four-step system that includes (1) informal verbal warnings, (2) a formal written warning with a copy entered in the employee's personnel file, (3) negative sanctions such as a 3-day suspension or docked pay, and (4) termination or discharge.

Research on the use of these systems suggests that, in general, certain types of infractions result in certain types of discipline. For example, infractions such as absenteeism and intoxication result in warnings or written reprimands, while infractions such as dishonesty and insubordination may often result in discharge (Wheeler, 1976). Two other points also seem clear. First, most managers are reluctant to use formal disciplinary procedures, and often choose less severe punishments than might objectively be called for (Wohlking, 1975). This reluctance is probably due to both personal reservations about "being a heavy" and the threat of legal actions and grievances. Second, even though a manager may decide against using the formal disciplinary system, he or she is still likely to feel that the subordinate was personally responsible for what transpired. If so, the manager may carry around suspicions, grudges, and hard feelings that might not surface openly, but that may show up in other ways such as in poor job assignments, low pay raises, and weak promotion recommendations.

Finally, we should also note how the subordinate reacts to the allegation that he or she has performed poorly. Latham, Cummings, and Mitchell (1981) suggest that the typical responses are to deny it, hide it, justify it, or allocate it elsewhere. Denial is an attempt to refute the accusation or challenge the basic nature of the charge. Hiding it involves covering up various aspects of the problem. Justifying it entails an open recognition that the problem occurred, but at the same time blaming it on circumstances beyond the employee's control. If these strategies do not work, the employee may attempt to pass the buck to someone else—to argue that it is really someone else's problem.

Thus, we are faced with a vexing situation. Managers are often likely to see the causes of poor performance in the subordinate's character, motivation, or ability, while subordinates are likely to see the same situation quite differently. It is clearly an area in which there is the potential for major disagreements, high emotions, and much conflict. It is also an area in which errors in judgment frequently occur. For example, one study reports that about half of the people who take their dismissal to arbitration get reinstated (Miner & Brewer, 1976). These data suggest that in many cases dismissal is an inappropriate response given the nature of the situation.

Highlighting the Role of Managerial Judgment

Most incidents of poor performance are neither severe nor clear-cut. Very few reach arbitration, and, except for flagrant violations (e.g., striking one's boss, being drunk on the job), the penalties are not well spelled out. What usually happens is that a subordinate misses a deadline, is tardy or absent occasionally, does not work overtime when needed, engages in horseplay, does sloppy work, or commits some other, less extreme violation of expected behavior. The task of correcting these problems can often be quite difficult, simply because there are few clear prescriptions or rules about how to proceed. A great deal thus depends on the quality of the judgments made by the manager.

527

Chapter 16:
The Line
Manager's Impact
on Employee
Performance

The manager's judgment comes into play at two distinct points. The first is in trying to determine why the behavior occurred. To ascertain the cause of the poor performance, the manager may solicit information from a variety of sources, including the subordinate in question. After this information is gathered, it must be processed, sorted, and evaluated. Eventually, a judgment must be reached regarding which factors were the primary causes. For example, an instance of poor performance might be judged as due to a combination of low skill and poor instructions.

After the cause of the poor performance is determined, the manager's judgment next comes into play in selecting a course of action to correct the problem. For example, if the subordinate's poor performance is seen as caused by low motivation, the manager might engage in a formal disciplinary procedure and orally reprimand the employee. If, on the other hand, the reason is perceived to be insufficient information or support, the manager might institute changes in the work setting. If lack of ability is seen as the cause, training might be appropriate.

Thus, dealing with poor performance involves a two-stage process. There is a diagnostic phase, in which the manager assesses the cause of the poor performance, and a decision phase, in which response is selected from a set of alternatives. Both phases entail active information processing and judgment on the part of the manager. A formal model of this two-stage process is described in the next section.

A Model of Diagnosing and Responding to Poor Performance

The model presented here is an elaboration of the two-stage process just described. The foundations for its development come from a variety of sources, and more detailed discussions of this literature can be found elsewhere (e.g., Green & Mitchell, 1979; Mitchell, Green, & Wood, 1981). The assumptions and hypotheses built into the model were mostly generated from attribution theory (see Chapter 4, "Perception and Personality") rather than from the literature on industrial discipline or performance appraisal. Therefore, a brief review of attribution theory and its relevance to performance appraisal issues may help to provide a better understanding of much of what follows.

As you may recall, attribution theory focuses on people's naive assumptions about the causes of their own behavior and the behavior of others. All of us try to figure out why we and other people do certain things. The process of determining the causes of behavior is an attribution process—we attribute our behavior, and the behavior of others, to various types of causes. By engaging in this attribution process, we are better able to understand and anticipate our own and others' actions.

The contributions of attribution theory to our knowledge about the problems of performance evaluation are threefold. First, research on the attribution process has shown that people are fairly systematic in their diagnoses of behavior (Ross & Fletcher, 1985). We know a fair amount about what sort of information is processed, and about how it is processed. Second, we have learned that there are a number of both more rational and less rational cognitive activities that go on. Both types of activities are built into the model we will present. Third, one major distinction that has been exceptionally helpful is the idea that causes of behavior can be grouped into two major classes: internal and external. Internal causes are factors associated with the person—the individual's abilities, effort, personality, and mood. External causes are factors associated with the setting—task difficulty, available information, and interpersonal pressures. Whether a manager makes an internal or external attribution about the cause of a performance problem is critical for understanding what response will be selected.

The model is presented in Figure 16-4. The two main stages are labeled links 1 and 2. Link 1 refers to the process of making an attribution, and link 2 refers to the process of choosing an appropriate response. For both of these stages there are some rational factors and some biases (i.e., nonrational factors) that affect the manager's judgments. The rest of this section briefly describes these "moderators" in more detail.

The most obvious rational factors helping a manager make attributions are *distinctiveness, consistency,* and *consensus* information. Distinctiveness refers to the extent to which a subordinate's poor performance on the present task is distinct from (as opposed to typical of) his or her performance on *other task*

FIGURE 16-4
A model of manager's responses
to poorly performing subordinates.

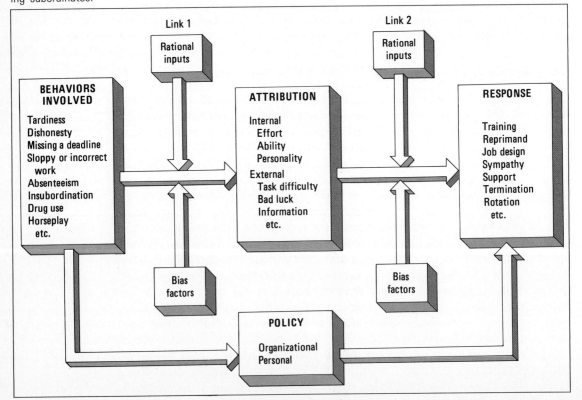

assignments. The less distinctive his or her current poor performance, the greater the likelihood of an internal attribution. Consistency refers to the extent to which the subordinate's present poor performance is consistent with his or her *past performance on this same task.* The more consistent the present poor performance is with that of the past, the greater the likelihood of an internal attribution. Finally, consensus refers to the extent to which the subordinate's poor performance is similar to the performance of *other subordinates* who have done the same task. When few others have performed poorly at the task (i.e., when there is low consensus), there is a greater likelihood of an internal attribution.

For example, suppose a subordinate fails to turn in a budget report on time. The manager gathers or recalls the information just described, and realizes that (1) this subordinate frequently misses deadlines on all sorts of tasks, (2) he is always late with financial reports, and (3) none of the other subordinates were late. In this case the manager is likely to attribute the poor performance to something about the subordinate (e.g., low ability or motivation). If, on the other hand, the subordinate has never missed a deadline before on any task, he always turns in financial reports on time, and everybody had trouble getting their reports in during this particular month, an external attribution is likely. Something about the financial situation this month (or perhaps too much work) is the probable attribution. (For a more detailed discussion of these attributional patterns see Chapter 4, pp. 82–84.)

Besides these rational informational cues, there are many other factors that can influence the attribution, and a great number of these introduce bias into the process. First, and probably most important, is the actor-observer bias. It has been well documented that people focus on external factors when explaining their own behavior but tend to focus on internal factors when explaining the behavior of others (Jones, 1979). It is the actor that is salient to the outside observer, but it is the environment that is salient to the actor. Therefore, a subordinate (actor) explaining his or her own behavior is likely to see it as caused by external events, while the manager (observer) is likely to see it as caused by internal dispositional factors.

Another nonrational factor influencing the attribution process is the self-serving bias. In general, people tend to attribute successes to themselves and failures to forces beyond their control. For example, several studies have shown that when a group fails, the individual group members say that they had relatively little impact on the group's product (e.g., Ross & Sicoly, 1979; Schlenker & Miller, 1977). Their stated contributions always add up to less than 100 percent. In contrast, when the group succeeds, everyone says that he or she made substantial contributions, and the totals add up to more than 100 percent. When we combine these two biases, we can see that in cases of poor performance it is very likely that managers will see the cause as being internal to the subordinate, while the subordinate will see the cause as being external. This difference in attribution is likely to lead to conflict, disagreement, and hard feelings.

It should be noted that anything that increases the distance (psychologically or physically) between the manager and the subordinate is likely to increase the magnitude of the actor-observer and self-serving biases. Therefore, the less the manager likes the subordinate, the less experience he or she

529

Chapter 16:
The Line
Manager's Impact
on Employee
Performance

has with the subordinate's job, and the more power the manager has, the more likely he or she is to make internal attributions for poor performance. Just the opposite is true for good performance. For example, the more prejudiced a male manager is against females, the more likely he is to attribute their success at work to luck or to an easy job (e.g., Garland & Price, 1977).

The second link in the model is the decision phase—the manager must select a response. If an internal attribution has been made, the response is likely to be directed at the subordinate (e.g., give a reprimand, provide training), and if an external attribution is made, a response directed at the task will be more appropriate (e.g., provide more support, change the task). Again, however, there are some more rational and less rational factors that can affect this response.

On the rational side is the fact that managers at this point usually engage in some sort of cost/benefit analysis. That is, they weigh the pros and cons of various responses. They consider the probability that a given response will (1) change the subordinate's behavior, (2) have a positive or negative impact on other employees, (3) make the manager feel good, (4) adhere to company policy, and so on. These are clearly important inputs to the decision.

But, again, there are some subtle biasing factors that enter into the picture. For example, there is now considerable evidence that the consequences of the poor performance can affect the response of the manager. If the missed deadline for the financial report results in a lost contract, the manager is much more likely to be punitive than if nothing adverse occurs. In many cases, the subordinate may have no control over the outcome; yet he or she is treated much more severely when something negative happens than when nothing negative happens (e.g., Mitchell & Wood, 1980).

Another source of bias in the response phase is likely to come directly from the subordinate, in the form of apologies, excuses, and external explanations. Even though a manager may have accurately diagnosed that a subordinate performed poorly because of low motivation, he or she is much less likely to be punitive and severe if the subordinate apologizes and promises it will never happen again. It is simply hard for a manager to be severe and punitive with someone who admits his or her mistake.

A final source of bias springs partly from the actor-observer phenomenon. Managers are not very likely to look at and understand ways that a task can be changed. They are much more apt to try to change the person. This bias occurs in part because it is easier to tell someone to "be different" (e.g., work harder) than it is to try to change the environment. Furthermore, we often do not have the appropriate vocabulary or knowledge that is needed for dealing with changes in the task.

Let us summarize the implications of what goes on in the two phases we have described. First, managers are likely to see the poor performance of subordinates as internally caused. Second, there is likely to be disagreement about this attribution. Third, in addition to the internal attribution, there are forces (such as outcome knowledge and ease of use) that push the manager toward a personal, punitive response. However, apologies and social or organizational constraints may make it difficult to use such responses. Thus, situations can arise in which a manager may unknowingly make an error of judgment about the causes of a subordinate's poor performance, and then feel frustrated because certain social or organizational norms prohibit what he or she feels should be done.

531

Chapter 16:
The Line
Manager's Impact
on Employee
Performance

One final point should be noted. There are times when the above process is *not* used. As described earlier, there are certain situations in which there exist either personal or organizational policies that deal with poor performance (e.g., three unexcused absences in a month require a written reprimand). Under these conditions, the attributional process may not be active. This possibility is represented in the model by the line that directly connects the behavior to the response.

Some Empirical Results Supporting the Model

A number of empirical studies have been conducted to test some of the basic propositions of this model (e.g., Mitchell, Green, & Wood, 1981). The methods used in these studies have varied widely. In some studies, critical incident interviews and surveys were conducted in organizations in order to gather information about the types of performance problems actually encountered by managers, as well as the managers' attributions for, and responses to, these problems. In other studies, special cases were created (based on the incidents gathered in the interviews and surveys) and then presented to managers in a written form or on film. For example, in one study managers saw a filmed interview between a nurse supervisor and her subordinate in which they discussed an incident where the subordinate nurse had administered the incorrect dosage of a drug. Embedded in the film were the experimental variables of interest (e.g., an apology either was or was not made; a serious outcome either did or did not occur). After seeing the film, the managers indicated what they thought the cause of the poor performance was, and they rated the appropriateness of various responses. Finally, some studies used live examples of poor performance. In these studies, people were actually hired to work as supervisors in a clerical setting. Their subordinates were confederates of the researchers who performed according to a preplanned script. Again, the design of the research allowed for several variables to be independently manipulated (e.g., the subordinates' past work history, apparent level of ability, and similarity to the supervisor.)

The results from these studies have strongly supported the model. The following is a list of some of the main findings that have been obtained:

1. People do attribute success to internal factors and failure to external factors. When they succeed, they say it was because of their effort or ability. Failure is attributed to bad luck or to a tough task.
2. Distinctiveness, consistency, and consensus information affect attributions in the manner predicted. When a subordinate has failed before on the task, has failed frequently on other tasks, and does poorly compared to peers, an internal attribution is made by the manager. The opposite conditions result in an external attribution.
3. Effort attributions on the part of the manager lead to more extreme responses than ability attributions. More specifically, success is more highly rewarded when it is attributed to effort than when it is attributed to ability. And failure is more severely punished when it is attributed to lack of effort than when it is attributed to low ability.

4. Internal attributions made by the manager result in more personal and punitive responses directed at the subordinate than do external attributions.
5. Negative or severe outcomes of poor performance increase the chances that negative responses will be directed at the subordinate.
6. Apologies on the part of the subordinate make it less likely that the manager will be punitive in comparison to situations in which no apology is made.
7. A manager who is dependent on the subordinate will want the subordinate to look good to others and will explain poor performance as externally caused.
8. Organizational policies can change or bypass the attributional process and directly dictate a response.

Thus, managers are active processors of information, and a variety of both relevant (e.g., past performance) and irrelevant (e.g., dependence) variables affect their judgments about subordinates. The task confronting us is to reduce the errors produced by the irrelevant variables in order to make the evaluation process more accurate and equitable. We turn now to a review of some techniques designed to attain these goals.

Strategies for Dealing with Poor Performance

Dealing effectively with a performance problem requires that a manager accurately diagnose the causes of the poor performance and then respond to it in an appropriate manner. As we have seen, however, various biases in the attribution process can lead to distortions and outright errors in diagnosis. One major problem is that managers often fail to appreciate the extent to which poor performance is the result of situational factors (cf. Ross, 1977).

It seems likely that managers can be trained to reduce these attributional errors. One way may be to encourage them to use a checklist that asks a series of questions designed to help them systematically ascertain the causes of a performance problem. Figure 16-5 shows such a checklist. Mager and Pipe (1970) offer a slightly different checklist that is also quite useful. This type of procedure may help to eliminate attributional errors resulting from the actor-observer and self-serving biases. (Notice that this is a type of aided analytic decision strategy similar to those discussed in Chapter 11, pp. 340–348.)

It is also important to make managers more aware of the extent to which the task environment can affect people's performance. Messy work areas can result in accidents. Lack of rules and disciplinary procedures may result in horseplay or fighting. Interruptions and distractions can reduce productivity. And poorly articulated goals can lead to missed deadlines. Indeed, such environmental factors can lead not only to poor performance, but also to lower job satisfaction and higher turnover (O'Connor, Peters, Pooyan, Weekley, Frank, & Erenkrantz, 1984). Given the natural inclination to focus on the subordinate instead of the environment as the cause of behavior, it is essential to train managers to evaluate *both* internal and external causes of poor performance.

Assuming that a manager has carefully examined all of the evidence and has

FIGURE 16-5
A checklist for diagnosing the causes of poor performance.

1. Is the cause internal or external?
   (a) What is previous performance on this task?
   (b) What is performance on other tasks?
   (c) How do other people do on this task?

2. If internal:
   (a) Is it an ability problem?
       (1) Has performance been good in the past?
       (2) Is the ability frequently used?
       (3) Does the person have the potential to learn?
       Arrange feedback, practice, training, transfer, or dismissal.

   (b) Is it an effort problem?
       (1) Is desired performance negatively rewarding?
       (2) Is poor performance positively rewarding?
       (3) Is performance important?
       (4) Are there personal or interpersonal obstacles?
       Arrange feedback, rewards, punishments, or dismissal.

3. If external:
   (a) Is the task too difficult?
       (1) What are the demands of the job?
       (2) Is there a simpler way?
       (3) Does the person need help?
       (4) Is the task intrinsically unpleasant?
       Arrange for job redesign, enrichment, or restructuring.

   (b) Are there extenuating circumstances?
       (1) What distractions and disruptions occur?
       (2) Is the person dependent on others?
       (3) Were the proper materials and information available?
       Counsel and provide support services.

made an accurate attribution for the performance problem, the next step is to choose a response. If an external attribution has been made, some sort of change will need to be made in the environment. The factors that block effective performance will need to be removed. This might involve something as simple as improving the quality of the support services supplied to the subordinate. Alternatively, it could require a major redesign of the subordinate's job.

If an internal attribution is made, on the other hand, the appropriate response depends on whether ability or effort (motivation) is seen as the primary cause of the problem. If ability is perceived to be the primary cause, action must be taken to achieve a better match between the abilities of the subordinate and the skill demands of the job. This might involve providing the subordinate with skills training so that his or her ability is improved. Or the subordinate might be assigned other duties that are more in line with his or her level of ability. If neither of these two alternatives is possible, dismissal may be the only viable solution. This, however, is an extreme response that is costly for both the organization and the subordinate. Therefore, it should be used only as a last resort.

Finally, if the poor performance is perceived to be due to a lack of effort, action must be taken to improve the subordinate's motivation. This might include establishing clearer performance expectations, providing accurate feedback about what is being done wrong, and arranging reward and punishment contingencies that encourage the desired behavior. Each of these strategies is briefly discussed below.

Establish Clear Expectations. If the performance problem is to be corrected, it is essential that the poor performer understand what *good* performance is. Every employee needs to know both what is expected, and how he or she is going to be evaluated.

The organization can take a role in clarifying these expectations by providing a formal job description as well as a carefully designed performance appraisal system. Notice, however, that it is important that the performance appraisal system be behaviorally anchored (see Chapter 15). If it is not behaviorally anchored, it will not provide the poor performer with sufficient information about how to improve his or her performance. For example, appraisals based on personality traits (e.g., being "committed," "energetic," or "conscientious") are poor devices for clarifying expectations because they do not tell the poor performer how to become more effective. Telling subordinates to be more "committed" or more "conscientious" does not tell them in any clear way how they are supposed to behave. Thus, organizations can help their managers deal with performance problems by providing them with behaviorally anchored systems for evaluating their subordinates' performance.

In addition, the manager can help to clarify expectations by (1) setting very specific performance goals, and (2) providing guidelines for how the subordinate should and should not behave. These guidelines should clearly indicate *what* behaviors are inappropriate, *why* they are inappropriate, and *what will happen* if these behaviors continue to occur. A combination of an accurate and detailed job description, a behaviorally based performance appraisal system, specific performance goals, and clear behavior guidelines from the manager will leave little doubt in the poor performer's mind about how he or she is expected to behave.

Provide Accurate Performance Feedback. Coupled with clear expectations about how they *should* behave, employees also require accurate feedback about how they *are* behaving. Although employees may understand at a conceptual level what behaviors are expected, they may not always be fully aware of whether or not they are actually meeting those expectations. For example, a salesclerk in a department store may understand that she is expected to be friendly toward customers, but may not realize that customers interpret her "friendliness" as impertinence. The result may be a lower than expected level of sales and a higher than expected level of customer complaints. Without some sort of feedback, this situation is unlikely to improve.

Unfortunately, managers are sometimes reluctant to give their subordinates negative performance feedback (Larson, 1984, 1986). Part of the reason for this is that they want to avoid creating any bad feelings or interpersonal unpleasantness. As a consequence, when evidence of an employee's poor performance first crops up, a manager may decide to do nothing about it in the hopes that the problem will go away by itself. Later, when the poor performance persists or gets worse, strong feelings of resentment and anger may have built up in the manager, and he or she may tend to "let the boom down"—

respond more vehemently and punitively than might objectively be called for.

Our recommendation is that managers learn to overcome their initial reluctance to give negative performance feedback. They should give feedback as soon as they see signs of performance problems. Giving feedback early is likely to have two benefits. First, the performance problem can be corrected more quickly. Second, the manager is more likely to be able to give the feedback in an objective and nonthreatening way. This will increase the chances that the employee will accept the feedback and respond positively to it (cf. Ilgen, Fisher, & Taylor, 1979).

Arrange Rewards and Punishment. Finally, correcting a performance problem requires that the proper reinforcement contingencies be operating. This means that the manager must attend to the way that both rewards and punishments are administered. More specifically, the manager must ensure that good performance is rewarded and not punished, and that there is nothing that will reward poor performance.

One way to reward good performance is simply to tell the subordinate that you like what he or she is doing. It is a mistake to assume that when an employee performs well no verbal reinforcement is needed. Good performance *does* need to be recognized and rewarded. This is especially true when there is a performance problem. It shows the employee very clearly what is desired and what will continue to get rewarded. It thus encourages the employee to replace the problem (and nonrewarded) behaviors with those behaviors that are desired. Managers often greatly underestimate the power of verbal rewards in this process.

535

Chapter 16:
The Line
Manager's Impact
on Employee
Performance

FIGURE 16-6
When it occurs, good performance needs to be recognized and rewarded.

THE WALL STREET JOURNAL

"You want recognition? OK — Hi!!"

With regard to punishment, there is a great deal of controversy over the proper use of discipline in organizational settings (e.g., Arvey & Jones, 1985). In general, employees seem to respond better when desired behaviors are rewarded than when undesired behaviors are punished. On the other hand, there is evidence that discipline can have a small but significant positive impact on performance (Beyer & Trice, 1984). Arvey and Ivancevich (1980) suggest that discipline is likely to be most effective when it is administered in a constructive and fair manner. Thus, while punishment should probably be used much less frequently than rewards, when it is used punishment should be (1) applied as soon as possible after the infraction or problem behavior has occurred, (2) administered consistently across employees and occasions, (3) accompanied by a clear explanation for why the employee is being punished, and (4) be neither too mild nor too severe.

In summary, the management of poor employee performance requires both an accurate attribution about the causes of the problem and an appropriate response. An external attribution implies a response directed at the environment, while an internal attribution implies a response directed at the employee. It should be clear that the success of this process depends heavily on the manager's ability to diagnose the problem and select a course of action. The quality of both the diagnosis and the response will be improved to the extent that the manager has an accurate understanding both of the attribution process and of the factors that influence employee motivation and performance in organizations.

MANAGING THE EFFECTIVE EMPLOYEE

At the beginning of the chapter we identified three problems that managers must learn to deal with if they are to be successful. Two of these have already been discussed: socializing the new employee and managing the poor performer. The third problem is that of managing the effective employee. It may seem strange to label effective employees as a "problem" for the manager, since achieving employee effectiveness is clearly a desirable goal. However, this label is useful because it calls attention to the fact that managers should be just as active in trying to maintain the good performance of their effective employees as they are in trying to socialize new employees and improve the performance of ineffective employees. Managerial diagnosis and action, therefore, continue to be important even when employees are performing well. Indeed, it is precisely when the manager *stops* diagnosing and actively managing the situation that employee effectiveness is most likely to decline.

Thus, many of the recommendations that were made in connection with managing both the socialization process and the poor performer also apply to managing the effective employee. For example, goal setting remains an important motivational strategy that should be systematically applied. Specific, difficult, yet obtainable goals will help to ensure that the effective employee continues to perform at a high level. Note, however, that while the manager should take responsibility for ensuring that goals are set, it may not be essential that he or she be the one to do the actual goal setting. Over time it seems quite reasonable that effective employees can learn to set their own performance

A PR Firm Shares the Wealth with Its Client

Sometimes, a consultant performs beyond one's expectations. Keene Corporation, a New York-based industrial products manufacturer, hired Ardrey, a New Jersey-based public relations firm, to handle their PR campaign for 1981. Keene was so pleased with Ardrey that, when fiscal year '81 was over, Keene asked Ardrey to participate in its internal incentive bonus plan.

"They're treating us just like family," beams William ("Doc") Ardrey, who heads the PR firm. "I've never heard of a PR agency being invited to participate in its clients' bonus plan, have you?"

But over at Keene, Ray Schumack, director of public relations and advertising, sees nothing remarkable about it. "We have goals; everything at Keene is done on a management-by-objectives basis. It's practiced to the nth degree, it's not just lip service. So we applied that principle to our product publicity program. Ardrey had a goal, and they exceeded it—it's that simple."

What *is* extraordinary, in Schumack's assessment, is applying MBO to a publicity program. "I've spent a lot of years in publicity work, and I know that in talking to a client, it's very difficult to come up with specific goals. One tends to talk in generalities— 'We're going to get your name in the paper,' 'maybe we could do a story on this or that.' As you go through the year, you discover that you'll do almost anything to collect your fee; then you have to ask if what you did was really helpful. Then the client doesn't know how to evaluate the results.

"We were looking for a system that pins things down. We get everybody to agree on what we want to do and how to do it. Then we find standards for measuring results."

Ardrey attended Keene's business planning meetings and visited Keene's product divisions as soon as Keene signed them, ultimately developing a list of potential news releases and feature articles. Keene okayed the list and developed a "point system": A major article placed in a prominent publication might be worth five points, a minor news release worth one point, and so on. At year's end, Ardrey had gone beyond its point objectives, so Keene awarded a bonus.

Ardrey says his 12-person company's bonus ran "in the four figures," and that it was spent on health club memberships for all 12.

Source: *Management Review,* August, 1982, p. 41. Reprinted by permission of the publisher, Copyright © 1980, American Management Association, New York. All rights reserved.

goals. Indeed, having employees set their own goals may occasionally be the more preferable strategy. Research suggests that managers sometimes set less difficult goals for their employees than the employees set for themselves (e.g., Latham, Mitchell, & Dossett, 1978). Furthermore, it seems likely that employees may be more committed to attaining the goals that they set for themselves. Regardless of who sets the goals, however, they should be stated in very specific terms so that it will be clear to both the employee and the manager when they have (or have not) been met.

Providing the effective employee with feedback about how well he or she is performing also is important. Even when employees are performing well, they still need periodic feedback both to keep them motivated and to keep their behavior oriented in the proper direction. Indeed, feedback is so important that if a manager does not openly volunteer it, employees will often seek it out by closely scrutinizing subtle cues in the manager's behavior and by comparing themselves to others (Ashford & Cummings, 1983). The danger in this is that employees may sometimes misinterpret the meaning of the cues. Thus, they may conclude that there is something wrong with the way they are performing, when in fact there is nothing wrong. Managers can avoid this problem by ensuring that their effective employees receive adequate performance feed-back. When employees are performing well on the job, the successful manager will make sure that they know it.

Finally, it is also essential that managers make certain that their employees continue to be reinforced for performing well. This means ensuring that the outcomes employees get from their jobs are commensurate with the quality of the performance they turn in, and that those outcomes match the employee's needs. If there is one thing that is constant in organizations, it is change. The environment changes, tasks change, and people change. Thus, outcomes that were rewarding yesterday may not be rewarding today, and new reward struc-tures that are set up today may not apply tomorrow. Furthermore, outcomes that are rewarding for one employee may not be rewarding for another. In order to be successful in coping with all of this, managers must actively monitor the rewards that are being received and make whatever adjustments are necessary to ensure that those rewards continue to fit both the employee and the employee's performance. This applies to the tangible rewards that employees receive, such as pay and promotion, as well as to those that are less tangible, such as recognition and praise.

Employee Development

Beyond these specific strategies, there are two somewhat broader issues that we would like to mention very briefly. The first concerns employee development. Employee development is essentially an extension of the socialization process discussed in the first part of the chapter. Here, however, we are talking about the continued socialization of the more experienced employee. The goal of employee development is to expand the employee's skills and experiences so that he or she can be promoted upward in the organization.

Employee development is an important element of every manager's job (Follett, 1941). It is especially relevant to the management of effective employees, since it is the effective employee who is most likely to be singled out as a candidate for further development. There are several things that managers can do to help develop their effective employees. One is to *enlarge* the employee's job. As discussed in Chapter 6, job enlargement involves the *horizontal* expansion of a job, that is, expanding the number of different types of tasks the employee is expected to do. Job enlargement implies expanding the scope of the job, while leaving the employee with roughly the same level of autonomy and responsibility. Alternatively, a manager might prefer to *enrich* the employee's job. In contrast to job enlargement, job enrichment usually involves both the *horizontal* and *vertical* expansion of a job. That is, the individual is given not only a wider variety of tasks to perform, but also greater discretion and responsibility for how to go about doing the tasks (Hackman & Oldham, 1980). Notice that while job enlargement gives the employee experi-ence with a greater variety of tasks, job enrichment also gives him or her greater experience in decision making concerning how to structure and set priorities for the work that needs to be done. Clearly, if an employee is going to be promoted to positions higher up in the organization, the added experi-ence that comes with job enrichment can be a valuable asset.

Both job enlargement and job enrichment give the effective employee broader experience by changing his or her existing job. In contrast, *job rotation* accomplishes this goal by moving the employee from one job to another. Job rotation has the advantage of giving the employee experience with a wide variety of tasks that may be difficult or impossible to incorporate into a single job (e.g., working in both marketing and finance). Job rotation also has the benefit of putting the employee in contact with people from many different areas, thereby giving him or her a better sense of the diversity of perspectives and concerns facing people in different parts of the organization. In other words, it helps the employee develop a generalist perspective.

In order to make effective use of job enlargement, job enrichment, and job rotation as strategies for employee development, the manager should have a fairly clear idea about the type of position that the employee might potentially be promoted into. Moreover, it is important that the manager be able to identify accurately both (1) the skills and experiences that are needed in order to perform well in the target position, and (2) the specific type of job changes that will be most helpful in providing those skills and experiences to the employee. Hall and Morgan (1977) add several further recommendations. First, they suggest that the developmental job changes be large enough to "stretch" the employee's skills and capabilities, yet small enough to be manageable. Additionally, they argue that the changes should last long enough for the employee to master the job, but not so long that the job becomes routine or boring. In other words, when the employee has mastered the new (or revised) job, it is time to consider making further changes. Finally, the changes should complement or supplement, as opposed to duplicate, the employee's previous experience.

It is important to note that these developmental job changes can and should be used as rewards for good employee performance. The manager should clearly explain to the employee that his or her job is being expanded or rotated because he or she has so far performed well, and that this change is intended to increase his or her promotability in the future. Thus, by making the developmental job changes openly contingent upon high job performance, a manager can further increase the probability that his or her effective employees will continue to be motivated to perform well in the future.

Mentoring

Even broader than the notion of employee development is that of *mentoring*. Schein (1978) defines a mentor as someone who acts as a combination of coach, role model, developer of talent, opener of doors, protector, and sponsor. The first three functions (coach, role model, and developer of talent) suggest that employee development is an important part of the mentoring role. However, mentoring goes beyond mere development. The mentor also acts as an advocate, using his or her own power and influence in the organization to smooth the way for the protégé's advancement (i.e., as an opener of doors, protector, and sponsor).

The importance of mentors and the mentoring process has only recently begun to be recognized and researched. Collins and Scott (1978) comment that "everyone who makes it has a mentor." While this claim may be somewhat overstated, there is evidence that a large percentage of successful

539

Chapter 16:
The Line
Manager's Impact
on Employee
Performance

middle- and upper-level managers have had mentors who have helped them advance in their careers (e.g., Missirian, 1982; Reich, 1985; Roche, 1979). Indeed, some authors view mentoring as so important that they suggest all managers should be thoroughly trained in the mentoring process, and that their performance as mentors should be evaluated during formal performance appraisals (e.g., Levinson, 1979). Again, this view may be extreme. Nevertheless, the point is well taken that a mentor can indeed be an important factor in an individual's career success.

It is beyond the scope of the present chapter to examine the mentoring process in detail (the interested reader is referred to Clawson, 1980; Hall, 1976; Kram, 1983; Missirian, 1982; Schein, 1978). Our purpose here is simply to call attention to the fact that in addition to developing their employees' skills, managers are also occasionally called upon to play that part of the mentoring role in which they act as advocates for their employees. In doing this they must draw on their external and hierarchical relationships with others in the organization. The ability of managers to influence others outside their own organizational unit in order to create opportunities for the advancement of deserving subordinates can be an important asset. If employees recognize the benefits, in terms of advancement, that the manager can confer, they are much more likely to try to please the manager by working hard to achieve whatever goals and objectives the manager would like to see accomplished. In a real sense, then, the manager's external power, that is, his or her ability to influence others outside his or her organizational unit, can significantly increase his or her internal power. Externally powerful managers have the potential to be more effective mentors, which in turn should enhance their ability to manage the effective employees who work under them (cf. Schein, 1978).

Summary

Some of the most important points made in the chapter are listed below.

1. Organizational socialization refers to the process by which employees come to acquire the values, attitudes, and patterns of behavior that are most desirable from the organization's point of view.

2. Line managers often have a great deal of latitude in structuring the socialization of new employees. They can determine whether the process is collective or individualistic, formal or informal, sequential or random, fixed or variable, serial or disjunctive, and oriented toward investiture or divestiture.

3. Specific strategies for increasing the likelihood that the socialization process will be successful include (1) ensuring that the new employees have the skills they will need to do well, (2) giving them a challenging first job, (3) setting specific performance goals, (4) providing adequate performance feedback, and (5) placing them in work groups that have high morale and exhibit patterns of behavior that are desired by the organization.

4. Poor performance can be defined as a deviation from expected or normative behavior. Dealing with poor performance involves a two-step process of diagnosis and action.

5. Attribution theory helps to explain the diagnostic process, and it points out where errors can occur. The actor-observer and self-serving biases frequently result in incorrect judgments about the causes of the performance problem.

6. The action or response chosen by the manager is often based on a cost/benefit analysis. However, apologies, social norms, and the consequences of poor performance may bias the response selection process.

7. Specific strategies for dealing with performance problems include establishing clear expectations, providing accurate performance feedback, providing adequate rewards for good performance, and, when needed, administering punishment for poor performance.

8. Diagnosis and action continue to be important even when managing the effective employee. Managers should be just as active in trying to maintain the good performance of their effective employees as they are in trying to socialize new employees and improve the performance of ineffective employees.

9. Two considerations relevant to managing the effective employee are employee development and mentoring. With regard to mentoring, managers may on occasion be called upon to act as an advocate for their employees, using their own power and influence in the organization to help smooth the way for their employees' advancement.

541

Chapter 16:
The Line
Manager's Impact
on Employee
Performance

IMPLICATIONS FOR RESEARCH

In this chapter we have made a large number of recommendations for managerial action. We have suggested, for example, that managers should set specific, difficult, yet attainable performance goals for their new employees, that they should be on the lookout for environmental factors when analyzing the causes of poor employee performance, and that they should give their employees adequate performance feedback—even those who are performing very well. However, behavioral evidence suggests that these recommendations are not always easy to put into operation. Thus, while the need for setting specific goals and for providing adequate amounts of performance feedback may seem obvious, managers sometimes have trouble actually doing these things. Overcoming the actor-observer and self-serving attributional biases when diagnosing the causes of performance problems can be even more problematic. An important research question is, therefore, how can we make it easier for managers to follow the recommendations outlined in this chapter? What sorts of strategies can be devised to help managers change *their own behavior* so that they will be more effective in managing the behavior of those who work for them?

Two possibilities suggest themselves. One is to provide managerial skills training. For example, preliminary research by Ivancevich and Smith (1981) indicates that training can be effective in improving managers' goal-setting skills. They conducted a study with sixty sales managers from one division of a large manufacturing company. They demonstrated that a 5- to 9-hour training program consisting of either lecture and role play, or lecture, modeling, role play, and videotaped feedback significantly increased the degree to which these sales managers actually set specific, challenging goals for their subordinates. What is more, after the managers were trained, their subordinates showed significant improvements in their sales productivity. These results are quite encouraging. What is needed is further research to determine whether similar types of training will help to improve the accuracy of managers' causal attributions, the quality of the performance feedback they give, and other essential managerial behaviors.

The second possibility for assisting managers in following the recommendations outlined in this chapter is to provide them with decision aids, such as the checklist for diagnosing the causes of poor performance shown in Figure 16-5. Whenever a manager tries to assess the causes of an employee's poor performance, he or she can review the checklist, systematically answer all of the questions, and thereby decrease the probability of overlooking important pieces of information and making serious attributional errors. The Vroom and Yetton model discussed in Chapters 12 and 14 can serve a similar function when the question is whether or not to involve subordinates in the decision-making process (see Figure 12-4 on p. 375).

We believe that such decision aids can be very effective—*provided they are used*. And there is the rub. In the bustling confusion of everyday organizational life, managers may find it awkward and/or excessively time consuming to make systematic use of these aids. Managers often have to diagnose the causes of poor performance, give performance feedback, and set performance goals, all on a moment's notice. Under these conditions it is easy to ignore formal decision aids, since their use typically requires extra time and effort.

Thus, research is also needed to determine how to get managers to use the decision aids that are available to them. To be most beneficial, this research should proceed on two fronts. One is to find ways to motivate managers to take the time to use the decision aids. The other is to devise better ways to package the aids themselves, so that they are more convenient to use and more readily available at the moment they are needed most (e.g., they might be written as computer programs that can run on the manager's desk-top computer). These two complementary lines of research, along with additional research on managerial skill training, should ultimately make it easier for managers to modify their own behavior in ways that will help them do a more effective job of managing others.

IMPLICATIONS FOR PRACTICE

Throughout this chapter our emphasis has been on implications for practice. We have suggested a number of concrete actions that managers can take in dealing with three major classes of problems: socializing the new employee, managing the poor performer, and managing the effective employee. Rather than repeating all of these recommendations here, we will simply reemphasize one major point: *Managing people in organizations requires constant attention, diagnosis, and action.* All too often managers slip into a pattern of "managing by exception"—devoting a great deal of attention and energy to correcting problem behavior, but devoting very little to managing those people and

543

Chapter 16:
The Line
Manager's Impact
on Employee
Performance

situations that are not causing problems. As we suggested in the chapter, this strategy is very shortsighted. The failure to manage effective performance actively only sets the stage for additional problems in the future. The squeaky wheel should be oiled. But so should those that do not squeak. For if they are not oiled regularly, they too will soon become a noisy irritation.

Discussion Questions

1. Why do you think it is hard for people to give negative feedback? Why is it unpleasant?
2. What effects do both poor performance and the feedback given to a poor performer have on the other members of a group?
3. Why do you think that actors and observers have different explanations for the causes of the actors' behavior?

CASE: MALPRACTICE OR MINOR MISTAKE?

You are the supervisor of the nurses working in the cardiac-care unit of a large Midwestern hospital. Halfway through one shift it is brought to your attention that a patient who had been well on the way to recovery was in the midst of a serious relapse. After a number of quick inquiries, the following situation emerged.

Jan Randolph, a relatively new nurse, had set up an IVAC unit (intravenous delivery) at the beginning of the shift to deliver some Inderol to the patient. Inderol reduces the rate of the heartbeat and must be delivered in very precise amounts. Later on in the shift, a physician was called when the patient's pulse was significantly slower and somewhat more irregular than it should have been, and the patient was showing signs of distress. While examining the patient, the physician noticed that the wrong size tubing had been put in the IVAC. As a result, the patient was receiving the drug at approximately five times the regular dosage. Shortly after the IVAC was taken down, the patient began to show signs of cardiac arrest and emergency procedures were instituted to save his life.

Later on in the shift you arrange for Randolph to come to your office, and the following discussion takes place:

Randolph: Hello, I heard you wanted to see me.
Supervisor: Yes, Jan, I wanted to talk to you about the problem we had on the ward this morning. Dr. Martin came to me in quite a state. He said that the wrong size IVAC unit had been used.
Randolph: I thought that was what you wanted to talk about.
Supervisor: Are you aware of what happened?
Randolph: Not really, I've been attending to my other duties.
Supervisor: Well, Dr. Martin says that the patient almost died because of the drug overdose. As it is, the patient is still in serious danger.
Randolph: I'm relieved that he's still alive. I heard it was touch and go.
Supervisor: Yes, apparently it was. What is your side of the story? Why did you use the wrong IVAC unit?
Randolph: Well, it was largely a result of circumstances beyond my control. We were very busy this morning. My patient load was heavy, and the nurse's aide who usually helps me was out today. Everyone seemed to need extra attention.
Supervisor: Didn't you double-check that the right amount of medicine was being delivered.

Randolph: No, when the ward is busy like that you hardly have time to get everything done, let alone double-check.

Supervisor: But don't you think this was a fairly serious mistake? After all, the patient almost died.

Randolph: Yes, but everything I do is potentially serious. I was doing the best I could under the circumstances.

Supervisor: Well, Jan, as your supervisor I really wish this incident had not occurred, and now I must make a decision about what to do about it.

Randolph: I realize that. I might add that I am sorry about what happened, and I feel badly about Mr. Hanke not receiving proper treatment. I'm also sorry for any of the problems I caused you or Dr. Martin. I will try very hard not to let something like this happen again.

Questions about the Case

1. What is your initial judgment about the cause of Jan Randolph's behavior?
2. What sort of additional information (if any) would you seek out before you made a decision? How might this information influence your judgment?
3. Do you think the apology would influence your judgment? How does what happened to the patient, Mr. Hanke, affect your opinion?
4. What sort of action is appropriate?

References

Aronson, E., & Mills, J. (1959). The effect of severity of initiation on liking for a group. *Journal of Abnormal and Social Psychology, 59,* 177–181.

Arvey, R. D., & Ivancevich, J. M. (1980). Punishment in organizations: A review, propositions, and research suggestions. *Academy of Management Review, 5,* 123–132.

Arvey, R. D., & Jones, A. P. (1985). The use of discipline in organizational settings: A framework for future research. In L. L. Cummings & B. M. Staw (Eds.), *Research in organizational behavior* (Vol. 7, pp. 367–408). Greenwich, CT: JAI Press.

Ashford, S. J., & Cummings, L. L. (1983). Feedback as an individual resource: Personal strategies of creating information. *Organizational Behavior and Human Performance, 32,* 370–348.

Beyer, J. M., & Trice, H. M. (1984). A field study of the use and perceived effects of discipline in controlling work performance. *Academy of Management Journal, 27,* 743–764.

Clawson, J. G. (1980). Mentoring in managerial careers. In C. B. Derr (Ed.), *Work, family, and the career: New frontiers in theory and research.* New York: Praeger.

Collins, E. G. C., & Scott, P. (1978, July-August). Everyone who makes it has a mentor. *Harvard Business Review,* pp. 89–101.

Feldman, D. C. (1976). A contingency theory of socialization. *Administrative Science Quarterly, 21,* 433–452.

Feldman, D. C. (1981). The multiple socialization of organization members. *Academy of Management Review, 6,* 309–318.

Follett, M. P. (1941). In H. C. Metcalf & L. Urwick (Eds.), *Dynamic administration: The collected papers of Mary Parker Follett.* Bath, UK: Management Public Trust.

Garland, H., & Price, K. H. (1977). Attitudes toward women in management and attributions for their success and failure in a managerial position. *Journal of Applied Psychology, 62,* 29–33.

545

Chapter 16:
The Line
Manager's Impact
on Employee
Performance

Gerard, H. B., & Mathewson, G. C. (1966). The effects of severity of initiation on liking for a group: A replication. *Journal of Experimental Social Psychology, 2*, 278–287.

Green, S. G. (1979). Causes of ineffective performance. *Proceedings of the Midwest Academy of Management*, pp. 38–48.

Green, S. G., & Mitchell, T. R. (1979). Attributional processes of leaders in leader-member interactions. *Organizational Behavior and Human Performance, 23*, 429–458.

Hackman, J. R., & Oldham, G. R. (1980). *Work redesign*. Reading, MA: Addison-Wesley.

Hall, D. T. (1976). *Career development*. Santa Monica, CA: Goodyear Publishing.

Hall, D. T., & Morgan, M. A. (1977). Career development and planning. In W. C. Hamner & F. L. Schmidt (Eds.), *Contemporary problems in personnel* (rev. ed., pp. 205–226). Chicago: St. Clair.

Ilgen, D. R., Fisher, C. D., & Taylor, M. S. (1979). Consequences of individual feedback on behavior in organizations. *Journal of Applied Psychology, 64*, 349–371.

Ivancevich, J. M., & Smith, S. V. (1981). Goal setting interview skills training: Simulated and on-the-job analyses. *Journal of Applied Psychology, 66*, 697–705.

Jones, E. E. (1979). The rocky road from acts to dispositions. *American Psychologist, 34*, 107–117.

Kram, K. E. (1983). Phases of the mentor relationship. *Academy of Management Journal, 26*, 608–625.

Larson, J. R., Jr. (1984). The performance feedback process: A preliminary model. *Organizational Behavior and Human Performance, 33*, 42–76.

Larson, J. R., Jr. (1986). Supervisors' performance feedback to subordinates: The role of subordinate performance valence and outcome dependence. *Organizational Behavior and Human Decision Processes, 37*, 391–408.

Latham, G. P., Cummings, L. L., & Mitchell, T. R. (1981, Winter). Behavioral strategies for enhancing productivity. *Organizational Dynamics*, pp. 5–23.

Latham, G. P., Mitchell, T. R., & Dossett, D. L. (1978). The importance of participative goal setting and anticipated rewards on goal difficulty and job performance. *Journal of Applied Psychology, 63*, 163–171.

Levinson, H. (1979). *Mentoring: Socialization for leadership*. Paper presented at the annual convention of the Academy of Management, Atlanta.

Locke, E. A., & Latham, G. P. (1984). *Goal setting: A motivaional technique that works*. Englewood Cliffs, NJ: Prentice-Hall.

Mager, R. F., & Pipe, P. (1970). *Analyzing performance problems; or, You really oughta wanna*. Belmont, CA: Fearon.

Matsui, T., Okada, A., & Kakuyama, T. (1982). Influence of achievement need on goal setting, performance, and feedback effectiveness. *Journal of Applied Psychology, 67*, 645–648.

Miner, J. B., & Brewer, J. F. (1976). The management of ineffective performance. In M. D. Dunnette (Ed.), *Handbook of industrial and organizational psychology* (pp. 995–1030). Chicago: Rand McNally.

Missirian, A. K. (1982). *The corporate connection: Why executive women need mentors to reach the top*. Englewood Cliffs, NJ: Prentice-Hall.

Mitchell, T. R., Green, S. G., & Wood, R. E. (1981). An attributional model of leadership and the poor performing subordinate. In B. M. Staw & L. L. Cummings (Eds.), *Research in organizational behavior* (Vol. 3, pp. 197–234). Greenwich, CT: JAI Press.

Mitchell, T. R., & Wood, R. E. (1980). Supervisors' responses to subordinate poor performance: A test of an attributional model. *Organizational Behavior and Human Performance, 25*, 123–138.

O'Connor, E. E., Peters, L. H., Pooyan, A., Weekley, J., Frank, B., & Erenkrantz,

B. (1984). Situational affective reactions and turnover: A field replication and extension. *Journal of Applied Psychology, 69,* 663–672.

Reich, M. H. (1985, March). Executive views from both sides of mentoring. *Personnel, 62,* 42–46.

Roche, G. R. (1979, January-February). Much ado about mentors. *Harvard Business Review,* pp. 14–28.

Ross, L. (1977). The intuitive psychologist and his shortcomings: Distortions in the attribution process. In L. Berkowitz (Ed.), *Advances in experimental social psychology* (Vol. 10, pp. 174–220). New Jersey: Academic Press.

Ross, M., & Fletcher, G. J. O. (1985). Attribution and social perception. In G. Lindzey & E. Aronson (Eds.), *The handbook of social psychology* (3d ed., Vol. 2, pp. 73–122). New York: Random House.

Ross, M, & Sicoly, F. (1979). Egocentric biases in availability and attribution. *Journal of Personality and Social Psychology, 37,* 322–326.

Sarason, I. G., Levine, H. M., Basham, R. B., & Sarason, B. R. (1983). Assessing social support: The social support questionnaire. *Journal of Personality and Social Psychology, 44,* 127–139.

Schein, E. H. (1968). Organizational socialization and the profession of management. *Sloan Management Review, 9,* 1–16.

Schein, E. H. (1971). The individual, the organization, and the career: A conceptual scheme. *Journal of Applied Behavioral Science, 7,* 401–426.

Schein, E. H. (1978). *Career dynamics: Matching individual and organizational needs.* Reading, MA: Addison-Wesley.

Schlenker, B. R., & Miller, R. S. (1977). Egocentrism in groups: Self-serving biases or logical information processing? *Journal of Personality and Social Psychology, 35,* 755–764.

Van Mannen, J., & Schein, E. H. (1979). Toward a theory of organizational socialization. In B. M. Staw (Ed.), *Research in organizational behavior* (Vol. 1, pp. 209–264). Greenwich, CT: JAI Press.

Wheeler, H. N. (1976). Punishment theory and industrial discipline. *Industrial Relations, 15,* 235–243.

Wohlking, W. (1975). Effective discipline in employee relations. *Personnel Journal, 54,* 489–501.

Wright, J. P. (1979). *On a clear day you can see General Motors.* Grosse Pointe, MI: Wright Enterprises.

Chapter 17

Change in Organizations

> There is nothing permanent except change.
> —HERACLITUS

Both the popular press and the social science literature are filled with stories about alienation, the "blue-collar blues," white-collar crime, sabotage at work, and other examples of malaise in the workplace. According to a national survey taken a few years ago, 36 percent of all employed Americans felt that their skills were not being adequately used, 50 percent complained about a lack of control over what they did, and only 41 percent reported that they had an interesting job. And for the first time there was a significant decline in job satisfaction (Hoerr, 1979). Other, more recent surveys show similar trends (e.g., Yankelovich & Immerwahr, 1983). The explanations offered for such problems are numerous: People are different today—they want different things from their jobs than they used to; organizations have gotten too big—they are less human; society is changing too rapidly—we cannot adjust.

There is some truth in each of these explanations. For example, people *are* different. Educational levels—and correspondingly, expectations and abilities—have risen. Similarly, people are generally more affluent and have greater security in this country than they had 50 years ago. The influence of the church and the family has also decreased, and there is some evidence that obedience to authority has declined as well. Finally, society has begun to emphasize cooperation and "self-actualization" over competition and hard work directed toward achieving organizational goals. All of these changes suggest that employees come into the workplace with a different set of values and expectations than they had in the past.

It is also true that organizations have gotten larger and more complex. In the process they have all too often failed to accommodate the changing values and expectations of their employees. Walton (1972) suggests the following set of discrepancies between employee expectations and organizational reality:

1. Employees want challenge and personal growth, but work tends to be simplified, and specialties tend to be used repeatedly in work assignments. This pattern exploits the narrow skills of a worker, while limiting his or her opportunities to broaden or develop.
2. Employees want to be included in patterns of mutual influence; they want egalitarian treatment. But organizations are characterized by tall hierarchies, status differentials, and chains of command.
3. Employee commitment to an organization is increasingly influenced by the intrinsic interest of the work itself, the human dignity afforded by management, and social responsibility reflected in the organization's products. Yet organizational practices still emphasize material rewards and employment security while neglecting other employee concerns.
4. What employees want from careers, they are apt to want right now. But when organizations design job hierarchies and career paths, they continue to assume that today's workers are as willing to postpone gratifications as were yesterday's workers.
5. Employees want more attention paid to the emotional aspects of organization life, such as individual self-esteem, openness between people, and expressions of warmth. Yet organizations emphasize rationality and seldom legitimize the emotional part of the organizational experience.
6. Employees are becoming less driven by competitive urges, less likely to identify competition as the American way. Nevertheless, managers continue to plan career patterns, organize work, and design reward systems as if employees valued competition as highly as they used to.

Finally, society itself has become more complex. The world around us is changing at an ever-increasing rate. We are becoming more and more dependent upon other cultures, economies, regional groups, and small segments of the workforce. A strike by the employees of even a single organization (e.g., city sanitation workers, police, transit employees) can seriously affect all of our lives. So too can the decisions of just one political leader in the Middle East. As these events unfold, communication media bring us instant reports transmitted by satellite from around the world. Through these reports, individual differences in life-style, norms, and habits become more apparent and acceptable. One consequence of this is that organizations are finding it more and more difficult to reconcile individual and group differences through a powerful "efficiency imperative." What is good for General Motors is not necessarily good for the country—much less the world as a whole.

If organizations are to survive, they must somehow come to grips with the changes that affect them. They must learn to deal with the changing demands of their members, the business environment, and society at large. The implication, of course, is that organizations themselves must be capable of change.

In this final chapter of the book we focus on the process and management of organizational change. It is appropriate that we end with this chapter, since implementing many of the ideas and recommendations made throughout the book implies changing the status quo—changing the organization from the way it exists now to some desired future state. In the following pages we will examine more closely both the process of change and specific strategies and techniques for accomplishing change.

PERSPECTIVES ON CHANGE

In thinking about the process of organizational change, two questions immediately come to mind. The first is, *why* do organizations change? We suggested a preliminary answer to this question in the introductory paragraphs—to survive. But this answer is too general to be very useful. It does not tell us, for example, why organizations change in some respects but not in others, nor does it clarify why some organizations change and others do not. To address these more specific issues requires a more detailed analysis of the motivation for organizational change. The second question that comes to mind when thinking about organizational change is, *what* is changed? What are the various organizational factors that can be modified to help the organization adapt and flourish? We take a closer look at both the "why" and the "what" of organizational change in this first section.

The Motivation for Change

Beer (1980) has suggested a number of factors that influence the likelihood that an organization will initiate some type of change. The first and most important factor is *dissatisfaction with the status quo*. If there is no dissatisfaction with the way the organization (or organizational unit) is currently operating— no matter how bad things may seem from the outside—there will be no motivation for change.

One source of dissatisfaction is evidence of deficiencies in the internal functioning of the organization, such as increases in absenteeism and turnover and decreases in morale and productivity. Dissatisfaction can also arise from perceived changes in the environment that make the organization's existing mode of operation inefficient or obsolete. The general proliferation of computerized ordering, shipping, and billing systems, for example, makes it more difficult for organizations that still use manual systems to compete on the basis of quick customer delivery. This change in the environment should thus stimulate dissatisfaction with existing manual systems, even though those systems may not have changed in their *absolute* level of efficiency.

Although dissatisfaction with the status quo is essential for motivating organizational change, it is not sufficient. Another important ingredient in the change equation is the perception that there is *an alternative way to manage or organize that will improve the situation.* Said differently, a potential solution to the problem must be seen. Thus, those individuals who are in a position to initiate change in the organization must perceive that there exist specific courses of action that can be taken to help relieve problems such as high absenteeism, low productivity, and slow customer responsiveness. If it is believed that there is no solution—that there is nothing that can be done to improve things—there will be no motivation to change, even though there may be great dissatisfaction with the current state of affairs.

In addition to perceiving that a solution exists, *the transition from the current (unsatisfactory) state to the desired (solution) state must be seen as manageable.* Not all organizational changes are equally easy to accomplish. When the desired solution state is substantially different from what currently exists, and when the change will affect a great many people, a significant amount of energy will usually be needed in order to mobilize and coordinate the change (e.g., as when all of the jobs in a manufacturing plant are redesigned in order to accommodate the introduction of new robot technologies and/or autonomous work groups). If the transition period is not managed well, the desired solution state may never be fully realized, or if it is realized, it may not operate as expected because of a lack of commitment on the part of the employees who are affected by the change.

Notice that the transition period can be conceptualized as a separate phase of the change process that is intermediate between, and distinct from, both the current state of the organization and the desired future state. This is illustrated in Figure 17-1. Circle A in Figure 17-1 represents the organization as it currently exists. Circle C represents the desired future state of the organization. The desired future state might involve redesigned jobs, new work technologies, new reporting relationships, new systems of reward, or even new values and norms of behavior.

In order to make the change from the current state to the desired future state, the organization must move through state B, the transition state. During the transition state a number of problems are likely to arise. These include

FIGURE 17-1
Organizational
change can be
conceptualized as
a transition state.
(*Adapted from
Beckhard & Harris,
1977.*)

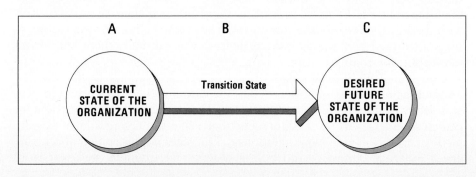

resistance to the change on the part of those who are most affected by it, increased political activity, and the possible loss of control over important organizational functions as old, well-understood control mechanisms are abandoned and newer, less familiar mechanisms are put in their place. All of these problems need to be addressed if the change is to be successfully implemented (Nadler, 1982). To the extent that they seem difficult or impossible to manage, there will be less motivation to implement the change in the first place.

Finally, even when the transition to the new organizational state appears manageable, it is important that the gains expected from the change be greater than the perceived costs (where costs are measured in terms of time, money, lost productivity, turnover, and so on). For example, imagine that three dentists who together own a small dental practice are considering buying a computerized medical records system for their office (i.e., the kind that runs on a personal computer). Suppose they know that their most experienced and highly valued nurse/secretary has a "computer phobia," and that there is a good chance she will quit her job rather than learn how to use the new system. If the cost of losing this person is judged to be too great in relation to the benefits that the new system will bring, there will be little motivation to implement this change.

To summarize, change is likely to occur in an organization only when there is dissatisfaction with the status quo, when it is perceived that there is an alternative way to organize that will improve the situation, when the transition to the desired future state seems manageable, and when the perceived costs of the change do not exceed its expected benefits. If one or more of these preconditions does not exist, there is little likelihood that a change will take place.

What Gets Changed

The various factors that can be changed in an organization fall into four major categories. One category involves *redesigning the jobs* that are performed by organization members. The jobs people perform may be expanded, contracted, or reorganized. Certain tasks might be added to a person's job, others might be dropped, and still others might be performed using new methods (e.g., new equipment) or in new sequences. The shift from a traditional assembly-line method of manufacturing to an autonomous work group method, for example, generally implies a substantial increase in the number and variety of tasks that an employee is expected to perform.

A second category of change involves *modifying the formal structure of the organization.* Organizational units might be created or eliminated, lines of authority and communication might be altered, the responsibility for making certain kinds of decisions might be moved to either higher or lower organizational levels, and control systems might be added, modified, or deleted. The introduction of a new layer of management or a new performance appraisal system are examples of the kind of change that alters the formal organizational structure.

The third category focuses on *changing the individual members of the organization.* Employees can be hired, transferred, promoted into new positions, and if need be, fired. Employee training also falls into this category. Training is designed to change employees by improving their ability to perform well on the job.

The final category has to do with changes directed toward *modifying the norms and informal social relations* that exist within the organization. At the group level of analysis, action can be taken to reduce intergroup conflict, to increase the cohesiveness within groups, and even to change group-supported values and norms of behavior. Attempts might also be made to modify the values and norms that are shared by *all* members of the organization. In this case the focus would be on changing the overall culture of the organization (see Chapter 9, pp. 279–280).

An Open Systems Theory Perspective

The four factors that can be changed in an organization—the jobs performed, the formal organizational structure, the members of the organization, and the informal social relations—correspond exactly to the four central elements in Nadler and Tushman's (1980) congruence model of organizations. We discussed the congruence model at the beginning of the book in Chapter 3, "Understanding Organizations" (see pp. 65–67). As you will recall, the congruence model is an elaboration of the open systems theory view. As such, it focuses on the interaction between the organization and its environment. Those factors in the environment that influence the organization are called inputs, while the effects that the organization has on the environment are called outputs. According to an open systems perspective, an organization creates outputs by acting upon and transforming inputs. The congruence model elaborates this transformation process. It suggests that the quality of an organization's outputs are a direct result of the way in which the four organizational elements fit together. When they fit together well, a state of congruence exists, and desirable outputs are expected. When they do not fit together well, a state of incongruence exists, and undesirable outputs are likely.

Our purpose in returning to the congruence model is to provide a broader framework for understanding the focus of organizational change. If an organization's outputs are indeed a result of the way in which its elements fit together, then organizational change should be oriented toward optimizing that fit. The implication is that when a change is contemplated for any one element of the organization, it is essential to diagnose carefully the fit between that element and those elements that are not changed.

Let's take an example. Suppose you are the newly hired chairperson of a large academic department in a private university. Your department has forty-one faculty members and nine secretaries. The department is structured so that each secretary works with either four or five faculty members. The secretaries all have their own offices near the faculty members they work with, and they are spread out over three floors of the building. Secretaries at your university earn substantially less than they would if they were working in the local business community, but you have heard no strong complaints about this, nor is there any evidence of union organizing activity.

Recently, you have noticed that your faculty members often make special requests for temporary typing support from outside the department. It seems that the departmental secretaries are barely able to keep up with their work load, and that during peak periods (e.g., when midterm and final exams must be typed) they often get so overloaded that extra outside help is needed. Because hiring temporary typists is an expense your department can ill afford, you decide to investigate the matter more closely.

After wandering from office to office for a few days, you discover what you believe is a major cause of the problem. It appears that most of the secretaries in the department arrive for work an average of a half hour late in the morning, that they take extra-long lunch breaks, and that they often leave 20 to 30 minutes early in the afternoon. Thus, you conclude that one reason the secretaries are so easily overloaded is that they are absent from work for as much as 1.5 hours per day.

In an effort to correct this problem, you are thinking about instituting a sign-in/sign-out procedure to monitor the hours that each secretary is on the job. This procedure would require that the secretaries stop by your office and sign in when they arrive for work in the morning, sign out before going to lunch, sign in again after lunch, and sign out once more when they go home at the end of the day. Your expectation is that if the hours the secretaries spend on the job are more closely monitored, they will be more likely to work the full time they are supposed to and thus be better able to keep up with their work load.

In analyzing this scenario, it should be clear that what is being contemplated is a change in the formal organizational structure. The sign-in/sign-out procedure is a formal system for monitoring and controlling the attendance behavior of the secretarial staff. Before introducing this change, however, it is important to consider how it is likely to fit with the other elements of the organization. Of particular concern is its likely fit with the needs and values of the secretaries. Notice that while the secretaries are currently working less than they are supposed to, they are also being underpaid in comparison to what they could be earning elsewhere. Perhaps they justify this underpayment by not working as hard as they otherwise might. Thus, they may view the present situation as being an equitable one—the university pays them less, but because their attendance is not closely monitored, it also permits them to work less.

What is likely to happen if the sign-in/sign-out procedure is instituted? While it may compel the secretaries to work longer hours, it is also likely to upset their sense of equity, since they will now be putting in more hours of work for the same low pay. This perceived inequity will probably generate a good deal of dissatisfaction, which may manifest itself in a number of ways. For example, the secretaries may show a greater propensity to take "sick days" without actually being sick, to quit their jobs in favor of better paying ones in the local business community, and/or to begin seeking union representation in order to improve their current pay.

Thus, what at first appears to be a solution to the problem may turn out to be no solution at all, since it fails to address the fit between two important organizational elements—the formal organizational structure and the individual members of the organization. If the secretaries start taking their time off as "sick days," the work load problem may still exist. And even if it does not, it may be eliminated at the expense of higher turnover and union activism. Thus, one set of problems will have been exchanged for another, which is hardly an acceptable solution.

To summarize, whenever an organizational change is being planned, it is important to examine how the change will affect the congruence among organizational elements. If the contemplated change involves altering the organizational structure, one should diagnose the likely impact of that change on the fit between the formal structure and each of the other three organizational elements (individuals, jobs, and informal social relations). Similarly, if the change has to do with the jobs being performed (as in the dental office example given previously), the likely fit between the redesigned jobs and the remaining organizational elements should be examined. Taking the congruence among organizational elements into account when planning a change will generally increase the probability that an effective change will be selected.

THE CHANGE PROCESS

Introducing any kind of change into an organization is a complex, multistep process. The process begins when a problem is recognized. An attempt is then made to discover the causes of the problem. Once the causes are determined, some sort of change is introduced. Finally, the effectiveness of the change must be evaluated. Each of these steps is discussed in greater detail in the following sections.

Problem Recognition

Some of the most easily recognized signs of problems appear in the routine organizational data-gathering process. Statistics on turnover, absenteeism, grievances, union disputes, and productivity all reflect the general health of an organization. These measures are usually part of any inclusive control system. When significant numbers of people begin to leave the organization, come to work irregularly, break regulations, and generally slack off, you can be fairly sure that (1) something is wrong, and (2) something needs to be done about it.

Besides these obvious signs of malaise, there are other, more subtle cues that one should pay attention to. Are there frequent arguments among coworkers? Do people seem tense? Does there seem to be less commitment and enthusiasm than previously? While less objective and countable, these impressions may also reflect problems. In some cases, they may be more important indicators than the objective factors.

Identifying the Causes

Once a problem is recognized, the next step is to discover its causes. For many kinds of problems, personal observation and informal chats with employees will provide sufficient information for a diagnosis. For other problems, however, rather large amounts of information may be needed before an accurate assessment can be made. To help gather this information, it is sometimes useful to employ a questionnaire. A wide variety of standardized question-naires are available for this purpose.

Some of these questionnaires are helpful for assessing the specific *structural and procedural characteristics of the jobs* being performed in the organization (e.g., Hackman & Oldham, 1980; McCormick, 1979; Tornow & Pinto, 1976). These instruments are designed to provide data on such diverse factors as the information flow and types of mental processes used in the job; the degree of variety, autonomy, and feedback found in the job; and the amount of time the employee is required to spend on such activities as planning, coordinating, and supervising others.

Other questionnaires assess *employees' reactions to their jobs*. These include measures of the degree to which employees perceive their jobs as meaningful, the extent to which they feel personally responsible for the work that gets done, and the degree to which they are satisfied with their jobs. The Job Descriptive Index discussed in Chapter 5 is a good example of a questionnaire assessing job satisfaction (see pages 122–123).

Finally, there are a number of questionnaires that focus on the *interpersonal relationships* that exist both within and between organizational units, as well as on such organization-wide issues as a firm's overall management style and/or climate (e.g., Likert, 1967). *Climate* refers to employee perceptions about the general way the organization deals with its members and the environment. It is a reflection of the overall atmosphere in the organization (Hellriegel & Slocum, 1974; see also Field & Abelson, 1982).

The effective use of any of these questionnaires requires a certain amount of training and expertise. In every case, however, when properly employed, these instruments can be quite helpful in identifying the specific causes of significant organizational problems.

Implementing the Change

Once the causes of the problem have been identified, the next step is to take action to remedy the situation. Usually this means making some sort of change, whether it be in the formal organizational structure, the jobs being performed, the individual organizational members, or the informal social relations. Nadler (1982) suggests that in order to implement an organizational change successfully, three main tasks must be accomplished: (1) motivation for the change needs to be generated among the individuals who must carry it out, (2) the transition state needs to be managed to ensure that control is maintained during and after the change, and (3) the political dynamics of the situation need to be managed so that they support the change. We discuss each of these three tasks in greater detail.

Generating Motivation for Change. Virtually every kind of change implies that at least some members of the organization will have to alter their behavior. The successful introduction of a new performance appraisal system requires that managers and supervisors take the time and energy to use the new system properly. The merger of two competing departments into one requires that the members of the newly created department now cooperate with their

Middle Managers and Supervisors Resist Moves to More Participatory Management

CORNING, N.Y.—When senior management at Corning Glass Works here began a program last year to foster a more participatory style of management, some supervisors were dubious. Now they're believers.

What turned them around were experiences like one at the company's plant in nearby Erwin, N.Y., where a die-manufacturing problem needed to be solved. Supervisors put five machinists in a room and gave them whatever information they needed. Five hours later, the team had a solution costing less than $200.

Under the old management style, says Bob Pierce, a department head, supervisors and engineers would have huddled, "and it would have come out as an edict" with uncertain results. Now, by getting workers involved, the people who actually have to carry out a decision "have a personal obligation to make it happen."

Corning has been fortunate. Getting plant supervisors and middle managers to give it a serious try is the essential first step in establishing a more participatory management style. But to hear executives tell it, that isn't an easy task at many companies. In fact, says Mark Andrews Jr., president of Mark Andy Inc., a small printing-press maker in Chesterfield, Mo., "It's like pulling teeth."

EAGER TROOPS

The aim of participatory management is to get first-line supervisors and plant managers to elicit ways of doing a better job from workers on the shop floor. Hourly workers who have been ignored for years usually like the idea of being listened to, and top executives who launched the program are eager for it to happen.

But mid-level employees, like the Corning supervisors in Erwin, are sandwiched in between. They worked hard to get into management and tend to guard their old-style authority jealously. They grew up in a system in which "management has all the answers"—even if it didn't—and they have long been taught that their job is to keep the hourly employees in the dark and the production lines humming.

Now, their bosses tell them, "We want more participation" from the workers, as well as better management and a steady flow of quality products, says Joseph Propersi, Corning's manufacturing-education manager. Managers in the middle are left wondering. "How do I do both?"

Faced with that dilemma, many managers and supervisors dig in to oppose the change. When one big telecommunications company started its program, middle managers boycotted an orientation meeting. At S. C. Johnson & Son Inc., in Racine, Wis., Philip Ricco, the productivity director, says he once watched a hard-bitten manager bluntly tell a boss: "I've been here longer than you, and I'll be here after you've gone, so don't tell me what really counts at this company."

Because of the central role middle managers and supervisors play in implementing a more participatory management style, attitudes like that obviously jeopardize the entire program. "People in the middle are the ones who make it go or don't go," says Mark Arnold, consulting services director of Organizational Dynamics Inc. in Burlington, Mass.

The problem of getting middle managers to make the transition to managing worker teams from the more traditional, autocratic management of individuals "is huge," says Mr. Ricco of S. C. Johnson. "It's *the* problem." Johnson, he says, has made more progress than most companies. Among other things, it holds working sessions three or four times a year to help middle managers focus on the company's overall strategy and goals, and it publishes a quarterly managers' newsletter.

At Florida Power & Light Co., middle managers became confused about their new roles, prompting the company to tailor special training sessions to help them along. But while such retraining can be useful, some managers and supervisors never get the message. They must learn how to run regular meetings of hourly workers, do their homework before the meetings and follow up on suggestions made by the worker teams. . . .

TRW Inc.'s valve division in Cleveland reassigned several first-line supervisors and managers to jobs one-time adversaries. And adding another layer of management to the organization demands that people follow the leadership of their new superiors.

In most circumstances, such changes cannot be accomplished simply by legislation. At some level, the individuals who must change their behavior have to accept and even want the change. They must be willing participants in the change process. Too often an organizational change will fail solely because those whose behavior is critical to the effective implementation of the change do not want it. There are very few changes that can be made in an organization that cannot be subverted by members who do not want or accept the change. New performance appraisal forms can be ignored or filled out mindlessly, political factions and infighting can prevent recently merged departments from performing effectively, and employees can quietly sabotage the efforts of newly appointed managers.

Thus, it is important to generate a motivation for change among those employees whose behavior is personally affected by it. Nadler (1982) recommends several strategies for doing this. The first is to *surface dissatisfaction with the present situation.* Just as dissatisfaction with the status quo is essential for management's motivation to introduce a change, dissatisfaction is also essential for the motivation of those who must carry it out. People need to be convinced that the old performance appraisal system is unreliable, that the existing departmental structure is counterproductive, and that the present management structure is insufficient for coping with important organizational problems.

Motivation for change can also be generated by *getting those who are affected by the change to participate in its design.* Participation builds a sense of "ownership," and it motivates people to want to make the change work (cf. Vroom & Yetton, 1973). Silverman and Wexley (1984) have demonstrated, for example, that when employees are involved in the development of the rating scales used in a performance appraisal system, they are subsequently more satisfied with the appraisal system, and are more motivated to improve their own performance when an appraisal reveals deficiencies. Similarly, Latack and Foster (1985) found that employees are more satisfied with major work schedule changes when they have an opportunity to participate in the decision to implement them.

Finally, Nadler (1982) also recommends that the *desired new behaviors be systematically rewarded.* Formal rewards such as pay, bonuses, promotions, official recognition, and job assignments should be carefully examined and restructured to reinforce the change. The same goes for informal social rewards. Thus, managers should be rewarded for making effective use of new performance appraisal systems. The members of a newly merged department should be reinforced for cooperating with one another. And employees should be rewarded for helping to ensure that new management structures succeed. Like any other behavior that takes place in an organization, change is strongly influenced by its consequences. Thus, change is most likely to occur when it is perceived to lead to positive consequences for those individuals who must actually do the changing.

Managing the Transition State. Change interrupts the normal flow of events in an organization. The larger the change and the more people involved, the greater the disruption. This disruption tends to undermine normal systems of management control. Depending on the type of change involved, customary sources of information and lines of communication may be lost. The meaning of certain performance measures may suddenly become ambiguous or irrelevant. And boundaries of authority and responsibility may temporarily become confused. If left unattended, these problems can paralyze an organization, and they can result in the ultimate failure of the change. The most effective strategy for dealing with these problems is to prevent them from occurring in the first place. This can be accomplished by carefully planning for the change in advance and by committing time, energy, and resources to managing the transition period.

In planning for the change, managers should develop for themselves, and communicate to their employees, a very clear picture of what things will be like once the change has been implemented (Beckhard & Harris, 1977). A *clear image of the future* gives employees a better understanding of their own role in the change and how they are expected to behave. It provides, if you will, a template to which they can match their behavior both during and after the change. Furthermore, it indicates how they will be personally affected by the change. Impending organizational changes often cause employees to worry about how their own future performance (and outcomes) will be affected. If manual systems are to be computerized, for example, people will naturally wonder whether they will be able to cope successfully with their newly redesigned jobs. Will they be able to learn the language of the computer? What will happen if their productivity drops off during the learning phase? How will their redesigned jobs affect their relationships with others? Will they suddenly be moved to a new location where they do not know anyone? Providing a clear image of the future will not only answer these questions for the desired future state (circle C in Figure 17-1), it will also answer them for the transition period and will clarify how the organization plans to help the employee make the transition (e.g., by providing computer training, by suspending normal performance criteria until it is certain that the employee has learned the skills necessary to perform well on the job, and so on).

It is also important to *commit sufficient resources to ensure the successful transition to the desired future state of affairs.* This may involve assigning personnel to help manage the change, as well as committing money for such things as employee training, consultation with technical experts, and the like. With regard to personnel, for large-scale changes it may be necessary to appoint a *transition manager.* The sole job of this individual is to oversee all of the details of the transition period. As Nadler (1982) suggests, it is frequently difficult for one person to manage the current state of the organization, prepare to manage the desired future state, and simultaneously manage the transition state. The reason is that there is simply too much to do. If a transition manager is appointed, he or she can be given the power and authority to make the decisions necessary to ensure that the transition takes place smoothly.

Finally, it may also be necessary to *build special feedback mechanisms that will operate during the transition period* and that will provide information on how the change is progressing. As noted previously, during a period of transition, normal lines of communication and feedback may break down. If they do, and there is nothing to take their place, one can lose sight of how the transition is proceeding. Consequently, if there are aspects of a situation that require additional attention, there may be no way of knowing it. Thus, efforts should be made to develop new ways to obtain information during the transition period. For example, surveys, special group meetings, and interviews conducted by an impartial party (e.g., a consultant) may be helpful for determining how well employees are coping with the transition—both technically and attitudinally.

Supporting the Change. Finally, it is also important to manage the political dynamics of the situation so that it supports the change. As we discussed in Chapter 13, political behavior is an inherent part of any organization. Political activity arises whenever there are important choices to be made in situations in which different groups have different preferences and there is uncertainty about which alternatives are objectively correct or best (see Figure 13-6 on page 418). Because change disrupts the normal course of events in an organization, it has the potential for generating an extremely high level of uncertainty. Consequently, it also has the potential for generating an extremely high level of political activity. It is unrealistic to expect that this political activity can ever be completely eliminated. Instead, the best that can be hoped for is to *manage the situation so that powerful groups within the organization will support rather than block the change.* This usually involves building a coalition of groups that are willing to support the change, and using such tactics as negotiation, compromise, and co-optation to influence those groups that may oppose it. It is often the case that organizational change is as much a political event as it is a technical event. Thus, the political aspects of the change process should not be ignored (cf. Pettigrew, 1978; Schein, 1985).

Evaluating the Change

The final step in any change process is to evaluate its effectiveness. This evaluation must be done on two levels. The first level concerns the implementation itself: Has the change to the desired future state actually been accomplished? For example, if the change involved introducing a new performance appraisal system, is the new system now being used conscientiously by line managers, or has it been ignored, not taken seriously, or rejected outright? If the answer is that it has been ignored, not taken seriously, or rejected, the transition to the desired future state has not been achieved. The implication is that something must have gone wrong in implementing the change. Either insufficient motivation was generated for the change, technical aspects of the transition phase were not well managed (e.g., perhaps more time should have been devoted to providing managers with performance appraisal training), or important political issues were not adequately handled (e.g., opposition from union groups or from certain factions within top management).

If, on the other hand, the change to the desired future state has been accomplished (e.g., the performance appraisal system is being used by line managers as intended), it is important to ask whether or not the problem that you originally set out to solve with the change has now been corrected. Has absenteeism decreased, morale risen, and/or productivity improved? If the answer to this question is *yes,* the change can be scored a success. If the answer is *no,* however, something must have been wrong with your original diagnosis of the situation. Perhaps some critical piece of information was overlooked. Or maybe an important fit with another element of the organization was not taken into consideration. Whatever the reason, it will be necessary to go back to the diagnostic stage and begin anew with a fresh and improved analysis of the problem.

ORGANIZATIONAL CHANGE STRATEGIES

So far we have discussed the overall process of organizational change. The next portion of the chapter is devoted to a more detailed description and evaluation of a number of important change strategies currently being used in organizations. We examine change strategies in each of the four areas covered by the elements of the congruence model: changing people, changing jobs, changing informal group relations, and changing the formal organizational structure.

Changing People

If after carefully diagnosing the causes of a problem it seems advisable to change one or more of the people employed by the organization, there are two basic courses of action that can be taken. The first is to replace the current employees with new ones. The second is to modify the way in which the current employees behave. The first option covers employee transfer and termination, while the second focuses on employee training.

Transfer and Termination. The impetus for both transferring and terminating employees often (but not always) stems from a perceived lack of fit between the person and the job. In the case of termination, this usually means that the employee is judged not to have the skills and abilities necessary to perform well on the job. If the individual seems incapable of acquiring the necessary skills and abilities, and there are no other jobs in the organization for which he or she is suited, there may be no choice other than termination. On the other hand, when it does seem possible to teach the employee the necessary skills, or when there are other jobs in the organization that appear to fit the individual's capacities better, training or transfer may be the more desirable alternatives. When feasible, these alternative courses of action will usually be preferred because they eliminate some of the costs associated with recruiting and selecting new employees.

It is important to recognize that the use of employee termination as an organizational change strategy is not limited to any one level of the organization. Even those who occupy positions at the very top are not invulnerable. When the organization as a whole performs poorly, those at the top are often in danger of losing their jobs. This is true for sports teams (head coaches), business organizations (presidents and CEOs), and universities (presidents and chancellors). The head of the organization is terminated by some governing body (e.g., the board of directors) because he or she is perceived to be incapable of improving the performance of the organization.

In comparison to termination, transfer is likely to be considered not only when the employee's skills and abilities are *deficient* with respect to the requirements of the job, but also when he or she has *outgrown* the job. In the latter case, there is a lack of fit between the person and the job because the job no longer challenges the skills and abilities of the employee. Thus, the goal of transferring the employee is ultimately the same in both situations—to improve the person-job fit.

It should be noted that in comparison to situations in which the person does not have sufficient skills to perform well on the job, it can sometimes be more difficult to recognize when the job does not fully use the skills of the person. In the former case, evidence of poor performance draws one's attention to the problem. In the latter case, by contrast, performance may not be a good indicator. The individual who has skills and abilities in excess of the job requirements may perform quite acceptably, and his or her performance may be hard to distinguish from that of employees whose skills are more closely matched to the job. A better indicator of this sort of problem may be evidence of low job satisfaction, such as absenteeism and signs that the individual is preparing to quit the job.

Training. Like termination and transfer, the impetus for providing employees with remedial training is usually to correct a perceived lack of fit between the person and the job. Training is basically learning. It is an attempt to provide the individual with experiences that will help him or her perform more effectively on the job. A training program is meant to structure these experiences in such a way that the appropriate skills and attitudes are acquired and developed. Thus, training can be defined as *an attempt by the organization to change the behavior of its members through the learning process in order to increase effectiveness.*

Training programs can be designed to help employees improve their skills in three distinct areas: technical, human, and conceptual (Katz, 1974). *Technical skill* refers to the employee's understanding of, and ability to use, the specific methods, processes, procedures, and techniques required to perform the tasks that make up the job. Thus, for example, it refers to those abilities that a pilot needs in order to fly an airplane, that a doctor needs in order to perform surgery, and that an accountant needs in order to prepare a financial statement. Seminars in which engineers are taught how to use new computer-aided design (CAD) equipment and workshops in which managers learn how to do certain types of departmental budgeting are examples of training programs that focus on technical skills.

Human skill refers to the employee's ability to work effectively as a group member and to motivate and lead others. Whereas technical skills focus on working with "things" and are usually highly specific to the particular job being performed, human skills focus on working with people and are applicable in almost any organizational setting. Training programs that help managers learn how to set specific performance goals for their employees (e.g., Ivancevich & Smith, 1981) or that teach them how to modify the situation to fit their leadership style (e.g., Fiedler, Chemers, & Mahar, 1976) are examples of this category. Taking a course in organizational behavior can also be thought of as a type of human skills training.

Finally, *conceptual skill* refers to the employee's understanding of the functioning of the organization as a whole. This includes understanding all the elements of the organization and how they relate to one another, as well as how the organization relates to its environment (e.g., the industry, the economy, the political environment). A job-rotation program that is designed to give managers experience in a variety of different areas within the organization is an example of a training program that focuses on developing conceptual skills. Specialized courses in organizational planning, policy, and strategic decision making may also fall into this category.

It should be noted that the relative importance of these three types of skills varies at different organizational levels. At the lowest levels of the organization, technical skills are extremely important, while conceptual skills are less important. The reverse is true at the highest levels. Thus, as one moves up the organizational hierarchy, technical skills become increasingly less important, while conceptual skills become increasingly more important. Human skills, on the other hand, are important at all organizational levels (Katz, 1974).

Every conceivable type of training method has been used to teach skills in these three areas, although certain approaches are better suited for teaching some skills than others. We will briefly mention a few of the more commonly used methods here. (For a more comprehensive review, see Wexley, 1984; Wexley & Latham, 1981.)

Training methods can be roughly divided into those that are used on-site and those that are used off-site. *On-site training* takes place at the work site, usually with a coworker or supervisor serving as the trainer. The most common form of on-site training is called *on-the-job training* (OJT). OJT is used primarily for improving an employee's technical skills. It usually involves assigning a more experienced or skilled employee to work closely with the individual who needs the training. The experienced employee provides guidance and instruction in order to help solve problems and to teach the less skilled employee the most efficient way to do the work. The less skilled employee is expected to learn by a combination of observation and practice. Apprenticeship programs and job-rotation programs are also forms of on-site training (recall that these were discussed in connection with socializing new employees in Chapter 16).

Off-site training, as the name suggests, is done away from the work site, most often in a classroom environment. Off-site training methods include lectures, discussions, audiovisual presentations, programmed instruction, equipment simulators (e.g., flight simulators for pilot training), case studies, role playing, behavioral modeling, and management games. Of these various methods, programmed instruction and case studies are often considered to be the most effective methods for ensuring the acquisition and retention of factual knowledge related to technical skills, while role playing and behavioral modeling are usually judged best for teaching interpersonal and human-relations skills. Case studies, discussions, and management games are generally the methods of choice for teaching problem solving and conceptual skills (cf. Carroll, Paine, & Ivancevich, 1972).

To summarize, whenever there is perceived to be a lack of fit between the person and the job, one strategy for correcting the situation is to change the person involved. This might consist of replacing the individual through either transfer or termination, or of attempting to change his or her behavior through some form of training. It is important to recognize, however, that changing the person is not the only way to correct a poor person-job fit. An alternative approach is to change the job.

Changing the Job

Whether one should try to correct a poor person-job fit by changing the person or changing the job depends to some extent on how widespread the problem is. When the problem is an isolated case and involves only one or at most a very few individuals, an attempt to change the person may be most appropriate. However, when the problem is more systemic in nature, involving many different individuals, person-oriented changes may not be feasible. This is especially true when the various jobs being performed underutilize the employees' skills and abilities. The person-oriented change that is most appropriate for such a situation (transfer), may simply not be possible when large numbers of individuals and jobs are involved. Under these circumstances, it may be necessary to take a different approach—to modify the jobs so that they better fit the people performing them. In this section we will consider three different types of job-oriented changes: changing work schedules, changing task characteristics, and forming autonomous work groups.

Work Schedules. One type of job-oriented change that has become increasingly popular in recent years is to modify the work schedule. An example of such a modification is the *4/40 workweek*. Under this work schedule, employees work a standard 40-hour week, but do so in four 10-hour days. This has the attraction of providing employees with longer weekends and therefore larger blocks of leisure time. Another example is called *flexitime*. Here employees are expected to work five 8-hour days, but they have some degree of flexibility as to exactly which set of 8 hours they work in a given day. Under this system, there is usually an established set of "core hours" during which all employees are expected to be on the job (e.g., from 10 A.M. to 2 P.M.). During this time group meetings, conferences, and other similar events can be scheduled. It is then up to each employee to decide which other hours to work in order to make a total of 8 hours. Some employees may prefer to arrive early and leave early (e.g., work from 7 A.M. to 3 P.M.), while others may wish to arrive late and leave late (e.g., work from 10 A.M. to 6 P.M.). Still others may wish to arrive early and leave late, taking a long break midafternoon so that they can go shopping, running, or attend to other personal needs.

Empirical research examining the effects of work-schedule changes on employee satisfaction and performance has produced mixed results. Concerning the 4/40 workweek, while many employees respond favorably to it, there are some who do not. Those who respond most favorably tend to be (1) younger employees, (2) those who work in low-level jobs, and (3) those who have rather low job satisfaction and commitment to begin with (Goodale & Aagaard, 1975; Ivancevich, 1974). The latter two points suggest that the 4/40 schedule may be satisfying to certain employees simply because it offers a partial escape from an unpleasant work situation. Evidence regarding the impact of the 4/40 work schedule on productivity seems to indicate that it does not significantly improve productivity at the individual level (e.g., Ivancevich & Lyon, 1977). On the other hand, even when individual productivity does not change, overall group or organizational productivity may increase in those jobs in which significant amounts of time are spent performing start-up or shut-down operations (Swierczewski, 1972). When the number of start-up/ shut-down cycles is reduced from five to four, more time is available for production.

Less research has been conducted on the effects of flexitime, but the results that are available are generally positive. Employees who work on a flexitime schedule are generally more satisfied with their jobs and less likely to be absent from work (Golembiewski & Proehl, 1978). Productivity gains can also be expected, but this is likely to occur primarily when there are limited physical resources that employees must share among themselves (e.g., when a group of programmers must share a small number of computer terminals; Ralston, Anthony, & Gustafson, 1985). The explanation for this is that a flexitime schedule tends to reduce the amount of time that employees spend waiting for resources currently being used by someone else. Under a flexitime schedule, employees can make informal arrangements among themselves to come in early or stay late in order to use equipment that must be shared.

Task Characteristics. In addition to changing the work schedule, one might also consider redesigning the tasks performed on the job. Scientific interest in task design dates back to the turn of the century and the work of Frederick W. Taylor (1911). We discussed Taylor's "scientific management" approach in some detail in Chapters 3 and 6. As you will recall, Taylor sought to find the "one best way" to design tasks, with the emphasis on efficiency and productivity. In pursuit of this goal, employers designed simpler jobs, with tasks that were more repetitive, and more boring to perform. Perhaps the best example of jobs that have been designed using this approach are those held by assembly-line workers in many modern factories. A basic assumption underlying this method of task design is that if employees are well paid, they will not mind the boring, repetitive work. As we have seen, however, this assumption reflects an overly simplistic view of human motivation.

Contemporary approaches to task design that take better account of employee motivation have emphasized the need to expand the scope of jobs, making them broader, more complex, and less repetitive—just opposite to the dictates of Taylor's scientific management. These newer approaches seek to expand jobs through either *job enlargement* or *job enrichment*. As we have discussed elsewhere, job enlargement focuses on expanding the job by increasing the number and variety of tasks that are performed, while job enrichment increases the employee's autonomy and responsibility.

One scientific theory of job enrichment that has received a great deal of attention is the model proposed by Hackman and Oldham (1980). We briefly introduced this model in Chapter 6 (see Figure 6-6 on page 175). The model focuses on the impact of five core job characteristics: *skill variety* (the degree to which the job requires the use of a number of different skills and talents), *task identify* (the degree to which the job involves the completion of a "whole" and identifiable piece of work), *task significance* (the degree to which the job affects the lives of others), *autonomy* (the degree to which the employee can make independent decisions about scheduling and work procedures), and *feedback* (the degree to which job activities provide the employee with clear information about the effectiveness of his or her performance). According to Hackman and Oldham (1980), these five job characteristics can significantly influence work motivation, job satisfaction, and performance, depending on the *growth need strength* of the employees involved. Growth need strength is defined as the degree to which the employee has a *need for personal accomplishment, learning, and development on the job.* For those employees who have a moderate-to-high growth need strength, it is predicted that high levels of these job characteristics will result in high levels of motivation, satisfaction, and performance. For those who have relatively low growth need strength, on the other hand, these job characteristics are not expected to be related to motivation, satisfaction, and performance.

FIGURE 17-2
Doing repetitious, boring work has often been the source of turnover and absenteeism on the job.

To get a better feel for this theory and its implications for how one might go about achieving a better person-job fit, let us consider two hypothetical jobs. The first is that of a word processor in one of the research departments of a large brokerage firm. The individual occupying this position is responsible for doing all of the word processing for the department. This includes preparing letters, technical reports, and other, more specialized documents. Most of the technical reports generated in this department contain text that is accompanied by statistical tables. The word processor is responsible for producing every aspect of these reports, including whatever graphics may be required. The person employed in this position negotiates the priority and production scheduling of the reports as they come in, and works closely with the investment analysts to make sure that all materials are error-free before they are distributed outside the department. If we were to rate this job on the five core job characteristics (perhaps using one of the questionnaires discussed previously), we might find a profile similar to that shown for job A in Figure 17-3.

Now consider the job of a word processor in a different brokerage firm. In this firm, all word processing is handled by a central word-processing department. The individual operators in the department handle documents from all parts of the organization. However, each operator specializes in one type of material (e.g., standard text, technical text, statistical tables, technical graphics). Since many documents contain two or more types of material (e.g., text plus tables), they are often subdivided and handled by different specialists. Decisions about how to subdivide the work are made by the word processing supervisor, who also does all the production scheduling. Once the specialists have completed their portions of the work, a separate "finishing operator" integrates the material and assembles the final product. If a document is

FIGURE 17-3
Job characteristics profiles for two jobs (higher values indicate that more of the job characteristic is present).

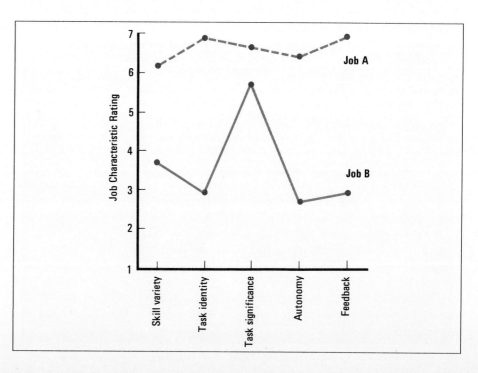

returned to the word-processing center for correction, it is the finishing operator who makes the necessary changes. In this way, the specialists are never interrupted with corrections. If we were to rate the specialist's job on the five core job characteristics, we might find a profile similar to the one shown for job B in Figure 17-3.

As the figure suggests, in comparison to the employee in job A, the word-processing specialist in job B uses a narrower range of skills (low skill variety), often does only a segment of the work required to produce a whole document (low task identity), has little control over decisions about how and when the work is done (low autonomy), and gets little feedback about the accuracy of his or her work (low feedback). Only the significance of the task comes close to approaching the level observed in job A. According to the Hackman and Oldham (1980) model, job B should be less motivating than job A, especially for individuals with a moderate-to-high growth need strength.

There is a substantial amount of research supporting the Hackman and Oldham (1980) model, especially with regard to its predictions concerning job satisfaction. Across a wide variety of studies conducted in both laboratory and field settings, ratings of the five core job characteristics tend to be positively correlated with job satisfaction. Moreover, these correlations are generally higher for individuals with a high growth need strength (Loher, Noe, Moeller, & Fitzgerald, 1985). The results are also supportive for the predictions concerning motivation. The performance predictions, on the other hand, have received only mixed support. While some studies do find that ratings of the five core job characteristics are correlated with performance, other studies find no correlation. It is difficult to know what to make of this, however. As Griffin (1982) points out, these contradictory findings may stem from the fact that performance has been operationalized differently in different studies, thus making the results hard to compare. Additional research examining the performance question is clearly needed.

Whether the performance predictions are ultimately supported or not, the job satisfaction and motivation results are sufficiently strong and consistent to suggest that changing the characteristics of the task can be a useful strategy for bringing about a better fit between the person and the job. For employees who have a moderate-to-high growth need strength, a better person-job fit will be achieved to the extent that the ratings on the five core job dimensions can be raised to a high level. Hackman and Oldham (1980) have suggested several strategies for accomplishing this.

The first strategy they recommend is to *combine tasks*. By putting together existing, fractionalized tasks to form larger, more complete modules of work, both skill variety and task identity can be increased. Thus, for example, rather than having different individuals do different parts of the word-processing job (e.g., text, tables, final assembly), one person would do them all.

A second strategy is to *form natural units of work*. This means organizing the items of work into logical or inherently meaningful groups. For example, in the word-processing department, each operator might be given permanent responsibility for the work coming in from one or more specific departments or business groups. This type of change can increase both task identity and task significance.

Yet another strategy is to *establish client relationships*. The employee is put in direct contact with those individuals (whether inside or outside the organization) who receive and use the results of his or her work. This might be done in the word processing center by having each operator manage his or her own working relationship with the people in the departments he or she serves. This will tend to increase the feedback that the operator receives, as well as the level of skill variety and autonomy in the job.

A fourth strategy is to *increase the vertical loading in the job.* This means giving the employee more responsibility for setting schedules, determining work methods, and deciding when and how to check on the quality of the work being produced. This will increase the amount of autonomy in the job.

A final strategy is to *open feedback channels.* In the word-processing center, this means ensuring that the specialists receive complete and timely information about the accuracy of their work. This might be accomplished by having the specialists make their own corrections, or if someone else does the corrections, by giving the specialists summary reports about the frequency and type of errors they have made. This will greatly increase the amount of feedback in the job.

If some or all of these changes were actually applied in the word-processing department, the job characteristics profile for job B in Figure 17-3 would come to look more like the one shown for job A.

Autonomous Work Groups. For some types of jobs, it may seem difficult to apply many of the change strategies recommended in the preceding section. For example, how does one go about combining tasks in an automobile assembly plant so that employees perform more complete, identifiable, and meaningful pieces of work? It would be silly to have each and every employee build an entire car. It would even be impractical to have each employee responsible for a major subassembly (e.g., body, engine, drive train), since each subassembly consists of a very large number of parts and involves too many separate tasks for a single person to handle efficiently.

When the smallest meaningful module of work involves more separate tasks and operations than one person can efficiently perform, the solution may be to design the work around relatively small, autonomous groups. In other words, apply the job change strategies discussed previously at the *group* level of analysis. Thus, for example, combine tasks so that the group performs a larger, more complete module of work. Form natural units of work so that the group produces a logical or inherently meaningful whole product. Establish client relationships between the group and those who use the group's product. Increase the vertical loading of the job so that the group can set its own schedule, determine its own work methods, and so on. And finally, open feedback channels so that the group as a whole is aware of the results of its effort.

The historical foundations for the autonomous work-group approach to job redesign can be traced to the research in the British coal-mining industry discussed in Chapter 3 (see pp. 60–61). More widely known, current examples of this approach are the changes that have been made in Sweden at Saab and Volvo (Gyllenhammar, 1977; Tichy, 1973, 1974). At Saab, for example, automobile engines are assembled by small groups of five to ten people. The group members all have related duties, and they decide among themselves how to assign tasks and distribute their effort. Because they rotate jobs, each group member must learn how to do all of the assembly tasks. Each group puts together the entire engine—cylinder block, heads, rods, crankshaft, and everything else. In addition to assembly, the group's responsibilities include inspection, quality control, housekeeping, and maintenance. They work at their own pace, and they determine when and how long they will spend on breaks. The only requirement is that they produce 470 engines over a 10-day span. Under this system, there has been higher job satisfaction, lower turnover and absenteeism, and improved work quality.

Of course, the use of autonomous work groups presents its own set of problems. Issues of group cohesiveness, work norms, and interpersonal relations suddenly become important. If, for example, there are strong feelings of animosity, distrust, and tension within the group, the group's productivity is likely to suffer. When such problems arise, ways need to be found to improve the informal group relations. It is this topic to which we turn next.

Changing Informal Group Relations

Whenever people work in groups, there is a need for good interpersonal relations. This is especially important when the tasks being performed are highly interdependent. High task interdependence implies a strong demand for both cooperation and coordination. These are facilitated by good interpersonal communication and by a positive, mutually supportive atmosphere. When these favorable interpersonal conditions do not exist, there is a lack of

FIGURE 17-4
One form of job enrichment is to do away with the assembly line and have people work in teams.

fit between the demands of the task and the informal group relations, and problems of both morale and productivity are likely to result. Systematic efforts to improve the informal social relations that exist within a group or organization are often called *organization development*.

The Philosophy of Organization Development. Organization development typically involves a long-term attempt to bring about a change toward greater interpersonal effectiveness within an organization or organizational unit. Figure 17-5 summarizes some of the most important characteristics of organization development. In most cases, an outside consultant with special expertise in organization development participates in the initial phases of the change process. However, the long-run goal is to help members of the organization learn to resolve interpersonal problems by themselves, without outside help. The change process may involve any number of more specific organization development techniques. Here we will examine three of these techniques: survey feedback, team building, and Grid organization development.

Survey Feedback. One commonly used organization development technique is call *survey feedback*. It is an approach that emphasizes data gathering and diagnosis as a prerequisite for problem solving. It begins with the consultant systematically collecting data about the problems affecting the group or organizational unit. This usually involves the use of questionnaires and/or group discussions, and it gets the client group actively involved in the data-generation process. The obtained data are then tabulated and organized by the

FIGURE 17-5
General characteristics of organization development. (*Adapted from Eddy, 1971.*)

1. The focus is on the total system of interdependent suborganizational groupings (work units, teams, management levels) rather than on individual employees. Team development is frequently a major component of the change process.

2. The approach to change is "organic." It seeks to establish a climate in which growth, development, and renewal are brought about as a natural part of the organization's daily operation, rather than superimposed unilaterally.

3. Experiential learning techniques (role playing, problem-solving exercises) in addition to traditional lecture methods are utilized. Subject matter includes real problems and events that exist in the organization, as well as hypothetical cases or examples. Often there is gathering and analysis of organization data—either formally or informally.

4. Emphasis is placed upon competence in interpersonal relationships rather than upon task skills. Much of the content and method is based on behavioral sciences rather than upon management theory, operations research, or personnel techniques, although these may be included as part of the program.

5. Goals frequently have to do with developing behavioral competence in areas such as communication, decision making, and problem solving, in addition to understanding the principles and theories.

6. The value system is humanistic. It is committed to integrating individual needs and management goals, maximizing opportunity for human growth and development, and encouraging more open, authentic human relationships.

7. There is less intention to refute the traditional structural-functional conception of the organization than to augment this conception with newer data and help remedy some of its major dysfunctions.

consultant, but they are not interpreted or evaluated. Instead, they are fed back to the client group for the purpose of problem solving. This feedback process is usually most effective when it occurs in small-group meetings, preferably meetings attended by a supervisor and all of his or her subordinates (Beer, 1976). Survey feedback can be used to help an organization deal with such issues as intergroup relations, role responsibilities, supervision, organizational policies, job satisfaction, and organizational commitment.

Survey feedback can help stimulate change in an organization in at least two different ways (cf. Nadler, 1977). First, the process of data collection by itself can help focus people's attention on areas in which there may be problems. It can get people to begin thinking about the problems and about ways to deal with them. It can do this in part because the data-collection effort serves as a signal that management considers the problem to be important. Thus, for example, if a questionnaire is distributed about the degree to which supervisors are perceived to be accessible (available) to their subordinates (e.g., Follert, 1984), supervisors are likely to conclude that management views supervisor accessibility as an important behavioral dimension. Consequently, they may become more conscientious about being accessible—even before receiving the results of the survey. (Note that a similar point was made in Chapter 15 in connection with our discussion of single versus multiple criteria in performance appraisal. See page 494.)

Second, once the data have been collected, feeding them back can motivate change by calling attention to problems that had not previously been recognized. For example, the supervisors in a given department may believe that they have a good, open working relationship with their subordinates. The subordinates, however, may feel otherwise. When this comes to light in the survey data, it can move the supervisors to work to redress the problem. Similarly, when supervisors suddenly find out that their subordinates feel anxious because of role conflicts or role ambiguity, or that tension has been created in the group because of uncertainties surrounding goals and objectives, action can be taken to change the situation.

It should be noted that simply feeding back the data does not by itself guarantee that it will be accepted and properly used. Nadler (1977) suggests that when survey data are fed back, two important issues need to be dealt with before the data can be effectively used as a basis for problem solving and change. The first concerns the *validity* of the data. When a consultant comes into a group meeting in order to feed back data that indicate some type of problem exists, people will often feel anxious and defensive. As a result, they may try to challenge the validity of the data, claiming that the situation is really not as bad as the data seem to suggest. One way to overcome this is to get the members of the group personally involved in the data-collection process. In this way, they are likely to be more accepting of whatever results are generated.

Once the validity issue is resolved, the second problem is to get the members of the group to *take responsibility* for both the data and their implications. When survey results indicate that employees feel their supervisors are too inaccessible, certain supervisors may try to avoid taking responsibility for the problem by claiming, "Well, that may be true for the company as a whole, but it doesn't really apply in my department." Or, "It's not my fault. Management gives me too many other things to do." These types of rationalization help the individual avoid the problem by locating it somewhere else. It is the job of the feedback consultant to see to it that those who receive the feedback confront the problems head on, taking "ownership" when the data indicate that this is appropriate. It is only when the data are perceived as valid, and when the appropriate group members take responsibility for the problems that are illuminated, that those individuals will begin in earnest to seek ways to solve the problems.

Team Building. When survey feedback is employed for the purpose of organization development, it is often used in conjunction with other techniques that are oriented toward helping the group find solutions to the problems that have been uncovered. These other techniques are generally classified together under the heading of *team building*. Thus, team building begins with an initial data-gathering phase, followed by one or more meetings of the client group. These team-building meetings are generally held off-site (e.g., at a local hotel) and may last 3 to 5 days. Early in the meeting, the consultant feeds back the survey data to the group, and the group categorizes and assigns priorities to the problems that are identified. Based on the priorities assigned, a problem-solving agenda is set for the remainder of the meeting. From this point on, the role of the consultant is to help the group critique the process of its interaction, to promote group norms conducive to confronting and resolving conflict, and to facilitate problem solving (cf. Beer, 1976).

One approach to team building is to apply what is called a "T-group" methodology. This involves having the group members spend several days together by themselves in an unstructured environment in order to examine their perceptions of one another and how they function as a group. Issues of power, status, and authority tend to carry over from the normal work environment and are likely to become important topics of discussion (Shepard, 1965). However, because the members of the group have to live with one another back on the job, it is often psychologically risky for them to be completely open and candid in expressing their feelings. As a result, this approach to team building is very difficult to use, and successful outcomes are hard to achieve.

Another team-building strategy is to spend time clarifying the roles and expectations of the various group members. As we saw in Chapter 9, when people do not understand their roles (role ambiguity), or when the various roles they are expected to play come into conflict with one another (role conflict), problems can occur. Among other things, these can lead to stress, antagonism, and poor interpersonal communication. The key to clarifying roles within work groups is to get the group members to exchange their role perceptions and expectations (cf. Dayal & Thomas, 1968). Beer (1976) comments that such exchanges can help groups resolve problems having to do not only with roles, but also with interpersonal relations, power, intergroup relations, and leadership.

Finally, team building may also be facilitated by examining the goals of both the individual group members and the group as a whole. Oftentimes group members may be unsure of what their goals are, or they may disagree about the importance of various goals. By focusing on goals during the team-building meeting, misunderstandings and disagreements can be resolved, and specific, agreed-upon goals can be set. As we have seen elsewhere in the book, when goals are specific, and when the members of the group all participate in setting them, commitment and performance are likely to increase.

Grid® Organization Development. In comparison to survey feedback, team building has a much narrower focus. It is oriented toward improving the functioning of specific work groups within the organization, as opposed to either large organizational units (e.g., divisions or plants) or the organization as a whole. Survey feedback is somewhat more versatile in this regard, in that it can be applied at any unit of analysis from the individual work group up to the entire organization. There are, however, organization development techniques that are specifically designed to deal with the organization as a whole. Grid organization development is one of these.

Grid organization development was designed by Blake and Mouton (1985) as a method for dealing with several important barriers to organization effectiveness, including *poor planning* and *poor communication.* According to this approach, poor planning in organizations results from a failure to develop a well-defined organizational strategy. Thus, Grid organization development is in part an attempt to help the organization evolve a strategy by generating a clear description of itself, its market niche, what its optimum organization structure should be, and what its primary goals and policies are. Once articulated, these can serve as a guide for decision making and action in the future. Poor communication, by contrast, is hypothesized to result from an ineffective management style, which in turn is assumed to reflect an inadequate understanding of human behavior in organizations. Thus, Grid organization development also attempts to teach managers relevant theories of human behavior and helps them improve their "human" skills so that they will have a more effective management style.

Blake and Mouton (1985) use a grid such as the one shown in Figure 17-6 to help managers understand their management style, and if need be, to change it. This model focuses on two independent behavior dimensions: concern for production and concern for people. (Note the similarity between these two dimensions and the initiation of structure and consideration dimensions discussed in Chapter 14.) Managers are rated on a scale from 1 to 9 on each dimension. According to Blake and Mouton (1985), managers are likely to be most effective when they score very high on *both* dimensions, that is, when they show high levels of concern for both production and people. This is the so-called 9,9 style of management. Part of the goal of Grid organization development is to change the style of the organization's management to the 9,9 position. Since the focus is on the style of management exhibited organization-wide, this process can be thought of as a method of changing the overall culture of the organization.

The implementation of Grid organization development involves a six-phase process. The first three phases focus on management style, while the last three focus on clarifying the organization's strategy. Phase 1 entails helping managers to identify their managerial style and learn how to become more effective leaders. Phase 2 involves a team-building process not unlike that described previously. Phase 3 focuses on resolving conflicts that may exist between groups. Phase 4 involves designing an ideal model of what the organization

FIGURE 17-6
The managerial
Grid. (*Adapted
from Blake &
Mouton, 1964.*)

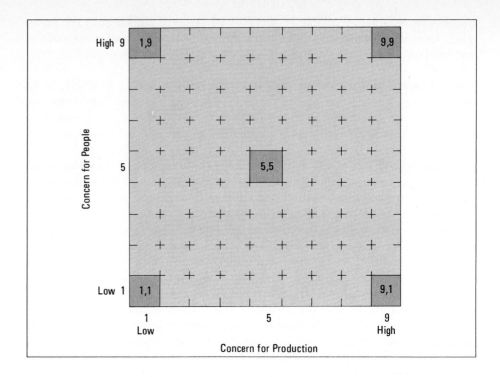

should look like, while phase 5 consists of attempts to implement that model. In Phase 6, the entire process is systematically evaluated in order to determine the rate at which the organization is progressing toward the dual goals of better planning and better communication.

Grid organization development is usually introduced in relatively small work groups, starting first at the level of senior management. Once implemented at the top, it is then repeated over and over again with groups at successively lower organizational levels. It can take as long as 5 to 6 years to implement this process throughout the entire organization.

Evaluating Organization Development. It is extremely difficult to evaluate the effectiveness of these various organization development strategies. The reason for this is that the empirical research that has been done in this area has often not been of very high quality. In many instances the research reports are little more than case studies describing the symptoms present in a particular organization along with the organization development intervention that was applied. Relatively few studies have been done using carefully controlled experimental designs. Studies infrequently use control groups for comparison purposes, and the organization development interventions are seldom assigned on a random basis.

Despite these shortcomings, a few studies have been done with sufficient rigor to warrant at least two tentative conclusions (Nicholas, 1982; Porras & Berg, 1978a, 1978b). First, there is evidence that both process (e.g., behavior, self-awareness) and outcome (e.g., performance) variables can be affected by organization development techniques. Second, organization development seems to have a stronger impact at the individual and small-group level of analysis than at the level of the overall organization. A great deal more empirical research will be needed before more specific conclusions can be drawn about the impact of these various organization development techniques.

Changing Formal Organizational Structures

To this point we have discussed strategies for changing three of the four elements that make up the Nadler and Tushman (1980) congruence model of organizations: people, task characteristics, and informal social relationships. The one remaining element in the model is the formal structure of the organization. Among other things, formal structure includes the manner in which the organization is differentiated, the average span of control at various organizational levels, the degree of formalization that exists, and the extent to which important decisions are made exclusively by top management. In addition, control systems, performance appraisal systems, and formal systems of reward also fall under the heading of formal organizational structure.

It is beyond the scope of this text to review in any detail the various strategies for changing formal organizational structures. This is the province of organization theory, and the interested reader is referred to any number of excellent texts on this topic (e.g., Galbraith, 1977). We do wish to emphasize, however, that the basic objective in changing organizational structure is essentially the same as the objective in changing any other aspect of the organization, namely, to achieve an optimal fit among organizational elements.

A central consideration is to optimize the fit with the tasks being performed. Thus, for example, Tushman and Nadler (1978) argue that the organization's tasks should be analyzed for their information processing requirements, and the formal structure of the organization should be adjusted to provide exactly the right amount of information processing capacity. Information processing capacity can be increased by moving to a more organic structure, while it can be decreased by moving to a more mechanistic structure (recall that these two organizational forms were discussed in Chapter 3, pp. 52–53).

Although it is essential to have a good fit between the formal structure of the organization and the tasks being performed, it is also important to consider the way in which aspects of the formal structure fit both the people involved and their informal social relationships. For example, does the reward system provide outcomes that are valued by the members of the organization? Does it reward cooperation and mutual support when such behavior is desired? As we have seen elsewhere, poor fits in these areas can cause just as many problems as a poor fit between the organization's structure and its tasks. The well-designed formal organizational structure will optimize each and every one of these fits.

CHANGE IN ORGANIZATIONS: A FINAL COMMENT

Throughout this chapter we have emphasized the point that organizational change should be directed toward optimizing the fit between organizational elements. In considering how this might be accomplished, we have examined a variety of strategies for changing people, jobs, informal social relations, and to a lesser extent, the formal organizational structure. Although we discussed these various change techniques separately, we do not mean to imply that organizational change should be approached in a piecemeal fashion, focusing on only one element at a time. Quite the contrary, the success of many change programs will depend on being able to modify several elements of the organization simultaneously. An example will help to illustrate this point.

Imagine the following situation. The manufacturing division of a small Midwestern maker of hospital diagnostic equipment is experiencing a variety of problems. The rates of absenteeism and turnover have become alarmingly high, quality-control problems are on the rise, and the company has recently been having difficulty meeting production quotas. After a careful analysis of the situation it is concluded that the primary cause of these problems is a poor person-job fit in the company's main fabrication and assembly plant. The company relies on an assembly-line method of production, with each person on the assembly line performing only a very small part of the overall assembly process. Jobs on the assembly line are highly repetitive, tedious, and boring. The employees who work on the line are extremely dissatisfied with their jobs, which is not surprising given the fact that most of them have a moderate-to-high growth need strength.

In order to alleviate the problems faced by this company, a decision is made to abandon the traditional assembly-line process of manufacturing in favor of an autonomous work-group method similar to that employed in the automobile assembly plants at Saab and Volvo. This new work arrangement should better fit the growth needs of employees, since it is likely to increase the skill variety, task identity, task significance, autonomy, and feedback in their jobs. However, if this change is to be truly effective, it will have to encompass more than just changing the job. A number of other changes will also have to be made (cf. Oldham & Hackman, 1980).

First, some attention will need to be devoted to changing the individuals who are to perform the redesigned jobs. At a minimum, technical training must be provided so that the employees can learn how to do those tasks with which they are currently unfamiliar. Furthermore, something will have to be done with employees who have a relatively low growth need strength. Although most employees are likely to welcome the change to the autonomous work-group system, those few who have a low growth need strength may respond negatively (e.g., resist the change and/or not perform well after it has been put into effect). Will these people be transferred to other jobs within the organization, and if so, where?

Another consideration is the way in which informal social relationships will have to change. Team building or some other similar type of intervention may be necessary in order to ensure that the individuals function well together in their new work groups. Some sort of group decision-making training may also be necessary, since an autonomous work-group method of manufacturing leaves many of the day-to-day operating decisions up to the group.

Finally, there are also several aspects of the formal organization that will need to be changed. Since it may no longer be possible to measure performance at the individual level of analysis, new performance appraisal and control procedures will be needed. More sophisticated methods of employee selection may also be required in order to obtain new employees who fit the more complex jobs that must be performed. Similarly, the reward system will have to be modified. Because the employees are being given more responsibility, not to mention a greater variety of tasks to perform, the absolute level of pay may have to be increased. Furthermore, if pay is based on performance, it will be necessary to alter the reward system so that pay is based on performance aggregated at the group level of analysis (again, because individual-level performance may be difficult to assess reliably). And finally, changes will have to be made in the method of supervision. The job of the first-line supervisor will have to change dramatically, since many of the supervisor's old responsibilities (e.g., assigning people to specific tasks, scheduling the work to be done) are likely to be taken over by the work group itself. The supervisor's job will have to be redesigned so that it supports (rather than overlaps or conflicts with) the efforts of the work group.

Thus, even when a change is directed toward improving the fit between two specific elements (e.g., between the person and the job), other aspects of the organization may need to be modified in order to support the change. Two important implications can be drawn from this. One is that the whole enterprise of introducing organizational change can sometimes be a very complex process. In order to ensure that a change is successful, one may need to take into consideration the relationships among a rather large number of variables. This is why it is often advisable to appoint a transition manager—someone whose sole responsibility is to manage the change. All by itself, managing a large organizational change project can be a full-time job.

Besides the sheer complexity of the problem, the necessity of modifying other organizational elements in order to support the primary change has a second important implication. If one or more key supporting changes are not or cannot be made, the success of the primary change is likely to be compromised. Thus, continuing with the example above, if senior management is unwilling to commit funds for team building and training in group decision making, some of the newly formed work groups may be left ill-prepared to deal with problems of internal conflict and/or the day-to-day operating decisions that must be made. As a consequence, they may function rather inefficiently. Or if the absolute level of pay is not increased, some employees may feel cheated and may respond by artifically restricting output. This, of course, would defeat the whole purpose of introducing the change in the first place. Thus, there are many potential barriers that can block the implementation and ultimate success of an otherwise well-intended change project. One needs to be aware of these barriers and take them into account whenever an organizational change is contemplated.

Summary

In this final chapter we have examined the process of implementing change in organizational settings. Some of the most important points made in this chapter are listed below:

1. Organizational change is motivated in part by a dissatisfaction with the status quo. In order to reduce this dissatisfaction, attempts might be made

to change the individual members of the organization, the jobs they perform, the informal social relations that exist among organization members, and/or the formal structure of the organization.

2. An open systems theory approach to organizational change suggests that when a change is contemplated, it should be directed toward optimizing the fit between the various elements of the organization.

3. The overall change process involves a number of steps. The problem must be recognized, its causes must be properly diagnosed, a specific change must be implemented, and the effectiveness of the change should be evaluated.

4. The effective implementation of a planned organizational change requires that a motivation to change be generated among those who will be personally affected by it. It may also be necessary to marshal political support for the change. Finally, sufficient time, energy, and resources should be devoted to managing the transition period.

5. Changes that target the individual members of the organization include transfer, termination, and training. Training programs may be oriented toward improving technical skills, human skills, and/or conceptual skills.

6. Job-oriented organizational changes include changing work schedules, changing the fundamental characteristics of the tasks that are performed on the job, and/or changing to autonomous work-group methods.

7. Changes designed to improve informal social relations within the organization are often referred to as organization development. Among the available organization development techniques are survey feedback, team building, and Grid organization development.

8. Organizational change can sometimes be an extremely complex process, with multiple changes being required in several areas simultaneously.

IMPLICATIONS FOR RESEARCH

Perhaps the most pressing need in the area of organizational change is for more sophisticated evaluation research, that is, better research designed to evaluate the overall effectiveness of various organizational change strategies. This is particularly true in the area of organization development. One review of the organization development literature found that (1) over 50 percent of the studies were correlational in nature (which means that it is impossible to draw causal inferences from them), (2) over 50 percent reported frequency or percentage data without any statistical comparisons, and (3) almost 95 percent relied solely on questionnaire or recall data rather than on objective measures (White & Mitchell, 1976). Although there has been some improvement in this overall pattern during the last decade (e.g., Vicars & Hartke, 1984), it is still the case that many studies in this area use questionnaire measures that are of uncertain reliability and validity, and too few make use of research methods involving control groups and random assignment of subjects to treatments. Thus, while the vast majority of evaluation studies published in the organization development literature claim to show that the particular change technique under investigation was successful (e.g., Golembiewski, Proehl, &

Sink, 1982), it is often difficult to have a great deal of confidence in these conclusions.

One particularly troublesome methodological problem is the fact that those individuals involved with the change often have fairly clear expectations about what sorts of results the change is "supposed" to produce. Over 80 percent of the research reported in the organizational change literature involves studies in which (1) the researcher is affiliated in one way or another with the organization in which the change occurs (and hence is likely to have a vested interest in the success of the change), and (2) the employees actually affected by the change are aware of the special arrangements that have been made. As we know from the Hawthorne studies discussed in Chapter 3 (see pp. 57–59), these extraneous factors have a powerful influence on behavior independent of whatever effect (if any) the treatment itself might have.

We should emphasize that this problem is by no means limited to organization development. It also applies to other types of organizational change research. For example, King (1974) demonstrated that the mere *expectation* that job enrichment would increase productivity led to greater performance improvements than did actual job enrichment.

This is a difficult problem to overcome because it is virtually impossible to introduce a change in an organization without the members of the organization being aware of it. Indeed, it might be argued that many organizational changes could not possibly have an effect *unless* the members were aware of them. The trick, then, is to develop a research method that allows people to be aware of the changes that are being implemented but at the same time rules out the possibility that a Hawthorne-like effect alone accounts for the observed results.

Thus, one very important direction for future research is to develop research methods that overcome this and other deficiencies commonly found in much of the existing organizational change literature. If this can be accomplished, the entire field will benefit. Not only will we be able to draw more confident conclusions about what sorts of organizational change interventions work in general, we should also be able to home in on answers to more specific questions, such as the types of situations in which various change techniques work best.

IMPLICATIONS FOR PRACTICE

Organizations are constantly trying to increase their effectiveness. They do this in part by changing—by introducing new ideas and new ways of doing things. The problem is that people often resist change; change can be threatening and can cause uncertainty. People know how things are now, but how will they be tomorrow? Will the employees' pay be decreased? Will they have to work longer hours? Will they be separated from their friends? These are real concerns for employees, and in order to implement change successfully, they must be dealt with.

There are several ways to facilitate change and make it more acceptable. One is to get people's input throughout the change process. What do they think the problem is? How do they think it should be corrected? Increasing participation in the planning stage should increase people's acceptance of and commitment to whatever change is ultimately adopted.

A second and related idea is to keep people informed. Let them know what is going on and why various things are being done. Information and participation can help to reduce some of the uncertainty and anxiety that often accompany change. Third, one should provide incentives for changing—make change attractive. People will be much more motivated to carry out the change if they see that doing so will lead to desired rewards. Fourth, the change should not be coercive. It is best if people engage in change programs because they want to. In some instances, employees might even be given a choice about whether or not to participate in a planned change (e.g., they might be given a choice between working in newly formed autonomous work groups or staying on a traditional assembly line). Change programs are more likely to be acceptable to employees when they contain some degree of flexibility.

Finally, organizations can take direct action to help employees cope with the emotional stresses that are often associated with change. For example, at AT&T there are employee discussion groups that meet regularly to talk about problems of stress. AT&T also offers training programs and seminars that include stress management segments. These sometimes include exercises designed to simulate the stress that accompanies change, followed by a discussion about ways to cope with it. The response to these efforts has been positive. As a result of such programs, people are "much more open" in talking about stress and "focusing on problem areas, and see some solution for those problems" ("Coping with Anxiety," 1979). Clearly it is important to deal not only with the content of change, but with the process of change as well.

Discussion Questions

1. Suppose the university decided to change its grading system from letter grades to numbers ranging from 0.00 to 10.00. How would you feel? How could such a plan be implemented successfully?
2. How is job enrichment different from job enlargement? Think of a job with which you are familiar. How would you enlarge it? How would you enrich it?
3. Do you think an organization has a prevailing climate? How would you go about changing climate? How would you know whether or not you were successful?

CASE: IMPLEMENTING CHANGE

The U.S. Navy decided to introduce a new management program called *Management by Objectives* (MBO). MBO is a method for establishing clear, concise performance objectives, along with realistic action plans for attaining those objectives. The Navy prepared detailed manuals describing the MBO process. The manuals contained instructions, forms, case examples, and other supplementary material. These manuals were sent out from Washington, D.C., to the top personnel at naval installations throughout the world.

A naval air station in the Northeastern part of the United States happened to be near a major urban university. At the school there were a number of organizational and industrial psychologists who had done contract work for the Office of Naval Research, and one of them, Dr. Colin Beard, was interested in the topic of motivation. Dr. Beard contacted the naval air station to see if he could help implement and evaluate the MBO program.

A couple of the squadron commanders were initially enthusiastic, so Dr. Beard arranged to meet with them the next day. He gathered together some materials on the subject and convinced one of his graduate students to accompany him.

The meetings were very cordial. Dr. Beard laid out what he wanted to do. He suggested that they gather data to describe the current level of motivation, satisfaction, and performance of two squadrons. Then one of the squadrons would set up the MBO program while the other would serve as a comparison group. In 3 months they would reassess performance, satisfaction, and motivation. If MBO worked, it would be implemented in the comparison squadron.

Well, this just would not do. Both squadrons were due to go on cruise in 3 months, and they both wanted the program. Neither commander wanted his squadron to serve as the comparison group. They were also hesitant about the measurement procedures and how their people would respond to a questionnaire. Dr. Beard explained that giving both squadrons the MBO program simultaneously would prohibit any sort of useful evaluation, but the commanders would not budge. Finally, Dr. Beard said that he just could not justify the amount of effort involved without the kind of research design he had suggested, so he recommended that they talk about it again after the two squadrons came back from their tour in 18 months.

The commanders agreed to this proposal, but they asked one last favor: Could Dr. Beard come and lead a couple of lecture/discussion sessions for the offices? "Sure,"said Beard, "I'd be glad to. How about next Tuesday afternoon?" "Yes, that's a good time for us," replied the commanders.

The attendance was high at the Tuesday session. Both commanders were there along with thirty other officers. Dr. Beard ran through the steps that were important in MBO. He particularly emphasized that differences in priorities should be *discussed and worked out jointly* between superiors and subordinates so that the rank order of objectives was clear to everyone. One of the commanders interrupted at this point to say: "We don't have any problems in priorities here. Everyone knows our first priority is to have our planes and pilots prepared for battle." Everyone in the audience directly behind the commander nodded their heads up and down.

Dr. Beard was slightly uncomfortable but he went on. He described how individual goals should be *jointly* set between the commanding officer and his or her immediate subordinates. This process should be a participative exchange and a flexible one. Finally, Dr. Beard illustrated how records of goal attainment could be used to show individual progress and performance.

At the end of the session, one of the commanders stood up and thanked Dr. Beard and turned to the rest of the men and said: "I know everyone here found this session helpful and informative. I'm sure each of us has some goals we want to set for our men. Let's get to it."

Questions about the Case

1. Do you think the commanders had the right idea about MBO? Where were they mistaken?
2. Should Dr. Beard have run the study without the research design he wanted?
3. Do you think some organizations are better suited for change than others? How would you have implemented a goal-setting program in the Navy?

References

Beckhard, R., & Harris, R. (1977). *Organizational transitions.* Reading, MA: Addison-Wesley.

Beer, M. (1976). The technology of organization development. In M. D. Dunnette (Ed.), *Handbook of industrial and organizational psychology* (pp. 937–993). Chicago: Rand McNally.

Beer, M. (1980). *Organization change and development: A system view.* Glenview, IL: Scott, Foresman.

Blake, R. R., & Mouton, J. S. (1985). *The managerial grid III.* Houston: Gulf.

Carroll, S. J., Paine, F. T., & Ivancevich, J. M. (1972). The relative effectiveness of training methods: Expert opinion and research. *Personnel Psychology, 25,* 495–509.

Coping with anxiety at AT&T. (1979, May 28). *Business Week,* p. 95ff.

Dayal, I., & Thomas, J. M. (1968). Operation KPE: Developing a new organization. *Journal of Applied Behavioral Science, 4,* 473–506.

Eddy, W. W. (1971, January-February). From training to organization change. *Personnel Administration,* pp. 37–43.

Fiedler, F. E., Chemers, M. M., & Mahar, L. (1976). *Improving leader effectiveness: The leader match concept.* New York: Wiley.

Field, R. H. G., & Abelson, M. A. (1982). Climate: A reconceptualization and proposed model. *Human Relations, 35,* 181–201.

Follert, V. (1984). A replicated factor analysis of a two dimension supervisor accessiblity scale. *Psychology, 21,* 8–19.

Galbraith, J. R. (1977). *Organization design.* Reading, MA: Addison-Wesley.

Golembiewski, R. T., & Proehl, C. W., Jr. (1978). A survey of the empirical literature on flexible workhours: Character and consequences of a major innovation. *Academy of Management Journal, 3,* 837–853.

Golembiewski, R. T., Proehl, C. W., Jr., & Sink, D. (1982). Estimating the success of OD applications. *Training and Development Journal, 37*(4), 86–95.

Goodale, J. G., & Aagaard, A. K. (1975). Factors relating to varying reactions to the 4-day workweek. *Journal of Applied Psychology, 60,* 33–38.

Griffin, R. W. (1982). *Task design: An integrative approach.* Glenview, IL: Scott, Foresman.

Gyllenhammar, P. G. (1977). How Volvo adapts work to people. *Harvard Business Review, 55*(4), 102–113.

Hackman, J. R., & Oldham, G. R. (1980). *Work redesign.* Reading, MA: Addison-Wesley.

Hellriegel, D., & Slocum, J. W. (1974). Organizational climate: Measures, research, and contingencies. *Academy of Management Journal, 17,* 255–280.

Hoerr, J. (1979, June 4). A warning that worker discontent is rising. *Business Week,* p. 152ff.

Ivancevich, J. M. (1974). Effects of the shorter workweek on selected satisfaction and performance measures. *Journal of Applied Psychology, 59,* 717–721.

Ivancevich, J. M., & Lyon, H. L. (1977). The shortened workweek: A field experiment. *Journal of Applied Psychology, 62,* 34–37.

Ivancevich, J. M., & Smith, S. V. (1981). Goal setting interview skills training: Simulated and on-the-job analyses. *Journal of Applied Psychology, 66,* 697–705.

Katz, R. L. (1974, September-October). Skills of an effective administrator. *Harvard Business Review,* pp. 90–102.

King, A. S. (1974). Expectation effects in organization change. *Administrative Science Quarterly, 19,* 221–230.

Latack, J. C., & Foster, L. W. (1985). Implementation of compressed work schedules: Participation and job redesign as critical factors for employee acceptance. *Personnel Psychology, 38,* 75–92.

Likert, R. (1967). *The human organization.* New York: McGraw-Hill.

Loher, B. T., Noe, R. A., Moeller, N. L., & Fitzgerald, M. P. (1985). A meta-analysis of the relation of job characteristics to job satisfaction. *Journal of Applied Psychology, 70,* 280–289.

McCormick, E. J. (1979). *Job analysis: Methods and applications.* New York: AMACOM.

Nadler, D. A. (1977). *Feedback and organization development: Using data-based methods.* Reading, MA: Addison-Wesley.

Nadler, D. A. (1982). Concepts for the management of organizational change. In D. A. Nadler, M. L. Tushman, & N. G. Hatvany (Eds.), *Managing organizations: Readings and cases.* Boston: Little, Brown.

Nadler, D. A., & Tushman, M. L. (1980, Autumn). A model for diagnosing organizational behavior: Applying a congruence perspective. *Organizational Dynamics,* pp. 35–51.

Nicholas, J. M. (1982). The comparative impact of organization development interventions on hard criteria measures. *Academy of Management Review, 7,* 531–542.

Oldham, G. R., & Hackman, J. R. (1980). Work design in the organizational context. In B. M. Staw & L. L. Cummings (Eds.), *Research in organizational behavior* (Vol. 2, pp. 247–278). Greenwich, CT: JAI Press.

Pettigrew, A. (1978). Toward a political theory of organizational intervention. *Human Relations, 28,* 191–208.

Porras, J. I., & Berg, P. O. (1978a). Evaluation methodology in organization development: An analysis and critique. *Journal of Applied Behavioral Science, 14,* 151–173.

Porras, J. I., & Berg, P. O. (1978b). The impact of organization development. *Academy of Management Review, 3,* 249–266.

Ralston, D. A., Anthony, W. P., & Gustafson, D. J. (1985). Employees may love flexitime, but what does it do for the organization's productivity? *Journal of Applied Psychology, 70,* 272–279.

Schein, V. E. (1985). Organizational realities: The politics of change. *Training and Development Journal, 39*(2), 37–41.

Shepard, H. A. (1965). Changing relationships in organizations. In J. G. March (Ed.), *Handbook of organizations* (pp. 1115–1143). Chicago: Rand McNally.

Silverman, S. B., & Wexley, K. N. (1984). Reactions of employees to performance appraisal interviews as a function of their participation in rating scale development. *Personnel Psychology, 37,* 703–710.

Swierczewski, T. (1972). *A study of one firm's installation of a four-day workweek.* Unpublished doctoral dissertation, City University of New York.

Taylor, F. W. (1911). *The principles of scientific management.* New York: Harper.

Tichy, N. M. (1973, Autumn). Job redesign on the assembly line: Farewell to blue-collar blues. *Organizational Dynamics,* pp. 55–60.

Tichy, N. M. (1974, Summer). Organizational innovations in Sweden. *Columbia Journal of World Business,* pp. 18–22.

Tornow, W. W., & Pinto, P. R. (1976). The development of a managerial job taxonomy: A system for describing, classifying and evaluating executive positions. *Journal of Applied Psychology, 61,* 410–418.

Tushman, M. L., & Nadler, D. A. (1978). Information processing as an integrating concept in organizational design. *Academy of Management Review, 3,* 613–634.

Vicars, W. M., & Hartke, D. D. (1984). Evaluating OD evaluations: A status report. *Group and Organization Studies, 9,* 177–188.

Vroom, V. H., & Yetton, P. W. (1973). *Leadership and decision making.* Pittsburgh: University of Pittsburgh Press.

Walton, R. E. (1972, November-December). How to counter alienation in the plant. *Harvard Business Review,* pp. 72–81.

Wexley, K. N. (1984). Personnel training. *Annual Review of Psychology, 35,* 519–551.

Wexley, K. N., & Latham, G. P. (1981). *Developing and training human resources in organizations.* Glenview, IL: Scott, Foresman.

White, S. E., & Mitchell, T. R. (1976). Organization development: A review of research content and research design. *Academy of Management Review, 1,* 57–73.

Yankelovich, D., & Immerwahr, J. (1983). *Putting the work ethic to work: A public agenda report on restoring America's competitive vitality.* New York: The Public Agenda Foundation.

Acknowledgements

Page 12, Figure 2-1:
By permission of *The Daily of the University of Washington*.

Page 21, Figure 2-2:
By permission of the Boeing Company.

Page 30, Figure 2-5:
Copyright © 1985 by King Features Syndicate, Inc. Reprinted by permission.

Page 42, Figure 3-1:
By permission of *The Daily of the University of Washington*.

Page 51, Figure 3-4:
Copyright © 1967 by the American Sociological Association. Adapted by permission of the publisher and Dr. Perrow.

Page 65, Figure 3-5:
Copyright © 1980 by American Management Association, New York. Adapted by permission of the publisher. All rights reserved.

Page 80, Figure 4-1:
Left, Ellis Herwig/The Picture Cube.
Right, Frank Siteman/The Picture Cube.

Page 86, Figure 4-4:
Copyright © 1980 by the American Psychological Association. Adapted by permission of Dr. Mitchell.

Page 98, Figure 4-7:
Copyright © 1982 by the American Psychological Association. Adapted by permission of Dr. Bray.

Page 101, Figure 4-8:
Copyright © 1974 by the American Psychological Association. By permission of Dr. Snyder.

Page 123, Figure 5-5:
By permission of Dr. Smith.

Page 128, Figure 5-8:
Copyright © 1976 by Academic Press. Adapted by permission of the publisher and Dr. Staw.

Page 133, Figure 5-11:
By permission of the American Cancer Society.

Page 164, Figure 6-3:
By permission of Johnny Hart and News America Syndicate.

Page 168, Figure 6-4:
Copyright © 1975 by the American Psychological Association. Reprinted by permission of Dr. Latham.

Page 169, Figure 6-5:
By permission of Weyerhaeuser Company.

Page 175, Figure 6-6:
Copyright © 1980 by Addison-Wesley Publishing Company, Inc., Reading, MA. Reprinted by permission of the publisher.

Page 177, Figure 6-7:
Copyright © 1977 by Academic Press. Adapted by permission of the publisher and Dr. Komaki.

Page 197, Figure 7-4:
Copyright © 1985 by Tribune Media Services. Reprinted by permission.

Page 202, Figure 7-5:
Copyright © 1985 by the American Psychological Association. Reprinted by permission of Dr. Lazarus.

Page 235, Figure 8-5:
By permission of Weyerhaeuser Company.

Page 238, Figure 8-6:
Copyright © 1984 by Prentice-Hall, Englewood Cliffs, NJ. Reprinted by permission of the publisher.

Page 269, Figure 9-4:
By permission of Penton Publishing, a Division of Penton, Inc.

Page 281, Figure 9-8:
Copyright © 1964, University of Chicago Press. Adapted by permission of the publisher.

Indexes

Author Index

Subject Index